W9-AFY-108

IE, NCSU

A. Bilkey

MATERIAL HANDLING SYSTEMS DESIGN

JAMES M. APPLE

GEORGIA INSTITUTE OF TECHNOLOGY

JOHN WILEY & SONS, New York • Chichester • Brisbane • Toronto

John Wiley & Sons, Inc.

All Rights Reserved

Reproduction or translation of any part of this work beyond that permitted by Sections 107 or 108 of the 1976 United States Copyright Act without the permission of the copyright owner is unlawful. Requests for permission or further information should be addressed to the Permissions Department, John Wiley & Sons, Inc.

10 9 8 7 6 5 4 3 2

Library of Congress Catalog Card Number: 77–190203

PRINTED IN THE UNITED STATES OF AMERICA

ISBN 0 471 06652 4

Preface

This book is intended to be a comprehensive practical reference on modern material handling for engineers, production managers, technicians, and others concerned with the movement of material in the industrial plant. Because of its logical development of topics, and the integration of both theory and practice, this volume should also prove useful in industrial engineering and technology courses, and seminars conducted for professional groups in industry.

In dealing with machines, equipment, and systems within a single volume the emphasis is necessarily on fundamentals. The basic concepts of material handling are examined at length so as to clearly delineate the handling function and underscore the key role it plays in almost every productive activity. Each of the various components of the handling system is studied independently and also as an integral part of a complete plant system. Since the movement of material within a plant costs money, all significant elements of material handling expense are explored in depth and routines formulated for cost determination. The economic factors essential to the evaluation of design alternatives are given special attention.

Whereas in the past many material handling problems were solved intuitively, quantitative techniques are now available that can deal with a broad range of problems analytically. Such operations research methods as linear programming, queuing theory, dynamic programming, and simulation are discussed in this book in the context of specific material handling situations. The analyst is thus equipped with up-to-date mathematical tools needed to wrestle with the most sophisticated industrial operations.

Ultimately the design of a material handling system resolves into the selection of the "hardware" that will actually do the job. The objective examination in these pages of representative types of equipment and machinery, their applications, and advantages and disadvantages will serve as a reliable guide to the handling implementation available.

Perhaps the greatest material handling development in modern times has been the introduction of automation. Fully automated material handling systems and the automatic warehouse have had a profound effect on the entire production process. The essentials of automation as applied to this field are investigated and forecasts made as to future developments.

This book reflects the author's more than thirty years of study, teaching, and practicing in the field of material handling. It also necessarily includes the contributions of many other people and organizations. Whenever possible an attempt has been made to accurately credit the sources of materials.

The author would like to take this opportunity to specifically thank some of those who have contributed most significantly to this volume:

—Prof. James R. Bright, Associate Dean, Graduate School of Business, University of Texas, for providing much of the impetus for my writing the book, and who contributed the original drafts of chapters 1, 2, 4, and 18

—Mr. Burr Hupp and his associates with Drake Sheahan/Stewart Dougall—for adaptations of material presented at the Material Handling Management Courses at Lake Placid, N. Y.

—Mr. Calvin Hunter of Clark Equipment Co. and Mr. Lawrence Feit, of Interlake, Inc., whose critical opinions were of great help in preparing the chapter on automated warehousing

—Mr. Andrew J. Briggs of the May Co., whose original writing forms the basis for much of the material in the chapter on warehousing

—Dr. Robert N. Lehrer, who provided academic research support for part of the preparation of the manuscript.

Appreciation must also be expressed for my students, whose thought-provoking questions aided the conceptualizing process; for my colleagues in industry and education whose goading forced me to finish the work; and for those of the office staff who translated my scribbles and muffled dictation into a presentable manuscript. Last, but by no means least, my thanks are due my wife and family, who cheerfully put up with me—and without me—as the manuscript took shape.

JAMES M. APPLE

Atlanta, Georgia
August, 1972

Contents

MATERIAL HANDLING SYSTEMS DESIGN

1

Introduction to Material Handling

Ever since the beginning of time, man has been faced with the problem of moving himself and the materials needed for his existence. Movement is the common denominator in all economic activities involving physical goods, and in much that supports intellectual activity. The steel mill and the supermarket, the automatic factory and the construction project, the library and the bank—all are engaged in moving things. Man himself frequently acts as a material handler throughout his daily life. However, over a period of years he has learned to apply mechanical principles such as the lever, the wheel, the pulley, and the inclined plane to make the job of moving, lifting, and carrying easier, faster, and safer. Basically, material handling is the art of implementing movement—economically and safely. Yet, strangely enough, it is only since World War II that material handling has been properly recognized as a basic industrial task deserving systematic analysis and refinement, and yielding rich rewards to the imaginative engineer. The proper application of material handling knowledge will result in the smooth integration of all of the processes in an enterprise into one efficient production machine.

Although the primary function of material handling—the movement of materials—is as old as man, there is still no definition that is universally acceptable. Although many have been written, they are primarily descriptive of the situations in which the handling takes place, what it moves, its objectives, and other qualifications as to what handling is or is not. Rather than become involved in any such justifications, this text will proceed on the basis that: *Material handling is handling material!*

However, it should be noted that Material Handling is concerned with: motion, time, quantity and space. The Material Handling Institute describes this as follows:

First, Material Handling is MOTION. Parts, materials and finished products must be moved from location to location. Material Handling is concerned with moving them in the most efficient manner.

Second, Material Handling is TIME. Each step in any manufacturing process requires that its supplies are on hand the moment it needs them. Material Handling must assure that no production process or customer need will be hampered by having materials arrive on location too late or too early.

Third, Material Handling is QUANTITY. Rate of demand varies between steps in the manufacturing process. Material Handling has the responsibility of being sure that each location continually receives the correct quantity of parts-pounds-gallons.

Fourth, Material Handling is SPACE. Storage space, both active and dormant, is a major consideration in any building as space costs money. Space requirements are greatly influenced by the Material Handling flow pattern.

Put these four elements together and you have the basics of Material Handling. It should be noted that these elements are not treated independently. They must be integrated and their composite performance determines the quality of the Material Handling system.[1]

THE PLACE OF MATERIAL HANDLING IN INDUSTRY

It has been said that for a manufacturing activity of any kind, whether it is a single machine, a group of machines, or an entire plant, it is possible to identify three basic functions which define the total activity. The functions are work performing, handling, and control. This concept is shown in Figure 1–1.

However, material handling embraces two functions: moving and storage. It includes movement between machines or work stations, between departments, between buildings, the loading and unloading of carriers, as well as much of the handling done *at* the work place. It includes storage of materials (and tools and supplies) between and around all of the above locations, including raw material and work-in-process storage. It also includes finished goods warehousing and the other storage-related activities that lie between the producer and the consumer. In the classic sense, material handling is the act of creating *time* and *place* utility, as distinct from manufacturing, which creates *form* utility.

Historically speaking, industry has tended to concentrate on the art and science of making things and to neglect the art and science of moving things. There are two notable exceptions: the science of transportation, and the science of motion study at the workplace. Interestingly enough, the former involves movement over miles, and the latter concentrates on

---

[1] The Material Handling Institute Inc., *Basic Concepts of Industrial Material Handling.*

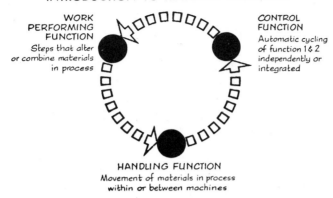

WORK
PERFORMING
FUNCTION
Steps that alter
or combine materials
in process

CONTROL
FUNCTION
Automatic cycling
of function 1 & 2
independently or
integrated

HANDLING FUNCTION
Movement of materials in process
within or between machines

Fig. 1–1.   Three basic functions of any manufacturing activity. (Courtesy of *Automation* magazine.)

activities within arm's reach. Here, engineering and organization skills have been systematically applied and are widely recognized as essential, but the gap between "miles" and "arm's length" has been long neglected. This is the gap that approximately embraces the field called *material handling*. Some idea of the total range of the levels of material handling activity can be obtained from a study of Figure 1–2, which indicates a range extending all the way from an individual workplace to the ultimate extent of movement from the sources of raw materials to distant customers.

MATERIAL HANDLING ACTIVITIES AND FUNCTIONS

In performing his duties, the material handling analyst becomes involved in a number of activities in which he has an interest or a responsibility for the effectiveness of material handling. Some of the activity areas in which he will normally work are as follows:

1. Packaging (consumer) at supplier's plant
2. Packing (protective) at supplier's plant
3. Loading at supplier's plant
4. Transportation to user plant
5. External plant handling activities
6. Unloading activities
7. Receiving
8. Storage
9. Issuing materials
10. In-process handling
11. In-process storage
12. Workplace handling
13. Intra-departmental handling
14. Inter-departmental handling
15. Intra-plant handling
16. Handling related to auxiliary functions
17. Packaging
18. Warehousing of finished goods
19. Packing
20. Loading and shipping
21. Transportation to consumer locations
22. Interplant handling

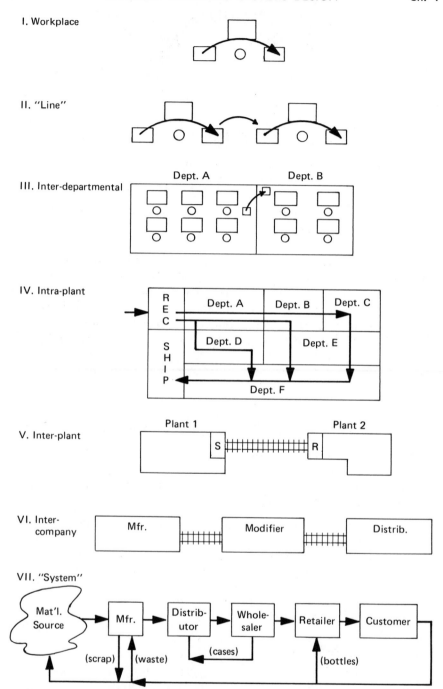

Fig. 1–2. The range of material handling.

Of course the type of enterprise and nature of its operations will determine the specific areas of activity, as well as the extent to which the material handling personnel will become involved.

In performing work in the activity areas listed above, attention will be centered on such matters as these:

1. Handling methods
2. Storage methods
3. Loading and unloading techniques
4. Packaging (consumer) methods
5. Packing (protective) methods
6. Testing of packages, packing and carrier loading methods
7. Material handling specifications and standards
8. Handling equipment feasibility
9. Equipment selection for both handling and storage
10. Auxiliary equipment evaluation and selection
11. Containers for shop, storage, packing, and shipping
12. Handling equipment repair and maintenance policies and procedures
13. Prevention of damage to materials and products
14. Safety of both personnel and product
15. Training of operating personnel and supervision in handling
16. Surveys to uncover improvement opportunities
17. Handling cost studies and cost control methods
18. Keeping up to date on handling equipment, methods, procedures, etc.
19. Related communication systems

Here again the nature of the enterprise and the types of operations being performed will suggest other duties to the material handling engineer. In general, his activities will cover any aspect of any operation in which handling is involved. In fact, in recent years, material handling has developed as a specialized area of the Industrial Engineering field, which is discussed later in this chapter.

OBJECTIVES AND BENEFITS OF BETTER HANDLING

In man's early history he turned to tools and machines to help him perform jobs that were beyond the ability of human muscles. The building of the pyramids, mining, the movement of stones for buildings or statues, the carrying of water from wells and rivers, the construction of ships and the loading of their cargoes forced him to develop cranes, hoists, sledges, wheelbarrows, and similar devices. With the Industrial Revolution and the rise of the factory system, man continued to develop handling equipment to do jobs where human and animal muscles were insufficient in either capacity or speed. As the factory system grew, the significance of labor cost also became more evident, and it was desirable to reduce material handling labor, which usually added to product cost, but contributed little if anything to value. Even today, the reduction of labor cost is still the reason most often cited for justifying material handling improvements.

However, the relative importance of labor cost as a manufacturing cost component is declining. For instance, a major electrical equipment manufacturing firm shows direct labor is 11 percent of manufacturing cost. An automotive engine plant has about a 7 percent labor cost, and a manufacturer of toiletries has a labor cost of only 4 percent. Industry now endeavors to improve handling because there are many benefits *other than labor savings* that arise in the modern industrial climate.[2] Of course, not all of these benefits appear in every material handling installation. Quite the opposite, indeed, for handling systems are frequently justified only on the basis of one or a few of the reasons. Nevertheless, both the manager and the engineer should always take a very broad point of view, in order to consider the *total* implications of a material handling situation. Benefits may emerge in the form of reduced costs, increased capacity, and improved working conditions.

Objective One: *Reduced Costs*

Cost-reduction programs have two broad goals: either to reduce the cost of material handling (and storage activities) or to reduce total production costs by improved handling procedures. The latter concept sometimes means increasing material handling costs in order to bring about a net reduction in total manufacturing costs. For example: A steel mill manufacturing pipe and bar stock from billets used a traditional method of moving materials between the rolling mill and a storage yard —an intra-plant railroad and locomotive crane system. In the early 1950's the firm developed a new system based on the straddle carrier (adopted from the lumber industry) and using heavy steel bolsters as a kind of rack-container, along with high-capacity fork-lift trucks to assist in loading the bolsters. All were under the control of a two-way radio system. Handling costs more than doubled, but unit production costs were lowered, because mill output increased approximately 20 percent as a result of the rapid response of the handling system to production demands. Also, the rolling mills realized a significantly higher utilization ratio because there was less waiting for material supply or removal. Other ways

---

[2] Note, however, that continuing wage increases and fringe benefits for labor provide new economic justification for further mechanization. In addition, federal government rulings, such as the 1965 decision to prohibit the use of Mexican *braceros* to harvest western crops, and requiring a minimum wage payment per hour for crop picking, have not only invited, but are forcing a new wave of mechanization.

in which cost reductions are realized through improved material handling are:

1. Reducing material handling labor.
2. Reducing the material handling work done by direct labor. High-skill and high-cost labor should not be assigned low-skill, low-cost work.
3. Reducing indirect labor associated with material handling activities, such as shipping and receiving personnel, production control personnel, tool room and storage personnel, inspectors, quality control, repair personnel, etc.
4. Reducing waste and damaged materials through more careful handling.
5. Reducing paper work and associated clerical help through handling systems that minimize control requirements.
6. Reducing the amount of material in the system by faster throughput and less in-process storage.
7. Reducing the amount of subsidiary materials such as packaging materials and other protective devices such as trays, racks, and special containers. This in turn reduces the amount of inspection work.

Objective Two: *Increased Capacity*

Increased capacity is frequently used as a justification for improving a handling system, where a firm needs more space or increased output. Material handling improvements can increase capacity in the following ways.

Better Space Utilization. Modern storage systems make use of "air rights" by means of racks, or containers that stack upon each other when full and nest completely when empty. Suppose materials are presently stored only to 6-foot heights. An improvement that will use the space up to a 12-foot height will double storage capacity! Frequently this can be done simply by the use of lift trucks. Handling systems, particularly cranes and conveyors, can operate in unused space above production activities. They can be arranged to operate outside buildings, in unused elevator wells, in unnecessary stairways, through underground passageways, or other unusable space. This can release prime space for production or storage. Sometimes the combination is extremely effective. For instance, the stacker crane (which can be thought of as a lift truck mast suspended from an overhead travelling crane) can be teamed up with special racks and automatic controls. This combination results in extremely high-density, compact storage operations up to heights of 70 feet. The net result is a great increase in space utilization and handling efficiency.

Many ingenious rack, container, and truck attachment systems have been developed for handling "difficult" materials such as bar stock, carpets and other long cylindrical shapes, coils, reels, tires, barrels, and items where instability or awkward shape had previously caused inefficient handling and the use of excessive space.

Improving the Layout To Reduce Travel or Excessive Waste of Space. By analyzing the flow of materials between operations, the volume involved, the flow paths, and the timing of materials movement, it is usually possible to reduce travel time and space needs. Rearranging equipment and providing handling systems that reduce the distance material must travel are useful practices. A study of aisle space, width, and location often reveals unnecessary use of space. The adoption of new forms of handling equipment such as the narrow aisle truck (in favor of the counter-balanced truck) can save considerable aisle space. The square feet of aisle space saved may be multiplied by 3, 4, or even more, when dealing with a warehouse by using the space released for vertical storage of unit loads or for racks of materials.

In some warehouse operations, a simple re-arrangement of stock to put "fast-moving" items close together may cut down the travel time of order pickers. Thus better handling concepts increase output, even when there is no change in the volume of space used.

Higher Equipment Utilization. Many pieces of expensive production equipment do not operate at their potential capacity because they are limited by the rate at which materials are supplied to, or removed from, the equipment or the work area. A proper handling system, or efficient control of an existing handling system can greatly increase production equipment utilization. For example, in a traditional automobile engine factory of 1948 the average transfer-type machine operated at 60 percent of theoretical capacity. After the systems were "automated" (i.e., provided with automatic, continuous feeding and removal of engine blocks throughout the sequence of machining operations) the equipment utilization jumped to 80 percent. This 33 percent increase in productivity was realized either as increased production or as a reduction in the number of machines required and, hence, a corresponding reduction of space, operators, and costs.

Providing a hand-lift truck to operators of heavy stamping presses at elevators and other such locations may increase equipment utilization because the operators will not have to wait for a lift truck or overhead crane to move material in their vicinity.

Faster Loading and Discharge of Common Carriers. The development of bulk conveyor systems for loading and unloading boats, barges, and railroad cars and the adaptation of portable conveyor systems and cranes to the loading of motor carriers greatly reduces loading time. Thus, the transportation unit can spend more time moving and less time sitting at the loading dock. This not only lowers operating cost but reduces the number of docks or terminal spaces required, with a corresponding reduction of loading crews and of supervision.

Objective Three: *Improved Working Conditions*

Safety to Men, Materials and Associated Equipment.   These may be enhanced by a proper material handling system. For instance, when Ford provided mechanized handling of engine blocks in its Cleveland plant in 1950, the accident rate was more than cut in half. Insurance costs, accident costs, lost time associated with accidents, etc., are all reduced by better handling. Material and equipment damage are also greatly decreased.

Easier Jobs.   Where heavy objects must be handled, the rate of output may be significantly affected by the physical ability and condition of the operators. Moreover, heavy work can only by done by men, and often only by young men. Many handling systems have been justified, in part, by the fact that they have taken the high effort out of the task, resulting in a steadier flow of work throughout the day and in higher production. It also may mean lower employee turnover, less training of replacement workers and better morale in the work force.

Lighter Work.   If the work is physically lighter, it may be possible to use operators of a different job classification, which can mean lower wage rates. At least one major in-process handling system was justified simply on the differential in wages between the existing male work force and the female work force that was to be used after the heavy manual effort was mechanized. The automatic 155-mm howitzer shell plant, built by U.S. Industries at Rockford, Illinois, in the closing days of World War II, was automated *specifically* so that women could do the work in the plant.

Foolproof Operation.   In some activities it is all too easy for an operator to become confused and to direct material to a wrong location, to use the wrong amounts, to mishandle or damage materials, or to otherwise disrupt production operation. Handling systems are sometimes installed to insure that such errors will not happen. In the mixing of fertilizers, foods, and other bulk products that are formulated to order, this may be a very attractive benefit.

Objective Four: *Improved Salability of a Product*

Handling systems often enhance the value of a product to the customer. The adoption of such a handling system may make the difference in the customer's decision to use one vendor instead of another. This may be accomplished by the following means.

Speed of Service. If the handling procedure can provide goods or materials promptly, according to the customer's desire, or with a significant time advantage over competitors, it may be the prime reason that business is obtained or retained.

Helping Customers Cut Costs. The development of the unit load has enabled vendors to help customers cut their costs since they need not handle individual items, or undertake the expense of palletizing on their own docks.

The reduction in packaging or packing materials and their cost is sometimes obtained through unit load techniques. This may enable the vendor to cut his cost to the customer. Also, the use of materials by the purchaser may be simplified by proper unit load design, thereby reducing the cost of unpacking and disposing of the packaging material. Unitizing by the vendor may be done at the end of his assembly lines, or other final operations.

The development of the "shipping" container, which contains from 640 to several thousand cubic feet, and is integrated into the receiving system and even into discharge at the production machine or the point of use, may offer great savings. This may appeal to the customer because it reduces his receiving costs and preserves the integrity of that particular lot of material. It may also eliminate the need for covered storage or locked storage. Because of great discharge speed, it may reduce the amount of material in the cycle of vendor-manufacturer-carrier-customer; and it may also reduce demurrage charges. Thus it may appeal to a number of people in the several phases of the economic system.

Sales Value of an Outstanding Installation. While it might be hard to prove that a handling system is justified in promotional value alone, a tremendous amount of publicity can accrue to a truly outstanding system. Several managers have been heard to argue vigorously that by taking prospective customers through their new factories, the visitors have become so impressed that an order was obtained because of the impression of efficiency, quality, and service conveyed by the installation. Also, an outstanding plant may obtain a tremendous amount of technical publicity in trade and professional journals that may attract customers as well as enhance the reputation of the firm in all circles. An outstanding plant is admired by employees as well as customers. It may improve the standing of the firm in the community, and make it far easier to hire and retain the best people, or to draw from a larger labor pool.

CONCLUSIONS

Obviously, modern handling methods offer many types of benefits carrying different degrees of importance to different organizations at different times. Therefore, one should *never be satisfied to think of handling only in terms of labor savings*. Indeed, one single criterion should never be used as the sole justification for the system. It is important to look at the entire range of benefits, so that the true value of the various alternatives being considered can be seen.

LIMITATIONS AND NEGATIVE ASPECTS OF MATERIAL HANDLING SYSTEMS

It is bad engineering and worse management practice to look only at benefits and to ignore limitations. Handling systems, at times, have consequences that may be distinctly negative. These too, should be evaluated before the changes are adopted. Some such possible disadvantages are:

Additional Capital Investment

It must be verified that the cost of the handling system is more attractively invested in the system under consideration than in any other part of the business. It should be assured that the gains expected are not based upon a more mechanized system vs. present practice, but rather the proposed new system vs. the *best version* of present practice.

Loss of Flexibility

If a proposed handling system is designed around a material of a limited size, shape, volume or rate of production, and geared to a particular sequence of operations, one should be aware of the impact of potential changes. Is the proposed system *flexible enough* to be economically and quickly adapted to the likely range of changes in the product or production technique? If not, changeover cost and time loss must be included in the evaluation, or it must be shown that the investment will be satisfactorily recovered before the proposed handling system will require modification. Many conveyorized systems come to economic grief on this failure.

Vulnerability to Downtime

Since a handling system is a composite of mechanical and electrical machinery and controls, it must be recognized that it may break down at times. What happens then? How long will it take to get it back into service, and what will be done while repairs are being made? If this is serious, the handling system must be redesigned to provide for more reliability, for alternate handling techniques in event of breakdown, or for in-process storage that can feed subsequent operations while the system is being repaired. All of these can result in additional costs that must be charged against the handling system.

Maintenance

If it is planned to install additional handling mechanization, almost surely it will be necessary to take on more maintenance. This may mean the addition of new maintenance skills, or a provision for obtaining them when needed. It may be that extra pieces of handling equipment should be provided for use during servicing, downtime, or breakdowns. It may be necessary to plan for periodic overhauls by skilled technicians. It may be necessary to carry a large supply of repair parts, or a new or enlarged maintenance facility and staff may be required.

Auxiliary Equipment Costs

Frequently a new handling system carries with it requirements that involve hidden or unrecognized costs for auxiliary equipment or service. For example, adopting a lift-truck system means more than taking on the mobile equipment, its power supply, and its maintenance. If it is decided to use liquid petroleum (LP) gas fuel, for instance, special fuel storage tanks and additional safety requirements will be required. What will this cost? Also, the lift-truck system will usually require pallets. How many will be needed and what will they cost? Their price may run three to four times the cost of the trucks! And once the pallets have been procured, how much will it cost to repair them? Very few managers appreciate that a pallet will cost about a dollar per year to own and maintain.

The point of identifying these drawbacks is neither to discourage nor disparage the adoption of modern handling methods, but to emphasize that a careful balance of the total benefits and limitations is required before wise decisions can be reached.

THE IMPORTANCE OF MATERIAL HANDLING

The actual size of the handling "task" would be difficult to measure in any terms. However, some idea of the size of the segment of business and industry which *is* materials handling can be obtained from a number of "educated guesses" which have been made over a period of time—plus a reasonable evaluation of the overall handling task. If one were to review the total literature in the field, he might conclude by averaging all of the estimates made by all of the experts, that material handling accounts for about 25 to 30 percent of production costs. However, the sources of such figures are lost in their repetition, and it might be wiser to recognize that they could very likely range from a low 5 to 10 percent, to a very high 85 to 90 percent, depending on the nature of the activity of which the handling is a part. Being realistic about the handling segment of industry, one might refer back to the list of material handling activities on page 5, and contemplate the *real* portion of the total cycle which *could* be categorized as handling. Reflect for a moment upon that portion of the individual production operations that is *really* productive effort! Then, looking down the list, begin to visualize and add the estimated percentage of *each* step in the activity, from top to bottom, which might be classified as *handling*. It is the author's personal opinion that if such calculation were to be made in the typical plant, the cost of handling would turn out to be closer to 60 to 80 percent! Why this relationship has never been properly recognized by management is beyond comprehension in light of the tremendous potential existing for cost improvement. Other measures frequently heard draw conclusions such as the fact that one out of ten in the labor force is occupied in handling; or, in a specific plant, fifty tons of material may be handled for each ton produced; or that the annual cost of handling is in the neighborhood of twenty billion dollars. A real answer can only be determined by an individual company devoting enough effort and attention to handling to permit an equitable determination of the number of people or dollars involved in handling.

Suffice it to say at this point, that the handling activity in a typical plant accounts for a *much* higher percentage of the total activity than is commonly recognized. With this in mind, the material handling engineer should expend every effort to determine as nearly as possible the *real* cost of handling in his plant as a basis for explaining to management the profit improvement potential of a worthwhile effort toward uncovering improvement opportunities. It might even be said that the material handling analyst has "a gold mine under his nose"!

MATERIAL HANDLING AS A CAREER

As material handling has grown in importance and its potentials recognized, there has gradually developed a "profession" of material handling. This is due in part to the increasing numbers of people involved; the efforts of such organizations as the International Material Management Society and the National Council of Physical Distribution Management; the several trade publications in the handling field; increased efforts of the educational community; the urging of such trade associations as the Material Handling Institute and the Conveyor Equipment Manufacturer's Association; and the increased impetus resulting from the growing number of equipment manufacturers. There is also an Association of Material Handling and Plant Layout Consultants, which attempts to solidify professional practices in the field. And, of course there are the professional societies, such as the American Institute of Industrial Engineers and the American Society of Mechanical Engineers, both of which have divisions dealing with material handling.

With the material handling field growing as fast as it is (see Figure 1–3), a broad array of opportunities exists for careers in the field. In general, they can be classified as follows:

1. Material handling equipment users—industry, business, commerce and government
2. Material handling equipment manufacturers
   a. General management
   b. Marketing
   c. Equipment design
   d. Manufacturing
3. Material handling equipment distributors
4. Material handling consultants
5. Teaching—full or part-time

These opportunities are described in more detail in Figure 1–4.

THE DEVELOPMENT OF MATERIAL HANDLING

As pointed out earlier in the chapter, the history of material handling can be traced back almost to the beginning of man, where prehistoric man used logs for rollers, levers for lifting, and slings for carrying heavy loads. Probably the earliest records of material handling activities are to be found in the murals and reliefs of ancient Egypt, which document the movement of such heavy loads as stone blocks and statues. Although it is not known exactly how the Egyptians erected their obelisks and giant statues, several theories have been proposed, based on archeological studies, pieced together with the primitive representations of the murals and reliefs. Actually it was not until the Middle Ages were coming to an end, and subsequently during the Renaissance, that descriptions and drawings on handling heavy loads became more numerous. In fact, it is these records which permit historians to speculate on the handling methods used in prehistoric times.

In ancient Rome, again, contemporary art and writings describe projects in which handling was a major part. In the days of Julius Caesar, one Marcus Eitrubius Pollio, an engineer and architect, wrote a manual

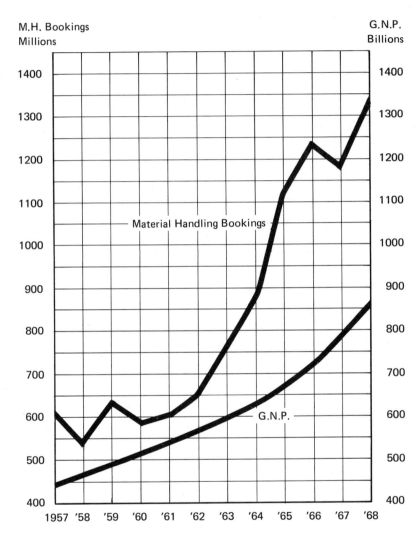

Fig. 1–3. Growth of the material handling field, as measured by equip-ment sales. (From *Careers With the Material Handling Equipment Manufacturers,* The Material Handling Institute, Inc., Sept. 1970.)

General Field	Typical Employers	Kinds of Positions	Duties
Industry at Large—Manufacturing	Mfgrs. of automobiles, appliances, locomotives, hardware, food, drugs, chemicals, basic metals, etc. No limit on kind of product. However, the materials handling opportunities are in the medium and larger sized companies.	Materials Handling Engineer	To study materials handling problems and devise better methods.
		Materials Handling Manager	Operate the materials handling activities of a plant. (Frequently embraces the m-h engineering job above.)
		Industrial Eng. Methods Eng., or Plant Layout Eng. (spending part time on m-h problems).	Improve existing m-h methods and develop m-h procedures for new activities.
Industry at Large—Distribution	Department Stores, Chain Stores of all types, (Oil, Drug, Grocery, etc.) Railroads, Airlines, Truck and Marine Carriers; Terminals for each type of carrier. Mail Order houses; industrial and public warehouses.	Warehouse Manager Engineering & Const. Manager Supt., Ass't Supt. Freight Supervisor Terminal Manager	Operate warehouses, shipping and receiving facilities, inter and intra building transportation. Also devise new methods for storage, handling and inventory control.
Materials Handling Equipment Manufacturers	1. Mfgs. of Industrial Vehicles, such as fork trucks, mobile cranes, hand trucks, tractors, etc. 2. Conveyors—roller, belt, chain, pneumatic and some 75 other types. 3. Overhead Equipment—Monorails, cranes, hoists, etc. 4. Related Equipment—containers, batteries, dockboards, elevators, weighing devices, and hundreds of others.	Design: Design Engineer, Mechanical, Hydraulic or Electrical Design Eng. Production: Positions typical of production operations for any machinery. Sales & Application Engineering: Salesman, Sales Manager, Application Engineer, Vice President of Sales.	Design standard and special materials handling devices and systems. Same as with any machinery manufacturer. Sell equipment and systems. Help to plan and develop adaptations of equipment to solve special customer problems.
Consulting	1. General Industrial Consultants 2. Management Consultants 3. Materials Handling Consultants	Materials Handling and Plant Layout Specialist	Make studies, determine costs, develop new handling procedures, and sell these programs to the clients' management. Frequently includes reorganization, retraining, and reassignment of personnel, wage studies, job evaluation, etc.
Government	Military Departments, Army, Navy, Air Force, Marines.	M-H research engineers with Bureau of Supplies and Accounts, Bureau of Ordnance, Transportation Corps, Quartermaster Corps, etc.	Design and develop handling and packaging procedures and standards for military affairs.
	Department of Commerce	Commodity Standardization	Work with industry to coordinate marketing and storage practices.
	Department of Agriculture	Marketing research	Develop better procedures for backward agricultural marketing activities.
	Post Office Department	Methods and operations research	Develop better mail handling and sorting procedures.
Teaching	Universities	Faculty: Full or part time	Teaching materials handling, packaging, work simplification, etc. Directing or conducting m-h research.
Manufacturer's Sales Representative	Self or other individual	Sales	Selling the products of several (as high as 10-20) manufacturers of m-h equipment.

Fig. 1–4. Opportunities for material handling employment. (From *Modern Material*

Typical Projects Done Recently	Comments
...mpare methods and select best procedure for stockpiling a chemical. 2. Analyze ...ge of the plant's finished goods and design a new warehouse. 3. Review and refine ...t layout to simplify the handling. Assist in development of a complete automa-...ystem for an automobile plant. 4. Develop new shipping method. ...y to day operation of intraplant transportation systems. 2. Development of an ...tive system for fork truck operators. 3. Development of a completely new ...o move billets and rolled products, to and from a steel mill rolling line. ...prove the method of removing bagged material from the bag packing machine. ...velop and run a work simplification program that saved $250,000 the first	Extremely broad work, taking one into every phase of a plant's activity. Excellent background for major operating and supervisory positions. Call for lots of imagination, energy, and tact. Can lead to important improvements in processing, purchasing and distribution.
...sign a standard warehouse for a national chain and develop standard storage ...andling methods; select standard handling equipment for 140 warehouses. ...velop a new layout for sorting, segregating, and pricing department store ...s. 3. Develop a new procedure for shipping and receiving steel in sheets, ...tural shapes, and bar stock. 4. Operate a 3500 man force of material ...ing personnel for a large department store	Over half the cost of distribution is in physical handling. Work in this field has tremendous possibilities.
...sign and sell a method for producing, virtually automatically, foam rubber ...resses. ...nveyorize the manufacture of military tanks. ...sign and install the handling system for a large new appliance plant. ...evelop an industrial truck that can automatically pick up, carry, stack and un-...rolls of sensitized paper in the dark. ...evelop and sell a fork truck-container system for feeding small parts to a pro-...on line. ...evelop a clamp truck for handling cotton bales. ...sign and sell a monorail system for automatically dispatching textile rolls from ...operation to any of 260 machines, and for automatically feeding these rolls ...any empty unit. ...sign a belt conveyor system capable of hauling ore and coal 108 miles across ...s.	Many excellent opportunities lie in work with the equipment manufacturers. This work offers almost unmatched variety since one deals with every kind of industrial activity. The materials handling industry is one of the most rapidly growing in America, and thus provides a future with lots of growth potential. The line between selling, developing, and installing a new handling concept is often vague; so the individual must be versatile.
...udy, evaluate and recommend the handling procedures best suited to various ...me of shipping dock activity for an association of motor truck terminal opera- ...prove the handling system in an old, multistory plant making machine tools. ...esign and install a handling and storage procedure for a grocery warehouse.	There is a serious need for good materials handling consultants.
...esign a unit load system for hundreds of military commodities. ...evelop and compare mechanical methods of handling supplies on beach heads and ...ombat zones by helicopter, fork truck, aerial cableways, portable conveyors, ...other devices. ...to develop standard container sizes for thousands of grocery and drug products ...der to simplify handling throughout the country. ...pare and evaluate methods of handling fruit from tree to warehouse; of hand-...cotton bales, etc. ...elop a system for handling mail sacks and packages in containers.	Excellent government openings for materials handling engineers are appearing. Furthermore, if mechanized handling is ever applied wholeheartedly to military operations, it will be a tremendous contribution to our national strength. This could become one of the most fascinating and important contributions in all materials handling work.
...evelop a materials handling course and a textbook. ...irect Research on m-h equipment design. ...un a materials handling seminar for local industry.	Teachers are needed badly, particularly for "practical" night school teaching of men in industry.
...gn and sell materials handling systems, frequently combining different ...pment to achieve a special job for a plant.	Excellent chance to build your business.

...es R. Bright, "Why Not Build Your Future in Materials Handling?"
...dling, Sept. 1953.)

titled "De Architectura." This was written about 30 B.C., although the author stated that his information was taken from Greek records of several hundred years previous. Although the original drawings were lost, the written descriptions provided enough detail so that they could be reconstructed in such a way as to describe the handling appliances of that time.

In the thirteenth and fourteenth centuries, tread mills were in use as a source of power for cranes in building construction as well as at dockside. And in 1436 it was recorded that the Venetians established a "progressive assembly line" for building warships.

Other early writers, such as San Gallo (1445–1516), left records showing how columns were erected and loads lifted in his time. And yet another early "engineer," by the name of Agricola, in his work entitled "De Re Metallica" describes in great detail the handling devices of the mid-sixteenth century, including wheel barrows, pulleys, tracked vehicles used in mining operations, jib cranes, bucket elevators, suction pumps, water wheels, etc.

It was during this period of the 1500's that embryo factory systems were developed for the making of armaments, armor, and cloth. In the 1600's and 1700's the factory movement blossomed in England with the development of iron foundries that produced as much as 100 tons a week, and Arkwright's cotton mill which turned cotton into thread by machinery.

Oliver Evans, in the 1780's, installed a system of belt conveyors for continuously handling grain and flour in his mill located near Philadelphia. This achievement was documented in his book entitled *The Young Mill Wright and Miller's Guide,* published in 1795. Thereafter the development of manufacturing processes and the related handling activities was rather rapid in many directions, encompassing the well-documented work of Eli Whitney, Eli Terry, and many others. In the 1880's, Frederick W. Taylor, "The Father of Scientific Management," performed what is probably his most widely known experiment with various sizes of shovels used for handling materials in a steel mill. And it will be remembered that Frank B. Gilbreth performed many of his experiments in the early 1900's on the movements of operators laying bricks and performing other construction tasks.

Probably Henry Ford gave material handling one of its greatest advances when he installed a moving belt conveyor as a work bench in 1914, and also began to move automobile chassis mechanically along a final assembly line.

A real interest in mechanical handling never really appeared until World War II, when a shortage of manpower forced industry to look elsewhere for handling the tremendous loads demanded by the war effort. The lift truck, which had been developed in the early 1900's, and was subsequently fitted with forks, became the work horse of the material handling effort. From that point on, the material handling industry began to move, with new items of equipment, new companies, and new demands by industry all adding to the explosive growth. What the observer sees today in the modern mechanized manufacturing plant is the result of a continual refinement of concepts, equipment, and systems into the smooth-working, highly integrated production complex.

THE ORGANIZATION DILEMMA

It might be concluded from the preceding portion of this chapter that material handling has had anything but an orderly growth or acceptance by industry as a whole. How is it then that material handling could have been so long neglected? Very likely a major reason lies in the many physical locations in the materials flow cycle at which handling activities occur, as well as the many organizational components in which various handling-related activities are located. It will be observed that these handling activities are performed at *many locations,* under *different authorities,* having *different degrees* of *engineering skill* and *economic support.* Also, handling is usually *obscured* by the prime function (such as production, assembly, inspection, distribution, etc.). Thus, handling procedures develop around custom, chance, or expediency. They are very likely to be formed without much thought as to their influence on adjacent operations, and little if any consideration of their influence on operations that lie beyond those activities that are the responsibility of any one individual. To further compound the problems, the handling activity is influenced concurrently by policies and decisions of different departments, such as product design, traffic, purchasing, production, and sales. As a result we see modern production operations sandwiched between handling methods of unknown vintage or questionable efficiency.

As suggested above, this picture has been changing rapidly since World War II. Increasing labor costs, the integration required in highly automatic production systems, and the economic necessity of keeping ever larger and faster production equipment and transportation vehicles operating near capacity have highlighted the need for improved material handling. In the production, warehousing and distribution fields, the computer is having a profound effect because the tremendous speed and other advantages of electronic data processing cannot be fully realized with antiquated handling procedures. The automation of information handling sharply highlights weaknesses in material handling.

Another factor encouraging material handling progress is that labor savings in production-type work frequently have reached a point of diminishing returns, leaving material handling standing revealed as the promising and fruitful opportunity for improvement. Thus, since the late 1940's, almost all medium- and large-sized firms, and many thousands of small firms, have been giving material handling increased management and engineering attention.

In addition, there are probably some other logical reasons for the "neglect" of material handling in the past. For instance, the simple lack of awareness on the part of management of the size, scope, and significance of material handling certainly has prevented the material handling engineer from making his full contribution. On the other hand there has been somewhat less than a concerted effort to improve the marginal professional status of material handling. As will be pointed out later in this chapter, worthwhile efforts are now being made in this direction. Also contributing to the dilemma has been the scarcity of printed material on the basic aspects of material handling, leaving the "handling fraternity" without valid sources of reference for tackling the myriad of problems facing it, not the least of which has been its own inability to adequately define the field of material handling.

To add to the general confusion, recent developments in the field of physical distribution and materials management have further clouded the situation. Probably because of the lack of progressive thinking on the part of material handling personnel, the physical distribution "people" have stepped in and "adopted" many of the activity areas which are logical segments of a total material handling function. At the same time, material-management proponents have added to their portfolio of purchasing, production control and inventory control all the other material-related activities that can be imagined. Certainly there is room at present for a concerted effort by top people in all three fields to cooperate more closely with each other, and to more clearly define the individual roles of each as well as their interrelationships. Some of the factors and problems underlying this dilemma are further emphasized in the following section.

Relationships to Other Organizational Functions [3]

In carrying out their duties, material handling personnel work in close association with many organizational functions and activities, such as the following:

Purchasing. Purchasing personnel can help reduce handling costs, by checking with material handling before ordering a sizable quantity of

---

[3] Portions of this section are adapted from G. B. Carson, H. A. Bolz, and H. H. Young, *Production Handbook*, The Ronald Press Co., 3d edition, 1972.

material in order to study the method or form in which the materials will be received. Also many savings can be realized if manufacturers will cooperate with suppliers, carriers, and customers in designing receiving and shipping methods to facilitate handling.

The proper exchange of information between purchasing, handling, and the carriers will open up many opportunities for handling cost reduction. Serious consideration should be given to selecting the mode of transportation as well as the vehicle and load configurations to facilitate loading and unloading. Careful attention should be also paid to the design of docks and related facilities, since they will greatly affect the efficiency of the handling activities involved in both receiving and shipping operations. Both the unloading and loading methods will be affected by arrangements which have been made (or not made!) in cooperation with purchasing and transportation personnel.

Inventory and Materials Control. These functions, which have been the responsibility of a coalition of production control and purchasing activities, have recently given a great deal of attention to the economics of inventory management, emphasizing the costs and financing of handling and storing materials and supplies. Item quantities and characteristics will of course dictate the nature of the storage method. In many cases however, purchase price considerations appear to have been a major factor in determining quantity, often overlooking the effect of item quantity on handling costs. Also, the effect of the scheduling activity in determining stock withdrawal quantities directly affects order characteristics.

The control of materials in storage is traditionally governed by accounting requirements, as this relationship is critical in raw materials inventory, with the result that accounting procedures frequently influence handling practices in storage operations. In such cases, it should be recalled that materials cost more to handle than do paper work, and therefore adjusting the accounting procedure to permit the most economical material handling activity may be worth considering.

If the raw materials and supply problem is studied in its entirety, with full consideration of quantity-price relationships, in-bound shipping charges, dollars tied up in inventory, quantity-storage relationships, and production-schedule-withdrawal relationships, it may be found that the controlling cost factor is the material handling expense, which may actually have been given the least amount of attention.

It is precisely the type of situation implied here that has fostered the development of the *material-management* concept, in an attempt to combine a number of previously independent, but intimately related, functions within the industrial organization.

Production Control. The material handling function must know production and shipping schedules far enough in advance to schedule handling labor and equipment in order to provide the service required. If changes in plans represent greater than normal fluctuations, changes in handling methods and facilities may be necessary or desirable. Also, planned changes in normal inventories of materials should be communicated to the material handling function to permit the planning of changes in storage facilities or methods.

The requirements of production control can frequently result in the addition of unnecessary handling operations to the manufacturing sequences, as well as to in-process storage. Whenever two operations producing parts at unequal speeds follow each other, a *balancing operation* must take place. In some cases this can be accomplished by multiple machines on one or the other of the operations, but more often it is necessary to create a production bank or float to level off the inequalities in production rates. Analysis of scheduling often indicates the cause of these apparently unnecessary handling operations.

Some of the *specific* ways in which material handling can cooperate with production control are:

1. Provide direct, mechanical paths for materials movement.
2. Move materials in lots, batches, or containers of a predetermined quantity or size.
3. Store or pack materials in containers holding a specific number of pieces.
4. Use containers (wire mesh) through which contents can be identified and/or counted.
5. Utilize two-way radio or TV to expedite movement and control of materials.
6. Make optimum use of mechanical handling in order picking, accumulation, loading.
7. Pace production with mechanical handling equipment.
8. Build production, inventory and accounting control features *into* the material handling system.
9. Move materials on a schedule and in lots to match production and to avoid rush delivery, partial loads, or duplicate moves.
10. Use move tags or orders as authority for all moves: avoid verbal orders.
11. Coordinate handling schedule with purchasing and manufacturing.

Industrial Engineering. As mentioned earlier in this chapter, the material handling function is frequently classified as a division of the broad field of industrial engineering. Also under the jurisdiction of industrial engineering are other organizational functions with which material handling is intimately related in carrying out its day-to-day activities. Some of them are briefly mentioned below.

Process engineering is involved with the design of the manufacturing process. This in turn establishes the number of machines, the operation sequence, the degree of mechanization and automation, and can seriously affect line balancing and in-process handling and storage operations. It is therefore advisable for the material handling engineer to work very closely with the process-engineering personnel.

Methods engineering is concerned with the design of individual workplaces, the operator methods used in performing the operations, and the interrelationships between the individual workplaces and the overall materials flow. The methods engineer can facilitate handling operations by paying careful attention to the principles of workplace layout, as listed in Chapter 12.

Work standards have been applied to production operations for many, many years, although their use in measuring and evaluating material handling methods is less common. Whenever practicable the material handling engineer should cooperate with work standards personnel in an attempt to establish work standards for material handling operations, for use as the basis for incentive plans for material handlers.

Plant layout is generally responsible for the development of the overall flow pattern and the physical arrangement of the facilities in the plant, with the layout frequently built around the flow pattern. It is therefore extremely important that layout personnel work closely with material handling.

Plant layout is concerned with the analysis, planning, and design of the physical facilities utilized in the production of goods or services. Material handling deals with that phase of the operations which involves the movement of materials used in carrying on the activities of the enterprise. No two aspects of industrial activity are more closely related. Actually, material handling is a major part of nearly all plant layout work. This close relationship is emphasized in the following definition of plant layout:

Plant layout may be defined as *planning* and integrating the paths of the component parts of a product to obtain *the most effective and economical* interrelationships between men, equipment, and the *movement of materials from receiving, through fabrication, to the shipment of the finished product.*[4]

It will be noted that the italicized words represent a definition of material handling. However, merely establishing the importance of this close interrelationship is not enough. The task remains to insure that

[4]J. M. Apple, *Plant Layout and Materials Handling*, 2nd ed., The Ronald Press Co., 1963, p. 3.

when physical facilities are designed, the necessary material handling plans are integrated into the project. In order to do this, it is necessary to understand something of the process involved in designing physical facilities, as well as the factors involved in handling the materials, throughout the *entire* cycle of activities.

From the above, it should be recognized that because of the close interrelationship between plant layout and material handling, the scopes of the two activities are just as closely interwoven. This close interrelationship can be observed by reviewing the activities with which the material handling engineer deals, as outlined on page 5. It will be concluded that it is difficult to distinguish the specific responsibility for any individual function. In general, the plant layout engineer would be *primarily* concerned with the activities related to the production facilities themselves, while material handling is more closely concerned with the need for interrelating and tying together the individual operations into an integrated system.

Objectives of Plant Layout and Material Handling

In much the same way that the scope of both plant layout and material handling are closely interrelated, so also are their objectives. Indicated below are some of the objectives of plant layout. Under each are listed some objectives of material handling associated with each plant layout objective.

1. Facilitate the manufacturing process
   a. Efficient flow of materials
   b. Minimum of production bottlenecks
   c. Quicker delivery to customers
2. Minimize material handling
   d. Larger unit loads
   e. Less damaged materials
   f. Better control of materials
   g. Automatic or mechanized handling
3. Maintain flexibility of arrangement and operation
   h. Flexibility of handling methods and equipment
   i. Coordinated material handling system
   j. Material handling planned for expansion
4. Maintain high turnover of work-in-process
   k. Shorter production time cycle
   l. Constant rate of production
5. Hold down investment in equipment
   m. Less idle time per machine
   n. Reduced handling between operations
6. Make economical use of floor area
   o. Better space utilization

    p. Higher production per square foot per employee
    q. Use of material handling equipment not requiring fixed floor space.
7. Promote efficient utilization of manpower
    r. Minimize manual handling
    s. Make effective use of containers
8. Provide for employee convenience, safety and comfort
    t. Safer working conditions
    u. Less fatigue
    v. Improved personal comfort
    w. Upgrading of employees

Again, as with the scope of material handling and plant layout, it can be seen that the objectives are so closely intertwined as to form an acceptable single list, i.e., with the objectives of plant layout, implemented in many cases, by carrying out the objectives of material handling. Then, achieving the plant layout objectives nearly always implies that a good job has been done in achieving the objectives of material handling.

Interrelationships Between Material Handling and Plant Layout

As has been indicated, the effective arrangement of physical facilities includes very close cooperation with the material handling personnel. The integration of the material handling phase requires consideration of the entire layout-planning procedure. It is presented in Figure 1–5, in abbreviated outline form. In the outline, each item represents a step in the overall planning process, or a factor of extreme importance to the planning process. The columns at the right represent the 10 major factors in analyzing a material handling problem. The check marks represent those factors in the material handling phase of the problem that are most likely to be involved in accomplishing the indicated plant layout planning steps. This visual representation emphasizes the close relationships existing between the layout and handling planning activities. It should be evident that the interaction of the two fields permeates the entire planning process.

The foregoing discussion of the many interrelationships between material handling and plant layout has emphasized the extreme importance of these interrelationships. It has also pointed out the almost complete dependence of an effective plant layout on an effective material handling system, and to a great extent, vice versa. The successful solution of a complex layout and handling problem can be attained only if proper and adequate attention is given to both phases of the problem. Their successful interrelationships must be approached through the careful planning of every aspect of the entire problem.

Steps in Plant Layout Planning	Factors in Material Handling Planning									
	Material			Move				Method		
	1. Characteristics	2. Quantity	3. Scope	4. Source & destination	5. Route	6. Frequency	7. Speed or Rate	8. Unit or load	9. Equipment	10. Manpower
1. Procure and analyze *basic data*										
A. Production quantities		✓				✓	✓	✓	✓	✓
B. Drawings, specifications, etc.	✓									
C. Production processes				✓	✓	✓				
D. Production standards						✓	✓			
E. Number of machines, etc.						✓			✓	
F. Manpower requirements									✓	✓
2. Determine *material flow* pattern										
A. Assembly, Operating, Process and other charts					✓	✓				
B. Building specifications				✓	✓	✓		✓	✓	
C. General flow pattern types				✓	✓	✓			✓	
D. Activity relationships				✓	✓	✓				
E. Flow pattern				✓	✓	✓			✓	
3. Establish *space requirements*										
A. Storage space	✓	✓		✓				✓	✓	✓
B. Service activity space									✓	✓
C. Production space				✓	✓					
4. Allocate activity *areas*										
A. Flexibility and expansion		✓	✓		✓				✓	
B. Area Allocation Diagram			✓	✓	✓					
5. Design *material-handling* system										
A. General material handling methods	✓	✓	✓	✓	✓	✓	✓	✓	✓	✓
B. Equipment types	✓	✓	✓	✓	✓	✓	✓	✓	✓	✓
C. Specific handling methods	✓	✓	✓	✓	✓	✓	✓	✓	✓	✓
6. Plan individual *work area methods*										
A. General materials flow					✓	✓	✓		✓	
B. Flow through work areas					✓	✓	✓			✓
C. Work area layouts						✓	✓		✓	✓
7. *Coordinate* planning activities										
A. Layout Planning Chart					✓	✓				
B. Flow Diagrams—major activity areas				✓	✓	✓				
C. Relations to master plan				✓	✓	✓			✓	
D. Service area relationships				✓	✓	✓			✓	✓
8. *Construct* master *layout*										
A. Relationship to land available				✓	✓	✓			✓	✓
B. Column spacing and aisle locations	✓				✓	✓			✓	
C. Final layout					✓	✓			✓	
D. Plot Plan				✓	✓	✓			✓	✓
9. *Evaluate* layout										
10. *Install* layout										

Fig. 1–5. Interrelationships between plant layout planning procedure and factors for analyzing a material handling problem.

Production. Since material handling exists primarily to *serve* the production function, the utmost in cooperation is necessary between the two, in order to produce the product in the most efficient way and at the lowest cost. One of the goals of the material handling function is to do just that, and all of the activities described in this book are directed towards this goal!

Plant Engineering. This activity is concerned with the design and maintenance of the physical facilities necessary to carry out production and the related functions. Therefore, their advice should be sought on all aspects of material handling that interface with the plant building, as well as the maintenance of material handling equipment.

Quality Control. The quality function interest in material handling activities is primarily from the point of view of protecting manufactured parts and products from unnecessary damage. Since this is also one of the objectives of the material handling activity, handling personnel should make every effort to plan for the protection of materials, parts, and products from unnecessary damage due to handling or related activities.

Sales and Distribution. The responsibility for getting finished goods into the hands of the customers offers many opportunities for the improvement of related handling activities. This will be discussed further in Chapter 18.

In establishing packaging and shipping requirements, it should be planned to unitize the product for mechanically loading carriers when practicable. The point at which the unitizing operation occurs in the production sequence can have a major effect upon the handling methods both before and after that point. In recent years the trend toward customer dictation of delivery schedules and loading methods has increased and, in many industries, manufacturers deliver unitized or specially packed products to customers on a precisely predetermined schedule. Automotive components, for example, are shipped in large, reusable compartmented cartons mounted on pallets or skids, to permit fork truck handling, while "drop" sides permit easy access of contents on the production line.

Safety. This activity is of special importance in the material handling function, since a large number of accidents occur in handling operations. In fact, two-thirds of the general causes of accidents are directly related to material handling. Therefore the material handling engineer should work closely with the safety engineer to design safety into both handling methods and equipment.

Employee Relations. Of particular interest to employee relations personnel are those menial, routine, monotonous, back-breaking jobs commonly found in material handling. Their interests are centered on the problems of minimizing such jobs—and when this type of work *is* found necessary, to make sure it is planned so that it can be carried out safely.

It can be seen that material handling is closely interrelated with many other organizational functions in carrying out its normal everyday activities. Many of the interrelationships pointed out above will have a serious effect on material handling, since they will very likely dictate some of its functions and activities. Also, the implied interrelationships will have an effect on the handling equipment selected, the amount of handling equipment required and the handling manpower complement.

RELATIONSHIPS BETWEEN MATERIAL HANDLING AND THE PHYSICAL FACILITIES

There are many interrelationships between the material handling activities of an enterprise and its physical facilities, such as the location, transportation facilities, plant layout, and several aspects of the building itself. In many cases the *location* of the facility will have a bearing on the material handling operations. For example, heavy industries such as steel, aluminum, glass, heavy chemicals, etc., would select locations to give them favorable relationships to their sources of raw materials.

Transportation considerations relate themselves directly to material handling activities in the plant through the nature of unloading or shipping operations, and plants which use only one type of transportation have far simpler handling problems than those using several types of carriers. Also, the increasing recognition of the high cost of handling in the distribution phase of industry has led to a much more careful selection of distribution facility locations.

Since the plant layout itself has a considerable effect on the cost of handling, the facility planning should involve the development of an efficient layout around a preplanned flow pattern. The flow of materials then becomes the basis for the layout and the processes are performed in their respective locations *along* the preplanned flow lines. Actually, the handling of materials is such an important operation that the handling system should be *designed* before the building is planned, in order that the two can be fully integrated, and it might be said that the building should be "wrapped around" the layout.

In designing the building itself, column spacing and aisle width may be a limiting factor in selecting the type of handling equipment, or determining the sizes of loads that can be moved efficiently. The design of floors in terms of capacity and surface finish should take into careful consideration the types of handling equipment which might be used. And when considering the possibility of overhead conveying equipment, the required support must be designed into roof trusses and columns.

Also, the anticipation of future conversion from manufacturing to warehousing, or vice versa, may dictate a design compromise that will favor the more important of the functions to be eventually served.

Other important building details, such as doors, loading docks, elevators, fire walls, and such "permanent" installations as toilets, offices, etc., should be given careful consideration in light of their possible effect on the handling activities.

Although single story plants have been in vogue for a considerable period of time, recent developments in vertical handling may make it considerably easier to move materials automatically and at less cost between floors, than by elevators, or even on a single floor, over a greater distance.

THE NEED FOR A NEW APPROACH TO MATERIAL HANDLING

It might be said that past approaches to material handling problems have frequently led to alleviating the problems rather than solving them. This is very possibly due to the rather narrow viewpoint from which the problem was analyzed, as well as the fact that the background of the analyst was likely to be equipment (hardware) oriented. This combination, of course, frequently resulted in a serious shortage of adequate analyses, although it did "alleviate" many handling situations—especially where expediency was the key word. However, with the ever-pressing need for increasing profits and the inherent savings potential which exists in every enterprise, there is certainly no excuse for such haphazard approaches to material handling problems. This is especially true in view of the wide variety of handling equipment available, its rapidly increasing capabilities, its complexity, and the new generation of analytical techniques available for studying handling problems. Nevertheless, it must be admitted that the analyst of the past has been able to get away with this superficial approach because there was usually so much room for improvement in a typical handling situation that *any* suggestion was likely to be helpful. That is, the answer proposed may not have been the best, but it was better than the existing method. Although this is a regrettable situation to say the least, it is *still* practiced in many companies, due to the lack of awareness of the size, scope, and significance of the material handling function. The next chapter will present a basic approach to material handling problems in an attempt to put an end to the slipshod practices of the past, which unfortunately are still being followed in too many instances.

2

A Basis for Material Handling Analysis

If it is true that material handling problems have been treated so naively in the past, it is obvious that there is a need to make a fresh start and follow a new approach, if the saving opportunities embedded in handling and related activities are to be uncovered. With the continual squeeze on profits caused by rising costs and increasing competition in nearly every business and industry, management is being forced to look everywhere and at every cost item for improvement opportunities. And, material handling has been shown to have tremendous savings potential. However, these savings cannot be realized if the haphazard approaches of the past are permitted to continue. In addition, the rapidly increasing variety of new handling devices on the market is a continual challenge to the material handling engineer in his search for better methods. Then too, there are available a multitude of new analytical techniques for examining handling problems. These are explored in Chapter 10.

Another reason for increasing the emphasis on the material handling function is to try to clear up the current confusion over the definition, scope, and importance of material handling that exists in many companies. This confusion can be overcome by an alert handling staff which will:

1. Better define the handling function in the plant.
2. Obtain more accurate handling costs.

3. Make a serious attempt to spell out the organizational responsibilities and authorities of the handling function.
4. Clarify the relationships between handling and other functions with which it must deal in carrying out its everyday activities.

Other factors which will give impetus to a new approach to material handling are the recent recognition of the function and its importance by management, the cost-price squeeze which urgently calls for some kind of action, and the increased efforts in an attempt to identify measures of material handling performance.

SCOPE OF THE MATERIAL HANDLING ACTIVITY

Actually there is no greater agreement on the scope of material handling than there is on its definition, since the extent of the material handling activity in a specific enterprise depends on a number of characteristics of the enterprise, such as:

1. Type of company—manufacturing, extractive, distribution, commercial, etc.
2. Product manufactured—size, materials used, precision required, perishability, etc.
3. Size of company—normally the larger the company, the more extensive the material handling activity.
4. Value of the product—expensive products, precision work, etc., would normally call for more careful handling operations.
5. Personalities of individuals involved—inevitably the personalities of the individuals who are concerned with the handling activity will have a great bearing on its functions and importance and on the attention given to it by management.
6. Value of activity being performed—which might be measured in terms of the labor content as compared with the contribution of other economic factors to the value of the product of activity.
7. Organizational structure of the enterprise—the organizational structure of the particular company will also affect the function and extent of the material handling activity.
8. Relative importance of material handling to the company—a consideration of and decisions on the above factors will normally determine the importance of material handling in the particular enterprise, which in turn will determine the emphasis to be placed on the function as well as its place in the organization.

One of the few general conclusions that can be drawn about material handling is that its scope is rapidly expanding and its importance is becoming more widely recognized. In a somewhat chronological sense, material handling activity in a company will frequently fit one of the three following stages of development: (1) conventional, (2) contemporary, or (3) progressive.

In the "conventional" interpretation of material handling, primary emphasis is on the movement of materials from one location to another, more likely than not, within the confines of the individual plant. The concern of the material handling engineer is merely to find the best way of moving something from point A to point B. His interest is usually in individual, isolated, independent material handling problem situations.

Usually, the analyst is working "with blinders on" and is merely "putting out fires" in the material handling area. More likely than not he finds himself busy jumping from fire to fire in order to meet the immediate needs of those who call for his services—with most of his attention given to those who shout the loudest. Very little attention is given to, nor is there much interest in, the possible interrelationships between the individual handling situations with which he is keeping himself busy. It can easily be concluded that the material handling function operating in this fashion is neither very efficient nor progressive.

From the "contemporary" point of view, there is a plant-wide concern, centering attention on the overall flow of materials in the enterprise. The engineer finds himself concerned with the interrelationships between *all* handling problems and with the possibility of establishing a general overall material handling plan. His effort is directed toward tying each problem and its solution into all others, in order to obtain a *totally integrated material handling plan*. This point of view is becoming more common in the typical manufacturing enterprise today . . . but, not nearly often enough!

The "progressive" (or *systems*) approach to material handling requires the analyst to visualize the material handling problems, the physical distribution activities and all closely related functions as *one*, all-encompassing *system*. This point of view involves a much broader consideration of *all* of the handling activities which would be involved in:

1. The movement of all materials *from all sources of supply*
2. All handling activities *within and around the plant* itself
3. The handling activities involved in the *distribution of finished goods* to all customers of the enterprise

This broader, more inclusive point of view has the theoretical goal of conceptualizing a total solution to the overall handling problem in terms of a "theoretical ideal system." It is then the task of the material handling engineer to design as much of the total system as is currently practicable, implement those portions which it is feasible to install, and continue to work on other portions of the "theoretical" system. Over a period of time many of them might be implemented, as means become available and their installation becomes practical and/or economical. While the "systems" approach may appear rather theoretical, it *does* serve as a worthwhile goal for the design of an overall material handling plan. The extent to which the total systems concept is carried out depends upon the importance of the material handling activity to the individual enterprise as well as the practical economics of extending the overall handling system "backwards" to the many customer locations. Obviously, the total implementation of such an approach is much simpler when the sources of supply, the manufacturing processes, and the customers are limited in number, complexity, and intervening distances. Nevertheless, the aggressive material handling engineer should do no less than work closely with his company's major suppliers toward the improvement of any material handling activities in which they might have a common interest. These would include such things as the method of packaging the raw materials at his vendor's plant, the method of loading and/or shipping these materials to his own plant, and the effect that these two would have on the unloading, storage and/or use of the materials at his plant.

The same philosophy applied to the finished goods portions of the handling-distribution cycle involves a similar degree of cooperation between the manufacturing plant and at least its *major* customers. Here again, investigation should include a serious consideration of the packaging, packing, loading, and shipping techniques and methods. In each case detailed attention would be given to facilitating the handling and/or storage activities of the customers who will receive the materials.

THE MATERIAL-FLOW CYCLE

These interrelationships between the various activity centers in the total material-flow cycle are shown diagramatically in Figure 2–1. From the systems point of view, the concern of the material handling analyst would be for the *total* materials flow as shown in the diagram, from *all* sources of *all* material and to *all* destinations. In many cases, the flow of materials would also include those activities necessary for efficiently handling scrap, waste, empty containers, returned goods, etc., back through the appropriate channels to the points at which they might re-enter the system. James A. Brown has suggested that

. . . all of industry is a mass flow of materials from their original sources—mine, forest, field and water—to the hands of the ultimate consumer. In the course of this flow, materials are picked up, moved, put down and stored—in many cases, *hundreds* of times—as they move through the total cycle on the way to becoming finished products. Some of the handling activities are easily recognized, while others are hidden within the production operations and/or related auxiliary activities. Nevertheless, they all create costs whose total represents a large portion of the production cost. In the overall process of

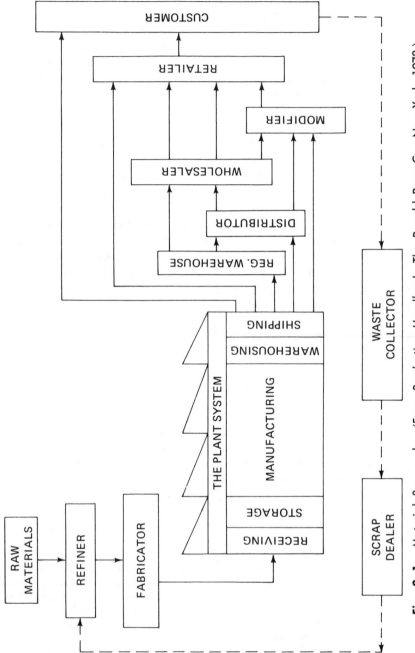

Fig. 2-1. Material flow cycle. (From *Production Handbook*, The Ronald Press Co., New York, 1972.)

becoming finished goods, the materials move through several phases of the total cycle: first, raw materials; second, work-in-process; and third, as finished goods in the distribution aspects of the cycle.[1]

As Figure 2–1 depicts, this should actually be considered one, overall, integrated material-flow cycle, with "subcycles" within each separate segment, such as: raw materials extraction, basic material processes, fabrication of major components, manufacture and assembly of complex products and the several stages of the physical distribution process.

Although the individual firm most often thinks primarily of its "own" material-flow cycle, it should not fail to recognize that it is actually only a segment of the whole. And—in analyzing and planning for the implementation of their own flow problems—careful thought should be given to the relationships between the several segments. In a particular enterprise, the scope of material handling should normally be based on the company's material-flow cycle, in somewhat the same fashion as depicted in Figure 2–1. The minimum practicable consideration in implementing the material-flow cycle would cover no less than the activities between receiving and shipping, including of course, all of the productive activities. However, under normal circumstances it should not be at all difficult to extend the company's material-flow cycle back to the vendor packaging and/or packing activity, and forward through the receipt of the goods by the customers.

As implied above, the only logical overall approach to the material handling problem is by way of the "systems" concept. The task is entirely too complex for a piecemeal approach! The complicated handling tasks of today not only deserve, but demand examination in a more organized fashion than has been practiced in the past. All of this begins, of course, with a proper recognition by management of the significant role played by material handling and the savings potential of a serious effort directed in its behalf. This involves no less than the development of a carefully planned program of analysis, leading to a proper problem solution and implemented with a carefully selected combination of equipment, techniques, and procedures to achieve optimum results. A detailed description of the systems concept in material handling is contained in Chapter 9.

THE MATERIAL HANDLING EQUATION

As the material handling system is analyzed, and probably subdivided into smaller, more "manageable" problem situations, the question is, "How shall the improvement of the specific material handling situation

[1] Adapted from James A. Brown and B. D. Beamish, "Improving Material Movement Through the Manufacturing Cycle," in a paper before the Economic Council of Canada, Toronto, May 1965.

be approached?" The common error is to assume that some kind of equipment will "solve" the problem. In fact, there is an almost magnetic attraction to beginning with a study of the available types of equipment in an attempt to find one that will alleviate the situation. This of course is usually a mistake. It is beginning at the wrong end of the material handling problem, for it is starting with an answer, rather than with the problem!

Rather obviously, the first question to be asked in any problem-solving approach is "Why?" Why do this at all? There are many startling examples of handling activities being performed for reasons that no longer make sense, and sometimes reasons that never made sense! For instance, in a chemical plant, a foreman studying a work simplification project decided to improve the method of moving ice into his building and to several reactor kettles. Two men and a pick-up truck were moving almost 70 barrels of crushed ice a day about ¾ of a mile. Drums were then man-handled to the second floor and dumped into the reactor vessel cooling chambers. After the foreman had designed an improved handling system, he naively raised the question as to "why" the ice was required. This was quickly traced back to specifications set by the process engineers, and then back to a pilot plant procedure. The pilot plant people followed it back to the laboratory. The laboratory chemists were appalled. "You don't need ice!" they said, "We just took a few ice cubes out of our laboratory refrigerator to cool the beakers while we worked on the reaction. All you need to do is cool the kettles to 50° F." And—this could be done simply by circulating the plant water supply through the cooling vessel. Yet this activity had been carried on for years before somebody asked "why"!

A simple, unsophisticated, yet useful, way to keep a material handling study in perspective, is the *material handling equation*. It has six obvious parts, of which the first is WHY. The "equation" can be represented as in Figure 2–2. The second part is WHAT or the *material* to be moved, and the problem here is to clarify the real object of the handling problem. *What* is to be handled?

First, it is necessary to distinguish between *primary* and *secondary* materials. If oil is in drums, or sugar in 100 lb. sacks, or electric motors in individual corrugated cartons, the test of primary versus secondary material may quickly reveal that one is not necessarily committed to moving drums but to moving oil, etc. Therefore, the range of solutions includes not only drum handling methods but other methods of moving and handling *fluids* such as pipe lines, pneumatic tubes, tank cars, and rubber "balloons." The same reasoning applies to sugar, motors, and other "contained" materials. Sometimes, for good reasons, it may be concluded that the primary material is indeed the individual carton

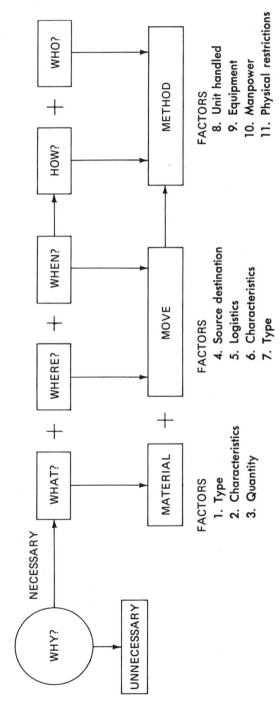

Fig. 2-2. Material handling equation. (Adapted from *Production Handbook,* The Ronald Press Co., New York, 1972.)

containing the motor. But unless this question is explored with vigor and imagination, improvements of the most valuable sort may be overlooked. For example:

A major chemical firm had a substantial drum handling problem on the docks at a large eastern port. The corporate handling analyst was asked to study possible methods of moving thousands of these drums through the port, but more efficiently. In the course of studying the problem he asked the manager "What is in these drums?" The manager replied that it was a dilute acid. Both men stared at each other as the word "dilute" began to register in their minds. The product was a very weak concentrate of acid, and in fact, they were shipping largely water! By shipping the acid in a more concentrated form, about half of the drums could be eliminated, as well as the folly of shipping water from Texas to the East Coast! No one had ever asked "What"!

Having identified the primary material, then ask whether the *form* can be changed to something that will simplify the handling? For example: gases, liquids, and slurries usually can be pumped and moved through pipelines far more economically than they can be moved in individual containers, at least over the short distances encountered in most industrial operations. Anything that will flow, also fills space better than the same material put into containers. It is usually far more economical to handle acid in tank cars than in individual carboys, provided the volume is adequate and the discharge conditions appropriate.

It might also be wise to consider whether an additional processing step could be added in order to make the material easier to handle. For instance, some agricultural and chemical products are pelletized in order to make them flow easier. This facilitates filling and feeding through hoppers. So, the question is: Will an additional processing step put this material into a form that facilitates the handling operation?

Another question might be, "Can the *shape* be changed to simplify handling?" If the material is stiffened by being coiled or processed, so as to *create* a flat surface, or compressed to provide stability or a smaller size, it may vastly simplify handling. It is much easier to handle a coil of sheet metal than it is to handle a long flat strip.

Another example of this concept is the so called "twin packing" technique in which several units, such as farm tractors, are partially disassembled and packed into a single large container. The idea is to disassemble removable elements and use *them* to fill in the voids, and to "nest" protruding elements within the container.

Then one might ask, "Will it help to change the size?" This is simply a matter of considering whether the physical dimensions can be altered so that handling is simplified. Examine clearances needed by doors, ceilings, containers, the workplace, etc. For example, a firm received 18 ft. lengths of bar stock which were unloaded from railroad cars, inspected, and stored. As material was needed the bars were withdrawn and desired lengths cut off. Rarely would exactly 18 ft. of a bar be consumed, and the small pieces left over were discarded. The material handling analyst asked why the bar stock was received in 18 ft. lengths? The answer was, "It has always been done this way." After a study of crane capacities, doorway clearances, storage techniques, stock selection procedures, etc., the analyst concluded that 36 ft. lengths were much more logical. This method was adopted with the following consequences: (a) The number of handlings was cut in half because each piece was twice as long. (b) The actual inspection time was greatly shortened because more footage was inspected with less movement. (c) As material was cut off a bar, the small end pieces were left over as before, but now there was only *one* piece to every 36 feet, instead of two. The net result was a saving of about $18,000 per year, simply due to the change in size.

Economies generally accrue when handling larger objects, hence larger loads and masses as one unit, but there are limiting factors, such as what is the optimum size for the *point of use?* Also, limitations arise in the dimensions and/or weight capacities of carriers, doors, floors, docks, aisles, elevators, and other handling devices.

Another interesting possibility is to *supplement* the material to simplify handling, which is sometimes expensive because an object is fragile or unstable. Proper protective enclosures can simplify handling. Or it may pay to add a base, pallet, or frame to an irregular object to provide stability or facilitate lifting.

Other shape qualities that make objects difficult to handle include such things as:

Square cartons: which tend to form unstable unit loads, since the separate stacks of cartons cannot be made to interlock with the adjacent stacks.

Fragile objects: which scratch, crush, or dent unless supplemented by protective frames and covers.

Awkward configurations: which form unbalanced shapes and tend to tip, fall, or roll.

In each case the solution is to alter, add, or remove elements in order to achieve a more easily handled shape.

The third part of the "equation" is WHERE which together with the "when," describes the *move.* First, it is necessary to determine and analyze the path over which material flows. Where did it originate? What is its destination? What path does it follow? Is there a handling device that will eliminate obstructions in the path? For example, in a pneumatic bulk conveying system the pipes can be laid over a rather tortuous path, across or under public thoroughfares, outside or inside buildings, etc. Whereas to move this bulk material in unit loads or individual containers might be very slow and cumbersome, indeed.

Another question is whether the job can be simplified by modifying the path. If material is to go down a long aisle, through doors and then wind back to an opposite point along the other side of the wall, it raises the question of whether a door or hole could be cut through the wall to eliminate the travel. If movement is difficult inside a building because of crowded conditions and/or multi-story operations, it might be possible to make the handling job easier by moving materials to the proper floor level *outside* the building.

Another possibility is to alter the origin or the destination of the move so as to simplify the path. For example, it may be found that high costs are incurred in taking material to an inspection station, spray booth, or other machine. Would it be advisable to move the machine or equipment causing the trouble to a more convenient location for *all* activities? Or, should another machine be installed to reduce travel distance and time?

The second part of the *move* is the WHEN, the fourth item in the material handling "equation," which suggests consideration of the volume, of the frequency of arrivals, the rate and manner of flow through the operations, etc. Costs are incurred because of surges in volume and pace. Operating complications arise in staffing and equipping for the peak or for the minimum material flow. If equipment is obtained to handle the peak, it is probable that men and equipment will be idle much of the time. On the other hand, if only the equipment needed to handle the minimum flow is provided, there will be times when bottlenecks and surpluses of materials will result in large cost increases. What, then *is* the compromise level for which to equip? Through a careful analysis, it must be determined when and how much the volume will fluctuate, determine the economics and operating implications of staffing and equipping for different levels, and prepare to deal with the kinds of problems that arise from the choices made. There must, of course, be agreement with management and operating people that this is the proper thing to do. If agreement is reached, the question then will become, "What can be done to modify and reduce these variations?" For example, a different purchasing procedure or timing of deliveries can often be effected. Traffic departments may be able to arrange more desirable incoming and outgoing schedules. It may be worthwhile to investigate customer schedules also, in order to determine whether *they* can modify their requirements to provide steadier flow through manufacturing operations.

The distinction of continuous vs. intermittent flow should also be considered, such as conveyorized handling piece-by-piece vs. the economies of batch handling with lift truck, crane, or hoist. Each has major implications for the operation it serves.

Thus, under this item of the material handling "equation," the goal is to smooth the flow of materials into a more uniform rate and timing. An important step is to get a policy decision on staffing and equipping the system for the proper level of handling capacity.

The fifth item in the "equation" is HOW—which implies the *method*. And, here it will be noticed that the "equation" uses the "chemical" $\rightarrow$ to imply or yield the method, not "equal" it. Having answered the multitude of questions arising from a consideration of the many factors suggested so far by the material handling equation, the analyst is *far* better prepared to consider the selection of an appropriate method, including the equipment [2]—*if* any. This aspect of the problem solution will be covered in Chapter 11, on equipment selection.

Along with the selection of the method, comes a consideration of the sixth and last item in the material handling "equation"—the WHO or the manpower required.

Having gone through the entire material handling "equation" it will be recognized that although it is far from adequate for the analysis of complex handling problems, it does describe a philosophy or approach that should not be forgotten. This philosophy is the basis for the detailed analysis procedure outlined in a later chapter, where the material handling "equation" will be further developed.

As has been pointed out, the material handling "equation" emphasizes the necessity of carefully analyzing both the MATERIAL to be handled *and* the MOVE to be made, *before* selecting the METHOD, or equipment. However, there are a large number of factors to be taken into consideration in selecting the proper method or equipment for implementing a specific move. Some are related to the material, some are related to the move, while others are related primarily to the equipment or method itself. In effect, the material handling problem-solving process usually requires that (1) the *characteristics* of the MATERIAL, and (2) the *requirements* of the MOVE, should be properly matched with (3) the *capabilities* of the METHOD, or equipment.

---

[2] It might be suggested parenthetically here that one of the *major* shortcomings in the alleged solutions to many material handling problems is the tendency of the analyst to jump from the "what" to the "how" in his rush to find a quick answer to the problem.

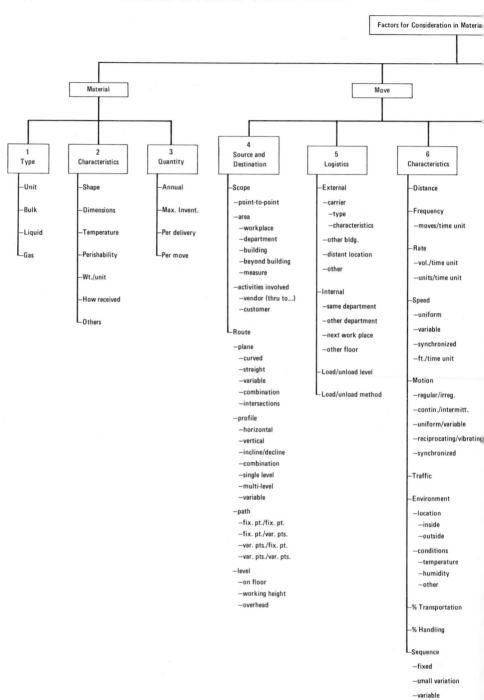

Fig. 2–3. Factors for consideration

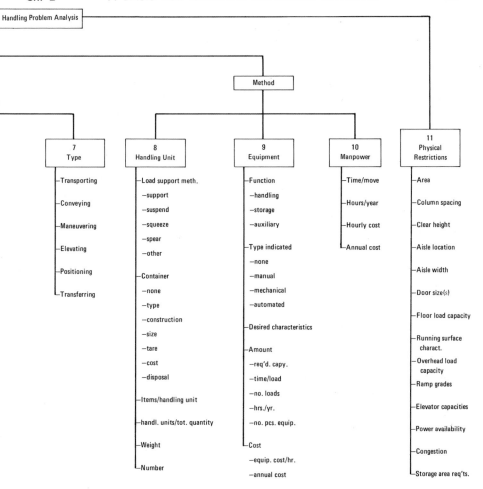

in material handling problem analysis.

FACTORS FOR CONSIDERATION IN ANALYZING MATERIAL HANDLING PROBLEMS

Before the problem analysis can proceed any further, it is advisable to delineate the factors necessary for the proper "consideration" of the Material, the Move, and the Method. This is suggested in Figure 2–3, in which some of the factors are shown classified under the eleven categories of basic data required for analyzing the problem.

The concepts developed in this chapter will be further discussed in Chapter 7, where the material handling equation and the "factors" will become the basis for a major portion of the material handling problem analysis procedure. In the *next* chapter, the principles of material handling will be discussed—as an additional aid to the identification, analysis, and improvement of material handling problem situations.

3

Principles of
Material Handling

One of the most important attributes of a good material handling engineer is his experience and its value as a resource in analyzing and designing solutions to material handling problems. But it takes years of exposure to a wide variety of situations to accumulate a worthwhile amount of experience. However, as is common practice in many fields, contemporary practitioners rely heavily on the experience of their predecessors, who have learned that certain fundamentals exist in their fields, whether in engineering, law, medicine, or material handling.

These fundamentals are developed over a period of years, and represent the accumulated experience of people who have practiced in the field. They are facts which have been tested. They are relationships which have been tried and found worthwhile. As these ideas, facts, and relationships were applied repeatedly and found to be useful, they were passed on to others in the field, and were frequently written down as guides for further application and testing.

"PRINCIPLE" DEFINED

A dictionary search of the various terms used to describe the word "principle" suggests that it might be defined somewhat as follows:

A principle is a prescribed guide to accepted procedures, established through past practice, which is taken for granted or accepted as authoritative by practitioners, and without which a system would be less effective.

Stocker has said:

Principles are organized knowledge. They represent the essence of accumulated knowledge with all the unnecessary details pushed aside, so that the understanding of a mass of facts is easier and its meaning quicker to grasp. In a sense, principles are the proverbs of materials handling, a guide to the busy man or student.

It has been proved that an inexperienced man placed in a new job involving materials handling can, with a knowledge of certain principles, find correct solutions faster, avoid criticism by his superiors, and otherwise benefit from the condensed experience of many other men.[1]

As useful as principles may be to the material handling engineer, they must be applied with extreme care and with a liberal amount of common sense. In fact, in many cases it will be found necessary to imply that they are only true, "all other things being equal," or "when practicable."

In considering the use of such principles, Morris [2] suggests that:

1. Taken literally, they may be used as general guides to action, with appropriate caution.
2. Their best use is perhaps as clues or suggestions as to what possibilities should be looked for and considered in a problem. They may be used as rough hypotheses to be tested in connection with particular instances.
3. Many problems are best treated first by the application of principles, before undertaking analysis.
4. Principles may help, and indeed may be the only resort, in those problems where analysis is too complex, too costly, or beyond the analyst's ability.

In spite of the possibility that such principles may be considered relatively ineffective or unscientific by some, it is felt that their proper application can be of extreme value in the analysis and solution of many material handling problems.

THE PRINCIPLES INTRODUCED

Principles of material handling may have been first published and explained in any detail by Harry E. Stocker.[3] Subsequent publication and discussion by Footlik and Carle,[4] Day,[5] Hall,[6] and others added to

[1] Harry E. Stocker, *Materials Handling*, Prentice-Hall, Inc., New York. Second edition, 1951, p. 7.

[2] Adapted from Wm. T. Morris, *Analysis For Materials Handling Management*, Richard D. Irwin, Inc., Homewood, Ill. 1962, p. 16.

[3] Stocker, *op. cit.*, pp. 11–72.

[4] I. M. Footlik, and J. F. Carle, *Industrial Materials Handling*, Lincoln Extension Institute, Cleveland, Ohio, 1968.

[5] J. B. Day, *Materials Handling Engineering*, Georgia Institute of Technology, Atlanta, Ga.

[6] Herbert H. Hall, list prepared for use by the College-Industry Committee on Material Handling Education, 1965.

the list of principles and their interpretations. Many extensive lists have been published, but most contained items which could not really be considered principles. Such statements are usually specific suggestions, and might well be considered as "corollaries." Some of them will be used as illustrations of the principles.

The principles presented here [7] represent an accumulation of experience equivalent to untold years of practice. They are adapted from those stated in the literature, with certain changes made for clarification and with several new ones added to round out the coverage of the field. In reviewing the principles it will be found that nearly every one applies to several aspects of material handling and aids in accomplishing one or more objectives.

In presenting the principles, each is stated and briefly described. Next, suggestions for putting the principle into use are spelled out—often in explicit detail—to facilitate their prompt and convenient application. Then, at the end of the presentation of the principles, some general suggestions are given on their use in analyzing and solving material handling problems.

1. PLANNING PRINCIPLE

All handling activities should be planned.

If there is one principle on which all should agree, it is that handling activities should be planned, and not left to chance, or to the vagaries of performance likely to result if operating personnel are left on their own to devise methods of handling. Remember: Handling may account for 25 to 80 percent of all productive activity! Management most certainly deserves to have this sizable portion of total activity planned—not left to chance.

Suggestions for Carrying out the Planning Principle

1. Avoid placing materials directly on the floor, without a pallet or other support underneath.

2. Assure adequate storage space at the workplace for the proper amount of material, both ahead of, and following the operation being planned.

3. Plan to use the same container throughout the system; avoid frequent changes of containers.

4. Consider floor load capacities, ceiling heights, truss capacities, column spacing, etc.

---

[7] Adapted from list by Hall as subsequently revised and "adopted" by the College-Industry Committee.

5. Comply with current aisle width, or alter if necessary and practicable.

6. Provide necessary clearances in and around each work place—for proper handling of materials and for maneuvering handling equipment.

7. Arrange for instructions for each operator in the correct method.

8. Place product on a packing base (pallet, skid, etc.) as early in process as is practical.

9. Plan for correct location of material supply and disposal in the work area.

10. Provide adequate means for scheduled scrap removal.

11. Plan for productive operations and inspections to be done *during* material movement.

12. Combine operations to eliminate intermediate handlings.

13. Do make judicious use of manual handling.

14. Plan to minimize walking.

15. Observe principles of motion economy (see motion study texts and workplace planning in Chapter 12.)

2. SYSTEMS PRINCIPLE

Plan a system integrating as many handling activities as is possible and coordinating the full scope of operations (receiving, storage, production, inspection, packaging, warehousing, shipping and transportation.)

Throughout this text, reference is made to the material handling *system*—a planned, integrated sequence of interrelated handling tasks—as opposed to "spot" solutions to isolated handling tasks. Each handling activity should be considered a portion of the whole handling system, and planned as an integral part of the system.

Suggestions for Carrying out the Systems Principle

1. Consider the entire scope of the handling activity, i.e., beyond the area under immediate consideration.

2. Plan flow *between* work areas.

3. Integrate operations into the handling system, such as: processing, inspection, packaging, etc.

4. Arrange for alternative handling methods—in case of emergency.

5. Move materials directly to production, whenever practical, rather than an intermediate storage area—to avoid re-handling.

6. Work closely with suppliers, customers, and carriers.

7. Be aware of future requirements—changes in product, process, volume, etc.—and allow for necessary flexibility.

3. MATERIAL-FLOW PRINCIPLE

Plan an operation sequence and equipment arrangement to optimize materials flow.

As has been previously suggested, material handling and plant layout are intimately interrelated. The material-flow pattern is actually the backbone of most production facilities, and one of the first steps in planning a material handling system is the design of the material-flow pattern. This may be largely determined by operation sequence, which in turn will determine the pattern of equipment arrangement.

Suggestions for Carrying out the Material-Flow Principle

1. Avoid crowded conditions.
2. Eliminate obstacles from material flow.
3. Carefully observe building and carrier restrictions.
4. Plan movement in a direct path. (Avoid backtracking, zig-zag flow, crooked paths.)
5. Arrange for alternate paths, in case of difficulty.
6. Be aware of cross traffic and take necessary precautions. Avoid traffic jams.
7. Keep related work areas close together.
8. Use product-type layout when possible.
9. Plan proper location of subassembly and feeder lines.
10. Combine operations to eliminate handling between them.
11. Plan for definite pick up and delivery locations.
12. Minimize moves between floors, buildings.
13. Process heavy, bulky materials close to receiving.
14. Move the greatest bulk and/or weight the least distance.

4. SIMPLIFICATION PRINCIPLE

Reduce, combine, or eliminate unnecessary movements and/or equipment.

Simplification is one of the by-words of efficiency, motion economy, and many other aspects of industrial operation. It should likewise be a goal in material handling. As used here, it implies, primarily, the reduction or elimination of moves as well as the elimination or reduction of equipment that is not being properly utilized.

Suggestions for Carrying out the Simplification Principle

1. Apply the principles of motion economy.
2. Reduce or eliminate long, awkward, or complicated moves.

3. Plan direct moves.

4. Deliver materials to the *correct* location (*spot*) the *first* time.

5. Avoid unnecessary handling.

6. Eliminate re-handling.

7. Plan to use materials out of original container (avoid switching containers, or taking items from containers and putting them on shelves or in bins).

8. Minimize number of moves per process. (Try to plan a maximum of one move *between* operations.)

9. Minimize walking.

10. Avoid use of a variety of equipment types and/or makes.

11. Provide proper number of containers.

12. Plan for adequate equipment capacity.

13. Do not mechanize for the sake of mechanization.

5. GRAVITY PRINCIPLE

Utilize gravity to move material whenever practicable.

This is certainly a very obvious principle—but one that is all too frequently overlooked because of its simplicity. Many material moves can be made efficiently by the proper application of the law of gravity.

Suggestions for Carrying out the Gravity Principle

1. Use roller or wheel conveyors, slides, chutes, etc., between operations.

2. Use ramps between varying work or floor levels.

3. Sloping floors (slight) can be utilized where considerable hand truck movement is in *one* direction.

4. Use chutes to connect conveyors at different levels.

5. Use spiral chutes to connect conveyors between floors.

6. SPACE UTILIZATION PRINCIPLE

Make optimum utilization of building cube.

Factory and warehouse space are expensive. Therefore, wasted space is wasted money. Inherent in this principle is that both square feet and cubic feet are to be given consideration. One *square* foot contains as many *cubic* feet as "clear" height will permit items to be stacked. In this way, a square foot can be "used" many times over—with 15-, 20-, 30-, 40-foot stacking of materials.

Suggestions for Carrying out the Space Utilization Principle

1. Move equipment and operations closer together (not too close).
2. Eliminate or condense "temporary" storage piles of materials.
3. Stack materials to use full cube available.
4. Use racks to permit higher stacking.
5. Use stacking containers to permit stacking, without racks.
6. Analyze space utilization to "find" additional square or cubic feet.
7. Remove slow-moving stock to less valuable space—outdoors, sheds, older buildings, farther away, etc.
8. Check on economic order quantities and economic lot sizes for possibility of reducing amount of materials required on hand.
9. Clean out storage areas and dispose of obsolete or useless materials.
10. Use narrow-aisle handling equipment to permit reduction of aisle widths.
11. Consider angle-stacking to permit narrower aisles with long materials.
12. Use handling equipment not requiring fixed floor space, i.e., mobile or overhead equipment.
13. Don't pile materials directly on floor—use pallets, skids, etc., to permit stacking.
14. Consider reinforcing floors to permit heavier floor loads and stacking to greater heights.
15. Use collapsible containers to save space required by empties.
16. Use palletless handling techniques to eliminate "lost cube" in pallets.
17. Consider possibility of nesting parts, products, containers.
18. Review possibility of increasing inventory turnover.
19. Design pallets, etc. to effectively utilize space between columns.

7. UNIT SIZE PRINCIPLE

Increase quantity, size, weight of load handled.

In general, the larger the load, the lower the cost per unit handled.

Wherever practical, individual items should be gathered and made up into unit loads. The entire following chapter is devoted to the unit-load concept, since it is one of the keystones of modern, efficient material handling. For further details, see Chapter 4.

Suggestions for Carrying out the Unit Size Principle

1. Examine every move of one item for possibility of making up unit loads.

2. Purchase materials in unit loads.
3. Work with vendors towards design of larger unit loads.
4. Use containers to consolidate items.
5. Use uniform, standardized containers.
6. Design pallet pattern to efficiently utilize pallets and storage space.
7. Design load size to make optimum use of handling equipment.

8. SAFETY PRINCIPLE

Provide for safe handling methods and equipment.

It should be obvious that all handling activities—in operation or being planned—should be safe, since an objective of material handling is to improve working conditions by providing safer work situations. A high proportion of all industrial accidents is in the material handling aspect of the production activity. A measure of this important relationship is the number of the "standardized" accident causes closely related to handling activities or equipment; for example:

1. Unsafe Conditions, Environmental Causes
   a. Inadequate guarding (of conveyors, trucks, etc.)
   b. Unguarded (equipment)
   c. Defective condition (of equipment)
   d. Hazardous arrangement (stacks of material, pallet loads, arrangement on trucks, etc.)
2. Unsafe Acts of Persons
   a. Operating without authority (trucks, etc.)
   b. Operating . . . at unsafe speed
   c. Making safety devices inoperative (governors, etc.)
   d. Using unsafe equipment (needing repair)
   e. Unsafe loading (machines, conveyors, cranes, trucks)
   f. Taking unsafe position or posture (in stacking, in RR cars, trucks, etc.)
   g. Working on moving equipment (trucks, conveyors, etc.)
3. Unsafe Personal Causes
   a. Improper attitude (taking chances, disregarding instructions)
   b. Lack of knowledge (poor instructions, new man, unskilled)

The above list represents 13 out of the 20 listed general causes of accidents! With the "cards stacked" against material handling activities, the engineer should lean over backwards to design safety into material handling methods and devices.

Suggestions for Carrying out the Safety Principle

1. Install adequate guards and safety devices on handling equipment.
2. Keep handling equipment in good operating condition.

3. Furnish mechanical handling equipment for difficult, hard, hazardous handling activities and to handle dangerous materials.

4. Do not permit handling equipment or devices to be overloaded or operated over rated capacity.

5. Examine 2-man lifting jobs for possible use of mechanical equipment.

6. Use mirrors at busy aisle intersections to permit seeing around the corners.

7. Keep aisles clear and uncluttered.

8. Install adequate lighting.

9. Maintain floors in good condition.

10. Avoid crowded conditions.

11. Provide good housekeeping.

12. Stack materials carefully.

13. Be sure operators are properly instructed in method and/or use of equipment.

14. Provide mechanized part feeding and removal devices.

15. Use remote emergency switches and controls.

16. Plan for removal of undesirable dust, fumes, smoke, etc.

17. Isolate inherently dangerous equipment, operations, etc.

18. Allow liberal factors of safety.

19. Use bright colors or moving lights to highlight handling hazards, moving vehicles, or danger areas.

20. Install "dead-man" switches on equipment requiring operators.

9. MECHANIZATION/AUTOMATION PRINCIPLE

Use mechanized or automated handling equipment when practicable.
Used judiciously, mechanized or automated handling devices and equipment can be of extreme value in increasing material handling efficiency. However, handling operations should not be mechanized for the sake of mechanization alone, nor should they be over-mechanized in terms of the function to be performed.

Suggestions for Carrying out the Mechanization/Automation Principle

1. Consider use of mechanization for:
   a. Large quantities or volumes of materials
   b. Frequent, repetitive moves, even though short
   c. Long moves
   d. High-effort, hazardous, difficult moves
   e. Two-man lifting/moving tasks
   f. Replacing excess manual handling

    g. Replacing a large number of persons doing handling

    h. Feeding and removing materials from machines

    i. Moving heavy containers

    j. Handling done by direct labor

    k. Scrap removal

    l. Reducing handling time

    m. Providing continuous, uniform, maximum controlled rate of movement

2. Do not overmechanize.

3. Design or select containers suitable for mechanical handling.

4. Use equipment that is self-controlled and self-programmed when practicable.

5. Consider mechanization of people flow and equipment movement—as well as material movement.

6. Mechanize communications to facilitate material movement.

7. Utilize automatic couplings, switches, transfers, etc.

8. Move heavy jigs, fixtures, tools, etc., by mechanical means.

10. EQUIPMENT SELECTION PRINCIPLE

In selecting handling equipment, consider all aspects of the MATERIAL to be handled, the MOVE to be made, and the METHOD(s) to be utilized.

This principle is primarily a reminder to be extremely careful in selecting and specifying handling equipment—by being *sure* that all phases of the problem are thoroughly analyzed. Chapters 7 and 11 will cover these factors in detail and discuss the importance of a complete analysis, as well as techniques and procedures for analysis.

Suggestions for Carrying out the Equipment Selection Principle

1. Select versatile equipment to carry out a variety of tasks and adjust to changing conditions.

2. Select standardized equipment to avoid a multiplicity of makes and models—and to minimize inventory of repair parts.

3. Consider changing material unit handled to improve handling method (i.e., bulk to bag; loose to containerized; individual item to pallet load; liquid to dry; dry to slurry, etc.).

4. Do not overlook the best procedure for the *present* method—before changing methods or equipment.

5. Prove that the move *is* necessary.

6. Compare costs on the basis of dollars per unit handled.

7. Consider indirect and intangible factors in justifying investments.

11. STANDARDIZATION PRINCIPLE

Standardize methods as well as types and sizes of handling equipment.

In almost any field of endeavor it is wise to standardize on the "one best way"—after it has been determined. This is not, however, meant to imply that methods, equipment, etc., should be "frozen" and adhered to indefinitely. A search for a better method should always be under way. The material handling engineer should constantly be on the alert for new developments which may replace current methods or equipment. Nor does standardization mean *only* one type or make of equipment must be used. It should be interpreted to mean the fewest practical number of types, makes, models, sizes, etc.

Any attempt at standardization should be preceded by a careful analysis. This will assure that the best *has* been determined, and that the wrong method, etc., is not standardized inadvertently, by a failure to make a thorough investigation.

Suggestions for Carrying out the Standardization Principle

1. Adhere to standard sizes of containers, etc.
2. Make dock heights a standard dimension.
3. *Plan* pallet sizes to fit carriers, products, bay sizes, and equipment.
4. Establish a system of pallet patterns.
5. Design new buildings to accommodate pallets, containers, equipment.
6. Purchase "standard" types of equipment.
7. Purchase "standard" sizes of equipment.
8. Record standardized methods.
9. Keep a manual of standardized methods, equipment, etc.
10. *Train* employees in standardized methods.

12. FLEXIBILITY PRINCIPLE

Use methods and equipment that can perform a variety of tasks and applications.

Equipment that can perform a wide range of handling tasks and which has a variety of uses and applications can often be more fully utilized than single-purpose, specialized units. Since industry requirements are subject to frequent change, flexibility should be carefully considered as an important characteristic of any handling equipment.

Suggestions for Carrying out the Flexibility Principle

1. Buy flexible equipment—lift trucks, roller and wheel conveyors, etc.
2. Specify adjustable speed drives.

3. Make use of attachments and accessories (for lift trucks, etc.).

4. Use gasoline-powered equipment (to permit operating farther from base than electric or L P gas).

5. Use four-way pallets, skids, containers.

6. Utilize trucks, etc. (mobile), in favor of conveyors (which may be fixed).

7. Carefully weigh use of special, single-purpose equipment.

8. Consider adjustable racks.

13. DEAD-WEIGHT PRINCIPLE

Reduce the ratio of mobile equipment dead-weight to pay load.

Excess weight of mobile equipment not only costs more money, but may require additional power and be slower to operate. It is therefore unwise to invest in a heavier-weight piece of equipment than is required by the task to be performed.

Suggestions for Carrying out the Dead-Weight Principle

1. Portable conveyors, dock boards, etc. should be made of lightweight aluminum, magnesium, etc.

2. Use lightweight pallets, skids, containers.

3. Purchase aluminum trailers to reduce tare weight.

4. Select lightweight equipment for light loads.

5. Use "walkie" type trucks (vs. counterbalanced, for elevator servicing).

6. Consider expendable materials for pallets, skids, containers.

14. MOTION PRINCIPLE

Equipment designed to transport materials should be kept in motion.

This principle implies that mobile equipment should be *kept moving*— that is, performing the function for which it was designed. It should not be tied up for unduly long periods of time for loading and unloading.

Suggestions for Carrying out the Motion Principle

1. Plan to reduce load/unload time to decrease turn-around time.

2. Use mechanized loading and unloading equipment.

3. Use tractor-trailer trains, loaded and unloaded by lift trucks, to free lift trucks for their intended purpose—lifting, stacking, maneuvering, etc. Tractor can return "empty"—or pull empty train of trailers for re-loading.

4. Maintain equipment properly to minimize downtime.

5. Use self-loading equipment—lift trucks, straddle carriers, etc.

6. Consider 2-way radio on vehicles to permit quicker dispatching.

7. Plan return loads for equipment.

8. Return mobile equipment promptly for re-use.

9. Study carefully use of load-carrier and platform-type trucks where carrying device is attached to motive unit.

10. Plan to *haul* loads, rather than carry them.

11. Utilize pallets, skids, etc. to hasten loading of trailers.

12. Use pallets or skids in place of "stationary," four-wheel hand trucks —which should be kept *moving*.

15. IDLE-TIME PRINCIPLE

Reduce idle or unproductive time of both handling equipment and manpower.

Idle time is undesirable in nearly any industrial or commercial activity, and especially so in the use of material handling equipment or manpower. Equipment and manpower are "making money" when fully utilized. Therefore, every effort should be made to plan methods and schedule equipment to permit full use of both resources.

This principle is very closely related to the motion principle and many suggestions made there are equally applicable here.

Suggestions for Carrying out the Idle-Time Principle

A. Manpower

1. Deliver materials at the proper rate.

2. Use indirect labor for material handling.

3. Install handling equipment to permit direct labor operators to spend full time on production.

4. Combine jobs, i.e. one man, 2 machines or jobs—load one while other is cycling.

5. Be sure operator is supplied with materials—not waiting.

B. Equipment

1. Schedule use of handling equipment.

2. Use radio for dispatching.

3. Transfer equipment to other areas where it can be utilized more fully (see also, motion principle suggestions).

16. MAINTENANCE PRINCIPLE

Plan for preventive maintenance and scheduled repair of all handling equipment.

The suggestions for application of several of the previous principles have implied the importance of preventive maintenance and scheduled repairs to the effectiveness of material handling activities. Probably very few phases of the material handling program can contribute more to overall plant efficiency than a well-organized maintenance and repair function.

Suggestions for Carrying out the Maintenance Principle

1. Anticipate repairs in order to avoid breakdowns that will take equipment out of service unexpectedly.

2. Require operators to make daily inspections of equipment and report findings.

3. Plan for detailed, major inspection and reporting on equipment condition at regular intervals.

4. Set up a regular lubrication schedule covering all handling equipment, using charts to assure adequate lubrication.

5. Establish a preventive maintenance program.

6. Provide adequate maintenance and repair facilities and personnel to handle normal requirements.

7. Work out a schedule and work load for repair work to permit its being done when equipment can be spared and at convenient times.

8. Maintain an adequate supply of repair parts and maintenance supplies.

9. Keep number of makes and models to minimum to reduce inventory of parts and simplify maintenance.

10. Paint all equipment on a scheduled basis to keep up appearance and promote care of equipment.

11. Require driver training for all mobile equipment operators.

12. Provide adequate instruction in proper operation of all non-mobile equipment.

13. Fix responsibility and delegate authority for the maintenance and repair function.

14. Send maintenance mechanics to factory training programs.

15. Check with manufacturers on required periodic maintenance—schedules, instructions, etc.

16. Alter maintenance schedules when production schedules change.

17. Avoid "over-maintenance."

18. Keep floor clean.

17. OBSOLESCENCE PRINCIPLE

Replace obsolete handling methods and equipment when more efficient methods or equipment will improve operations.

As with any other type of physical equipment, material handling devices are subject to obsolescence, as well as depreciation. And, in a similar sense, so are handling methods. New ideas, techniques, methods and equipment are reported every day, and the material handling engineer must be continuously alert to be sure he is aware of the latest developments.

Physical depreciation is not difficult to observe and to take into consideration in an analysis—but obsolescence is a less obvious characteristic. Many old, or even "ancient" pieces of equipment "still work," and even at relatively low costs for maintenance and repairs. However, new equipment may be faster, higher capacity, more efficient, etc., and result in a lower cost per unit handled—even though it does require a capital investment.

Suggestions for Carrying out the Obsolescence Principle

1. Establish a definite replacement policy.
2. Set up a replacement program and budget.
3. Beware of old equipment that "still works."
4. Carefully study all alternatives.
5. Rent or lease new equipment for a try-out period.
6. Establish a planned, periodic equipment evaluation program.
7. Keep up with what is new:
   a. Periodicals, journals, etc.
   b. Books, handbooks
   c. Equipment shows, expositions
   d. Technical society meetings
   e. Conferences, short courses
   f. Plant visits
   g. Manufacturer's representatives

18. CONTROL PRINCIPLE

Use material handling equipment to improve production control, inventory control and order handling.

Since material handling equipment is used to move materials through the plant and the production processes, its use can have a great effect on the control of the items being moved. In many cases, handling equipment provides a direct mechanical path for the movement, and thereby facilitates the control of the material.

Suggestions for Carrying out the Control Principle

1. Provide direct, mechanical paths for materials movement.
2. Move materials in lots, batches, containers of a predetermined quantity or size.

3. Store, or pack, materials in containers holding a specific number of pieces.

4. Use containers (wire mesh) through which contents can be identified and/or counted.

5. Utilize 2-way radio or TV to expedite movement and control of materials.

6. Make optimum use of mechanical handling in order picking, accumulation, loading.

7. Pace production with mechanical handling equipment.

8. Build production, inventory, and accounting control features into the material handling system.

9. Move materials on a schedule and in lots to match production, to avoid rush delivery, partial loads, duplicate moves.

10. Use move tags or orders as authority for all moves—avoid verbal orders.

11. Coordinate handling program (schedule) with purchasing, manufacturing.

19. CAPACITY PRINCIPLE

Use handling equipment to help achieve full production capacity.

In many ways, this principle is a summation of all the preceding ones, in that a major objective of material handling is to increase production capacity. Nearly every one of the foregoing principles will contribute in some way to higher production levels. However, the emphasis here is on those facets of operation and the other principles that are directed specifically towards increasing or making full use of production capacity.

Suggestions for Carrying out the Capacity Principle

1. Use mechanical handling equipment to assure a uniform, paced rate of flow.

2. Operate equipment at optimum rate.

3. Plan to utilize return runs of handling equipment.

4. Fully load or use containers, vehicle, conveyors.

5. Make full use of building cube and floor load capacity to obtain additional *square* feet.

6. Reduce times between operations and departments with mechanical equipment.

7. Efficiently utilize carrier capacity by judicious combination of load weight and volume.

8. Change size, shape of unit loads to utilize space, equipment capacity, manpower.

9. Use area over aisles (mezzanines, balconies) for additional storage space.

10. Make use of rented storage facilities during peak seasons to free own space for production.

11. Use outdoor storage space for materials not requiring protection from weather—or easily protected.

12. Pool handling equipment for better utilization.

13. Establish one-way aisles to ease traffic congestion.

14. Widen aisles to speed materials movement.

15. Utilize automatic door openers, dock levelers, couplings, etc.

16. Eliminate storage *areas* by using overhead *space,* moving storage, processing during movement, etc.

17. Use additional safety devices to permit greater speed of movement.

20. PERFORMANCE PRINCIPLE

Determine efficiency of handling performance in terms of expense per unit handled.

As pointed out above, there are many objectives of material handling. However, an effective handling method may achieve one or several of these objectives. The primary criterion for measuring the efficiency of a handling technique is dollars. Although efficiency could be measured in terms of total cost (and sometimes is) or equipment performance (as judged against selected criteria), the most effective means of measurement is in terms of dollars per unit handled. This is usually the ultimate measure from the point of view of management.

It should be pointed out that there *are* cases where maximum economy is *not* the overall goal. Some material handling devices may be installed to provide higher production rates, safer working conditions, or reduced physical effort. Time or effort saved may be the primary criteria, and the cost of handling may be of little or no interest.

Suggestions for Carrying out the Performance Principle

1. Carefully study all characteristics of the material to identify all possible units which *could* be used as a basis for comparison.

2. Select a common, convenient, standard unit.

3. Use the same unit for as many control purposes as possible.

4. Avoid changing the unit from department to department, time to time, etc.

Material Handling Check Sheet

General

Plant _____   Location _____

Dept. _____   Operation _____

Observer_____   Date _____

Indicators of Improvement Opportunities	Check		Remarks
	Yes	No	
1. Crowded conditions			
2. Poor housekeeping			
3. Cluttered aisles			
4. Excess mat'ls. in process			
5. Empty floor space			
6. Materials piled *on* floor			
7. Unused space overhead			
8. Damaged materials			
9. Excessive scrap			
10. Long moves			
11. Complex flow patterns			
12. Backtracking			
13. Cross traffic			
14. Related operations far apart			
15. Obstructions to materials movement			
16. Traffic jams			
17. Floor poorly maintained			
18. Excess inter-floor handling			
19. Inadequate scrap removal			
20. Excessive mat'ls. at work place			
21. Unnecessary handling			
22. Re-handling			
23. Idle handling equipment			
24. Idle production equipment			
25. Operators waiting for mat'ls.			
26. High indirect labor cost			
27. High handling cost			
28. Unexplainable delays			
29. Poor flow pattern			
30. Crooked aisles			
31. Narrow aisles			
32. Aisles not marked			
33. Poor utilization of bay size			

Fig. 3–1. Material handling check sheet—General.

Material Handling Check Sheet Material Handling Methods			
Plant _____		Location _____	
Dept. _____		Operation _____	
Observer _____		Date _____	

Indicators of Improvement Opportunities	Check		Remarks
	Yes	No	
1. Moving one item at a time			
2. Not using gravity			
3. Insufficient storage at workplace			
4. Poor flow between work areas			
5. Stock control difficulties			
6. Production bottlenecks			
7. Scheduling difficulties			
8. Moving loose materials			
9. Production machines idle			
10. Materials delivered to wrong place			
11. Slow materials movement			
12. Haphazard handling methods			
13. Difficult manual handling tasks			
14. Unsafe handling methods			
15. Unsafe handling equipment			
16. Overmechanized handling methods			
17. Overloaded handling equipment			
18. Underloaded handling equipment			
19. Operators waiting for mat'ls.			
20. Heavy physical exertion			
21. Low production			
22. Excessive loading & unloading time			
23. Crowded work places			
24. Individual handling operations not coordinated			
25. Building restrictions impede handling operations			
26. Carrier restrictions impede handling operations			
27. Heavy cross-traffic			
28. Large, heavy items moving long distances			
29. Communications (paper work) delays mat'l. handling			
30. Manual coupling; uncoupling trailers, etc.			
31. Non-standardized handling equipment			
32. Unplanned handling methods			
33. Excess variety of handling equipment			
34. Non-standard in-process handling containers			
35. Zig zag flow paths			
36. Insufficient mechanization of handling			
37. No plans for scrap removal			

Fig. 3–2. Material handling check sheet—Material Handling Methods.

Material Handling Check Sheet

—Storage and Warehousing—

Plant _____ Location _____

Dept. _____ Operation_____

Observer _____ Date _____

Indicators of Improvement Opportunities	CHECK		Remarks
	Yes	No	
1. Poor housekeeping			
2. Lack of space			
3. Traffic congestion			
4. Excess storage at work areas			
5. Stock bins (shelves, slots) overflowing			
6. Stock bins, etc. empty			
7. Unused overhead space			
8. Small items in large space			
9. Large items in small space			
10. Materials piled *on* floor			
11. Cluttered docks			
12. Disorganized order accumulation area			
13. Difficulty locating items			
14. Difficult access to goods			
15. Customer complaints			
16. Damaged goods			
17. Paper work holding up production, storage; shipping			
18. Unnecessary paperwork			
19. Insufficient illumination			
20. Aisles too narrow			
21. Aisles too wide			
22. Narrow aisle equipment used in wide aisles			
23. Wide-aisle equipment used in narrow aisles			
24. Non-standard containers; pallets			
25. Pallets used when not needed			
26. Man container & pallet sizes			
27. Containers, etc. don't fit column spacing			
28. Leaning stacks			
29. Outdoors materials stored indoors			
30. Indoor materials stored outdoors			

Fig. 3–3. Material handling check sheet—Storage and Warehousing.

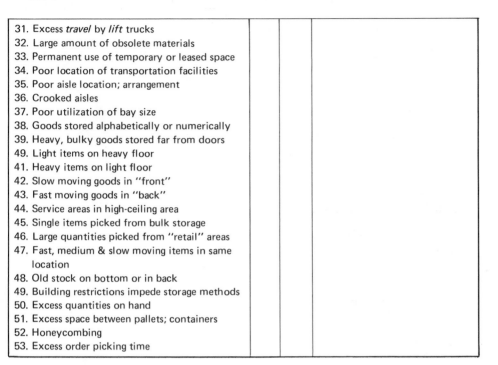

31. Excess *travel* by *lift* trucks
32. Large amount of obsolete materials
33. Permanent use of temporary or leased space
34. Poor location of transportation facilities
35. Poor aisle location; arrangement
36. Crooked aisles
37. Poor utilization of bay size
38. Goods stored alphabetically or numerically
39. Heavy, bulky goods stored far from doors
49. Light items on heavy floor
41. Heavy items on light floor
42. Slow moving goods in "front"
43. Fast moving goods in "back"
44. Service areas in high-ceiling area
45. Single items picked from bulk storage
46. Large quantities picked from "retail" areas
47. Fast, medium & slow moving items in same location
48. Old stock on bottom or in back
49. Building restrictions impede storage methods
50. Excess quantities on hand
51. Excess space between pallets; containers
52. Honeycombing
53. Excess order picking time

Fig. 3–3. *(Continued)*

USING THE PRINCIPLES

Merely stating the principles of material handling and indicating their advantages and some suggestions for their application does not assure that they will be properly used in analyzing or solving handling problems.

Perhaps the best way to utilize the principles effectively is by means of check sheets. Principles can be divided or sorted into interest areas, restated for more specific types of activity, and used in examining an area for the purpose of finding improvement possibilities. Such check sheets are shown in Figures 3–1 to 3–4, on which some of the ideas from this chapter have been abbreviated and adapted in such a way that they are easy to spot in practice, as an aid in helping to point out material handling difficulties.

Similar check sheets should be made up for other specific areas of activity and for specific plants—to reflect their individual differences in processes and modes of operation. In some cases, check sheets have been reproduced on pocket-size cards for easy reference by foremen, supervisors, etc.

Material Handling Check Sheet

—Manpower Utilization—

Plant _____   Location _____

Dept. _____   Operation _____

Observer_____   Date _____

Indicators of Improvement Opportunities	Check Yes	Check No	Remarks
1. Manual feeding of machines			
2. Manual removal of finished parts			
3. Excess manual handling			
4. Large no. of men doing handling			
5. Production operators idle			
6. Production operators handling materials			
7. Hard, hazardous work done by hand			
8. Difficult handling tasks			
9. Safety hazards			
10. Excess injuries			
11. Unnecessary handling			
12. Two-man lifting jobs			
13. Frequent, short, repetitive moves by hand			
14. Frequent employee complaints			
15. Operators walking for materials			
16. Heavy physical exertion			

Fig. 3–4. Material handling check sheet—Manpower Utilization.

CONCLUSION

While all may not agree that the preceding are *the* principles of material handling, it is felt that they do represent the more important concepts in the field. Along with the suggestions for application, they fairly well cover the scope of material handling and should serve as worthwhile guides for material handling planning and analysis.

Nearly every one implies or involves one or more of the aspects of the definition of material handling (motion, time, quantity, space) and most of them reflect the characteristics of the definition of a principle, stated at the beginning of the chapter.

4

The Unit Load Concept

INTRODUCTION

In the previous chapter, one of the fundamental principles of material handling, the *unit size principle,* suggested that the larger the load handled, the lower the cost per unit handled. It was pointed out that there were also many other advantages to be gained from handling "unit loads." This chapter will develop the unit load concept and discuss means by which unit loads are built and handled.

If the above implies that a larger load is more desirable than a smaller one, it is logical to ask "What is the right size for a package or load?" The spread of lift truck application throughout industry in the 1940's and 1950's removed the major consideration of size and weight, since the load was no longer limited to what a man could handle. With the fork truck and other mechanical handling devices, loads of almost any size, shape, and weight can be moved. In this regard, Glen R. Johnson, Jr., has said:

A study of precedent would show that the size, weight, and bulk of individual packages used in commerce today are the result of their being handled conveniently by one man. Of course, marketing demands reflect their influence on package sizes. But, when we come down to the selection of methods, techniques, systems or equipment for material handling, our choice is always guided by whether we want to handle one piece on one trip or one piece in a continuous flow from one point to another, or several pieces at a time either in a continuous flow or intermittently. The unit load principle implies that materials should be handled in the most efficient, maximum size unit, using mechanical means to reduce the number of moves needed for a given amount of material.[1]

[1] Glen R. Johnson, Jr., "Unit Load Theory and Practice," before U.S. Dept. of Commerce Trade Center, Cargo and Material Handling Seminar, Bangkok, Thailand.

A unit load has been defined by Professor James R. Bright as:

A number of items, or bulk material, so arranged or restrained that the mass can be picked up and moved as a single object too large for manual handling, and which upon being released will retain its initial arrangement for subsequent movement. It is implied that single objects too large for manual handling are also regarded as unit loads.

It can be seen that two major criteria are (1) a large number of units and (2) a size too large for manual handling. However, in the overall material handling and physical distribution activity, these two criteria as well as the balance of the above definition, and the "unit size principle," leave some room for misunderstandings, since it is obvious that either a "handful" or a "carload" both bear a relationship to the unit load concept.

In order to place the balance of this chapter in proper context with the total handling task, as well as to other chapters in the text, Figure 4–1 attempts to present the entire range of "containers" which might be found in the handling-distribution system. Although the sketches indicate containers from the smallest "parts bin" to the largest, truck-trailer-size "shipping container," it should be emphasized that there is no commonly accepted classification covering this range of containers and related devices—the sizes are variable within wide ranges; most sizes are not standardized; and the border lines between the categories shown overlap considerably in practice. However, it will be seen that each of the types shown *does* permit the handling of a large number of parts as one "unit."

In summarizing the unit load concept, Johnson has stated that it should:

1. Perform a minimum number of handlings and eliminate manual handling.
2. Assemble materials into a unit load for economy of handling and storage.
3. Assemble materials into unit loads as soon as possible and keep in that form as long as possible.
4. When necessary, redesign packages or cartons for better assembly into unit loads and retain the unit load form to use all possible cube and prevent product damage.
5. Make the unit load as large as possible considering the limitations of building, handling equipment, production areas, volume of material required, and common carrier dimensions and capacities.[2]

2 Johnson, *loc. cit.*

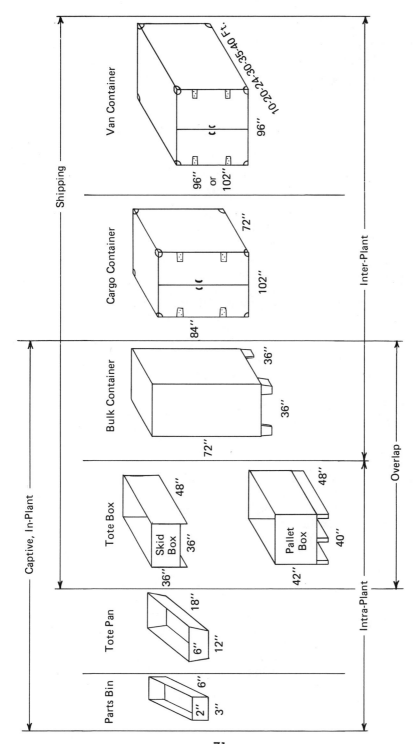

Fig. 4-1. Container types used in manufacturing and physical distribution.

This chapter will be concerned primarily with the type of unit load commonly built upon or around a skid, pallet, or equivalent devices (sheet pallets, trays, etc.). Other types of unit loads and containers are discussed elsewhere in this text.

ADVANTAGES OF UNIT LOADS

The advantages of the unit load concept are many and varied, and interrelated with many phases and aspects of the overall handling system. Some of the more common advantages are as follows: [3]

1. Permits handling of larger loads
2. Reduces handling costs
3. Faster movement of goods
4. Reduces time for loading and unloading
5. Reduces packaging costs
6. Maximum use of cubic space
7. Reduces pilferage in transit and storage
8. Less time wasted in tracing stray items
9. Reduces product damage
10. Reduces physical inventory time and cost
11. Better coordination of deliveries to production
12. Safer handling
13. Better customer service
14. Reduces transportation costs
15. Lower insurance rates for goods in transit
16. Reduces time and expenses of labeling individual items
17. Unitization permits uniform stock placement, resulting in uncluttered aisles
18. Production operators need not waste valuable time in helping others move materials
19. Items themselves need not be uniform as unitizing medium provides uniformity
20. Irregular items can become stable loads
21. Provides basis for overall handling system within physical distribution cycle
22. Provides basis for handling system within plant
23. Unitized loads stabilize stacks of materials
24. Unitizing medium can protect loads from foreign elements
25. Unitizing medium can provide uniform temperature and moisture control of goods
26. Maximum accessibility of stored goods
27. Reduces handling of individual items

---

[3] Partially adapted from (1) *Powered Industrial Trucks,* Industrial Truck Association, and (2) *Pallets and Palletization,* National Wooden Pallet and Container Manufacturers Association.

While certain of the above advantages accrue primarily to loads unitized by means of pallets, skids, etc., it can be concluded that there are sufficient advantages to any type of unitization to encourage an investigation of its applicability in any portion of the handling cycle. Figure 4–2 indicates the types of savings which can be realized from a unitization program.

DISADVANTAGES OF UNIT LOADS

In spite of the overwhelming evidence in favor of applying the unit load concept, there are, nevertheless, some disadvantages, such as:

1. Cost of unitizing
2. Cost of de-unitizing
3. Equipment required
4. Space required
5. Lack of flexibility
6. Wasted cube within unit load
7. Tare weight of unitizing medium
8. Problem of returning empty containers
9. Possible damage due to mishandling of large unit
10. Common carriers are not uniform in size
11. Transfer equipment often not available on both "ends" of the move

BASIC WAYS TO MOVE A UNIT LOAD

Since the unit load concept implies a fairly large quantity and/or volume, a primary consideration in its application should be the way in which the load will be lifted and carried. This is usually accomplished in one of the following ways:

1. A Lifting Device Under the Mass. This is by far the most common method of moving unit loads. It involves providing a method of getting under the load such as a pallet, pieces of dunnage between loads, or the use of racks so that one can get under the load at will. This approach is suitable for loads having at least one major flat surface, a center of gravity well inside the base, and which is essentially a stable load. If the load has an unbalanced weight distribution or is particularly long and awkward, there must be some auxiliary restraining device to make it safe or even practical. Incidentally, this leads to one of its basic disadvantages, since the spacing device will obviously occupy otherwise usable cubic feet in the storage area.

2. Inserting the Lifting Element into the Body of the Unit Load. Spearing the load, as one would spear a doughnut, is a useful technique,

In Receiving and Storing (Many Materials)

Material	Non-Unitized Load Handling Method	Man-Hours	Unitized Load Handling Method	Man-Hours	Labor Saved Percent
100-lb. bags (80,000 lb.)	Loose bags, eight high in car. Palletize in car. Haul and stack with fork truck.	32	On pallets in car Fork truck unloads, hauls, stacks.	1.25	96
300 boxes 80-500 lb. Mixed load (30,000 lb.)	Sort boxes to pallets for each source as remove from truck. Haul and stack with fork truck.	12	On pallets from suppliers. Fork truck unloads and stores.	0.75	94
Castings (112,000 lb.)	Loose castings in car. Place in skid boxes. Haul by fork truck to storage area and manually stack castings.	62	In wire mesh bins. Unload car with fork truck, used to stack in storage.	1.25	98
Four barrels (2,400 lb.)	Unload barrels from truck or freight car and move to storage with two-wheel hand truck.	0.1	On pallet. Unload and store with fork truck.	0.025	75
Dimensioned lumber 16-20 ft. long (40,000 lb.)	Men and crane unload pieces to four-wheel cart, pulled to storage by fork truck. Driver sets spacers. Truck stacks.	12	Strapped bundles weighing 2-6,000 lb. received in car. Spacers in bundles permit fork truck unloading, stacking.	0.4	97
Finished lumber 16-20 ft. long (32-40,000 bd. ft.)	Manually unload car on trailer to four-wheel carts, pulled to storage by fork truck. Driver sets spacers. Truck stacks.	24	Same as for dimensioned lumber.	0.33	98

For Many Cost Elements (Incoming Castings)*

Cost Element	Requirement For Non-Unitized Load	Requirement For Unitized Load	Savings Percent
Labor			
Loading castings at supplier	32 man-hours	2½ man-hours	92
Unloading, moving to storage at A-C	30 man-hours	1¼ man-hours ⎞	
Stacking castings in storage at A-C	32 man-hours	Included above ⎱	98
Loading into skid boxes for A-C production.	26 man-hours	Not required	100
Storage Space			
Area at supplier's plant	1200 sq. ft.	400 sq. ft.	66
Area at A-C	1200 sq. ft.	400 sq. ft.	66
Shipping Charges (3⅓ cars to transport loose castings vs. 1 car for unitized loads)			
Freight	$346	$246	28
Switching at supplier	$ 75	$ 22.50	70
Switching at A-C	$ 75	$ 22.50	70

Summary of Savings Per Shipment
   Labor 116 hours — $373, space — 1600 sq. ft., shipping charges — $205

*These are major cost elements saving around $14,000 per year on incoming shipments of castings, based on 112,000 lb. lots formerly received loose in boxcars. Now the customer provides the supplier with wire mesh pallet containers. Not shown are costs to recycle 33 pallet containers: $8.50 return freight and labor to handle empty containers. Pallet containers are also considered an improvement over palletized shipments requiring 2 ½ man-hours for supplier to strap.

Fig. 4–2. Unitization program brings savings like these. (From *Modern Materials Handling,* November 1961, pp. 76, 77.)

particularly adapted to "circular" unit loads such as wheels, coils, rolls, reels, pipe. Occasionally it is used for pieces of machinery or other objects having voids large enough to take forks or a ram, such as building tiles, blocks, etc. It is often possible to construct an artificial opening for a ram or forks into a conventional unit load and thus eliminate a pallet.

3. Squeezing the Load Between Two Lifting Surfaces. An instinctive human reaction is to carry an object by squeezing it between the hands, and this principle is incorporated in many lift truck attachments, as well as in tongs and grabs used with overhead handling systems. The clamp or grab usually has the advantage of handling without using an auxiliary lifting platform.

A basic advantage of the squeeze technique is that under some conditions it is possible to pick up, move, and release unit loads without preparation other than orderly stacking. For example, the large cartons, containers, or crates used for refrigerators, hot water heaters, television sets, etc., can be squeezed, lifted and stacked without auxiliary devices. However, it should also be noted that it is necessary with some attachments to leave space between adjacent stacks so that the clamp attachment will fit on each side of the load.

4. Suspending the Load. In some instances, when none of the foregoing systems are practical or economical, it is possible to suspend the load from a hook or with a sling. A suspended load does not present the danger of falling off the lifting surface. It can also be lifted up and over other materials without disturbing them, and higher stacking is often possible.

Although the suspended load is not carried rigidly and may require more care in handling, this freedom of movement may be a distinct asset in manipulating a load into tight quarters or getting it into a precise position.

On the other hand, suspension has at least two major disadvantages. The suspended load may require special rigging, and an additional operator may be needed to secure the load and attach the lifting device. A push-button or remote control crane can help overcome this objection.

Loads are most commonly suspended by (1) mechanically hooking into the object to be lifted, (2) looping slings around the load, or (3) gripping the load with a clamp. Two other devices should also be mentioned. A magnet at the end of the cable may eliminate some of the rigging difficulty and also permit instantaneous pickup and release within control of the operator. Vacuum cups are frequently used for handling large flat sheets of glass, metal, or other fairly stiff, low-porosity material, enabling the lifting of large fragile objects without marring or damaging them.

In practice many variations of those outlined above will be found in use, and it could be safely said that there is practically no limit to the ways to move unit loads except the imagination of the material handling engineer. Several of the methods described are illustrated in Figure 4–3.

TYPES OF UNIT LOADS AND RELATED DEVICES

In implementing the above methods, there are five basic unit load techniques, which are briefly defined here and covered in more detail later.

1. Unit Load on a Platform.

    a. Skid—a platform on "legs," spaced to enable a platform lift truck to move underneath; usually used for very heavy loads, and where tiering is not required.

    b. Pallet—usually a double-faced platform of minimum height, designed for insertion of forks between the two surfaces.

2. Unit Load on a Sheet.

    a. Flat sheet—corrugated cardboard, chip board, or plywood.

    b. Molded sheet, especially formed to facilitate building the load and leaving hollow spaces for fork entry

    c. Flexible sheet used as a "sling" between the forks, particularly for materials packed in bags.

3. Unit Load on a Rack.

    a. Specially designed to hold parts in a desired position or relationship.

    b. May have wheels to provide mobility.

    c. Trays may be considered a special form or rack.

    d. Often equipped with inserts, pegs, or holes to orient parts or as dividers between layers for ease of handling, inspection, disposal, etc.

4. Unit Load in a Container. Full or partial enclosure to suit requirements, such as a box, bin, crate, or "balloon."

5. Self-contained Unit Load. (*Not* requiring auxiliary aids.)

    a. Bundle—awkward objects tied together for handling ease.

    b. Bale—compressed to reduce size and improve handling.

    c. Fastened unit load—items rigidly fixed in position by a unitizing material such as strapping, tape, glue, etc.

    d. Interlocked unit load—items designed, shaped, and arranged so as to provide their own restraint, such as pigs of aluminum, cast so as to interlock in building a stack.

    e. Unrestrained load—items so arranged and handled as to provide a unit load, and usually requiring special clamps or forks for handling such items as cartons, bricks, concrete blocks, cases, drums, etc.

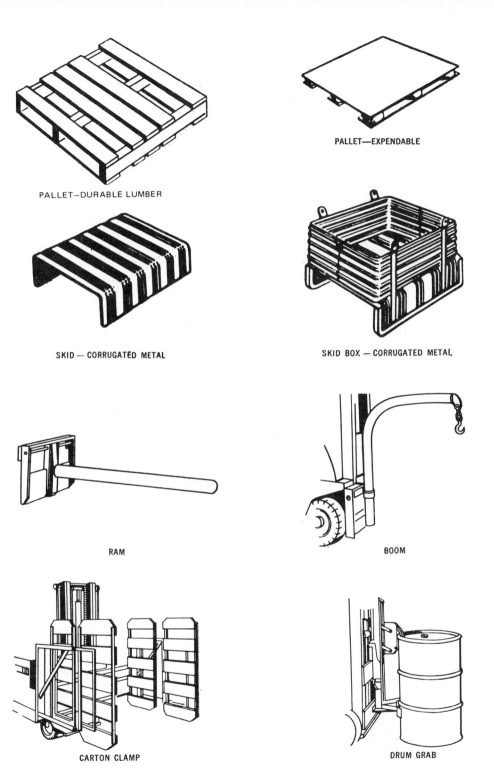

PALLET—EXPENDABLE

PALLET—DURABLE LUMBER

SKID — CORRUGATED METAL

SKID BOX — CORRUGATED METAL

RAM

BOOM

CARTON CLAMP

DRUM GRAB

Fig. 4–3. Some basic ways of moving a unit load. (From *Modern Materials Handling Directory*.)

Some of these are illustrated in Figure 4–4.

The imagination of the handling engineer will easily "invent" a multitude of variations of those suggested.

RELATIONSHIPS BETWEEN UNIT LOADS AND OTHER FACTORS

One item of extreme importance in considering the unit load concept is the very close relationship between the unit load itself and a number of other aspects of the handling-distribution system. Among these factors are:

1. Common carriers—legally restricted in both width and length, thereby becoming a prime basis for the dimensional aspects of the total handling system.
2. Shipping containers—some of which are available *only* in standardized sizes.
3. Supports—such as the pallet, skid, etc.—which also come in "standardized" sizes.
4. Cartons—which do *not* come in standard sizes, and thereby become one of the significant variables.
5. Pallet racks—which come in a variety of types, sizes, and configurations, both fixed and adjustable.
6. Column spacing—which *should* be determined by the more rigidly fixed dimensions of carriers, pallets, etc.
7. Aisle widths—which are also flexible and determined by a combination of the above plus a consideration of the handling equipment used, or to be used. (Obviously the building layout will be affected by the column spacing and aisle widths.)
8. Building size, construction, and features—such as length-to-width ratio, clear stacking height, floor load capacity, door locations, and docks.
9. Handling equipment—including such factors as equipment type, size, load capacity, and speed.
10. Consumer package sizes—which although often dictated by advertising and sales promotion considerations, should actually be an integral part of the physical distribution system.
11. Shelves, coolers, and freezers in retail store—likewise a link in the physical distribution system and closely related to package sizes and cartons, as well as the physical characteristics of the store building. (Shelf *depth* is standardized)
12. Consumer storage facilities—such as refrigerator and freezer dimensions, cupboard sizes, closet dimensions, etc.
13. Disposition of auxiliary devices—such as pallets, skids, cartons, containers, etc.

While the above may seem somewhat distantly removed from the subject of unit loads, the significance of some of the above factors and their

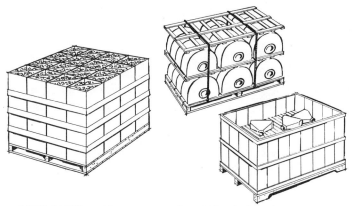

LAYER PACKS provide protection with vertical or horizontal separators.

LOADS ON WHEELS can be moved by truck or by hand, can be stackable.

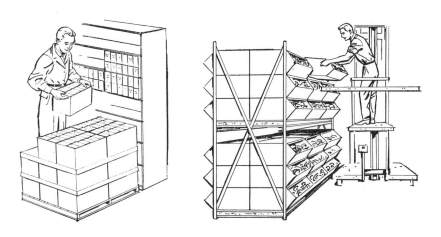

Fig. 4–4. Types of unit loads. (From *Modern Materials Handling,* November 1961.)

79

interdependence can be seen in Figure 4–5. The material-handling engineer should seriously consider nearly all of the above in his efforts to implement any segment of the total handling-distribution system. Other factors of interest in implementing the unit load concept are discussed in a subsequent section of this chapter on planning the unit load system.

PALLETS AND PALLET CONTAINERS

Introduction

Since the key to most unit load applications is a pallet, skid, or a container based on the pallet or skid, the material handling engineer should be well acquainted with the basic concepts embodied in such devices.

The definitions of significance in this discussion are:

1. Pallet. A horizontal platform device used as a base for assembling, storing, and handling materials in a unit load. Pallets may be classified as flat pallets, box pallets, and post pallets, the latter having either fixed or detachable corner posts to help restrain the load.

2. Skid. Usually a non-stackable, single-faced device with only two horizontal runners or stringers serving as supports for the deck surface, and elevated above the floor to allow lifting by a platform truck.

The National Wooden Pallet and Container Manufacturers Association has assigned the following type numbers to represent common combinations of features and characteristics.

1. Single-faced, non-reversible
2. Double-faced, non-reversible, flush stringer
3. Double-faced, reversible, flush stringer
4. Double-faced, non-reversible, single wing
5. Double-faced, non-reversible, double wing
6. Double-faced, reversible, double wing

In order to clarify the above classifications of pallet characteristics and types, some of them are illustrated in Figure 4–6.

Materials and Construction. Pallets, skids, and pallet and skid boxes are commonly made of wood, plywood, steel, lightweight metals, corrugated or chip board, plastic, or rubber. As is implied by their materials of construction, they are either expendable, general purpose, or special purpose. They are also contructed in either a "rigid" fashion or made collapsible to permit their return by common carrier in a minimum of space. Some of these types are shown in Figure 4–7.

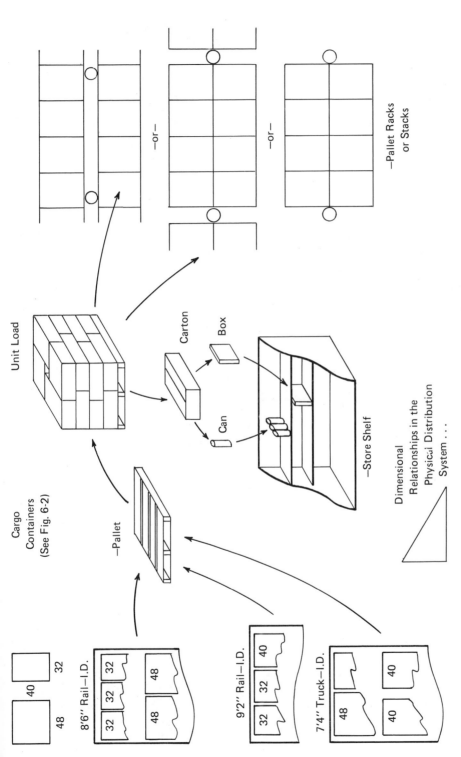

Fig. 4-5. Dimensional relationships in the handling-distribution system.

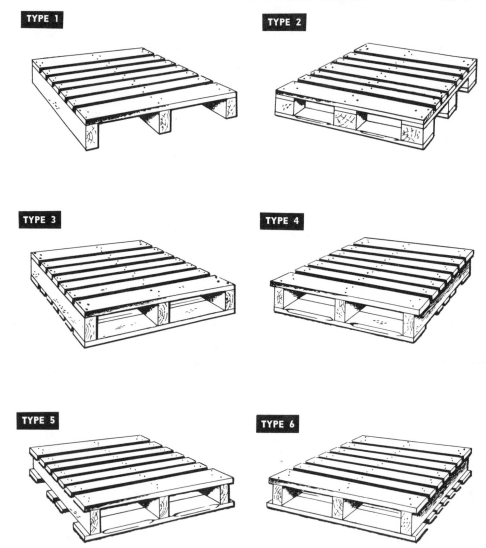

Fig. 4-6. Common pallet types. (From the *Technical Handbook on Pallets and Palletization,* 1968—National Wooden Pallet and Container Manufacturers Assoc.)

Pallet Costs. As with any other industrial equipment, pallets incur a cost for their use which is significant enough to be included in any calculation of system costs or saving. As a rule of thumb, the cost of a good lumber pallet may be estimated as about $5.00, with the cost of ownership estimated at approximately $1.00 per year, including depreciation

PALLET BASKET — WIRE MESH

SKID BOX — METAL PANEL

SKID BOX — CORRUGATED METAL

SKID BOX — WOOD

DEMOUNTABLE SECTIONS

DROP-BOTTOM SHOP BOX

SKID-MOUNT DUMP HOPPER

PALLET — CORRUGATED METAL

PALLET — WIRE MESH

PALLET — ALUMINUM

PALLET — DURABLE WOOD

PALLET — DURABLE WOOD

PALLET — EXPENDABLE FIBERBOARD

SKID -- CORRUGATED METAL

SKID — COMB. WOOD AND METAL

Fig. 4–7. Pallet and skid variations. (From *Modern Materials Handling Directory*.)

and maintenance. If it is desired to calculate a more accurate cost, the Douglas Fir Plywood Association suggests the following tabulation of cost items.

1. *Depreciation*

$$\frac{\text{initial cost per pallet}}{\text{expected useful life}} \quad = \quad \$\underline{\qquad}/\text{pallet}$$

2. *Average interest* (where applicable) $\underline{\qquad}/\text{pallet}$

3. *Insurance and taxes* (where applicable) $\underline{\qquad}/\text{pallet}$

4. *Maintenance*

$$\frac{\text{maintenance cost/year}}{\text{number of pallets}} \quad = \quad \$\underline{\qquad}/\text{pallet}$$

5. *Freight costs* (if dead-headed)

$$\frac{(\text{No. trips}) \, (\text{aver. miles}) \, (\text{frt. rate/ton mi.}) \, (\text{pallet wt.})}{(2000 \text{ lb./ton}) \, (\text{no. of pallets})} = \$\underline{\qquad}/\text{pallet}$$

Total Cost/Pallet/Year $

This calculation may be reduced to cost per pallet per trip, with the results used to determine the advisability of using expendable pallets. However, it will frequently be found that the cost of an expendable pallet is higher than the cost per trip of a high-grade returnable pallet.

As an example of the type of savings one might expect from a unitizing program, one study, made over a four-year period, shows the following, itemized by source of savings: [4]

Raw materials supplier	$.053/case
Manufacturer	.067/case
Distribution center	.092/case
Retail store	.041/case
Total savings	$.253/case

A more detailed analysis indicates the following man-hours per car unloading: [5]

Floor loaded (manual)	7.7
Partly palletized (manual at doorway)	4.1
Partly unitized (sheet pallet)	5.1
Fully unitized (pallets)	1.5
Fully unitized (sheet pallets)	3.5

Yet, in spite of the savings, the same study concluded the following, on the extent of unitized shipping:

Floor loaded	69%
Pallets	14%
Sheet pallets	3%
Combination	14%

[4] *Modern Materials Handling*, August 1969, "First Complete Study Shows a Pallet Can Save $500."

[5] Gordon C. Thomas, "What is Really Happening in Unit Load Shipping," *Modern Materials Handling*, March 1965.

Pallet Selection

Because there are so many kinds of pallets available, the selection problem is not a simple one. Perhaps a first step is to review the factors which should be considered in selecting a pallet appropriate for the unitizing task. These are listed in Figure 4–8, tabulated in two columns: one pertaining to the *kind* of pallet, and the second referring to the pallet *size*.

While a detailed discussion of each of the items in Figure 4–8 is beyond the scope of this text, serious consideration of each will suggest its relationship to the pallet-selection problem. It will be recognized that many of the factors are similar to or the same as were listed earlier in this chapter, in the discussion of the relationship between unit loads and other factors. Only a careful analysis of such factors can assure the selection of the proper pallet, but the task is somewhat simplified in the knowledge that only a few of the factors are of primary importance. In most cases, these will probably be:

1. Carrier size—which is relatively fixed, with the typical highway trailer permitting only about 7 ft. 8 in. of usable width, and a standard box car allowing about 9 ft. 2 in.
2. Item size—although theoretically variable, is frequently fixed at the time when the palletizing problem arises.
3. Building shape—which will have some influence, since it will determine the number of multiples of the pallet size which will fit in each direction.
4. Bay size—determined by column spacing and which is also theoretically variable, but which *may* be fixed in existing facilities.

Some of these factors are shown in Figure 4–5 with their relationships to other items in the total system.

Another significant factor in selecting the pallet is the group of "standard" sizes which have been adopted by the American National Standards Institute and are as follows:

	Rectangular		Square
R–1	24″ × 32″	S–1	36″ × 36″
R–2	32″ × 40″	S–2	42″ × 42″
R–3	36″ × 42″	S–3	48″ × 48″
R–4	32″ × 48″		
R–5	36″ × 48″		
R–6	40″ × 48″		
R–7	48″ × 60″		
R–8	48″ × 72″		
R–9	88″ × 108″		

It should be obvious that the selection of one of the above sizes would be preferable to an "odd" size, since they are becoming more widely accepted, and have been selected for optimum carrier utilization. The

Kind of Pallet   *Size of Pallet*

1. *Purpose*
   —unitize only
   —stack
   —customer service

2. *Item handled*
   —weight   —dimensions
   —density   —shape
   —stacking height   —load "plan" view
   —nature of material
   —nature of package

3. *Handling System*
   —truck ⎫
   —conveyor ⎬ capabilities, limitations
   —crane ⎭
   —auxiliary equipment   —compatibility with auxiliary equip.
   —compatibility of pallets with
    system
   —characteristics   —compatibility with handling equip.
   —storage system (block, racks)   —size

4. *Carrier*
   —characteristics
      —open, closed
      —heated, refrigerated
   —load capacity
   —availability
   —tariff rate

5. *Physical Facilities*
   —clear height   —building shape
   —elevator capacity   —aisle widths
   —environment (wet, dry, cold, hot)   —bay size
   —floor surface   —door openings

6. *Disposition of Pallet*   —elevator size
   —expendable
   —returnable
   —pool

7. *Common Practice*
   —scope
      —company
      —industry
      —U.S.
   —use
      —captive
      —non-captive

8. *Pallet Characteristics*
   —rough, smooth
   —solid or open deck
   —moisture content
   —variety of lumber
   —type of fasteners

Fig. 4–8.   Factors for consideration in pallet selection.

percent utilization of two carrier sizes for each of the standard pallet sizes (except the 88" × 108") is shown in Figure 4–9.

In spite of the reasons for using standard pallet sizes, there will always be that occasion where some special or unusual reason will require a variation and the argument for standardization should not interfere with the efficiency of a handling system if it is to be captive within the system. The engineer should not hesitate to consider special sizes, types, and varieties, but with proper consideration of the many factors previously suggested.

Pallet Pools

One of the potential values of using pallets is the possibility of joining a "pallet pool." In theory, this involves joint ownership of pallets by participating companies, with proper arrangements for such problems as supply, exchange, maintenance, and administration. A pallet pool can normally provide the advantages of pallet use without the disadvantages such as investment, return freight, repairs, etc.

Cornelis Hillenius describes the pallet pool operation as follows:

First one needs participants. In Holland a participant is a company willing to sign a contract containing his promise to pay for the purchase of a certain number of pallets. For this number of pallets he is partaking in the pool. After three years he can renew the contract and pay again for the contracted number of pallets. This is all. No further administration.

The shippers, who are the participants in the pallet pool, present the loaded pallet, loaded by themselves mostly with homogeneous goods at a railway station and then receive the same number of empty pallets from the railway. The goods are transported on the pallet, loaded by the shipper to the station of destination and if possible to the consignee, if he is also a partner in the pallet pool. If the consignee is a partner the pallets are delivered with the goods and the railways receive back an equal number of empty pallets from him. If the consignee is not a partner in the pool, the pallets are unloaded and the railways take the empty pallets back with them.[6]

While the pallet pool has been successful in European countries, it has not been implemented on a large scale in the United States except among grocery manufacturers and wholesalers. Its future development depends upon many factors, some of which are difficult to resolve among extremely large numbers of people spread over a wide geographical area.

If a pallet pool is to be established, the basic requirements are:

1. There must be a legal and binding contract between the participants, namely the shipper and receiver, and possibly the carrier. The contract must stipulate the rules of the pool.

[6] Cornelis Hillenius, "Packaging and Palletization; The Pallet Pool and the Modulus System," an unpublished paper.

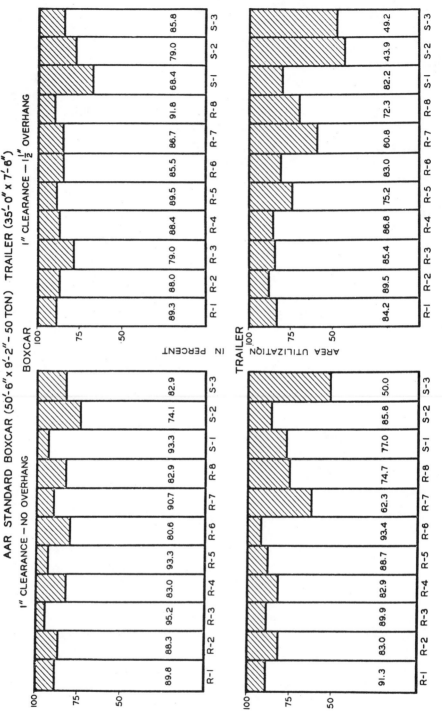

Fig. 4-9. Utilization of American standard pallet sizes, in percent. (From *Material Handling Engineering Directory*.)

88

2. Both shipper and receiver must use precisely the same type and size of permanent wooden pallets made to rigid specifications. Standardization of pool pallets by some uniform means is necessary.

3. Each participant need only own enough pool pallets to service their time cycle movement to customers, because the pallets are immediately replaced upon shipment, upon receipt, or upon the return of carrier equipment by exchange with pallets of equal quality and condition.

4. All pool pallets must bear a common identification mark. It should show the name of the initial purchaser and the pallet supplier.

5. The shipper, receiver, and carrier must agree in legal contract to be responsible for the pallets when in their custody. They must repair pallets when damaged, using specified materials or replace them when lost or stolen.[7]

PLANNING THE UNIT LOAD SYSTEM

Introduction

Having discussed the unit load concept and its interrelationships with other factors in the overall system, and having reviewed pallets and containers as the basis for many unit loads, the problem is now to design the unit load system itself. Here again it is necessary to give proper consideration to a rather lengthy list of factors which should be investigated to determine their relationship to the design of the overall unit load system. Although some of the factors have been considered previously, in the discussion of other aspects of the unit load concept, a rather exhaustive list is presented here for *final* review during the design stage:

A. Handling Task
    1. Material
    2. Quantity
    3. Duration of job
    4. Destination
    5. Disposition at destination
    6. Origin
    7. Loading technique
    8. Space utilization objective
    9. Efficiency of proposed unit load
B. Handling Cycle
    10. Conditions en route
    11. Storage requirements en route
    12. Environment en route
    13. Handling en route
    14. Handling aids

[7] "Exchange Pallets For Profits," in *Material Handling Engineering*, Presidential Issue, Oct. 1966, p. 43.

C. Physical Limitations
   15. Aisles
   16. Doors
   17. Carriers
   18. Ceiling height
   19. Column spacing
   20. Shipping docks
   21. Elevators, ramps, etc.
   22. Machine arrangement and working space
   23. Storage space dimensions
D. Weight Limitations
   24. Floor load limit
   25. Carrier floors
   26. Shipping dock floors and ramps
   27. Stacking heights
   28. Elevators
E. Economic Considerations
   29. Cost of handling equipment
   30. Cost of handling aids
   31. Cost of expendable unitizing materials required
   32. Labor cost
   33. Time requirements to prepare unit load
   34. Cost of handling system.

The analyst should determine the answers or accumulate the data implied by the above factors in order to have such information available during the design process. He might be wise to devise a form providing a space to record pertinent data, with provisions for remarks concerning relationships between specific factors and the various phases of the unit load system. Reference to Figure 4–15 presents another point of view for the systems study, and suggests potential cost reduction opportunities in the several phases of the system.

Criteria for Unit Load Design

In carrying out the design of the unit load system, it should be remembered that the load resulting from the design process must measure up to such criteria as:

A. Minimum weight
B. Low cost
C. Mechanical strength
D. Disposable (or expendable)
E. Universal in application
F. Optimum size
G. Low maintenance
H. Ease of de-unitizing

I. Ease of identification
J. Versatility
K. Transportable by conventional equipment
L. Interchangeable
M. Optimum shape
N. Easy to store
O. Stackable
P. Meet customer requirements
Q. Cost of unitizing

Many other criteria will suggest themselves to the analyst as he becomes more intimately acquainted with the many factors which are so closely interrelated in the unit load design process.

Elements of Unit Load Cost

As previously implied, the unit load will have some costs associated with its construction. These may be classified as follows: [8]

Labor
1. To assemble or disassemble load
2. To move material, consolidate and transfer load
3. To maintain inventory of unit load aids
4. To maintain and repair unit load aids
5. Training
Space
1. For assembling and disassembling loads
2. Storage space
3. Transfer and carrier space
Equipment and Materials
1. Assembly and disassembly equipment (staplers, strappers, balers, palletizers, etc.)
2. Handling equipment—cranes, lift trucks, pallets, containers, etc.
3. Expendable materials—strapping, dunnage, wood frames, paper, fasteners etc.
4. Return of handling aids—containers, pallets.
5. Attrition of permanent handling aids through damage and loss.

As pointed out previously, these costs must be balanced by any saving from the unit load system.

Designing the Unit Load

As might have been expected from a consideration of the long lists of various kinds of factors involved in making unit load decisions, the actual

[8] Charles W. Wood, "Planning for Unit Loads," *Transportation And Distribution Management*, Vol. III, No. 3, p. 11.

process of designing the unit load is rather complex. Although many so called "unit loads" are devised by assembling a large number of items and placing them on or into any container or support which is handy, they are likely to be much less efficient than a properly designed unit load. For example, the common practice of using "cast off" containers, such as 55-gallon drums or other cylindrical containers easily obtainable, may cause more difficulties in handling and storing operations than the benefits gained from "unitizing," even though such devices do achieve one of the unit load objectives—handling a number of items at a time.

It is suggested here, as it will be in many other situations throughout this text, that a logical procedure be followed in approaching a complex task. Therefore, as an aid in designing a unit load, the following is suggested as an overall approach.

1. Determine applicability of the unit load concept
2. Select the type of unit load
3. Identify the most remote source of a potential unit load
4. Establish the farthest practicable destination for the unit load
5. Determine the size of the unit load
6. Establish the configuration of the unit load
7. Determine the method of building the unit load

Each of the above will be discussed briefly in an attempt to guide the designer toward the most appropriate unit load for the material to be handled.

1. Determine Applicability of the Unit Load Concept. The previous portion of this chapter suggests that there are a number of factors to be considered in designing a unit load, and that some of them are related to the decision as to whether or not the situation at hand is amenable to solution by the unit load concept. Among these decision factors are the following:

A. Is the commodity unitizable?
(1) Material type—solid, liquid, bulk, etc.
(2) Material condition—sturdy, fragile, etc.
(3) Size
(4) Cube
(5) Shape
(6) Densities
(7) Chemical characteristics
(8) Stackability
(9) Unitizing costs
B. Is the volume of sufficient magnitude to warrant unitizing?
C. Is there a high enough frequency of movement?
D. Is the distance great enough to justify unitization?
E. Is the route to be taken practical for unit load handling?

F. Are the modes of transportation suitable to unit load handling?
G. Are the physical characteristics of the storage space at the destination receptive to unit loads?
   (1) Floor load capacity
   (2) Clear stacking height
   (3) Elevators
   (4) Ramps
H. What is the final disposition of the unit load?
I. What is the life expectancy of the system in which the unit loads will be used?
J. What are the potential handling methods?
   (1) At the source
   (2) At transfer points
   (3) At the destination
K. Can the costs of unitizing be justified?
L. What is the possibility of redesigning consumer packages to permit better unitization?
M. What will be the effect of the unit load on the physical distribution cycle?
N. Will the unit load be acceptable to the customer?

A serious consideration of the above questions, and a sincere attempt to determine answers to them will prove extremely helpful in determining whether or not the unit load concept should be further considered.

2. Select the Type of Unit Load. The previous discussion of unit load types will provide a background from which to select the type most appropriate. As an aid in selecting *the* type of unitizing device, R. T. Hartmann [9] has classified materials as follows:

A. Materials Not Strong Enough To Withstand Crushing: All materials which must be protected from crushing. They may be handled without any protection at all or packed in a carton. The strength of this protection will determine how many articles may be stacked one upon the other inside a container. Examples: Automobile components, made-up textiles, electrical appliances and components, light engineering products, glassware, plastic and rubber molded goods, toys, boots and shoes, pottery, hollow-ware, pharmaceuticals.

B. Materials Strong Enough To Withstand Crushing: Materials, strong in themselves and of regular shape, capable of being built into unit loads. When unitized such materials must be capable of withstanding the crushing load of other unit loads. Examples: Casks and drums, lumber and timber, sheet materials, such as steel, aluminum, hardboard, asbestos, cement, insulation board, plaster board, plywood.

[9] Adapted from R. T. Hartmann, "Palletization," *Higher Productivity*, May–June 1958, pp. 24–30.

C. Materials Strong in Themselves of Irregular Shape Suitably Packed For Unit Loads: Articles requiring intermediate battens, cartons, or cases —not to protect the material but to provide the right form for stacking— with the battens, cartons, or cases carrying the weight of the loads when stacked. Examples: Castings and forgings, goods in cases, crates, or cartons.

D. Bagged Materials Forming a Flat Surface Under Load: Materials of a nature sufficiently fluid to compress to a regular shape, thereby supporting the load above. It should be noted that some bagged materials should be placed on reversible pallets to provide an adequate bearing surface. Examples: Grain, powder, and materials with similar characteristics.

E. Bagged Materials Which Do Not Form Flat Surfaces Under Load: Materials which are not sufficiently fluid to compress to a regular shape, the articles being of a nature that will not settle down to form a flat surface to support stacked loads. Examples: Forgings, molded or machined parts, nails, nuts and bolts, small castings.

F. Large Irregular Loose Materials: Materials of a shape that will not stack or nest, or that need handling in a way to protect them from damage. Examples: molded plastics, sheet metal stampings, etc.

G. Small Irregular Loose Materials: Materials not needing protection, but whose size necessitates an enclosure, such as a box. For example: Cullet, forgings, machined and molded parts, stampings, scrap.

H. Materials Handled Hot from Production Processes: Irrespective of size, shape or weight, such material needs handling in a corrugated metal pallet box, if the container is to have a reasonable life. Examples are castings and forgings.

Hartmann then goes on to recommend the general category of unitizing device or devices applicable to each classification, as follows:

Class	Unitizing Device
A	Fixed and movable post, extension post, box, wire mesh
B	Flat pallets
C	Flat pallets
D	Flat pallets
E	Fixed and movable post, extension post, box, wire mesh
F	Fixed and movable post, extension post, box, wire mesh
G	Box, wire mesh, tilting box
H	Corrugated metal box (gondola)

It can be seen from the above, that the selection of the proper type of unit load and unitizing device and/or material is not a simple one. In fact, the successful development of efficient unit loads probably depends more upon experience than on any other factor.

An interesting approach to the decision-making process is illustrated in Figure 4–10.[10] While such an approach will not "solve" the problem, it does depict the thinking process which must be followed in the selection of a unit load device.

3. Identify the Most Remote Source of Potential Unit Load. One of the primary considerations in the design of a unit load handling system should be the extent to which the concept can be applied to the *total* handling system, of which the move being planned is only a portion. For this reason it is suggested that the analyst consider the possibility of applying the concept as far back in the total handling system as might be practicable. This suggests no less than a consideration of the outside source of the material being considered for unitization. It implies the advisability of working closely with the supplier, in the hope that some form of unitization may be developed at *his* plant, that can be subsequently handled in the same unit load—or a portion of the unit load—in the handling task under consideration.

4. Establish the Farthest Practicable Destination for the Unit Load. In the same context as suggested above, the potential of applying the unit load concept on the "distribution end" should also be considered. In this case, the analyst should work with the customer or customers, with the objective of designing a unit load for more efficient shipping and subsequent handling, storage and disbursing by the customer. In this type of situation, the unitization might begin during the final assembly process, at which point the product might be built on a base which would serve as a foundation for the unit load throughout the entire shipping and distribution cycle—as is commonly done with appliances.

5. Determine the Size of the Unit Load. Enough consideration has already been given to the dimensional factors in unit load design and a review of the preceding discussion is suggested. Possibly the most important of these factors, in many cases, is the size of the item to be unitized—since some combination of its dimensions will become the ultimate dimensions of the unit load. Although it has been previously implied that container sizes *might* be determined by the material-handling analyst, this is frequently not the case. Therefore, the analyst is forced to design a load around product dimensions determined by someone else, and possibly with little or no concern for the consumer package, carton, pallet, etc. Although such an approach may not result in an optimum unit load size, it does make it easier for the analyst to structure the load, with charts, tables, etc., as pointed out in the next section.

[10] F. C. Bacon, "Design of Efficient Unit Loads," an unpublished project report at Georgia Institute of Technology.

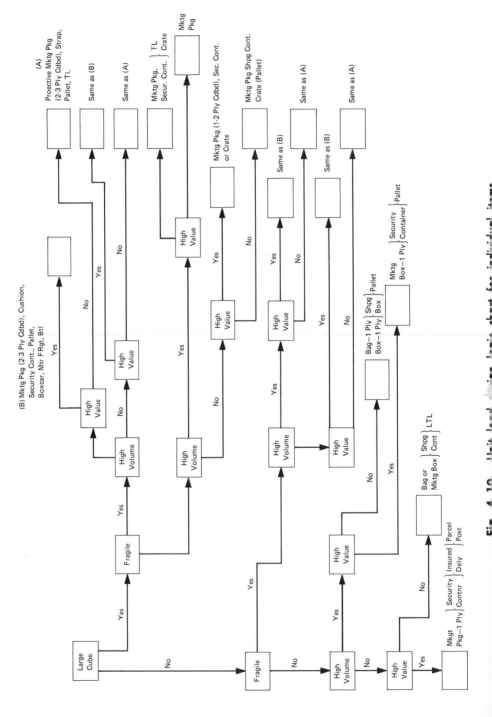

Fig. 4-10. Unit load design logic chart for individual items.

One other aspect that should be considered is the "deep" pallet [11] or the "wide" pallet. That is, should the pallet be—for example—48 in. (deep) × 40 in. or 40 in. × 48 in. (wide)? Some of the details of this situation are pointed out in Figure 4–11.

Careful consideration of such factors will gradually result in the selection of an equitable size and shape for the proposed unit load. It should again be emphasized that the analyst would be wise to *also* give consideration to "standard" pallet and/or shipping container sizes. This is another of the many phases of material handling in which the experience and judgment of the analyst are of considerable value in resolving the problem. There are no magic formulae for determining unit load sizes and configurations. However, it will be found that a little pencil and paper work will normally resolve the problem.

6. Establish the Configuration of the Unit Load. The configuration of the unit load includes the shape and the pattern of loading, both of which are determined by a number of the factors previously discussed. The configuration of course will vary primarily with the characteristics of the item to be unitized, including its shape and dimensions. If the items to be unitized are irregular or unstackable, the analyst is left pretty much on his own initiative to design a workable unit load. In many cases the unit load device will require auxiliary attachments such as sides, ends, or corner posts to restrain the load. Or, as previously suggested in the Hartmann classification, the items may be unitized *within* some kind of container.

However, if the items to be unitized are at all regular in form and shape, such as cartons, bags, blocks or bricks, the story is quite different. Such items can be built into a geometric configuration, as can bricks, resulting in a pallet pattern.

Common Pallet Patterns. A pallet pattern consists of (1) an arrangement of cases or cartons into a pattern which becomes one layer of a unit load, and (2) the number of layers making up the load. This is a significant factor in the number of cases in a unit load. Gordon C. Thomas has suggested [12] that the desirable number of cases from the manufacturer's point of view may not be the same as for the warehouse or distribution center. This is due to the fact that the manufacturer is concerned with a relatively small number of items to be shipped in relatively large quantities and with a relatively simple product mix. On the other hand, the problem of the distribution center involves the handling of several thousand items to be located and arranged in a large area so that they

[11] A pallet is normally described by identifying its stringer length as the first dimension.

[12] Adapted from Gordon C. Thomas, "What to Consider When You Switch to a Pallet Pool," *Modern Materials Handling,* April, 1965, p. 62.

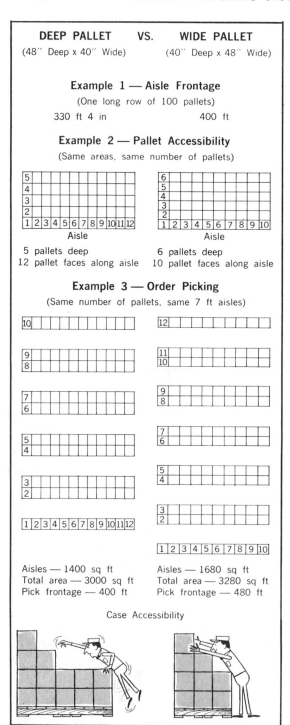

DEEP PALLET VS. WIDE PALLET

(48″ Deep x 40″ Wide) (40″ Deep x 48″ Wide)

Example 1 — Aisle Frontage

(One long row of 100 pallets)

330 ft 4 in   400 ft

Example 2 — Pallet Accessibility

(Same areas, same number of pallets)

5 pallets deep
12 pallet faces along aisle

6 pallets deep
10 pallet faces along aisle

Example 3 — Order Picking

(Same number of pallets, same 7 ft aisles)

Aisles — 1400 sq ft
Total area — 3000 sq ft
Pick frontage — 400 ft

Aisles — 1680 sq ft
Total area — 3280 sq ft
Pick frontage — 480 ft

Case Accessibility

Fig. 4–11. Comparison of deep pallet vs. wide pallet. (From "The Case of Deep vs. Wide Pallets," *Modern Materials Handling*, October 1961, p. 101.)

can be picked in small batches with a very high mix and shipped out in truck loads to a large number of destinations. In the course of trying to alleviate this apparent difficulty, it has been found that it increases efficiency for both producer and customer if orders are made up of either full unit loads or full layers, without hurting the customers' inventory level. Actually the customer gains in reduced cost of order preparation, order processing, receiving, storing, picking, and shipping. The manufacturer also gains in terms of reduced costs for order receiving, order processing, order picking, shipping, production planning, and sales forecasting.

Thomas also points out that the pallet pattern chosen will affect many things, including the following:

At the Manufacturer	At the Customer
Order processing	Order writing
Order picking	Order picking
Package design	Ceiling heights
Ceiling heights	Storage area heights
Handling equipment	Rack heights
Shipping habits	Receiving habits
Production schedules	Stock rotation
Warehousing	Physical inventories

General types of pallet patterns are commonly referred to as block, brick, row, and pin-wheel. These types along with several variations are shown in Figure 4–12.

Selecting the Pallet Pattern. Again the analyst is faced with a number of factors to consider before he can choose the pallet pattern to be used. Some of these are:

1. Carrier—
    Type
    Size
2. Pallet—
    Type
    Size
3. Item—
    Dimensions
    Shape
    Weight
    Density
    Orientation of items in container
    Items per container
    Fragility
    Ordering habits (or requirements)
4. Containers—
    Dimensions
    Shape

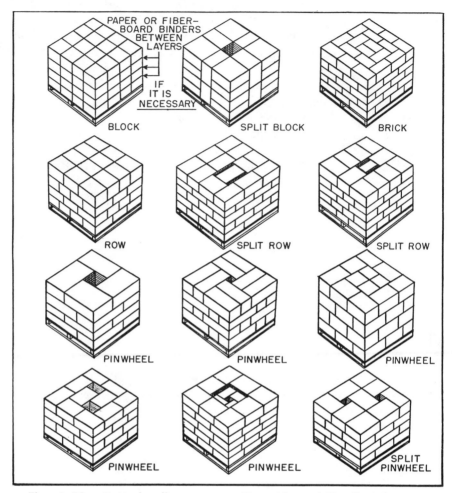

Fig. 4–12. Typical pallet patterns. (From *Material Handling Engineering Directory*, 1961–62.)

Weight
Strength
Permissible orientation of container for interlocking
Overhang
Underhang
Containers per layer
Carton length to width ratio
Amount of interlock (or overlap)
5. Handling equipment—
Available equipment
Attachments required

    Desirability of voids
    Alignment of voids
    Need for restraint
    Need for bracing
    Method of storing
6. Industry practice
7. Warehouse layout
8. Characteristics of movement

It will be observed that many of these are judgment factors, and working them into the selection process will depend on the knowledge and experience of the analyst. However, the fact that a regular object has rectangular dimensions considerably simplifies the final resolution of the pallet pattern selection. Although in the past many pallet patterns have been designed by trial-and-error methods, there are available a number of chart-type techniques which considerably simplify the problem. In general these consist of a matrix of container sizes such as that shown in Figure 4–13, accompanied by a chart of pallet patterns which have been determined by experimental methods, such as that shown in Figure 4–14. Much of the original research in this area was conducted by the U.S. Naval Research and Development Facility, under the direction of C. J. Heinrich.

An even more detailed analysis of these relationships has been made by Somer and Ringrose [13] of Phillips (Netherlands). Their method is illustrated in Figure 4–15.

7. Determine Method of Building the Unit Load. Previous sections of this chapter contain lists of factors for consideration at various stages in the development of the unit load. A review of these factors will suggest that a relative few are of primary significance when it comes to actually building or constructing the unit load itself.

Among these factors are:

1. Nature of items to be unitized—shape, weight, configuration, density
2. Quantities involved—for determination of manual, semi-mechanized, automatic
3. Customer wishes and capabilities—distribution warehouse, retailer, consumer, etc.
4. Methods of handling—shipping *and* receiving at destination
5. Cost of building the unit loads—labor, materials, equipment
6. Disposition of unitizing medium—integral, re-used, expendable

A consideration of the above and the resolution of the implied questions will assist in selecting the method to be used in building the load.

---

[13] T. J. Somer, and M. Ringrose, *Pallet Pattern Guide,* a private publication of N. V. Phillips Gloeilampenfabriken, Eindhoven, Netherlands.

6	1/2	7	1/2	8	1/2	9	1/2	10	1/2	11	1/2	12	1/2	13	1/2	14	1/2	15	1/2	16	1/2	17	1/2	18	1/2	19	1/2	20	1/2	21	1/2	22	1/2	23	1/2	24	1/2
5	29	29	29	29	29	29	29	29	27	27	27	27	27	23	23	23	23	23	23	23	23	23	23	23	23	14	14	14	14	14	14	14	14	14	14	14	14
1/2		29	29	29	29	29	29	29	27	27	27	27	27	23	23	23	23	23	23	23	23	23	23	23	23	14	14	14	14	14	14	14	14	14	14	14	14
6		29	29	29	29	29	29	29	27	27	27	27	27	23	23	23	23	23	23	23	23	23	23	23	23	14	14	14	14	14	14	14	14	14	14	14	14
1/2			29	29	29	29	29	29	29	27	27	27	27	23	23	23	23	23	23	23	23	23	23	23	23	13	13	13	13	14	14	14	14	14	14	14	14
7						29	29	29	29	29	29	29	29	23	23	23	23	23	23	23	23	23	23	23	23	14	14	14	14	14	14	14	14	14	14	14	14
1/2						29	29	29	29	29	29	29	27	23	23	23	23	23	23	23	23	23	23	14	14	14	14	14	14	14	14	14	14	14	14	12	12
8						29	29	29	26	26	26	26	26	22	22	22	22	22	22	21	21	19	19	19	19	14	14	14	14	14	14	14	14	12	12	12	12
1/2						28	28	28	25	25	25	25	25	22	22	22	22	19	19	19	19	14	14	14	14	14	14	14	14	14	14	14	12	12	12	12	12
9							25	25	25	25	25	25	24	22	22	20	19	19	19	18	18	18	14	14	14	14	14	14	14	14	14	14	12	12	6	6	6
1/2									25	25	25	25	25	21	21	20	18	16	16	16	14	14	14	14	14	14	14	12	12	12	12	6	6	6	4	4	4
10										25	24	24	21	21	21	20	18	16	16	16	14	14	14	14	14	14	14	14	6	6	6	6	4	4	4	4	4
1/2												21	21	20	20	20	16	16	16	16	16	14	14	14	14	10	10	10	6	6	6	6	4	4	4	4	4
11														17	17	17	15	15	12	12	12	12	10	10	10	10	6	6	6	6	4	4	4	4	4	4	4
1/2														17	17	17	15	15	12	11	11	11	9	9	10	10	6	6	6	6	4	4	4	4	4	4	4
12														17	17	17	15	11	11	11	11	8	8	8	8	8	6	6	6	6	4	4	4	3	3	3	3
1/2															16	16	15	11	11	11	8	8	8	8	8	8	6	6	6	6	4	4	4	3	3	3	3
13																8	8	8	8	8	8	8	8	8	8	6	6	6	6	6	4	4	4	3	3	3	3
1/2																		8	8	8	8	8	8	8	6	6	6	6	6	6	4	4	4	3	3	3	3
14																		8	8	8	8	8	8	8	6	6	6	6	6	6	4	4	3	3	3	3	3
1/2																			5	5	5	5	5	5	5	5	5	4	4	4	3	3	3	3	3	3	3
15																				5	5	5	5	5	5	5	5	4	3	3	3	3	3	3	3	3	3
1/2																					4	4	4	4	4	4	3	3	3	3	3	3	3	3	3	3	3
16																						4	4	4	4	4	3	3	3	3	3	3	3	3	3	3	3
1/2																							4	3	3	3	3	3	3	3	3	3	3	7	7	7	7
17																								7	7	7	7	7	7	7	7	7	7	7	7	7	7
1/2																									7	7	7	7	7	7	7	7	7	7	7	7	7
18																										7	7	7	7	7	7	7	7	7	7	7	7
1/2																											7	7	7	7	7	7	7	7	7	7	7
19																												7	7	7	7	7	7	7	7	7	7
1/2																														7	7	7	7	7	7	7	7
20																															7	7	7	7	7	7	7
1/2																																7	7	7	7	7	7
21																																	7	7	7	7	7

CHART FOR 40" X 48" PALLET

INSTRUCTIONS

1. LOCATE LENGTH OF CONTAINER AT TOP OF CHART.
2. LOCATE WIDTH OF CONTAINER ALONG SIDE OF CHART.
3. THE BOX AT THE INTERSECTION OF THE TWO DIMENSIONS CONTAINS A NUMBER WHICH REFERS TO A SPECIFIC PALLET PATTERN.
4. BY REFERRING TO THE PALLET PATTERN DIAGRAM WHICH CORRESPONDS TO THE NUMBER IN THE BOX, THE PATTERN FOR THE CONTAINER SIZE MAY BE DETERMINED.

Fig. 4–13. Pallet size matrix. (From *Warehouse Operations,* General Services Administration, February 1966, U.S.

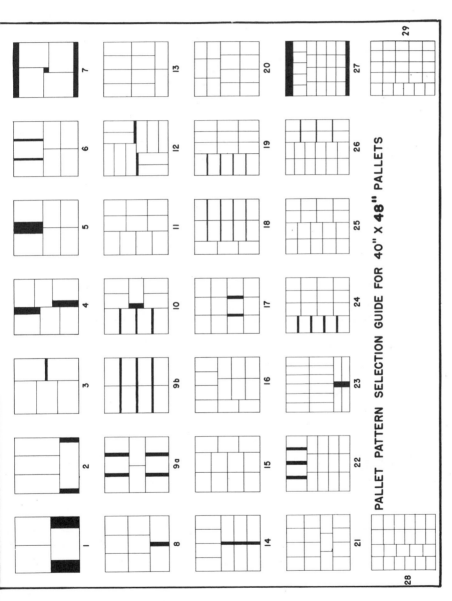

Fig. 4–14. Pallet pattern chart. (From *Warehouse Operations*, General Services Administration, February 1966, U.S. Government Printing Office, Washington, D. C.)

PALLET PATTERN SELECTION GUIDE FOR 40" X 48" PALLETS

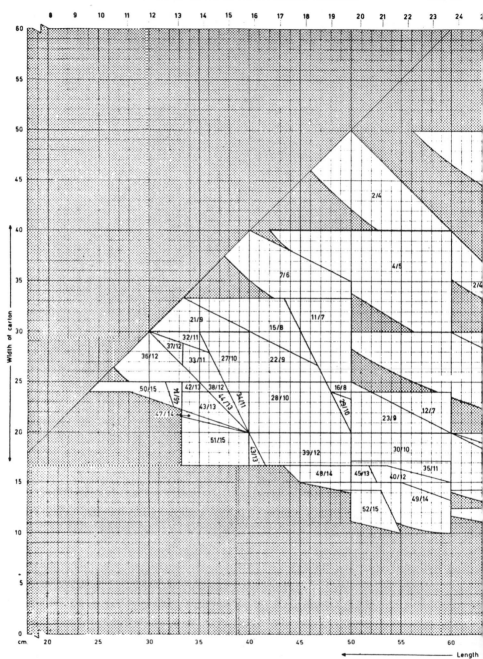

Fig. 4–15. Pallet pattern efficiency—numeric designations indicate
4–13). (From T. J. Somer and M. Ringrose, *Pallet Pattern*

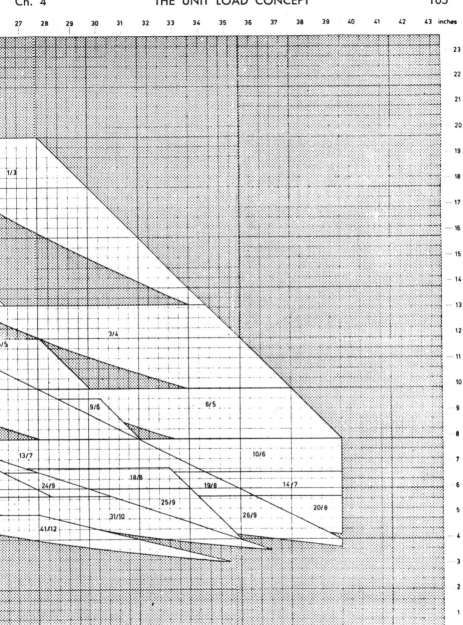

pallet pattern numbers (by different system than in Figs. 4–12 and
Guide, a publication of N. V. Phillips, Netherlands.)

Unitizing Aids. In the process of constructing the unit load it is likely that some unitizing aids will be required other than a pallet or skid. In some cases a pallet frame may be required to restrain the load; a guide or jig might be used in assuring the proper shape of the load; securing materials and supplies will often be necessary; and, if the quantity is large enough, palletizing equipment will be required. Some of these items will be discussed in more detail in the sections that follow.

Methods of Building Unit Loads. There are three general methods of constructing unit loads:

1. Manual
2. Semi-mechanized
3. Palletizers

In addition to building the load, there is the additional task of securing the unitized material to assure its safe transportation. Then there is the probability that the unit load will be disassembled at the receiving end, in which case provision must be made for this activity.

The manual construction of unit loads consists primarily of one or more operators arranging the materials into the desired pallet pattern, either on the floor, on a pallet, or on a slip sheet. In some cases a unitizing guide is used, which is essentially a two-sided box or frame against which the load is stacked to assure its proper alignment, size and configuration.

In the semi-mechanized method of building unit loads, a device is used which requires an operator to accept items for palletizing, usually from a conveyor, and then arrange them into the pallet pattern for each layer. The palletizer then transfers the layer to a pallet, lowers the load for the next layer while the operator repeats the layer-making procedure until the unit load is complete. A typical semi-mechanized palletizer is shown in Figure 6–78.

The automatic pallet loader or palletizer (Figure 6–77) is a machine which accepts cartons, bags, drums, or pails; arranges them into layers; places them on a pallet and discharges the complete unit load for removal by a conveyor, lift truck, or crane. The operation of the palletizer is somewhat as follows:

The basic process of forming a load in the machine consists of feeding a row of packages at a time onto a stripper plate. When a complete layer is assembled, the plate is withdrawn to deposit the layer on the empty pallet or the previous layer underneath. The pallet is lowered a distance equal to the height of the layer, the plate returns and the next layer is formed. Containers come off the metering conveyor at a uniform speed and spacing, and oriented in the same direction. A control unit (for example, a control cartridge combined with a photo cell counter) automatically governs the series of movements required for the particular pattern involved. As packages enter the loading area, the control unit signals the turning device, generally a retractable pin or arm, whenever one of them must be turned 90° to conform to the pattern. When a row has been formed, a pusher or ram device transfers it onto the stripped plate. If alternate layers require different row formations, as in interlocking patterns, controls also regulate this automatically. Usually some combination of stripper bar and pusher bar aligns and compacts each layer as it is deposited on the pallet. The controls count the number of containers in each row, number of rows in each layer, and number of layers in a complete load. They actuate the discharge of the fully loaded pallet and the insertion of an empty one in the pallet elevating mechanism.[14]

The total complement of palletizing equipment usually includes the following basic units: [15]

1. Pallet magazine
2. Pallet dispenser and positioner
3. Product in-feed conveyor
4. Pattern forming mechanism
5. Stripping mechanism
6. Elevator table and full load discharge mechanism
7. Full-load storage conveyor
8. Control system

Current models of pallet loaders are capable of providing the user with an infinite variety of pallet patterns, which may be changed by the operator in less than a minute, by inserting a "program selector." Maximum pallet and load sizes vary somewhat with different makes of palletizers, but a typical maximum load size is 50" × 60" × 84" high. The typical palletizer will handle up to 70 cartons per minute, weighing to 150 pounds each, and build them into a unit load up to about 4000 lbs.

As pointed out above, semi-automatic palletizers are somewhat less sophisticated, and generally include three basic features: [16]

1. They require an operator to form the pattern for each layer instead of controlling it automatically. However, they eliminate the lifting and take most of the effort out of the manual job.
2. By simpler design and a minimum of automatic controls and drives, they reduce initial costs drastically.
3. They aim at a maximum of flexibility in pallet patterns, carton sizes, and pallet sizes, with simple manual change-over from one size or pattern to another.

Special purpose palletizers are also available for handling such items as bagged material, open cases such as bottled goods, drums, kegs, pails, and so forth. It should be pointed out that although the term palletizer is commonly used to describe such equipment, it is somewhat of a misnomer, since most machines can build unit loads on a pallet, a sheet, or

14 "Mechanized Pallet Loaders," *Modern Materials Handling,* Oct. 1956, p. 107.
15 FMC Corporation, *FMC 406 Bag Loader For Bags and Pails,* Bulletin MH 201.
16 "Mechanized Pallet Loaders," *Modern Materials Handling,* Oct. 1956, p. 113.

on no support at all. There are also devices available known as de-palletizers, which operate by either of two general techniques: [17]

1. Removal of successive layers of products from the top of the unit load.
2. Removal of successive layers from the bottom of the unit load.

In general, these de-palletizers operate at a somewhat lower speed, about 30–40 cartons per minute.

Securing the Unit Load. As stated above, some unit loads are self-restraining while others require a method of securement to keep them from coming apart during subsequent movement and transportation activities. Among the various methods of securement commonly used are:

1. Steel strap
2. Wire
3. Tape—cloth or paper
4. Adhesives
5. Chip board or paper sheets
6. Dunnage
7. Storage aids—containers, bolsters, balloons, etc.
8. Interlocking or bonded loads
9. Truck attachments—clamps, etc.

Frequently the material being unitized will require or suggest either one or a combination of the above, or other techniques as applicable to the situation at hand.

Suggestions for Developing Unit Loads. Past experience of those who have dealt with the unit load process has suggested some rules of thumb which might be considered guides in the development of unit loads. Some of them are as follows: [18]

1. Consult package designer before establishing a unit load type and configuration.
2. Items smaller than fifteen per layer should be placed in containers
3. Consider the further unitizing of unit loads.
4. Do not stack cartons on their sides.
5. Consider reusable unit loads.
6. Consider disposable unit load materials and supplies.
7. Use jigs to guide building of unit loads.
8. Voids should be aligned parallel to the short dimension of the pallet.
9. Case length-to-width ratio should be fractional, not *even* multiples (i.e. 2½ to 1, not 2 to 1).

---

[17] Donald K. Morgan, "De-Palletizing Unit Loads," *Automation*, June 1966, p. 71.
[18] Partially adapted from T. J. Somer and M. Ringrose, *op. cit.*, and G. C. Thomas, *op. cit.*

10. Case interlock should be a minimum of 30% for a case of less than 10 lbs.; 20 to 25% for 10 to 40 lbs.; and 12 to 15% for over 40 lbs.
11. Packages in cartons should be oriented with case dimensions for added strength.

A review of this chapter will suggest other guidelines to be followed in designing and constructing unit loads.

PALLETLESS HANDLING

Another development in unit load handling is that which includes no pallet or other support in the final unit load. This method commonly makes use of a clamp type attachment on a fork lift truck. Unit loads of this type are most commonly made up of single items, such as rolls, bales, etc. or cartons, bags, etc., arranged in an optimum pattern so they can be picked up, moved, and stacked using the squeezing action of the clamp attachment. This technique is illustrated in Figure 4–16.

This technique, which was pioneered on cartons by the Procter and Gamble Company, under the direction of A. M. Spinanger, has the following advantages:

1. Lower operating costs
2. Lower initial investment
3. Safety and orderliness
4. Compatibility with other handling systems
5. Flexibility (since the warehouse is not limited to a single size unit load)
6. Well suited to high-turnover case goods

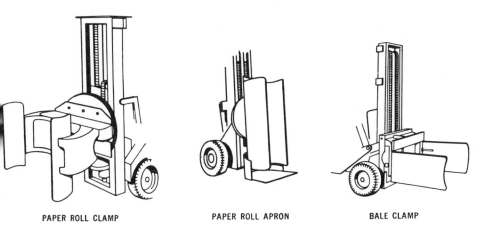

PAPER ROLL CLAMP   PAPER ROLL APRON   BALE CLAMP

Fig. 4–16. Palletless unit load attachments. (From *Modern Materials Handling Directory*.)

There are also some admitted disadvantages, such as:

1. Palletless systems not in universal use
2. Pallets are necessary for less than unit loads
3. Mixed loads cannot be stacked effectively
4. Floor loaded trucks must be unloaded manually

Other types of palletless handling techniques are indicated or implied by some of the attachments shown in Figure 4–3.

One of the obvious factors in the decision to use a palletless handling method is the cost involved. An illustration of typical costs suggested by the experience of Procter and Gamble [19] is shown in Figure 4–17.

UNIT LOAD EFFICIENCY

While the efficiency of the unit load in terms of pallet utilization has been suggested on the pallet size selection chart previously discussed, there are other ways in which efficiency might be determined. C. J. Heinrich suggests that the following information be obtained.

1. External dimensions
2. Internal dimensions
3. Tare weight
4. Designed weight capacity of commodities
5. Gross weight
6. Container costs

With this information and other data on hand, it is possible to calculate the following ratios:

1. $\dfrac{\text{Tare Weight}}{\text{Gross Weight}} = \%$

2. $\dfrac{\text{Tare Weight}}{\text{Load Capacity}} = \%$

3. $\dfrac{\text{Tare Weight}}{\text{Gross Cube}} = \text{lb/cu ft}$

4. $\dfrac{\text{Tare Weight}}{\text{Useable Cube}} = \text{lb/cu ft}$

5. $\dfrac{\text{Load Capacity}}{\text{Useable Cube}} = \text{lb/cu ft}$

6. $\dfrac{\text{Load Capacity}}{\text{Gross Cube}} = \text{lb/cu ft}$

7. $\dfrac{\text{Load Capacity}}{\text{Interior Floor Areas}} = \text{lb/sq ft}$

8. $\dfrac{\text{Useable Cube}}{\text{Gross Cube}} = \%$

9. $\dfrac{\text{Useable Cube}}{\text{Cost}} = \text{cubic feet/dollar}$

Heinrich suggests that the above ratios can be interpreted in terms of families of curves by types of container, and that it will also be possible to interpolate from such curves or charts in situations where actual data are not available.

[19] Procter and Gamble Company, *The Right Combination—a Report on Low Cost Warehouse Materials Handling*, 1964.

A. Wages Per Day	Wood Pallet	Palletless Clamp
1. Deposit pallets on dock	$ 4.60	None
2. Handle unit loads in warehouse	$ 33.00	$34.00
3. Handle pallets when empty	$ 5.90	None
4. Wage overhead at 20%	$ 8.70	$ 6.80
Subtotal	$ 52.20	$40.80
B. Pallet Expense Per Day		
1. Repair and maintenance	$ 26.60	None
2. Depreciation	$ 23.30	None
Subtotal	$ 49.90	$ 0.00
C. Clamp Expense Per Day		
1. Added maintenance	Base	$ 1.70
2. Added depreciation	Base	$ 3.50
Subtotal	$ 0.00	$ 5.20
D. Space Expense		
1. Pallet Storage Space	$ 9.60	None
Total Variable Costs	$111.70	$46.00

Annual Operating Expense Difference

Clamp vs. Wood Pallet $16,500

Fig. 4–17. Handling system operating expense comparison (10,000 cases per day, or 333 unit loads). (From *The Right Combination,* Procter and Gamble, 1964.)

CONCLUSION

This chapter has attempted to introduce the unit load concept with its multitude of advantages and has presented a wide variety of complex factors to be given consideration in its application. Considerably more detail can be found in some of the references cited, or may be obtained from the literature of manufacturers furnishing unit load equipment, materials, and supplies.

5

Equipment Concepts

In the material handling equation it was suggested that an analysis of the *materials* to be handled and the *moves* to be made should indicate the *method*. Chapter 7 will present the procedure by which such an analysis can be made. However, before becoming involved in problem-solving details, it is felt that a brief introduction to material handling equipment will prove helpful in comprehending the overall objective of the handling analysis—to design a *method*. And the method, nearly always, includes some type of handling equipment. Therefore, one of the major tasks of the material handling engineer is to become acquainted with the large and ever growing field of handling equipment, although it would be next to impossible for an individual to become intimately acquainted with *all* the types. The engineer's salvation lies in the fact that in a typical industry, business, or field of activity, only a fraction of the total is commonly applicable. Probably about 100 types—along with their attachments, accessories, etc.—will serve to implement a vast majority of industry's handling problems.

It should also be pointed out that in relatively few cases can a single piece of equipment do a complete job. Each type and variety of equipment has specific uses and advantages, and in most instances, two or more are combined into the solution of a single problem. More likely than not, a material handling system will include not only several pieces of equipment, but also more than one of the commonly designated handling "systems," since a handling problem large enough to be classified as a system will usually include many kinds of *moves*, and require several types of equipment. For example, a handling cycle might involve the use of an overhead crane or hoist to load a tractor-trailer train, which might be unloaded onto a conveyor by a fork lift truck. In fact, it is likely that an integrated group of carefully selected types of handling equipment will make up the most efficient system in a large majority of cases.

As the reader studies this and the following chapters, he should constantly keep in mind that the successful solution of most handling problems involves a proper matching of:

1. *Material* characteristics
2. *Move* requirements
3. *Method* (equipment) capabilities

—within the existing or contemplated physical facilities and environment, and against related costs.

THE PLACE OF EQUIPMENT IN THE HANDLING SYSTEM

As implied several times previously, equipment is not *always* required in order to solve a handling problem. Usually the simplest and most economical method should be utilized, which may not require any equipment. In fact, the work-simplification approach suggests the following general procedure:

1. *Eliminate* the move.
2. *Combine* the move with some other function: processing, inspection, storage, etc.
3. *Change the sequence* of activities to shorten, eliminate, or alter the move requirements.
4. *Simplify* the move to reduce the scope, extent, distance, method, equipment, etc.

Then—after having accomplished the above—the equipment would be selected, *if* necessary.

THE ROLE OF MANUAL HANDLING

A factor frequently overlooked in the rush to mechanize or automate is that manual handling *may* be the easiest, most efficient, and least expensive method of moving materials. So, even before attempting to select a piece of handling equipment the analyst should very carefully explore the possibility of manual handling methods.

Some of the characteristics which would generally tend to favor manual handling are:

1. Material Type
   a. Unit

2. Material Characteristics
   a. Small
   b. Light
   c. Fragile
   d. Costly
   e. Safe to handle
   f. Solid, or containerized
   g. Scrap
3. Material Quantity
   a. Small, low volume
   b. Single items, one at a time
4. Move Source and Destination—close together
5. Move Logistics
   a. Workplace (small area)
   b. Multi-plane
   c. Level to level
   d. Variable profile
   e. Complex path
   f. Working height
   g. Complicated move
6. Move Characteristics
   a. Short distance
   b. Infrequent
   c. Low rate
   d. Non-uniform rate
   e. Variable speed
   f. Irregular
   g. Intermittent
   h. Variable
   i. Low percentage of handling
   j. Variable sequence
7. Move Type
   a. Maneuvering
   b. Positioning
8. Handling Unit—same as items 1 and 2
9. Equipment
   a. Probably none
   b. Operator controlled
10. Manpower
    a. Relatively small amount of operator time required
    b. Low hourly rate
11. Physical Restrictions
    (As implied by other characteristics of the problem, above; otherwise, not applicable)

It should be pointed out that all the above characteristics do not imply *only* manual methods. Some of them, usually in combination with other characteristics or because of the nature of the material, will require mechanical devices. Only after it has been proved that manual handling is more costly, too dangerous, too slow, etc., should the analyst turn his attention to mechanical equipment.

NON-POWERED EQUIPMENT

Included with the several hundred types of material handling equipment are a number that are non-powered and/or manually operated or controlled, i.e., not "mechanized." The following list indicates some of the situations in which non-powered or manual equipment may fit into the handling system: [1]

1. Where handling volume is limited, or handling activity can be extended over a long period of time.
2. Where building limitations preclude use of heavier or bigger devices.
3. Where service conditions, such as confined areas, explosive atmospheres, or quiet surroundings necessitate the advantages of non-powered equipment.
4. Where equipment is used not only for handling, but for semi-live storage or display.
5. When investment capital is limited.
6. When the required flexibility, utility, mobility, and portability can only be obtained in a non-powered floor device.
7. Where the maintenance facilities are minimal or nonexistent.
8. Where the mobile equipment must be tailored to the product or need.
9. Where the operating efficiency of non-powered equipment is higher than that of any other type.
10. When loads are relatively light and equipment is to be manually moved.
11. For stand-by use.
12. For durable, low-cost operation.

The above possibilities should be checked before mechanized or powered equipment is seriously considered.

BASIC HANDLING EQUIPMENT TYPES

In general, it can be said that there are three "basic" types of material handling equipment: conveyors, cranes and hoists, and trucks. As will be pointed out later, there *are* sub-classifications under each, plus additional categories for accessories, attachments, and other related equipment. However, since the three basic types form a convenient framework for discussing handling equipment, they are briefly described as follows:

Conveyors

These are gravity or powered devices commonly used for moving uniform loads continuously from point-to-point over fixed paths, where the *primary function is conveying*.

[1] Caster and Floor Truck Manufacturer's Association, *Engineering and Purchasing Planbook*, 1959, pp. 16–18.

A. Common examples:
1. Roller conveyor
2. Belt conveyor
3. Chute
4. Trolley conveyor
5. Bucket
6. Pneumatic

B. Conveyors are generally useful when:
a. Loads are uniform
b. Materials move continuously
c. Route does not vary
d. Load is constant
e. Movement rate is relatively fixed
f. Conveyors can bypass cross traffic
g. Path to be followed is fixed
h. Movement is from one fixed point to another point
i. Automatic counting, sorting, weighing, dispatching is needed
j. In-process storage or inspection are required
k. Necessary to pace production

l. Process control is needed
m. Controlled flow is required
n. Handling hazardous materials
o. Handling materials at extreme temperatures or under adverse conditions
p. Handling is required in dangerous areas
q. Manual handling and/or lifting is undesirable
r. Integrating machines into a "system"
s. Handling between work places
t. Flexibility is required to meet changes in production processes, volume or pace
u. Conveyors can be installed overhead to save floor space
v. Necessary to make constant visual check of production processes

Cranes and Hoists

These overhead devices are usually utilized to move varying loads, intermittently, between points within an area fixed by the supporting and guiding rails, where the *primary function is transferring.*

A. Common examples:
1. Overhead travelling crane
2. Gantry crane
3. Jib crane
4. Hoist
5. Stacker crane
6. Monorail

B. Cranes and hoists are most commonly used when:
a. Movement is within a fixed area
b. Moves are intermittent
c. Loads vary in size or weight
d. Cross traffic would interfere with conveyors
e. Units handled are not uniform

Industrial Trucks

These are hand or powered vehicles (non-highway) used for the movement of mixed *or* uniform loads, intermittently, over various paths having suitable running surfaces and clearances, where the *primary function is maneuvering or transporting.*

A. Common examples:
   1. Fork lift truck   4. Tractor-trailer train
   2. Platform truck   5. Hand stacker
   3. Two-wheel hand truck   6. Walkie truck
B. Industrial trucks are generally used when:
   a. Material is moved intermittently
   b. Movement is over varying routes
   c. Loads are uniform *or* mixed in size and weight
   d. Length of move is moderate
   e. Cross-traffic would prohibit conveyors
   f. Clearances and running surfaces are adequate and suitable
   g. Most of the operation consists of handling (or maneuvering, stacking, etc.)
   h. Material can be put up into unit loads

Each of the above types will be further detailed on the following pages, but attention should be centered here on—

1. The basic capabilities of each type
2. Their relationships to the "factors" to be considered in analyzing handling problems

These interrelationships are shown in Figure 5–1.

BASIC HANDLING SYSTEMS [2]

In addition to the basic handling equipment types outlined above, handling activities may be classified in terms of types of *"handling systems,"* which is sometimes helpful in conceptualizing production situations and problem solutions. However, it should be pointed out that the word "system," as used here, does *not* mean the same as the word "systems" in the "systems approach"—discussed in Chapter 9. Nevertheless, the term "handling system" *is* fairly common, and will be understood here as a classification of handling methods according to some characteristic of the situation useful in solving the handling problem. Handling systems are as varied in their makeup as are the operations to which they may be applied, and different plants in the same industry may even use different systems for the same general purpose. The "systems" as described here may be used exclusively in a plant, *or* as components of an integrated and more all-encompassing plant material handling system. The equipment types referred to are described in Chapter 6. The basic systems are:

[2] This section has been adapted and condensed from a similar section in *Production Handbook*, 1972 edition, The Ronald Press Co. Refer to it for additional details.

TASK and EQUIPMENT CHARACTERISTICS / EQUIPMENT TYPE	CONVEYORS — Moving uniform loads continuously from point to point over fixed paths where primary function is transporting	CRANES and HOISTS — Moving varying loads intermittently to any point within a fixed area	INDUSTRIAL TRUCKS — Moving mixed or uniform loads intermittently over various paths with suitable surfaces where primary function is maneuvering
MATERIAL			
Volume	high	low, medium	low, medium, relatively high
Type	individual item, unit load, bulk	indiv. item, unit load, variety	indiv. item, unit load, variety
Shape	regular, uniform, irregular	irregular	regular, uniform
Size	uniform	mixed, variable	mixed, or uniform
Weight	low, medium, heavy, uniform	heavy	medium, heavy
MOVE			
Distance	any, relatively unlimited	moderate, within area	moderate, 250–300 ft.
Rate, Speed	uniform, variable	variable, irregular	variable
Frequency	continuous	intermittent, irregular	intermittent
Origin, Destination	fixed	may vary	may vary
Area covered	point to point	confined to area within rails	variable
Sequence	fixed	may vary	may vary
Path	mechanical, fixed pt. to fixed pt.	may vary	may vary
Route	fixed, area to area	variable, no path	variable, but over defined path
Location	indoors, outdoors	indoors, outdoors	indoors, outdoors
Cross traffic	problems in by-passing	can by-pass, no effect	can by-pass, maneuver, no effect
Primary function	transport, process/store in move	lift & carry, position	stack, maneuver, carry, load, unload
% Transport in operation	should be high	should be low	should be low
METHOD			
Load support method	none, or in containers	suspension; pallet, skid, none	from beneath; pallet, skid, container
Load/unload characteristics	automatic, manual, designated points	manual, self, any point	self; any point on available path
Oper. accompany load	no	may or may not, usually does	usually does; may be remote
BUILDING CHARACT.			
Cost of floor space	low, medium	high	medium, high
Clear height	if enough, conv. can go overhead	high	low, medium, high
Floor load capacity	depends on type conv. & mat'l.	depends on activity	medium, high
Running surfaces	not applicable	not applicable	must be suitable
Aisles	not applicable	not applicable	must be sufficient
Congested areas	fair	good	poor

Fig. 5–1. General characteristics of basic material handling equipment types. (From *Production Handbook*,

1. *Equipment* Oriented Systems

These are commonly described in terms of the three basic types suggested above; conveyors, cranes and hoists, and industrial vehicles. It will be seen in examining Figure 5–1 that each of these groups is applicable to certain types of handling situations. Equipment-oriented systems are further classified as follows:

A. *Industrial truck systems.* *Platform trucks and skids* constitute one system. The low lift trucks will pick up, transport, and set down skid-loaded materials, and while the low lift trucks are primarily used for moving, the high lift type is used for stacking, maneuvering, positioning, etc.

The *fork truck and pallet system* is simliar to the platform truck and skid system, except that forks require less clearance than the platforms, making it possible to use pallets, which are shallower than skids, and thereby saving space in tiering. Double-faced pallets make possible wider load distribution, another space saving feature. Also, fork lift trucks can usually stack higher than the platform trucks.

The *tractor-trailer system* is economical for hauling large quantities of materials for distances *over* 250–300 feet. The cost per ton for handling materials in this way is very low, as one tractor can move many loaded trailers at one time. Loading and unloading may be done by cranes, hoists, platform lift, or fork trucks—or even by hand.

B. *Conveyor Systems.* Conveyors and conveyor systems are more adaptable to mass movement than the unit systems. The application of control devices, programming systems and careful layout can often reduce the time and manpower used in material handling. Conveyors become uneconomical when they must be loaded and unloaded frequently or when complicated installations must be changed frequently.

C. *Overhead Systems.* In some cases overhead cranes and monorail equipment are used in operations where floor space utilization or product characteristics make the use of fork lift trucks or conveyors undesirable, and where travel distances and paths are reasonably restricted. Overhead systems are particularly useful in the production of large and/or heavy parts or products, produced in relatively low quantities, such as large engines, turbines, building trusses, large castings, machine tools, aircraft, etc.

2. *Material* (Load) Oriented Systems

These are commonly identified as: unit handling systems; bulk handling systems; and liquid handling systems. Here again it can be seen that certain types of equipment fit better into one category than another, while some are entirely impractical in a particular category.

A. *Unit handling* systems are generally more flexible and require less investment than many other approaches. They are particularly applicable to operations where non-repetitive handling sequences are found, or where a variety of products and materials are handled. However, they can also be applied in highly repetitive, large volume operations with considerable success. The unit load concept was further developed in Chapter 4.

B. *Bulk handling* systems usually ignore the identity of the individual particles, pieces, or items handled. Typical materials are coal, grain, ore, gravel, stone, powdered materials, etc. Bulk systems handle a flow of material on a continuous basis by means of various types of conveyors, power shovels, scoops, cranes, drag lines, and construction equipment. Fork lift trucks may also be used to handle bulk materials in bulk handling containers. Front end loaders and scoop attachments on lift trucks are common for handling operations such as the loading and unloading of bulk materials from freight cars.

Highway trucks, railroad cars, and ships are also adapted to accommodate the handling of bulk materials with special truck bodies and freight cars equipped with rapid loading and unloading devices.

Also bulk materials are "shapeless" and often confined in storage and transit by containers, such as sacks, tanks, bins, hoppers, skid boxes, barrels, etc. Once the material is confined, the handling problem is really no different than in the case of any other unit load. Finer varieties of bulk materials are also handled by pneumatic equipment.

C. *Liquid materials* are in a class almost by themselves, and require rather specialized handling equipment. Because of the extreme differences in material characteristics and handling equipment used with liquid materials, it is impractical to cover them in this text. The interested reader should refer to published materials in this specialized field, commonly covered by the chemical engineer.

3. Method (Production) Oriented Systems

These are commonly described or defined in terms of the types of production in which they are used.

A. The *manual* system implies the use of manual handling methods because of the nature of the operations, such as low volume, wide variety, extreme fragility, etc. Such situations would normally imply that anything other than manual handling would be undesirable or uneconomical.

B. *Mechanized* or *automated* systems imply increasing volume and/or standardization of product and therefore the use of more sophisticated, complex or mechanized equipment as the situation warrants. These systems make extensive use of conveyors, automatic controls, transfer machines, and other methods of mechanically and/or automatically handling parts or products between operations.

C. *Mass production handling systems* imply the presence of high volume which make it possible to apply complex material handling machinery economically. In mass production the basic manufacturing machinery is usually no different from that which is used in other production applications. The advantages of mass production are derived from the ability to control and manage repetitive handling operations automatically by the use of mechanical, electrical, electronic, photo-electric, and magnetically controlled equipment.

D. *Job shop handling system* describes the conventional concept of a "job shop" involving metal working operations on a small volume basis, although many semi-production operations also fall into this category. The manufacture of machine tools, heavy aircraft, glass tableware, pottery, furniture and many other everyday items is based on job shop type operations. In such cases, the volume is seldom enough to justify large investments in automatic handling equipment. The unit load system, with portable conveyors or sectional conveyor units, is usually used, although by establishing flexible or adaptable handling systems suitable to several similar products, and requiring the application of similar handling techniques, at least a part of the facility can approach the efficiencies of mass production. In some cases, efficient in-process inventory management can build up handling quantities to a level approaching small run mass production. Thus, the handling efficiency of a job shop is more dependent upon good management than on equipment applications.

In general *job shop type bulk* handling operations incorporate several types of handling equipment into an integrated system. As in the case of job shop unit handling systems, management is more critical than in mass production applications.

4. Function Oriented Handling Systems

These attack the problem of classifying handling equipment and activities on the basis of the function performed by the equipment. This method of classification, which appears useful from a problem-solving point of view is outlined later in this chapter, and divides equipment into the following categories:

A. Transportation systems
B. Elevating systems
C. Conveying systems
D. Transferring systems
E. Self-loading systems

While the above classification of handling systems will neither "solve" any problems nor cover every situation, it should prove helpful as background for a discussion of specific equipment types.

EQUIPMENT CLASSIFICATIONS

Having presented the three basic equipment types, and the several handling "systems," it is now advisable to further delineate the kinds of equipment in each type and/or system. It can be rightly concluded from the preceding that the problem of classifying equipment is not a clear-cut matter, since there are several possible bases for classification. Most of the existing classifications consist primarily of a further breakdown of the three basic types. As an insight into the complexity of the handling equipment field, and as partial guides to understanding the breadth of the field, a few of the more common classifications are presented. Based on the "three basic types" classification, but breaking it down into sub-groups is the following: [3]

11. Cranes, derricks, hoists and winches
12. Conveyors
13. Industrial trucks, tractors, trailers, stackers . . . and wheeled devices
14. Fixed track equipment (other than conveyors)
15. Elevating devices
16. Industrial storage facilities
17. Shipping containers
18. Packaging materials and equipment
19. Materials and equipment not listed above

The above classification (devised and copyright by John R. Immer) contains much more than just equipment. In fact, in its complete form, it is called a system for classifying material handling *information*. Other major headings are:

20 Industry	40 Material handled
30 Types of operation	50 Systems of organization

Each is sub-divided into a large number of topics, all of which are assigned numerical codes for the purpose of filing any material handling related information.

A second classification, developed by H. H. Hall, covers a far broader equipment range: [4]

---

[3] *Materials Handling Engineering Directory and Handbook,* Industrial Publishing Co. Cleveland, Ohio, 1965, pp. A/10–A/20.

[4] H. A. Bolz and G. E. Hagemann, *Materials Handling Handbook,* The Ronald Press Co., N.Y., 1958, pp. 1–5 to 1–16.

1. Conveyors
2. Cranes, elevators, and hoists
3. Positioning, weighing, and control equipment
4. Industrial vehicles
5. Motor vehicles (highway)
6. Railroad cars
7. Marine carriers
8. Aircraft
9. Containers and supports

It is felt that the above classification, in its entirety, is one of the most inclusive, even though it does not contain all known equipment types. However, it will serve as a very complete listing, and as a basis for a filling system of equipment data.

One author [5] has tackled the problem on the basis of the *function* performed by the equipment. While this method of classification appears more useful from a problem-solving point of view, it too includes debatable areas, especially where a type of equipment is capable of performing more than one function. However, since it does perform a helpful service in guiding the problem solver, the functions are described below.

1. *Transportation systems*
   Horizontal motion over fixed or variable, level or nearly level routes by pulling or pushing, on surface riding vehicles.
2. *Elevating systems*
   Vertical motion over fixed vertical or steeply inclined routes with continuous or with intermittent motion.
3. *Conveying systems*
   Horizontal, vertical or compound motions, through the air, over fixed routes by gravity or by power.
4. *Transferring systems*
   Horizontal, inclined or declined motions, through the air, over fixed routes or limited areas, with intermittent motion.
5. *Self-loading systems*
   Intermittent motion with machines that pick up, move horizontally, set down and, in some cases, tier loads without other handling. Also known as Unit-Load Systems.

One further "classification" (Figure 5–2) worthy of mention divides the entire list of equipment types into—

1. discontinuous movement
2. continuous movement
3. potential movement

[5] D. O. Haynes, "Master Chart of Basic Materials Handling Systems," *Distribution Age,* April, 1953.

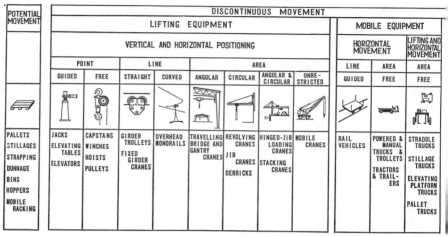

POTENTIAL MOVEMENT	DISCONTINUOUS MOVEMENT											
	LIFTING EQUIPMENT								MOBILE EQUIPMENT			
	VERTICAL AND HORIZONTAL POSITIONING								HORIZONTAL MOVEMENT		LIFTING AND HORIZONTAL MOVEMENT	
	POINT		LINE		AREA				LINE	AREA	AREA	
	GUIDED	FREE	STRAIGHT	CURVED	ANGULAR	CIRCULAR	ANGULAR & CIRCULAR	UNRE-STRICTED	GUIDED	FREE	FREE	
PALLETS STILLAGES STRAPPING DUNNAGE BINS HOPPERS MOBILE RACKING	JACKS ELEVATING TABLES ELEVATORS	CAPSTANS WINCHES HOISTS PULLEYS	GIRDER TROLLEYS FIXED GIRDER CRANES	OVERHEAD MONORAILS	TRAVELLING BRIDGE AND GANTRY CRANES	REVOLVING CRANES JIB CRANES DERRICKS	HINGED-JIB LOADING CRANES STACKING CRANES	MOBILE CRANES	RAIL VEHICLES	POWERED & MANUAL TRUCKS & TROLLEYS TRACTORS & TRAIL-ERS	STRADDLE TRUCKS STILLAGE TRUCKS ELEVATING PLATFORM TRUCKS PALLET TRUCKS	

Fig. 5–2. Material handling equipment classification. (*Material.* Copyright; reproduced by permission of the Controller

A significant feature is the series of sketches used to help identify each category. The groups are divided on the basis of the functional and mechanical features of each equipment type.

For the purposes of this text, handling equipment will be classified as shown in Figure 5–3, which contains 140 of the more commonly used equipment types. Many of them are covered in the next chapter, where selected types are: (1) defined, (2) their characteristics listed, and (3) illustrated.

TRENDS IN HANDLING EQUIPMENT

Early handling equipment was simple, manually operated, and relatively uncomplicated. As equipment manufacturers have developed their lines and competed in serving the market, equipment lines and types have multiplied, become more complicated, more sophisticated and more mechanized. In reviewing equipment progress over a period of years, it has become apparent that several trends are developing. Some of these are:

    A. General
        1. Engineered handling systems are replacing mechanization of individual handling tasks.
        2. Handling is being integrated into the processes.
        3. Automatic and remote controls are being built into equipment.
        4. Communications capabilities are being integrated into equipment.

	CONTINUOUS MOVEMENT							
	CONVEYING EQUIPMENT							
	TRANSPORTING				FREE ROLLING	SLIDING	PROPELLING	VIBRATING
WING CHANISM	POWERED CONVEYORS				LINE	UNPOWERED	POWERED	POWERED
	CONTINUOUS CARRYING	LINKED CARRIERS	DETACHABLE CARRIERS	CONTINUOUS PROPULSION	UNPOWERED	INTERMITTENT	CONTINUOUS	CONTINUOUS
ERHEAD OWLINE ROLLEY NVEYORS — FLOOR OWLINE ROLLEY NVEYORS OT TUGS	FLAT BELT; TROUGHED; CLOSED BELT; SLAT; CARRIER & CHAIN CONVEYORS.	BUCKET, EN MASSE, APRON AND PAN CONVEYORS, CROSSBAR CONVEYORS.	OVERHEAD TROLLEY CONVEYORS OVERHEAD CHAIN CONVEYORS	POWERED ROLLER CONVEYORS PNEUMATIC CONVEYORS AIR FILM CONVEYORS	ROLLER, WHEEL AND BALL TRACKS	CHUTES	SCREW CONVEYORS SPIRAL ELEVATORS	VIBRATORY FEEDERS, SCREENS, ELEVATORS
IN CONVEYORS OF THIS TYPE THE TRANSPORT- NG MECHANISM TRAVELS FORWARD WITH THE MATERIAL CONVEYED				IN CONVEYORS OF THIS TYPE THE TRANSPORTING MECHANISM DOES NOT ITSELF TRAVEL FORWARD				

ndling, No. 2, Ministry of Technology, London, 1965. British Crown
r Britannic Majesty's Stationery Office.)

5. Receiving and shipping are being given increased attention.
6. More attention is being given to the maintenance aspects of equipment.
7. Storage and order picking activities are being mechanized and automated.
8. Specialized pieces of equipment are being developed for specific tasks.
9. Equipment is frequently designed for versatility, flexibility, and adaptability.
10. Trend toward larger plants and fewer of them, more highly mechanized and automated.
11. Tendency to make use of vertical space.
12. Application of handling know-how to waste materials.
13. More handling "installations" being done on a "turn-key" basis.
14. Mechanization of assembly and inspection operations.
15. Better cooperation among parties—user, manufacturer, consultant, carrier.
16. Increasing flexibility of transfer machines.
17. Greater use of continuous processing.
18. More mechanization in warehousing.
19. More "build-it-yourself" equipment components.
  B. Conveyors
   1. Higher speeds.
   2. Larger capacity.
   3. Flexible, adaptable.
   4. More emphasis on controls.

C. Cranes
  1. Remote, electronic control.
  2. Computer control on stacker crane systems.
D. Trucks
  1. Electric
     a. Improved controls.
     b. Better motors.
     c. Fuel cells.
     d. Longer operating hours.
  2. Gasoline, etc.
     a. Better engines.
     b. Hydrostatic transmissions.
     c. Higher torque at lower speeds.
     d. Individual drive wheels.
  3. Both
     a. Higher travel and lift speeds and heights.
     b. More economical operation.
     c. Increased up-time.
     d. Power steering and brakes.
     e. "One-shot" lubrication.
     f. Automatic transmissions.
     g. Adjustable, "luxury" seats.
     h. More attachments.
     i. Smaller, lighter (1 to 1 ratio of load to vehicle).
     j. Operator to ride *with* load for stock picking.
     k. Riderless trucks and tractors; electronically guided.
     l. Increased capacity (100,000 lbs.).
     m. Better visibility.
     n. Increasing use of side-loading trucks.
E. Bulk Handling
  1. Computer control of batching and weighing.
  2. Belt conveyors moving more material faster, farther, and at lower cost.
  3. Pneumatic conveyors more widely used for smaller operations.
  4. New construction materials and techniques used on containers and conveyors to reduce cost and extend applications.
F. Miscellaneous
  1. Growth in application of air casters and pallets.
  2. Increased use of air freight.
  3. Wider use of industrial robots.
  4. Automatic loading and unloading of carriers.
  5. More extensive use of work feeders.
  6. Greater acceptance of intermodal containerization.

In designing handling systems or selecting handling equipment, the above trends should be kept in mind. When possible, they should be used as guides to the development of proposed problem solutions.

I. Conveyors
  A. Belt
    1. closed
    2. flat
    3. portable
    4. telescoping
    5. trough

  B. Bucket
    1. conveyor
      a. gravity discharge
      b. pivoted bucket
    2. loader (portable)
      (Bucket elevator—
      (See Sec. II B)

  C. Cable (aerial tramway)

  D. Chain
    1. apron
    2. arm
    3. car type
    4. cross-bar
    5. drag
    6. en-masse
    7. flat-top
    8. flight
    9. pallet
    10. power and free
    11. pusher bar
    12. rolling
    13. slat
    14. sliding
    15. suspended tray
    16. tow
      a. over-head
      b. flush
      c. under-floor
    17. trolley
      a. cable
      b. chain

  E. Chute

  F. Magnetic

  G. Pneumatic
    1. pipeline
    2. air-activated gravity
    3. tube

  H. Roller
    1. accordion
    2. gravity
    3. live
    4. portable
    5. rack
    6. spiral

  I. Screw
    (Trolley, See ID 17)

  J. Vertical Reciprocating

  K. Vibrating

  L. Wheel
    1. gravity
    2. live
    3. rack
    4. spiral

II. Cranes, Elevators, Hoists, Monorails
  A. Cranes
    1. jib
      a. floor mount
      b. top and bottom
      c. wall mount
    2. portable
    3. travelling
      a. bridge
        —top-running
        —under-running
      b. gantry
        —double leg
        —single leg
    4. stacker
      a. crane
      b. storage machine
    5. mobile
      a. aerial (helicopter)
      b. crawler
      c. rail
      d. rubber-tired

  B. Elevators
    1. bucket
      a. continuous
        —external discharge
        —internal discharge
        —super capacity
      b. spaced
        —centrifugal discharge
        —positive discharge
    2. floor-to-floor
    3. freight
    4. lifts
    5. portable

  C. Hoists
    1. chain
    2. powered
    3. skip

  D. Monorails

III. Industrial Vehicles
  A. Non-Powered
    1. dolly
    2. wheelbarrow
    3. 2-wheel hand truck
    4. 4-wheel hand truck
      a. box
      b. platform
      c. special
    5. hand lift (jack)
      a. pallet
      b. skid
    6. lift table
    7. semi-live skid
    8. stacker (See II B5)
    9. trailer

  B. Powered
    1. crane
    2. fork lift
    3. front-end loader
    4. narrow aisle
      a. general
      b. order picker
    5. platform
    6. platform lift
    7. reach
    8. side loader
    9. straddle carrier
    10. straddle crane
    11. straddle truck (out-rigger)
    12. tractor
    13. tractor-trailer train
    14. walkie
    15. special
      a. die handling
      b. personnel carrier
      c. ram

IV. Containers and Supports
  A. Shop Containers
    1. bags
    2. boxes
    3. cartons
    4. crates
    5. pallet boxes
    6. skid boxes
    7. tote boxes
    8. trays

  B. Bulk Containers
    1. barrels
    2. drums
    3. tanks
    4. special

  C. Shipping Containers
    1. bulk
    2. freight
    3. liquid

  D. Supports
    1. bins
    2. frames
    3. pallets
    4. racks
    5. shelves
    6. skids

V. Auxiliary Equipment
  A. Air Film
  B. Ball Table
  C. Communications
  D. Batteries
  E. Controls
  F. Crane Attachments
  G. Dock Boards
  H. Dock Levelers
  I. Lift Truck Attachments
  J. Packaging
  K. Pallet Loader
  L. Pallet Unloader
  M. Positioner
  N. Ramp
  O. Shrink-Film Packaging
  P. Weighing
  Q. Work Positioner

Fig. 5–3. Classification of handling equipment.

CONCLUSION

This chapter has attempted to acquaint the reader with the equipment phase of the handling problem solution. Basic handling systems have been identified, types of equipment have been classified and equipment functions have been described. The place of equipment in the system has been discussed, along with suggestions to aid in choosing between manual, non-powered and mechanized methods.

Because of the rapidly growing material-handling industry, and its continual introduction of new equipment types and variations, the handling engineer must make a concentrated effort to keep up with the field. Some of the ways he can do this are:

1. Trade publications
2. Sales literature
3. Trade expositions
4. Sales engineers
5. Training courses, conferences
6. Professional society meetings
7. Texts and handbooks

Further details on many types of equipment will be found in Chapter 6, and the sources listed at the end of that chapter.

6
Selected Material Handling Equipment

There are about 570 types of material handling equipment currently on the market, with more being introduced continually. For any *one* person to be knowledgeable on this wide range of subject matter is almost impossible. This chapter will not even attempt such coverage, but will briefly introduce, describe, and illustrate a reasonable number of the types commonly used in industry. And, at that, many of those common in the rather specialized industries—such as chemical, mining, construction, etc.—will have to be omitted because of space limitations.

Those presented in this chapter are selected from the list of about 140 outlined in the classification in Figure 5–3, which is abbreviated here as Figure 6–1. Due to space limitations, only about 80 types are presented.* The numbering system in Figure 6–1 is used to identify the illustrations in this chapter.

In presenting each type of equipment, an attempt has been made to be brief yet understandable. Pictures and drawings are used when appropriate. The characteristics listed include: (1) advantages, (2) uses, (3) applications, and (4) limitations. It is understood that nearly *all* types of handling equipment have a number of common advantages:

1. Relieving manpower of high-effort tasks
2. Safer handling; less accidents
3. Reduced handling cost
4. Increased production
5. Reduced product damage

The reader should also understand that the equipment characteristics suggested on the following pages are only presented as guides, to give an

---

* The author has reviewed about 2000 photos to select those in this chapter. *All* were selected to show as clearly as possible in one photo:
    (1) what the equipment looks like, for identification purposes (2) how it works, or is built (3) how it is used (4) uncluttered backgrounds.
Therefore, some do show older models of equipment, as it was not possible to get satisfactory photos of current models. However, for the purposes of *understanding* the equipment, this is a relatively unimportant point.

I. Conveyors
A. Belt
  1. flat [6-2]
  2. portable [6-3]
  3. trough [6-4]
B. Bucket
  1. gravity discharge
  2. pivoted bucket (Bucket elevator-see Sec. II B)
C. Chain
  1. apron [6-5]
  2. arm [6-6]
  3. car type [6-7]
  4. drag [6-8]
  5. flat-top [6-9, 6-9]
  6. flight [6-11]
  7. power and free [6-12]
  8. slat [6-13]
  9. tow
    a. over-head 6-14]
    b. flush
    c. under-floor [6-15]
  10. trolley [6-16]
D. Chute
E. Pneumatic
  1. pipeline [6-18]
  2. air activated gravity [6-19]
  3. tube [6-20]
F. Roller
  1. gravity [6-21]
  2. live [6-22]
  3. portable
  4. rack [6-23]
G. Screw
  (Trolley, See IC 10)
H. Vibrating [6-25]
I. Wheel [6-26

II. Cranes, Elevators Hoists, Monorails [6-27]
A. Cranes
  1. jib
    a. floor mount [6-28]
    b. top and bottom [6-29]
    c. wall mount
  2. travelling
    a. bridge [6-30]
    —top-running [6-31]
    —under-running
    b. gantry [6-32]
  3. stacker
    a. crane [6-33]
    b. storage machine [6-34]
  4. mobile [6-34A]
B. Elevators
  1. bucket
    a. continuous [6-35]
    —external discharge
    —internal discharge
    b. spaced [6-36]
    —centrifugal discharge
    —positive discharge
  2. portable [6-37]
C. Hoists [6-38, 6-39]
D. Monorails [6-40]
III. Industrial Vehicles
A. Non-Powered
  1. dolly [6-41]
  2. 4-wheel hand truck [6-42]
  3. hand lift (jack) [6-43]
  4. semi-live skid
  5. stacker (See II B 2)
  6. trailer (See III B 10)

B. Powered
  1. crane [6-44]
  2. fork lift [6-45, 6-46]
  3. narrow aisle
    a. general
    b. order-picker [6-47]
  4. platform (load carrier) [6-48]
  5. platform lift [6-49]
  6. reach [6-50]
  7. side loader [6-51]
  8. straddle carrier [6-52]
  9. straddle truck (out-rigger) [6-53]
  10. tractor-trailer train [6-54, 6-55]
  11. walkie [6-56, 6-57]
IV. Containers and Supports
A. Shop Containers
  1. pallet boxes [6-58]
  2. skid boxes [6-59]
  3. tote boxes [6-60]
B. Bulk Containers [6-61]
C. Shipping Containers [6-62]
D. Supports
  1. frame [6-63, 6-64]
  2. pallet
  3. rack [6-65, 6-66, 6-67]
  4. skid [6-68]
V. Auxiliary Equipment
A. Ball Table [6-69]
B. Crane Attachments [6-70, 6-71, 6-72, 6-73]
C. Dock Boards [6-74]
D. Dock Levelers [6-75]
E. Lift Truck [6-76] Attachments
F. Pallet Loader [6-77, 6-78]
G. Ramp [6-79]

idea of the application possibilities of individual equipment types. The data tabulated are an attempt to document a combination of observations, experience, and data gleaned from many reference sources. Of course there are the inevitable errors of misinterpretation, as well as the not-so-obvious misstatements due to a lack of agreement in the "trade" on everything from names of equipment types to the variations in specifications. For physical details on equipment, the reader *must* inquire of the equipment manufacturers.

Many of the definitions have been adapted from *Conveyor Terms and Definitions,* by the Conveyor Equipment Manufacturer's Association, as well as similar publications of other trade associations. Much of the detail under each has been obtained from literally hundreds of periodical articles and manufacturer's bulletins, as well as from the several reference books listed at the end of the chapter.

I. CONVEYORS

I A1: Flat Belt Conveyor. An endless fabric, rubber, plastic, leather, or metal belt operating over suitable drive, tail end, and bend terminals and over belt idlers or slider bed for handling materials, packages, or objects placed directly upon the belt (Figure 6–2).

Characteristics

1. Top and return runs of belt may be utilized
2. Will operate on level, incline up to 28 degrees, or downgrade
3. Belt supported on flat surface is used as carrier of objects or as basis for an assembly line
4. Belt supported by flat rollers will carry bags, bales, boxes, etc.
5. Metal mesh belts are used for applications subjected to heat, cold, or chemicals
6. High capacity
7. Capacity easily adjusted
8. Versatile
9. Can elevate or lower
10. Provides continuous flow
11. Relatively easy maintenance
12. Used for:
    —Carrying objects—units, cartons, bags, some bulk materials
    —Assembly lines
    —Moving people
13. Limitations
    —Fixed path
    —Relatively high cost
    —Elevating angle limited
    —Straight line flow between pulleys
    —Up to 72 in. wide

Fig. 6–2. Flat belt conveyor carrying orders to packing area. (Courtesy of Logan Company.)

—Up to 800 ft per min
—Problems with horizontal turns

I A2: Portable Belt Conveyor. A portable conveyor in which a belt is used as the conveying medium. Used for loading or unloading trucks; between machines; scrap handling, etc. Belt may be cleated for inclines (Fig. 6–3).

I A3: Troughed Belt Conveyor. A belt conveyor with the edges elevated on the carrying run to form a trough by conforming to the shape of troughed carrying idlers or other supporting surface (Fig. 6–4). Provides a greater capacity than flat belt for bulk materials—up to 2000 tons per hr! Used primarily for bulk materials and those which would slide or fall off flat belts.

I B1: Bucket Conveyor—Gravity Discharge. A type of conveyor using gravity discharge buckets attached between two endless chains and which operate in suitable troughs and casings in horizontal, inclined, and vertical paths over suitable drive, corner, and take-up terminals.

Characteristics
1. Simple
2. Relatively low cost

Fig. 6–3. Portable belt conveyor moving parts from machine to skid box. (Courtesy of Rapistan, Inc.)

3. Buckets of iron or steel
4. Specific type should be selected for material to be handled, and application.
5. Buckets rigidly attached to chains, and act as flights on horizontal runs.
6. Used for:
    —Moderate capacities—100 ft/min, 100–125 tons/hr
    —Combining vertical and horizontal paths
    —Limited space
    —Minimum degradation of material
    —Bulk materials—coal, sand, etc.
    —Non-abrasive materials
7. Limitations
    —Normal particle size 2–3 in.
    —Normal lifts to 100 ft; can go to 300 ft
    —100 to 300 ft/min
    (*See also* II B1, Bucket Elevator)

Fig. 6–4. Troughed belt conveyor. (Courtesy of Rex Chainbelt, Inc., Conveyor Division.)

I B2: Bucket Conveyor—Pivoted. A type of conveyor using pivoted buckets attached between two endless chains which operate in suitable guides or casing in horizontal, vertical, or inclined, or a combination of these paths over drive, corner, and take-up terminals. The buckets remain in the carrying position until they are tipped or inverted to discharge.

Characteristics

1. Massive, slow-moving
2. Path can be vertical, horizontal or combination
3. Commonly a rectangular, run-around path
4. Low maintenance (some in use 40–50 years!)
5. Buckets fed by hoppers
6. Buckets tripped to discharge
7. Used for:
    —Power plants; coal and ashes
    —Cement mills
    —Ceramic industry
    —Stone crushing plants
    —Abrasive materials
8. Limitations
    —40–60 ft/min
    —200–300 tons/hr common
    —Higher cost than regular bucket conveyor
(*See also* Bucket Elevator, II B1)

I C1: Apron Conveyor. A conveyor whose carrying surface consists of overlapping metal aprons, attached at their ends to two strands of chain running in steel guides. Beaded slat edges and turned-up ends result in a minimum of spillage. Called pan conveyor when carrying surface has turned-up, vertical ends (Fig. 6–5).

Fig. 6–5. Apron conveyor handling castings. (Courtesy of FMC Corporation, Link Belt Division.)

Characteristics

1. Discharges over head end
2. Can operate at 45 degrees—with cleats
3. Rugged; long life
4. Minimum maintenance
5. Minimum lump breakage
6. Used for:
   —Severe service
   —Heavy, bulk materials
   —Greasy, oily materials
   —Feeding crushers, breakers, etc.
   —Hot forgings and castings, etc.
   —Turnings and chips
   —With holes in aprons, can drain wet materials

—With stainless steel aprons, handle food materials
—Conveying submerged materials for quench or cooling
7. Limitations
    —Relatively slow speed
    —60–100 ft per min
    —100–300 tons per hr
    —One way travel
    —Inclines to 45°

I C2: Arm Conveyor.   A conveyor consisting of two endless chains, to which are attached projecting arms, or shelves, to support packages or objects and carry them in a vertical or inclined path (Fig. 6–6).

Characteristics
    1. Makes economical use of floor space
    2. Continuous motion

Fig. 6–6. Arm conveyor lifting barrels. (Courtesy of FMC Corporation, Link Belt Division.)

3. Can raise or lower objects
4. Usually loads on up side and discharges on down side
5. Can have manual or automatic load and discharge stations
6. Appropriate design variation should be selected for intended use
7. Special arms can be designed for specific load configurations
8. Usually serves two or more floors
9. Used for:
    —Barrels, drums, rolls
    —Elevates, empties, lowers filled containers in bottling plants, refineries, etc.
10. Limitations
    —40–50 ft per min
    —Relatively low volume
    —Loads must be adaptable to spaced supports
    —May require safety devices

I C3: Car-Type Conveyor. A series of small cars attached to and propelled by an endless chain or other linkage running on a closed track (Fig. 6–7).

Fig. 6–7. Car-type conveyor carrying molds in a foundry. (Courtesy of FMC Corporation, Link Belt Division.)

Characteristics

1. Endless, so loads continue over fixed path until removed
2. Some cars have tilt tops for unloading
3. Can also be automatically loaded
4. Frequently synchronized with other handling or process equipment
5. Design can include processing during movement
6. Operates in horizontal plane—except for slight incline
7. Cars usually permanently attached to drive chain or cable
8. Cars may be propelled by pusher dogs on chain or cable—against lugs on cars
9. Used for:
    —Unusually heavy or irregular loads
    —Large, heavy objects
    —Foundry pouring and cooling lines
    —Built to a smaller scale, for containers in canning and bottling
    —For assembly; to return fixtures to starting point
    —For testing during transportation
10. Limitations
    —Fixed path

I C4: Drag Chain Conveyor.   A conveyor having one or more endless chains riding in and resting on the bottom of a trough, where the material is propelled by the chain links (Fig. 6–8).

Characteristics

1. Load usually carried on upper run
2. Trough may be wood, concrete, steel
3. Material above chain level moved by its cohesiveness with material below
4. Chain usually cast malleable iron or steel
5. Chain may be reversed when worn
6. Movement usually horizontal to slight incline
7. Heavy duty
8. Simple in design
9. May require lubrication, depending on material
10. Little maintenance, easy repair
11. Used for:
    —Bulk materials
    —Hot materials
    —Abrasive materials
    —Quenching hot metal
    —Timber, logs, lumber
    —Packages
    —Cars—by putting 2 wheels on chain
12. Limitations
    —Slow: 50–200 ft per min

—300–1000 cu ft/hr
—High chain pull due to friction
—Wear calls for adjustment
—Fixed path
—May degrade materials
—Relatively high cost
—Can't turn horizontal corners

Fig. 6–8. Drag chain conveyor for moving pulp wood. (Courtesy of Jeffrey Manufacturing Co.)

I C5: Flat-Top Chain Conveyor. A chain with specially designed links or with flat plates attached to the upper side of the chain links so as to form a continuous, smooth, level top surface on which articles are conveyed (Figs. 6–9, 6–10). A common variation is not actually chain driven, but consists of flat hinge-like plates so designed that the hinge barrels are driven by sprockets.

Characteristics
1. Chain may ride on its rollers (rolling) or slide on ways (sliding)
2. Carrying strand of chain rides in continuous tracks or ways
3. Top plates can be rectangular or crescent shaped
4. Serves as a continuous moving table
5. Crescent type can turn horizontal curves

Fig. 6–9. Flat-top chain conveyor moving rolls of steel. (Courtesy of Jervis B. Webb Company.)

6. Can be installed in multiple widths for wider objects or to provide several lanes of similar items
7. Used for:
   —Bottles
   —Cans
   —Specially designed heavy-duty variation used in 2 parallel lines, straddling a pit for moving cars through assembly operations
8. Limitations
   —"Regular" type usually limited to small light loads
   —Normally operate on horizontal plane or slight incline

I C6: Flight Conveyor. A conveyor comprising one or more endless strands of chain with spaced transverse flights or scrapers attached which push the material along a trough (Fig. 6–11).

Characteristics

1. May be several hundred feet long
2. Similar in operation to drag chain (I C4)
3. Operates on downward slope to retard material flow
4. Can move materials in both directions
5. May discharge over end or through gates in bottom
6. Trough bottom may be removable—for replacement
7. Wood trough used for light material

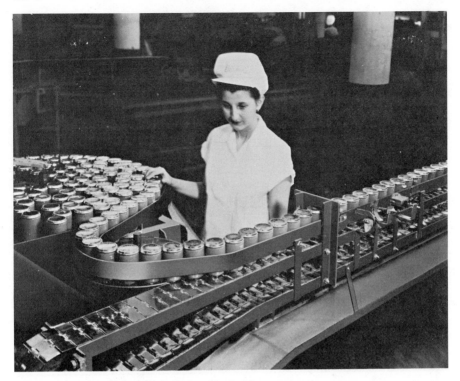

Fig. 6–10. Smaller version of flat-top chain conveyor in a cannery. (Courtesy of FMC Corporation, Link Belt Division.)

8. Can handle 2 or more materials by means of longitudinal partitions which divide trough into channels, with flights slotted to match
9. Rugged, long-life, low maintenance
10. Can be single or double chain drive
11. Causes little dusting
12. Does not degrade material
13. Wide range of sizes, capacities, and design
14. Used for:
    —Coal, ashes, sand, gravel, ore, etc.
    —Wood chips, sawdust, log butts
    —Chemicals
    —Some fruits and vegetables; grain
    —Loading bunkers and bins
    —Under floor to remove metal chips from machining lines
15. Limitations:
    —Operates to 35°–45°, but at reduced capacity
    —Not suited to abrasives

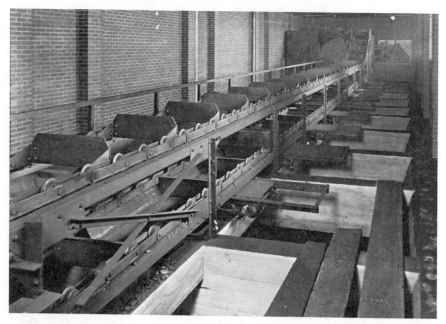

Fig. 6–11. Flight conveyor. (Courtesy of Jeffrey Manufacturing Co.)

—Large lumps may cause difficulty
—Low forward speed of material movement
—Speeds to 100–150 ft per min
—Usually custom designed

I C7: Power and Free Conveyor. Power and free conveyors are a combination of powered trolley conveyors and unpowered monorail-type free conveyors (Fig. 6–12). Two sets of tracks are used, usually suspended one above the other. The upper track carries the powered trolley conveyor, and the lower is the free monorail track. Load-carrying free trolleys are engaged by pushers attached to the powered trolley conveyors. Load trolleys can be switched to and from adjacent unpowered free tracks.

Characteristics

1. "Free" trolleys move by gravity or by "pushers" supported from trolley conveyor on upper level
2. Interconnections may be manually or automatically controlled
3. Track switches may divert trolleys from "power" to "free" tracks
4. Dispatching may be automatically controlled
5. Gravity "free" tracks may be installed between two "power" tracks for storage
6. Speeds may be varied from one "power" section to another

Fig. 6–12. Power and free conveyor, showing "power" rail above and "free" rail below. (Courtesy of Jervis B. Webb Co.)

7. Can include elevating and lowering units in "free" line
8. Can recirculate loads on all or sections of system
9. Can be computer controlled
10. Used for:
   —Temporary storage of loads between points on machining, assembly, and test lines
   —Routing loads to selected points
   —Overhead storage for later delivery of loads to floor level
   —Integrating production, assembly, and test equipment
   —Provides for surge storage against a breakdown in one area
11. Limitations:
   —Relatively expensive
   —Costly to re-locate

I C8: Slat Conveyor. A conveyor whose carrying surface consists of spaced wood or metal slats, fastened at their ends to two strands of chain running in a suitable track or guide (Fig. 6–13).

Fig. 6–13. Slat conveyor. (Courtesy of FMC Corporation, Link Belt Division.)

Characteristics

1. Slats made of wood, metal or combination
2. Slats only ¼″–½″ apart provide a relatively continuous surface
3. Slats can serve as base for fixtures or be built as specially designed supports for specific objects
4. Slats can be mounted at work level or flush to floor—where slow speed permits foot traffic to cross over
5. A variation uses rollers as slats
6. Sturdy, heavy duty, low maintenance
7. Inclines in a relatively short horizontal distance
8. For inclines over 10° requires cleats; then can operate to 30–40°
9. Used for:
    —Heavy, unit loads (crates, cartons, drums, rolls, bags, etc.)
    —Hot materials—castings, forgings, molds
    —Wet materials
    —Warehousing—goods to and from storage

10. Limitations:
   —Speeds to 50–70 ft per min
   —Relatively high cost
   —Not good for small or sticky materials
(*See also* flat belt I A1 and flat top chain, I C5)

I C9: Tow Conveyor.   An endless chain:

a. Supported by trolleys from an *overhead* track
b. Running in a track *flush* with or on the floor
c. Running in a track *under* the floor

Characteristics

GENERAL

1. Performs somewhat same function as tractor-trailer train (III B10)
2. Carts usually 3 ft × 5 ft; can be larger
3. Cart can be specially designed for specific loads
4. Track *can* be equipped with sidings
5. Rugged; easy maintenance
6. Automatic programmed pick-up and release of carts
7. Carts removed from conveyor become "free" and portable to any point
8. Can include moderate inclines and declines
9. Can make use of carts required for other purposes
10. Requires no operator
11. Paces activity
12. Relatively low cost per ton handled
13. Used for:
   —Boxes, barrels, crates, cartons, freight
   —Warehousing:
      —Loads between receiving, storage, shipping
      —Order picking—operator attaches free cart to conveyor (or picks one up)
   —Intra-plant moves
   —Assembly lines (especially b and c)
   —Continuous moving storage
14. Limitations:
   —Follows fixed paths
   —Loads from 500 lb to 4000 lb/cart
   —Lengths from 500 ft to over 5000 ft
   —15–20-year life
   —Speeds of 100–150 ft per min
   —For warehouse use, building should be 80–100,000 sq ft
   —Incline slope may be limited by loads falling off
   —Capacity depends on chain *and* drive

SPECIFIC

I C9a: Overhead (Fig. 6–14)

Characteristics

1. Track 8 or 9 ft from floor
2. Frees floor; no interference with other traffic
3. Track may dip to lower level for more convenient access to carts
4. Unwheeled "carts" may be used for overhead transporting, with dips to working level as required
5. Carts connected to conveyor by hook and chain—or link
6. Cheaper to install than under-floor
7. Limitations
   —Obstructs overhead space
   —Slower than under-floor
   —Connection to conveyor may jerk cart and disturb load
   —Speeds to 150 ft per min; usually 100, with 1000 lb warehouse carts; 50–60 ft per min in manufacturing operations

Fig. 6–14. Overhead tow-line moving stock-picking carts. (Courtesy of Rapistan, Inc.)

I C9b: Flush

Characteristics

1. Carts connected to conveyor by chain to special link on chain
2. Easily installed in existing buildings
3. Lower cost; low maintenance
4. Car rides on tracks mounted on floor

5. Often called floor conveyor
6. Limitations
   —Interferes with cross traffic
   —Speed to 50 ft per min (10–15 most common)

I C9c: Underfloor (Fig. 6–15)

Characteristics

1. Carts connected to conveyor by pin through slot in floor to pick up device on chain
2. Commonly installed in new buildings
3. Greater speed than overhead
4. Pick-up action smoother than overhead
5. Limitations
   —Tracks clogging with refuse, etc.
   —More difficult access for maintenance
   —Speeds to 160 ft per min; usually 60–90 ft per min with 1500–2000 lb per cart

I C10: Trolley Conveyor. A series of trolleys supported from or within an overhead track and connected by an endless propelling medium such as chain, cable, or other linkage, with loads usually suspended from the trolleys (Fig. 6–16).

Characteristics

1. Trolleys run (a) on flanges of structural tracks, or (b) inside rectangular or round tubes
2. Multiple-wheel trolleys or multiple-trolleys with load bar between used to distribute weight of large loads
3. Load carriers suspended from trolleys and usually designed for optimum handling of object being moved
4. Propelling medium can be chain, cable, or solid link
5. May use sprocket wheel or caterpillar drive
6. Functions in 3 dimensions (horizontal, vertical, incline)
7. Track 8 or 9 ft above floor
8. Track may be elevated for move, then dip for access to operator or process
9. Track easily routed around obstructions
10. Frees floor space; no interference with other traffic
11. Entire length can be used; i.e., no "return" run
12. Relatively inexpensive to install and relocate
13. Salvage value high
14. Low operating and maintenance cost
15. Relatively unlimited length and path
16. Can follow complicated paths
17. Easy to alter, shorten, lengthen path
18. Paces activity
19. Can be made automatic and/or computer controlled

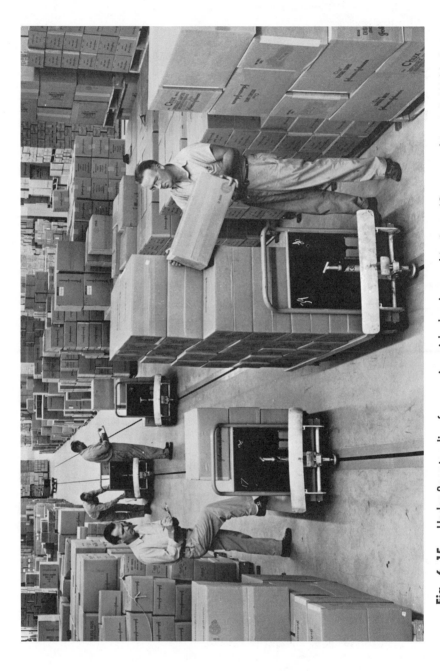

Fig. 6–15. Under-floor tow line for carrying picked orders to shipping. (Courtesy of Jervis B. Webb Co.)

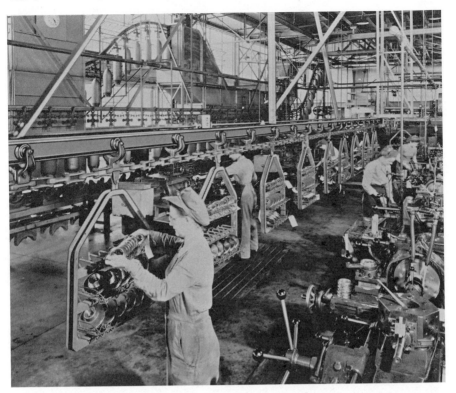

Fig. 6–16. Trolley conveyor. (Courtesy of Material Handling Systems, Division of American Chain and Cable Co.)

20. Loads can be automatically switched to or from conveyor
21. *Can* be hung from floor mounted supports
22. Used for:
    —Moving nearly any material or load
    —Overhead moving storage
    —Intra-plant movement
    —Inter-plant movement
    —Inter-floor movement
    —Recirculating materials
    —Order picking, with goods *on* conveyor and picker selecting
      as items go past him
    —Moving objects through continuous processes such as paint-
      ing, baking, degreasing, etc.
23. Limitations
    —Obstructs overhead space; cuts lighting
    —Fixed path
    —May narrow the aisles
    —Can't always run track to point desired

—Load capacity determined by track, trolley, and structural
support capacity
(*See also* Power and Free Conveyor I C7 and Tow Conveyor I C9)

I D: Gravity Chute. A slide made of metal or other material and
shaped so that it guides objects or materials as they are moved from one
location to another (Fig. 6–17). May be used on horizontal or declined
planes, or as a spiral between extreme levels.

Fig. 6–17. Gravity chute. (Courtesy of Logan Co.)

Characteristics

1. Usually slopes downward to utilize gravity
2. Running surface may be wood, metal, composition
3. May be straight, curved, or spiral; open or closed
4. Spiral can be multiple flight
5. Frequently custom designed and home made
6. Low cost—no power, low maintenance
7. Makes economical use of space (spiral)
8. Rate of descent determined by:
    —Contacting surface
    —Atmospheric conditions
    —Pitch
    —Length
9. Can be variable pitch; portable
10. Used for:
    —Many kinds of materials and objects
    —Inter-floor moves
    —Inter-level moves
    —Warehouses, stores, terminals, industry
    —Loading and unloading carriers
    —Fire escapes
    —Between machines; storage ahead of a machine
    —From machines to container on floor
11. Limitations
    —Horizontal or down only
    —May require fire doors
    —Best for relatively uniform objects
    —Not good for tall objects or open containers
    —Relatively short distances covered

I E: Pneumatic Conveyor.   Pneumatic conveyors can be divided into 3 major categories:

1. *Pipeline.* A system of vertical and horizontal pipes (Fig. 6–18) which carry particles of solid materials by means of air pressure in the system, and classified as:
    a. Positive pressure—uses a positive displacement blower to create the positive air flow in the pipeline. Materials are injected into the air stream via air locks and blown via the pre-set conveying path to a storage silo or process bin.
    b. Negative pressure (vacuum)—employs a positive displacement blower to create the vacuum in the line, a suitable intake mechanism, such as a nozzle or hopper, and a receiving station in which conveyed particles are separated from the moving air stream by tangential or cyclonic action and discharged or distributed to storage or process.
    c. Combination—employs the principles of both types. The vacuum part of the system is generally used to unload or reclaim

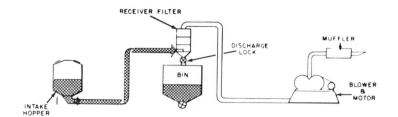

vacuum

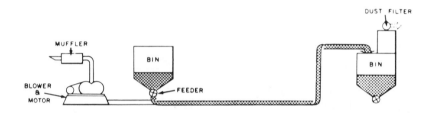

pressure

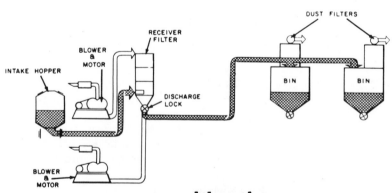

combination
vacuum-pressure

Fig. 6–18. Three basic types of pneumatic conveyors. (Courtesy of Fuller Company.)

152

materials from storage. Particles are drawn to the receiving station and discharged into the pressure part of the system. From here they are distributed to single or multiple storage silos.

d. Closed loop—similar to (a) but with air vented back to the source, rather than to the atmosphere.

2. *Air-activated.* A rectangular duct with an air-permeable bottom in which low-pressure air from a plenum below fluidizes the pulverized material, causing it to flow by gravity, down the duct (Fig. 6–19).

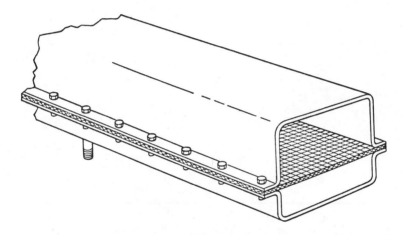

Fig. 6–19.   Air-activated gravity conveyor. (Courtesy of Fuller Company.)

3. *Tube.* A tubular system, up to 15 sq in. in cross-section, through which small packages or containers fitted with air-seal rings are moved by air pressure (Fig. 6–20).

Characteristics

A. *General*

1. High pressure systems *can* handle metal parts 2″ long by 4″ in diameter; also wood chips
2. Can handle materials with densities from 75 to 250 lb/cu ft
3. Self-cleaning
4. Flexible—easy to add to, change, or adapt to variations in volume, operating procedures, or layout
5. Minimum maintenance
6. Savings due to price differential between purchase of materials in bulk and purchase of materials in bags or small containers—by elimination of packaging costs.[1]

[1] Items 6–10 are from M. N. Kraus, *Pneumatic Conveying of Bulk Materials,* The Ronald Press Co., 1968, p. 4.

Fig. 6–20. Pneumatic tubes for carrying small tools. (Courtesy of Lamson Division, Diebold, Inc.)

7. Savings due to reduced freight rate of bulk materials
8. Savings due to reduction of labor costs for handling and storage of bags or small containers.
9. Reduction of losses due to torn sacks, spillage, residual materials in discarded bags or containers.
10. Used for:
    a. Delivery of dry materials via pipelines to remote plant areas which are economically inaccessible via mechanical conveyors
    b. Storage of bulk materials in large capacity bins and silos in plant areas otherwise unavailable for storage of packaged materials
    c. Increased plant safety due to elimination of man-handling bags

or containers and elimination of dust when one is opening and
dumping containers

   d. Reduced product contamination due to handling of materials
in a closed system

   e. Elimination of fire protection systems usually required in areas
where material in bags or bulk containers would be stored

11. Limitations

   a. Relatively high initial investment

   b. Uni-directional

   c. Limited to selected materials (usually dry and granulated,
pulverized, crushed, pelletized, etc.)

   d. Distances limited—even with boosters

      —Vacuum to 1500 ft

      —Pressure to one mile

   e. Capacity limited

B. *Specific* [2]

  1. Pipelines

    a. Positive pressure

     1. Uses minimum air for a maximum amount of material

     2. Pressure source pushes material

     3. Conveying path may be changed manually by flexible hose
and selection station, or automatically by remote controlled
diverter valves

     4. Used for:

      (a) Granular or fibrous materials

      (b) Moving material from single entry point to several or
widely scattered discharge points

    b. Negative pressure

     1. Pressure source pulls material

     2. Leakage is inward

     3. Minimum dusting

     4. Used for:

      (a) Unloading carriers

      (b) Delivering materials to processes

      (c) Picks up from bulk containers or several scattered entry
points for discharge at a single point

    c. Combination

     1. Negative pressure brings material to an intermediate station

     2. Positive pressure moves material to discharge points

     3. For multiple entry *and* discharge points

    d. Closed loop

     1. Conveying medium is recycled and permits accurate tem-
perature and moisture control

[2] Portions adapted from *Transvair Pneumatic Conveying Systems*, Young Machinery
Co., Muncy, Pa.

  2. Minimum product loss or contamination
  3. Used for:
     (a) Hazardous chemicals
     (b) Hygroscopic materials
     (c) Dusty materials
  2. Air-activated
     1. Easily shut off and started up
     2. Can go around corners
     3. Requires calculated slope
     4. Can divide flow into two or more streams as it moves
     5. Used for:
        (a) Bins, to aid discharging
        (b) Relatively short distances
        (c) Relatively low volumes
        (d) "Fluidizable" materials
  3. Tube—used in factories, stores, banks, hospitals, etc. to convey small parts and tools, money, samples for testing, mail, blueprints, etc.

I F1: Roller Conveyor—Gravity. A conveyor which supports the load on a series of rollers, turning on fixed bearings, and mounted between side rails at fixed intervals determined by the size of the object to be carried, which is usually moved manually or by gravity (see variations which follow) (Fig. 6–21).

Characteristics
  1. Rollers usually cylindrical tubing with a bearing on each end
  2. Rollers range from ¾" to 3½" in diameter with length governed by load
  3. Curved sections used for turns
  4. Rollers may be tapered for turns, or arranged differentially
  5. Tight corners may use ball table (see VA)
  6. Requires 3 rollers under load at all times
  7. Rollers may be troughed or formed to conform to shape of load
  8. "Standard" roller spacing is 3", 4", 6"
  9. Inexpensive, easy to install, minimum maintenance, long life
 10. Runs can include switches, spurs, gates, scales, deflectors, up-enders, processing and packaging equipment
 11. Can be arranged in spiral (chute) form
 12. Belt boosters used between levels
 13. In spite of apparent simplicity often the basis for highly engineered installations
 14. Used for:
     —Almost any load with rigid riding surface that will contact 3 or more rollers
     —Moves between areas, machines, buildings

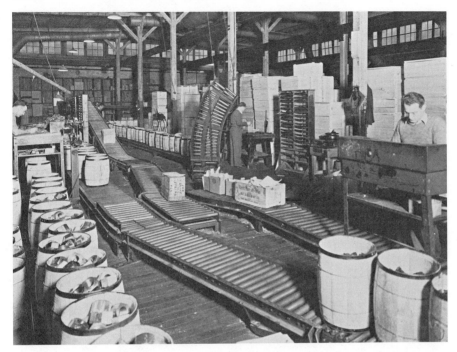

Fig. 6–21. Gravity roller conveyors showing switch and lift sections. (Courtesy of Logan Company.)

—Storage between work stations
—Warehouses, docks, foundries, steel mills, canneries, manufacturing, assembly, packaging
—Loading and unloading carriers (portable sections and accordion type)
—Bases for a handling system
—Integral segment of composite handling system

15. Limitations
—Relatively short distances
—Frequently require guard rails to restrain loads
—Normal capacity 70–750 lb per roller
—Can be designed to handle 10 tons!
—Best for objects with rigid riding surfaces (can be overcome by closer roller spacing or putting items on trays or in containers)
—Distance may be limited by amount of fall required to utilize gravity for movement
—Heavy loads might accelerate beyond control

(*See also* Wheel Conveyor, 1 I)

I F2: Roller Conveyor—Live. Similar to gravity roller, except that power is applied to some or all of the rollers to propel the loads (Fig. 6–22).

Fig. 6–22. Live roller conveyors. Note drive belt under rollers. (Courtesy of Rapistan, Inc.)

Generally used for same purposes as gravity rollers (I F1) except for features noted below. Therefore, also similar to belt conveyor except better for heavy duty.

Characteristics

1. Power usually applied by
   —Chain on sprockets
   —Belting (underneath) held up against rollers at intervals by other rollers or other devices
2. Can move objects on level runs, up slight grades, or restrain descent on down grades
3. Permit controlled flow—articles are spaced
4. Inclines possible to about 10°; declines to 17°
5. Curves can be powered

6. More rugged than belt conveyors

7. More expensive than gravity or belt conveyors

I F3: Portable Roller Conveyor. A short (up to about 20 ft) section of roller conveyor mounted on legs or stands, and often with wheels. Primarily intended for temporary use at a location. Also useful in loading and unloading carriers.

I F4: Roller Rack. A storage rack in which the storage surface is composed of sections of roller conveyor, usually sloping slightly toward the discharge end (Fig. 6–23).

Fig. 6–23. Gravity conveyor rack with wheels supporting pallets and separate rollers guiding pallets at entry to rack. (Courtesy of Interlake, Inc.)

Characteristics

1. Provides moving storage

2. Assures first-in, first-out storage

3. Permits relatively large number of "openings" per lineal foot of rack front, therefore . . .

4. Commonly used for order selection, thereby drastically reducing walking distance per item picked by about 50%
5. Can pick 100–300 items/hr (vs. 50–100 by manual methods)
6. Every item fully visible and in reach
7. Easy inventory control
8. Partially depleted lanes are useless space
9. Requires ¾"–1" drop per foot of length
10. Lanes should be about 30 ft long to avoid large accumulated loads and long settling time
11. Lanes *can* be powered

I G: Screw Conveyor.   A conveyor consisting of a continuous or broken-blade helix or screw fastened to a shaft (usually a pipe) and rotating in a trough so that the revolving screw advances the material (Fig. 6–24).

Fig. 6–24. Trough-type screw conveyor. (Courtesy of Jeffrey Manufacturing Co.)

A *ribbon* conveyor has the screw attached to the shaft with arms or spokes so as to leave a space between the screw and shaft.

A *paddle* conveyor has the screw or ribbon interrupted and shaped as individual paddles.

Characteristics

1. Feeding can be from top, end, or bottom
2. Discharge is from end or bottom

3. Screw is driven from one end
4. Screw can be right or left hand
5. *Can* be both, to deliver at both ends from the middle, or to bring 2 materials together at the middle
6. Screw is designed to accommodate specific materials and/or functions
7. Usually runs on horizontal or incline, but at a reduced capacity
8. *Can* be used vertically as an elevator
9. To turn corners, one discharges into another at a lower level—with a gear arrangement between them for drive purposes
10. Relatively low cost
11. Compact and can operate in close quarters
12. Used for:
    —Almost any pulverized or granular material but may need special screws for some
    —Adaptable to almost any temperature
    —Controlling material flow
    —As a mixer or blender
    —Feeders for process equipment
13. Limitations
    —Commonly made in 10–12 ft sections
    —Certain amount of degradation of materials
    —Length limited by torque capacity of shaft and drive
    —Operate at 10–120 ft per min
    —Handle up to 10,000 cu ft per hr

I H: Vibrating (Oscillating) Conveyors. A trough or tube flexibly supported and vibrated at a relatively high frequency and small amplitude to convey bulk material or objects (Fig. 6–25). An oscillating conveyor is similar in construction, but has a relatively lower frequency and larger amplitude of motion. Material is moved by being lifted or ratcheted forward.

Characteristics
1. Vibration induced electrically or mechanically
2. Handles gently; does not break up materials
3. Self cleaning
4. Rugged; used for 24-hr duty
5. Low maintenance; little wear on trough
6. Mechanical models handle at a greater distance and at a lower cost
7. Used for:
    —Wide variety of materials—but not sticky or tacky
    —As a feeder
    —Hot or cold materials
    —Gaseous, abrasive, toxic materials
    —Screening, blending, separating, cooling, drying
    —Strict control of hazardous materials (mechanical type, less control)

Fig. 6–25. Oscillating (vibrating) conveyor. (Courtesy of FMC Corporation, Link Belt Division.)

        —Oscillating type used widely for handling hot castings, sand, etc.

  8. Limitations:

        —Moves material at a fixed rate of flow

        —Materials can be 5–400 lb per cu ft

        —Handles cubes up to 4–5 ft³

        —Tube diameters 4–26 in.

        —Trays: 5–60 in. wide

        —Relatively costly

        —Moves material at 30–50 ft per min

        —Conveying speed varies with material

        —Upward slope limited

        —Regular substantial foundation

        —Limited length per drive unit

11: Wheel Conveyors. A conveyor which supports the load on a series of skate-like wheels, mounted on common shafts in a frame or on parallel spaced rails, and with the wheels spaced to accommodate the size of the load to be carried (Fig. 6–26). Also adapted to live, rack, and spiral versions as in the roller conveyor.

Characteristics

    1. Characteristics very similar to the roller conveyor

    2. Objects usually moved by hand or gravity

Fig. 6–26.   Gravity wheel conveyor.   (Courtesy of Rapistan, Inc.)

3. Wheels 2 in. diameter and up and staggered on shafts
4. Lighter weight construction than roller conveyor
5. Frequently made of aluminum with plastic wheels
6. Easily portable
7. Less expensive than roller
8. Requires about 50% as much grade as rollers, except when used for storage
9. Easy to set up and put away
10. Low maintenance
11. Comes in 5 ft and 10 ft sections
12. Number of wheels per foot determines load capacity
13. Must have 6 wheels under load
14. 1½–3 in. pitch per 10-ft section advisable
15. Used for:
    —Warehousing
    —Frequently carried in trucks for use in unloading and loading
    —Ideal for curves, due to differential characteristics of construction
    —Single wheeled rails useful in flow rack construction—on two sides of a "lane"
    —Single rails useful as guides
16. Limitations (*See also* Roller Conveyors, I F1)
    —Better for solid, smooth-bottom objects
    —Less load capacity than rollers
    —Not as good for spirals as rollers
    —Usually for less extensive use than rollers
    —Usually for lighter weight items than rollers

II. CRANES, ELEVATORS, HOISTS, MONORAILS

II A1: Jib Crane. A lifting device travelling on a horizontal boom which is mounted on a column or mast which is fastened to:

a. Floor (Fig. 6–28)
b. Floor *and* a top support (Fig. 6–29)
c. Wall bracket or rails

Characteristics

1. Can rotate to 360°
2. Inexpensive and versatile
3. Adapted to portable use by an outrigger-equipped wheeled stand
4. Sometimes mounted on wheels and top and bottom rails along a wall or dock
5. Heavy duty (hammer-head type) used for loads up to 350 tons
6. Used for:
    —Serving individual work places in machine shops, etc., anywhere within its radius
    —Loading and unloading carriers

Fig. 6-27. Some common types of overhead handling equipment. (By permission of and copyright by Dresser Crane Hoist and Tower Division of Dresser Industries.)

Fig. 6–28. Heavy duty floor-mounted jib crane lifting 15,000-lb. steel coils. (Courtesy of Dresser Crane Hoist and Tower Division, Dresser Industries, Inc.)

        —Handling molds in a foundry
        —Supplementing an overhead travelling crane
    7. Limitations
        —About 15 tons
        —Move distance limited by length of boom—usually to 25 ft

II A2a: Bridge Crane. A lifting device mounted on a bridge consisting of one or two horizontal girders, which are supported at each end by trucks riding on runways installed at right angles to the bridge. Runways are installed on building columns, overhead trusses, or frames. Lifting device moves along bridge while bridge moves along runway.

Characteristics

    1. Covers any spot within the rectangular area over which the bridge travels, i.e., length of one bay

Fig. 6–29. Jib crane, top *and* bottom mounted, using older style track. (Courtesy of Cleveland Crane and Engineering, Division of McNeil Corporation.)

2. Can be provided with "cross-over" to adjacent bay
3. Provides 3-dimensional travel
4. Designed as:
   —Top-running, where end trucks ride on top of runway tracks (Fig. 6–30)
   —Bottom-running, where end trucks are suspended from lower flanges of runway tracks (Fig. 6–31)
5. Hoist can also be top or bottom running
6. Bottom-running usually limited to about 10 tons
7. Bridge propelled by hand, chained gearing or power
8. Two hoists (light and heavy duty) may be mounted on one crane
9. Usually designed and built by specialist companies
10. Does not interfere with work on floor
11. Can reduce aisle space requirements
12. Can reach areas otherwise not easily accessible
13. Craneways can extend out of building
14. Can be pendant or radio controlled from the floor
15. Used for:
    —Low to medium volume
    —Large, heavy and awkward objects

Fig. 6-30. Top-running bridge crane. (Courtesy of Dresser Crane Hoist and Tower Division, Dresser Industries.)

Fig. 6–31. Under-running bridge crane. (Courtesy of Cleveland Crane and Engineering, Division of McNeil Corporation.)

  —Machine shops, foundries, steel mills, heavy assembly and repair shops
  —Intermittent moves
  —Warehousing and yard storage
  —With attachments such as magnets, slings, grabs, buckets, etc. can handle an extremely wide range of loads
16. Limitations
  —Capacities to 1000 tons
  —Spans to 125 ft
  —Bridge speeds from 200–500 ft/min
  —Hoist speeds to 80 ft/min
  —Movement is relatively slow
  —Expensive
  —Confined to area covered by craneway
  —Heavy framework required to support ways
  —Usually requires an operator in cab—sometimes 1 or 2 "hookers"

II A2b: Gantry Crane. A crane, commonly of bridge type, which is supported by a structure spanning an intervening space, on:

—Legs travellings on tracks on the floor, or . . .

—*One* leg (as above) and one rail mounted on columns or a wall (single-leg gantry: Fig. 6–32).

—2 legs in fixed positions

—2 legs, on wheels; i.e., portable (1- to 3-ton capacity)

Fig. 6–32. Single-leg gantry crane. (Courtesy of Cleveland Crane and Engineering, Division of McNeil Corporation.)

Characteristics

1. Use indoors and outdoors
2. Relatively easy to change location of operation
3. Can be cab-, pendant-, or radio-controlled
4. Cantilever type has bridge extending beyond legs
5. Many other variations for special purposes
6. Long life
7. Low maintenance
8. Used for:
    —Short moves
    —Loading and unloading carriers
    —Unit as well as bulk materials
    —Outdoor storage operations

—Same purposes as bridge crane, usually
—Situations where overhead runways are impractical due to length, cost, alignment, interference with other operations, old buildings, etc.
—Supplement bridge crane
9. Limitations
    —Scope of move confined
    —Capacities to 300 tons
    —Lengths of 200–300 ft or more
    —Fairly expensive
    —Requires trained operator
    —Requires organized work activity

II A3a: Stacker Crane. A device with a rigid upright mast or supports, suspended from a carriage, mounted on an overhead travelling (bridge) crane—or equivalent—and fitted with forks or a platform to permit it to place in or retrieve items from racks on either side of the aisle it traverses (Fig. 6–33).

Fig. 6–33. Stacker crane. (Courtesy of Cleveland Crane and Engineering Division of McNeil Corporation.)

Characteristics

1. Requires "aisles" only 4″–6″ wider than load
2. Little if any obstruction of aisle when in raised position or out of aisle
3. Serves both sides of aisle
4. Saves both square feet and cubic feet
5. Permits high selectivity
6. Reduces order selection time
7. Can be manned, pendant, electronic, card, or even computer controlled
8. Can be transferred from aisle to aisle by transfer bridge
9. Operator may ride in cab with load-carrying device
10. Helps assure orderly storage operations
11. Minimizes inventory control problems
12. Usually requires one operator
13. Used for:
    —Handling unit or containerized bulk loads
    —Storage and warehousing operations (1 cu ft/ton in steel storage operations)
    —Adaptable to "automatic" warehousing operations
    —With attachments can handle a wide variety of loads
    —Excellent for long loads (metal bars, shapes, sheets, pipes, tubes, etc.)
14. Limitations
    —Usually 200–300 storage positions
    —Travel limited by crane support
    —Lift limited by clear height available
    —Relatively high maintenance
    —Practical height to 25 ft
    —Bridge span to 150 ft (40 ft–70 ft common)
    —Capacity to 15 tons (some, over)
    —Loads to 40 ft long
    —Travel speed to 350 ft per min
    —Lift speed to 100 ft per min
    —Lifts per hour to 60
(*See also* Storage Machine, II A3b)

II A3b: Storage Machine. This device (Fig. 6–34) is an outgrowth of the stacker-crane concept and commonly consists of a mast or upright supports:

—Suspended from a crane bridge
—Fastened to rack-mounted rails
—Suspended from a top-mounted monorail
—Supported from the floor, on a wheeled "truck"
—Supported between top *and* bottom rails or tracks

Fig. 6–34. Storage machine—based on stacker crane principle. Stacker device operates between rows of racks by card, tape, or computer control. (Courtesy of Hartman Engineering/Manufacturing Division, Hartman Metal Fabricators, Inc.)

Integral in the uprights are forks or a platen device which moves up and down the support to permit it to place in or retrieve items from the racks on either side of the relatively narrow aisle it traverses. It may be:

—Captive, within the aisle it serves
—Portable, by means of a "transfer car" or device at the end of the aisles, to permit it to be moved from one aisle to another
—Mobile, by means of its own wheels and power to move to any racks located on a suitable running surface

Characteristics
1. Permits random storage
2. Provides high selectivity
3. Requires minimum building, heat, light—only as required by product
4. Can be manual, electronic, punched card, or computer controlled

5. Permits automatic perpetual inventory
6. Can guarantee first-in, first-out stock rotation
7. Some can stack loads 2 deep, therefore increasing output by 25% (but doubling aisle width)
8. Cost breakdown, approximately:
    —Racks, 40–50%
    —Stacker and controls, 15–35%
    —Conveyor and related equipment, 15–20% (all, plus building cost)
9. About 10% are computer controlled (1970)
10. Used for:
    —Storage of materials and supplies
    —Finished goods warehousing
    —In-process storage
    —Nearly any load on pallet or in container
11. Limitations
    —High cost ($100–200 per storage opening)
    —High maintenance
    —Loads between 500 lb and 5 tons
    —Fire protection a problem
    —Optimum stacking height 60 ft (some go to 165 ft)
    —Aisle lengths to 300 ft
    —Commonly have 5–6000 storage positions (some planned for 100,000!)
    —Horizontal speed to 500 ft per min (300 optimum)
    —Vertical speeds to 100 ft per min
    —40 transactions per hour (20 in, 20 out) common

II A4: Mobile Crane. A self-propelled tracked or wheeled [3] vehicle upon which is mounted a boom and other equipment to permit swivelling 360° to pick up, carry, and deposit a load (Fig. 6–34A)

Characteristics
1. May be mobile via crawler (caterpillar), rail, rubber tire, or air
2. Gasoline or diesel powered
3. Capacities up to:
    — 50 tons—tires
    —100 tons—crawler
    —250 tons—rail
4. Used for:
    —Bulky, irregular shaped loads
    —Intermittent moves
    —Outdoors
    —Loading and unloading trucks and rail cars
    —Fixed (rail) or varying paths
    —Maintenance

---

[3] Except for the helicopter—with a winch attachment—known as an "aerial crane."

Fig. 6–34A. Mobile crane. (Courtesy of FMC Corporation, Link Belt Division.)

   5. Limitations
        —Commonly requires a crew of 2–5 men
        —Slow
        —Reach limited to boom and load restrictions
        —Requires much space
  (*See also* III B1)

II B1: Bucket Elevator. A type of conveying device for carrying bulk materials in a vertical or inclined path, consisting of an endless belt, chain, or chains to which buckets are attached, and operating between head and boot terminal machinery in a supporting frame and/or casing. Bucket elevators are classified as:

   a. Continuous (Fig. 6–35)
     1. External discharge
     2. Internal discharge
     3. Super capacity
   b. Spaced [4] (Fig. 6–36)
     1. Centrifugal discharge
     2. Positive (perfect) discharge

   [4] Pivoted bucket and gravity discharge spaced bucket elevators are listed as conveyors—under I B1, I B2.

Fig. 6–35. Continuous bucket elevator. (Courtesy of FMC Corporation, Link Belt Division.)

Fig. 6–36. Spaced bucket elevator. (Courtesy of Conveyor Division, Rex Chainbelt, Inc.)

Characteristics

  A. General

    1. Buckets loaded by scoop action in boot, or by chute above
    2. May or may not have casing
    3. Some operate at an incline
    4. Selection should be carefully based on material and application
    5. Buckets made in a variety of shapes, sizes, weights and materials
    6. Chains are usually malleable iron
    7. *Continuous* type: less spillage, chute-fed, larger capacity, lower power requirements
    8. *Spaced* types have scoop loading and operate partially loaded
    9. *Belt* types are of higher speed and capacity, smoother and quieter
    10. Chain types are heavier duty and for more abrasive materials
    11. May or may not have enclosing casing

B. Specific

1. External discharge
   - —100–175 ft per min
   - —Lumpy and abrasive materials
   - —Buckets loaded directly
   - —Buckets nearly continuous, almost touching
   - —Back of preceding bucket serves as chute
2. Internal discharge
   - —Free flowing, non-abrasive materials
   - —Gentle handling of small articles such as stampings, castings, plastic chips, pellets, bolts, nuts, rivets, seeds, granular chemicals, shelled nuts, etc.
   - —Buckets loaded from chute
   - —Buckets continuous, overlapping
3. Super-capacity
   - —Larger buckets, to 6 ft long
   - —Volume handling of large lumpy materials
   - —10–12 in. lumps
   - —200% capacity of normal bucket elevator
   - —1000 tons per hour
   - —Optimum efficiency at 30–70° incline

(*See also* Bucket Conveyor, I B1, 2)

4. Centrifugal discharge
   - —200–400 ft per min
   - —150 tons per hr
   - —Buckets dig into material in boot
   - —For free flowing, fine and loose materials with small to medium lump size
5. Positive (gravity) discharge
   - —120 ft per min
   - —For light, fluffy, fragile or sticky materials
   - —Boot fed.

II B2: Portable Elevator. Sometimes known as a stacker, the portable elevator (Fig. 6–37) consists of a base, on wheels or casters, a vertical frame or mast, a lifting and lowering mechanism, and a load-carrying platform or forks. Lifting is accomplished by hydraulic or mechanical action, and power may be manual, or electric—by means of batteries or alternating current. The mast may be telescopic or non-telescopic. Designed to fill the gap between the hand lift (III A3)) and the fork lift (III B2).

Characteristics

1. Inexpensive
2. Uncomplicated
3. Light weight

Fig. 6–37. Portable elevator (stacker). (Courtesy of Hyster Company, Lewis-Shepard Division.)

    4. Maneuverable
    5. Simple to operate
    6. Long life
    7. Compact
    8. Versatile
    9. Minimum maintenance
  10. Used for:
      —Narrow aisles
      —Relieving more expensive equipment
      —A table, with adjustable height
      —Personnel lift; maintenance work, etc.
      —Die handling
      —With special attachments, for handling coils, rolls, drums, barrels, etc.
  11. Limitations
      —250–5000 lbs. (usually under 1 ton)

—Lifts to 40 ft
—Needs good floors
—Limited travel speed and distance

II C: Hoist. A device for lifting or lowering objects (Figs. 6–38, 6–39), suspended from a hook on the end of retractable chains or cables. Usually supported from overhead by a hook or traveling on a track.

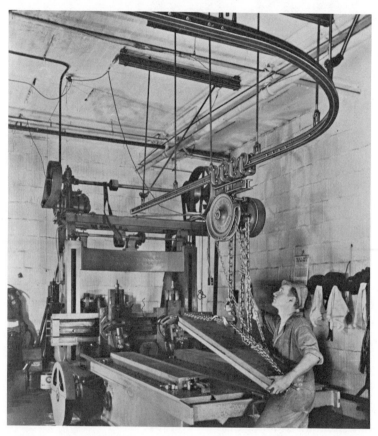

Fig. 6–38. Chain hoist on monorail track for loading heavy material onto planer bed. (Courtesy of Eaton Corp., Handling Systems Division.)

Characteristics

1. Rugged and dependable
2. Simple and inexpensive
3. Easy installation
4. Versatile
5. Operate by hand (chain), air, or electricity (pendant switch box)

Fig. 6–39. Electric-powered hoist on overhead crane. (Courtesy of Eaton Corp., Yale Hoisting Equipment Division.)

6. Used for:
   —Relatively light loads
   —Intermittent moves
   —Varying loads
   —Serving a machine or work place

—Transfers between work places
—To supplement overhead travelling crane
7. Limitations
    —Load capacity
    —Relatively slow
    —Requires overhead support
    —Travel distance
    —Manually operated
    —Path fixed by track

II D: Monorail. A handling system [5] on which loads are suspended from wheeled carriers or trolleys that are readily rolled along an overhead track (Fig. 6–40). The carrier wheels usually roll along the top surface of the lower flange of the rail forming the track, or in a similar fashion with other track shapes.

Fig. 6–40. Monorail with special carrier for moving items from warehouse to packing area. (Courtesy of Cleveland Crane and Engineering, Division of McNeil Corporation.)

---

[5] Extracted from: *Material Handling With Monorails,* Monorail Manufacturer's Association, 1967.

Characteristics

1. Relatively low installation cost
2. Low operating cost
3. Little maintenance
4. Track may be pipe, T, I, flat bar or other formed structural shape
5. Can be hand or motor propelled on both travel and lift
6. Motor may be controlled by pendant switches, from integral cab, or automatically
7. Removes traffic from floor
8. Releases floor space
9. Makes use of overhead space
10. Easily extended
11. Switches, spurs, transfer bridges, drop sections, swinging sections, cross-overs, turntables provide flexibility
12. Used for:
    —Point-to-point moves
    —Fixed path handling
    —Low-volume moves
    —Intermittent handling tasks
    —Semi-live storage (on spur tracks)
    —Loading and unloading carriers
    —Handling through processes (paint, bake, dry, plate, test)
    —Connecting buildings
    —Pouring metal (from ladles suspended from monorail carrier)
13. Limitations
    —Low volume
    —Low speed
    —Travel limited by rail
    —Building must support load
    —Manual—3 tons
    —Power—20 tons

III. INDUSTRIAL VEHICLES

III A1: Dolly. A small low platform-type load carrier with one or more rollers, casters, or wheels (Fig. 6–41).

Characteristics

1. Similar to platform truck—but usually smaller wheels and no "handle"
2. Inexpensive
3. Sturdy; long life
4. Usually 3- or 4-wheeled
5. Can handle up to 60–80 tons! (but usually for much lighter loads —to 2–3000 lbs)
6. Used for:
    —Low volumes

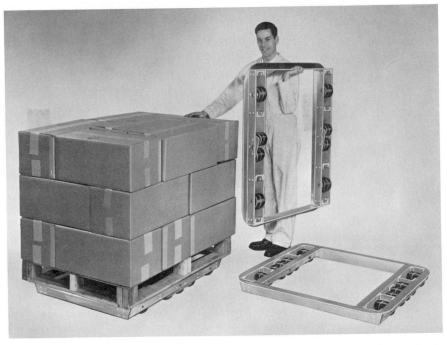

Fig. 6–41. Pallet dolly. (Courtesy of Magnesium Corporation of America.)

  —Short distances
  —Intermittent moves
  —Variable paths
  —Wide variety of loads
  —Supporting pallet for loading and moving out of carrier unable
    to support lift truck
  —Dolly platform frequently built to accommodate load (rolls,
    etc.)
 7. Limitations
  —Need good floor
  —Requires manpower to move, usually
  —May be hard to load
  —Travel distance limited

III A2: Four-Wheel Hand Truck.   A rectangular load-carrying platform
with 4 or 6 wheels, for manual pushing, usually by means of a rack or
"handle" at one or both ends. Some have 2 larger wheels at center of
platform also, for easy maneuverability (Fig. 6–42).

Characteristics

 1. May be fitted with box or other special "body" for variety of
    handling tasks

Fig. 6–42. Four-wheeled hand truck. (Courtesy of Hyster Company, Lewis-Shepard Division.)

2. Inexpensive
3. Versatile
4. Used for:
   —Manual handling of large loads
   —Supplementing mechanical handling
   —Low-frequency moves
   —Low-volume movement
   —Short distances
   —Relatively light loads
   —Temporary storage; in-process storage
   —Handling awkward shapes
   —Weak floors
   —Small elevators
   —Narrow aisles
   —Crowded areas
5. Limitations
   —Requires manpower
   —Capacity limited—about 4000 lbs.
   —Slow

III A3: Hand Lift Truck. Essentially a wheeled platform (Fig. 6–43) that can be rolled under a pallet or skid, and equipped with a lifting device designed to raise loads just high enough to clear the floor and

Fig. 6–43. Hand lift truck (jack). (Courtesy of Hyster Company, Lewis-Shepard Division.)

permit moving the load. Propulsion is by hand and lift is by hydraulic or mechanical means. Platform type is used for handling skids, and fork type for handling pallets.

Characteristics

1. Low cost
2. Durable, minimum maintenance
3. Light weight
4. Compact
5. Simple to operate
6. Versatile
7. Used for:
    —Loading or unloading carriers
    —Supplementing powered trucks, spotting loads
    —Moderate distances (50–200 ft)
    —Intermittent, low frequency of use
    —Low volume moves
    —Increasing utilization of powered equipment
    —Captive use in a local area (economical)
    —Loading and unloading elevators
    —Tight quarters; narrow aisles
8. Limitations
    —Requires aisle space
    —Low clearance height

—Requires manual effort
—Cornering a problem on narrow aisles
—Bumpy "ride"

See also Chapter 5, Equipment Concepts, regarding the place of manual equipment in the handling system.

III A4: Semi-Live Skid.   A platform with two wheels at one end and two legs at the other, for use with a lift jack, which is basically a handle with two wheels attached, that fits into a socket at the leg end.

Characteristics

1. Inexpensive
2. Durable
3. No power required
4. Empties easily moved by using legs as "handles"
5. Used for:
    —Short moves
    —Medium weights
    —Maneuvering loads
    —Supplementing powered equipment
    —In and around crowded work area
    —Infrequent moves
6. Limitations
    —Requires manpower
    —Slow
    —Fairly hard to move any distance

III A5: Trailer.   A load-carrying platform, mounted on four wheels or casters. Designed to be towed individually or in trains, with "steering" by (1) two casters on front, (2) fifth wheel (turntable) or (3) four-wheel steer, with two interconnected fifth wheel turntables. Couplers connect trailers. (*See also* I C9a,c; III B10a,b, Tractor-Trailer Train.)

Characteristics

1. Inexpensive
2. Light weight—can be wood or metal
3. Adaptable, with specially designed superstructures, to an extremely wide variety of tasks.
4. Running gear governed by use, floor conditions, and space restrictions
5. Hauled by tractor, conveyor tow-line (I C9) or sometimes lift truck—one tractor can handle 3 trains of 4 trailers each
6. Handle up to 20 tons
7. Used for:
    —Supplementing lift trucks, between docks and storage areas (receiving or shipping)

—High volume
—Long distances (over 300 ft.)
—Varying routes
8. Limitations
    —Must allow space for trains to clear corners
    —Need smooth surface

III B1: Crane Truck. A self-propelled wheeled vehicle designed to accommodate a crane for lifting and carrying objects (Fig. 6–44).

Fig. 6–44. Crane truck. (Courtesy of Eaton Corp., Industrial Truck Division.)

Characteristics

1. May be gasoline, diesel, LP (liquid petroleum), gas, or battery-powered
2. Capacities to 10,000 lbs
3. Used for:
    —Lifting, loading, positioning, maneuvering loads
    —Handling awkward shapes with slings, chains, etc.
    —Short moves
    —Maintenance and repair work
    —Yard work

4. Limitations
    —Not practical for long moves
(*See also* II A4, Mobile Crane)

III B2: Fork Lift Truck: A self-loading, counterbalanced, self-propelled, wheeled vehicle, carrying an operator, and designed to carry a load on forks (or other attachment) fastened to telescoping mast which is mounted ahead of the vehicle to permit lifting and stacking of loads (Figs. 6–45, 6–46).

Fig. 6–45. Fork lift truck. (Courtesy of Materials Handling Division, White Motor Corp.)

Characteristics
1. May be powered by gasoline, diesel, battery, or LP gas engine
2. Mast may be tilted forward or backward to facilitate loading and unloading
3. Operator may ride in center or at back end of truck—or, with special attachments, on the lifting mechanism, with the load
4. Operator may sit or stand
5. Used with a wide variety of attachments to provide an extremely flexible and adaptable handling device
6. Carries own power source—therefore useful away from power lines
7. Wheels and tires can be provided for a variety of floor conditions or operating locations—wood, concrete, highway, yard

Fig. 6–46. Heavy-duty (70,000 lb.) lift truck stacking shipping containers. (Courtesy of Clark Equipment Co.)

8. Wide range of capabilities
9. Electric type especially useful where reduced noise, and/or no fumes are desired
10. Used for:
   —Lifting, lowering, stacking, unstacking, loading, unloading, maneuvering
   —Variable and flexible paths
   —Medium to large units loads
   —Uniform shaped loads
   —Low to medium volume of material
   —Intermittent moves
11. Limitations
   —Usually requires skid, pallet or container
   —Gas—noisy, fumes, high maintenance
   —Electric—slower, high initial cost, low maintenance
   —Requires suitable running surface
   —Requires adequate clearances
   —Requires skilled operator
   —Requires maintenance facility
   —Power source tied to vehicle (vs. tractor-trailer train)
   —Usually uneconomical for moves over 300 ft

　　　—Travel speed limited to 6–10 mph
　　　—Lift speed limited to 80 fpm
　　　—Grades limited
　　　—Lift heights up to 20 ft
　　　—Loads limited to 130,000 lbs
　　　—Relatively high deadweight to load capability
　　　—Efficiency depends on operator

III B3a: Narrow-Aisle Truck. In general, refers to any one of several types of powered trucks which are capable of operating in a "narrow" aisle (6 ft. down to 30 in.), by virtue of one of the following features:

1. Outriggers (straddle *truck*) (see Fig. 6–53)
2. Extendable forks (reach truck)
   a. Pantograph (see Fig. 6–50)
   b. Sliding forks
   c. Moving mast (see Fig. 6–51)
3. Four-way travel
4. Side loader design (see Fig. 6–51)
5. Rotating mast
6. Side-motion fork attachment
7. "Narrow" construction (see Fig. 6–47)

Characteristics (General)

1. Uses less aisle space
2. Relatively maneuverable
3. Indoor models usually electric
4. Used for:
   —Order picking
   —Congested areas
   (*See* details under specific trucks)
   —Reach truck (Sec. III B6)
   —Side loader (Sec. III B7)
   —Straddle truck (Sec. III B9)
   —Order-picking truck (Sec. III B3b)

III B3b: Order-Picking Truck. A truck designed or adapted to facilitate the order-picking process by making it easier for the operator to control the truck lift and travel while selecting orders (Fig. 6–47). Variations include:

1. Walkie tractor, with trailer (see Fig. 6–54)
2. Walkie tractor, with pallet, rack, or container (see Fig. 6–57)
3. Walkie rider, to permit easy "leading" through aisles and riding between picking locations (see Fig. 6–54)
4. Straddle, with operating controls on a platform between the mast and forks. Vehicle sometimes only 26"–30" wide, with guide rollers

Fig. 6–47.   Order-picking truck, with controls on platform. Note guide wheels on outriggers, and rails to eliminate steering in narrow aisle. (Courtesy of Hyster Company, Lewis-Shepard Division.)

or wheels on chassis which engage rails on bottom of racks to eliminate need for steering. Operator rides on platform and can pick both sides of the narrow 36″ (±) aisle. (See Figs. 17–16, 17–17.)

III B4: Platform Truck (Powered).   A fixed-level, non-elevating, load-carrying powered industrial truck supporting the load on a platform (Fig. 6–48). Smaller-capacity models are referred to as load carriers or burden carriers, for handling lighter loads and "pick up" use.

Characteristics
1. Straight frame—carrying surface above wheels
2. Drop frame—carrying surface closer to floor with smaller wheels at end opposite power source (see Fig. 6–48)
3. Operator normally stands
4. May be gas, diesel or battery powered
5. Versatile
6. Adaptable—with special chassis or attachments

Fig. 6–48. Platform (load carrier) truck. (Courtesy of Elwell-Parker Electric Co.)

7. Used for:
   —Heavy loads
   —Occasional use
   —Relatively long loads with offset driver's seat—wall board, pipe, wood, etc.
   —Bulky loads
   —Maintenance work—carrying tools to work or work to shop
   —Where platform lift or fork lift is not warranted by handling volume

8. Limitations
   —Not self-loading or unloading
   —Power unit stays with load
   —Vehicle idle during load and unload
   —Capacities to 80,000 lbs

III B5: Platform Lift Truck (Powered). A truck designed to handle loads on skids by means of an elevating platform which lifts the skid (Fig. 6–49). Common types are (1) low-lift, up to 24-in. lift and (2) high-lift, over 24-in. lift. The forerunner of the fork lift truck.

Characteristics

1. Skids can be loaded or unloaded while truck is busy carrying
2. May be gas, diesel, or battery powered

Fig. 6–49. Platform lift truck. (Courtesy of Raymond Corp.)

3. Operator usually stands at rear
4. Some have 4-wheel steering
5. Low lift lifts only enough to clear floor with load
6. High lift can stack
7. Used for:
    —Low lift: hauling
    —High lift: tiering skids
    —Carrying racks of parts
    —Handling between work areas
    —Delivery of materials from storage to production
8. Limitations
    —Requires skids
    —Capacity to 100,000 lbs
    —Limited lift height

III B6: Reach Truck. A variation of the straddle truck in which the forks "reach out" for the load on a pantograph-type device which permits the forks to travel forward in order to engage the load, lift it, and then retract it to the mast for travelling (Fig. 6–50).

Fig. 6–50.   Narrow-aisle reach truck that can turn a right angle in a 6-ft. aisle.   (Courtesy of Raymond Corp.)

Characteristics

1. Uses less aisle space
2. Maneuverable
3. Weighs about 2000 lb. less than counter-balanced equivalent
4. Some models can stack loads 2 deep on racks
5. Used for:
    —Warehousing
    —Narrow aisles
    —Tight quarters
    —Low floor load areas
    —Loading/unloading vehicles
6. Limitations.
    —Can normally reach 24″–36″

—Reach takes 3–9 seconds
—Requires good floor conditions
—Lifts up to 16–18 ft

III B7: Side Loader Truck. A powered, 4-wheel truck, which picks up the load from the side by means of a mast with forks centrally mounted in a "bay" at the center of the truck chassis (Fig. 6–51). This arrangement permits the mast to travel transversely across the chassis and, in the extreme outboard position, lift loads within reach of the forks. The load is then "retracted" and placed on the chassis or deck for carrying.

Fig. 6–51. Side-loading lift truck. (Courtesy of Raymond Corp.)

Characteristics

1. No need to turn into the load
2. May be gas, diesel, or battery powered
3. Fast load pick up
4. Very maneuverable, for size of load
5. Quick, safe transport and stacking

6. Can climb 15–20% grade
7. One-man operation, even for most large loads
8. Some have pneumatic tires for outdoor use
9. Can travel on highway—about 25 mph
10. Truck width equals load plus about 3 ft
11. Heavy duty models have jacks for stabilizing while loading and unloading
12. Can have guide rollers for use in narrow aisles
13. Used for:
   —Narrow aisles
   —Long loads, 40 ft or more
   —Storing long loads (pipe, lumber, steel shapes, sheet metal, bar stock, etc.) on racks or piles
   —With attachment can tandem store 2 loads deep, therefore eliminating 2 aisles out of 5
   —Yard storage work
14. Limitations
   —Lifts 2 tons up to 30 ft
   —Lifts 10,000 lbs to 20 ft
   —Usually can work only one side of the aisle
   —Requires skilled operator
   —Requires skilled maintenance personnel
   —Relatively expensive

III B8: Straddle Carrier. A truck whose inverted frame has four wheels mounted on "legs," which permits the vehicle to straddle a load, pick it up with hydraulically operated load-carrying shoes, mounted within its frame, and then move with the load (Fig. 6–52).

Characteristics
1. Self-loading and unloading
2. Loads or unloads in 3–4 secs, practically "on the run"
3. May travel on highway—up to 60 mph
4. Travels backward and forward
5. Very versatile
6. May be 2- or 4-wheel steer
7. Large types can stack shipping containers 3 high
8. Pneumatic tires
9. Used for:
   —Long loads
   —Bulky loads
   —Fast movement of large loads
   —Shipping containers
   —Customer delivery (on highway)
10. Limitations
   —Load must be placed on skids, bolsters or trays
   —Lifts up to 70,000 lb

Fig. 6–52. Straddle carrier handling steel bars—60,000-lb. capacity. Note bolsters on ground at right which are clamped between carrier's load-carrying shoes. (Courtesy of Clark Equipment Company.)

—Load size 8 $\times$ 8 $\times$ 40 ft or even more
—Large
—Expensive
—Usually for outdoor use
—Requires skilled operator
—Requires skilled maintenance personnel

III B9: Straddle Truck (Outrigger). A variation of the lift truck where vehicle is equipped with wheeled outrigger arms extending forward on the floor along either side of the load. Arms perform the function of a counterbalance and keep the truck from overturning (Fig. 6–53).

Characteristics

1. Uses less aisle space
2. Can be equipped with reach attachment
3. Generally battery powered, therefore quiet, no fumes, low operating cost

Fig. 6–53. Straddle truck (also known as narrow aisle truck) with outriggers which straddle the winged skids, to balance load. Note also extension forks. (Courtesy of Clark Equipment Company.)

4. Operator rides, usually in stand-up position at rear of truck
5. Maneuverable
6. Relatively lightweight—about 2000 lb less than counter-balanced truck of equal capacity
7. Used for:
    —Narrow aisles (6½ ft)
    —Tight quarters
    —Low capacity floors
    —Loading elevators, trucks, etc.
    —Warehousing—stacking, picking, etc.
8. Limitations
    —Lifts to 18 ft
    —Loads to 6000 lb
    —Usually requires wing-type pallets, or . . .
    —Requires space alongside pallets or under racks to accommodate outriggers

III B10: Tractor-Trailer Train. A handling system consisting of a 3- or 4-wheeled, self-propelled vehicle designed for pulling loaded carts or trailers. Common versions are:

    a. Rider type (see Fig. 6–54)
    b. Walkie type
    c. Electronically guided type (see Fig. 6–55)

Fig. 6–54. Electric tractor hauling two 4-wheel hand trucks. Driver can also walk and "lead" truck by handle. (Courtesy of Eaton Corp., Industrial Truck Division.)

Characteristics
    1. Motive power is not tied up while trailers are being loaded or unloaded
    2. One power unit pulls several load units
    3. One tractor can keep three sets of trailers in use—one loading, one unloading, and one in transit, if loading and unloading labor is available at terminal points
    4. Low cost movement of large quantities
    5. Flexible route
    6. Three-wheeled-type tractor extremely maneuverable
    7. Electronically guided type requires no operator and follows a path described by a wire embedded in the floor (or a line, or tape) and can be programmed for automatic dropping of trailers and signalling arrival or sounding horn at intersections.

Fig. 6–55. Electronically controlled tractor-trailer train, following white line on floor via photo-electric scanner (can also follow wire embedded in floor). Can be programmed to stop, blow horn, drop trailer, etc. (Courtesy of Barrett Electronics Corp.)

8. Used for:
   —Greater volume than fork lift truck
   —Distances over 300–400 ft
   —Warehousing operations to haul loaded trailers from order picking area to order assembly area, and from receiving to storage
   —Receiving and shipping, in conjunction with fork lift truck for loading and unloading carriers
   —Specific loads, with specially designed trailers, such as platforms, boxes, racks, etc
   —Order picking where driver can also pick orders
   —Collecting or delivering loads to a number of locations, as on a route
9. Limitations
   —Requires a fairly wide aisle for turning corners and maneuvering
   —Total load may be 20–25 tons/tractor

—Must have enough material to be moved to necessitate large
  volume handling
—Electronically guided (No. 7, above) will travel 150–200 ft per
  minute with 15,000–20,000 lb *total* load

III B11: Walkie Truck.   A term applied to many of the "basic" truck
types previously described, when designed to be power-propelled, and
usually power-operated, but with the operator walking and operating the
truck by means of controls on the handle (Figs. 6–56, 6–57). Common
types are:

  a. fork lift
  b. narrow-aisle
  c. order picker
  d. pallet
  e. platform
  f. reach
  g. skid
  h. stacker (portable elevator)
  i. straddle (outrigger)
  j. tractor

Designed to fill the gap between the "hand" trucks and the rider
trucks, although some are designed as "rider-walkies."

Fig. 6–56. Walkie-type lift truck. (Courtesy of Hyster Company, Lewis-
Shepard Division.)

Fig. 6–57. Walkie-type jacklift. (Courtesy of Hyster Company, Lewis-Shepard Division.)

Characteristics
1. Smaller ⎫
2. Lighter ⎬ than rider-types
3. Slower ⎭
4. Usually battery powered
5. Used for (see also "rider" types):
    —Lighter loads
    —Shorter hauls (up to 250 ft)
    —Congested areas
    —Occasional use
    —Servicing elevators
    —Low floor load areas
    —Supplement rider trucks
6. Lower cost
7. Adaptable
8. Dependable

9. Limitations
   —Slower
   —Capacity to 20,000 lbs
   —Lift to 170 in

IV. CONTAINERS AND SUPPORTS

IV A1: Pallet Box. A pallet upon which a box, or equivalent, has been constructed to contain the load (Fig. 6–58). Box may be permanent, detachable, collapsible, or expendable.

Fig. 6–58. Pallet box with drop front for ease of access. (Courtesy of General Box Co.)

Characteristics

1. Permits unitizing items that will not stack upon themselves, or of bulk materials
2. Provides easy access to stored materials through openings in one side of pallet box
3. May be made of wood, sheet metal, formed wire mesh, corrugated board, etc.
4. Permits stacking otherwise unstackable materials
5. Easy to inventory
6. Can be stored outside
7. Minimizes packing of individual items
8. Many types have low first cost
9. Can be built to meet specific requirements
10. Increase flexibility of storage
11. Re-usable
12. Used for:
    —In-process storage
    —Inter-plant shipment
    —Protecting contents
    —Making better use of cube
    —Reducing freight cost
13. Limitations
    —Added tare weight
    —Uses up some of building cube
    —Empties occupy valuable space
    —Subject to damage
    —Require maintenance

IV A2: Skid Box. Same as pallet box, except on a skid instead of a pallet (Fig. 6–59).

IV A3: Tote Box. Any one of a number of varieties of relatively small containers (Fig. 6–60) for handling materials through the shop (sometimes known as shop boxes).

Characteristics

1. May be made of sheet metal, wire, wood, fiber board, corrugated board, or plastic
2. Permit easy handling of small parts
3. May be consolidated into unit loads
4. May be easily stacked or placed in racks
5. Custom liners or inserts permit safe handling of odd shaped or fragile items
6. Some are stackable
7. Used for
    —Consolidating items

Fig. 6–59. Skid boxes (note drop bottom and elevating rack). (Courtesy of Union Metal Manufacturing Company.)

         —Protecting items
         —In-process handling and storage
    8. Limitations
         —Cost
         —Weight

IV B: Bulk Container. Any one of a number of types of containers for unitizing bulk materials such as powdered, granular, or liquid—usually 100 to 200 cu ft capacity (Fig. 6–61).

Characteristics
    1. May be closed or open
    2. Made of metal, plastic, rubber, wood, wire mesh, corrugated, etc.
    3. May be lined
    4. Easy to inventory
    5. Some are collapsible (for return)
    6. Re-usable
    7. Easy to handle by mechanical means
    8. Stackable
    9. May be non-corrosive
   10. Used for:
         —Protection of contents—loss, weather, contamination
         —Inter-plant handling

Fig. 6–60. Steel containers (tote boxes), one type of a large variety of small containers. (Courtesy of Republic Steel Corp., Manufacturing Division.)

—Elimination of smaller containers such as bags, with attendant handling
—Increasing use of storage space
—Reducing freight cost
11. Limitations
—Some are costly
—May require maintenance
—Some non-collapsible
—Added weight
—May require specialized handling equipment
—Some loss of building cube

IV C: Shipping Container. A large container designed for consolidating material or goods to facilitate shipment by common carrier—usually 500–2500 cu ft; sometimes classified as pallet, cargo, and van containers (Fig. 6–62).

Characteristics
1. Common sizes: 8′ × 8′ × 10′–20′–30′–40′; "pallet" sizes 50–100 cu ft
2. Sealed by shipper
3. Handled as a unit—usually direct to customer

Fig. 6–61. Stainless steel bulk material container. (Courtesy of Tote Systems Division, Hoover Ball and Bearing Co.)

4. Reduced pilferage, damage, contamination, etc.
5. Reduced handling time (vs. individual items)
6. Reduced packaging and packing costs
7. Lower insurance rates
8. May be made of metal, wood, plastic, rubber, etc.
9. Some are collapsible
10. Some have drop bottoms
11. Many are designed for attachment *to* carriers
12. Used for:
    —Over the road, rail, sea or air shipment
    —Bulk, liquid, or unit materials
13. Limitations
    —Cost of containers
    —Maintenance
    —Cost of returning empties
    —Paperwork involved
    —Added tare weight

IV D1: Pallet Frame. A device or devices (Figs. 6–63, 6–64), usually for attachment to a pallet, where the frame characteristic of the device both contains the load and supports another load.

Fig. 6–62. Shipping container being unloaded from truck for transfer to flat car. (Courtesy of Seatrain Lines.)

Characteristics
1. Permits unitizing of goods not otherwise easily unitized
2. Permits stacking of goods not otherwise stackable
3. Allows access to loads on bottom of stack
4. Used for:
   —"Soft" items: tires, bags, etc.
   —Bulky goods: brooms, mops, etc.
   —Fragile goods
5. Limitations
   —Cost
   —Maintenance
   —Return cost

Fig. 6–63. Pallet-mounted frame permits stacking of crushable loads. (Courtesy of Tier-Rack Corp.)

IV D2: Pallet. A horizontal platform device used as a base for assembling storing and handling materials as a unit load. Usually consists of two flat surfaces, separated by stringers. (For details, see Figs. 4–6, 6–41, 6–50, 6–63, 6–65, 6–66, 6–79.)

Characteristics

1. May be expendable, general purpose, or special purpose
2. May be single or double faced
3. May be flush stringer, single or double wing
4. May be one-way, two-way, or four-way
5. Made of wood, plywood, metals, corrugated, plastic, etc.
6. Protects goods being moved from damage, pilferage, etc.
7. Facilitates inventorying
8. Promotes cleanliness and good housekeeping
9. Keeps material off floor, therefore easier to handle
10. Used for:
    —Fork-truck-based systems
    —Unitizing items

Fig. 6–64. Integral platform and uprights form stacking device for rolled roofing. (Courtesy of Paltier Corp.)

        —Utilizing building cube
        —Increasing load size
        —Reducing handling of individual items
        —Minimizing packaging of individual items
  11. Limitations
        —Cost ($3–5 each)
        —Ownership (about $1/pallet/year)
        —Occupies space (10–15 cu ft/pallet)
        —Fire hazard

IV D3: Rack. A framework designed to facilitate the storage of loads, and usually consisting of upright columns and horizontal members for supporting the loads, and diagonal bracing for stability (Figs. 6–65, 6–66, 6–67).

Characteristics
  1. May be classified as:
    Selective
      a. Bolted
      b. Lock-fit
      c. Palletless

Fig. 6–65. 8-high pallet racks of structural steel, being served by a side loading truck. (Courtesy of Frazier Industrial Co.)

    d. Special
       (1) Cantilever
       (2) Bar stock
       (3) A-frame
       (4) Custom
Bulk
    e. Drive-in
    f. Drive-through
    g. Live
Portable
    h. Integral unit
       (1) Rigid
       (2) Knock-down
       (3) Collapsible
    i. Pallet attachments
       (1) Bolt-on (special or adapted pallet)
       (2) Snap fit (standard pallet)
    j. Independent of pallet

Fig. 6–66. Sliding racks move to one side on rails to eliminate aisles. (Courtesy of Dexion, Inc.)

Fig. 6–67. Drive-in pallet rack. Note rail support arms for pallets, permitting truck to drive *into* rack—or *through*, if not against a wall, or blocked at other end. (Courtesy of Interlake, Inc.)

2. Made of metal, wood, pipe, etc.
3. May be fixed or adjustable in "shelf" height
4. Usually built for pallets, but may be used or adapted for skids, rolls, drums, reels, bars, boxes, etc.
5. May have "shelves" for storage of loads, but may be designed for drive-in or drive-through applications
6. Facilitate inventory taking
7. Rugged; minimum maintenance
8. "Live" racks are designed for loads to "flow" to the unloading position
9. Cantilever racks best for long items
10. Used for:
    —Increasing utilization of storage space
    —Increasing selectivity of goods stored

—Protecting goods
—Control of inventory
—Improving housekeeping
11. Limitations
    —Wasted space in unused openings
    —Cost

IV D4: Skid. A load-carrying platform (Fig. 6–68) supported from the floor by two parallel stringers or supports. (For details, see Chapter 4.)

Fig. 6–68. Metal skid for handling heavy loads. (Courtesy of Eaton Corp., Handling Systems Division.)

Characteristics

1. Similar to the pallet (*q.v.*)
2. Usually heavier and stronger than pallets
3. Usually for use with heavier loads
4. May be wood or metal
5. May be built into a shipping container for ease of handling
6. Used for same general purposes as pallets (*q.v.*)
7. Semi-live skids have 2 wheels and 2 "legs" for use with skid jack. (*See* Section III A4.)

8. Limitations
> —Not as applicable to stacking as pallets, due to having only one face
> —Cost
> —Space occupied lost to storage

V. AUXILIARY EQUIPMENT

V A: Ball Table. A group of ball transfers [6] over which flat-surfaced objects may be moved in any direction (Fig. 6–69). The same objective

Fig. 6–69. Ball table (with lift section) for easy maneuvering of packing boxes. (Courtesy of Standard Conveyor Co.)

is sometimes accomplished with a caster table, substituting casters for the ball transfers, for moving appropriate objects. Used for right-angle turns in roller, belt, and similar conveyors.

V B: Crane Attachments. Any one of a large number and wide variety of attachments to facilitate handling with cranes, hoists, and monorails. Include such devices as slings, tongs, clamps, grabs, magnets, buckets,

---

[6] A device in which a larger ball is mounted and retained on a hemispherical face lined with smaller balls.

Fig. 6–70. "C" hook coil grab. (Courtesy of Mansaver Division, American Chain and Cable Co.)

ladles, etc. Several are shown in the accompanying illustrations (Figs. 6–70, 6–71, 6–72, 6–73).

V C: Dock Board.   A specially designed platform device (Fig. 6–74) to bridge the gap between the edge of the dock and the carrier floor.[7] Sometimes known as bridge plates. (*See also* V G.)

Characteristics

   1. Made in formed shape to provide strength and side guards
   2. Usually lightweight metal
   3. Often designed with "loops" to permit moving by fork truck
   4. Sometimes fastened to edge of dock
   5. Some can be slid along a rail from one location to another
   6. Often have pins to lock lateral position
   7. Have non-skid surfaces
   8. May be flared for narrow (shallow) docks
   9. Should be carefully selected for intended use

---

[7] Carrier floors vary from 44″ for rail cars, to 48″ for pick-up trucks, to 52″ for highway trucks, plus special-type bodies of even lower design.

Fig. 6–71. Turnover grab handling coated roll stock for cans. (Courtesy of Mansaver Division, American Chain and Cable Co.)

V D: Dock Levelers. A platform-like device (Fig. 6–75), built into the dock surface (or edge) and hinged to permit raising and lowering to accommodate truck height when bridging the gap between dock and truck floor.

Characteristics

1. Permits extension of dock floor into carrier
2. Adjust up and down, left and right, or for vehicle tilt
3. May be counterbalanced or hydraulically operated
4. May be automatic; i.e., adjustment to truck initiated upon "bumping" by vehicle
5. Has "lip" to level out vehicle end of platform

Similar functions are performed by related devices such as:

1. *Truck Leveler.* A ramp or elevator-like device, built into the floor of the truck "well," upon which the back wheels of the truck are

Fig. 6–72. Motororized telescoping-leg horizontal coil grab. (Courtesy of Mansaver Division, American Chain and Cable Co.)

driven, so the rear end of the vehicle can be raised to dock level. Angle of incline from truck to dock is less than with dock board. Eliminates dock obstructions.

2. *Lifting Dock.* An elevator-like device designed to lift and lower loads between ground level and carrier floor level when a dock is not convenient or available. May be portable or built-in at door, rail siding, etc.

3. *Lifting Tail Gate.* A tail gate device attached to the rear of a truck and so constructed that it can be extended level with the truck floor and then lifted from or lowered to the ground as an elevator.

V E: Lift Truck Attachments. Any one of a large number (over 50) and wide variety of devices designed for attaching to lift trucks—to permit their adaptation to many tasks. Some of the more common types are listed below, and several are shown in the accompanying illustration (Fig. 6–76).

Fig. 6–73. Coil tray grab with telescoping-leg design. (Courtesy of Man-saver Division, American Chain and Cable Co.)

Common Lift Truck Attachments

A. Appliance stacker
B. Boom
C. Cab
D. Clamp
    1. Bale
    2. Barrel
    3. Carton
    4. Drum
    5. Roll
E. Crane
F. Crate grab
G. Die handler
H. Drop-bottom box dumper
I. Dumping hopper
J. Load inverter
K. Load stabilizer
L. Lowering mast
M. Maintenance platform
N. Overhead guard

O. Push-pull
P. Ram
Q. Remote control
R. Revolving carriage
S. Roller platform
T. Shovel (scoop)
U. Side-loader
V. Side-shifter
W. Snow plow
X. Special forks
    1. Brick
    2. Block
    3. Tile
    4. Extended
    5. Folding
    6. Retractable
Y. Swing-shift
Z. Vacuum

Fig. 6–74. Dock board. (Courtesy of Equipment Company of America.)

V F: Pallet Loader (Palletizer). An automatic or semiautomatic machine (Figs. 6–77, 6–78), consisting of synchronized conveyors and mechanisms to receive objects from conveyors and place them onto pallets according to a prearranged pattern. Basic types are (1) "stripper" and (2) "suction head."

The pallet *unloader* (depalletizer) performs the opposite function, and unloads the items, feeding them out in "single file."

Characteristics

1. Receives cartons, crates, bags from conveyors
2. Interchangeable devices direct construction of various pallet patterns
3. Built-up load leaves palletizer on a conveyor for removal by lift truck, etc.
4. Can build unit loads without pallet
5. Eliminates manual labor and carton damage
6. Palletizes 60–70 cases per minute
7. Limitations—pallets 36″ × 36″ to 48″ × 60″
   —Cartons L = 6″ to 60″; W = 6″ to 45″; H = 3″ to 20″

Fig. 6–75. Dock leveler. (Courtesy of General Box Co.)

—Loads to 50″ × 60″ × 84″ high
—Carton weight to 150 lbs
—Hydraulic and electronic maintenance required
—Possible jams

V G: Ramp. A portable device for placement at the door of a carrier or building (Fig. 6–79) and bridging the vertical distance to the ground level with a sloping runway—the ramp.

Characteristics
1. A portable loading dock
2. Usually lightweight metal
3. Formed to provide strength and side guarding
4. Hydraulic lift to carrier height on heavy-duty models
5. Used for:
   —Providing easy access to carrier without a raised dock
   —Provides access to a dock from ground level

CONCLUSION

This chapter has attempted to present a review of some of the more common types of material handling equipment used in business and in-

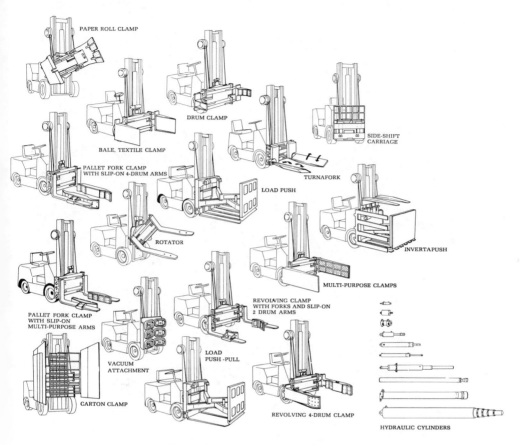

Fig. 6–76. Typical lift truck attachments. (Courtesy of Cascade Corp.)

dustry. Only about one sixth of the total number of types are presented here. For information on other types, or more details on those contained in this chapter, the reader is referred to the following sources.[8]

1. Association of Lift Truck and Portable Elevator Manufacturers, *Mechanical and Hydraulic Hand Lift Trucks,* 1957.
2. Bolz, H. A., and Hagemann, G. E., *Materials Handling Handbook,* The Ronald Press Co., 1958.
3. Caster and Floor Truck Manufacturers Association, *Engineering and Purchasing Planbook,* 1959.
4. Conveyor Equipment Manufacturer's Association, *Belt Conveyors for Bulk Materials,* 1966.

[8] Some of which are unfortunately out of print, but available in libraries.

Fig. 6–77. Automatic pallet loader. (*Top*) Cartons arrive via roller conveyor and are automatically arranged into a pallet pattern. Pusher bar (*upper right*) pushes pattern onto pallet, under lid at left. Successive layers are placed on pallets coming in from bottom. (*Bottom*) Magazine at right, with full pallet load discharged at left, for take-away by conveyor or lift truck. (Courtesy of Lamson Division, Diebold, Inc.)

Fig. 6–78. Semi-automatic pallet loader. Bags are supported on air cushion, permitting easy postitioning by operator. (Courtesy of Shields Conveyor Co.)

5. Conveyor Equipment Manufacturer's Association, *Conveyor Terms and Definitions*, 1966.
6. Haynes, D. O., *Materials Handling Equipment*, Chilton, 1957.
7. Haynes, D. O., *Materials Handling Applications*, Chilton, 1958.
8. Hudson, W. G., *Conveyors and Related Equipment*, Wiley, 1954.
9. Industrial Publishing Co., *Material Handling Engineering Directory and Handbook*, biennial.
10. Industrial Truck Association, *The Handbook of Powered Industrial Trucks*, 1957.
11. Keller, H. C., *Unit Load and Package Conveyors*, The Ronald Press Co., 1967.
12. Kraus, N. W., *Pneumatic Conveying of Bulk Materials*, The Ronald Press Co., 1968.
13. Modern Materials Handling, *Annual Directory and Buying Guide*.

Fig. 6–79. Portable loading ramp made of magnesium alloy. (Courtesy of Magline, Inc.)

14. Monorail Manufacturer's Association, *Material Handling with Monorail,* 1959.
15. Stoess, H. A., *Pneumatic Conveying,* Wiley, 1970.
16. Woodley, D. R., *Encyclopaedia of Materials Handling,* 2 vols., Pergamon, 1964.

7

General Analysis Procedure

It might safely be said that most material handling problems are not analyzed—they are solved! In entirely too many cases, the typical material-handling "man" will make a superficial review of the physical aspects of a problem situation—a walk through the area—and *announce* his "solution." "Buy a lift truck!" or "Buy a belt conveyor!" This is *not* analyzing the problem, and furthermore, it is doing a great injustice to himself, his superiors, the material handling profession, and the material handling equipment manufacturers.

Actually, he is only briefly assessing the obvious physical aspects of the situation, reviewing in his mind the several kinds of material handling equipment with which *he* is familiar, and proclaiming the one *he* feels will be of some help in *alleviating* the problem.

To a certain extent, this approach has been successful in the past, for a number of reasons:

1. There *is* a tremendous amount of room for improvement in almost any material handling situation.
2. He *does* know something about a few pieces of handling equipment—and a few things about material handling in general.
3. Many material handling problems *can* be improved to some extent by *any* one of a number of possible solutions.
4. He has made an "impression" by virtue of his quick "solution."

One might ask what is wrong with this approach, if it is helpful in correcting material handling difficulties. Why bother spending any more time on such problems?

There are several very important reasons why the above approach is wrong, and should not be condoned by good management, competent material handling men, or material handling equipment sales representatives:

1. Such "quickie" solutions may later prove to be wrong, or at least not the best.
2. Management deserves the best solution to the problem—at least a studied solution. The correct solution might save considerably more money and avoid the unnecessary interim costs of the "quickie" solution.
3. The problem may not even have been identified properly or completely. Possibly the *wrong* problem may have been solved! Or there may be *no* problem!
4. *All* the pertinent facts have not been obtained.
5. The analyst is *not* sufficiently familiar with the large majority of the more than 500 types and kinds of material handling equipment available.
6. The solution to the problem may not even require any equipment.
7. Material handling equipment manufacturers are not happy to sell and install equipment where the applications may later prove to be wrong.
8. A limited point of view probably has restricted potential methods of approach.
9. The observed problem may only be a symptom of a larger problem, not apparent without complete analysis.
10. Possibly, the observed situation could be eliminated, rather than "solved."
11. Company time and money has been wasted in implementing an "un-solution to a non-problem"!

The above observations certainly point out the fallacy of hasty solutions to material handling problems. Much more worthwhile results, as well as additional savings can be obtained by a proper approach to the analysis and solution of problems involving material handling activities. The balance of this chapter will outline an orderly approach to such situations, in the form of a problem solving "procedure."

It should be recognized that a material handling problem "solved" by the hasty method implied above has *not* dealt with the entire range of factors inherent in such a problem. It has only dealt with the *what* (material) and the *how* (equipment) aspects of the material handling equation. A more thorough analysis would have considered *all* of the pertinent factors involved, as pointed out in the discussion of the material handling equation in Chapter 2. Every handling problem should be analyzed in terms of the three major phases: *material, move,* and *method.* These phases, and the subdivisions of each, are recalled below:

Material
    1. Type
    2. Characteristics
    3. Quantity

Move
    4. Source and Destination
    5. Logistics
    6. Characteristics
    7. Type

Method
    8. Handling Unit
    9. Equipment
    10. Manpower
    11. Physical restrictions

These interrelationships were shown graphically in Figure 2–3 with the major sub-divisions of each factor, and this framework—the *material handling equation*—forms the underlying format of the detailed analysis procedure presented below.

PROCEDURE OUTLINED

In analyzing and searching for the best solution to a material handling problem, it would seem appropriate to follow a carefully thought out and detailed procedure. This should help assure that no significant factor is overlooked, and that the answer obtained is carefully developed and hopefully, the best. The procedure to be developed consists of the following steps.

Definition
    I. Identify the problem(s)
    II. Determine the scope of the problem(s)
    III. Establish objective(s)
    IV. Define the problem(s)

Investigation
    V. Determine what data to collect
    VI. Establish work plan and schedule
    VII. Collect data
    VIII. Develop, weigh and analyze data

Solution
    IX. Develop improvements
    X. Prepare justification

XI. Obtain approvals

XII. Revise as necessary

Installation

XIII. Work out procedures for implementation

XIV. Supervise the installation

XV. Follow up

In this and following chapters, the above steps will be described in detail and in many cases, documented with illustrations, examples, forms, charts, etc. However, it should be noted that *this* chapter does not *complete* the procedure implementation. Subsequent chapters will further develop details and provide additional information necessary for carrying out some of the steps.

It should also be mentioned it is not always necessary to follow such a procedure in a 1, 2, 3 fashion. Some problems, because of their nature, will not require of all the steps, and in other cases, it may be found necessary to perform some steps out of sequence due to the problem requirements or limitations. Nevertheless, in every case, it will be wise to check *each* step, to be sure no important item or factor has been overlooked.

PROCEDURE DESCRIBED

The original version of this analysis procedure was based on one developed by Burr W. Hupp, of Drake Sheahan/Stewart Dougall. It has been subsequently expanded and detailed by the addition of ideas and contributions adopted from many sources. *This* version of the procedure is directed primarily at the material handling *problem*, while a more detailed procedure, developed in Chapter 9, deals with the more complex nature of handling *systems*.

As an aid in carrying out the problem solving procedure, a Material Handling Analysis—Problem Solving Guide is included at the end of the chapter. It consists of an approximate outline of the chapter, presented in the form of a guide to assure including each part of the procedure.

Step I: Identify the Problem

The first—and one of the most important—steps in analyzing a material handling problem is the identification of the problem. It stands to reason that if the problem is not correctly and properly identified, it cannot be accurately defined, nor can its scope be determined.

In some cases, of course, the general problem may already be known, and may be so obvious to all concerned, that it needs no further identification. Or, it may have been observed and pointed out by another interested person. If either of the above are true, the second step—determine scope—can be carried out immediately.

However, if the objective is the rather general and common one of "improving material handling," then some systematic approach may be helpful in identifying individual problems, or at least in finding a starting place.

One method of "finding" problems is to tour the plant and observe what is going on from a "material handling point-of-view." It requires a very concentrated effort to visually separate out every aspect of the activity that involves material handling and that is open to *any* question in the way of improvement.

Since this may not be too easy, it may be helpful to rely on a comparison of what is observed, with the past experience of others in the material handling field. One of the easier ways to approach this is by the use of check sheets such as were included at the end of Chapter 3.

In use, the check sheets should be reviewed, and if any indicator (or anything closely resembling it) is spotted, a check mark should be entered in the "yes" column. Comments and/or observations may be indicated in the right-hand column, for further investigation or as reminders of specific items spotted in the plant. Then, each check mark should be further investigated, until the situation observed can be properly identified as a material handling problem. Each problem area so identified then becomes a prospect for a material handling improvement project and should be so recorded on a "list" of material handling projects to be further analyzed. Such a project list, developed from the check sheets, is shown in Fig. 7–1. This in turn might point out the need for a more specialized sheet, such as those at the end of Chapter 3.

Plant *ACME MANUFACTURING*   Department *SEVERAL*   Date *AUGUST 15*

1. Look into *crowded conditions* in final assembly stock area.
2. Check on piles of material *temporarily stored* (?) on receiving dock.
3. Investigate reasons for apparent *backtracking* of cabinets from assembly to finishing.
4. Find out why South aisle in machine shop is *vanishing* (being filled up with stock containers and blocking traffic.)
5. Check into excessive amount of material handling *equipment* in *repair* shop.
6. Why are cartons *rehandled* so many times from receiving to storage to assembly stock area to point of use?
7. Does poor material handling contribute to the *scrap* pile outside the shipping dock?
8. Why are 4 *men* used to unload cabinets from box car?
9. Has material handling contributed to the recent increase in *indirect* labor payroll?

Fig. 7–1. Material handling project list.

In general, it will be found that the conscientious use of check sheets will result in many of the following benefits:

1. Uncover areas of possible improvement.
2. Identify the problem, or problem area.
3. Point out possible solutions, or directions of approach.
4. Indicate magnitude of problem, scope, etc.
5. Make a record of the existing situation (or basis for comparison).
6. A final check against a proposed method; follow-up.
7. Guide or plan for future analysis efforts.
8. Aid in starting up a new M.H. program.

Following the above, or a similar procedure, should aid in properly identifying or ferreting out material handling problem situations.

Step II: Determine Scope of Problem

Having identified a material handling problem, the next step is to determine its *complete* scope. Too many times a material handling problem is solved "out of context" and the related activity areas overlooked or ignored. This means that one should not apply the "quick and easy" spot solution to a *portion* of a problem. Instead, its entire scope or range *must* be identified, and the problem analyzed and solved within its complete framework, and in proper perspective to all related activities and phases. The analyst should review the entire scope of the material handling function—as listed below:

1. Packaging at supplier's plant
2. Packing at supplier's plant
3. Loading at supplier's plant
4. Transportation to user plant
5. External plant transportation activities
6. Unloading activities
7. Receiving of goods
8. Storage of incoming materials
9. Issuing materials to production
10. In-process handling
11. In-process storage
12. Workplace handling
13. Intra-departmental handling
14. Inter-departmental handling
15. Intra-plant handling
16. Handling related to auxiliary functions
17. Packaging
18. Warehousing of finished goods
19. Packing
20. Loading and shipping

21. Transportation to customer locations
22. Inter-plant handling

These activities are listed on the Problem Solving Guide at the end of the chapter. For the problem at hand, a check mark should be placed in front of each activity which *might* be involved or related to the analysis or solution of the problem. Alongside each activity, indicate any ideas, suggestions, or comments which might be helpful later on in relating the activity to the problem solution. These notes should be carefully reviewed as the analysis proceeds, to be sure the solution is compatible with the overall handling system and that all related activities are encompassed by the solution.

Step III: Establish Objectives

After the problem has been defined it will be considerably easier to establish the objectives. They should be clearly stated, and in terms that will make it possible to check on the degree to which they are achieved in the proposed solutions. A clear statement of the objectives will also facilitate auditing the problem solution, *after* it has been installed in order to see if the "solution" is solving the problem.

Step IV: Define the Problem

Only after the complete scope of the problem has been determined, will it be possible to properly define the entire problem. An important benefit of defining the problem at this (later) point is that it serves to review previous thinking and establish parameters or boundaries within which the investigation should proceed.

Step V: Determine What Data To Collect

Once the problem has been carefully and completely defined, it can be determined what data must be collected. The Material Handling Analysis—Basic Data Required Form (Fig. 7–2) should be reviewed and the required data carefully and accurately recorded. The check sheets might also be reviewed for ideas and suggestions as to what data will be needed to further investigate the situations uncovered when it was filled in.

It will be noted that the "basic data" form carries out the theme of the material-handling equation. It contains all of the major factors and their sub-divisions, and significant data are called for under each. This form should prove extremely helpful in determining *what* data to collect. It should be reviewed carefully along with notes made in the problem definition and in establishing the scope of the problem.

MATERIAL HANDLING ANALYSIS—BASIC DATA REQUIRED

IDENTIFICATION

Company _____ Plant _____ Compiled By _____

Building _____ Location In Building _____ Date _____

Statement of Problem _____

_____

_____

(Should be accompanied by Process Chart and/or Flow Diagram)

(Check and/or fill in, as applicable)	Remarks, Explanation, etc.
MATERIAL—Part No(s). _____	

Description _____

1. Type

   Unit _____ Liquid _____
   Bulk _____ Gas _____

2. Characteristics

   Shape _____
   Dimensions _____
   Temperature _____
   Perishability _____
   Weight/Unit _____
   How Received _____

3. Quantity

   Annual _____ Maximum Inventory_____
   Per delivery _____ Per move _____

MOVE

4. Source and Destination

   External
      Carrier
         Type _____
         Characteristics _____
      Other building _____
      Distant location_____
      Other _____
   Internal
      Same dept. _____
      Other dept._____
      Next workplace _____
      Other floor _____
      Load/unload level_____
      Load/unload method_____

5. Logistics

   Scope
      point-to-point _____
      area
         ☐ workplace
         ☐ department
         ☐ building
         ☐ beyond building
         ☐ measure
      activities involved (*list,* from p. 5)

Fig. 7–2. Material handling analysis—basic data required.

234

Route

plane
- ☐ curved
- ☐ straight
- ☐ variable

- ☐ combination
- ☐ intersections

profile
- ☐ horizontal
- ☐ vertical
- ☐ incline/decline
- ☐ combination

- ☐ single-level
- ☐ multi-level
- ☐ variable

path
- ☐ fixed pt./fix. pt.
- ☐ fix pt./var. pts.

- ☐ var. pts./fix. pt.
- ☐ var. pts./var. pts.

level
- ☐ on floor
- ☐ working height
- ☐ overhead
- ☐ other (_____)

6. Characteristics

Distance _____

Frequency _____ moves/ _____ (time unit)

Rate _____ vol/ _____ (time unit)

units/ _____ (time unit)

Speed
- ☐ uniform
- ☐ variable

- ☐ synchronized
- ☐ ft./ _____ (time unit)

Motion
- ☐ regular
- ☐ continuous
- ☐ uniform
- ☐ reciprocating
- ☐ synchronized

- ☐ irregular
- ☐ intermittent
- ☐ variable
- ☐ vibrating

Traffic

Environment

location
- ☐ inside
- ☐ outside

conditions
- ☐ temperature (°F)
- ☐ humidity (%)
- ☐ (other)_____

%Transportation in move _____ %

%Handling in move_____ %

Sequence
- ☐ fixed
- ☐ small variation
- ☐ variable

7. Type of Move

- ☐ transport
- ☐ convey
- ☐ maneuver

- ☐ elevate/lower
- ☐ position
- ☐ transfer

METHOD

8. Handling Unit

Load support method
- ☐ support
- ☐ suspend
- ☐ squeeze
- ☐ spear
- ☐ other

Fig. 7–2. *(Continued)*

Container
- [ ] none   tare _____
- [ ] type _____   cost $ _____
- [ ] construction _____   disposal _____
- [ ] size _____ X _____ X _____

Weight _____

Items/handling unit _____

Handling Units/total quantity _____

9. Equipment

Function
- [ ] handling
- [ ] storage
- [ ] auxiliary

Type indicated
- [ ] none
- [ ] manual
- [ ] mechanical
- [ ] automated

Desired Characteristics _____
_____
_____
_____
_____
_____

Amount
- required capacity _____ (tons, pcs., etc.)
- time/load _____ min.
- number of loads _____
- hrs./yr. _____ hrs.
- no. pcs. of equipment _____

Cost
- equipment cost/hr $ _____
- annual cost $ _____

10. Manpower
Time/move required _____

Hours/year _____ hrs.

Hourly cost $ _____

Annual cost $ _____

11a. Physical Restrictions

Area _____ ft^2

Column spacing _____ X _____

Clear height _____ ft

Aisle(s) width _____ ft

Door(s) sizes _____

Aisle locations _____

Running surface characteristics _____

Congestion _____

Storage area requirements _____ ft^2

11b. Storage Area Restrictions

Floor load capacity _____ lbs./ft^2

Overhead load capacity _____ lbs./ft^2

Ramp(s) grade _____ %

Elevator capacity _____ lbs.

Power supply _____ volts

Electric Supply _____ kW

Fig. 7–2. *(Continued)*

236

It should be emphasized that this form will not *solve* any problems. It will serve as a guide to the organized collection of the necessary data, and will also be found useful as a check sheet and reminder to be sure some items are not overlooked. Its use may also suggest other information that may be required in the analysis procedure. This may be particularly true of data relating to materials flow, layout, etc. If this review of the problem *does* indicate that other specific data will be required, make the necessary notes at the appropriate place on the "basic data" form.

It should be remembered that this form should *not* be used for a problem of too large a scope. Instead, the problem should be subdivided into smaller units, and a separate basic data form used for each.

In addition to the specific types of data called for on the basic data form, other types of information will be required. This will be especially true if the problem is a complex one and involves a sizable segment of the company or plant. General information such as the following may be necessary or helpful:

1. A study of the organization chart, to determine responsibilities for the various phases of the problem.
2. A review of the company objectives to shed light on thinking that could affect any proposed solution.
3. An examination of company policies in such areas as capital expenditures, purchasing, inventory, personnel, labor relations, overtime, etc., to provide an insight into aspects of the problem solution which might arise at a later stage in the analysis.
4. A discussion of long-range plans to help in making decisions on such things as:
   a. production volume changes
   b. product design changes
   c. material changes
   d. funds available
   e. expansion probabilities

Step VI: Establish Work Plan and Schedule

The next step in the analysis procedure is to plan the procedure and work schedule by which the problem is to be solved. Of course, the extent to which such a plan is worked out, will depend upon the scope and complexity of the problem. Establishing the method of procedure may include or involve the following:

A. Cultivating contacts with proper persons
   1. Meet those who will be concerned with the problem and get to know them: production supervision, quality control, product

engineers, plant engineers, industrial engineers, material handling operating personnel, purchasing, etc.

2. Be sure *they* understand what is being done and why—and how *they* can benefit from the project.
3. Talk with and listen to the work force; note *their* points of view, problems, and observations; but be sure to check for accuracy.
4. Talk to each one in his own language.
5. Develop cooperation by reciprocity.

B. Grouping similar or related materials, problems, activity areas for convenient treatment as a *single* problem,

— OR —

C. Breaking overall problem into individual processes, departments, activity areas or functions to facilitate their analysis as *separate problems*.

D. Preparing plans for studying the problem, including:
   1. What is to be done: from review by check sheets (see end of Chapter 3), basic data required, etc.
   2. Who is going to do what
   3. What additional data are required
   4. Where to get necessary data

E. Establishing a detailed work schedule with appropriate time allowances for each major activity. Use critical path method networks if applicable, or at least the Gantt chart approach.

F. Distributing work schedule for comments, suggestions, revision if necessary and finally, approval by appropriate authorities.

G. Assigning responsibilities for each portion or phase of the project.

Other items may be found necessary or advisable, depending on the extent, complexity or scope of the project.

Step VII: Collect Data

The actual collection of the necessary data is the next step in the overall problem solving procedure. This may be accomplished somewhat as outlined below:

A. Review sources of data:

   1. Management personnel
   2. Personal observation and/or own background
   3. Own department
   4. Related departments, functions, etc.
   5. Vendors, sales representatives, etc.
   6. Other plants
   7. Competitors
   8. Courses and conferences
   9. Books and periodicals
   10. Commercial literature

B. Establish project relationships with other company functions and activities to plan necessary degree of cooperation in obtaining data.

C. Carefully *observe* the activity under analysis to be sure it is thoroughly understood and to find out:

1. Who does what
2. Details of methods used (charts, diagrams, etc.)
3. Equipment used
4. Problems encountered
5. Discrepancies between operators and/or shifts

—OR—

D. Carefully *plan* the activity under "synthesis," etc.

E. Obtain complete, accurate data on the *material, move,* and *method* (actual or proposed) and record it in convenient form (such as on the "basic data" form), entering appropriate notes in the right-hand columns. Be sure to check the source and accuracy of all data recorded, especially that on quantities. If necessary, design special forms for data collection on plant operations where insufficient data exists. Also, do not overlook cyclical and seasonal variations, or occasional unusual demands due to sales contests, vacations, material supply, etc.

F. Secure supplementary data deemed necessary on such items as:

1. Schedules
2. Layouts
3. Flow patterns
4. Building drawings or details
5. Equipment details

G. Obtain layout of the area under study.

1. If a layout exists, be sure it is carefully checked for completeness and accuracy.
2. If no layout exists, make one—and be sure it is complete and accurate.

H. Obtain or plan data on material *flow.* This covers the *move* phase of the material handling equation, and techniques will be considered in detail in Chapters 8 and 10. Be sure to use any or a combination of these techniques, many of which are extremely useful in analyzing the flow of materials. Some of them are:

1. Bill of material
2. Assembly chart
3. Production routings
4. Operation process chart
5. Multi-product process chart
6. Process chart
7. Flow process chart

    8. Flow diagram
    9. From-to chart
  10. Activity relationship chart
  11. Activity relationship diagram
  12. String diagram
  13. Memo-motion pictures

I. Procure information on each item of present material-handling equipment, noting make, type, size, capacity, special features, attachments, age, past performance, maintenance records, etc.

J. Secure data on all personnel involved in the project activity, including all details on job classifications, wages, etc.

K. Tabulate all information pertinent to storage aspects of the project. The Storage Analysis Sheet (Figure 7–3) will be found useful in this phase of the analysis for "converting" the inventory to square feet and/or cubic feet, by filling in consecutive columns across the sheet.

L. Examine procedures and techniques for communication and control related to the handling problem. Gather data on communications equipment, utilization, and effectiveness. Also, if advisable, chart flow of paperwork and note carefully the relationships to the control of materials and their flow. Use the Procedure Chart technique shown in Chapter 8.

Additional data, information, records, etc. may be necessary in specific situations, depending on the nature of the problem and its interrelationships with other phases of company operation. It should be noted that in the above analytical work, it is important to establish the extremes or ranges, as well as the most common operating conditions. It usually is desirable to omit extremes in designing a handling system, since the attempt to accommodate every possible variation makes many a system hopelessly complex and expensive.

Step VIII: Develop, Weigh, and Analyze Data

After the data have been collected, it becomes necessary to study, weigh, and analyze all of the facts, figures, and information accumulated. Although the details of such a procedure will not be discussed here, a general procedure and some suggestions may be helpful in the analysis process:

    A. Sort and classify all data into major aspects of the problem—material, move and method—and if necessary, into the major subdivisions.

    B. Check all data for completeness and accuracy of each item of information.

    C. Summarize data on each aspect of the problem.

COMPANY Acme Mfg. Co.   STORAGE ANALYSIS SHEET

☒ Incoming Stock
☐ In-Process Materials
☐ Finished Parts
☐ Finished Product

PRODUCT Widgets

Analyzed By: T.A.F.
Date: Sept 12

ANNUAL PROD'N. 100,000

No.	ITEM OR PART Description	No. per assy.	Size in inches L	W	Ht	Wt	QUANTITY Max. Inv.	Mo. Reqt.	Norm. Rec't.	RECEIPT Freq.	Carr. Type	HANDLING UNIT Type	L	W	Ht	Wt	Items/ Hdlg. Unit	Hdlg. Units For Max. Invent.	no. hdlg. units high	no. base units	Bulk or Pallet sq.ft. per base unit	sq.ft. for max. no.hdlg. units	cu.ft. for max. no.hdlg. units	Shelf	bin	STOR. LOC.
1	Base	1	4	8	1	3 lb.	5000	9000	2500	2/mo.	rail	pall. box	5	3	21	9 77	750	12	3	4	15	60	450			A-6
2	Bolt	4	2	3/8	–	2 oz	20 m	36 m	18 m	2/mo.	rail	keg – pall.	1 42	2 48	63 54	150	500 24	40 3	1 3	1	15	15	135			A-6
3	Pin	2	1	1/8	–	1/4 oz.	20 m	18 m	20 m	1/mo.	trk.	ctn.	8	5	4	16	1000	20	1	1	–	–	1	2 ft³		A-3
4	Rod	1	6 1/2	1/2	–	1/2 #	5 m	9 m	5 m	2/mo.	trk.	wd. box	12	6	3	50	100	50	1	1	–	–	1		7 ft³	A-4

Fig. 7-3. Storage analysis sheet.

D. Determine practicable ranges of all data and eliminate, for special examination, items that appear to be out of line.

E. Average, weight or otherwise treat data to yield information of the most useful form.

F. Develop charts, graphs, tables, etc. to properly present each type of data in terms most appropriate to the problem.

G. Check carefully for inconsistencies, omissions, errors, unnecessary activities, irrelevant data, etc.

As the above analytical work proceeds, it is possible that the analyst may find himself thinking in terms of possible solutions. This is not only unavoidable, but advisable, in that such thinking may possibly lead to the need for even more data that should be gathered and analyzed before any final conclusions are reached.

After all the data have been weighed and analyzed, they should be summarized in appropriate form for use in developing improvements. The Material Handling Analysis Re-Cap Sheet (Figure 7–4) will be found helpful in collecting and analyzing the data.

Step IX: Develop Improvements

The solution to almost every material handling problem is usually a process of comparing the facts and data accumulated with the analyst's own personal background and knowledge of the field of material handling. And, as pointed out in the beginning of this chapter, the hasty "answer" from too rapid a review of these two phases of the problem can easily result in basing the solution on incomplete data and insufficient experience or background. The detailed considerations outlined in this chapter will "force" a more complete and careful accumulation and the analysis of necessary data. If this has been done, then possible solutions have been running through the mind of the analyst and have been at least partially evaluated during the analysis process.

The problem is now one of carefully comparing data for all of the possible alternative solutions. Since it is neither practical, nor even possible to describe such a detailed process in writing, a rough guide may facilitate the process of developing the improved method.[1]

A. Re-define problem (if necessary) to reflect findings to date.

B. Investigate, evaluate, and summarize effect of anticipated changes in:

1. Capacity or Sales Volume
   a. Will it increase production volume?
   b. Will it cause a change in emphasis within the product line?

[1] Adapted from Burr Hupp, *Analysis of Material Handling Problems in Industry,* privately circulated.

			1	2	3	4	
11. Physical Restrictions		ELEVATOR CAPACITY	—				
		FLOOR CONDITION	Gd.				
		OVERHEAD LOAD CAPACITY	—				
		FLOOR LOAD CAPACITY	—				
		AISLE WIDTH	9'6"				
		CLEAR HEIGHT	24				
		COLUMN SPACING	—				
METHOD	**10. Manpower**	NUMBER OF MEN	—				
		HOURS PER YEAR	54				
	9. Equipment	NO. OF UNITS	—				
		CAPACITY	4M				
		TYPE	F.T.				
	8. Handling Unit	HANDL. UNITS PER TOT. QUANTITY	44				
		ITEMS/HANDL. UNIT	36				
		WEIGHT	2M				
		CONTAINER	Pall				
		LOAD SUPPORT METHOD	Spr.				
MOVE	**7. Type**	TRANSP., CONVEY, MANEUVER, ELEVATE, LOWER, POSITION, TRANSFER	T/M				
	6. Characteristics	SEQUENCE	—				
		% HANDLING	20				
		% TRANSP.	80				
		ENVIRONMENT	—				
		TRAFFIC	—				
		MOTION TYPE	INT.				
		SPEED	—				
		RATE	340/hr				
		FREQUENCY	1/hr				
		DISTANCE	80'				
	5. Logistics — Route	LEVEL	FL.				
		PATH	VP-VP				
		PROFILE	Hor.				
		PLANE	Str.				
	Scope	AREA	50x100				
		POINT TO POINT	✓				
	4. Source and Destination	LOAD/UNLOAD METHOD	F.T.				
		LOAD/UNLOAD LEVEL	Trk.				
		EXTERNAL—INTERNAL	E				
MATERIAL	**3. Quantity**	QUANT./MOVE	1600				
		MAXIMUM INVENT.	5M				
		ANNUAL USAGE	20M				
	2. Characteristics	WEIGHT/UNIT	55				
		DIMENSIONS	10x46 x12				
		HOW RECEIVED	Trk				
	1. Type	UNIT, BULK, LIQUID, GAS	U				
		MOVE NUMBER (from PROCESS CHART)	1	2	3	4	

Fig. 7–4. Material handling analysis—re-cap sheet.

c. Is it possible that anticipated material handling, or other cost reductions, will permit price reductions which will broaden markets and materially increase demand?

d. Are new products going to be introduced?

e. Will production requirement changes absorb existing storage space?

f. Will they increase or change raw material, in-process, or finished goods storage requirements?

g. Are purchasing changes tending to change raw material storage patterns?

h. Will trade customs or company policy change finished goods storage volumes or turnover rates?

i. Will changes in distribution methods, such as the opening of new distribution warehouses, affect storage volumes, sizes of shipments, or shipping units?

2. Product Design

a. Will they change the type or nature of material purchases; for instance, packaging and storage?

b. Will they alter production, storage or inspection methods?

c. Will new packaging methods alter the size, shape or weight of the finished item or require different methods of handling or storage?

3. Processing

a. Will it be an addition to or will it displace existing equipment?

b. Will it change operation sequence?

c. Will it necessitate structural changes?

d. Will it inherently require loading or unloading of product in a different form or by different methods?

e. Will it affect space for other operations?

f. Will it change flow rates, volumes, or production balance?

g. Will it change in-process storage patterns?

4. Tooling

a. Will it change production rates?

b. Will it eliminate or add operations at other work stations?

c. Will it affect flow paths or other operations by improving quality?

d. Will it affect operation sequence?

e. Will it change in-process storage patterns?

C. Review sources of ideas and data (see step VIIA above).

D. Select possible solutions from those suggested or conceived during the analysis.

E. Re-examine auxiliary activities, such as scrap removal, packaging materials supply, etc.

F. Make detailed plans for proposed methods.

1. Remember that methods, equipment and layout must be considered together.
2. Develop the basic handling method most applicable to layout possibilities and volume requirements.
3. Organize departmental layouts and methods.
4. Design work stations layouts and methods.
5. Look for the optimum degree of mechanization.
6. Plan for safety and comfort.
7. Include service operations in methods planning.
8. Predict maintenance problems and provide necessary space and equipment.

G. Select equipment. This topic is considered in detail in Chapter 11; review the procedure outlined there.
H. Check proposed methods against principles of material handling to be sure none have been violated, or that all deviations are justifiable.
I. Determine the required structural changes.
   1. Develop a detailed layout around the proposed new handling methods and equipment.
   2. Specify all required changes whether it is new construction, bracing to hold overhead equipment, or enlarging a door.
   3. Secure cost estimates.
J. Plan controls for the system.
   1. Develop methods for scheduling and controlling operations.
   2. Design necessary forms and chart paperwork flow.
   3. Determine the practical degree of mechanization of controls.
   4. Include requirements in equipment studies.
K. Provide a suitable communications system.
   1. Determine scope and means of communication network.
   2. Include new requirements in equipment studies.
L. Review the proposed plan again and again.
   1. Each step may suggest improvements in steps already considered.
   2. The objective is the optimum balance between cost and gains.
   3. All parts of the plan must fit together into an integrated whole.
M. Develop operating procedures.
   1. Prepare a complete, written operating plan.
      a. Describe each operating step including how the operation is to be performed, as well as the equipment and manpower required.
      b. Provide information on the proposed new equipment and how it is to be used.
      c. Spell out control procedures so that there can be no confusion.

      d. Determine and specify the training required for satisfactory personnel performance.

      e. Be sure that the finished plan is a clear and complete manual for use by operating personnel when the new methods are installed.

  2. Determine manpower requirements.

      a. Chart the proposed organization, if applicable.

      b. Prepare a detailed manpower requirement table, including relief and service personnel.

      c. Determine proposed labor costs.

The above should prove helpful in synthesizing the new method and in assuring that no major factor is overlooked.

Step X: Prepare Justification

The above should complete the formal and technical work involved in the problem solution. If any difficulties should arise in the latter stages of the procedure, it will be necessary to return to the appropriate step or steps in the procedure and re-check or re-calculate as needed. Then, having developed the new method and worked out all the details, it is now necessary to prepare the justification of the plan for management review and approval. The following outline summarizes the major steps to be carried out: [2]

  A. Compare the costs of the present and proposed operation.[3]

    1. Summarize labor and any special operating costs with the *proposed* methods.

    2. Summarize labor and any special operating costs under *present* methods.

    3. Reconcile present costs with proposed costs by adjusting present manpower requirements to meet proposed volume.

    4. Determine the savings (or losses) resulting from the new methods.

  B. Summarize required capital investment for the proposed methods.

  C. Determine the rate of return on the investment according to company policy.

  D. Review to make sure a different method will not bring a greater return.

  E. Evaluate gains other than dollar savings, such as:

    1. Improved service.

    2. Increased volume.

    3. Satisfactory control.

---

[2] *Ibid.*, pp. 14–15.

[3] Comparison of alternatives and cost analysis are covered in Chapters 13, 14, and 15. They should be studied carefully before undertaking this portion of the analysis.

    4. Savings from related operations.
    5. Increased profits from greater volume.
    (See also Chapter 14, on intangible factors.)

F. Review the solution in terms of the problem definition and objectives.
    1. Is it still an unquestioned necessity? Does it:
        a. Provide a required control over service, quality or personnel?
        b. Make it possible to meet expanded sales volume?
        c. Facilitate changes in production methods, product lines, or emphasis?
        d. Overcome a physical obstacle in the plant?
    2. Is it economically sound?
        a. Savings exceed cost of installation.
        b. Profits increased by increased volume.
        c. Cost of additional building eliminated.

G. State the justification clearly and explicitly.

H. Put the accumulated material together into a final project report, as required by company policy, including the following:

Body of Report
    1. Statement of request
    2. Description of proposed facility
    3. Need for facility
        a. Problem description
        b. Scope
        c. Definition of problem
    4. Present method
    5. Method of investigation
    6. Alternatives considered
    7. Proposed method
    8. Specifications
        a. Purchasing
        b. Design
        c. Construction
        d. Installation
    9. Required structural changes
  10. Anticipated results
  11. Financial analysis
        a. Justification (return on investment, etc.)
        b. Intangibles
  12. Human and public relations aspects
  13. Affect on related functions and activities
  14. Disposition of existing facilities
  15. Party responsibilities
        a. Company
        b. Vendor(s)

     c. Consultants
     d. Architects
     e. Builder
     f. Sub-contractors
16. Effect on future plans
17. Potential vendors
18. Approvals
19. Procedure for implementation
     a. Operating procedures
     b. Forms
     c. Communications
     d. Equipment installation
     e. Manpower needs
     f. Timing
     g. Schedule

Appendix

1. Data
2. Charts, graphs, etc.
3. Drawings
4. Photos
5. Layout
6. Diagrams
7. Spread sheets
8. Calculations
9. Specification details
10. Manpower requirements
11. References

Contents will of course vary with the individual problem, as well as with company policy or practices.

If desired or called for, plans should be made for an oral presentation of the project report. If approval by several members of management would be advisable or helpful, then *all* should be invited to review and approve the project. In many cases, an awareness of the problem, and an invitation to be "in on the act" will prove helpful in the successful installation and operation of the proposed plan. Appropriate visual aids should be prepared for the more important phases of the project, including slides, photos, tables, charts, layouts, mock-ups, models, etc.

Step XI: Obtain Approvals

A most necessary step in the procedure is the approval of the proposal. It is hoped that after the presentation has been made, management approval will be obtained.

Step XII: Revise as Necessary

This step has been included as a separate item because in many cases immediate approval of the original proposal may be withheld. If there are questions, points of disagreement, or items requiring further investigation, they should be handled expeditiously. If changes become necessary, they should be made, and approvals sought on the revisions and/or the entire project.

Step XIII: Work out Procedure for Implementation

Once the necessary approvals have been obtained, it becomes necessary to make plans for the implementation of the proposal. This might require the following:

A. Obtain up-to-date, firm quotations and delivery dates on all items to be purchased, since this may have been done for use in the proposal— or the proposal may have been based on estimates. In either case, if it was done during early stages of the investigation, it is wise to re-check with vendors.

B. Evaluate quotations and make a "spread sheet" if desirable. This should show items of equipment and their details down the left side, and vendors across the top. Intangible factors (see Chapter 14) should also be evaluated.

C. Select vendors for all components of the system and issue purchase orders.

D. Establish manpower (plant personnel) requirements, and budget both time and money required by their participation in the installation of the project.

E. Establish a time schedule for the installation. This may take the form of a CPM network or a Gantt chart, or both.

Other activities may be necessary, depending on the nature and complexity of the project. However, the above outlines the primary steps in planning for the installation.

Step XIV: Supervise Installation

Having made plans for the installation of the project, the material handling engineer should supervise its installation. He has spent many hours working out exactly how the new method will benefit the company, and should be sure that the installation is made in accordance with his plans. If any changes are found necessary, he should be consulted. Such changes should be approved by him—and others of management, if necessary.

Step XV: Follow Up

The last step in the general procedure is one of the most important. The material handling engineer should carefully observe the operation of the new installation over a period of time, *and* on all shifts. The success of the entire project may be jeopardized if those involved in its operation do not perform as planned, or as expected of them. It is up to the material handling engineer to see to it that everything works at it was planned; that everyone does what he is supposed to do; and to take corrective actions, if they are found necessary.

THE MATERIAL HANDLING ANALYSIS PROBLEM-SOLVING GUIDE

The above procedure may appear to be rather a long and drawn out way to solve a material handling problem. To a certain extent *it is!* But this is purposely so, to assure a complete and detailed analysis in order to find the best solution to the problem. Documented experience, based on the analysis of thousands of handling studies, has brought out many of the common errors that can be avoided by a proper analysis procedure. Some of the more obvious are:

1. Failure to examine the full range of benefits and liabilities.
2. Blind devotion to a given type of equipment.
3. Failure to consider impending events that will affect the size or life of the handling project, or invalidate other assumptions.
4. Hidden waste in equipment elaborations that add little benefit to handling performance.
5. Failure to create a full system, or a system appropriate to the environment, thus increasing costs in other parts of the system.
6. Failure to use imagination.

Since the procedure described in this chapter is pretty long to be "memorized," and then hope that nothing has been overlooked in the analysis, the Material Handling Analysis—Problem Solving Guide may prove helpful. The guide is shown in Figure 7–5 and will serve as an aid in organizing the attack and assuring that all steps in the procedure and all phases of the problem are properly covered. The guide—actually an outline of the entire analysis procedure discussed on the preceding pages —may be filled in and used as a "progress chart" during the problem analysis and solution. For example, as much of the form as is practicable can be filled out at the start, that is, sections I, II, III, and IV. Sections V through XV can be used to note and record progress *as* each succeeding step is carried out.

Company _____ Plant _____

Building _____ Area _____

Compiled by _____ Date _____

I. Identify the Problem (brief statement)

_____

_____

_____

II. Determine Scope of Problem (check *each* activity thought to be involved or related to problem at hand)

_____ 1. Packaging at supplier's plant
_____ 2. Packing at supplier's plant
_____ 3. Loading at supplier's plant
_____ 4. Transportation to user plant
_____ 5. External plant transportation activities
_____ 6. Unloading activities
_____ 7. Receiving of goods
_____ 8. Storage of incoming materials
_____ 9. Issuing materials to production
_____ 10. In-process handling
_____ 11. In-process storage
_____ 12. Workplace handling
_____ 13. Intra-departmental handling
_____ 14. Inter-departmental handling
_____ 15. Intra-plant handling
_____ 16. Handling related to auxiliary functions
_____ 17. Packaging
_____ 18. Finished goods warehousing
_____ 19. Packing
_____ 20. Loading and shipping
_____ 21. Transportation to customer locations
_____ 22. Inter-plant transportation

III. Establish Objective(s) (state carefully)

_____

_____

_____

Fig. 7–5. Material handling analysis problem-solving guide.

IV. Define the Problem (*complete* definition)

_____

_____

_____

V. Determine Data to be Collected

A. Review Preliminary Survey Check Sheet and note item numbers for which data must be collected.

General _____ Equipment _____
Material _____ Manpower _____
Move _____ Costs _____
Method-General _____

B. Review Basic Data Required form and indicate any *additional* data required.

Material _____
Move _____
Method _____

C. Any data required on

Organization _____ Co. Policies _____
Co. Objectives _____ Long Range Plans _____
(other) _____

	Assigned to:	Target Date	Date Compl.
VI. Establish Work Plan and Schedule			
A. Contacts to make			
B-C. Problem properly divided or grouped			
D. Plans made			
E. Work schedule established			
F. Work schedule approved			
G. Responsibilities assigned			
H. _____ (other)			
VII. Collect Data			
A. Sources reviewed			
B. Cooperative relationships arranged			
C-D. Activity observed or planned			
E. Basic data accumulated			
F. Supplementary data accumulated			
G. Layout procured or made			
H. Material flow analyzed			
I. Data on materials handling equipment on hand			
J. Data on personnel tabulated			
K. Storage data compiled			
L. Communications investigated			

Fig. 7–5. *(Continued)*

	Assigned to:	Target Date	Date Compl.
VIII. Develop, Weigh and Analyze Data			
A. Sorted and classified			
B. Checked for completeness and accuracy			
C. Summarized			
D. Ranges, etc., determined			
E. Averages, weights, established			
F. Charts, graphs, tables, etc., prepared			
G. Data double-checked			
IX. Develop Improvements			
A. Cost comparisons made			
B. Anticipated changes investigated			
C. Idea sources reviewed			
D. Possible solution selected			
E. Auxiliary activities re-examined			
F. Detailed plans of proposed methods made			
G. Equipment selected			
H. Solution checked against principles			
I. Structural changes determined			
J. Controls planned			
K. Communications planned			
L. Plans reviewed			
M. Plans written out			
N. Operating procedures developed			
X. Prepare Justification			
A. Cost comparisons made			
B. Capital investment summarized			
C. Rate of return determined			
D. Calculations reviewed vs. other methods			
E. Intangible gains evaluated			
F. Solution reviewed vs. other methods			
G. Justification clearly stated			
H. Report prepared			
I. Oral presentation ready			
J. Visual aids on hand			
XI. Obtain Approvals			
A. Management approval received			
B. _____ (others)			
XII. Revise as Necessary			
A. Revisions made			
B. Revisions approved			

Fig. 7–5.   *(Continued)*

	Assigned To:	Target Date	Date Compl.
XIII. Procedure for Implementation			
A. Quotations received			
B. Quotations evaluated			
C. Vendors selected and P.O. issued			
D. Installation manpower needs determined			
E. Time schedule established			
XIV. Supervise Installation			
A. Personnel assigned to supervise			
B. Changes authorized			
C. Installation satisfactory			
XV. Follow Up			
A. Personnel assigned to follow up			
B. Corrective action necessary			
C. Corrective action taken			
D. Installation functioning properly			

Remarks, Comments, Suggestions

_____

_____

_____

_____

Fig. 7–5. *(Continued)*

CONCLUSION

This chapter has presented an overall description of the procedure for analyzing a material handling problem. It has not, nor will it, *solve* any problems. It has only outlined a logical approach to a problem, with the hope that following it will facilitate finding the solution. In many cases, the details of the procedure are contained in other chapters. Their contents should be reviewed at the time their subject matter is referred to in the procedure, or at least before starting to apply the procedure.

Actually, the overall material handling problem-solving procedure is not complete until the reader has covered the related chapters which deal with detailed analytical approaches to specific phases of the overall procedure.

8

Basic Analytical Techniques

One of the most important steps in the analysis of a material handling problem is that of obtaining accurate data. And probably one of the most neglected phases of data gathering is the "move" aspect of the problem—which is really not that difficult to document. It does require a lot of detail work to make an accurate record of *all* the "moves," and it also requires that many different kinds of data be gathered on the several aspects of the move. Of the many aspects of the move, one of the most important is the *route* over which the move is made. Also of interest are the *volume* moved, the *distance* travelled, the *frequency* with which the move is made, the *rate* at which the material travels, and the *cost* of the move.

Another problem, and possibly the most confusing to the analyst, is that the project most likely involves a large *number* of moves—not just one or two. These moves may take the material through a complex, integrated handling cycle, occurring over a relatively long period of time. For example, the project may actually "begin" at a vendor's plant, progress through several departments of the manufacturing plant under analysis, and "end" in the customer's storage area. In any case, it is usually a series of a large number of moves, interspersed with a lesser number of related activities such as production operations, inspections, storages, etc.

One of the easiest ways of beginning the analysis of a complex series of moves is by graphical means. This chapter will deal primarily with a number of the more commonly used graphical techniques. While many of them are covered in motion study texts, it is felt that their use is important enough in material handling to warrant their inclusion here—with emphasis on their applications in analyzing handling problems.

SOURCES OF DATA REQUIRED

Before beginning the discussion of techniques, it should be emphasized that all available data related to the "move" is to be accumulated. This will include data on such factors as are indicated in the chart below, along with possible sources of the data:

Aspects of the Move	Basic Data Sources							
	Schedule	Bill of Materials	Routing	Layout	Job or Move Orders	Plot Plan	Vendors	Customers
—Scope			√	√		√	√	√
—Source/destination			√	√		√	√	√
—Route/distance			√	√		√	√	√
—Frequency	√	√			√			
—Speed/Rate	√	√			√			
—No. of moves	√	√			√			
—Area covered			√	√				
—Path			√	√	√			
—Location			√	√	√			
—Operations in Transit			√		√			

Additional information on other aspects of the "Move" may be obtained from:

    Carrier dimensions
    Maps
    Building drawings
    Control procedures

Appropriate data on each move, as well as on every aspect of each move, should be obtained and its accuracy checked with a reliable source. With these data at hand or available, most of the following analytical techniques can be constructed and used, when combined with personal observation of the problem at hand, or a synthesis of the proposed method.

The following chapter will cover a number of the so-called "quantitative" techniques, which make greater use of mathematics and statistics, and often with the assistance of a computer.

GRAPHICAL TECHNIQUES

Among the most useful techniques for recording and/or analyzing the move are several graphical methods in common use. These include the:

1. Assembly Chart
2. Operation Process Chart

3. Multi-Product Process Chart
4. Process Chart
5. Flow Diagram
6. Flow Process Chart
7. From-to Chart
8. Procedure Chart
9. Critical Path Network

Each of these will be explained briefly and illustrated. Further details on some of them may be found in texts on motion study, plant layout and critical path methods. No attempt will be made here to evaluate the techniques, since practice and experience will indicate which ones are most useful in specific situations. Also, their method of construction and the type of data required for each suggest their individual applications.

1. Assembly Chart

The Assembly Chart is a graphical representation of the interrelationships between components of a product (see Figure 8–1). It shows:

1. What components make up the product
2. Relationships between parts
3. Sequence in which components are assembled
4. A preliminary idea of the materials flow.

Construction. An Assembly Chart may be constructed in the following manner:

1. Using the bill of materials and the production routing for the assembly process, determine the *last* operation and represent it with a ½ circle in the lower right corner of a piece of paper. Briefly describe the operation alongside the circle—at the right.
2. Draw a horizontal line from the circle toward the left to indicate each component assembled at the operation just recorded. Components should be listed in order of assembly (or disassembly), last item at bottom, etc. At the end of each line, indicate the part number, name, pieces/assembly, etc., on the left side of the sheet.
3. If any component is a subassembly or a part of one, draw *its* horizontal line only part of the way to the left, insert a ⅜-inch circle to represent the subassembly operation, and draw lines from it—to the left—to indicate each component of the subassembly, as above.
4. When the last assembly operation and its components are completely recorded, draw a short vertical line from the top of the circle, and enter a second ½-inch circle to represent the "next-to-last" assembly operation. Indicate the components to the left, as in steps 3 and 4.
5. Continue in the above manner until the product has been "disassembled" and all components have been recorded at the left side of the sheet, from bottom to top. (The "disassembly" method of

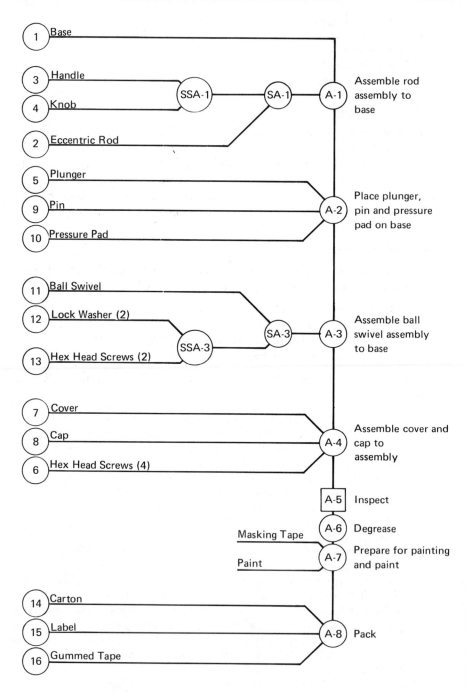

Fig. 8–1. Assembly chart for Powrarm.

drawing the chart is usually easier than starting at the beginning and working down—although the analyst may prefer the other approach.)

6. Check the chart against the bill of materials to be sure no component has been omitted. Enter assembly operation numbers from the routings *in* the circles.

2. Operation Process Chart

The Operation Process Chart is an extension of the Assembly Chart, and adds the operations from the production routing to each component "line." (See Figure 8–2.) It can be useful in showing:

1. Operations necessary on each component.
2. Sequence of production operations.
3. Sequence of component production and assembly.
4. Which components are more complex and require more attention in analysis or planning.
5. An approximation of the relative space requirements for each component production area.
6. Relationships between components which are purchased and those which are fabricated.
7. A more accurate impression of the materials flow pattern than the Assembly Chart.

Construction. An Operation Process Chart is made as follows:

1. Starting at the lower right corner of a piece of paper, record assembly operations, as on the Assembly Chart. Purchased (complete) components are represented by short lines to the left, with part numbers and names shown on the lines.
2. When a component will require operations on it, draw a horizontal line to the far left, then up toward the top of the sheet. Indicate operations from production routings, by ½-inch circles (or squares for inspect) in reverse order, toward the top. At the top, draw a short horizontal line to the right to identify the component. Enter operation numbers from the routing in the circles.
3. Continue in this manner, using Figure 8–2 as a guide, until all components have been charted. All *fabricated* parts should be along the top, usually with the *major* component (chassis, base, etc.) on the right. All *purchased* parts should be within the *body* of the chart.
4. Sub-assemblies are handled in much the same manner as on the Assembly Chart (Figure 8–1), although they may "break out" differently with the added information from part routings.
5. Check chart against bill of materials and all routings to assure that there are no omissions of parts or operations.

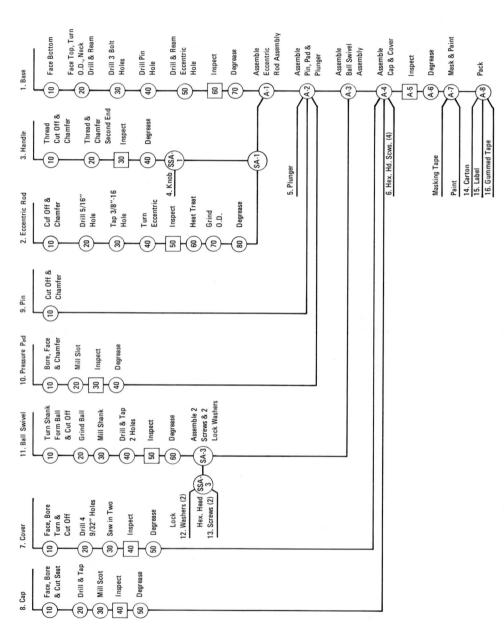

Fig. 8–2. Operation process chart for Powrarm.

3. Multi-Product Process Chart

Closely related to the Operation Process Chart is the Multi-Product Process Chart. (See Figure 8–3.) It is particularly useful in showing production relationships (or lack thereof) between components of a product, or individual products, materials, part or jobs. It is particularly helpful in a job shop situation.

Construction. A Multi-Product Process Chart is made as follows:

1. Down the left side of a sheet of paper, list the departments, processes or machines through which the items being studied must pass during their fabrication. They may be listed from top to bottom in:
   a. "geographical" sequence, as they occur in the plant
   b. *or,* in as logical a sequence as possible, all factors being considered. (Exact order is not necessary, since the *construction* of the chart will show up any serious errors in arrangement or layout.)
2. Across the top, list the components, products, etc., being studied. (For more than 20 to 25 items, divide items into similar groups and work with groups, or use the From-To chart, discussed later). They should be arranged, in a logical order, by similarity of processing operations required. Here too, constructing the chart will indicate errors in the arrangement.
3. From the production routings, record the operations on each item, *opposite* the proper department, process, or machine and *under* the proper item, by a circle containing the operation number from the routing.
4. Connect the circles in sequence, even though back-tracking may be shown.
5. Study the resulting chart for:
   a. Backtracking—indicating the possibility of rearranging departments, etc.
   b. Similarity of "flow patterns"—indicating desirability of processing parts in the same area, at the same time, etc.
   c. "Clues" to arrangements that will produce an efficient flow pattern.

Note: The above three charts can be made much more valuable if quantitative data are incorporated in their construction to show number of pieces, weights, number of moves, distances, etc.

4. Process Chart

The Process Chart is a *tabular* record of the steps in a process, using process symbols to represent each step, and containing sufficient descrip-

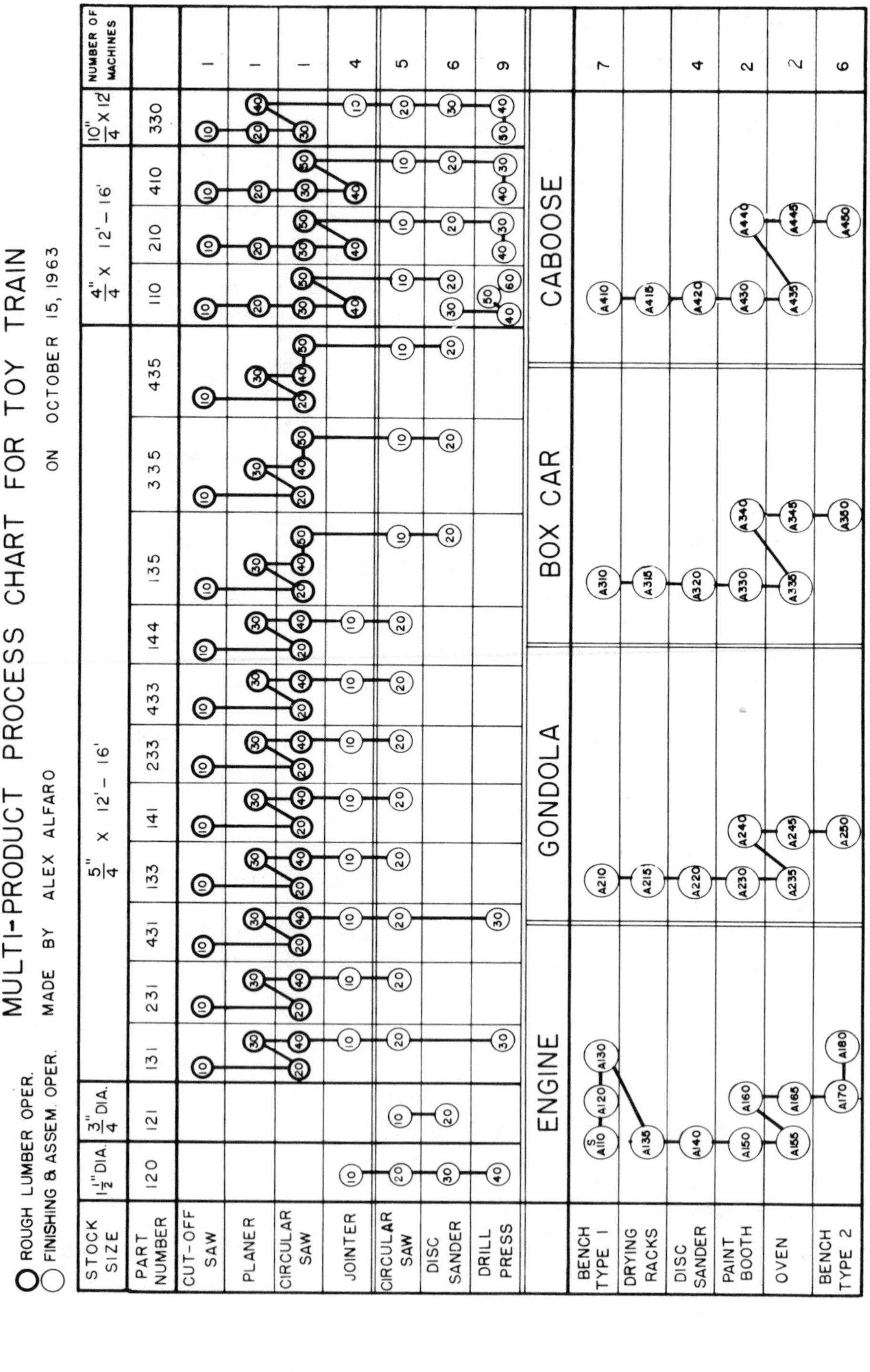

Fig. 8–3. Multi-product process chart.

tive material to tell what happens at each, along with related significant data (see Figure 8–4).

Construction. Directions for making Process Charts are contained in many motion study texts and handbooks. They are outlined briefly below:

1. Most commonly, a printed form is used, with the following process symbols printed in columns at the left:

    ○ Operation: object under observation is changed in physical form, or does work.

    ⇨ Transportation: object moves, or is moved.

    ☐ Inspect: object is examined for identification or inspected or checked for quality, quantity, or characteristics.

    ▽ Store: object is in storage awaiting authorized removal.

    D Delay: object is waiting for next planned action.

2. Fill in data called for at top of form.
3. Decide on item to be followed. Only *one* material (or person) can be followed at one time on the same Process Chart. If it is desired to follow several items (or persons), use the Flow Process Chart, which is explained later in this chapter. *Do not skip* from material to man to material, etc.
4. Identify first step—most likely a "store"—and enter a number 1 *inside* the symbol on the form (each *type* of symbol is numbered consecutively, to aid in tying in with other charts and data).
5. Briefly describe step and enter any other desired data in columns to right.
6. Repeat steps 4 and 5 to end of process. Connect symbols with a solid line.
7. Summarize data in table at top of form.
8. Study Process Chart for improvement possibilities and make chart of proposed improved method.
9. Use record of *moves* as a basis for cost determination as explained in Chapter 15.

5. Flow Diagram

The Flow Diagram is a *graphical* record of the steps in a process, made on a layout of the area under observation. It is frequently used as a supplement to the Process Chart (see Figure 8–5, which "matches" Figure 8–4).

Construction. The Flow Diagram is made as follows:

1. Obtain a layout of the area involved in the activity under observation.
2. Record on the layout, as near the point of occurrence as possible, the process symbol that best describes the activity—as with the

PROCESS CHART

PART NAME ___Gizmo___

PROCESS DESCRIPTION ___Machine base and assemble, and finish___

DEPARTMENT ___Machine shop, Assembly, and Finishing___

PLANT ___XYZ Products Co.___

RECORDED BY ___I. M. Looking___   DATE _____

	SUMMARY	
		NO.
○	OPERATIONS	
⇨	TRANSPORTATIONS	
☐	INSPECTIONS	
D	DELAYS	
▽	STORAGES	
	TOTAL STEPS	
	DISTANCE TRAVELED	

STEP	Operations Transport Inspect Delay Storage	DESCRIPTION OF PRESENT METHOD				
1	○⇨☐D▽	in storage at receiving				
2	○⇨☐D▽	to position at mach 2	walkie	6'		
3	○⇨☐D▽	at mach. 2				
4	○⇨☐D▽	into mach. 2	hand	4'		
5	①⇨☐D▽	turn				
6	○⇨☐D▽	to table	hand	4'		
7	○⇨☐D▽	on table				
8	○⇨☐D▽	to mach. 3	hand	4'		
9	②⇨☐D▽	drill				
10	○⇨☐D▽	to table	hand	4'		
11	○⇨☐D▽	on table				
12	○⇨☐D▽	into mach. 4	hand	3'		
13	③⇨☐D▽	drill				
14	○⇨☐D▽	to skid	hand	4'		
15	○⇨☐D▽	on skid				
16	○⇨☐D▽	to Assembly Dept.	walkie	10'		
17	○⇨☐D▽	at end of assembly bench				
18	○⇨☐D▽	onto bench to assy. position	hand	5'		
19	④⇨☐D▽	assemble				
20	○⇨☐D▽	to inspection position	hand	3'		
21	○⇨☐D▽	inspect				
22	○⇨☐D▽	to skid at end of assy. bench	hand	8'		

Fig. 8–4. Process chart. (From James M. Apple, *Plant Layout and Materials Handling*, The Ronald Press Co., New York, 1963, p. 165.)

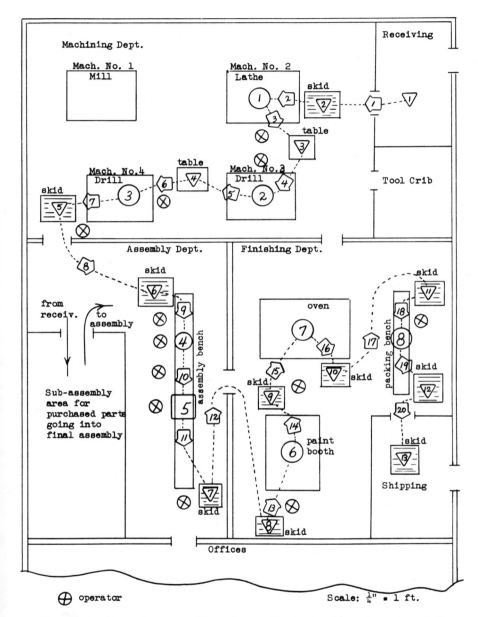

Fig. 8–5. Flow diagram. (From James M. Apple, *Plant Layout and Materials Handling,* The Ronald Press Co., New York, 1963, p. 167.)

Process Chart—or if a Process Chart has been made, transfer symbols from it to the Flow Diagram.
3. Number symbols, in the same manner as with the Process Chart, or to match the Process Chart.
4. Connect the symbols with a line, to show the path(s) travelled by the object(s) under observation.
5. Study the Flow Diagram, along with the Process Chart, for improvement possibilities.
6. Use chart for explaining the process to others.

6. Flow Process Chart

The Flow Process Chart is a combination of the Operation Process Chart (Figure 8–2) and the Process Charts (Figure 8–4) of each component of the product or assembly. It presents the most complete graphical representation of the overall process (see Figure 8–6).

Construction. The Flow Process Chart is developed in the following manner:

1. Obtain an Operation Process Chart for the process being studied.
2. Obtain Process Charts for each component of the product.
3. Re-draw the Operation Process Chart, inserting all process symbols from each Process Chart on the appropriate vertical line representing each component.
4. Enter any additional desired data alongside proper symbols, such as distance, quantity, time, cost, etc.
5. Study resulting chart for any possible improvement in the overall process, inter-relationships between operations or individual processes, etc.

7. From-To Chart

The basic From-To Chart is a matrix technique for summarizing material travel between related activities (see Figure 8–7). It is extremely useful for:

1. Determining relative locations of activities.
2. Establishing material flow patterns.
3. Showing degree of self-sufficiency of each activity.
4. Pointing out possible production control problems.
5. Planning interrelationships between several products, parts, materials, etc.
6. Depicting quantitative relationships between activities and the related handling between them.
7. Comparing alternative flow patterns.
8. Shortening distances travelled during a process.

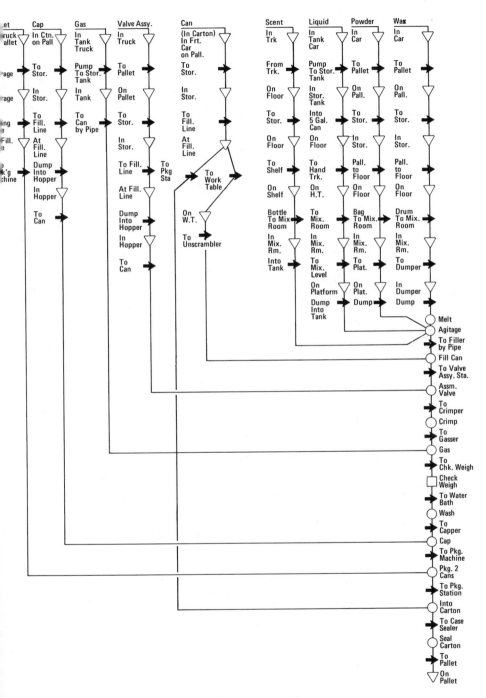

Fig. 8–6. Flow process chart.

PLANT _Acme Manufacturing Co._   TRIAL NO. _1_   DATE _June 7_

FROM-TO CHART

FROM (Contributor) \ TO (User)	1 Rough Stores	2 Mill	3 Lathe	4 Drill	5 Bore	6 Grind	7 Press	8 Hone	9 Saw	10 Final Inspection	TOTALS
1 Rough Stores		2	8	2		1	4				17
2 Mill			1				1		2	1	5
3 Lathe		2		4	1		1			3	11
4 Drill		1					2	1	1	5	10
5 Bore				1							1
6 Grind				1						1	2
7 Press				2						6	8
8 Hone										1	1
9 Saw			2			1					3
10 Final Inspection											
TOTALS		5	11	10	1	2	8	1	3	17	58 / 58

Fig. 8-7. From-to chart. (From James M. Apple, _Plant Layout and Materials Handling_, The Ronald Press Co., New York, p. 171.)

The From-To Chart is also commonly referred to as a Travel Chart or Cross Chart, although in some cases, the latter two are constructed and applied in somewhat different manners.

The From-To Chart has great potential as an analytical tool, but it has not yet been fully developed. Most current applications are relatively unsophisticated, tabulating only the number of moves and frequently the distances or volumes involved. The basic chart is described below, followed by a brief discussion of possible variations.

Construction. The From-To Chart is developed as follows:

1. Draw a matrix similar to that shown in Figure 8–7, with as many rows *and* columns as there are activities under consideration.
2. Enter activity titles or names in the *same* order across the top, *and* down the left side. Sequence may represent "geographical" arrangement in the plant, logical arrangement of process flow, or proposed sequence. (As in the case of the Multi-Product Process Chart, the exact sequence is not important, as the *use* of the chart will point out errors and suggest changes in sequence.)
3. Entry of data *into* the matrix can be done in several ways, depending on objective or desired results of the analysis. Figures may represent:
   a. Number of moves between activities.
   b. Quantity of material moved/time period.
   c. Weight of material moved/time period.
   d. Combination of quantity times weight/time period.
   e. Percent of total *through* each activity to each subsequent activity.
   f. Move time.
   g. Move cost.
4. Prepare basic data for entry into matrix by tabulating values representing information to be charted, in terms of moves *from* each activity *to* each activity.
5. For each move of material, *from* one activity *to* another, enter a tally mark *in* the appropriate square of the matrix. This must be done for each part, product, or material included in the analysis. Numbers in each square represent the total number of moves from and to the activity. They can be cross-checked in the "Totals" column.
6. Analyze the From-To Chart for better arrangements of activities to reduce handling, cost, distances, production control problems, etc. For instance, in the above example:
   a. All entries below the diagonal indicate back-tracking, i.e., backwards from the order indicated by the numbers representing activities.
   b. All entries in the upper right or far right indicate items "skipping" past several activities to get to *their* next activity.

c. Items moving from one activity to an adjacent activity result in the marks falling in the cells *along* and *above* the diagonal. This represents "straight-line" flow.

By "inspection" then, it is seen that a better solution can be devised, by rearranging the columns and rows to put the larger numbers of tally marks closer to the diagonal, and fewer marks below the line. Also those further away from the line can be moved closer to the line.

A more quantitative approach to the analysis is obtained by taking "moments" around the diagonal, and aiming for the lowest total, using distance from the diagonal as the "moment arm," i.e., the number of squares *away* from the diagonal.

As indicated previously, numbers in the cells can represent other values than just the number of moves. This would make the From-To chart considerably more useful. For further details, the analyst should study the references given below.[1]

Recent research has seen the From-To Chart used as the basis for data arrangement for "computerized" plant layout algorithms. An early example is the CRAFT [2] program developed by Armour and Buffa at U.C.L.A. A more recent study by Gani, Devis, Deisenroth, and Apple at Georgia Tech uses the From-To chart in their PLANET [3] program.

8. Procedure Chart

One of the most important aspects of handling is the communication of information pertaining to the movement of materials, since it is frequently the communication or lack of it that determines the efficiency of the handling activity. The Procedure Chart is a technique used primarily to show the movement or flow of written or oral communications between departments or persons and to show product flow as it is tied in with these communications.

The Procedure Chart makes use of certain conventions and symbols to aid in recording the paperwork flow, as follows:

—— Solid line represents the movement of a written form of communication. A separate line is used for *each* piece of paper insofar as practical.

[1] For more detailed discussion see (1) H. A. Bolz and G. E. Hagemann, *Material Handling Handbook*, The Ronald Press Co., 1958, pp. 2.46–2.53; (2) James M. Apple, *Plant Layout and Materials Handling*, The Ronald Press Co., 1963, pp. 168–172 for a somewhat different interpretation and instructions; (3) Richard Muther, *Systematic Layout Planning*, Industrial Education Institute, 1961, pp. 4–14 to 4–20; (4) Richard Muther, *Practical Plant Layout*, McGraw-Hill Book Co., 1955, pp. 178–191.

[2] G. C. Armour, *A Heuristic Algorithm and Simulation Approach to Relative Location of Facilities*, an unpublished doctoral dissertation, U.C.L.A., 1961.

[3] M. D. Deisenroth, *Quantitative Utilization of Activity Data for Initial Layouts*, an unpublished master's thesis at Georgia Institute of Technology, 1970.

~~~ Wiggly line is verbal communication.

– – – Dashed line represents the movement of a product, container, or equipment.

◯ Circle (large) represents *action taken,* and should be larger than other symbols so as to be dominant.

▽ Triangle (large with small inside) represents *product stored.*

☐ Square (large) represents *checking or inspecting.*

⌈LS⌉ ⌈M⌉ ⌈R⌉ ⌈T⌉ A flag (with key initials in it) attached to a large "action"
◯ ◯ ☐ symbol represents a *form originated* at that time.

▽ Triangle (small) represents *paperwork filed.*

▼ Triangle (small and filled in) represents *paperwork destroyed.*

Construction. The Procedure Chart is constructed as follows:

1. Prepare a form similar to that shown in Figure 8–8.
2. The horizontal rows represent "steps" in the procedure. Ordinarily there should be only one dominant symbol in a row, except in cases where action is being taken simultaneously at several places, or where the symbol, etc., is self-explanatory.
3. The vertical columns represent "Places of Performance"—activities, locations, persons, department, etc. All symbols in a column indicate action taken, etc., by that person, department, etc.
4. The direction of "flow" is always *in* at the top of a symbol and *out* at the bottom and generally from the upper left to the lower right of the chart.
5. The number of lines leaving a symbol at the bottom always equals the number of lines entering the symbol at the top except for lines representing verbal communication.
6. Each line is identified by a key or code which is explained in the legend at the bottom of the chart.
7. The routine "filing" and "form destroyed" symbols are smaller than the dominant "action taken" symbols. As a general rule it is not necessary to amplify the smaller symbols with notes on the chart. Symbols alongside each will serve to identify forms filed or destroyed.
8. Alternate paths may be shown by the same type of line as that used for the regular route with the alternate path so identified.
9. Comments or notes are made on the Procedure Chart when necessary to make the meaning of a step clear. These notes are as brief as possible and are located on the same horizontal row as the step being described. They are located at the left of the row in the space provided.

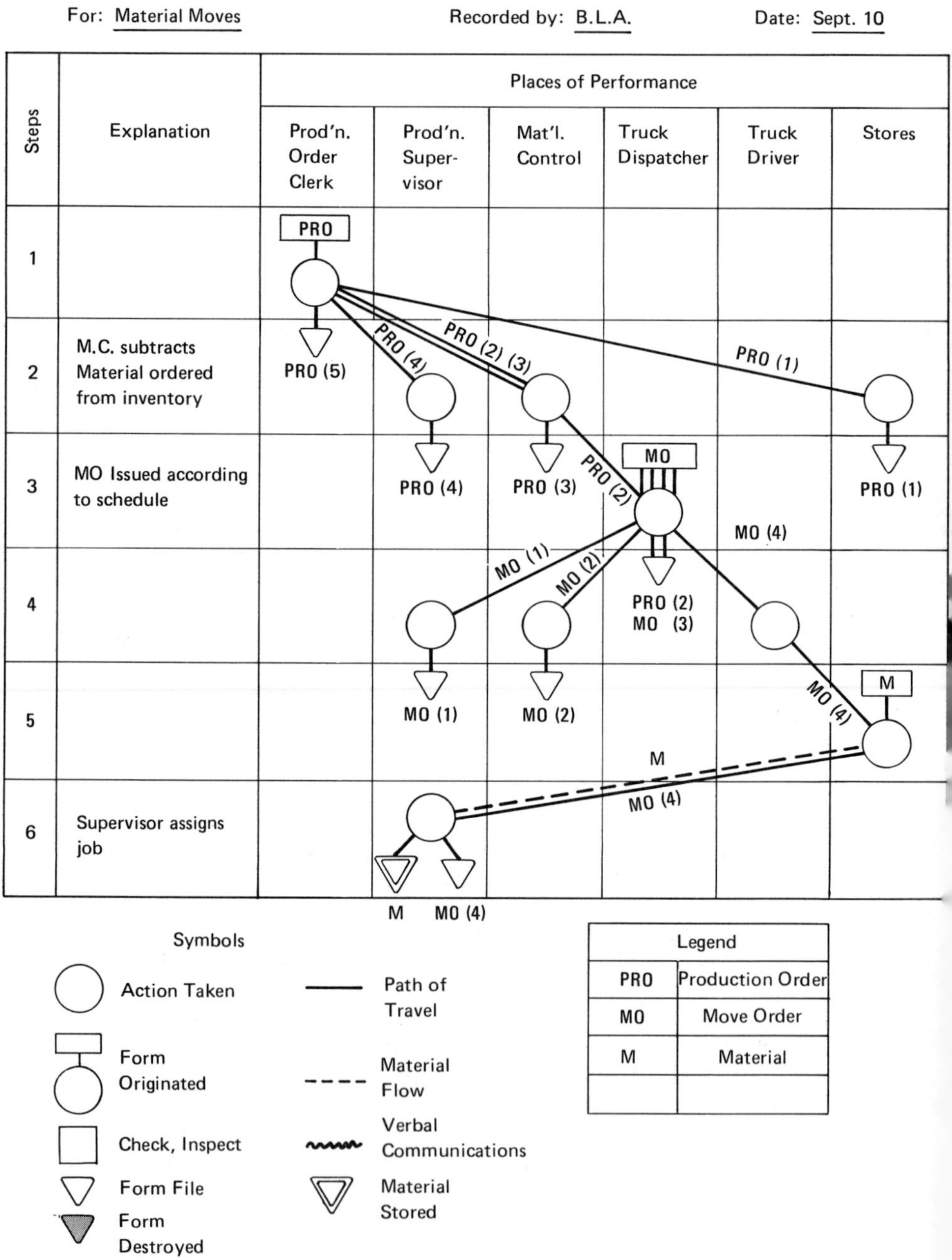

For: Material Moves   Recorded by: B.L.A.   Date: Sept. 10

Fig. 8–8. Procedure chart.

10. The chart should be a complete enough document in itself so that it can be read by anyone with ordinary familiarity or a brief explanation of this means of presentation, without referring to anything else. However, if the chart is used in a report to be read by laymen, it may be desirable to include a "Discussion of Procedure"—a verbal description of the steps, referring to the steps on the Procedure Chart.

11. Some suggestions for checking the completeness and accuracy of the chart are as follows:
   A. Each form must be "originated."
   B. Places of performance should not be repeated, nor contain both department and sections of departments.
   C. Each copy of a form should eventually be either filed or destroyed.
   D. There should be a line for each copy of each form.
   E. The number of lines entering a place of action or temporary file must equal the number leaving.
   F. No two major "action taken" symbols should occur at the same step—unless they are self-explanatory.
   G. The chart should read from the top to the bottom—no upward flow—and generally from upper left to lower right.
   H. The number of items "permanent filed" and "destroyed" should equal the number "originated."

It is frequently surprising to find that the use of a Procedure Chart will show that the "material handling" problem is *not* a "material handling" problem. It is a communications or paperwork problem! While the Procedure Chart is not a commonly used technique, it is presented here in sufficient detail to permit its use, because it is felt that it has a great potential in solving handling and related problems.

9. Critical Path Methods (CPM)

One of the more recent techniques that is basically a graphical tool is known as the Critical Path Method. While it has not often been used in *analyzing* material handling problems, it is extremely useful in the *planning* and *installation* of complex handling systems. CPM is ideally a *project* management tool—an outgrowth of the well-known Gantt chart.

CPM makes use of a network-type diagram to graphically represent interrelationships between phases or elements of a project. Time estimates for each activity in the project are used to determine the "critical path," or that specific sequence of activities governing the minimum total time required by the project. An example of a CPM network is shown in Figure 8–9.

A technique based on the CPM Concept is PERT (Program Evaluation and Review Technique). Where CPM estimates are made at a

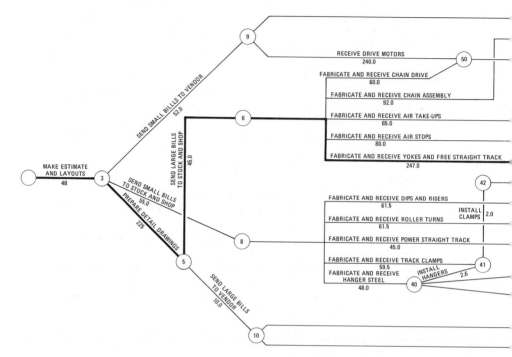

Fig. 8–9. Critical path network diagram for

single facility, dollar, or investment level, PERT estimates are over the *range* of possible resource levels which may be required to complete an activity. This duration uncertainty results in a range of project times with a related range of project costs. The probabilities of the various estimates being true and the related uncertainties involved must be taken into consideration. Statistical methods are used to developed optimum combinations, with calculations programmed on a computer.

For additional details on CPM, PERT, and other network techniques the reader should consult any of the numerous books available on the subject.

CONCLUSION

This chapter has reviewed some of the more common graphical techniques useful in the analysis of material handling problems. A single problem may make use of several of them, depending on the type of data on hand or the results desired from the analysis.

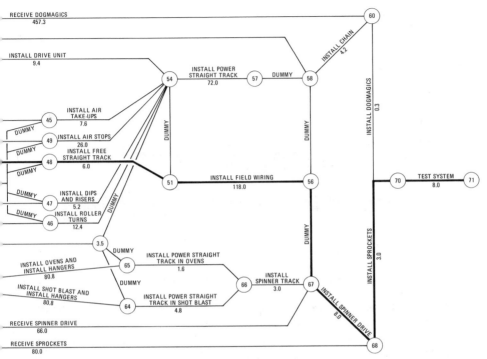

fabrication and installation of trolley conveyor.

Another whole area of analysis, making use of more sophisticated mathematics, is covered in Chapter 10, "Quantitative Analytical Techniques." This group may be categorized under the general heading of operations research and makes use of techniques, some of which are classified as mathematical programming, simulation, etc. Several of the more common techniques will be presented briefly.

9

The Systems Concept
in Material Handling

WHAT IS THE SYSTEMS CONCEPT?

Probably no other word in use today has more different interpretations than the word "system." It may be best then to begin with a dictionary definition and develop the topic on that basis. Webster's Seventh New Collegiate Dictionary defines a system as: "a regularly interacting or interdependent group of items forming a unified whole." And along somewhat similar lines, Webster's Third New International Dictionary says that a system is: "a complex unity formed of many often diverse parts subject to a common plan or serving a common purpose," with one interpretation suggesting that a system is "a set of objects joined in regular interaction or interdependence."

Any system must have a reason for its existence: its *objective.* In accomplishing this objective there are *restraints* under which the system must operate. If there is an *input* into one end of the system, it is expected that there will be an *output* at the other end. If this happens, and it must if the system has a real objective, then there will be some change or *process* within the system. To accomplish an orderly input-process-output relationship there must be some form of *control.* This control is provided by *feedback* within the system. The complete system will then have for its parameters:

1. Objective
2. Input
3. Restraints
4. Process

5. Feedback
6. Control
7. Output

The preceding parameters do not define a *complete* system, for in addition there must also be integration, organization, and communication.

Size is not necessarily a characteristic of a system. The material handling system can and should encompass the entire enterprise but it can be made up of micro systems, each involving materials movement between any two points. In fact it is desirable and generally recommended that efficient micro systems be incorporated into macro systems. However, it must be remembered that sub-optimizing, without regard for the *entire* system can be dangerous. In order for a macro material handling system to be effective from an overall enterprise view point, it should include the following characteristics:

1. Involve the entire enterprise.
2. Provide for handling material, *and* the relevant data.
3. Include all phases of movement from incoming raw materials to outgoing finished goods.

If, when planning the material handling system, all phases of the enterprise are *not* considered, some important part of the system may be overlooked, for the entire enterprise, from the raw material to the consumer, must be considered for the systems approach to be successful. Provision must be made to handle the physical material as well as all the information related to the handling system.

Remember also, that once the system has been built to *satisfy* all the requirements and meet the objective, the system is not the same any more. The *operation* of the components *changes* the system. Many unexpected and sudden changes may occur when the system goes into operation, since the system includes both men and physical objects and the human factor may be the cause of changes, variations, or even failures.

Now, having defined a material handling system and delineated the systems concept, it is possible to summarize what is meant in relationship to material handling and/or physical distribution activities by describing a system as [1]:

1. A larger-scale, result-oriented point of view . . .
2. which consciously exploits gaps between traditional categories of knowledge . . .
3. in an attempt to discover and sort out the tangle of factors and find relevant and reliable interrelationships . . .

---

[1] Partially adapted from Hare, Van Court, Jr., *Systems Analysis: A Diagnostic Approach,* 1967, Harcourt Brace & World, Inc., New York.

4. to make it easier to diagnose, conceptualize, design, and evaluate complex combinations of sophisticated hardware, information flow, and organizational interrelationships.

Contrary to popular opinion, "systems" is neither a method nor a rigid procedure. It is a structure for thought. It involves the recognition that no part of some whole is completely independent of the other parts. Therefore activity in one part of the whole will affect, perhaps indirectly, and only after considerable delay, the state of the other parts.

With this recognition of practically universal interdependence, the systems approach requires that any proposed action be evaluated in terms of its direct effect plus all the ramifications of its interactions with the other parts of the whole. The result is that problems *must* be considered from a broad viewpoint. The effect on the *whole* must guide the analyst and not simply the effect on the single part which may appear to be the primary cause of the problem. In material handling this suggests that an orderly approach be followed in attacking alternative solutions to assure consideration of all factors and all possible alternative solutions. All the ramifications of each alternative must also be considered. The final solution must then be based on the integration of the material handling system into the entire operation.

Then it may be concluded that a *material handling system* is:

1. A carefully and thoroughly researched solution to a handling problem . . .
2. usually resulting in an integrated composite of facilities, activities, and information flow . . .
3. encompassing as much of the total problem scope and environment as is feasible and economical . . .
4. with the objective of providing movement and/or storage of materials and subject to some form of regulated control.

The balance of this chapter will be devoted to a discussion of the application of the systems concept to material handling problems.

INTERPRETATION OF THE SYSTEMS CONCEPT

Actually the systems approach is little more than a rigorous and orderly way of appraising a problem of a complex nature . . . in a "let's stand back and look at this situation from all its angles "[2] frame of mind, asking:

1. How many distinguishable elements are there to this seeming problem?
2. What cause and effect relationships exist among these elements?

[2] P. G. Thome and R. G. Willard, "The Systems Approach—A United Concept of Planning," in *Aerospace Management*, Fall–Winter, 1966, p. 25.

3. What functions need to be performed in each case?
4. What trade-offs may be required among resources once they are defined?

Challenges of this magnitude as a rule are characterized by the following orders of difficulty:

1. A complex goal (involving a major system composed of hardware, computer programs, facilities, personnel, and data).
2. A constantly changing environment (which affects objectives, constraints, and criteria).
3. Limited resources for advanced development (money, man-power, facilities, and time).

According to Herman A. Affel, Jr.,

Eventually a system engineer reduces functional relationship to mostly hardware relationships, though some of the functional black boxes in his design may turn out to be people interfacing with equipment.

The system has many components which contribute to the common purpose: The designer's objective is to organize them in an optimum way so that they will transform a given set of inputs into a desired overall output.

The system engineer looks at the functional parts of a system, at the information or material flow between them and at the delays that may be encountered in various parts as the system is subjected to various loadings. He looks for bottlenecks, for trouble at interfaces. He includes in his considerations the psychology as well as the economics, the social sciences as well as the physical sciences, and procedural techniques as well as the diverse technical advances of the age. Most frequently, the system engineer provides a structure which is as formal as possible, for trying to measure the effectiveness of various possible solutions. The economic consequences of gross mistakes can be severe.

If there is anything that characterizes the environment in which a system engineer lives and works it is the multifaceted nature of a problem that appears to overwhelm when it is first presented . . .

Trying to solve big problems with many interrelated functions, piece-by-piece, may not always be successful—because the system engineer may never discover the true relationships of many parts of the problem. But one thing is certain: Trying to solve an enormous problem all at once is an overwhelming task. So system engineering is usually a team affair, to share this load. A reasonably vigorous technical framework is needed to allow a group of designers to become more than the apocryphal committee which designed the camel.[3]

SYSTEMS SCOPE IN THEORY AND PRACTICE

In many cases, the original thinking and the preliminary conceptual design of a system is represented by a flow chart, as shown in Figure 9–1.

[3] Herman A. Affel, Jr., 'System Engineering," *International Science* and *Technology*, Nov. 1964, p. 8.

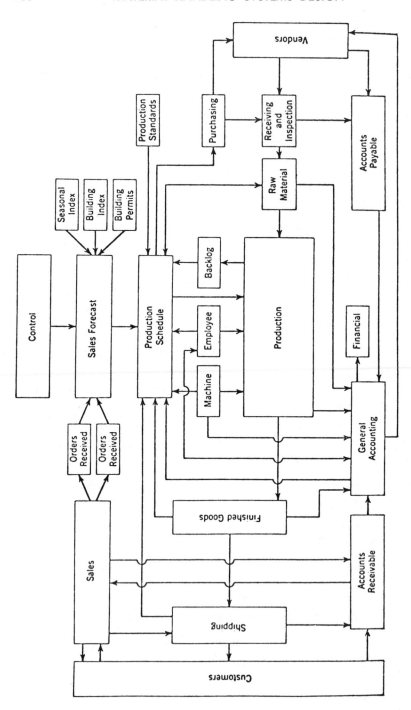

Fig. 9–1. Typical flow chart representing the interrelationships between functions in a production organization. (From E. S. Buffa, *Operations Management*, 2d ed., by permission of John Wiley & Sons, Inc., p. 416.)

This flow chart of course represents the system only in a "gross" fashion, in that detail of many interrelationships are not accurately shown.

In its ultimate, theoretical framework, a true system would very likely encompass any and all interacting elements within the universe. However, in real life the scope of a system is usually limited by a combination of practical and economical restrictions. Even the world's most complex systems project to date—the Apollo Moon Shots—recognizes only a small portion of the universe!

A more down to earth example of a nearly "perfect" system, in the most complex sense of the word, in both scope and depth, is illustrated in Figure 9–2. Here the material (water) makes a complete, closed loop— from spigot to drain to ground to rain. Think, for a moment, how complicated a material handling engineer might have made such a system, by merely deciding to unitize (containerize) the water at some point or points in the flow!

So, it should be emphasized that to be successful, a material handling system need not encompass the entire universe, nor must it cover either the *entire* "mine to consumer" route, nor complete coverage of *all* factors in total depth. The typical material handling system might extend only from a plant receiving department to its shipping dock. However, in situations where the analysts have given more than passing thought to the systems concept, a serious attempt would be made to cooperate closely with both suppliers and customers in order to extend the handling system from the plant in those two opposite directions.

HOW DOES THE SYSTEMS CONCEPT DIFFER FROM COMMON PRACTICE?

It will be remembered, from Chapter 2, that from the "traditional" point of view, the material handling analyst was concerned with problem areas as if they were individual, isolated, independent, unrelated situations. His primary objective was to move item X from point A to point B. And, from the "contemporary" point of view, he looked at material handling with plant-wide concern, as if flying in a helicopter, several hundred feet over the plant and with the roof removed! From this vantage point, he could view the overall materials flow and see the interrelationships between *all* handling activities, with the idea of establishing an overall material handling plan which would tie each problem solution into all others.

Finally, from the "progressive," or *systems* point of view, the analyst might visualize himself as being in a space ship, 150 miles over the plant, and able to see not only the intraplant movement of materials, but the

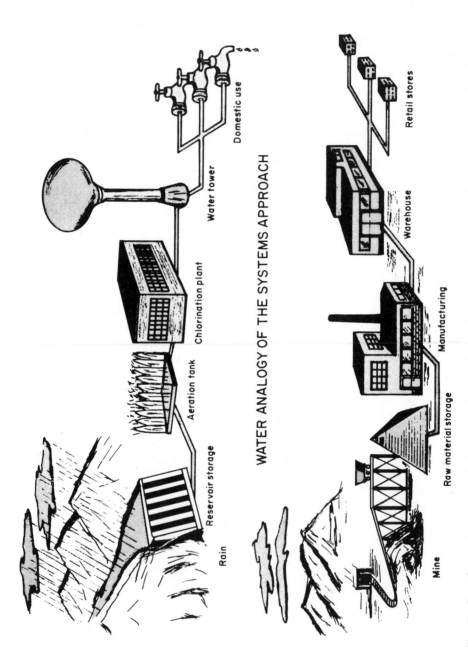

WATER ANALOGY OF THE SYSTEMS APPROACH

Fig. 9–2. The systems concept. Note continuous flow with water; vs. need for discrete flow in application to manufacturing situation below. (From E. R. Sims, Jr. "Why Buy a System?", *Material Handling Engineering*, January 1961, p. 22).

incoming flow of materials *from suppliers,* as well as the outgoing flow of finished goods to *customers.* He would now visualize the material handling and physical distribution problems as one system, with his concern expanded to cover all activities, from *all* sources of supply to *all* customers. He would then attempt to conceptualize a total system in terms of a theoretical ideal, implementing each segment as means became available. A review of Figure 2–1, the material flow cycle, will show the general relationships implied in the application of the systems approach to material handling and physical distribution problems.

The "Ideal Systems" Approach

In the "Ideal Systems Approach" as described by Nadler,[4] the analyst would:

1. Aim for the "Theoretical Ideal System"
   a. May never attain it
   b. Represents farthest possible extreme of perfection
   c. Equals instantaneous moves, at zero cost
2. *Conceptualize* the "Ultimate Ideal System"
   a. Based on valid costs
   b. Will attain this—but in the future
   c. Requires further research and development; non-existent (but feasible) equipment, etc.
3. *Design* the "Technologically Workable Ideal System"
   a. Technology *is* available
   b. Could be installed
   c. Cost or other conditions may prevent some components from being installed now.
4. *Install* the "Recommended System"
   a. Will work now
   b. Cost in line
   c. No obstacles

It should be observed that if the above philosophy is carried out, a higher-level solution will be achieved than if the problem is approached from the "old-fashioned" point of view or even the conventional point of view. In fact, Nadler concludes by stating that: "If your guide for planning a system is a perfect system, your final system will be better than if your guide was something less." This is the same as stating that, if you don't aim for the moon, you'll never get there. Figure 9–3 depicts Nadler's concept of the ideal systems approach.

---

[4] Adapted from Gerald Nadler, "What Systems Really Are," in *Modern Materials Handling,* July, 1965.

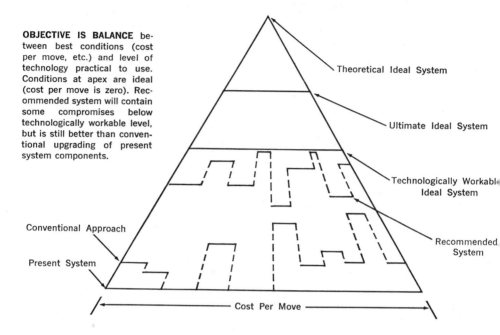

OBJECTIVE IS BALANCE between best conditions (cost per move, etc.) and level of technology practical to use. Conditions at apex are ideal (cost per move is zero). Recommended system will contain some compromises below technologically workable level, but is still better than conventional upgrading of present system components.

Theoretical Ideal System

Ultimate Ideal System

Technologically Workable Ideal System

Recommended System

Conventional Approach

Present System

Cost Per Move

A BETTER SYSTEM RESULTS here because you first analyze system characteristics to know what the extreme limits to progress CAN be, and in what direction you SHOULD go. With the ideal established, you have a guide which is also a blueprint to further system changes.

Fig. 9–3. The ideal-systems approach. (From G. Nadler, "What Systems Really Are," *Modern Materials Handling,* July 1965.)

WHY THE SYSTEMS CONCEPT IS IMPORTANT IN MATERIAL HANDLING

Although the systems concept was first applied to such complex situations as military logistics and space exploration, it is rapidly becoming common practice in other areas of application. Of interest here is the entire field encompassed by the terms material handling *and* physical distribution. A. W. Fasold suggests that there are three categories of changes which have come about and that have made it almost necessary to apply the systems approach to complex handling and distribution problems. He outlines these changes as follows: [5]

A. Changes in Management Thinking
　　1. Increased costs
　　2. Growth of mechanization

[5] A. W. Fasold, adapted from a presentation, "The Systems Concept . . ." at the Materials Handling Management Course, Lake Placid, New York, 1967.

3. Trend toward systems purchasing by the government during World War II (as opposed to purchasing components)
4. Need for a common understanding between customer and supplier for efficient integration of equipment
5. Recognition of handling as a part of an overall system, combining production, handling, inspection, control, storage and warehousing into one, integrated activity.
6. Use of computers to enhance the problem-solving capability of systems engineers.

B. Changes in the Material Handling Market
1. The market is continuing to grow more complex.
2. Material handling activities are becoming more entwined with other functions.
3. Complex systems, while highly productive, are extremely expensive.
4. Such systems are not easily altered, revised or changed.

C. Changes in the Material Handling Industry
1. The increased complexity of the problems has brought about a number of mergers of material handling manufacturers as a means of assembling teams of experts to solve the problems.
2. Selling is frequently done on the basis of problem-solving capability, rather than either price or products produced.
3. Internal communications between many divisions of a single company becomes important to both vendor and customer.
4. Advertising programs and sales organizations are being switched from product orientation to capability orientation.

Allan Harvey [6] suggests that the systems approach, in its efforts to deal with the pressures of competition and the squeeze on profits, accomplishes the following:

1. Usually results in better solutions than those obtainable by traditional approaches.
2. Provides for a continuous feedback of necessary information.
3. Frees the enterprise from the perils of organizational complexity.
4. Provides decisions based on the full knowledge of their impact on total costs.
5. Provides a vehicle for the application of new techniques and technologies, in both problem solving and problem implementation.
6. Puts a firm foundation under the corporate information and control procedures.
7. Frequently forces the development of new equipment concepts to implement unusual handling problems, vs. forcing problem solution around the capabilities of existing handling hardware.

[6] Allan Harvey, "Systems Can *Too* Be Practical," *Business Horizons,* Indiana University, Summer 1964, p. 68.

He continues by reiterating the fact that both *things* and *facts* flow through a company. Only when these flows are integrated can the business become an entity. And he concludes by stating that "Only the systems approach can give management the kind of information and control it needs to maximize growth and profitability." In addition to the above somewhat intangible advantages of the systems approach, the following benefits may also be obtained:

1. Provides continuous flow
2. Reduces space requirements
3. Requires less supervision
4. Reduces indirect labor costs
5. Reduces both in-process and finished goods inventories
6. Reduces delay between work stations
7. Improves production control
8. Reduces damage due to handling
9. Provides for efficient coordination of handling activities linking vendors, manufactures, distributors and customers

INDICATORS OF A NEED FOR THE SYSTEMS APPROACH

The above reasons for and advantages of the systems approach imply certain indicators of situations in which this approach is worthy of consideration. Among them are:

1. Information and control procedures in need of overhaul
2. Organizational difficulties interfering with progress
3. Decisions being made on incomplete or inaccurate data and/or costs
4. Potential for meaningful use of some of the newer analytical techniques and technologies
5. Problem at hand extremely complex and difficult to solve
6. Potential improvement by adopting continuous flow principle
7. Space at a premium
8. Supervision difficult
9. High indirect costs
10. High in-process and finished goods inventory
11. Inventory control difficulties
12. Scheduling problems
13. Delays between operations and work stations
14. Product damage due to handling
15. Possibility of better coordination with vendors and/or customers
16. Competitive pressures
17. Anticipated expansion of product line or volume
18. Proposed changes in data processing system
19. Present operations never really *studied* in depth—for uncovering improvement possibilities
20. Loss of orders due to stock-outs

21. Unsatisfactory customer service
22. Potential advantages of physically linking production and handling operations
23. Apparent need for expansion or re-modeling
24. Present equipment obsolete, inflexible, high operating cost
25. Good possibility of implementing a portion of a potential future system
26. Inefficient material flow and/or plant layout
27. Other organizational functions automating

Management should carefully evaluate the current problem against such indicators.

And, in conclusion, Allan Harvey suggests that the nature of problem situations requiring the systems approach: [7]

1. Will have a critical impact on the competitive position
2. Involves long-term commitments
3. Cuts across organizational lines
4. Involves complex trade-offs

STEPS IN SYSTEMS DEVELOPMENT

As has been previously indicated, some types of handling problems are of a more complex nature than others. This suggests that the best solution may not always be easily attainable, nor will the relatively straight-forward problem-solving procedure, outlined in Chapter 7, adequately cover the complex interrelationships with the possibility of many overlapping aspects which might be found in a multiple problem situation. The systems approach involves a much more sophisticated analysis of a material handling or physical distribution problem situation, and the approach to its solution will usually require a more thorough and rigorous investigation, due to the fact that in most cases, a problem demanding the systems approach is directed more toward a total materials flow cycle (Figure 2–1), than to the solution of an individual problem situation. In reality the system design procedure will usually follow the same pattern as in Chapter 7, "General Analysis Procedure," except that the complexity of a systems-type situation demands a more detailed treatment, and requires a procedure consisting of several more steps, as well as greater care in carrying them out. A suggested approach to the systems-type of problem situation is as follows:

Phase I—Definition
    1. Identify problem(s)
    2. Determine cause(s) of problem(s)

[7] Allan Harvey, "When Systems Approach Pays Off," *Automation*, June, 1968, p. 20.

3. Establish scope and range of functions and activities affected
4. Establish constraints
5. Set objectives
6. Develop design and evaluation criteria
7. Define problem(s)
8. Make feasibility study

Phase II—Investigation
9. Determine information and data needed
10. Establish work plans and schedule
11. Collect data, facts and information
12. Verify data, etc.
13. Develop, analyze, interpret and evaluate data.
14. Re-define problem(s)

Phase III—Synthesis
15. Conceptualize system possibilities
16. Structure alternative systems
17. Simulate potential systems
18. Select feasible system

Phase IV—Design
19. Define proposed system
20. Establish specifications
21. Develop and design components
22. Develop budget for implementation
23. Prepare justification report and/or presentation
24. Obtain approvals
25. Revise as necessary
26. Evaluate design progress

Phase V—Implementation
27. Organize for procurement
28. Procure equipment and facilities
29. Install equipment
30. Plan for orientation and training of operators and managers
31. Prepare for human and public relations considerations
32. Start-up and de-bug
33. Audit performance

Figure 9-4 will be helpful in visualizing the differences between the "standard" problem-solving procedure and the "systems" approach to a problem situation. It will be noted that the first *14* steps of the above procedure parallel the first *8* steps of the problem analysis procedure. Therefore, the first 14 steps will not be discussed in *this* chapter. It is with Phase III, System Synthesis, that the present procedure begins to diverge and develop into a more rigorous analysis of the problem. The following discussion is concerned with those steps which are substantially *different* in the "systems" approach from those in the "problem" approach.

	COMPLEX PROJECT—*SYSTEM*
DEFINITION	1. Identify problem(s)
	2. Determine cause(s) of problem(s)
	3. Establish scope and range
	4. Establish constraints
	5. Set objectives
	6. Develop design and evaluation criteria
	7. Define problem(s)
	8. Make feasibility study
INVESTIGATION	9. Determine information and data needed
	10. Establish work plan and schedule
	11. Collect data, facts and information
	12. Verify data, etc.
	13. Develop, analyze, and evaluate data
	14. Re-define problem(s)
SYNTHESIS	15. Conceptualize system possibilities
	16. Structure alternatives
	17. Simulate potential systems
	18. Select feasible system
DESIGN	19. Define proposed system
	20. Establish specifications
	21. Develop and design components
	22. Develop budget for implementation
	23. Prepare justification
	24. Obtain approvals
	25. Revise as necessary
	26. Evaluate design progress
IMPLEMENTATION	27. Organize for procurement
	28. Procure equipment and facilities
	29. Install equipment
	30. Plan for orientation and training
	31. Prepare for human and public relations
	32. Start-up; de-bug
	33. Audit performance

INDIVIDUAL PROJECT—*PROBLEM*	
1. Identify problem(s)	**DEFINITION**
3. Determine scope of problem(s)	
3. Establish objectives	
4. Define problem(s)	
5. Determine what data are needed	**INVESTIGATION**
6. Establish work plan and schedule	
7. Collect data	
8. Develop, weigh and analyze data	
9. Develop improvements	**SOLUTION**
10. Prepare justification report	
11. Obtain approvals	
12. Revise as necessary	
13. Work out procedures for installation	**INSTALLATION**
14. Supervise the installation	
15. Follow up	

Fig. 9–4. Approaches to material handling projects.

SYSTEM SYNTHESIS

This section will discuss the steps involved in systems synthesis and follows the numbering system of the preceding outline. Steps 1–14, which are problem oriented, are dealt with in Chapter 7, pages 230–242.

Conceptualize System Possibilities

One of the distinguishing features of the systems concept is that it requires the analyst to stretch his imagination far beyond the boundaries within which he is accustomed to working. This provides an opportunity to conceptualize a large number of alternative possibilities for solving the problem. The "conceptualizing" is frequently done with the aid of a flow chart, such as that shown in Figure 9–1, which is subsequently converted to the format shown in Figure 9–5 where each symbol represents a step, activity, or function in the potential system. The conventions (diamonds and rectangles) in Figure 9–5 are those used in the General Purpose Systems Simulation (GPSS) method of notation.

It should be pointed out that if the total problem appears too large to be manageable as a single system, it will either be necessary or advisable to divide it into subsystems. This will very likely require a separate new flow chart for each subsystem, and probably additional flow charts for the several alternatives for implementing each alternative or subsystem.

Structure Alternative Systems

It is in this step that the systems approach becomes more pronounced by virtue of the fact that it may very likely involve the simulation of the proposed solutions or alternatives, probably with the aid of a computer. The flow chart is the most common preliminary step in structuring a problem solution for computer simulation. If this step is carried out in the manner implied the procedure would be somewhat as follows:

a. Sketch a preliminary flow chart of the entire system.
b. For each step, function, or activity shown on the flow chart, determine the parameters, characteristics, factors for consideration, etc., required to reach the system objectives.
c. Establish the constraints to be met or complied with by the system, in reaching the desired objective.
d. Develop a block diagram of the system logic—which is the next step beyond the flow chart in preparing the system description for use with the computer. A typical block diagram is shown in Figure 9–6.

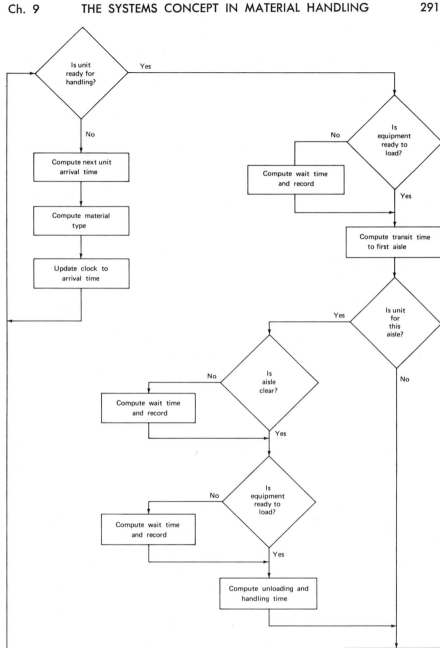

Fig. 9–5. Typical flow chart. (From *Production Handbook,* The Ronald Press Co., New York, 1972.)

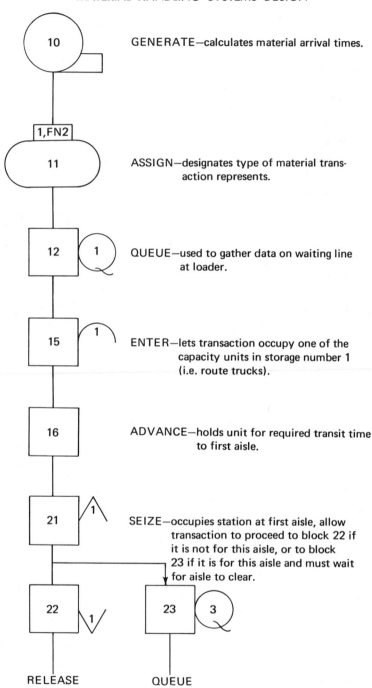

Fig. 9–6. Portion of block diagram in GPSS. (From *Production Handbook*, The Ronald Press Co., New York, 1972.)

Simulate Potential Systems

At this point, the block diagram must be prepared for use in the computer, somewhat as follows:

a. Convert "model" to computer language. (The block diagram, as shown in Figure 9–6 is frequently referred to as a "model.") When it is complete in terms of the logic flow, its meaning must be converted to a computer language. There are a number of different computer languages used in simulation, depending on the type of problem, the programmer, and the type of computer equipment available. One of the more common computer languages useful in the material handling field is "General Purpose System Simulation," commonly referred to as GPSS. Figure 9–7 represents the conversion of several steps from the preceding block diagram into the GPSS language.

b. Prepare computer input. This step involves the process of punching a card (or preparing a tape) to represent each of the steps in the computer language. If done on punched cards, the result will be as depicted in Figure 9–8.

c. "Run" the model on the computer. In this way, the model is manipulated, or "put through its paces" to check the reasoning, parameters, constraints, and results as a means of testing the proposed system. Several sets of data will probably be utilized in making the computer run.

d. Analyze results. The analysis of the computer runs would normally include a comparison of simulations using the several sets of data and/or of several alternative systems or sub-systems. This step also includes the "debugging" of the model, and making corrections necessary in both the simulation model and computer program.

Select Feasible System

Having structured and/or simulated several possible alternative solutions, it now becomes necessary to evaluate the various alternatives. This involves an investigation of the following, among others:

1. The mechanical feasibility of each alternative
2. Relative costs
3. Potential savings
4. Return on investment
5. Feasibility of implementing some of the alternatives at a future date
6. Degree to which each alternative meets the objectives of the system
7. Relative ease of supervising, maintaining each of these alternatives

GENERAL PURPOSE SYSTEMS SIMULATOR II

PROGRAMMER: M.D.D.
PROGRAM TITLE: M.H. SIMULATION
PROJECT NO: 1234   VERIFY

DATE: ____
PAGE ____ OF ____

LOCATION	NAME (LEFT JUSTIFIED)	X	Y	Z	SELECTION MODE	NEXT BLOCK A	NEXT BLOCK B	MEAN TIME	MODIFIER	REMARKS
1	JOB									
1	FUNCTION	RN1	D4							
.20	.60	1	.90	3	1.0	4		1	FN1	
10	GENERATE					11				
11	ASSIGN	1	FN2			12				
2	FUNCTION	RN1	D11							
.03	.07	2	.12	3	.19	4	.26	5	.35	6
.44	.54	8	.64	9	.82	10	1.0	11		
2	FUNCTION	RN1	D3							
12	QUEUE	1	0	1		15				
15	ENTER	1				16				
16	ADVANCE	2				20				
20	QUEUE	2				21				
2	QTABLE	2	0	1	PICK 100	22				
21	SEIZE	1				22	23			
22	RELEASE	1				30				
23	QUEUE	3				31				

21	SEIZE	1			FN	3		
2	QTABLE	2	0	1	100			
20	QUEUE	2			21			
16	ADVANCE				20	2		
15	ENTER	1			16			
1	QTABLE	1	0		100			
12	QUEUE	1			15			
11	ASSIGN	1	FN2		12			
10	GENERATE				11	1	FN1	

Fig. 9–8. Typical section of card deck. (From *Production Handbook*, The Ronald Press Co., New York, 1972.)

On the basis of an evaluation of such factors, the preliminary selection should be made of the system which appears to be feasible at this point in the analysis.

SYSTEM DESIGN

Reference to Figure 9–4, Approaches to Material Handling Projects, will show that the design *segment* of the systems procedure also differs considerably from that required for the analysis of a more limited problem. Therefore, Step 9 of the previous procedure, "Develop Improvements," is replaced *here* by the following 8 steps. It will be noted that the major cause of the difference is the greater complexity of the systems-type problem.

Define Proposed System

Although it will be remembered that the problem-definition phase of the analysis deals with the definition of the *problem,* it is now necessary to define the *system* by which it is proposed to solve the problem, on the basis of the facts, factors, and conclusions drawn from the preceding portion of the analysis. By this time it should be possible to accurately define and describe the system in terms of its scope, its re-defined objectives which might consist of a written description, a detailed step-by-step outline, and a flow chart or block diagram similar to those used in structuring the alternative systems during the synthesis phase of the problem analysis.

Establish Specifications

It is now necessary to detail carefully the functional specifications to be met by the system, as well as each individual segment of the system. Such specifications may be in terms of physical dimensions, overall configuration, output per hour, or cost per unit. Comparable specifications should be established for the information portion of the system involving paper work, records, etc. It should also be done for those control aspects of the system for which functional or operating specifications would be desirable or necessary. It is possible at this point that some of the equipment items will be fairly well identified, so that *their* specifications may also be recorded. At all times, it is necessary to keep in mind the importance of integrating the information phase of the system and other phases of plant operation with the assistance of the electronic data processing personnel.

Develop and Design System Components

At this point, the actual design process takes place. That is, the "hardware" aspects of the system are developed in the form of blueprints; the control system is designed and specified in an appropriate manner; and the information system is developed and reduced to a form capable of implementation.

The design process involves detailed preparation for the fabrication or procurement of all segments of the system. It will be necessary to establish the responsibilities of the user, the vendors, and the consultant (if one is assisting with the design process). An important phase of the functional design is the establishment of performance requirements to be used as guides by the vendors and also as bases for measuring the effectiveness of the components.

It may be found necessary during the design process to indicate the need for prototypes of selected portions of the system and to specify the terms and conditions under which any pilot operations may be necessary.

Another aspect of the design procedure will concern itself with establishing areas for measuring system performance in terms of labor content, costs, or other units which may serve as values against which to judge performance.

It should not be forgotten that all of the above applies not only to the "hardware" aspects of the proposed system, but also to the information and control phases as well.

Develop Budget for Implementation

Having structured the proposed system in terms of functional specifications and preliminary design details, it will be necessary to prepare a budget for the implementation of the proposed system. The specifications and preliminary design should provide an adequate basis for discussion of the project with potential suppliers. Quotations should be requested from selected suppliers with their full knowledge that the figures are tentative, and are to be used only as a basis for preliminary project approval. Upon receipt of quotations from interested suppliers, it will be necessary to study and evaluate them in relationship to the specifications; after which it will be possible to prepare a preliminary budget.

Prepare Justification Report and/or Presentation

Typical information to be included in the justification of the proposed plan, for management review and approval, is outlined below:

1. Comparison of costs between present and proposed methods of operation.
2. Summary of capital investment required for the proposed method.
3. Determination of rate of return on investment, according to company policy.
4. Review of applicable intangible gains.
5. Review of proposed solution in terms of original problem definition and objectives.
6. Presentation of the justification clearly and accurately.

Company policy will usually determine whether the problem solution will be presented in the form of a report, an oral presentation, or a combination of the two. In any case, the preparation will involve about the same information and data as in Step X in Chapter 7 (p. 246). The contents will vary, of course, with the individual problem as well as with company practice. If desired, plans should be made for an oral presentation of the report using appropriate visual aids, such as slides, photos, charts, mock-ups, models, etc.

Obtain Approvals

Approval is not only necessary, but usually advisable as a means of creating an awareness of the problem among higher levels of management. In fact, the acceptance, as well as the successful operation, of the proposed plan may hinge on whether management personnel affected by the plan were or were not given an opportunity to be part of the decision-making group.

Revise as Necessary

In many cases immediate approval of the original proposal may be withheld pending a further investigation of several items or questions by the review group. If such changes become necessary, they should be made, approved and incorporated into the problem solution.

Evaluate Design Progress

Since the system development procedure has very likely involved a large amount of time and money up to this point, it would appear worthwhile to evaluate the progress being made on the overall program at strategic points during the development progress. Accomplishments should be checked or measured against the original system objective, as well as the development schedule.

SYSTEMS IMPLEMENTATION

The complex analysis procedure also requires a more detailed consideration of the implementation phase than does the limited problem situation. For this reason the following steps are outlined in considerable detail.

Organize for Procurement

It is implied that the implementation of a complex system involves more than just "buying" and therefore justifies whatever efforts are necessary to organize the procurement process, since the completed system may cost hundreds of thousands or even millions of dollars. This would involve making detailed plans for the investigation of each major segment of the system, arranging contacts with the several parties who might be involved in the procurement process both inside and outside the buying organization, and properly scheduling all procurement efforts to assure coordination of the several parties. Specific assignments should be made, but with *one* individual in overall control of the procurement process.

It is to be concluded from the above that the user cannot expect to buy a complex system "off the shelf." A successful system usually results only from a carefully specified, designed, and installed combination of integrated components.

Procure Equipment and Facilities

After the above preliminary work, it is necessary to actually procure equipment required for the proposed system. This will involve all of the activities suggested in Step XIII of the Problem Analysis Procedure, on page 249.

A complex system may also require the development, installation and testing of a prototype or pilot installation which must be built, run, checked out, and revised as necessary prior to the completion of the procurement activity.

It may also be wise to include, as part of the purchase order, a statement regarding vendor follow-up at predetermined intervals—or requiring "proper operation" for a specified period of time (without breakdowns) before final payment is made. Customer and supplier responsibilities should also be spelled out as a part of the purchase order.

Install Equipment

Probably the first step in planning for the installation of the equipment is to construct a critical path network (see Figure 8–8) to insure that equipment is installed in the right sequence and on schedule. If the installation is to be made in a new building, it will be necessary to plan for the site to be ready to receive the equipment. On the other hand, if the equipment is to be installed in an existing building, it will be necessary to develop plans so that operations can continue during the installation as much as is practicable.

Allan Harvey [8] suggests that the following situations may develop into "problems" during the installation process, and necessary steps should be taken to avoid any difficulties which may arise:

1. Delivery of equipment
   a. Changes in delivery will have to be negotiated with the vendor.
   b. Availability of building resources such as utilities, receiving dock, elevators, etc.
   c. Equipment protection during the time it is waiting for installation.
   d. Responsibility for such things as construction equipment, cranes, utilities, insurance, building permits, building code and resolving any problems involving changes.
2. Agreements with architects and contractors relating to the coordination of trades involved in the installation, and the resolution of any differences which may arise.
3. Inspection of selected components at predetermined stages of the installation.
4. Clarification of the roles of the several parties during the installation.

[8] Allan Harvey, adapted from the outline of a presentation, "The Systems Concept . . . ," at the Materials Handling Management Course, Lake Placid, New York, June, 1967.

5. Integration of the information system with the physical system; particularly if several vendors are involved, and priorities and procedures must be worked out.
6. Move sequence and/or schedule problems involving parallel operations of several vendors and their respective phasing out procedures will have to be resolved.

The resolution of such problems must be carefully and tactfully handled during the installation process. And it should go without saying, that the system design coordinator must be on hand during the entire installation. It would be extremely unwise for him to be absent long enough to permit deviation from design plans as they may become expedient during the installation process.

Plan for Orientation and Training of Operators and Managers

The proper operation of a complex handling system requires the development of proper training plans for all those who may be concerned with its operation. Because the installation will most likely be considerably different from previous methods, detailed plans must be made for the careful training of those who will operate the equipment as well as for the orientation of any management personnel who will be associated with it. This involves development of preliminary operating procedures, discussions with appropriate personnel, and then finalization of procedures and training plans.

Prepare for Human and Public Relations Considerations

One consequence of the installation of a complex system is the possible reduction of personnel—or change in job classifications. Planned efforts should be directed toward smoothing over any such situations. In fact, the installation of a new "system" provides an opportunity to change operating methods and job classifications, as well as to re-assign personnel.

It may also be desirable to consider any possible public relations aspects of the proposed installation. If the human relations or public relations aspects might suggest negative reactions, steps should be taken to overcome such possibilities. In a good many cases, it will be advisable to "capitalize" on the prestige value of a new, expensive, and complex installation. Those aspects worthy of promotion should be promulgated among operating personnel, management personnel, customers, vendors, the community in general, and stockholders, to take advantage of the "publicity" value of the installation.

Start-Up . . . and De-bug

No system is immune to the unpredictable difficulties which are bound to develop during the start-up process. Regardless of the efforts taken to assure proper operation, situations will arise that have not been foreseen. For this reason, it is necessary to set up a procedure for handling these difficulties, including schedules for their correction and assigning responsibilities for carrying out remedial work. It will be helpful at this time if a procedure is also established for logging the various types of problems encountered, and recording downtime caused by each. Such data will be extremely helpful in the correction process.

The last step in the start-up procedure involves carrying out whatever tests were previously specified to be met, prior to the acceptance of the system. After the installation has been operating for a sufficient period of time without serious difficulties, and management is satisfied with the performance, it is appropriate to officially "accept" the completed installation. Arrangements should also be made for subsequent performance evaluations at scheduled intervals to insure that design criteria and objectives are achieved. Agreement must be reached between parties on any point where performance does not meet expectations.

Audit System Performance

The final step in the total procedure for the analysis and design of a complex system involves an audit of the operation at a predetermined time (or times) as a means of assuring that the system is operating properly and as a basis for subsequent improvement in the system. In preparation for such an audit, it will be found desirable to pay close attention to:

1. Establishing responsibility for specific segments of the system
2. Assigning personnel to each
3. Observing, evaluating, and paying particular attention to:
   a. Equipment warranties
   b. Unforeseeable events which could not have been known until the system was in operation, such as: maintenance, safety hazards, or such mechanical difficulties as materials build-up on components.
   c. Operating or other conditions which may change after the installation has been made.

During the audit of the new system, it will again be necessary to pay close attention to the responsibilities of the several parties involved. Some areas of concern might be:

1. The customer should carefully review all contractual arrangements in order to be sure that all parties have carried out their respective duties and responsibilities.
2. Since the supplier is at a disadvantage, he will very likely be motivated to correct any difficulties in order to gain acceptance and preserve his reputation.
3. The customer can lose a considerable amount of money if the system does not operate properly; therefore, problems of contingent liability should be carefully explored and settled.
4. With problems of safety, the vendor could become liable.
5. All back-up systems should be checked out to be sure that they will operate properly in case of a breakdown.
6. A continual watch should be made in order to assure that the original problem analysis was complete, and that some oversight or neglected aspect of the problem has not resulted in a sub-optimal solution to the problem.
7. In order to assure adequate follow-up over a reasonable period of time, personnel should be specifically assigned to perform necessary inspections and evaluations, with reports made to appropriate personnel.

It should be emphasized that the audit of the system is not only the last step in the problem-solving procedure, but in many cases, one of the most important. It is only by a thorough and careful audit that it can be shown that the problem was properly defined, thoroughly investigated, effectively solved, and efficiently implemented. It should also be recognized that a properly conducted audit provides an ideal basis for uncovering subsequent improvement possibilities and for updating the system.

One of the most important phases of the system audit is that of evaluating the net accomplishments of the total system installation. Such an evaluation may ask such questions as:

1. To what degree does the system performance meet the pre-determined objectives?
2. Is the installation over-mechanized?
3. Is the pay-off up to expectations, or must it await a higher level of output than (a) that for which it was designed, or (b) that obtainable during the break-in period?
4. Is there a need for re-calculating selected data, or determination of post-operation facts in order to obtain proper information for a true evaluation?
5. Is it possible that some of the justification for the system may be "written off" in terms of company pride for the installation, or in terms of some of the many other intangible advantages gained from the installation?

As this point, it should be obvious that there is a considerable difference between the analysis of an individual problem of relatively limited scope and a complex handling situation requiring the development of a system. The above discussion has attempted to point out those phases of the analysis and design which are different—primarily in terms of detail—for the complex problem than for the limited problem. Although both procedures are similar, as shown in Figure 9–4, it is felt that the detail brought out above will permit a more effective solution of the complex problem situation.

Perhaps the preceding discussion can be clarified with the aid of Figure 9–9, which depicts the procedure in diagrammatic form. The dotted lines indicate either:

1. Feedback of information and/or data, or
2. Need for either re-checking previous steps, or looking ahead to subsequent steps, for guidance at a given point in the analysis.

The dotted lines are only meant to be suggestive of such interrelationships—and do not imply a procedural sequence.

WHO WILL DEVELOP THE SYSTEM?

Because of the complexity, size, and scope of many handling/distribution systems, it is unlikely that the typical user will have the in-house capability for developing and designing the system by himself. Therefore, in all probability, the task will be divided amongst several parties, such as the user himself, a consultant, and a supplier. And it is more than likely that some combination of these three will have a hand in designing the system.

According to Norman M. Sullivan,[9] the user has three choices:

1. Staff up to meet the situation. This may be the ideal solution; particularly if management is embarked on a long-range project involving continued use of this built-up staff.
2. Engage a professional consultant. The consultant might not only help him develop a system, but might help him in evaluating the proper approach, and setting up the organization required.
3. If the general class of equipment the system will require is apparent, he may call in an engineering-oriented supplier with adequate study staff, skilled and experienced in his particular field.

And of course there is always the possibility that the group developing the system may be made up of some combination of the above three

[9] Norman M. Sullivan, "The Systems Point of View," an unpublished paper.

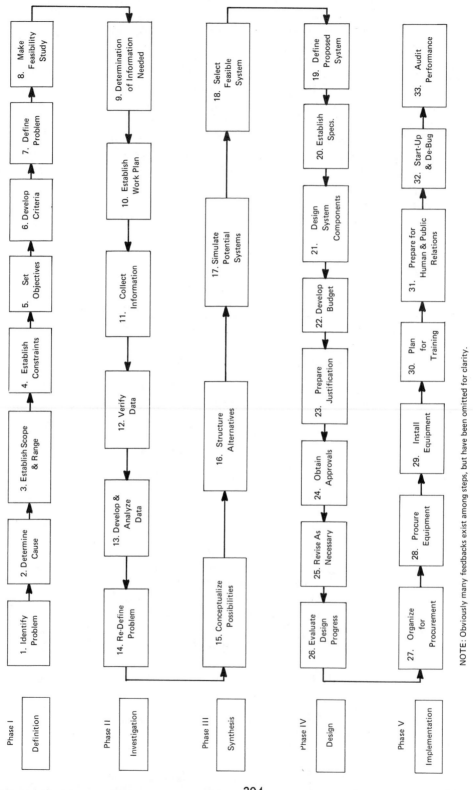

Phase I	Phase II	Phase III	Phase IV	Phase V
Definition	Investigation	Synthesis	Design	Implementation

1. Identify Problem
2. Determine Cause
3. Establish Scope & Range
4. Establish Constraints
5. Set Objectives
6. Develop Criteria
7. Define Problem
8. Make Feasibility Study

9. Determination of Information Needed
10. Establish Work Plan
11. Collect Information
12. Verify Data
13. Develop & Analyze Data
14. Re-Define Problem

15. Conceptualize Possibilities
16. Structure Alternatives
17. Simulate Potential Systems
18. Select Feasible System

19. Define Proposed System
20. Establish Specs.
21. Design System Components
22. Develop Budget
23. Prepare Justification
24. Obtain Approvals
25. Revise As Necessary
26. Evaluate Design Progress

27. Organize for Procurement
28. Procure Equipment
29. Install Equipment
30. Plan for Training
31. Prepare for Human & Public Relations
32. Start-Up & De-Bug
33. Audit Performance

NOTE: Obviously many feedbacks exist among steps, but have been omitted for clarity.

304

groups. In fact, Sullivan suggests that this "team" will vary in make-up from project to project depending on the nature of the problem at hand. Figures 9–10 and 9–11 indicate two approaches to systems development,

User	Supplier
1. Establish Objectives	8. Equipment Application Engineering
2. Determine Range of Affected Functions	9. Hardware Specifications
3. Data Development & Analysis	10. Equipment Design Engineering
4. Synthesize System, Paperwork & Controls	11. Equipment Manufacturing
5. Systems Structuring & Layout	12. Field Installation
6. System Pre-check & Preliminary Justification	13. Start-up
7. Functional Specifications	
14. Operational Audit	

Fig. 9–10. Approach to systems development: Example 1. (From Norman M. Sullivan, "Working with the Supplier," unpublished paper; courtesy of Rapistan, Inc., Grand Rapids, Mich.)

User	Consultant	Supplier
1. Establish Objectives	2. Determine Range of Affected Functions	8. Equipment Application Engineering
	3. Data Development & Analysis	9. Hardware Specifications
	4. Synthesize System, Paperwork & Controls	10. Equipment Design Engineering
	5. Systems Structuring & Layout	11. Equipment Manufacturing
	6. System Pre-check & Preliminary Justification	12. Field Installation
	7. Functional Specifications	13. Start up
	14. Operational Audit	

Fig. 9–11. Approach to systems development: Example 2. (From Norman M. Sullivan, "Working with the Supplier," unpublished paper; courtesy of Rapistan, Inc., Grand Rapids, Mich.)

depending on the nature of the project, and based on Sullivan's 14 steps in systems development. Sullivan further suggests that there is a variation in the degree of involvement in the systems development procedure, varying at any particular point in time during the term of the project development. This relationship is shown in Figure 9–12 in which an area of overlap is seen.

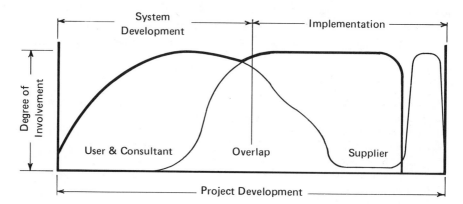

Fig. 9–12. Chart showing varying degrees of participation of user, consultant, and supplier at different points in time. (From Norman M. Sullivan, "Working with the Supplier," unpublished paper; courtesy of Rapistan, Inc., Grand Rapids, Mich.)

In a somewhat similar arrangement, in Figure 9–13, the 33 steps previously defined and described are listed, along with a legend to indicate the amount of involvement by the user, consultant, and supplier.

If the user were to turn to a supplier of engineered handling equipment, the supplier would generally make a survey of the situation which would take from one to three days and would be done at no charge. Very likely he would come up with one of the following recommendations:

1. He sees no solution to your problem with his type of equipment, and would, therefore, go no further.
2. He sees a possible solution to the problem and would continue further on one of the following approaches:

   a. he might request specific information from your staff people as to present and projected volume, handling and shipping requirements.
   b. he might recommend that a consultant be brought in to analyze the management aspects of your business so that management goals become better defined. The consultant might also gather marketing information and provide an overall approach to defining the system.
   c. the supplier might offer to have his engineer develop the management data needed on a per diem basis.[10]

Depending on the outcome of the above, subsequent steps in the project development would be worked out by the parties concerned.

[10] "Systems Planning: How to Get Started," *Materials Handling Engineering*, April 1965, p. 81.

AREAS OF RESPONSIBILITY / STEPS IN SYSTEMS DEVELOPMENT		CUSTOMER	CONSULTANT	SUPPLIER*	OTHERS
DEFINE	1. Identify problem(s)	P	S, A	A	
	2. Determine cause(s) of problem(s)	S	P	A	
	3. Establish scope and range	J	J		
	4. Establish constraints	P	S	A	
	5. Set objectives	P	S		
	6. Develop design and evaluation criteria	S	P		
	7. Define problem(s)	S	P		
	8. Make feasibility study	S	P	A	
INVESTIGATE	9. Determine information and data needed	S	P	A	
	10. Establish work plans and schedule	P	A		
	11. Collect data, facts and information	P, S	P, A		
	12. Verify data, etc.	S	P		
	13. Develop, analyze, interpret, evaluate data	S	P		
	14. Re-define problem(s)	S	P		
SYNTHESIZE	15. Conceptualize system possibilities	S	P	A	
	16. Structure alternative systems	A	P	S	
	17. Simulate potential systems		P	S	
	18. Select feasible system	S	P	A	
DESIGN	19. Define proposed system	S	P	A	
	20. Establish specifications	J	J	A	
	21. Develop and design system components	A	A	P	
	22. Develop budget for implementation	S	P		
	23. Prepare justification	S	P	A	
	24. Obtain approvals	J	J		
	25. Revise as necessary	J	J	J	
	26. Evaluate design progress	S	P	S	
IMPLEMENT	27. Organize for procurement	S	P		
	28. Procure equipment and facilities	A	A	P	
	29. Install equipment	A	A	P	
	30. Plan for orientation and training	A	P	A	
	31. Prepare for human and public relations	S	A	P	
	32. Start up and de-bug	S	A	P	
	33. Audit systems performance	P	A	S	

*Supplier may also serve as consultant

P = Primary responsibility   J = Joint
S = Secondary (= Primary if no consultant)   A = Advisory

Fig. 9–13. Roles of parties involved in systems development.

Another approach to the relationship between the user and potential outside assistance is shown in Figure 9–14.

A trend of interest to the systems purchaser is the growing development of their capabilities by leading equipment suppliers through the acquisition of companies or services furnishing related equipment or services. As a result, some of the larger concerns are attaining their goal of total capability and total responsibility for handling an entire system order or contract.

	Make Inhouse Application	System Study	
		Inhouse	Outside Assistance
Within user's capability?	Consider if Yes	Consider if Yes	Use if No
Workload of user's capable people	Consider if Available	Consider if Available	Use if not not Available
% of product cost in study area	1% _____50%		
Need for improvement—small or large?	Small _____1% _____ 500% Large		
One project or multiduplicating projects?	Give consideration if multiple project. May still go outside		Consider when one project

Fig. 9–14. A method of checking factors influencing choice between inhouse or outside help in systems development. (From H. A. Zollinger, "Use Systems Approach When Solving Material Handling Problems," *Automation*, April 1968, p. 87.)

THE ROLE OF THE COMPUTER IN THE SYSTEMS CONCEPT

The concept that material handling activities should be considered not independently, but as a part of the total flow cycle, has become much more apparent since the computer entered the scene. In fact, with a computer involved in the system, it is difficult to visualize material handling as being outside the scope of management decision making. Actually computers are there because when used properly, they can integrate management functions in a way which has never previously been possible. Bruce Whitehall has said that: [11]

[11] Bruce Whitehall, "Computers in Handling Systems," *Mechanical Handling*, October 1968, p. 1551.

With their ability to grasp, correlate, and assess factors at a speed and comprehensiveness which the human brain cannot compete with, they are herald of the super-system, into which management services such as materials handling, are absorbed into one common stream of data flow . . . materials handling men are, in fact, faced with a new challenge, that of getting their data organized with a precision that meets the requirements of a computer.

In general, computers perform three basic functions: [12] (1) receive data on location or at remote locations, (2) process data, (3) store data. In regard to the modes in which computers operate, Paul Mann states that:

Most computers are used for off-line data storage and processing. This is the type used for computerized inventory control and order picking programs. You have a general purpose unit fed by card or magnetic tape. The information on these cards or tapes comes from people punching in information. The output is generally in printed form for manual use, such as order picking.

More sophisticated materials handling systems use real-time, on line computers. These take data from physical devices, such as scales, or sensing switches on conveyors; interpret this information with stored programs; and issue specific instructions to activate equipment such as batchers, conveyors, stacker cranes.

Computers are used in carrying out or assisting many types of operations and management activities related to the material handling function. Among the more common of these operations are:

1. Inventory control
2. Process control
3. Material control
4. Distribution control
5. Production control
6. Warehousing control
7. Communications
8. Warehouse layout
9. Solution to handling/distribution problems

Several of these applications are cited below. For example, in one computer-oriented material handling system reported in *Material Handling Engineering*, the operation takes place in three areas:

Direct Materials Flow. Controls automatically recognize the identifying code of carriers transported along the conveyor line, and operate diverters which direct the carriers to the programmed destination. (An identification code is magnetically transferred to a carrier when it is released from storage, and that code is read at each point in the system where a decision is to be made regarding destination.) The computer has stored in it a complete set of part

[12] Paul Mann, "Computers Tell Handling Systems What to Do," *The Presidential Issue, Material Handling Engineering*, October, 1966, p. 80.

numbers as well as the route along which each part is to be directed. This route can be modified simply by typing new instructions from the on-line keyboard.

Records Inventory Data. Since the computer directs the flow of parts being manufactured, it contains all the data necessary to construct an inventory for all parts at any stopping point in the system. The computer is programmed to type out any of this data upon request from the operator. The data appears in such a form that part numbers and quantities in each section of the plant can be scanned in a short period of time.

Monitors Machine Activity. While performing these other tasks, the computer is also able to sense when each of more than 50 die casting machines completes a cycle, when any one is malfunctioning, and for what reason. The computer has recorded the quantity of parts that are cast in one cycle, and thus keeps a running record of the number of parts made. The operator pushes a button when the machine is not producing parts: one button for hydraulic failure, one for electrical, and one for "other." The computer prints a one-line statement when the machine is down, including time and reason, and keeps a record of all time spent active, or if down, the amount of time down for each type of failure.[13]

Another system of computerized manufacturing control installed at the Chrysler corporation, is described as follows:

Chrysler's overall plan will put the headquarters computer system on-line with 7 other computer systems, at assembly plants from coast to coast. Then computer subsystems, at headquarters and plants, will instantly collect inventory control and operations data and send it to the headquarters random access file. These files will become a central data bank, under computer control.

Into the computer's files will flow facts collected at the source, about actions when they occur, that affect plant operations (quality, production, manpower, materials and costs), parts inventories (the availability and movement of parts from supplier plants into assembled products). Thus, the headquarters computer will have all the facts it needs to prepare accurate summary reports for group management. And, through the computer network, the plans for production schedules, manning assignments and material control.

All this will be made possible by computer subsystems: 1) for inventory control centered at headquarters, and 2) for operations control within each assembly plant.

These subsystems will include networks of terminals for instant data collection, replies to inquiries and instant reporting for off standard conditions. They will tap the random access files of their own computers to prepare summary and exception reports for management and subordinates concerned with inventory or operations control.[14]

---

[13] "Systems Planning: Computers Play Many Roles," *Material Handling Engineering,* October, 1967, p. 85.

[14] "For Your Top Management—Company-Wide Control as Never Before," *Modern Materials Handling,* October, 1967, pp. 36 f.

A "computerized" distribution center is described by Allan Harvey, as follows:

The subsystem shown [Figure 9–15] links a distribution center with a number of plants and its corporation headquarters. At headquarters there is a central computer with files of production schedules, inventory, and orders on hand. Throughout this network are transacters that communicate directly with the central computer. In addition, the distribution center has its own computer that is linked directly with the central computer. Customer's orders are received, entered into the central computer through a keyhole cathode ray tube device. The computer determines whether the order can be filled from available finished goods inventory. If not, the computer examines the production schedule, other shipping requirements, and assigns an "available" date.

If required, it releases production orders to the plant. Once an item is released for production, it is followed through its manufacturing operation by inputs back to the central computer from the transacters which are located at key points in the manufacturing process. The flow through the plants is controlled up to the time when it is shipped to the distribution center. When the merchandise arrives at the receiving dock, a transacter is used to inform the central computer of the receipt. One of the files in the central computer memory bank is a complete operating model of the distribution center. This makes it possible to relate on-line information about the status of any order to the total flow through the distribution center. It also identifies and keeps track of each element of work by specific tasks and by times.

When the transacter at the receiving dock informs the central computer that an item has arrived, the computer specifies the tasks involved in putting that merchandise in stock. It transmits each identified task to the distribution center computer which then assigns it to one of a number of computer-controlled fork lift vehicles. They communicate directly with the distribution center computer, which in turn is on-line with the central computer.

These vehicles are unmanned and the computer identifies which vehicle is available and assigns to it the task of picking up the load of merchandise and carrying it—automatically guided by the computer—to the appropriate pallet rack location. Automatically, the fork lift mechanism is raised and the pallet load put into the appropriate rack.

The transacter on the vehicle then transmits a message to the distribution center computer identifying the location of this merchandise. Thus, the fact that the merchandise is in the distribution center, and where it is located, is communicated instantaneously to the distribution center computer which immediately inserts these data into the memory of the central computer at headquarters.

Orders as they are received are entered into the central computer and each line item on each order is checked against the inventory of finished goods in the distribution center. If the merchandise called for by a particular order is available to be shipped, that order is instantaneously put into an order file in the central computer. It reviews such orders each evening and selects those that are to be released to order-picking the following day. The criteria used in that selection include marketing policy, customer priorities, transportation costs, and financial policy considerations.

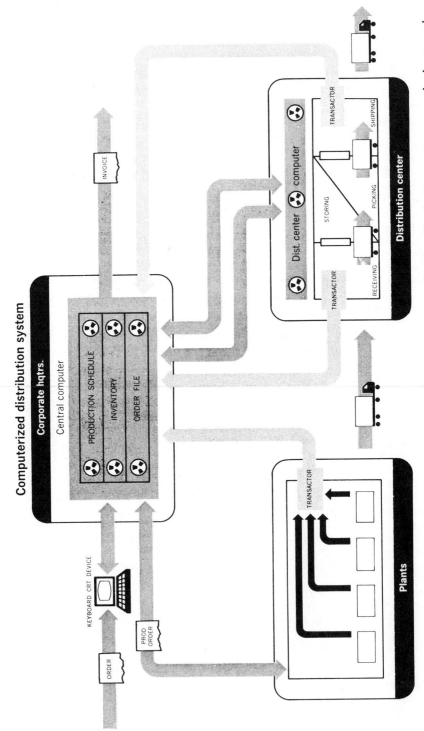

Fig. 9–15. Schematic diagram of computerized distribution system, linking distribution center, several plants and the computer center, at corporate headquarters. (From Allan Harvey, "For Materials Handling Systems: New Computers for Real-Time Use," *Material Handling Engineering*, March 1969, p. 122.)

Having determined what orders are to be released the next day, the central computer then analyzes the items on those orders and determines how they are to be picked to optimize the operations of the distribution center, including the materials handling equipment used. This equipment includes computer-controlled vehicles to which carts are attached. On these carts the picked merchandise is assembled by order while the cart is in transit from location to location.

Finally, having batched the orders in accordance with these criteria, the central computer releases the batches to the distribution center computer which prints the orders up and assigns each batch a code number. The operator on the designated order-picking vehicle puts the assigned batch code number into his input console which then receives from the computer the tasks involved in picking the orders associated with that code number. The distribution center computer then guides the stock picking vehicle and its picking cart through the distribution center from one location to another, and at each specified location raises the vehicle platform to the proper elevation and informs the operator via a display console exactly what to pick. As the vehicle travels to the next location, he puts what he has picked in the appropriate place on the cart, in accordance with the instructions on the display console. Thus, while the vehicle is travelling, the operator is assembling individual line items into orders.

In addition, the distribution center computer performs some other functions related to minor decisions concerning physical inventory stock replenishment requirements and any emergency conditions that arise during the day. This computer also prints out packing lists and labels which are associated with the orders that are being picked. When the order picking vehicle has picked the last item in its current batch of orders, it is automatically directed to the shipping area where the order is checked. The information is put into the transacter which immediately transmits the data to the central computer indicating that the order is complete. An invoice is generated at the same time and forwarded automatically to the customer.[15]

The above illustrations should amply document the extent of computer involvement in handling/distribution systems, and suggest the extreme importance of integrating computer capabilities into complex systems.

The use of computers in analyzing and solving problems has been referred to previously, and is further developed in other chapters.

STAGES IN DEVELOPMENT OF A COMPLEX SYSTEM

It should have become increasingly apparent by now that the development of a complex system is not an easy task, and that as pointed out earlier, nearly every system is composed of subsystems. Then, it may be wise to think in terms of subsystems when developing a more complex system, consisting of a large number of interrelated functions. From this point of view, then, one of the smallest subsystems in a manufacturing/

---

[15] As told by Paul Mann, Jr., "For M. H. Systems: New Computers for Real-Time Use," *Materials Handling Engineering*, March, 1969, p. 123.

handling/distribution system would be the individual workplace, and the subsequent development of a total system might proceed somewhat as follows:

1. Individual operation and its work area.
2. Two related operations with necessary handling, to, between and from.
3. Several related operations and required handling.
    a. One piece of standard handling equipment to accomplish all handling tasks.
    b. Several pieces of standard handling equipment, each selected to optimize one or more handling tasks.
    c. A system of several pieces of standard handling equipment, tied together with custom-designed devices.
    d. A custom system designed to tie *all* operations and *all* handling into an entity (such as a transfer machine).
4. Several interrelated transfer machines or other systems.
5. An automatic manufacturing activity.
6. An automatic production function.
7. An automatic production and distribution system.

If reference is made here to Figure 2–1 (Materials Flow Cycle), it will be seen that an individual work area, within the manufacturing phase of the cycle, might be the smallest subsystem practical for consideration in the overall cycle. At subsequent stages in the development of the total system, the efforts might proceed as outlined above, until the ultimate is accomplished, or a point is reached at which further development is impractical at a given point in time.

NEED FOR A MASTER PLAN

A complex system is not usually developed, designed, and implemented in one continuous process. More likely than not, a considerable period of time may elapse between the conceptualization and implementation of such a system. For that reason there is a great need in the early stages in the planning process for at least outlining a long-range master plan covering the potential development and implementation of the total system. While this need not necessarily be in great detail, it should be available as a means of identifying end objectives and delineating the path by which they will be reached.

Actually the situation is a little different from what one might experience in acquiring a new home. For example, if one were walking up to a nearly finished, brand new home being considered for purchase, he might be greatly misled or even discouraged by the existing appearance of the yard, drive, walks, etc. presently consisting of a mire of mud and a clutter of leftover odds-and-ends of building materials. However, the potential owner would find himself visualizing the house as a future "home," and in his mind's eye, he would picture it as it *will* look, when completely finished and beautifully landscaped—say five to ten years hence. This is the essence of long-range planning! In fact, an architectural rendering of the home would show an infinitely more detailed plan to assure the potential buyer what the house *will* look like when the construction and landscaping have been fully implemented.

But, it is entirely possible that one could not afford to carry out the "dream plan" in one giant step. In fact, even if he could it would take 3 to 5 years for the plants to reach maturity and match the architectural rendering. So, he might tackle the job a little at a time, with logical, easy, and/or inexpensive items first, with the subsequent addition of other features each time he could see his way clear to do so. But he would *always* be working toward the master plan—as specified by the architect—even though slight variations might be made over the years as a result of new thinking, new materials or acceptable modifications of the overall plan.

Eventually, however, by following the master plan (modified and adapted to the passing years) the "dream plan" will become a reality, even though somewhat different from the original picture.

Now, if this line of thinking is applied to the development of a handling/distribution system, it will be recognized that a long-range plan is *the* guide to the eventual development and *total* implementation of a system which might not have been totally feasible at the time of conception. Nevertheless, the original long-range plan, modified by subsequent events, becomes a useful tool in the eventual implementation of the total system.

LESSONS LEARNED TO DATE

Most of the complex systems which have been developed to date have been the product of hard work, detailed planning and team effort, along with a goodly portion of "blood, sweat and tears." However, over a period of time, some "lessons" have been learned by systems planners which are worthy of note. Some of the more important are:

1. It is vitally important to define objectives properly.
2. Optimum results depend on early planning.
3. There are many "grey" areas of fact, costs, and feasibility.
4. It takes nerve to tackle large problems.
5. Some far-out thinking will be helpful in getting attention.
6. Don't expect too much, too soon.
7. People acceptance is essential to proper operation.

8. Even the best systems have "bugs."
9. Think simple before you think complex.
10. Carefully consider improving the present method first—but from the systems point of view.

These guide lines should be considered seriously by those who would attempt to develop complex systems in handling or distribution if they expect success in meeting their objectives.

CONCLUSION

This chapter has attempted to define and explain the systems concept as it applies in the field of material handling and physical distribution. Inevitably this interpretation will not be universally acceptable. However, it is hoped that the concepts expressed here will give the reader a reasonable idea of what the systems concept is, and how it can be interpreted or applied to a handling/distribution problem situation. Other chapters offer more detail on specific procedures and techniques useful in systems planning.

REFERENCES

1. AFFEL, HERMAN A., JR., "Systems Engineering," *International Science and Technology,* November, 1964, pp. 18–26.
   Discusses the role of the systems engineer and how it relates to the entire enterprise.
2. HARVEY, ALLAN, "Systems Can Too Be Practical," *Business Horizons,* Summer, 1964, pp. 59–69.
   Discusses the advantages and disadvantages of material-handling systems.
3. HARVEY, ALLAN, "The Systems Engineering Approach to Materials Handling," Materials Handling Conference of the American Society of Mechanical Engineers, Cleveland, Ohio, June 9–12, 1968.
4. "How to Plan Whole-System Service," *Modern Materials Handling,* January, 1965, pp. 42–45.
   Ways to integrate systems into the entire organization.
5. "MHE Guide to Systems Engineering," *Material Handling Engineering,* April, 1965, pp. 71–109.
   Reports covering all phases of systems as related to material handling.
6. NADLER, GERALD, "What Systems Really Are," *Modern Materials Handling,* July 1965.
   Author's opinion on the essential elements of a system and how to develop the best system.
7. "Systems Concept: Another Management Revolution," *Steel,* June 15, 1964, pp. 25–27.
   History and development of the systems concept. Systems engineer qualities are enumerated.

8. "Systems Concept Gets Big Boost," *The Iron Age*, June 18, 1964, p. 67.
   Discusses the complexity and advantages of systems.

9. "Urgently Needed: System Balanced Policies," *Modern Materials Handling*, January 1965, pp. 38–41.
   Discusses the system function of incoming and outgoing materials storage.

10. WEISS, M. D., "Organizing for Systems Engineering," *Control Engineering*, May 1963, pp. 89–94.
   Discusses the science of systems engineering and the outside sources available to implement it.

11. "Why Buy A System?," *Material Handling Engineering*, January 1961, pp. 68–75.
   Discusses the results of hardware vs. the idea approach. Consultants' role is also discussed.

12. YOUNG, A. W., "Material Handling Climbs Aboard the Systems Bandwagon," *The Iron Age*, November 11, 1965, pp. 142–144.
   Electronic data processing applied to the idea and equipment of systems. Automated warehouses discussed.

10

Quantitative Techniques for Material Handling Analysis

This chapter [1] will review and briefly analyze many of the so-called "quantitative techniques" which it is felt are applicable to material handling analysis and planning. Selected techniques are evaluated as to their applicability and each technique is presented in such a way that the reader can:

1. Understand what it is
2. See how it "works"
3. Relate it to some phase of material handling
4. Compare it with the other techniques
5. Evaluate it for possible use

[1] This chapter is based on two theses submitted to the Georgia Institute of Technology, as follows:
1. J. R. Buchan, *An Evaluation of Selected Quantitative Methods Useful in Plant Layout*, 1966.
2. D. L. Totten, *Applications of Quantitative Techniques in Facilities Planning*, 1967.

They were "companion" theses in that the former was an attempt to identify, explain, and evaluate selected quantitative techniques felt to be useful in material handling analysis. The second work surveyed the profession to determine the extent to which the techniques had been used, and were found useful. It also documented each technique by means of carefully selected and evaluated examples or case histories. Many of these examples are referred to within this chapter by the traditional thesis notation ( ), and listed at the end for those who want to investigate them further.

It is not the purpose here to present sufficient information for application of the techniques. The references at the end of this chapter will indicate sources for obtaining additional information on both theory and application. The primary purpose of this chapter is to present the techniques and provide an intelligent background for the selection of those applicable to analytical work in this field.

The techniques and models in this chapter apply primarily to activity location and material handling design. Some of them also apply to system evaluation. This limitation does not imply a lack of relevance for other models such as line balancing, machine loading, scheduling, sequencing and plant location, but reflects a necessary limitation in the scope of this chapter.

TECHNIQUES FOR EVALUATION

The problems considered here are concerned with the optimum location of equipment or with the movement of materials. When discussing a particular technique, the measure of effectiveness used is traffic distance unless otherwise indicated.

Some of the procedures discussed are based upon classical mathematics; others have been developed recently from the area of operations research. Not all guarantee an optimal solution. It is hoped that the analyst will be able to determine which procedures can be presently used, and which ones will require further study and development before being useful in his situation.

The techniques are roughly divided into four types: (1) linear deterministic, (2) non-linear deterministic, (3) linear probabilistic, and (4) non-linear probabilistic. The techniques to be discussed are:

1. Linear programming
2. Assignment techniques
3. Transportation programming
4. Transshipment programming
5. The traveling salesman technique
6. Integer programming
7. Dynamic programming
8. Queuing theory
9. Conveyor analysis
10. Simulation

This chapter draws upon a wide range of sources. Only those sources directly quoted are referenced, and they are listed at the end of the chapter.

LINEAR PROGRAMMING

Linear programming has become the most frequently applied of the quantitative techniques used in operations research. It is a mathematical technique for determining the best allocation of limited resources or capacities to accomplish a desired objective, e.g., minimizing costs or maximizing profit. The technique requires that the variables of a problem be fairly constant and their values known. The relationship among the variables must represent a linear or straight-line relationship to one another. The technique is thus applicable mainly in static conditions.

Linear programming has been and can be applied to optimize non-automatic material handling, that is, almost any material handling activity other than that accomplished by conveyors. There are several important prerequisites that must be met before any attempt can be made to improve the material handling activity through use of linear programming. These prerequisites are, as adapted from Metzger (1):

1. *An adequate inventory and material control system.* This implies a well-ordered storage and warehousing situation, with a designated place or area for everything.

2. *A measure of material handling between the various locations.* It is necessary to have a measure of handling, including loading, unloading, moving loaded, and moving empty, between the various departments, storage areas, warehouses, or internal shipping and receiving points in the plant, in order to develop the material handling schedules. Distance, cost, or time may be used as a measure, according to Metzger.

3. *An indication of average material movements per day.* The mathematical solution is based upon average material movements. The average moves per day can be simply a listing of origins, destinations, and number of moves.

4. *A daily indication of material requirements for the following day.* This is the necessary preplanning information to allow optimum schedules to be prepared. In most industrial operations the work for the following day is known; hence most, if not all of the material requirements can be determined.

5. *The relationships involved in handling and moving materials must be linear.*

If these prerequisites can be met, the analysis of a problem can proceed. This analysis takes the form of five phases, which are:

a. An initial survey to identify the various loading and unloading stations, and to determine the average number of material moves required per day.

b. Preparation of handling time data between every possible origin and destination, and time requirements for loading and unloading at the various locations.

c. Determination of the minimum "dead heading" requirements via linear programming.

d. Development of round trips and subsequent schedules for the handling equipment.

e. Daily implementation and scheduling to realize the continued benefits in optimum utilization of the material handling equipment and personnel.

Linear programming is most commonly solved by the simplex method. The transportation, transshipment, and assignment techniques are all special cases of the general linear programming procedure, and all can be solved by this widely known procedure.

The general linear programming problem is to find an optimum solution to the linear function

$$Z = e_1 x_1 + e_2 x_2 + \cdots + e_j x_j + \cdots + e_n x_n$$

subject to the linear constraints

$$x_j \geq 0 ; \quad j = 1, 2, \ldots, n$$

which also satisfy m linear inequalities

$$
\begin{aligned}
a_{11} x_1 + a_{12} x_2 + \cdots + a_{1j} x_j + \cdots + a_{1n} x_n &\leq b_1 \\
a_{21} x_1 + a_{22} x_2 + \cdots + a_{2j} x_j + \cdots + a_{2n} x_n &\leq b_2 \\
\cdot \\
\cdot \\
\cdot \\
a_{i1} x_1 + a_{i2} x_2 + \cdots + a_{ij} x_j + \cdots + a_{in} x_n &\leq b_i \\
\cdot \\
\cdot \\
\cdot \\
a_{mi} x_1 + a_{mx} x_2 + \cdots + a_{mj} x_j + \cdots + a_{mn} x_n &\leq b_m
\end{aligned}
$$

where a_{ij}, b_i, and e_j are given restraints. If m is greater than n, the problem has an infinite number of solutions. Another way of expressing the general linear programming problem is to optimize the effectiveness function

$$E = \sum_{j=1}^{n} e_j x_j$$

subject to the constraints

$$\sum_{j=1}^{n} a_{ij} x_j \{\leq, =, \geq\} b_i \quad i = 1, 2, \ldots, m$$

and

$$x_j \geq 0 \quad j = 1, 2, \ldots, n$$

The simplex method is most commonly used to solve the linear programming problem and may also be used to solve the assignment technique, transportation programming, and the transshipment problems.

Although the mathematical computations in the simplex method are relatively simple and essentially a mechanical repetition of a sequence of precisely defined steps, it may be long and tedious. The real problem is to recognize that a problem can be solved by linear programming and to construct a model that will lead to a useful solution.

Evaluation

Linear programming has found wide use in distribution, location, allocation, replacement, product mix, and planning models. As in virtually every other mathematical model used in facilities design, linear programming lacks a valid unit of measurement. In most problems, time or costs are the values optimized but these values are usually arbitrarily chosen —so it may be questionable if time or costs were the best measurement to use.

The mathematical computations in linear programming are relatively simple and can easily be accomplished manually for small or medium problems. Large problems frequently require the use of a computer to handle the large volume of computations.

Assignment Technique

The assignment technique is a special case of the general linear programming procedures, in which it is usually desired to assign n jobs to n facilities. The effectiveness of each facility for each job is given, and the objective is to optimize the measure of effectiveness in assigning each facility to one job, only. Since one item can be assigned to one and only one box, the assignment problem can be expressed mathematically as that of job optimizing the effectiveness function.

$$E = \sum_{i=j}^{n} \sum_{j=1}^{n} e_{ij}x_{ij}$$

subject to the constraints

$$\sum_{i=1}^{n} x_{ij} = 1 \qquad j = 1, 2, \ldots, n$$

$$\sum_{j=i}^{n} x_{ij} = 1 \qquad i = 1, 2, \ldots, n$$

As in the linear programming technique, optimization will require the minimization or maximization of the measure of effectiveness chosen. The user of the assignment technique has control of the assignment x_{ij}, but the effectiveness coefficients, e_{ij}, are not directly under his control.

Although the assignment technique may also be solved by the simplex method, the most efficient routine to date for solving the assignment technique was first proposed by Kuhn and is known as the "Hungarian method." This method requires that the problem be set up in the form of a square effectiveness matrix. However, problems of a matrix form that is not square, or which have prohibited assignments, are often encountered and may be converted into a square matrix.

Example

Management wants to add three new pieces of equipment, say A, B, and C, to an existing layout. The product size is such that a lift truck can carry only one at a time. Truck movement is restricted by aisles to rectangular directions. Figure 10–1 shows the candidate locations for the possible new machines at X, Y, and Z. It also shows the existing machines and their locations as 1, 2, 3, 4, and 5.

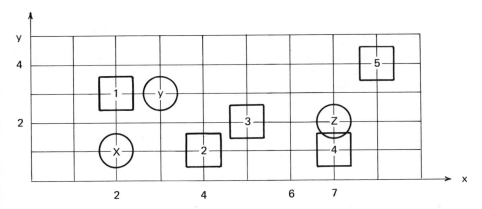

Fig. 10–1. Squares show the locations of existing machines; the circles indicate the candidate areas.

Table 10–1 gives the expected traffic between the new and existing machines. Notice that each of the new machines does not have a material-handling relationship with all of the existing machines.

Table 10–1.   Traffic Matrix

New Machines	1	Existing Machines 2	3	4	5
A	25	8	4	0	30
B	0	7	10	12	8
C	8	5	60	0	16

Taking rectangular distances from Figure 10–1 yields the following distance matrix:

Table 10–2.   Distance Matrix Developed from Figure 10–1

Candidate Areas

Existing Machines	X	Y	Z
1	2	1	6
2	2	3	4
3	4	3	2
4	6	7	2
5	9	6	3

Matrix multiplication of the traffic matrix and distance matrix develops the effectiveness matrix:

$$\begin{bmatrix} 25 & 8 & 4 & 0 & 30 \\ 0 & 7 & 10 & 12 & 8 \\ 8 & 5 & 60 & 0 & 16 \end{bmatrix} \begin{bmatrix} 2 & 1 & 6 \\ 2 & 3 & 4 \\ 4 & 3 & 2 \\ 6 & 7 & 2 \\ 9 & 6 & 3 \end{bmatrix} = \begin{bmatrix} 352 & 241 & 280 \\ 208 & 183 & 96 \\ 410 & 209 & 236 \end{bmatrix}$$

In terms of the layout problem, this matrix multiplication operation "says," if new machine A is placed in candidate area X, the measure of effectiveness will be:

$$25(2) + 8(2) + 4(4) + 0(6) + 30(9) = 352 \text{ handling unit-feet/time unit}$$

Figure 10–2 puts the effectiveness matrix into the context of the problem and shows the results of application of the Hungarian method.

Candidate Areas

		X	Y	Z		X	Y	Z
New	A	352	241	280		[0]	⊠	39
Machines	B	208	183	96		1	87	[0]
	C	410	209	236		90	[0]	27

Fig. 10–2. Effectiveness matrix is shown on left. Other matrix indicates results from Hungarian method.

Therefore, a feasible and optimal layout solution is to:

Assign A to Candidate X
Assign B to Candidate Z
Assign C to Candidate Y

The problem-solving technique can easily be expanded to include any finite number of new machines to be located in the same number of candidate areas. The method is well suited to computer calculation.

Evaluation of Assignment Method

The assignment method has demonstrated value in certain types of handling and layout problems. The required mathematical data are relatively easy to apply. Situations involving unequal numbers of machines and candidate areas, as well as prohibited assignments, can be easily handled. However, this procedure does have limitations. It is not possible to consider cases where machines are not independent. If two machines are to have direct material handling contact, there is no way to incorporate this requirement into the model except by increasing generality.

Another shortcoming is the inability to consider the efficient use of floorspace. A small machine may be assigned to a large area, resulting in a large amount of wasted floorspace. This can be controlled partially in the cost matrix.

Finally, the assignment method is based on the assumption of deterministic traffic data. If the data are actually nearly deterministic, the procedure is satisfactory. However, if the traffic data are subject to relatively large random variation, the solution may not be optimum at all times since the layout solution is sensitive to variation in traffic.

TRANSPORTATION PROGRAMMING

The transportation problem deals with the distribution of a single commodity from various sources of supply to various points of demand in such a manner that the total transportation costs are minimized. The cost may be expressed in terms of distance, time, or dollars.

The technique for solving this type of problem allows movement only from sources to destinations. The problem is structured as follows, with the notation explained as the structure is developed. There are m origins or sources, with each source i possessing a_i items, $(i = 1, 2, \ldots, m)$. There are n destinations, with destination j requiring b_j items, $(j = 1, 2, \ldots, n)$. There are $(m)(n)$ costs, one associated with moving one item from each source to each destination. The transportation problem is to empty the sources and fill the destinations so that the total cost is minimized.

The following conditions are required:

1. The total capacity of all sources must equal the total requirement of all destinations, or

$$\sum_{i=1}^{m} a_i = \sum_{j=1}^{n} b_j$$

2. The total number of items shipped to all destinations from any source must be equal to the capacity of that source, or

$$\sum_{j=1}^{n} X_{ij} = a_i ; \qquad i = 1, 2, \ldots, m$$

3. The demand of every destination must be fully satisfied by the total of the items shipped from all sources, or

$$\sum_{i=1}^{m} X_{ij} = b_j ; \qquad j = 1, 2, \ldots, n$$

4. The number of items shipped from any source must be non-negative, or

$$X_{ij} \geq 0 \text{ for all } i \text{ and } j.$$

The cost equation is of the form

$$Z = \sum_{i=1}^{m} \sum_{j=1}^{n} C_{ij} X_{ij} = C_{11} X_{11} + C_{12} X_{12} + \cdots + C_{mn} X_{mn}$$

where C_{ij} is the cost of shipping one item from source i to destination j and X_{ij} is the number of items shipped from i to j.

Example

In this example assume that an in-plant material-handling system consists of identical fork-lift trucks which move identical containers from three storage areas to four service areas. The containers are handled one at a time by a truck and are not reusable. The cost of handling is expressed in time units. A tabular statement of the problem is:

Source	Containers Available	Destination	Containers Required
1	10	1	9
2	5	2	4
3	8	3	3
		4	7
	23 Containers		23 Containers

Handling costs are as follows (in seconds):

$C_{11} = 62$	$C_{14} = 51$	$C_{23} = 66$	$C_{32} = 55$
$C_{12} = 18$	$C_{21} = 15$	$C_{24} = 54$	$C_{33} = 16$
$C_{13} = 39$	$C_{22} = 41$	$C_{31} = 37$	$C_{34} = 26$

The problem is put into matrix form for solution as shown in Figure 10–3. The numbers in the small boxes are the handling costs, C_{ij}. All the stated conditions are satisfied and the problem is ready for solution.

Destination	A	B	C	TOTALS
1	62	15	37	9
2	18	41	55	4
3	39	66	16	3
4	51	54	26	7
TOTALS	10	5	8	23

Fig. 10–3. Transportation problem in matrix form with costs included.

The solution procedure used here (Figure 10–4) is an adaptation of the Vogel approximation method as described by Sasieni (2):

Destination	A	B	C	TOTALS
1	62 / 3	15 / 5	37 / 1	9
2	18 / 4	41	55	4
3	39 / 3	66	16	3
4	51	54	26 / 7	7
TOTALS	10	5	8	23

Fig. 10–4. Solution to the transportation problem.

Metzger (1) approaches the in-plant material handling problem in a different way. The same assumptions regarding the types of trucks and containers as in the previous illustration apply except that the containers are not expendable and are subsequently removed from the delivery point for re-use. In this problem some departments always send out filled containers while others always receive filled containers. The material handling activity must not only distribute the filled containers but also take care of the empty containers. Metzger states the problem as one of determining the most economical distribution of empty containers.

Evaluation of the Transportation Problem

The transportation programming model was originally developed to calculate minimum cost schedules for moving goods from warehouses to destinations. Many large plants have a similar problem on a smaller scale such as distributing parts and supplies from storage areas to assembly areas. Manpower or personnel assignments, machine loading, and other problems have algebraic equations that are identical in form to those of the transportation programming technique. The technique as a distribution problem permits shipment only from source to destination which may not be realistic in all cases. The number of applications of transportation programming to facility design problems has been limited but the opportunities are there.

The approach used by Metzger is currently in wide use, as attested by the many cases which have been published. The example used here illustrates a very important aspect of the transportation problem, namely, that mathematical programming is usually applicable to only a relatively small portion of the total problem. One of the really serious shortcomings associated with the transportation problem, which is shared by virtually every other mathematical model in material handling, is the lack of a really valid unit of value measurement. Time was the value measure optimized in this example, but it is questionable if time is the best measure to use. The same question applies to the other readily available units of measure.

The demonstrated usefulness of the transportation problem solution justifies further research into its application to material handling. The solution procedure is simple and can easily be done manually for most small- to medium-size problems. Large problems can be easily solved on a computer.

TRANSSHIPMENT PROGRAMMING

The typical, or "standard" transportation problem permits shipment only from source to destination. Transshipment problems include the possibility of any source or destination acting as an intermediate point in seeking an optimal solution. Shipments are not restricted to direct connections between origins and destinations but may follow any sequence. This is far more realistic in a distribution problem since it is common for destinations to transship material to other destinations in order to meet abnormal demands in the other destinations. In such a case a location may serve as both a source and as a destination and the distinction as to which it should be designated may not be clear.

An ordinary m-source and n-destination transportation problem, when converted into a transshipment problem by removing the restrictions on the sources and destinations to permit them to receive as well as send, becomes one of $m + n$ sources and $m + n$ destinations (3). Changing from an ordinary transportation problem to a transshipment problem results in a larger problem, but it can still be solved by the standard transportation method, with a few small changes.

To set up the transshipment problem, designate the sources and destinations as terminals (T). As before, the amount shipped from T_i to T_j is X_{ij} with cost per unit c_{ij}. Obviously $X_{ii} = c_{ii} = 0$ since no terminal will ship to itself. Assume that at m terminals the total shipped out exceeds the total shipped in and at the remaining n terminals the total inshipment exceeds the total outshipment. Let the total inshipment at $T_1, T_2, \ldots, T_m$ be $t_1, t_2, \ldots, t_m$, respectively, and the total outshipment at $T_{m+1}, T_{m+2}, \ldots, T_{m+n}$ be $t_{m+1}, t_{m+2}, \ldots, t_{m+n}$, respectively. The constraints for the transshipment problem are

$$\sum_{i=1}^{m} a_i = \sum_{j=m+1}^{m+n} b_j$$

where a_i is the excess of outshipment over inshipment at terminal i, and b_j is the excess of inshipments over outshipments at terminal j. The objective, or total cost, function is

$$Z = \sum_{i=1}^{m+n} \sum_{j=1}^{m+n} c_{ij} X_{ij}$$

The differences in the transshipment problem and an $m + n$ square transportation problem are:

(1) in the transshipment constraints there are no X_{ii} terms and
(2) $b_j = 0$ for $j = 1, 2, \ldots, m$ and $a_i = 0$ for $i = m + 1, m + 2, \ldots, m + n$.

The t_i and t_j in these constraints may be considered as algebraic substitutes for X_{ii} and X_{jj} (4). The transshipment problem has the form shown in Table 10–3. All t's are placed on the main diagonal with a negative sign so that the t's, as well as the X_{ij}'s, may be constrained to non-negative values. The procedure for solving this problem is identical with that used for solving a transportation problem.

Example

The transportation problem previously used can be solved as a transshipment problem with the addition of the cost (time) data shown in Table 10–4.

Figure 10–5 shows the tableau resulting from the addition of these data to the solution to the foregoing transportation problem. Computation reveals that the old solution is not optimal for the transshipment problem. Figure 10–6 shows the optimal solution obtained by this technique.

Table 10–3. Format for the Transshipment Problem

Terminals		t_j			Capacity
		$1 \ldots m$	$m+1$	$m+n$	
	1	$-t_i \ldots X_{im}$	$X_{i,m+1} \ldots$	$X_{i,m+n}$	a_1
	.	. .		. .	.
	.	. .		. .	.
	.	. .		. .	.
t_i	m	$X_{m,1} \ldots -t_m$	$X_{m,m+1} \ldots$	$X_{m,m+n}$	a_n
	$m+1$	$X_{m+1,1} \quad X_{m+1,m}$	$-t_{m+1} \ldots$	$X_{m+1,m+n}$	0
	.	. .		. .	.
	.	. .		. .	.
	.	. .		. .	.
	$m+n$	$X_{m+n,1} \quad X_{m+n,m}$	$X_{m+n,m+1}$	$-t_{m+n}$	0
Requirement		$0 \ldots 0$	$b_{m+1} \ldots$	b_{m+n}	$\sum a_i = \sum b_j$

Table 10–4. Inter-Terminal Time Values for Transshipment Problem

		To						To		
		1	2	3	4			A	B	C
	1	0	22	73	54		A	0	33	59
From	2	22	0	38	42	From	B	33	0	66
	3	73	38	0	31		C	59	66	0
	4	54	42	31	0			Sources		

Destinations

A graphical representation of the optimum flow provided by the solutions to the transportation problem and the transshipment problem is shown in Figure 10–7. The total time (cost) required by the two solutions is not the same. The transportation problem required

$$Z = \sum_{j=1}^{n} \sum_{i=1}^{m} X_{ij}C_{ij} = 3(62) + 5(15) + 1(37) + 4(18) + 3(39)$$
$$+ 7(26) = 669 \text{ time units}$$

while the transshipment problem required

$$Z = 8(18) + 2(39) + 5(15) + 1(16) + 7(26) + 4(22) = 583 \text{ time units}$$

a saving of 86 time units.

TERMINALS	$T_1(A)$	$T_2(B)$	$T_3(C)$	$T_4(1)$	$T_5(2)$	$T_6(3)$	$T_7(4)$	CAPACITY
$T_1(A)$	0 / −0	33	59	62 / 3	18 / 4	39 / 3	51	10
$T_2(B)$	33	0 / −0	66	15 / 5	41	66	54	5
$T_3(C)$	59	66	0 / −0	37 / 1	55	16	26 / 7	8
$T_4(1)$	62	15	37	0 / −0	22	73	54	0
$T_5(2)$	18	41	55	22	0 / −0	38	42	0 ;
$T_6(3)$	39	66	16	73	38	0 / −0	31	0
$T_7(4)$	51	54	26	54	42	31	0	
REQUIREMENT	0	0	0	9	4	3	7	23

Fig. 10–5. Tableau of transshipment problem containing transportation problem solution.

TERMINALS	$T_1(A)$	$T_2(B)$	$T_3(C)$	$T_4(1)$	$T_5(2)$	$T_6(3)$	$T_7(4)$	CAPACITY
$T_1(A)$	0 / −0	33	59	62	18 / 8	39 / 2	51	10
$T_2(B)$	33	0 / −0	66	15 / 5	41	66	54	5
$T_3(C)$	59	66	0 / −0	37	55	16 / 1	26 / 7	8
$T_4(1)$	62	15	37	0 / −0	22	73	54	0
$T_5(2)$	18	41	55	22 / 4	0 / −4	38	42	0
$T_6(3)$	39	66	16	73	38	0 / −0	31	0
$T_7(4)$	51	54	26	54	42	31	0 / −0	
REQUIREMENT	0	0	0	9	4	3	7	23

Fig. 10–6. Tableau of optimum solution to transshipment problem.

Evaluation of the Transshipment Problem

The greatest advantage the transshipment problem has over the transportation problem is its much more realistic statement of the distribution problem. It is very well suited for comparing alternative locations of terminals such as departments or machines, though a dif-

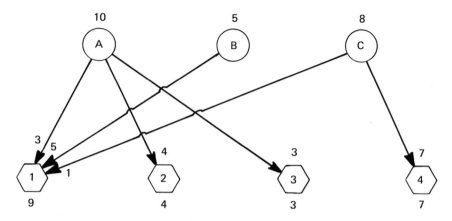

Transportation Solution

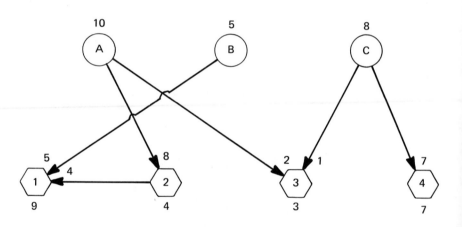

Transshipment Solution

Fig. 10–7. Comparison of optimum solutions to transportation and trans-shipment problems.

ferent tableau must be solved for each alternative. Similarly, it can be used to decide which of a limited number of candidate areas to use as terminals or machine locations based on some cost measure.

The major disadvantage of the model is that it requires about twice as large a solution matrix as does the transportation problem. However, this disadvantage is not serious in view of the ease of finding a solution by computer programs.

In summary, the transshipment programming procedure appears to be an excellent tool for use in quantitative analysis of material handling problems. However, there is at present little published information on actual problems solved or applications of the technique.

THE TRAVELING SALESMAN TECHNIQUE

A "traveling salesman" problem solution involves finding an optimal route between a series of locations under the condition that each location is visited only once and a return is made to the point of origin, without backtracking. An optimal route is defined as one for which either total distance traveled, total cost of travel, or total time of travel, is a minimum. The problem takes its name from the often-cited illustration of the traveling salesman who starts from home and visits $n - 1$ specified locations before returning home. It is a routing problem which involves sequencing locations in order to minimize the travel between them.

The problem of locating facilities can be expressed in certain cases as a variation of the traveling salesman problem. Other variations include the truck dispatching problem, the combinatorial problem, and some machine sequencing problems.

Analysis of the Problem

Although efficient methods and procedures are known for solution of problems of a similar nature, such as assignment and transportation problems, there is less known about efficient methods for solving the traveling salesman problem.

The problem may be stated as follows:
Determine

$$X_{ij}(i, j = 1, 2, \ldots, n)$$

which minimize

$$T = \sum_{ij} a_{ij} X_{ij}$$

subject to

$$X_{ij} = (X_{ij})^2, \text{ i.e., } X_{ij} \text{ is either 0 or 1.}$$

$$\sum X_{ij} = \sum_j X_{ij} = 1$$

$$X_{i_1 i_2} + X_{i_2 i_3} + \cdots + X_{1_{r-1} i_r} + X_{i_r i_1} \leq r - 1$$

$$X_{ii} = 0$$

where a_{ij} are specified real numbers representing cost or distance, X_{ij} is 0 or 1 and $(i_1, i_2, \ldots, i_r)$ is a permutation of the integers 1 through r. The problem is one of finding a permutation $P = (1, i_2, \ldots, i_n)$ of the integers from 1 through n such that the value of the quantity

$$a_{1i_2} + a_{i_2i_3} + \cdots + a_{i_n1}$$

is minimized.

In general there are $(n-1)!$ possible routes which can be taken when visiting $n - 1$ locations once each and returning to the point of origin. The number of possibilities for a 15-location tour would be 653,837,184,000 different routes. The real problem is to find an *efficient* method of selecting the optimum sequence since even a modern high-speed computer would require an unreasonable amount of time to evaluate each permutation in a problem as small as ten locations.

At the present time, there is relatively little theory on the travelling salesman problem. In fact, early attempts at solution yielded only such general theorems as: "In the Euclidean plane, the minimal path does not intersect itself" (5).

Methods of solving the problem can be sub-divided into three major segments: beginning point, solution generation, and termination rule. When the latter step results in stopping only if a tour is optimal, the method is referred to as *exact*. If the rule results in an iteration stopping with less than an optimal tour, the method is called *approximate*.

One of the procedures that leads to a "near-optimal" solution, developed by Dantzig, Fulkerson, and Johnson (6), outlines a linear programming approach that sometimes enables one to find an optimum route and prove it so. Their approach is to start with a small number of linear constraints that are satisfied by all paths. The problem is then solved by the standard simplex technique. If the solution is not a "tour," that is, does not visit every location once with no overlap or back-tracking, new constraints are added to eliminate the solution and obtain a new one. This continues until a "near-optimal" solution is reached and then each remaining possibility is evaluated manually, using a map.

Barachet (7) has developed an intuitive procedure which takes a feasible solution and obtains successively shorter routes by applying the following theorems:

1. A route of minimum length does not cross itself.
2. If the protruding angles formed by three consecutive sections are obtuse angles, these three sections make up a route of minimum length.
3. If all the points make up a convex polygon, the route of minimum length corresponds to this convex polygon.

4. A circuit including $N-k$ consecutive sections which are common with a minimum circuit obtained for the case of K-consecutive sections is longer than the latter or equal to it.

Barachet points out that the procedure is essentially intuitive and leaves doubt as to whether or not the minimum route will be obtained.

Croes (8) has an interactive procedure similar to the approaches used by Dantzig and by Barachet, though it is less intuitive than Barachet's methods. It is cumbersome for computer computation.

Dacey (9) has developed a procedure for obtaining an initial near-optimal feasible solution which will occasionally also yield an optimal solution. If a solution is not optimal, better solutions can be obtained by one of the previous methods.

A rule of thumb for obtaining approximate solutions to the problem is to use the "nearest location" approach. The criterion is simply to select the nearest unvisited location as the next location to visit. Good results are frequently obtained by this method.

Example

This example is chosen to show the similarity and differences between the traveling salesman problem and a transportation or assignment problem. In the transportation problem the permutations need not be cyclic but in the traveling salesman problem they must be. A solution to the assignment problem will also be a solution to the traveling salesman problem if, and only if, the assignment matrix is symmetric and the elements on the main diagonal are all zero.

Given the matrix of transportation costs below (10), it is desired to determine the minimum trip cost from some starting location through each other location once and back to the origin (Figure 10–8). The infinite costs on the main diagonal are to insure that no assignment will be made there. Subtracting the minimum from each row and column yields Figure 10–9.

		To				
		A_1	A_2	A_3	A_4	A_5
	A_1	∞	2	5	7	1
	A_2	6	∞	3	8	2
From	A_3	8	7	∞	4	7
	A_4	12	4	6	∞	5
	A_5	1	3	2	8	∞

Fig. 10–8. Cost matrix of relationships between locations.

The matrix is examined for some "next best" solutions to the assignment problem to try to find one that satisfies the additional restrictions. The smallest non-zero element is 1, so each element of value 1 has its row and column deleted and the resulting 4 × 4 matrix is searched for an optimal allocation solution and a feasible traveling salesman solution.

		A_1	A_2	A_3	A_4	A_5
	A_1	∞	1	3	6	0
	A_2	4	∞	0	6	0
From	A_3	4	3	∞	0	3
	A_4	8	0	1	∞	1
	A_5	0	2	0	7	∞

Fig. 10–9. Solution to assignment problem.

The best solution is found to be Figure 10–10. The best sequence is

$$A_5 \rightarrow A_1 \rightarrow A_2 \rightarrow A_3 \rightarrow A_4 \rightarrow A_5$$

and the total cost is $1 + 2 + 3 + 4 + 5 = 15$.

		A_1	A_2	A_3	A_4	A_5
	A_1	∞	1	3	6	0
	A_2	4	∞	0	6	0
From	A_3	4	3	∞	0	3
	A_4	8	0	1	∞	1
	A_5	0	2	0	7	∞

Fig. 10–10. Solution to traveling salesman problem.

Evaluation

The traveling salesman problem is useful in problems such as truck dispatching, determining the assignment of machines to candidate locations if the product is manufactured in cyclic sequence, or for laying out an assembly line so that time is minimized or the production rate maximized. Another valuable use is in determining the most economical sequence of n operations to be done in some sequence on a single machine. However, the lack of an uncomplicated general solution procedure that guarantees an optimal solution may reduce the importance of the traveling salesman procedure in the area of facility design. There are a few published examples where the application of some solution procedure to a traveling salesman-type problem has yielded substantially good results. One of the best is a case study by Hare and Hugli dealing with the production of kitchen units (11). The reader is advised to check current technical literature for the most recent developments in solving the traveling salesman problem, since later efforts have resulted in better solution procedures than are documented in most text books.

However, the technique does have a significant value in special cases where the product passes through a series of operations without backtracking and the problem is to determine the sequence which minimizes the distance, time, or cost of travel.

INTEGER PROGRAMMING

The integer programming technique is a special case of the general linear programming procedure that requires the variables to take on only integral values. The problem is called an all integer problem if all the variables are restricted to integer values and a mixed integer problem when only certain specific variables must be integers. The integer problem retains the usual linear constraints of the linear programming problem.

Contrary to intuition, rounding the variables of an optimum simplex solution to the nearest integer does not provide an optimum integer solution (12), for example, a routing problem solution which states that a particular truck should make 6.39 trips. The problem of calculating feasible integral solutions remained unsolved until 1958 when Ralph Gomory (13) devised an algorithm for producing optimum integral solutions to all integer programming problems.

The Add K Machines Model

The formulation of the layout program requires the definition of the integer, variables W_{ij} and Z_{ij}, which are restricted to values of zero or one as follows:

$$W_{ij} = \begin{cases} 1 \text{ if } j\text{th new machine is located at } x = i \\ \\ 0, \text{ otherwise} \end{cases}$$

$$Z_{ij} = \begin{cases} 1 \text{ if } j\text{th new machine is located at } y = i \\ \\ 0, \text{ otherwise} \end{cases}$$

The objective function for adding two new machines to an existing layout is

$$\text{Min } F = \sum_{j=1}^{K} \left\{ \sum_{i=1}^{N_x} C_{ij} W_{ij} + \sum_{i=1}^{N_y} d_{ij} Z_{ij} \right\}$$

where N_x = number of discrete units in the x direction contained in the candidate area.

N_y = number of discrete units in the y direction contained in the candidate area.

C_{ij} = total traffic-distance in x direction for jth new machine located at $x = i$.

d_{ij} = total traffic-distance in y direction for jth new machine located at $y = i$.

This objective function is subject to restrictions which:

1. Insure that the variables take on only values of zero or one, and
2. Guarantee that no two machines are placed on top of one another.

The first restriction is stated as

$$\sum_{i=1}^{N_x} W_{ij} = 1 \qquad \text{for } j = 1, 2, \ldots, K$$

$$W_{ij} \leq 1 \qquad \text{for } i = 1, 2, \ldots, N_x \quad \text{and} \quad j = 1, 2, \ldots, K$$

$$\sum_{i=1}^{N_y} Z_{ij} = 1 \qquad \text{for } j = 1, 2, \ldots, K$$

$$Z_{ij} \leq 1 \qquad \text{for } i = 1, 2, \ldots, N_y \quad \text{and} \quad j = 1, 2, \ldots, K$$

The constraints insuring that no two machines are assigned the same location are:

$$\sum_{j=1}^{K} W_{ij} \leq 1 \qquad \text{for } i = 1, 2, \ldots, N_x$$

$$\sum_{j=1}^{K} Z_{ij} \leq 1 \qquad \text{for } i = 1, 2, \ldots, N_y$$

There is an assumption that no new machine will have length longer than the discrete interval or width wider than the discrete interval. In other words, this procedure assumes that any new machine will require not more than one discrete interval.

Because of the current relative lack of applicability of this technique, no example will be given. Those readers desiring more information should check items 14, 15, and 16 in the bibliography at the end of the chapter.

Evaluation

Integer programming is not widely used in the facility design area. Although it is a very promising tool, more efficient methods are needed to obtain solutions, as even the small problems generally require the use of a computer. It is useful, however, when many machines must be arranged in a limited number of candidate areas. Any type of movement may be used with this model since it is not restricted to straight line or rectangular movement. The model lends itself to computer calculation with existing algorithms, but more efficient computer programs are needed. Manual computation is quite tedious and cumbersome. Further work in developing more efficient computer algorithms should lead to an even more useful model. The model guarantees an optimum solution.

DYNAMIC PROGRAMMING

Dynamic programming is a relatively new technique concerned with decision situations involving effectiveness functions of many variables which may be subject to constraints. An essential difference between dynamic programming and other approaches is that the dynamic programming approach changes one problem in n variables into n problems, each in one variable. As a result, problems exhibiting a large number of variables are reduced to a sequence of problems with only a single variable.

Dynamic programming is a computational technique developed to a considerable extent by Richard Bellman (17) and his associates at the Rand Corporation.

Consider a discrete process in one dimension, say x, with a finite number of stages, say n. Decisions are successively made, one at each stage, and the process assumes a different state at each stage. Enumerate the stages in a fixed order, 1, 2, . . . , n. The first decision q_n is taken when the process is in the nth stage. The state of the process is denoted by p_n. As a result of the decision q_n, the process attains the state p_{n-1} and $n - 1$ stages remain. When the process is in state p_i, there are i stages remaining. The state p_i is a result of the decision q_{i+1} when the process was in the state p_{i+1}. The state p_i may be expressed as a function of p_{i+1} and q_{i+1} as:

$$p_i = T(p_{i+1}, q_{i+1})$$

The Return Function

The evaluation of a sequence of decisions requires a criterion as a basis of evaluation. A quantity called the return function, which may be return on investment, profit, savings in time, distance, money, or any given value measure, measures the return from a sequence of decisions. The return function is dependent upon a series of states and decisions and may be expressed as

$$R(p_1, p_2, \ldots, p_n; q_i, q_2, \ldots, q_n)$$

The problem is to maximize or minimize the return function. The total return from the sequence of decisions depends upon the returns associated with each individual decision, where the returns are denoted by $g_1(p_1,q_1)$, $g_2(p_2,q_2)$, . . . , $g_n(p_n,q_n)$.

The following assumptions are made:

1. The returns from all individual decisions can be interpreted in terms of a common parameter.
2. The total return of the sequence of decisions is a sum of the individual returns.

Therefore,

$$R(p_1, p_2, \ldots, p_n; q_1, q_2, \ldots, q_n) = g_1(p_1, q_1)$$
$$+ q_2(p_2, q_2) + \cdots + g_n(p_n, q_n)$$

The Functional Equations

In place of considering a particular quantity of resources and a fixed number of activities, the return function considers the entire family of such problems in which the number of resources may assume any positive value and n may assume any integer value.

What seems to be a static process is artificially given a time-like property by requiring the allocations to be made one at a time. Viewed in this way, the allocation process appears to be dynamic.

The maximum of $R(p_1,p_2, \ldots, p_n; q_1,q_2 \ldots, q_n)$ depends upon p_n and n. Allowing p_n to range over $n = 1,2, \ldots$, a sequence of functions, $\{f_n(p_n)\}$ is generated, defined by the relation

$$f_n(p_n) = \max_{q_1, q_2, \ldots, q_n} [g_1(p_1, q_1) + g_2(p_2, q_2) + \cdots + g_n(p_n, q_n)]$$
$$i = 1, 2, \ldots n, n = 1, 2, \ldots, n$$

Consider the decision q_n. Associated with the decision is the return $g_n(p_n,q_n)$. As a result of the decision, the process changes from p_n to p_{n-1} and now has only $n-1$ stages. The return from the remaining $n-1$ decisions must also be a maximum with an initial state p_{n-1}. This may be expressed as

$$f_n(p_n) = \max_{q_n} [g_n(p_n, q_n) + f_{n-1}\{T(p_n, q_n)\}]$$

which is a basic functional equation in a general form.

The Optimality Principle

The preceding development has depended on a very general technique called *The Principle of Optimality* (17):

An optimal policy has the property that whatever the initial state and initial decision are, the remaining decisions must constitute an optimal policy with regard to the state resulting from the first decision.

The Computational Scheme

Allow p_n to take values at intervals, say Δ, over a certain useful range; p_n may take values $\Delta, 2\Delta, \ldots, k\Delta$. This is followed by computations of $f_n(p_n)$, $n = 1,2,3, \ldots$. For $p_n = k$, using the relation

$$f_1(k) = \max_{q_1} [g_1(k, q_1)]$$

$f_1(\Delta), f_1(2\Delta), \ldots$, are calculated with k taking values $\Delta, 2\Delta, \ldots$. The values of $f_1(\Delta), f_1(2\Delta), \ldots$, and the corresponding decisions $q_1, q_2, \ldots$, are recorded and retained.

Using the equation

$$f_n(p_n) = \max_{q_n} [g_n(p_n, q_2) + f_{n-1}(p_{n-1})]$$

the values of $f_2(\Delta), f_2(2\Delta), \ldots$, are computed, retaining the maximum value and the corresponding q_2 values. The procedure is repeated with $n = 3,4, \ldots$.

The typical tabulation takes the form shown in Table 10–5.

Table 10–5. Tabulation of Computational Algorithm

P_n	q_1	$f_1(p_n)$	q_2	$f_2(p_n)$	q_3	$f_3(q_n)$	$\cdots$	q_n	$\cdots$	$f_n(p_n)$
o										
Δ										
2Δ										
.										
.										
.										
$k\Delta$										

Example

Assume a problem of the transportation type (18) with the addition of quadratic costs of shipping and a "set-up cost" for shipment from a source to a destination. The term "set-up cost" means a cost which is independent of the quantity shipped, but which is not incurred if nothing is sent. The cost and demand values are shown in Table 10–6.

Table 10–6. Cost Values Between Sources and Destinations

To Destination	From Source 1			From Source 2			Demand
	Set-Up	x	x^2	Set-Up	x	x^2	
1		1.0		2	3.1		10
2	1	2.0			4.1		25
3		3.0	0.01		2.1	4	45
4		1.5			1.1	0.1	15
5		2.5			2.6		5
6	10	5.0	−0.01		3.0		15
7		3.0		5	1.0	0.2	20
8		6.0			2.0		15
9	8	6.0	−0.05		2.0		10
10		6.0			5.0	0.01	20

Each function $q_{ij}(X)$, where X is the number of items shipped, has the form

$$g_{jj}(X) = A_{ij}X + B_{ij}X + C_{ij}(X)$$

where C_{ij} = "set-up" cost. $C_{ij} = 0$ if $X = 0$; $= C_{ij}$ for $X > 0$.
A_{ij} = cost of shipping one unit from source i to destination j.
B_{ij} = quadratic cost factor of shipping one unit from source i to destination j.

Thus, the cost of sending X items from Source 1 to Destination 3 is $3X + 0.01X^2$ and from Source 1 to Destination 6 is $5.0X - 0.10X^2 + 10$ if $X > 0$, 0 if $X = 0$.

If 100 units are to be shipped from Source 1 and 80 units from Source 2, the optimal solution is shown in Table 10–7. The calculation required two minutes of computing time and four minutes of output time on the RAND Johnniac computer.

Evaluation

The dynamic programming technique offers considerable advantage over conventional mathematical procedures in solving multistage decision problems. By its nature the approach yields relative maxima or minima. In addition, the technique provides a family of optimization functions which can be used with a wide range of problems.

The functional equations technique provides a computational procedure which retains the advantages of the method of direct enumera-

**Table 10–7.   Solution to the Transportation Problem
Using Dynamic Programming**

To Destination	From Source 1	From Source 2	Cost	Cumulative Cost
1	10	0	$ 10.00	$ 10.00
2	25	0	51.00	61.00
3	5	40	99.25	160.25
4	15	0	22.50	182.75
5	5	0	12.50	195.25
6	0	15	45.00	240.25
7	20	0	60.00	300.25
8	0	15	30.00	330.25
9	0	10	20.00	350.25
10	20	0	120.00	470.25

tion and simultaneously eliminates the major bulk of the computations encountered in direct enumeration.

Most, if not all, problems encountered in facilities planning will be multidimensional. That is, more than one resource and constraint will be involved. The computations involved in multidimensional problems are very tedious so that a computer is desirable for most problems of practical size. A number of computer programs are available.

The literature contains very few applications of dynamic programming to either material handling or plant layout activities. However, the technique appears to be particularly potent for work in this area due to the ability to reduce the number of variables to controllable proportions.

QUEUING THEORY

A number of models of material handling flow systems include factors which are characterized by a distribution of a random variable. The most general, and probably most effective, analytical approach to such random flow systems is waiting line analysis, or queuing theory. Queuing theory refers to the mathematical and physical investigation of a class of problems characterized by several attributes: (1) there is an input of units entering the system; (2) the units moving through the system are discrete; (3) the units which have begun to require service are ordered in some fashion and receive service in that order; (4) a mechanism exists that governs the time at which a unit receiving service has its service terminated; and (5) at least one of the two mechanisms, arrival or service, is not completely determined, but can be considered a probabilistic system of some sort.

The reason the variables are random, rather than functionally dependent on time, is that arrivals are generally random events in time (that is, the exact instant they will occur is unpredictable) and service times are also random variables. Therefore, most applications of waiting line theory are concerned with averages, such as the average length of the line at any instant, and the average idle time of the service facility in a given time period. Though the times of arrivals and departures cannot be predicted with exactness, they can be predicted in terms of means, variances, and probabilities.

The Single-Channel Waiting Line

A single-channel waiting line consists of a single line formed in front of a single-service mechanism. In a material handling system, this situation might be represented by units of product brought into live storage prior to an operation. In general, the mean time of an operation can be controlled but the time for any particular cycle is subject to uncontrollable random fluctuation. Also, the mean rate at which units arrive can be controlled, but again, there will be random fluctuations beyond control.

The arrival process is analyzed in detail by Morris (19) and Faller (20). The following is a tabulation of useful relationships taken from Sasieni (21) where $1/\lambda$ is the mean time between arrivals and $1/\mu$ is the mean service time per unit.

$$E(m) = \frac{\lambda^2}{\mu(\mu - \lambda)} \quad \text{average queue length}$$

$$E(m|m > 0) = \frac{\mu}{\mu - \lambda} \quad \text{average length of non-empty queues}$$

$$E(n) = \frac{\lambda}{\mu - \lambda} \quad \text{average number of units in system}$$

$$E(w) = \frac{\lambda}{\mu(\mu - \lambda)} \quad \text{average waiting time of an arrival}$$

$$E(w|w > o) = \frac{1}{\mu - \lambda} \quad \text{average waiting time of an arrival that waits}$$

$$E(v) = \frac{1}{\mu - \lambda} \quad \text{average time an arrival spends in the system}$$

$$\sigma_n^2 = \frac{\lambda\mu}{(\mu - \lambda)^2} \quad \text{the variance of } n$$

All these relationships assume that arrivals occur in Poisson fashion, service times occur in exponential fashion, and the system is in a steady-state condition.

A queuing model can be generalized to make λ and μ functions of the number of units in the system and also to describe a system in which the largest permissible number of units in the system is N. The procedure for generalizing is included in the reference by Morris. The generalized models are similar to but more complex than the model cited here. For example, the expected number of units in a system which can contain at most N units is

$$E(n) = \left\{ \frac{\left[1 - (N + 1)\left(\frac{\lambda}{\mu}\right)^{N} + N \left(\frac{\lambda}{\mu}\right)^{N+1} \right]}{\left(\frac{\mu - \lambda}{\mu}\right)\left[1 - \left(\frac{\lambda}{\mu}\right)^{N+1} \right]} \right\} \frac{\lambda}{\mu}$$

and the same assumptions hold as before. Unless N is relatively small, the generalized models will yield results very little different from the simpler models given earlier.

Example

Any time services are demanded in a non-regular manner, or arrivals occur in a non-regular manner, the system capacity can be overtaxed from time to time. An example is the case where the output of one or more machines is the input of another machine. If the output of the first machine is approximated by a Poisson distribution and the process is in steady state, then these equations can be applied to determine the storage capacity required between machines. Assume that records show that the first machine has an output of 2.2 units per minute on the average and the output rate of the second machine is 2.5 units per minute on the average. If there are no items lost in machine two, that is, the input equals the output, then the servicing rate, μ, is 2.5 units per minute and the arrival rate, λ, is 2.2 units per minute. Then $E(n) = \dfrac{\lambda}{\mu - \lambda} = \dfrac{2.2}{2.5 - 2.2} = 7.33$ units, the average number of units in the system. The variance is $\sigma_n^2 = \dfrac{\lambda\mu}{(\mu - \lambda)^2} = \dfrac{(2.2)(2.5)}{(0.3)^2} = 61.1$ and the standard deviation is $\sqrt{\sigma_n^2} = 7.8$. A storage area large enough to accommodate

$$E(n) + 2(\sigma_n) = 7.33 + 2(7.8) = 22.9 \text{ units}$$

will be large enough to handle storage of units between machines 94 percent of the time (22). However, 6 percent of the time there will be congestion in the storage area.

Multi-Channel Waiting Lines

The preceding model has the disadvantage of not being completely realistic, though in many cases it serves well enough as an approximation. A more realistic model can be obtained by considering the case where a finite number of channels is available.

The assumptions used to obtain the single-channel model hold except that the number of service channels is greater than one. If all service channels are busy, the arriving unit joins a waiting line and waits until a channel is freed. This means that all incoming units have a common waiting line (23). A waiting line will exist only if the number of units n awaiting, or in, service is greater than k, the number of service channels available.

As long as at least one channel is free, the situation is exactly the same as the single-channel model. For varying n, the following situations arise:

$$n = o \qquad \lambda_n = \lambda \mu_n = 0$$
$$1 \leq n < k \qquad \lambda_n = \lambda \mu_n = n\mu$$
$$n \geq k \qquad \lambda_n = \lambda \mu_n = k\mu$$

In the special case $k = 1$, we obtain equations on page 344 which describe the system. For $1 \leq n < k$

$$P_n = \frac{1}{n!} \left(\frac{\lambda}{\mu} \right) P_0$$

and for $n \geq k$

$$P_n = \frac{1}{k! k^{n-k}} \left(\frac{\lambda}{\mu} \right)^n P_0$$

and

$$P_0 = \frac{1}{\left[\sum_{k=0}^{k-1} \frac{1}{n!} \left(\frac{\lambda}{\mu} \right)^n \right] + \frac{1}{k!} \left(\frac{\lambda}{\mu} \right)^k \frac{k\mu}{k\mu - \lambda}}$$

The above equations are valid only if $k > \dfrac{\lambda}{\mu}$; otherwise stability is never achieved and the queue builds up indefinitely. For the general case of k servicing channels, the probability of an arrival waiting is the probability that a given instant there are at least k units in the system.

$$P(n \geq k) = \sum_{n=k}^{\infty} P_n = \frac{\mu(\lambda/\mu)^k}{(k-1)!(k\mu - \lambda)} P_0$$

The formulas given below, expressed in terms of P_0 for brevity, are taken from Sasieni (24):

$$E(m) = \frac{\lambda\mu(\lambda/\mu)^k}{(k-1)!(k\mu-\lambda)^2} P_0 \qquad \text{(average queue length)}$$

$$E(n) = \frac{\lambda\mu(\lambda-\mu)^k}{(k-1)!(k\mu-\lambda)^2} P_0 + \frac{\lambda}{\mu} \qquad \text{(average number of units in system)}$$

$$E(w) = \frac{\mu(\lambda/\mu)^k}{(k-1)!(k\mu-\lambda)^2} P_0 \qquad \text{(average waiting time for arrival)}$$

$$E(v) = \frac{\mu(\lambda/\mu)^k}{(k-1)!(k\mu-\lambda)^2} P_0 + \frac{1}{\mu} \qquad \text{(average time an arrival spends in the system)}$$

Table 10–8 gives a numerical illustration of the case $k = 3$ and $\lambda/\mu = 2$.

Table 10–8.   Probability of n Units in System When $k = 3$ and $\lambda/\mu = 2$

n	0	1	2	3	4	5	6	7
Stations busy	0	1	2	3	3	3	3	3
Units waiting	0	0	0	0	1	2	3	4
P_n	0.111	0.222	0.222	0.148	0.099	0.066	0.044	0.029

Example

A production department has three identical machines in operation. Production units arrive in Poisson fashion at an average rate of 20 units per 8-hour day. The production rate of each machine has an exponential distribution, with mean service time of 40 minutes. Units are processed in the order of their appearance.

$$\lambda = \frac{20}{8} = 2.5 \text{ arrivals per hour}$$

$$\mu = \frac{60}{40} = 1.5 \text{ units serviced per hour}$$

$$P_0 = \frac{1}{1 + \frac{5}{3} + \frac{1}{2}\left(\frac{5}{3}\right)^2 + \frac{1}{6}\left(\frac{5}{3}\right)^3 \frac{9}{4}} = 24/139$$

The expected number of idle machines

$$3P_0 + 2P_1 + P_2 = 3(24/139) + 2(24/139)\left(\frac{5}{3}\right) + (24/139)\left(\frac{1}{2}\right)\left(\frac{5}{3}\right)^2 = 4/3$$

The probability of one idle machine at a specified instant is $(1/3)(4/3)$ $= 4/9$. The expected working time for one machine is $(1 - 4/9)8 =$ $(5/9)(8) = 40/9$ hours per day. The average time an arriving unit spends in the system is

$$E(v) = \frac{1.5(5/3)^3}{2[3(1.5) - 2.5]^2}(24/139) + \frac{1}{1.5} = 49.0 \text{ minutes}$$

Other values could be similarly determined and, with appropriate cost parameters, an optimum policy could be determined.

The models discussed here assume Poisson arrival and service distribution. However, there are other types of distributions associated with queuing lines. The Erlang family of distributions is probably the most common and is discussed in the cited literature.

Evaluation

The major problem involved in using queuing, or waiting line, theory is the assumption of a Poisson input, or arrival, rate and output, or service, rates. The question of how much error is introduced by this assumption is difficult to assess and where it occurs in the system is frequently hard to locate.

Waiting line analysis is a very well-developed field; what is presented here is only the barest introduction. The mathematical formulation of various models is widely published and understood. The application of queuing theory to material handling problems is not extensively published, except in conveyor theory. One of the difficulties appears to be that most practical applications require a considerable amount of accurate cost information which is difficult to obtain.

Useful application of queuing models requires, as do all mathematical models, a balance of experience in material handling and experience in mathematical analysis in order to achieve effective recommendations for the improvement of material handling systems. There are important insights into material handling procedures to be gained from the use of analytical methods in addition to the improvement expected as a result of applying the model.

In summary, in view of the vast quantity of literature published on queueing theory, the present most critical need is for the development of an understanding of the kind of cost information required to meaningfully apply optimization techniques. Very little of the current literature uses cost figures in conjunction with queuing models, therefore it is difficult to determine if the true value of queuing models in material handling is proportional to the literature generated about it. Certainly it appears to be a fruitful area for investigation with specific material handling objectives in mind.

CONVEYOR ANALYSIS

Conveyors comprise a large portion of the linkages between production centers in current production systems. Most are used for both transportation and in-process storage. Morris (25) classifies conveyors into four major categories:

1. Constant-speed, irreversible belt conveyors which simply transport and store material.

2. Controlled movement systems, which are reversible. These are operator controlled and move away from the work station for storage and into the work station for recovery.

3. Power and free systems, consisting of parts carriers which can be connected to and disconnected from the moving portion of the conveyor at will.

4. Closed-loop, irreversible, continuous operating systems with parts carriers which cannot be removed.

The first three types may be called open-loop systems and the fourth type a closed-loop system. The operating characteristics of the open-loop systems are quite easy to predict, on theoretical grounds at least, lending an aura of confidence to their use. Open-loop conveyors are generally quite flexible in use whereas closed-loop systems are not. On the other hand, closed-loop systems are generally simpler and lower in cost per unit length than open-loop systems (26).

Since most open-loop systems can be mathematically described quite easily, in terms of arrival and service rates, this section will be devoted to closed-loop systems.

Design Considerations

Kwo (27) lists three considerations basic to closed-loop conveyor operation. They are (1) the uniformity principle, (2) the capacity constraint, and (3) the speed rule. The uniformity principle states that it is necessary to try to load and unload the conveyor uniformly over the entire loop. The capacity constraint dictates that the accommodations furnished by the conveyor should be at least equal to the accommodations required. The speed rule defines a range of permissible speeds for the conveyor. The lowest speed is set by the higher of either the loading or unloading rate and the highest speed is restricted by the electromechanical limits of the conveyor or by the speed of the human materials handler, whichever is lower.

Uniformity Principle. Let

N_T = number of elementary cycles considered
T = cycle times
W = revolution time
N_W = 2, 3, . . . , integer
T_L = loading time in elementary cycle
T_u = unloading time in elementary cycle.

The conditions which must be met simultaneously are:

$N_T T/W = N_W$, a positive integer not equal to one; and $N_W \neq N_T$

$$N_T T_L/W = \text{a positive integer,}$$

or

$$N_T T_u/W = \text{a positive integer}$$

with

$$T_L + T_u = T$$

The above indicates that after an interval of time $N_T T$, all things return to what they were at the start. This interval may be one elementary or N_T elementary cycles. Since neither accumulation by loading nor depletion by unloading can continue indefinitely, after some time lapse the accumulation must equal the depletion. N_T cannot be equal to N_W, since if they were, any section of the conveyor would get the same loading-unloading effect from cycle to cycle and uniformity would never be achieved. The same reasoning rules out $N_W = 1$. The second equation states that the total accumulation (or depletion) in the time interval $N_T T$ must be such that it can be shared evenly by the entire conveyor. This means that the time lapse over which there is net gain (or loss) of parts must be an integral multiple of the revolution time.

Capacity Constraint. Let

m = total number of carriers on the conveyor
q = capacity of a carrier
v = velocity of the conveyor
L = length of the conveyor
W = revolution time of the conveyor
S = spacing between carriers
K = accommodations required per unit time
$$mqv/L = mq/W = qv/S \geq K$$

The left hand side of this equation is the number of racks passing by any point in a unit time. This is the potential capacity of the conveyor.

Speed Rule. Let

r_L = loading rate
r_u = unloading rate
t_L = average time to load a part
t_u = average time to unload a part
v_c = maximum allowable speed of conveyor

$$\max\ (r_L, r_u) \leqq v/S \leqq \min\ (1/t_L,\ 1/t_u,\ v_c/S)$$

The speed rule is generally invalidated for the upper and lower bounds in the above equation since there is usually reserve carrier capacity available and materials handlers are allowed to move with the conveyor for a short distance when necessary. For these reasons the uniformity principle and capacity constraints are much more significant than the speed rule. In practice, the speed rule is used only as a check to insure feasibility of a suggested speed.

Kwo does not consider the effect of random variation on the individual station, but merely states that in practice the materials handler is allowed to move with the conveyor when necessary to overcome delay. However, Reis, Dunlap, and Schneider (28) do consider the role of the individual station. They include graphs indicating delay time and bank sizes needed for various capacity stations.

Disney (29) discusses the conveyor system utilizing parallel loading and unloading stations with a sensor-controlled ordered entry discipline. There is apparently no current publication combining all these possibilities in a single system.

Example

This example is adapted from work done by Kwo (27). Suppose the following is known:

1. Output of loading area, A, is 6 parts per minute.
2. Input to unloading area, B, is 2 parts per minute.
3. The distance from A to B is 1,200 feet.
4. Carrier spacing of four feet is to be used.
5. Reserve live storage capacity is to be 480 parts.

Assume that economic lot size considerations require A to produce in batches of 720 parts requiring a two-hour production run. The loading time will be 720 parts/6 parts/min. = 120 min., and similarly the unloading time will be 360 minutes for an elementary cycle time of 120 + 360 − overlap of 120 = 360 min. or 6 hours. Then:

$$N_T = 1, \ T = 360, \ T_L = 120, \ T_u = 240,$$

and

$$WN_W = 360, \ N_W = 2,3, \ldots, \ \text{integer.}$$

From $N_T T_L / W$, $120/W = $ a positive integer; $240/W = $ integer, so that W may be either 1, 2, 3, 4, 5, 8, 10, 12, 15, 20, 24, 30, 40, 60, or 120. Assume that 60 feet per minute is the maximum allowable conveyor speed. Since the distance between A and B is 1,200 feet, the conveyor must be at least 2,400 feet long. Therefore, $L/W = 2,400/60 = 40$. No value for W less than 40 need be considered.

Choose the revolution time, W, equal to 60 minutes, for simplicity. The operating capacity requirements are, for loading, 6 parts per minute; unloading, 2 parts per minute. The accumulation rate is $6 − 2 = 4$ parts per minute for the first 120 minutes and $− 2$ parts per minute for the remaining 240 minutes. The peak accumulation will be $120(4) = 480$ parts.

As a first try, let the conveyor length, L, be the minimum possible, 2,400 feet. The conveyor speed is then $v = L/W = 2,400/60 = 40$ feet per minute, a reasonable figure. From the pre-determined conveyor spacing for 4 feet and chosen length of 2,400 feet, $m = L/S = 2,400/4 = 600$ carriers. The pre-determined maximum reserve capacity requirements, when converted to a one-minute interval basis, are $480/60 = 8$. The total capacity requirements on a per-minute interval basis are the sum of the maximum operating capacity requirements, the pre-determined reserve capacity requirements, and twice the smaller of the two rates. This is $K = 8 + 8 + 4 = 20$.

The total number of parts each carrier is to accommodate, from the expression for K, $q = KW/m = 20(60)/600 = 2$ parts per carrier, which appears to be a reasonable number.

The parameters of the conveyor are then: $W = 60$ minutes, $T = 360$ minutes, $L = 2,400$ feet, $m = 600$, $q = 2$, $S = 4$ feet, and $v = 40$ feet per minute. These parameters should be applied to the various combinations of equipment available to arrive at a minimum cost facility which satisfies the parameters.

Evaluation

In general, the conveyor design problem is considerably more complex than the example given here. A regularly recurring recommendation throughout existing literature is to test the proposed conveyor system design over a wide range of system parameters through simulation. This recommendation apparently reflects the lack of adequate testing of the conveyor models developed. In addition, most conveyor models require consideration of a number of possibilities which result in poorly defined reactions in the system such as interference and imbalance.

The existing mathematical models do not replace traditional design techniques but they do aid in evaluating costs of production, costs of delay, bank capacity, conveyor accommodation requirements, and so forth. However, with the models available, almost any type of closed loop conveyor system can be planned with a reasonably high assurance that the system will do its intended job satisfactorily.

SIMULATION

In most practical problems it is too expensive and time-consuming to experiment with full-scale, potential solutions to layout problems or material handling systems. Simulation takes a real system and attempts to duplicate it on paper or with computers, by procedures which generate data representative of the effectiveness of various alternative solutions at relatively low cost and in a short period of time.

To simulate a system, a fairly good knowledge of the parts or components of the system and their characteristics is required, although knowledge of the parts of a system does not imply any knowledge of the system behavior. Simulation sums the behavior of the parts and helps to explain and predict the dynamic behavior of the system.

A major difference between one type of simulation and another is the presence or absence of chance or stochastic processes and their associated probability distributions in the simulation. Where probability distributions are explicitly included, the analysis is frequently called Monte Carlo simulation (30), because the technique has to do with evaluating elements of chance, which have a major role in industry in the nature of rejects, breakdowns, and so on. Basically, Monte Carlo analysis is a simulated sampling technique, in which the sample data are synthetically generated when actual samples are unavailable.

The data are commonly generated by some random number generator in order to replace the actual items to be sampled with their theoretical counterpart, as described by some probability distribution. The generator could be a random number table, a pair of fair dice, or any unbiased source of values. The data of interest are tabulated as a probability density function. If the data have a known probability distribution, the density can be computed mathematically and no real or observed information is needed. If the probability distribution is not known, it is necessary to take actual samples or to use historical information to approximate the probability density for specified values. For example, if records show that the number of breakdowns per hour in a group of machines is as follows:

Number of breakdowns/hr	0	1	2	3	4	5	6	7 or more
Frequency	893	227	189	101	41	11	2	0

The total number of observations is 1464 and the relative frequency is:

$$X = 0 \quad 1 \quad 2 \quad 3 \quad 4 \quad 5 \quad 5 \quad 7 \text{ or more}$$

Probability of X breakdowns per hour $= 0.61 \; 0.15 \; 0.13 \; 0.07 \; 0.03 \; 0.01 \; 0.00 \; 0.00$

Then a set of random numbers used to generate sequences of breakdowns would have 61 percent of its numbers indicating zero breakdowns, 15 percent indicating one breakdown, and so on.

Thus, a properly designed set of random numbers can be used to generate sequences of numbers which have the same statistical characteristics as the actual system being simulated. As long as the statistical model continues to represent the facts of the system, an infinite amount of simulated experience is available, usually at much lower cost than actual experience.

In summary form, the steps in the Monte Carlo method of simulation are:

1. Pick the measure of effectiveness.
2. Decide which variables significantly affect this measure.
3. Determine the proper probability density functions to represent the variables.
4. Choose the candidate solutions to the problem.
5. Generate a set of random numbers.
6. For each set of random numbers, enter the probability density function to determine the corresponding value of the data of interest.
7. Insert the values of the data of interest in the model of the measure of effectiveness, and compute.
8. From a run of figures computed in step 7, select the best alternative.
9. Make some confidence statements concerning the choice in step 8.

When a problem does not involve too many variables, simulation can be done manually. In general, a computer is faster and more economical for problems of practical size.

Example

Schiller and Lavin (31) provide an example of simulation as a means of determining the warehouse dock space required by a department store chain which was planning to consolidate three warehouses into a single unit. The problem was to determine the dock space required to handle the truck traffic at the new warehouse, which fell into the framework of waiting-line analysis but was sufficiently complex to be more easily solved by simulation than by analysis.

A study of truck arrival patterns at the existing warehouses showed that arrivals were effectively described by a Poisson probability distribution with no significant variation among days of the week or weeks of the month. Although the number of arrivals in the mornings was significantly higher than arrivals in the afternoon, there was no difference in the number of arrivals in half hour periods during the morning. The afternoon half hour intervals were also homogeneous.

The study of service times at the dock showed that one class of truck was *loaded* only and a second class *unloaded* only. There were two groups of unloadings, both negative exponentially distributed with means of 10 and 45 minutes. In the case of trucks being loaded, service time was negative exponential after a mean holding time of 18 minutes.

The company wanted facilities which would be adequate for the pre-Christmas peak season. The arrival and service time data were modified to reflect what was believed to prevail during this season. Warehouse facilities having 12, 15, 18, and 21 docks were then simulated and showed the rate at which the mean line length would build up during the morning, resulting in a heavy load on the system during the 11:00 A.M. to 12:00 A.M. period. The result of the simulation was the plotting of the probability distributions of line length and waiting time during this period, as shown in Figures 10–11 and 10–12. From these, management could make a decision as to the consequence of providing various numbers of docks at the new warehouse.

Evaluation

Simulation is most helpful where formal mathematical analysis is not possible or convenient, although it shares the disadvantage common to all models, in that it focuses on certain characteristics of the system and largely ignores others.

Monte Carlo simulation has one outstanding advantage. In addition to being useful in problems for which no "analytical" solution exists, it is useful when the analyst can't develop a mathematical solution. Some of the more elegant solutions to complex analytical problems are beyond the mathematical training of many people. In such cases, Monte Carlo methods of picking a solution to the problem are possible (30).

In general, it is useful to make a reasonable effort to treat a problem analytically before turning to simulation, since it is a sampling technique and is subject to the same difficulties encountered in any sampling plan. The factors to be tested, the level at which they will be tested, the number of samples to be taken, and the analysis of variance must all be carefully

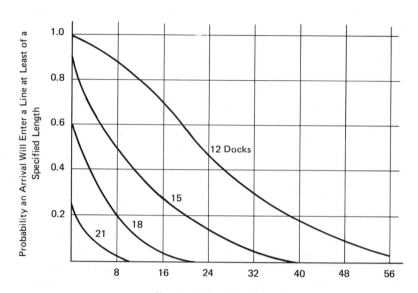

Fig. 10–11. Probability of line length for a specified number of docks.

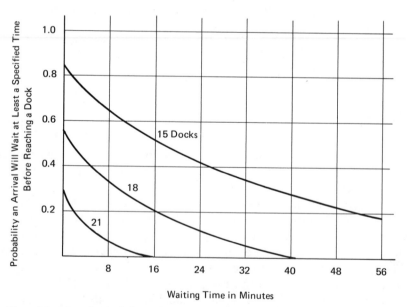

Waiting Time in Minutes

Fig. 10–12. Probability of an arrival waiting with a specified number of docks.

planned in advance. Most simulation problems can be handled effectively on a computer, although it is inefficient use of computer time; however, small problems can be done manually.

SUMMARY

The quantitative techniques discussed in this chapter represent some of the most powerful tools currently available for use in facilities planning. However, the list of the techniques is by no means a complete one. Continued development of new concepts together with quantitative analytical tools will continue to expand the capabilities of the facilities designer.

At the present time, six of the techniques covered in this chapter "guarantee" optimal solutions when appropriate assumptions and constraints are satisfied. They are:

1. Linear programming
2. Assignment technique
3. Transportation problem
4. Transshipment problem
5. Integer programming
6. Dynamic programming

The traveling salesman technique provides a solution that is near optimal and sometimes optimal. Queuing theory and simulation cannot guarantee optimality, due to their probabilistic nature. Conveyor analysis generally requires that its solution be tested by simulation or actual operation. The algorithms available for solving quadratic programming

Table 10–9. Characteristics of Solution Procedures for Each Technique

	Transportation Programming	Assignment Techniques	Transshipment Programming	Traveling Salesman Technique	Integer Programming	Dynamic Programming	Waiting Lines	Conveyor Analysis	Monte Carlo Simulation	Quadratic Models
Guaranteed optimal	x	x	x		x	x				x
Computer solution required				x°	x	x			x°	x
Computer solution desirable	x	x	x	x	x	x	x	x	x	
Number of added machines considered	m	m	m	m	m	m			m	m
Number of candidate locations Number of machines added		x	x		x	x			x	
Consider prohibited assignments	x	x	x	x				x		

* Choice depends upon size of the problem.

problems do not guarantee an optimal solution. In all cases, a computer solution may be either required or desired for a problem of practical size.

As a possible guide to the selection of the most appropriate technique for analyzing a particular problem, Table 10–9 provides a tabular summation of the characteristics of each technique and Table 10–10 lists the type of data each can use.

Table 10–10. Data Characteristics for Each Technique

	Transportation Programming	Assignment Techniques	Transshipment Programming	Traveling Salesman Technique	Integer Programming	Dynamic Programming	Waiting Lines	Conveyor Analysis	Monte Carlo Simulation	Quadratic Models
Handling between machines allowed				x			x	x	x	
Routing fixed	x	x	x	x				x		
Movement direction: Straight line						x		x	x	
rectangular						x		x	x	
arbitrary	x	x	x	x	x	x		x	x	
Candidate areas: discrete	x	x	x	x	x	x		x	x	x
continuous										x
Measure: deterministic	x	x	x	x	x	x		x	x	x
stochastic						x	x	x	x	

Even this group of techniques does not permit a solution to all facilities design problems. In many cases one or more of them will be found useful as powerful tools to guide and assist in developing a solution or in improving an existing situation. However, the ingenuity of the analyst is likely to continue to be the moving force in layout planning until these and similar techniques are more thoroughly tested in real-world problem situations, and analysts are trained to use them.

Recommendations for Applications of Techniques

Linear programming, assignment, transportation programming, and *transshipment programming* techniques are recommended when static conditions and straight line relationships exist. The techniques may be used as allocation models for selecting among alternate ways of performing a task or choosing the best combinations of existing facilities or resources in order to optimize effectiveness. They are recommended when more than one machine is to be added to a layout with discrete candidate areas. They are also useful when the number of candidate areas is greater than or equal to the number of new machines to be added. The computational procedures are relatively simple and large problems can be readily solved on a computer. Each model guarantees an optimal solution, providing it is used correctly. Recommended applications include:

1. Optimum locations of facilities.
2. Optimum use of facilities or resources.
3. Improved lines or product mixes.

The techniques may also be used for transportation problems in which it is desired to:

1. Minimize transportation and distribution costs.
2. Establish an optimum route.

Integer programming is useful when there are more machines than candidate areas to place the machines. Any type of movement, straight line, rectangular, or a combination of the two may be used with the model. It is not well suited to manual computation but does guarantee an optimal solution when used correctly.

Dynamic programming is recommended for solving linear programming type of problems listed above when a multistage decision process is involved. Situations may be frequently encountered which require one to make a series of decisions with the outcome of each decision depending on the results of a previous decision in the series. Specifically, dynamic programming has been applied to procurement problems, equipment replacement policies, production and distribution problems, allocation and inventory problems.

The *traveling salesman technique* is recommended for finding the optimal route from a given location, visiting a specified group of locations with no backtracking, and returning to the point of origin. The technique has also proved useful when scheduling a machine over a given set of repeated operations. Small problems can be solved with a combination of graphical and computational procedures while larger ones can be solved on a computer. Some of the more recent solution procedures result in "near-optimal" solutions.

Queuing theory analysis is recommended to analyze situations in which some service is performed under random demand and waiting lines or queues form due to irregularity of demand, service or both. The technique may be used for solving the problem where the number of service facilities is subject to control, but the timing of the customers is not. An example is the determination of the number of dock facilities needed for loading and unloading trucks. Queuing theory may be used to solve scheduling problems where the timing of customer arrivals is subject to control but the amount of service facilities is not. A sequencing problem in which the order of units to be processed so that the service time is minimized may be also solved by queuing theory. Queuing theory has also been used successfully to solve line balancing problems when the arrivals are subject to control and all units require the same multiple operations.

Waiting-line models are widely documented and are recommended for the analysis of storage space requirements, material handling equipment requirements, the quantity of materials required at a given point, and the scheduling and dispatching of material handling equipment within a production system, when the needs of the system occur in Poisson fashion and the needs are satisfied in an exponential manner. Most computations can be done manually, though large problems may require a computer. The probabilistic nature of waiting lines prohibits an absolute optimal solution but a relative optimal solution can be achieved.

Conveyor models are developed primarily for closed-loop, irreversible conveyor systems. Most such models are useful as part of a simulation procedure, since the interactions of system components result in extremely complex mathematical relationships. Very few conveyor problems can be solved manually and computer computation is almost mandatory. If the system relationships can be computed, an optimum, or near optimum, solution can be achieved.

Simulation is recommended whenever the number or complexity of system components creates a mathematically unmanageable problem. This technique is also a useful procedure for simpler problems where the mathematical ability of the analyst is limited. There is no guarantee of optimality except through an exhaustive repetitive procedure which is seldom economical.

Quadratic and quadratic integer programming are not practical as facility design tools at the present time, as the computational methods are still too cumbersome and there is no guarantee of optimality.

CONCLUSION

Although surveys have shown that there is comparatively little industrial application of the techniques described here, their potential is extremely challenging. As further experimentation takes place, and results are documented, more analysts will be encouraged to use and experiment with these approaches. It is hoped that some readers of this text will do so and will report their successes to encourage further efforts along these lines.

For the student interested in the application of quantitative techniques to facilities design problems, there are many interesting situations offering challenging opportunities for further investigation. Among them are the following:

1. Develop a procedure for designing material-flow patterns.
2. Develop a model or technique for handling stochastic traffic-distance data.
3. Develop a procedure for evaluating the relative efficiency of alternative material handling plans or systems.
4. Develop a method of predicting and controlling material handling costs.
5. Develop useful relationships between the distance traveled, handling equipment used, and the total cost of material handling.

This chapter has attempted to explore the application of quantitative techniques to handling and facilities design problems. Further details on these techniques can be found in the references listed in the bibliography.

REFERENCES CITED

1. METZGER, ROBERT W., *Elementary Mathematical Programming*, John Wiley and Sons, Inc., New York, 1958, p. 212, et seq.
2. SASIENI, MAURICE, ARTHUR YASPAN, and LAWRENCE FRIEDMAN, *Operations Research—Methods and Problems*, John Wiley and Sons, Inc., New York, 1959, p. 198, et seq.
3. CHUNG, AN-MIN, *Linear Programming*, Charles E. Merrill Books, Inc., Columbus, Ohio, 1963, p. 273.
4. CHUNG, p. 274.
5. ACKOFF, RUSSELL L., *Progress in Operations Research*, Vol. 1, John Wiley and Sons, Inc., New York, 1961, p. 153.
6. DANTZIG, G. B., D. R. FULKERSON, and S. M. JOHNSON, "Solutions of a Large-Scale Traveling-Salesman Problem," *Journal of Operations Research Society of America*, 2, 393–410 (1954).
7. BARACHET, L. L., "Graphic Solution of the Traveling-Salesman Problem," *Operations Research*, 5, 841–845 (1957).
8. CROES, G. A., "A Method for Solving Traveling-Salesman Problems," *Operations Research*, 6, 791–812 (1958).
9. DACEY, MICHAEL F., "Selection of an Initial Solution for the Traveling-Salesman Problem," *Operations Research*, 8, 133–134 (1960).
10. SASIENI et al., p. 266f.

11. Hare, Van Court, Sr., and Wilfred C. Hugh, "Applications of Operations Research to Production Scheduling and Inventory Control II," Proceedings of the Conference on "What is Operations Research Accomplishing in Industry?", 56–62, Case Institute of Technology, Cleveland, Ohio, 1955.

12. Danskin, J. M., "Linear Programming in the Face of Uncertainty: Example of a Failure," Second Symposium on Linear Programming, Paper No. 3.

13. Gomory, Ralph E., "All-Integer Programming Algorithm," (IBM Research Center, Research Report RC–189, January, 1960).

14. Gomory, Ralph E., "An All-Integer Programming Algorithm," Industrial Scheduling, J. F. Muth and G. L. Thompson, eds., Prentice-Hall, New York, 1963, pp. 193–206.

15. Balinsky, M. L., and R. E. Quandt, "On an Integer Program for a Delivery Program," Operations Research, 12:2, March 1964, pp. 377–383.

16. Moodie, C. L., and D. E. Mandeville, "Project Resource Balancing Techniques," Journal of Industrial Engineering, 17:7, July, 1966, pp. 377–383.

17. Bellman, Richard E., and Stuart E. Dreyfus, Applied Dynamic Programming, Princeton University Press, Princeton, N.J., 1962, p. 15.

18. Bellman, p. 89f.

19. Morris, William T., Analysis for Materials Handling Management, Richard D. Irwin, Inc., Homewood, Illinois, 1962, p. 63.

20. Feller, William, An Introduction to Probability Theory and Its Applications, 2nd ed., John Wiley & Sons, Inc., New York, 1957, p. 400 et seq.

21. Sasieni et al., p. 133.

22. Richman, Eugene, and Salah Elmaghraby, "The Design of In-Process Storage Facilities," Journal of Industrial Engineering, Vol. VIII, No. 1, January-February, 1957, p. 9.

23. Feller, p. 400f.

24. Sasieni et al., p. 138.

25. Morris, p. 129.

26. Helgeson, William B., "Planning for the Use of Overhead Monorail Non-Reversing Loop Type Conveyor Systems for Storage and Delivery," Journal of Industrial Engineering, Nov.-Dec., 1960, Vol. XI, No. 6, p. 488.

27. Kwo, T. T., "A Method for Designing Irreversible Overhead Loop Conveyors," Journal of Industrial Engineering, Nov.-Dec., 1960.

28. Reis, Irvin L., Lloyd L. Dunlap, and Morris H. Schneider, "Conveyor Theory: The Individual Station," Journal of Industrial Engineering, Jul.-Aug., 1963, Vol. XIV, No. 4.

29. Disney, Ralph L., "Some Results of Multichannel Queueing Problems with Ordered Entry—An Application to Conveyor Theory," Journal of Industrial Engineering, Mar.-Apr., 1963, Vol. XIV, No. 2.

30. Bowman, Edward H., and Robert B. Fetter, Analysis for Production Management, Richard D. Irwin, Inc., Homewood, Illinois, 1961, p. 344.

31. Schiller, Donald H., and Marvin M. Lavin, "The Determination of Requirements for Warehouse Dock Facilities," Operations Research, April, 1956.

11

Equipment Selection Procedure

The selection of the proper piece of material handling equipment is an extremely complex and difficult task, partly due to the fact that there are so many different kinds of equipment from which to choose. It has been estimated that there are approximately:

240 types of conveyors, etc.
 60 types of trucks and vehicles
100 types of cranes and hoists
 70 types of containers and racks
100 types of auxiliary equipment

570 types of material handling equipment

Fortunately, only about 60 to 80 of them are in common use. However, it is frequently possible that the problem at hand can best be solved by one of the 500 or so lesser known types or variations—with which the material handling engineer is not familiar. For instance, it is quite possible that a problem could be *alleviated* with a troughed belt conveyor. But it might be *solved* with a "zipper" conveyor—a specialized type of closed belt conveyor. So unless the material handling engineer has a tremendously wide background and depth of knowledge, it is very possible that he will often select a piece of equipment that is less than the best for the task at hand.

The only solution to this dilemma—and it cannot be more than a partial solution—is to study the trade magazines, sales literature, etc.; attend the trade expositions; talk to sales engineers; attend conferences and training courses; read books; and attend professional society meetings. In this way, over a period of years, it is possible to accumulate a fairly wide knowledge of the equipment available.

Nevertheless, each material handling problem *must* be solved, and most require some kind of equipment in their implementation. And it will be recalled, that the overall goal in selecting *a* piece of equipment, is to properly match:

—the *material* characteristics
—the *move* requirements
—the *method* (equipment) capabilities or requirements

consistent with the physical restrictions within which the activity takes place—and of course within cost constraints that would be acceptable. The following pages are intended to serve as a guide to the selection of the most appropriate equipment for the problem at hand.

EQUIPMENT SELECTION GUIDE LINES

In other portions of this text, in relation to other aspects of the material handling problem situation, there are suggested many factors, ideas, indicators, concepts, principles, etc. equally applicable to the equipment selection process. Some of them are listed in Table 11–1 as *very* general guide lines for the selection of handling methods. While these characteristics are not infallible, they should be helpful in guiding the analyst in his thinking, during the analysis process.

PLACE OF EQUIPMENT SELECTION IN THE PROBLEM-SOLVING PROCEDURE

In review, it will be recalled that the following 9 steps in the analysis procedure must usually take place *before* the equipment is selected.

    I. Identify the problem
    II. Determine the scope of the problem
  III. Establish objective
    IV. Define the problem
    V. Determine what data to collect
    VI. Establish work plan and schedule
  VII. Collect data
 VIII. Weigh and analyze data
    IX. Develop improvements (which includes selecting the equipment, as section IX G)

Table 11–1. Equipment Selection Guidelines

No Equipment	Equipment			
	A. *General*	B. *Manual*	C. *Mechanized*	D. *Automated*
1. Low volume	1. Loads over 50 lb. (or other predetermined limit)	1. Relatively light loads	1. High volume	1. High volume
2. Low rate of flow	2. Two-man handling tasks	2. Limited volume	2. Continuous movement necessary	2. High percentage of handling in operation
3. Non-uniform flow	3. Travel time exceeds lifting and placing time	3. Physical restrictions	3. Much handling required	3. Uniform product; material
4. Small items	4. Unused space above floor	4. Equipment equally useful for storage	4. Direct labor performing handling tasks	4. Stable product
5. Short distances		5. Limited capital	5. Need for controlled rate of flow	5. Practicable to combine movement with production or other operations
6. Limited area		6. Minimum maintenance facilities	6. Increased capacity	6. Maintain process control
7. Infrequent handling		7. Stand-by use	7. Hazardous materials	7. Reduce cost
8. Occasional handling		8. Wide variety of small or infrequent handling tasks (requiring flexibility of manual equipment)	8. Operators waiting for materials	8. Limited number of paths
9. Varying paths		9. Efficiency of manual methods relatively high	9. Manual handling undesirable	9. Moves relatively fixed
10. Small percentage of time spent in handling		10. Low cost operation	10. Production bottlenecks	10. Relatively fixed material flow pattern
11. Little cost attributable to handling		11. Complex flow pattern	11. Unit loads practicable	
12. Complex flow pattern			12. Dependable handling necessary	
13. Obstacles in flow path			13. Limited space	
14. No alternative			14. Wasted cube	
			15. Flexible types of equipment adaptable to handling tasks	

Obviously, until the first 8 steps have been accomplished, it is not possible to intelligently select the equipment, for it is during those steps that the information and data are accumulated and developed for use in the equipment selection process. Too much emphasis cannot be placed on the importance of the careful and complete collection of information on the material and move aspects of the problem—before attempting to determine what equipment to use.

EQUIPMENT SELECTION CRITERIA

It should be apparent to the thorough analyst that the piece of handling equipment selected should possess certain desirable characteristics or meet certain criteria if it is to be best suited to the handling task. Many such characteristics or criteria have been stated or implied throughout this text. Some of these, as suggested by the principles of material handling, imply that the equipment selected should:

1. Fit into the handling system.
2. Combine handling with other functions (production, storage, inspection, packing, etc.)
3. Optimize materials flow.
4. Be as simple as is practicable.
5. Utilize gravity wherever possible.
6. Require a minimum of space.
7. Handle as large a load as is practical.
8. Make the move safely, in terms of both manpower and material.
9. Use mechanization judiciously.
10. Be flexible, adaptable.
11. Have a low dead-weight-to-pay-load ratio.
12. Utilize a minimum of operator time.
13. Require a minimum of loading, unloading and rehandling.
14. Call for as little maintenance, repair, power and fuel as possible.
15. Have a long, useful life.
16. Be capable of capacity utilization.
17. Perform the handling operation efficiently and economically.

Using the above as a basis, and adding items from other aspects of the handling problem analysis procedure, the Preliminary Material Handling-Equipment Evaluation Sheet (Figure 11–1) has been developed. Each alternative under consideration can be informally "rated," or a more precise approach can be taken, as with the indeterminate costs and intangible factors to be dealt with in Chapter 14. This evaluation sheet is intended to be used in the equipment selection process—probably *before*, or along with, the more formal analysis techniques used for the cost and related factors.

PRELIMINARY MATERIAL HANDLING EQUIPMENT EVALUATION SHEET					
Project Title: _____ Project No.: _____					
Analyst(s): _____ Date: _____					
		Alternatives			
	Characteristics for Evaluation	A	B	C	D
EQUIPMENT CHARACTERISTICS	1. Compatibility with handling system				
	2. Degree of complexity				
	3. Utilization of gravity				
	4. Space requirements				
	5. Safety				
	6. Degree of mechanization				
	7. Flexibility				
	8. Adaptability				
	9. Load/unload time				
	10. Maintenance requirements				
	11. Depreciation rate; time				
	12. Degree of standardization				
	13. Durability				
	14. Quality				
	15. Operating cost				
	16. Supervision requirements				
EQUIPMENT UTILIZATION	17. Possibility of performing other functions *during* movement				
	18. Optimization of materials flow				
	19. Capacity for job at hand				
	20. Amount of operator time required				
	21. Percent of time equipment will be used				
	22. Expected percent of down time				
	23. Effect of further developments on equipment				
	24. Relative contribution to production efficiency				
	25. Effect on quality				
VENDOR CHARACTERISTICS	26. Availability of equipment				
	27. Manufacturer's reputation				
	28. Availability of service				
	29. Quality of service				
	30. Availability of parts, etc.				

Fig. 11–1. Preliminary material handling equipment evaluation sheet.

EQUIPMENT SELECTION PROCEDURE

Actually, no "formal" procedure exists for the selection of handling equipment. The problem is basically little different from any other selection problem, although in most selection problems, a careful analysis is more the exception than the rule. However, because of the potential consequences, and the amount of money often involved, it is incumbent upon the handling engineer—and his reputation—to do the very best job he can in selecting *the* proper handling equipment. The material that follows is an attempt to outline the thinking process involved and to guide the analyst in his efforts. The steps to be discussed are:

1. Relate all factors pertinent to the problem
2. Determine appropriate degree of mechanization
3. Make a tentative selection of equipment type
4. Narrow the choice
5. Evaluate the alternatives
6. Check the selection for compatibility with the rest of the system
7. Select the specific type of equipment
8. Prepare specifications
9. Procure the equipment

The following pages amplify these steps and suggest methods and techniques for implementing them.

1. Relate All Factors

As has been emphasized many times, there are three major aspects of a material handling problem: the *material,* the *move* and the *method.* Previous discussion has pointed out that there are some 70 to 80 sub-factors under these 3 phases—many of which must be taken into consideration in solving the problem. The Material Handling Analysis—Re-cap Sheet (page 243) is an attempt to do just this. But it will *not* select the equipment. If the material handling analyst has the proper background, the re-cap sheet—*while* it is being filled in—will *guide* his thinking toward the equipment type by focusing his attention on those pieces of equipment (with which he is familiar) that come closest to matching the *characteristics of the material* and the *requirements of the move.*

2. Determine Degree of Mechanization

It has been suggested previously that the mechanization of the handling operation is—in general—a worthwhile objective. However, a warning should be sounded against "mechanization for the sake of mechanization." Therefore, before a decision can be made on the equipment to be used for a specific handling situation, some consideration must be given to a determination of the appropriate degree of mechanization. And, it should be realized that, in general, when moving from a lower level of mechanization to a higher level, the "unit" cost will be reduced. However, it is also true that if the degree of mechanization is increased to an excessively high level, the total of the capital investment and operating costs will very likely *raise* the "unit" cost. Therefore, there is an optimum level of mechanization although it is not necessarily the same for every handling operation in the entire process. Only by means of a complete engineering and economic analysis can the optimum level be reached for each handling task in the system.

The concept of "levels of mechanization," developed by Prof. James R. Bright, and shown in Figure 11–2, was intended to apply to manu- facturing processes. A variation was later developed by M. S. Bazaraa for application to material handling, and is shown in Figure 11–3. Then, Figure 11–4 shows the concept of Bazaraa's levels of material handling mechanization in their relationships to some of the characteristics of a material handling problem. The white spaces show the range of mecha- nization levels appropriate to each characteristic, or factor. Obviously, the figure is not intended to resolve the problem, but it *does* show the thinking process involved in making the decision on the appropriate level of handling mechanization.

It should be observed that very few of the so-called automated han- dling systems in existence reach the top level of either classification. The selection of *the* level of mechanization becomes a problem of economic feasibility. After the total handling system has been conceptualized, it is necessary to make engineering economic analyses of each move. Only after such an investigation can it be determined:

1. What is *possible* now.
2. What is economically *feasible*.
3. What *will* be possible and/or economical at a later date.
4. What to *install* today.

The procedure to be followed in making the feasibility study should also be investigated in an engineering economy or similar text.

3. Tentative Selection of Equipment Type

In addition to the above consideration of material handling problem "factors" and levels of mechanization, the equipment selection process *still* depends largely on the analyst's knowledge of handling equipment, as pointed out in Chapters 5 and 6. The chart showing the characteristics of basic handling equipment types (Figure 5–1), and the "thinking

Initiating Control Source	Type of Machine Response			Power Source	Level Number	LEVEL OF MECHANIZATION
From a variable in the environment	Responds with Action	Modifies own action over a wide range of variation		Mechanical (Nonmanual)	17	Anticipates action required and adjusts to provide it.
					16	Corrects performance while operating.
					15	Corrects performance after operating.
		Selects from a limited range of possible pre-fixed actions			14	Identifies and selects appropriate set of actions.
					13	Segregates or rejects according to measurement.
					12	Changes speed, position, direction according to measurement signal.
	Responds with signal				11	Records performance.
					10	Signals pre-selected values of measurement. (Includes error detection)
					9	Measures characteristics of work.
From a control mechanism that directs a pre-determined pattern of action	Fixed within the machine				8	Actuates by introduction of work piece or material.
					7	Power Tool System, Remote Controlled.
					6	Power Tool, Program Control (sequence of fixed functions).
					5	Power Tool, Fixed Cycle (single function).
From man	Variable				4	Power Tool, Hand Control.
					3	Powered Hand Tool.
				Manual	2	Hand Tool.
					1	Hand.

Fig. 11-2. Levels of mechanization. (From James R. Bright, *Automation and Management*, Division of Research, Harvard Business School, 1958.)

Classification		Level	Description	Examples	Characteristics
Manual Control	Manual Power	1	Hand		Man carries load.
		2	Hand Equipment		Equipment carries load.
		3	Mechanized Hand Equipment		Uses mechanical advantage.
	Gravity	4	Gravity Equipment		Positive control of object.
	External Power	5	Power Equipment, Hand Control		Power does work; man controls power.
		6	Power Equipment, Remote Hand Control		Control remote from load.
Automatic Control	External Power	7	Power Equipment, Program Control		Control according to program.
		8	Power Equipment, Feedback Control		Automatic correction, according to signal.
		9	Adaptive System Equipment		Integrated system of signals and actions.
		10	Fully Automated System Equipment		

Fig. 11–3. Levels of mechanization for material handling equipment. (From *Production Handbook*, The Ronald Press Co., New York, 1972; based on material in Bazaraa thesis, Georgia Institute of Technology.)

process" represented therein—along with the experience of the analyst—must be relied upon in choosing the equipment type best suited to each individual move, or to the process as a whole. Referring to Figure 5–1, it will be seen that the intent was to correlate the significant factors in the material handling *problem,* with the general capabilities of the 3 basic

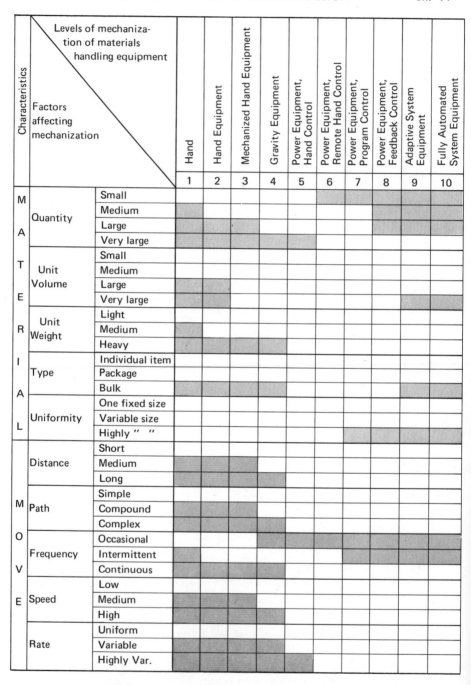

Fig. 11–4. Relationships between the factors and the degrees of mechanization. (From Bazaraa thesis, Georgia Institute of Technology, Atlanta, Georgia.)

types of handling equipment. The chart can be used by noting those factors in the vertical columns applicable to the problem being analyzed and then further investigating that type showing the largest number of relationships. For a more positive analysis, the applicable problem characteristics can be circled or checked in the columns. The column showing the most circles or checks indicates the type of equipment warranting additional consideration.

4. Narrow the Choice

The general guide lines indicated in Fig. 5–1 are further amplified in the Material Handling Analysis—Equipment Selection Guide (Fig. 11–5). On the left hand side of the guide will be found most of the factors and subfactors (over 100!) affecting the handling problem. Again they are grouped under the three major phases, material, move, and method (equipment). The top of the chart indicates 30 of the more common types of equipment, classified in the three major groups—conveyors, cranes and trucks. Each check mark indicates that the equipment *under* which it appears, is compatible with the *factor* opposite it in the left hand column. Such a chart cannot accurately depict relationships between the 500 plus equipment types and over 100 problem characteristics. But it *will* serve as a *guide* to general types of equipment, since it again depicts the thinking process involved in the selection problem. No such "crutch" can compare with personal knowledge, nor can it indicate logical adaptations which may make an equipment type applicable, but it might be helpful in pointing out possibilities with which the analyst may not be familiar. Figure 11–6 is a commercial chart developed along the same lines for a "family" of bulk material conveyors, and with the characteristics directed specifically toward the materials and equipment types peculiar to such problems.

In addition to the above-mentioned charts, there *are* other sources of help in narrowing down the equipment alternatives to the most appropriate type or types. Among them are:

1. The books, handbooks, etc., listed in Chapter 6.
2. Manufacturer's literature
3. Manufacturer's representatives

And, it might logically occur to the alert analyst, that such a gargantuan task of data assimilation is a proper task for a computer. Actually, it is. In an experiment [1] performed at the Georgia Institute of Technology, it was proved that the equipment selection problem, as depicted

---

[1] A research project, financed in part by the International Material Management Society, and reported in "Can You Computerize Equipment Selection," in *Modern Materials Handling*, Nov. 1966.

Material Handling Analysis—Equipment Selection Guide

Characteristics of the Handling Problem	Apron	Belt	Bucket	Chain	Chute	Flight	Monorail	Pneumatic	Power & Free	Roller	Screw	Slat	Tow	Trolley	Wheel	Bridge	Gantry	Hoist	Jib	Mobile	Stacker	Crane	Pallet-Lift (Hand)	Pallet-Lift (Walkie)	High Lift (Walkie)	High Lift (Rider)	Hand Platform	Straddle Carrier	Tractor Trailer
Conveyors / Cranes / Trucks																													
MATERIAL																													
Type																													
Indiv. Item	×	×			×		×	×	×	×		×	×	×	×	×	×	×	×	×	×	×	×	×	×	×	×	×	×
Packaged		×		×			×		×	×		×	×	×	×	×	×	×	×	×	×	×	×	×	×	×	×	×	×
Unit	×	×					×		×	×		×	×	×	×	×	×	×	×	×	×	×	×	×	×	×	×	×	×
Bulk			×		×	×		×			×		×																
Nature																													
Fragile							×		×			×	×	×		×	×	×	×	×	×	×	×	×	×	×	×	×	×
Sturdy		×		×		×	×		×	×	×	×	×	×	×	×	×	×	×	×	×	×	×	×	×	×	×	×	×
Bulky	×		×		×		×		×	×		×	×	×	×	×	×	×	×	×	×	×	×	×	×	×	×	×	×
Weight/Load																													
1-100 lbs.	×	×	×	×	×	×	×	×	×	×	×	×	×	×	×	×	×	×	×	×	×	×	×	×	×	×	×	×	×
100-1000 lbs.							×		×	×		×	×	×		×	×	×	×	×	×	×	×	×	×	×	×	×	×
Over 1000 lbs.							×		×			×	×	×		×	×	×	×	×	×	×		×	×	×		×	×
Quantity-Total																													
High									×			×	×	×												×			×
Medium	×	×	×	×	×	×	×	×	×	×	×	×	×	×	×											×		×	×
Low	×	×	×	×	×	×	×	×		×	×				×	×	×	×	×	×	×	×	×	×	×		×		
MOVE																													
Load Handled																													
Uniform	×	×	×	×	×	×	×	×	×	×	×	×	×	×	×	×	×	×	×	×	×	×	×	×	×	×	×	×	×
Variable	×	×	×	×	×		×	×		×	×	×	×	×	×	×	×	×	×	×	×	×	×	×	×	×	×	×	×
Unit Load							×		×			×	×	×		×	×	×	×	×	×	×	×	×	×	×	×	×	×
Rate/Speed																													
Uniform	×		×	×		×	×				×	×	×	×							×								
Variable	×		×	×	×	×	×	×	×	×	×	×			×	×	×	×	×	×	×	×	×	×	×	×	×	×	×

374

Frequency																													
Regular	X	X	X	X	X	X		X	X	X	X	X	X	X	X						X								
Irregular							X	X								X	X	X	X	X	X	X	X	X	X	X	X	X	X
Continuous	X	X	X	X	X	X		X	X		X	X	X	X	X														
Intermittent	X	X	X	X	X	X	X	X	X	X	X	X			X	X	X	X	X	X	X	X	X	X	X	X	X	X	X
Distance																													
Short—																													
Under 100 ft.	X	X	X	X	X	X	X	X		X		X			X	X	X	X	X	X	X	X	X	X	X	X	X	X	X
Medium—																													
100-300 ft.	X	X	X	X		X	X	X	X	X	X	X	X	X	X	X	X			X	X		X	X	X	X	X	X	X
Long—over																													
300 ft.		X					X	X	X	X			X	X		X				X								X	X
Area Covered																													
Fixed	X	X	X	X	X	X	X	X	X	X	X	X	X	X	X	X	X	X	X	X	X								
Variable																						X	X	X	X	X	X	X	X
Large													X	X		X				X						X		X	X
Medium													X	X		X	X			X	X	X		X	X	X		X	X
Small																X	X	X	X	X	X	X	X	X	X		X		
Path																													
Fixed	X	X	X	X	X	X	X	X	X	X	X	X	X	X	X														
Variable																X	X	X	X	X	X	X	X	X	X	X	X	X	X
Straight	X	X	X		X	X	X	X	X	X	X	X	X	X	X														
Curved		X		X			X	X	X	X			X	X	X														
Combination		X		X			X	X	X	X			X	X	X	X													
Obstacles				X			X	X	X	X			X	X	X	X	X	X	X	X		X	X	X	X	X	X	X	X
Course																													
Fixed Pt./Fix. Pt.	X	X	X	X	X	X	X	X	X	X	X	X	X	X	X	X				X									
Fix. Pt./																													
Variable Pt.																X	X	X	X	X	X	X	X	X	X	X	X	X	X
Var. Pt./Var. Pt.																X	X	X	X	X	X	X	X	X	X	X	X	X	X

Fig. 11–5. Material handling analysis—equipment selection guide.

Material Handling Analysis—Equipment Selection Guide

Characteristics of the Handling Problem	Conveyors															Cranes						Trucks							
	Apron	Belt	Bucket	Chain	Chute	Flight	Monorail	Pneumatic	Power & Free	Roller	Screw	Slat	Tow	Trolley	Wheel	Bridge	Gantry	Hoist	Jib	Mobile	Stacker	Crane	Pallet-Lift (Hand)	Pallet-Lift (Walkie)	High Lift (Walkie)	High Lift (Rider)	Hand Platform	Straddle Carrier	Tractor Trailer
Course (continued)																													
Var. Pt./Fix. Pt.																X	X	X	X	X	X	X	X	X	X	X	X	X	X
Two-Way							X			X						X	X	X	X	X	X	X	X	X	X	X	X	X	X
Direction/Plane																													
Horizontal	X	X		X		X	X	X	X	X	X	X	X	X	X	X	X	X	X	X	X	X	X	X	X	X	X	X	X
Vertical			X					X								X	X	X	X		X								
Incline	X	X	X	X	X	X	X	X	X	X	X	X	X	X	X	X	X	X	X	X				X	X	X		X	X
Single-Level	X	X				X		X	X		X	X	X	X						X		X	X	X	X	X	X	X	X
Multi-Level		X						X													X			X	X	X			
Combination		X						X	X				X	X		X					X			X	X	X			
Level																													
On Floor	X	X		X		X		X	X	X	X	X	X		X	X	X			X	X	X	X	X	X	X	X	X	X
Working Height		X		X		X		X	X	X	X	X			X	X	X												
Overhead	X	X	X		X		X	X	X	X	X		X		X	X	X	X	X	X	X	X	X	X	X	X	X	X	X
Level/Level										X	X	X		X	X				X										
Location																													
Inside	X	X	X	X	X	X	X	X	X	X	X	X	X	X	X	X	X	X	X	X	X	X	X	X	X	X	X	X	X
Outdoors	X	X	X				X	X		X	X	X	X	X	X	X	X	X	X	X	X	X				X		X	X
Between Bldgs.	X	X					X	X		X	X		X	X	X							X				X		X	X
Beyond Bldgs.				X		X	X			X		X				X						X				X			
Oper. in Transit	X	X					X		X	X			X	X	X														
Cross Traffic							X		X	X			X	X	X	X	X	X	X	X	X	X	X					X	X
% Handl. in Oper																													
Low							X								X	X	X	X	X	X	X	X	X	X	X		X		
Medium		X		X	X	X	X	X	X	X	X	X	X	X	X			X	X		X	X		X	X	X	X	X	X

FACILITIES																							
Aisles																							
Under 6 Ft.	n.a.	n.a.	n.a.	n.a.	n.a.	n.a.	n.a.	n.a.	n.a.	n.a.	n.a.	n.a.	n.a.	n.a.	n.a.	n.a.			✕	✕		✕	✕	
Over 6 Ft.	n.a.	n.a.	n.a.	n.a.	n.a.	n.a.	n.a.	n.a.	n.a.	n.a.	n.a.	n.a.	n.a.	n.a.	n.a.	n.a.			✕	✕		✕	✕	
Column Spacing																								
Close	n.a.	n.a.	n.a.	n.a.	n.a.	n.a.	n.a.	n.a.	n.a.	n.a.	n.a.	n.a.	n.a.	n.a.	n.a.	n.a.			✕	✕		✕	✕	
Wide	n.a.	n.a.	n.a.	n.a.	n.a.	n.a.	n.a.	n.a.	n.a.	n.a.	n.a.	n.a.	n.a.	n.a.	n.a.	n.a.			✕	✕		✕	✕	
Truss Height																								
Under 12 Ft.	✕	✕								✕	✕	✕	✕	✕	✕	✕	✕	✕	✕	✕	✕	✕	✕	✕
Over 12 Ft.	✕	✕								✕	✕	✕	✕	✕	✕	✕	✕	✕	✕	✕	✕	✕	✕	✕
Floor Load Cap'y.																								
Under 200 lbs.	✕	✕					✕		✕	✕	✕	✕	✕	✕	✕	✕	✕	✕	✕	✕	✕	✕	✕	✕
Over 200 lbs.	✕	✕					✕		✕	✕	✕	✕	✕	✕	✕	✕	✕	✕	✕	✕	✕	✕	✕	✕
EQUIPMENT																								
Powered	✕		✕	✕		✕	✕	✕	✕	✕	✕	✕	✕	✕	✕	✕	✕	✕	✕	✕	✕	✕	✕	✕
Operator Req'd.		✕			✕		✕	✕	✕	✕	✕		✕											
Mobile										✕	✕	✕		✕										
Self Load./Unload			✕												✕	✕								
Tiering/Stacking									✕								✕		✕	✕		✕	✕	✕
Elevate/Lower								✕									✕		✕	✕		✕	✕	✕
Positioning																	✕		✕	✕		✕	✕	✕
Transferring	✕					✕				✕							✕		✕	✕		✕	✕	✕
Controls																								
Manual	✕	✕	✕	✕	✕	✕	✕	✕	✕	✕	✕	✕	✕	✕	✕	✕	✕		✕	✕		✕	✕	✕
Automatic	✕															✕	✕		✕	✕		✕		✕
Remote	✕																✕							✕

Fig. 11–5. (Continued)

377

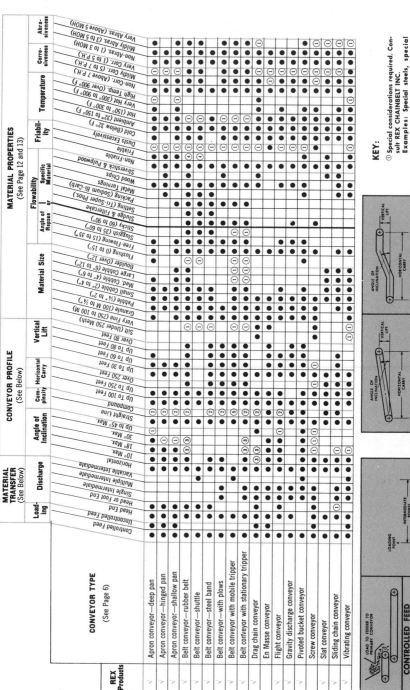

Fig. 11–6. Conveyor selecto-guide. (From Conveyor Division, Rex Chainbelt, Inc.)

KEY:

① Special considerations required. Consult REX CHAINBELT INC. Examples: Special steels, special belts, enclosures, etc.

② In combinations of inclined and horizontal units only.

③ Investigate maximum operating angle for material handled.

④ At controlled belt speeds.

⑤ Tripper must be located on horizontal section.

by Figures 5–1 and 11–5 and 11–6, *can* be structured as a computer "routine." This was, in fact done, but for a limited "repertoire" of equipment (only 17 types)—and was proved workable. However, the practical problems of implementing such a program with over 500 equipment types has so far proven impractical, primarily due to the tremendous technical task of reducing the 500 plus types to comparable data profiles—and the forbidding task of keeping such a "file" up-to-date. The block diagram depicting the computer program is shown in Figure 11–7, and a sample printout of "suggested" equipment possibilities is shown in Fig. 11–8.

As the reader views the figures in this chapter, he will gain an insight into the tremendous complexity of the problem. However, he should not become discouraged, since a reasonable amount of practical experience will fairly well qualify him in a particular company. And—the guides presented here should prove helpful as a means of gaining knowledge.

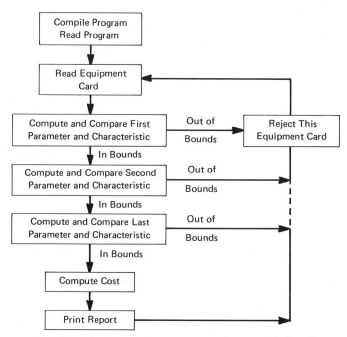

Fig. 11–7. Flow diagram of computerized material handling equipment selection program.

5. Evaluate Alternatives

Having narrowed the choice to a relatively few types or pieces of equipment, its now necessary to carefully evaluate the alternatives. This consists of determining the cost of each alternative, as well as comparing

```
PROBLEM NUMBER 3
WEIGHT = 3000    CONTAINER =  1    UNLOAD LEVEL  = 84    AISLE WIDTH   = 144
LENGTH =   42    UNIT RATE  = 32   CURVES NUMBER =  3    FLOOR LOAD    = 500
WIDTH  =   30    DISTANCE  = 200   GRADES NUMBER =  2    OBSTACLES     =  2
HEIGHT =   48    LOAD LEVEL =  6   GRADE PERCENT = 10    FLOOR TYPE    =  3

   B C  I     L M L F F M M I O T A A A N C
   A A  N     D A I O O A A N U I T T T E O
   L P  C     A X F R R X X N U I T T T T S
   A A  H     D T K K G S R R E A A A A T
   N G        L   R P A A T C C C W B
   C I  L     S L W A E D D Y H H H E A
   E T  B     T F P G I D E U U P G S
   Y S        R T D T D E D S S E 1 2 3 T E

1 30  90000 15 144 99 30 33 18 11 2 68 3 1 3 4 48 $ 6000  TOWMOTOR MODEL 5103015  ATTACHMENT FOR
1 30 121500 24 144 75 36 39 18 10 4 77 3 1 3 5 61 $ 6500  TOWMOTOR MODEL 5023024  ATTACHMENT FOR
1 40 163000 24 144 75 36 39 18 10 2 77 3 1 3 5 71 $ 7000  TOWMOTOR MODEL 5024024  ATTACHMENT FOR
1 40 163000 24 144 70 36 39 18 10 7 88 3 1 3 4 70 $ 7200  TOWMOTOR MODEL 6014024  ATTACHMENT FOR
1 50 203750 24 144 70 36 39 18 10 1 88 3 1 3 4 77 $ 7500  TOWMOTOR MODEL 6015024  ATTACHMENT FOR
--------------EQUIPMENT FILE EXHAUSTED--------------
```

Fig. 11–8. Computer printout of material handling equipment selection program.

the intangible aspects of each. The Preliminary Material Handling Equipment Evaluation Sheet (Figure 11–1) may be found helpful at this point. More detailed procedures are developed in Chapter 14.

6. Check Selection for Compatibility

During the equipment selection process, constant attention should be given to the compatibility of the equipment types under consideration with other equipment in use, or to be used. It must be remembered that the material handling *system* is a composite solution to a number of interrelated handling problems. Each segment of the system must be carefully integrated with all of the other segments—and a major aspect of the overall solution is the handling equipment.

In general, it can be said that a material handling system consists of a solution which ties together all interrelated handling operations and equitably integrates all phases of the entire problem into the overall implementation of the flow of materials through the plant.

This phase of the selection process also suggests that *compatible* equipment also implies a consideration of simplification (reduction of equipment varieties) and standardization (reduction of models and makes).

7. Select Specific Type of Equipment

Next, on the basis of the preceding analyses, it should be possible to select the specific type of material handling equipment. In review, the overall procedure has guided the analyst gradually through several important steps. Help has been given along the way:

1. *The material handling equation* focused attention on the three major phases of the problem: material, move, and method.
2. The 11 primary subfactors were spelled out and detailed.

   —material type   —move type
   —material characteristics   —handling unit
   —quantity   —equipment
   —source and destination   —manpower
   —logistics   —physical restrictions
   —move characteristics

3. The *Material Handling Check Sheets* helped in identifying the specific problem.
4. The *Problem Solving Guide* outlined the entire procedure.
5. The *Basic Data Required* form facilitated the accumulation of the necessary facts, figures and information.
6. The *Process Chart, Flow Diagram,* etc. were used in analyzing the move portion of the problem.

7. The *Storage Data Sheet* was useful in gathering information on the storage aspects of the problem.
8. The *Preliminary Material Handling Equipment Evaluation Sheet* served as an aid in comparing equipment alternatives against the less quantitative aspects of the problem.
9. The *Material Handling Analysis Re-cap Sheet* made it possible to condense all the important data collected into a convenient format.
10. The *Equipment Selection Guides* and related data were of assistance in selecting the types of equipment for the job.
11. The *Equipment Operating Cost Determination* form (Chapter 14) will put the cost aspect in sharper focus and result in comparative hourly costs for the operation of the equipment.
12. The *Re-cap of Comparative Costs* form (in Chapter 14) will assure proper consideration of *all* cost factors, as well as of the intangible factors.

Experience, of course, is still the most helpful ingredient in the equipment selection process—and the analyst will obtain this only by working in the field. It might be encouraging to know that there *are* men who, by reason of their long experience, are able to take an "educated look" at a handling situation, and withdraw from their fund of knowledge *the* best piece of equipment for the job. In fact, if one were to observe such an individual "in action," he would note an almost computer-like observation and thinking process as the "expert" views and assimilates the problem, and then "selects" the equipment.

8. Prepare Specifications

Having selected the equipment type most appropriate to the problem solution, it must now be procured, and the first step is that of detailing the performance specifications to assure that the several competitive bids to be obtained will be compatible, that is, on the same or equivalent piece of equipment.

A careful study of the type of equipment selected will be necessary to familiarize the analyst with what details *should* be specified, and the permissible variations he can allow. This is extremely important, so that the bidders will have *some* leeway and also so that a desired bidder is not "boxed out" by the specifications. However, if the specifications are too "loose," the resulting piece of equipment may not perform as required. As the analyst grows in experience, and his knowledge about equipment increases, it will be possible for him to write specifications to "fit" those pieces of equipment he *knows* will do the job—even to the makes and models. To a certain extent, this is "boxing in" those makes or models that *will* be acceptable, and "boxing out" those he does not choose to consider. In such a situation, a careful balance must be maintained in order to be fair to all qualified competitors and so as not to arouse the animosity of possible future suppliers. If the equipment being specified requires design work, it should be done at this point. Carefully detailed drawings are a necessary part of many specifications and will help assure compatible bids. Figures 11–9 and 11–10 illustrate the types of forms useful in comparing specifications and technical details of alternative pieces of equipment.

In complex, integrated systems, where several suppliers may have to work together, and where much design work is necessary, extra care must be taken in the first broad system specifications. If the vendors are not allowed enough freedom in designing *their* portions of the system, it is possible that the material handling engineer might have inadvertently limited the flexibility and imagination of the vendor's design engineers.

Again, experience is the by-word, and in this regard it is frequently advisable to call in a consultant. His broad background and experience in various industries and situations makes him eminently qualified to aid in conceptualizing the system, in writing the specifications, and in fact, in coordinating the implementation of the entire project.

9. Procure Equipment

Once the specifications have been determined, the procurement process can begin. If the material handling engineer does not have a knowledge of sources of supply, he should consult the trade magazines and directories. Two outstanding sources of such information are the *Material Handling Engineering Directory and Handbook* referred to elsewhere in this text and the annual equipment issue of *Modern Materials Handling* magazine.

After prospective suppliers have been selected, formal requests for quotations may be issued, accompanied by the final specifications and drawings. In many cases, the analyst may also want to work with local distributors and have their sales representatives call on him to discuss the problem.

In either case, quotations should be requested in writing, and when received, should show evidence of including all items covered by the specifications. Upon their receipt, the engineer should evaluate them carefully. It will probably be found desirable to again use the Equipment Operating Cost Determination form, and the other equipment evaluation techniques from Chapter 14, or comparative analysis forms similar to Figs. 11–9 and 11–10, now that specific makes and models are

Low- and High-Lift Power-Operated Platform Trucks
Walkie and Rider Types—Gasoline and Electric Types

Name of Manufacturer								
Model No.								
Technical Data:								
1. Rated capacity								
2. Lowered height								
3. Maximum lift								
4. Size of platform								
5. Service weight								
6. Over-all length								
7. Over-all width								
8. Underclearance at center								
9. Height of driver's platform								
10. Wheel base								
11. Drive wheel or wheels— type and size								
12. Turning radius—inside								
13. Turning radius—outside								
14. Intersecting aisles								
15. Rt. angle stack—aisle req.								
16. Top speed—forward loaded								
17. Top speed—forward unloaded								
18. Top speed—reverse loaded								
19. Top speed—reverse unloaded								
20. Lift speed—loaded								
21. Lift speed—unloaded								
22. Driver control position								
23. Type of lift								
24. Driver's vision								
25. Type of drive coupling								
26. Hand and/or foot controls								
27. Type of steer								
28. Ampere-hour capacity of battery for 8 hr.								
29. Weight of battery								
30. Price of battery								
31. Walkie Only — Position of hand control								
32. Walkie Only — Location of raising & lowering buttons or levers								
33. Walkie Only — Length of steer handle in fully extended position								
34. Walkie Only — Position of regular brakes								
35. Walkie Only — Position of dynamic brakes								
36. Degree of grade it will climb with full load								
37. Complete truck price, less battery								
38. Type and capacity of charger recommended								
39. Price of charger								

Fig. 11–9. Form for analyzing manufacturers' specifications. (From H. A. Bolz and G. E. Hagemann, *Materials Handling Handbook,* The Ronald Press Co., New York, 1958.)

	BIDDER A		BIDDER B	
GENERAL:				
1. Capacity	20/5 Ton		20/5 Ton	
2. Span	90'0''		90'0''	
3. Lift	35'0''		35'0''	
4. Total Net Weight	88,000 lbs.		77,000 lbs.	
HOISTS:	**Main Hoist**	**Aux. Hoist**	**Main Hoist**	**Aux. Hoist**
1. Hoist Speed	25 FPM	54 FPM	25 FPM	54 FPM
2. HP of Hoist Motor and Rating	40 HP 30 M. -55° C.	20 HP	40 HP	20 HP
3. Computed HP Required	39 HP	19.7 HP	39 HP	19.7 HP
4. Number and Parts of Rope	8 parts 5/8''	4 - 1/2''	8 - 9/16''	4 - 3/8''
5. Type of Wire Rope	6/19 Improved Plow Steel	6/19 Improved Plow Steel	6/19 Improved Plow Steel	6/19 Improved Plow Steel
6. Diameter of Hoist Drum	20''	15''	15''	10''
7. Material in Drum	Welded Steel	Cast Iron	Cast Iron	Cast Iron
8. Type of Bearing	Hyatt Roller	Hyatt Roller	Hyatt Roller	Hyatt Roller
9. Make & Type of Gears & Pinions	Spur Gears Welded Steel Forged Steel Pinions	Spur Gears Welded Steel Forged Steel Pinions	Spur Gears Welded Steel Forged Steel Pinions	Spur Gears Welded Steel Forged Steel Pinions
10 Material of Gears and Pinions	Gears SAE 8630 Pin. SAE 8742 Heat Treated Hardened	Gears SAE 8630 Pi. SAE 8742 Heat Treated Hardened	Gears SAE 1040 Pinions SAE 1045	Gears SAE 1040 Pinions SAE 1045
TROLLEY:				
1. Trolley Speed	200 FPM		125 FPM	
2. HP of Trolley Motor and Rating	7½ HP		3 HP	
3. Computed Running HP Required	3.5 HP		1.96 HP	
4. Service Factor Used	2.14		1.53 HP	
5. Diameter of Trolley Wheels	13½''		12''	
6. Spread of Trolley	8'0''		7'0''	
7. Type of Bearings	Hyatt 5214		Hyatt 5212	
8. Make & Type of Gears & Pinions	Welded Spur Gears - Forged Steel Pinions		Welded Spur Gears - Forged Steel Pinions	
9. Material of Gears and Pinions	Gears SAE 8630 —▸ Pinions SAE 8742 Heat Treated — Hardened		Gears SAE 1040 Pinions SAE 1045	
10. Weight of Trolley complete	18,400 lbs.		13,000 lbs.	
BRIDGE:				
1. Bridge Speed	300 FPM		300 FPM	
2. HP of Bridge Motor and Rating	25 HP		20 HP	
3. Computed Running HP Required	8.85		8.75	
4. Service Factor Used	2.83		2.29	
5. Girder Section at Center of Span	Top-28 x ¾'' Bot.-28 x ½'' Webs-60 x ¼''		Top-28 x 5/8'' Bot. - 28 x 3/8'' Webs - 54 x 5/16''	
6. Number & Dia. of Bridge Wheels	4 - 24''		4 - 21''	
7. Maximum Wheel Load	50,600 lbs		44,000 lbs.	
8. Wheel Base	13'8''		12'3''	
ELECTRICAL:				
Control —				
Make & Type of Hoist Control	Semi-Magnetic Drum		Drum Control	
Make & Type of Aux. Hoist Control	Semi-Magnetic Drum		Drum Control	
Make & Type of Hoist Limit Switches	Motor Circuit		Control Circuit	
Make & Type of Trolley Control	Drum		Drum	
Make & Type of Bridge Control	Drum		Drum	
Make & Type of Overload Protection	Overload Relays		Fuses	

Fig. 11—10. Form for comparative analysis of overhead crane bids. (From Frank M. Blum, "How to Evaluate Crane Bids," Harnischfeger Corp., Milwaukee, Wisconsin.)

being considered. The procedures in Chapter 14 might also prove very helpful in evaluating the intangible factors.

A word should also be said here about the "make or buy" problem. Since many items of material handling equipment are not "shelf" items, but custom-designed devices, consideration might be given to developing and building the equipment within the plant. At least, if an appropriate plant capability exists, their personnel should be given an opportunity to "bid" on the equipment. More detailed information on the "make or buy" problem can be found in an engineering economy text.

The final decision on the source of the equipment will most likely be made by the material handling engineer, in conjunction with those other plant personnel who usually participate in such matters. However, the "burden of proof" rests on the material handling engineer. His work should be complete, accurate, and up-to-date. It is *his* reputation that is at stake in the final solution of the problem.

LEASE VS. PURCHASE

It would be wrong to conclude the equipment selection process without giving consideration to the lease vs. purchase question. Since leasing is becoming increasingly popular, the pros and cons should be reviewed carefully, in relation to company investment policies. Some aspects for consideration of the problem are outlined below:

A. *Factors to be considered in leasing*
   1. Availability of working capital
   2. Ability to borrow
   3. Earnings from equipment investment
   4. Tax consequences
   5. Condition of financial ratios
   6. Operating conditions (special requirements vs. standard equipment)
   7. Maintenance facilities available
   8. Down time probabilities
B. *Advantages of leasing*
   1. Retention of working capital
   2. Protection of credit rating
   3. Service and repairs furnished
   4. Payments are a business *expense* (vs. a capital expenditure)
   5. Technological advances become the problem of the lessor
   6. Avoid cost of inflation
   7. Tax advantages
   8. Possible lower net cost (including return on capital investment)

   9. Easier to sell management (than purchasing)
  10. Flexibility in use of equipment (may lease for a short time)
  11. Simplifies accounting
  12. Aids modernization without "using up" capital
C. *Disadvantages of leasing*
   1. Prestige of ownership gone
   2. Possible dispossession (cancellation or non-renewal of lease)
   3. Restricted freedom of action (on possible desired modification of equipment)
   4. Higher cash outlay
   5. Leasing of less value if company *has* sufficient cash
D. *Types of leases*
   1. Straight: lessor retains ownership
   2. Lease-option (to buy): actually a financing plan
   3. Lease with full maintenance
   4. Fleet lease: several pieces of equipment
   5. Power package lease: battery and charger
   6. Master lease: permits leasing of additional equipment without renegotiating of lease
   7. Package lease: covers a variety of equipment
   8. Rental: for short-term, indefinite needs
   9. Time payments: similar to lease-option

The above items should all be given proper consideration from both an operating and financial point-of-view, and by a thorough investigation with local distributors.

CONCLUSION

This chapter has presented an orderly approach to the analysis of one of industry's most perplexing problems: how to select the right piece of handling equipment. As was stated at the outset, the selection process is often a nebulous and complex task. In order to avoid the mistakes of the snap judgment or off-the-cuff types of decisions, a rather detailed procedure has been described. Although it may appear to be a forbidding process, the only proper approach to such a complex problem situation is an orderly one. It is felt that the procedure and the several forms presented will literally serve as "crutches" to help the analyst along the way. At the *least*, they will help him to organize his thinking along proper channels. At the *most*, they may permit him to reach a solution to a difficult problem which might otherwise be unattainable because of its complexity and the myriad aspects to be examined and evaluated. Hopefully, the procedure will have gradually steered him closer to a correct solution. It is felt that little if any further *written* advice can be added to help solve equipment selection problems. From here on, the "one best way" depends on the analyst continuing to expand his knowledge of equipment, its characteristics, and its applications.

Rather obviously, the procedure itself will not *solve* any problems, nor will it select any equipment. Each problem differs from others, and certainly it will be found necessary to vary the procedure or redesign some of the suggested forms to better fit individual problems. However, the thinking process outlined here will be found helpful in guiding the analyst toward a better solution to the problem. Constant use of the procedure will inevitably make it easier for the analyst to cope with such problems, and will eventually make it possible for him to carry out some of the steps "in his head." Again, experience is the most helpful tool in the guarantee of a proper solution.

12

Material Handling
at the Workplace

As pointed out previously in this text, the typical concept of material handling envisions in-plant handling and more specifically that movement of materials necessary to implement the progress of work from one operation to the next. Of course it may also include such related activities as the movements of materials into and out of storage, or between departments or buildings. And in the more recent interpretations, material handling is concerned with complex, integrated handling systems, as discussed in Chapter 9.

However, one aspect of material handling which has been long neglected is that which is carried on at the workplace. This oversight has probably been "excused" because:

1. Such handling appears to be a minor part of the overall system.
2. It does not always involve the large, expensive equipment types most frequently pictured as "material handling equipment."
3. The material handling engineer may feel it is outside his area of responsibility, while . . .
4. The methods engineer feels that anything above and beyond the more common hand motions performed at or near a workplace is beyond the scope of his responsibility.
5. The types of equipment that can be used to improve the handling may not be known to the methods or process engineer.

So, material handling at the workplace has remained an orphan—someone else's responsibility. However, the material handling engineer should be vitally interested in extending his efforts toward the integration of the overall handling system as far into every operation as he possibly can. This chapter will examine the workplace as an area of utmost importance, and one which should be of extreme interest to the material handling engineer, if for no other reason than the default of others in the manufacturing planning processes.

Some of the reasons for considering the handling of materials at the workplace are:

1. The growing interest in separating out the *real, total* material handling content of a production activity
2. Drawing attention to that percentage of the activity and costs which are material handling
3. Arousing interest—by virtue of this percentage—in considering improvement opportunities
4. Properly allocating cost components

It will be argued by some that such a detailed breakdown will only result in a shuffling of cost components from one category to another, and that the total cost will remain the same. This of course may be true, except that the procedure *should* result in a more accurate knowledge of cost components, and this in turn should lead to more intelligent improvement efforts.

WHAT IS MATERIAL HANDLING AT THE WORKPLACE?

Material handling at the workplace may be defined as that handling which must be done *after* the material has been delivered and set down for use at the workplace, and *before* it is picked up to be removed to the next operation. In diagrammatic form, this would appear as in Figure 12–1.

The "workplace" is considered to be that area in which an operator performs a specific operation, or operations; it is usually spelled out as *an* operation on a production routing or operation sheet; and is usually a unit of work upon which a time standard has been set.

The following characteristics of material handling at the workplace suggest some of the unique aspects which separate it from "traditional" material handling:

1. The distances involved are relatively short
2. The number of moves is usually high, i.e., it is a function of the number of cycles performed
3. The greater portion of the cycle time required at an individual workplace is taken up *by* material handling

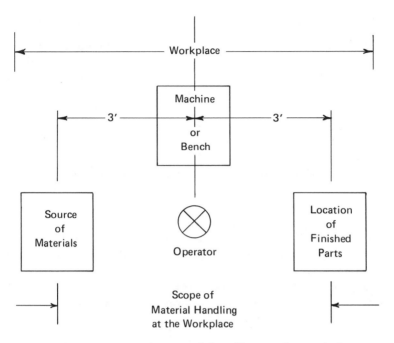

Fig. 12–1. Scope of material handling at the workplace.

4. Much of this material handling is *commonly* classified as direct labor!
5. Much of the handling activity at the workplace is subject to improvement by traditional material handling techniques and devices

The above emphasizes the uniqueness of this handling problem and suggests an entirely new area for investigation and the identification of cost improvement possibilities.

Actually, there may be some disagreement that the activity under discussion is *really* material handling. In the normal recordkeeping procedures of industry, the work activity being considered here is mostly classified as "production," and the time spent in handling the material is a part of the operation cycle; is included in the standard time; and is paid for as direct labor. However, since the *handling* part of the activity is subject to improvement by material handling techniques and devices, it will be considered here as *material handling*—regardless of how it is classified in the cost system. Furthermore, in the concept of direct costing, it is conceivable that such handling activities *should* be separated out and classified as material handling costs, instead of being buried under the broad cover of direct labor.

CONSIDERATIONS IN MATERIAL HANDLING AT THE WORKPLACE

Although the distances involved in handling materials at the workplace are generally relatively short, the *number* of these moves is the factor which emphasizes their importance. For example, a fork truck or conveyor may deliver a container of 1,000 items to an operator, at the start of his shift, in a matter of a few minutes. But the handling and processing of these 1,000 pieces may occupy the operator for an hour, a day, or a week. Since it is probable that each individual item must be handled by the operator—into, through, and out of the workplace—the total time involved in *handling* the materials *at* the workplace may run into many hours. Consider a relatively simple situation, such as that depicted in Figure 12–2.

The total cycle time—as determined by time study (or other means) —is .30 minute. Of the total, .05 minute is *actual* processing time—during which the *form* of the material is being physically *changed*, and is truly *direct* labor.

If the operator did no more (or less) than pick up the item, put it into the machine, and dispose of it to the proper location, his activities—and related times—might be as follows:

	Material Handling	Actual Processing
1. *Pick up part* from container on left, with both hands	.06 min.	—
2. *Place part* into fixture	.08	—
3. PROCESSING, controlled by machine	—	.05 min.
4. *Remove part* from fixture	.04	—
5. *Place part* into container on right, with both hands	.07	—
	.25 min.	.05 min.

This would make the actual processing time .05/.30 × 100 percent, or 16⅔ percent of the total. The balance, or 83⅓ percent, *could* be classified as material handling. For the 1,000 parts mentioned above, the total times would be:

$$1,000 \times .05 \text{ min} = 50 \text{ min processing}$$
$$1,000 \times .25 \text{ min} = 250 \text{ min material handling}$$

The 250 minutes, or 4⅙ hours, spent in handling materials at the workplace is actually non-productive time, or indirect labor, and is well worth the serious attention of the material handling engineer, in cooperation with the process and/or methods engineers.

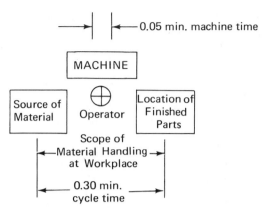

Fig. 12–2. Time relationships in material handling at the workplace. (From *Production Handbook,* The Ronald Press Co., New York, 1972.)

While it is inevitable that materials must be handled—either manually or mechanically—it is obviously important that the total costs involved be kept to a practical minimum.

The costs of material handling may be considered as consisting of:

1. Human energy, either properly utilized or wasted in handling
2. Man-hours consumed by the handling activity
3. Costs of equipment utilized in handling
4. Costs of manpower used in handling
5. Costs of injuries attributable to material handling
6. Cost of materials damaged or scrapped due to material handling

All of these costs are commonly considered part of factory overhead or burden—which is always a prime target for cost reduction. Any effort resulting in the reduction of *these* material handling costs will result in a corresponding reduction in factory overhead.

PHASES OF MATERIAL HANDLING AT THE WORKPLACE

As can be imagined from the preceding discussion, material handling at the workplace can become a quite involved and extremely complex area for investigation. Subdividing it into its several phases will help to visualize and analyze its complexities and its interrelationships with the productive activities. These phases are:

1. *Preparatory*—handling of materials *adjacent* to the workplace and prior to their use at the workplace.
   a. Bringing materials closer to or into the workplace or machine

    b. Re-arranging, re-stacking, sorting, or separating materials

    c. Unwrapping, untangling, or unpacking materials

2. *Feeding*—placing or directing materials *closer to* the work place or point-of-use (sometimes combined with positioning).

    a. Placing materials in work area or surface

    b. Feeding materials toward point-of-use

3. *Positioning*—orienting materials *into* the workplace or point-of-use.

    a. Positioning materials in proper location for operation

    b. Placing materials into fixture, jig, machine

4. *Manipulating*—handling or holding materials within or through the workplace—during the operation, assembly, inspection, etc.

    a. Actually performing the operation

    b. Assembling, disassembling, etc.

    c. Transferring from machine station to station, spindle to spindle

    d. If manual = direct labor

    e. If mechanical = overhead

      (The above portion is *not* regarded as material handling.)

5. *Removing*—taking materials *out of* the workplace or machine.

    a. Taking materials out of the jig, fixture, etc.

    b. Disposing material to a location for moving to next workplace

6. *Transporting*—moving materials *away* from the workplace.

    a. Moving a part to the next workplace

    b. Usually *this* is "traditional" material handling

It should be noted that the major concern of material handling at the workplace is for the preparatory, feeding, positioning, and removing phases, since manipulating is usually a part of direct labor, and transporting is part of "material handling."

ADVANTAGES OF PROPER WORKPLACE HANDLING

If proper planning is applied to the several types of work involved in material handling at the workplace, it should be found that:

1. Highly skilled personnel will spend more time on actual production
2. Less skilled personnel can take over much of the required manual handling
3. Employee fatigue will be reduced
4. Production will be increased
5. Many handling activities can be mechanized
6. Operations will be safer
7. Employee morale will be higher
8. Less material will be spoiled or damaged
9. Housekeeping will be improved around the workplace
10. Flow of materials will be smoother
11. Handling will be more efficient, due to less congestion in work area

It would certainly appear that such benefits are worth the effort of investigating the material handling activities in and around the workplace.

RELATIONSHIPS BETWEEN PLANT LAYOUT AND THE WORKPLACE

It has been stated that material handling can be no more efficient than is permitted by the overall plant layout—and a good plant layout is designed around a well-planned flow pattern. This suggests that an efficient handling system would result from a design that properly coordinates the activities along the flow pattern, with the handling methods and equipment necessary to implement the movement of materials into and out of individual workplaces.

Assume a typical flow pattern, as indicated in Figure 12–3. Each line represents the path to be followed by a product component, or several components.

As shown, the planned direction of materials flow in each line has been determined, and should be adhered to in each subsequent planning step. One of these steps is the *design* of the individual workplaces required to produce the part that will move along each flow line. It is important that each individual workplace be properly designed and properly placed in its respective flow line, to insure the smooth flow of materials. For example, if the flow line on the left (Figure 12–3) flows from "north" to "south," then the flow of material through *any* workplace on the line should also flow from north to south, regardless of which "side" of the line it is planned for. And this is primarily dependent upon whether the workplace is *planned* for a right-to-left, or left-to-right flow of material. This concept is illustrated in Figure 12–4.

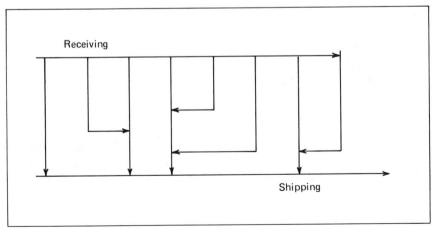

Fig. 12–3. Material flow pattern.

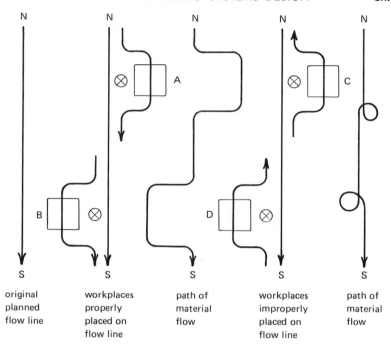

Fig. 12–4. Relationships between material flow pattern and workplace material flow.

In Figure 12–4, workplace "A" has been planned for N-S, or left to right, flow and "fits" in its proper relationship to the planned materials flow. Workplace "B" has been planned for N-S flow also, but right to left movement—since it is on the *other* side of the line. However, it too "fits" into the overall flow pattern.

But workplaces "C" and "D" have *not* been planned to fit properly into the line. The parts being handled prescribe reverse circular paths through the workplaces. Suppose, for example, that each "backward" pass through a workplace (C and D) takes an extra .01 minute, because of a required transfer of the part from one hand to the other, due to the design of the workplace. If 1,000,000 units per year pass through such a workplace, 10,000 extra minutes or 167 extra hours are being paid for. If an hour costs $5.00 (labor + overhead), this represents an annual loss of $835 per workplace. Certainly such situations should not be permitted to creep into a layout. It can be readily seen that the improper placement of a workplace on a flow line will result in backtracking and unnecessary, and therefore, costly handling. For these reasons, it is evident that each individual workplace is an integral part of the overall plant layout and its materials flow pattern.

RELATIONSHIPS BETWEEN MATERIALS STORAGE AND THE WORKPLACE

Another situation related to material handling at the workplace is the storage of items to be used at the workplace. There are many ways of implementing this problem, including the following:

1. *Centralized Storage:* in which all parts used at a workplace are stored in one central "stock room" or similar area, until needed. They are then delivered to the appropriate workplaces. This method requires movement into the storage area; storage; and movement out again. Frequently, such an area is some distance from the workplaces and results in excess handling.
2. *Decentralized Storage:* in which several smaller "stock rooms" are utilized. Nearly the same conditions exist as above; although move distances may be somewhat shorter.
3. *Moving Storage:* in which parts are placed on a conveyor that "circulates" between the source of the parts and the area in which they are to be used. It also circulates *among* the workplaces being served. Figures 12–5 and 12–6 illustrate this method of in-process storage.
4. *Moving Workplace (to storage):* in which the materials remain in a fixed position and the tools and/or operators move *to* the materials. This is common where the material or part is large, or heavy, or cannot easily be moved. Another common example is in a mine, quarry, or similar situation, where the material is "fixed" in its location. And in other cases, the operator and workplace are moved to the materials location.
5. *Point-of-Use Storage:* in which materials to be used at a specific point, are stored *at* the point. In its ideal application, materials are delivered directly from the incoming common carrier and set down *at* the workplace in the position in which they will be used. In practice, this "ideal" plan is frequently interrupted by necessary receiving inspection and stock storage activities. Figures 12–7, 12–8, and 12–9 illustrate this concept, with the latter showing the re-stocking of the area. In the situation shown, the *entire* inventory of parts used at the workplace is stored in the pallet boxes and racks adjacent to the bench. Working stock is on the first two "levels," while reserve stock is placed above.

PLANNING AN EFFICIENT WORKPLACE

It should be remembered that each workplace is a miniature "factory" with its own "receiving," "production," and "shipping" areas. One of the big problems in planning workplaces is that of tying each one into the

Fig. 12–5. Refrigerator parts on an overhead storage (bank) conveyor. (Courtesy of FMC/Link Belt Division.)

overall flow pattern. To aid in reaching this objective, the following general procedure will serve as a guide:

1. Determine direction of general flow of material or activity through the plant or department from the overall flow pattern.
2. Based on the above, determine the desired direction of flow through the workplace, i.e., left-to-right, right-to-left, front-to-back, or back-to-front.
3. Determine items be contained in the workplace, such as machine type, bench, stock containers, conveyors, etc.
4. Make a rough sketch of the major pieces of equipment in the workplace in their approximate desired positions and indicate direction of material flow (from No. 2 above) by an arrow.

Fig. 12–6. Wheel-type conveyors serving as moving storage between operations. (Courtesy of The Logan Company.)

5. Indicate sources of materials used in the workplace, and the direction from which they come.
6. Indicate the destination of the materials from the workplace, and the directions to which they must go.
7. If applicable, indicate method of waste or scrap disposal and direction to which it must go.
8. Sketch in any material handling equipment serving the workplace or area.
9. Check the sketch against the principles of motion economy and workplace layout (below) to assure consideration of necessary factors.
10. Indicate distance between items in the workplace on the sketch.
11. Record workplace plan to scale and in detail on an Operation Chart or similar form.
12. If practical at this point, indicate desired method operator should follow in performing the operation, as illustrated in Figures 12–10A, 12–10B, and 12–10C.

Following the procedure should help to assure the proper integration of each workplace into the overall materials flow pattern. Further design

Fig. 12–7. Point-of-use storage. (From James M. Apple, *Plant Layout and Materials Handling,* The Ronald Press Co., New York, 1963.)

effort is required to implement the workplace *handling* activities. This is discussed in a following section of this chapter, on workplace handling equipment.

PRINCIPLES OF WORKPLACE LAYOUT

One of the easiest ways to eliminate, minimize, or improve material handling at the workplace is through the application of the "principles of workplace layout," which have been adapted from well-known principles

Fig. 12–8. Typical assembly line work station using portable tray-trucks to furnish subassemblies made in bays at rear and as pictured in Fig. 12–7. (From James M. Apple, *Plant Layout and Materials Handling,* The Ronald Press Co., New York, 1963.)

of motion economy and supplemented by other factors closely related to the design and arrangement of a workplace. They are stated as follows:

1. Plan for tools, gages, materials, and machine controls to be located close to and in front of operator.
2. Plan a definite place for tools, gages, and materials.
3. Plan to use gravity when possible to feed and remove materials.
4. Plan to pre-position materials and tools within the workplace.
5. Plan for delivery of materials directly to point of use.
6. Arrange material so operator is not required to "prepare" or reposition it.
7. Plan prompt and efficient removal of materials from workplace.
8. Provide adequate means for planned scrap removal.
9. Plan location of materials within workplace to permit obtaining them with the most efficient sequence of motions.
10. Plan proper height relationships between material supply, point-of-use, and disposal.
11. Plan each workplace in proper relationship to preceding and following operations.
12. Plan storage for a practicable minimum of incoming materials at workplace as well as for finished work awaiting removal.

Fig. 12–9. Restocking point-of-use materials supply. (From James M. Apple, *Plant Layout and Materials Handling,* The Ronald Press Co., New York, 1963.)

13. Leave sufficient space at workplace for efficient material delivery, storage and removal.
14. Select appropriate handling equipment (covered in a following section).
15. Be sure handling equipment at workplace is properly integrated into overall handling system.
16. Avoid placing materials directly on the floor, without a pallet or other support underneath.
17. Plan to use the same container throughout the system; avoid frequent changes.

18. Provide necessary clearances in and around each workplace for proper performance of the operation, and for maneuvering handling equipment.
19. Place product on packing base (pallet, skid, etc.) as early in the process as is practical.
20. Combine operations in order to eliminate intermediate handlings.
21. Make judicious use of manual handling.
22. Plan to minimize walking.
23. Use containers, racks, etc., to hold items so as to prevent damage to work already completed.

Faithful attention to the above principles of workplace layout can often result in worthwhile economies with little or no expense—since many of them are concerned only with the arrangement of facilities within the workplace for more efficient handling.

IMPLEMENTING WORKPLACE HANDLING

In implementing the material handling at the workplace, the problems may be most conveniently considered in terms of the six phases of workplace handling. They are restated below, with suggestions and comments to aid in improving the handling activities within each.

1. *Preparatory:* handling of materials adjacent to the workplace.
   a. Work with vendors for packaging to prevent tangling, mixing, etc.
   b. Use unit packs, dispensing packages, etc.
   c. Put materials down in the *right* position the *first* time.
2. *Feeding:* placing or directing materials closer to the workplace or machine.
   a. Use gravity chutes, conveyors, etc., to move materials closer to point of use.
   b. Use feeders for individual pieces, sheets, coils, bars, etc. to increase both efficiency and safety in loading.
   c. Plan mechanical feeding if practicable to assure a uniform, constant, regulated, and uninterrupted flow.
   d. Use hopper-shaped bins
3. *Positioning:* orienting materials into the workplace or point of use.
   a. Use indexing devices and similar aids assuring positive alignment.
   b. Apply vibratory or rotary parts feeders.
   c. Make use of special containers, racks, trays, etc. to pre-position items.
4. *Manipulating:* handling or holding materials within or through the workplace.
   a. Review principles of motion economy (in any motion study text).

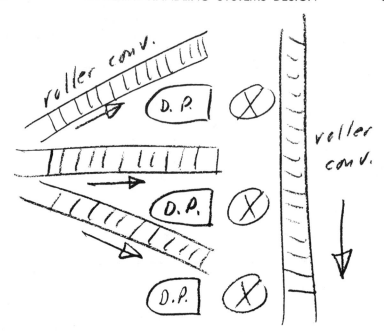

Fig. 12–10 A. Preliminary sketch of a work area plan. (From J. M. Apple, *Plant Layout and Materials Handling*, The Ronald Press Co., New York, 1963.)

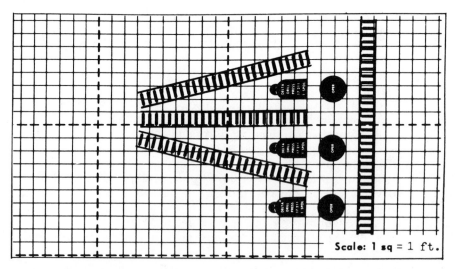

Fig. 12–10 B. Layout of area with commercial templates. (From J. M. Apple, *Plant Layout and Materials Handling*, The Ronald Press Co., New York, 1963.)

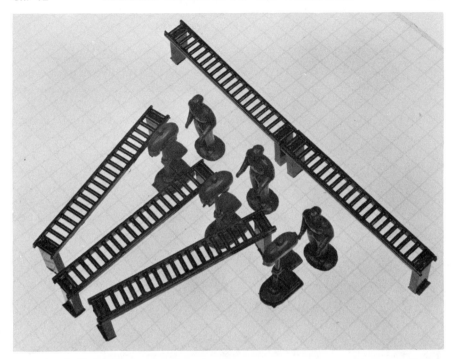

Fig. 12–10 C. Same work area as above, but in scale models. (From J. M. Apple, *Plant Layout and Materials Handling*, The Ronald Press Co., New York, 1963.)

    b. Review principles of workplace layout on previous pages.
  5. *Removing:* taking materials out of the workplace or machine.
    a. Allow space for a normal amount of finished material.
    b. Plan for removal at proper intervals to avoid congestion.
    c. Arrange for mechanical removal of materials.
    d. Plan for prompt removal of chips, turnings, scrap, etc.
  6. *Transporting:* carrying materials away from the workplace.
    a. Use mechanical devices or aids.
    b. Use gravity where practicable.
    c. Move materials promptly to avoid accumulation.
    d. Move materials in unit loads where practicable.

Many other ideas will come to mind as the analyst reviews the above, along with the principles of motion economy and workplace layout. Trade magazines and practical experience will also provide a background of resources to the material handling engineer.

WORKPLACE HANDLING EQUIPMENT

As suggested above, an important source of ideas for implementing work place handling is the wide variety of devices already on the market. Many of these are every-day, garden-variety production aids—but, are often overlooked as being useful as material handling devices. Some may be adapted from their originally intended purposes, while others can be combined or supplemented with custom designed devices. Some of the many kinds of equipment available are listed in Fig. 12–11, classified by the phases of workplace handling. Many of them are illustrated (in some other context) throughout this book. (See Figures 6–3, 6–7, 6–16, 6–20, 6–22, 6–28, 6–29, 6–30, 6–32, 6–38, 6–39, 6–40, 6–59, 6–60, 6–69.) Some of the more specialized devices and/or unusual applications are pictured at the end of this chapter.

INDUSTRIAL "ROBOTS" [1]

One of the most interesting devices for use in material handling at the workplace is the industrial "robot," or universal transfer device. Basically, it is a one-armed machine, capable of picking up items, manipulating or maneuvering them, and putting them down again—all with high precision of both location and motion path. Their capacity will equal or exceed that of the human operator in lifting capacity, reach, and continuous speed of operation. The hydraulically powered, computer-controlled arm has 3-dimensional capability, and can have many types of gripping devices attached to the end. An electronic control unit, with a memory, permits the device to be "taught" repetitive operations. Such devices currently cost about $20,000 to $25,000—but will very likely go down to under $15,000.

Some of the advantages and benefits of the universal transfer device are:

1. Monotonous operations need no longer be performed by human beings
2. Pacing of operators is easily possible
3. Work can be done in unpleasant or dangerous environments
4. Operations can be planned without regard to human limitations and frailties—such as: dexterity, sex, seniority, vacations, coffee breaks, carelessness, fatigue, etc.

[1]Adapted from D. F. Bowman, "Industrial Robots," *Plant Engineering*, Oct. 17, 1968.

1. PREPARATORY—handling of materials adjacent to the work place

—sorters
—sheet separators
—unstackers

—special racks, trays, etc.
—hand lift trucks
—conveyors

2. FEEDING—placing or directing materials closer to the work place or point-of use

—dial feed
—bar feeds
—reel feeds
—strip feeds
—sheet feeds

—conveyors
—trucks
—cranes
—magazine feeders

—hoppers
—gravity
—rotary
—vibratory
—chutes

3. POSITIONING—orienting materials into the work place or point of use

—mechanical positioners
—mechanical hands
—robots
—index tables

—rotary tables
—turnovers
—up-enders
—rotary chucks

—manipulators
—transfer machines
—work loaders

4. MANIPULATING—handling or holding materials within the work place

—robots (universal transfer devices)
—Unimate
—Versatran
—etc.

—work holders
—work positioners (see No. 3 above)
—manipulators
—assembly machines

5. REMOVING—taking materials out of the work place or machine

—ejectors
—chutes
—shuttles
—conveyors

—mechanical hands
—indexing devices
—rotary tables
—unloaders

—robots
—ball transfers

6. TRANSPORTING—carrying materials away from the work place

—conveyors
—chutes

—trucks
—cranes

7. MISCELLANEOUS
—vacuum lifter
—standard workplace
  equipment (benches, etc.)

—pallet loaders
—depalletizers
—automated equipment

Fig. 12–11. Workplace handling equipment classification.

5. Operations can run around-the-clock
6. Quality is improved through uniformity of activity and elimination of breakage and other damage.

Capabilities permit the devices to follow either continuous or point-to-point paths—with up to about 200 locational spots in the cycle. Some typical applications are shown on the chart in Figure 12–12.

INDUSTRIAL ROBOT APPLICATIONS—
JOB IMPROVEMENTS AND SAVINGS

Plant & Application	Labor Saving	Productivity	Quality	Environment/ Safety
Automotive Press Feeding	1 man/shift 2-10 hr. shifts/day 2.5 men/day	100% increase 570 parts/hour to 1150 parts/hour	Less die wear	Eliminates hand feeding
Automotive Forge Feeding	1 man/shift 2 shifts/day 2 men/day	(Line controlled)	Consistent time cycle	Removes man from hot job. 2200°F parts.
Automotive Injection Molding	1 man/shift 3 shifts/day 3 men/day	(Line controlled)	Better molding due to exact timing.	Removes man from hot job.
Metal Working Machine Unload	1 man/shift 2 shifts/day 2 men/day	(Line controlled)	Decreased damage to precision parts.	
Glass Rod Transfer Tube Transfer	2 men/shift 4 shift/week 8 men/day	Increase 15%	Decrease in breakage of fragile parts. Also reduces scratching.	Eliminates hand feeding of breakable material.
Glass Flat Glass Transfer	2 men/shift 3 shifts/day 6 men/day	(Line controlled)	Less breakage.	Removes men from high heat area. Part 600°F.
Glass Lehr Loading	1 man/shift 4 shift/week 4 men/day	Increase up to 20%.	Less breakage. Better heat control through accurate loading.	Increases operator safety.
Plumbing Fixtures Frit Spray	1 man/shift 2 shifts/day 2 men/day	Increase 30%	Consistent coating coverage. 40% material saving.	Removes person from toxic atmosphere.
Brick Plant Kiln Car Setting	2 men/shift 2 shifts/day 4 men/day	Increase 25%	Less marking of brick. Better firing through accurate positioning.	Removes operator from dusty, back-breaking job.

Fig. 12–12. Applications and benefits of universal transfer devices. (From D. F. Bowman, "Industrial Robots," *Plant Engineering*, Oct. 17, 1968.)

Figure 12–13 indicates cost relationships, and suggests economic feasibility on 1-, 2- and 3-shift basis.

Figures 12–14 to 12–22 illustrate some of the applications of universal transfer devices and other workplace handling equipment.

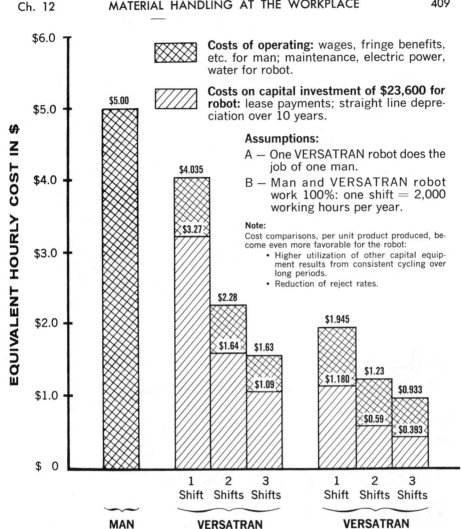

Fig. 12–13. Cost relationships of universal transfer devices. (Courtesy of Versatran Division, AMF, Inc.)

Fig. 12–14. Versatran removing cartons from conveyor and placing them in position in shipping crate. (Courtesy of Versatran Division, AMF, Inc.)

Fig. 12–15. Unimate removing die casting from machine. Subsequently, it starts the next cycle, turns the part over, quenches it in a tank of water, and places it on a conveyor. (Courtesy of Unimation, Inc.)

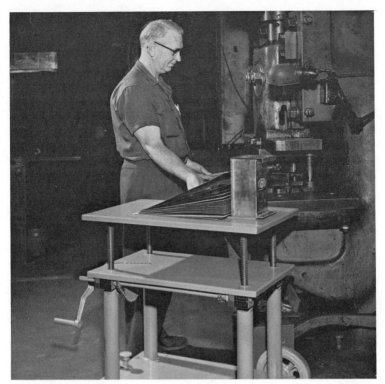

Fig. 12–16. Magnetic sheet separator used to facilitate handling metal blanks into press. (Courtesy of Hamilton Tool Co.)

Fig. 12–17. Belt conveyors for taking work to operators from dispatcher (off picture, to right) and returning finished work to be re-directed. (Courtesy of Rapistan, Inc.)

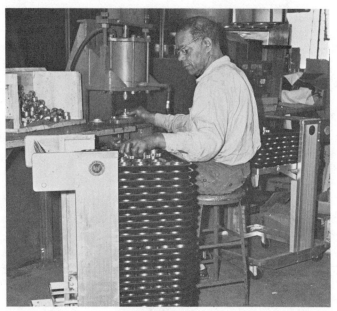

Fig. 12–18. Lowerator for maintaining uniform work level of parts, both into and out of operation. (Courtesy of AMF, Inc.)

Fig. 12–19. Specially designed castered cart for (1) holding part in position, (2) at proper level, and (3) providing means for moving between work stations. (Courtesy of Faultless Division, Bliss and Laughlin Industries.)

Fig. 12–20. A combination of (1) roller conveyor (2) live wheel conveyor, and (3) trolley conveyor with a special carrier and guide for moving goods from picking area of warehouse to packing department. (Courtesy of Rapistan, Inc.)

Fig. 12–21. Portable, cleated-belt conveyor for removing forgings from press and placing in skid box for transfer to next operation. (Courtesy of Rapistan, Inc.)

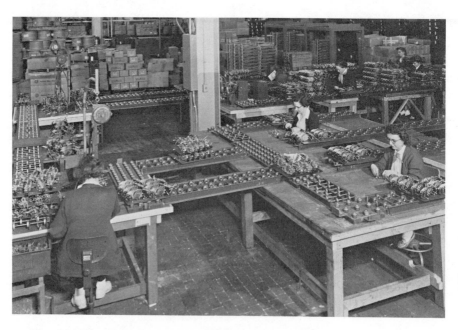

Fig. 12–22. Wheel conveyors move parts containers into, through, and out of related work places. (Courtesy of The Logan Company.)

CONCLUSION

Material handling has been recognized as one of the few remaining sources of worthwhile savings in the manufacturing phase of industry. While much headway has been made in the *general* field of material handling, relatively little attention has been focused on the material handling that occurs *at* the individual workplace. A review of the concepts and suggestions in this chapter should be helpful in minimizing workplace material handling.

13

Material Handling
Cost Concepts

It could be said that there are only two major functions in production:

1. Processing—in which the materials under consideration are changed in physical form
2. Material handling—in which the materials are brought to, moved through, or removed from the processing activities.

In a typical manufacturing situation, processing and material handling may account for 50 percent of production costs, although, of course, this will vary considerably with the specific industry. The material handling portion will be about one-half of the total, or 25 percent of the total production cost, on the "average." However, as pointed out in Chapter 1, this will vary from less than 10 percent to over 90 percent, depending on the particular situation.

In any case, material handling is a major factor in the cost of production, and would appear to be a big enough problem for many people to be concerned about—and many are, but not nearly enough. In fact, one survey [1] states that of over 70 "Grade A" plants, a vast majority kept *no* separate handling cost records. Only five kept identifiable handling cost accounts and were willing to report on them.

DIFFICULTIES IN DETERMINING MATERIAL HANDLING COSTS

The best and most common excuse for not keeping material handling cost records is that it is difficult—if not impossible—to determine them

[1] "Those Hidden Handling Costs," *Factory,* August 1958.

accurately. It is certainly *not* impossible, and really not difficult, although finding accurate costs does require a different point of view than is prevalent in many instances today. For example, Prof. Byron W. Saunders has said:

There appears to have grown up around the subject of materials handling costs, a certain mysticism which would seem to be unwarranted. The topic of this paper indeed suggests that the materials handling costs are in some manner a different type of cost than other production costs and that it is necessary to reassess our concepts concerning them. On the contrary, it is believed that materials handling cost should be treated just as any other direct costs and so evaluated. To do this may require some adjustment of the accounting methods which evaluate manufacturing processes and systems.

Stated another way, the fact that materials handling costs have become entwined with the concepts of overhead and thereby lost their identity apparently is the principal reason for unfamiliarity with the problems of materials handling costs. The fact that handling labor (unless it is an integral part of a productive operation) is called indirect labor, hence overhead, contributes in no small measure to this loss of identity.[2]

And along the same lines, Allen K. Strong has stated:

Very few companies, even today, recognize materials handling as a major function in their organization. They do not realize that their accounting procedure does not reflect the true cost of moving material through the plant. The accountant actually works for the tax collector, and it has been traditional to lump jobs requiring common labor into "Indirect" along with the oilers, sweepers, janitors, etc. Many so-called direct labor or production jobs contain high percentages of materials handling time that is traditionally a part of the job and is buried in the piece work rate.[3]

It can be concluded from the above, that a major part of the problem is a mental one—a preconceived notion that material handling costs are different, as well as difficult to separate from other indirect costs. Probably the most "difficult" aspect of the entire problem is that it does require hard, detailed work. Some of the commonly heard excuses for *not* accurately determining handling costs are:

1. Most material handling costs are "buried" in indirect labor costs
2. Much material handling is hidden within direct labor cost, i.e., *within* that portion of time allowed for performing an operation, and classified by time study and accounting as *direct* labor
3. Handling-equipment operating costs are "difficult" to determine
4. Complex interrelationships exist between handling and other activities
5. Hard to identify material handling costs

[2] B. W. Saunders, "Some Basic Concepts Relating Materials Handling Costs to Overall Production Costs," A.S.M.E. Paper No. 55–A–170.

[3] A. K. Strong, "Organizing Materials Handling for Effective Cost Reduction," privately circulated.

6. Not under one authority
7. Records not set up properly; incomplete
8. Varying concepts of what material handling really is
9. Accounting department may not be willing to undertake such analysis
10. All operations not adequately sub-divided
11. Material handling activities mixed in with other work
12. Material handling methods vary with time and conditions
13. Material handling costs may not relate compatibly to other productive measures
14. May cost more to determine material handling costs than it is worth

So, it might be concluded that if it is *this* difficult, it can be overlooked in favor of doing something easier—which is exactly what entirely too many people have been doing for entirely too long!

REASONS FOR DETERMINING ACCURATE MATERIAL HANDLING COSTS

But material handling is *too* large a segment of production, and too much money is involved, to ignore it in a well-managed plant. Instead, it should be considered a prime target for cost improvement, and an especially fruitful one *because* it has been neglected for so long. Some of the specific reasons for attacking material handling costs are: [4]

1. Have an *accurate* record of production costs.
2. Recognize *all* material handling costs, so that continuing day-by-day operating controls can be maintained over handling efficiency.
3. Uncover opportunities for cost and/or methods improvement.
4. Serve as a basis for economic evaluation and cost comparison when improved methods are suggested.
5. Detect *all* savings which can result from a proposed handling project.
6. Justify large investments in automation and other intensive mechanization, by isolating handling costs involved in the operations covered by proposed equipment.
7. To help minimize material handling costs.
8. To more accurately reflect material handling cost in total cost.
9. To prevent material handling costs from distorting overhead cost.
10. For budget purposes.
11. Basis for determination of material handling efficiency.
12. Direct labor now spent in material handling can be more efficiently utilized on production.

[4] Frederick Golden, "Pinning Down the Cost of Materials Handling," A.S.M.E. Paper No. 57–A–267: adapted and supplemented.

13. Justify installation of additional material handling equipment or personnel.
14. Aid in determining need for changes in material handling.

The progressive plant manager should recognize that the above reasons for knowing material handling costs are valid in his operation. And since material handling in itself may account for such a large portion of his production costs, the above reasons should add emphasis to his desire to begin immediately to rectify the long-ignored area of material handling costs.

NEED FOR AN ORGANIZED APPROACH

Certainly no problem as complex and, at the same time, as significant as this should be approached in a haphazard manner. The importance alone is enough to suggest a planned, orderly attempt to determine material handling costs.

Another reason for such an approach is the large number of inter-relationships between material handling and other functions in the organization. Chapter 1 has pointed out the extremely broad scope of the material handling function—from supplier to customer. Needless to say, such an extended area of coverage demands close attention to all phases of analysis to insure complete and adequate cost figures. Many of the interrelationships between these functions and activities are by way of the dollars involved. Many of the material handling costs will be affected by the way in which the related functions are carried out.

The balance of this chapter will discuss some of the major concepts useful in determining and accumulating material handling costs. The following two chapters (14 and 15) will suggest techniques helpful in analyzing and using such costs.

SCOPE OF MATERIAL HANDLING COSTS

One of the most confusing aspects of determining material handling costs is that of classifying them into logical groupings as a basis for study and analysis. Referring back to the scope of material handling activities may serve as a possible starting place for such classification. In Chapter 1, 22 activities were identified in the over-all range of the material handling function. However, within many of the items on that list is a secondary classification.

A. *Specialized* material handling activities
B. *Mixed* material handling activities

C. *Borderline* material handling activities
D. Material handling activities commonly classified as *distribution* costs

Each of these classifications is a source of specific interest and of distinctive problems in the analysis of material handling costs. Each is presented here to acquaint the analyst with the peculiarities of these phases of the cost problem:

A. *Specialized Material Handling Activities.* Those handling tasks which are definitely classified as material handling activities; are easily identified as such; are easily isolated; and are easily measured. The activites within this classification are usually assigned full-time personnel and equipment, and the related costs are commonly classified as material handling cost, but usually as indirect costs. This classification might include such activities as:

1. Unloading operations
2. Receiving activities
3. Storage operations
4. Materials issue
5. Materials distribution to production
6. Inter-departmental handling
7. Loading operations
8. Inter-plant handling

B. *Mixed Material Handling Activities.* Those handling tasks which are usually *within* some other area of activity; are usually classified (cost-wise) as an inseparable portion of the other activity; which are difficult to isolate; and are therefore, "difficult" to measure. The material handling activities within this classification are most commonly performed as a part of another job—frequently by production personnel, *and* the related costs are probably classified as *direct* costs (although not always) as shown below. The classification would include the material handling *done* within the following activities:

1. In-process handling
   —by production operators
2. Intra-departmental handling
   —from one work area to another within the same department, by the machine operator
3. Workplace material handling (see also Chapter 12)
   —*preparatory* to use of material in machine
   —handling *into* the machine
   —handling *within* the production cycle—but *not* in changing the physical characteristics of the material
   —handling *from* the work place, but not to the next workplace
4. In-process storage
   —handling to and from an intermediate storage area by production operators

5. Service and auxiliary operations
   —handling of materials to and from other related areas and activities, such as tool room, tool crib, production control, supervision, salvage, maintenance, etc.
   —handling to, through, and back from quality control, which occupies a substantial amount of the "productive" time of machine operators.

C. *Borderline Material Handling Activities.* Those in which the classification will most likely vary from plant to plant, depending on the nature of the industry and the accounting classifications. It might include such activities as:

1. Packaging }
2. Packing   } at vendor's plant

   —which may or may not be a specific charge to the user plant

3. Packaging }
4. Packing   } at "our" plant

   —which may or may not be classified as direct labor in the accounting system

D. *Material Handling Activities Commonly Classified as Distribution Costs.* Which incidentally may also include packaging and packing. This category may include:

1. Loading by vendor
   —according to our specifications
2. Transportation to our plant
   —which may be by vendor truck, user truck, or common carrier
3. External material handling
   —at our plant, and before entering our building, such as in yards, on docks, etc.
4. Finished goods warehousing
5. Shipping operations
   —such as labelling, rate calculations, sorting, etc.
6. Transportation from user plant
   —which may be by customer truck, our truck, or common carrier

Figure 13–1 visually portrays their several interrelationships.

CONSEQUENCES OF MORE ACCURATE COST ANALYSIS

While the above has not *solved* any problems, it has raised several of great importance to the accurate determination of material handling costs. In every one of the situations pointed out:

Scope of Material Handling	SPECIALIZED definitely matl. hdl'g & easily isolated and measured	MIXED with other activities & difficult to isolate	BORDERLINE depends largely on plant acct'g system	usually considered DISTRIBUTION costs
1. Packaging) at vendor's			X	
2. Packing) plant to our specifications			X	
3. Loading by vendor				X
4. Transp. to user plant				X
5. External material handling				X
6. Unloading	X			
7. Receiving	X			
8. Materials storage	X			
9. Materials issue/distribution	X			
10. In-process handling		X		
11. In-process storage		X		
12. Work place handling		X		
13. Intra-dept. handling		X		
14. Inter-dept. handling	X			
15. Intra-plant handling	X			
16. Service & auxil. operations		X		
17. Packaging			X	
18. Finished goods warehousing				X
19. Packing			X	
20. Loading and shipping	X			
21. Transportation from plant				X
22. Inter-plant handling	X			

Fig. 13–1. Activities within the scope of material handling classified as to kinds of problems involved in determining costs.

1. An aspect of material handling is involved.
2. A management decision must be made as to whether it shall be included in material handling costs or not.
3. Cost improvements are possible by careful analysis of many of the areas pointed out—which might have been otherwise overlooked or neglected.

It should be apparent that much of the concern here is with actual material handling costs that are currently being "disguised" as overhead, or "hidden" within direct labor. It is up to the material handling engineer to clarify such relationships and aid management by ferreting out as many of these *real* material handling costs as can be honestly classified and measured. This will certainly require more careful record keeping than has been practiced in the past. It will also require better reporting of activities and better analysis—with the help of techniques such as work sampling, standard data, and statistics. In many cases, the computer will be found not only helpful, but necessary.

However, one apparent contradiction is also a distinct possibility. Accurate accounting for material handling costs may result in the discovery that there is *more* material handling activity than had been recognized. Nevertheless, much of it may be eliminated, simplified, or merely re-assigned to material handling personnel from production operators, who will now be busy getting out production, instead of handling. And the *new* costs will more truthfully reflect the *real* cost relationships.

FACTORS AFFECTING MATERIAL HANDLING COSTS

In working toward the more accurate delineation of material handling costs, it may be helpful to classify them into their basic types, and then sub-divide each into its components. This will permit a closer look at the complex interrelationships pointed out previously. Factors affecting material handling cost may be classified as follows:

1. *Direct Costs*—commonly associated with the operation of a piece of equipment, and the most easily measured, such as:
   a. Equipment
      —capital investment
      —fixed charges
      —variable charges
   b. Manpower
      —full time on material handling (specialized)
      —part-time on material handling (mixed)
      —"borderline" activity (requiring management decision to further classify)
      —distribution activity (also requiring management decision)
2. *Indirect Costs*—associated with the investment or operation, but not in direct relationship; measurable, but presenting more difficulty in reducing them to dollars.
3. *Indeterminate Cost Factors*—although related, these factors cannot be definitely or precisely determined or fixed. They are vague, imponderable, frequently not known in advance, or do not lend themselves to the determination of an exact cost figure; may have to be estimated.

4. *Intangible Factors*—in the ordinary sense, these defy quantification or calculation of a dollar value and therefore cannot be included as items in a *cost* comparison. (Although some engineering economists *will* reduce them to a cost factor.)

Direct Costs

Direct costs are those that can be charged directly to a specific piece of handling equipment or to an activity, usually on the basis of time allocated, and frequently on a full-time basis.

Equipment. One of the two major categories of direct costs is that associated with the equipment utilized in the handling activity, and may include:

CAPITAL INVESTMENT [5]

1. *Invoice price of equipment*—this figure is the estimated total of the invoices received from manufacturers of equipment and is obtained from the proposals of the various bidders.
2. *Installation charges*—all labor, materials, burden and other costs involved in removing the equipment from the receiving carrier, then placing and conditioning it ready for operation.
3. *Maintenance facilities*—the invoice prices, installation, costs, etc. required for equipment needed to maintain and repair the handling devices.
4. *Fueling and/or power facilities*—invoice price, installation costs, etc. for facilities necessary to provide power and/or fuel. If equipment is propelled by internal combustion engines, gasoline facilities or L.P. tanks must be provided; if batteries are the source of power, then charging equipment and battery handling devices must be provided.
5. *Alterations to present facilities*—labor, material, and burden involved in any necessary alterations to present property; altering door openings, strengthening floors, installing overhead structures, etc.
6. *Freight and other transportation*—all transportation charges on equipment, material, etc., necessary for the installation.
7. *Design work*—all labor, material and burden involved in engineering work required on the equipment and its installation.
8. *Supplies*—all expendable items needed to install the handling equipment.
9. *Other charges*—any capital costs not included in the previous categories.

[5] Adapted from Robert C. Brady, "Financial Factors in Selection of Handling Equipment," *Flow Magazine*, April, 1955.

10. *Credits*—the net realizable income from selling items which are abandoned. This figure will be the difference between sale price and the cost of preparing the abandoned items for sale. This could be a debit if the book value exceeds the net amount realized from the sale.

This account possibly warrants further discussion. If the items which can no longer be used in the operations under consideration can be profitably used elsewhere, the accountant should transfer the book value to the new location and thus make no charge or credit here.

There might be another point of view. If the book value for items abandoned does not equal exactly the net realizable salvage value, an error has been made in the depreciation rate and the difference should be adjusted to earned surplus. In that case again neither a debit nor a credit should be considered here.

Other accounting systems may call for a different treatment of some aspects of the capital cost, and the material-handling engineer should consult his Accounting Department for exact procedures. The sum of these ten accounts will be the estimated increase in assets or the total capital investment, or the cost of *owning* the equipment.

FIXED CHARGES [6]

1. *Depreciation*—the rate of depreciation for each class of equipment is a policy dictated by the income tax laws, top management, or the board of directors. Normally the word depreciation connotes two different elements of cost: depreciation and obsolescence. Depreciation is deterioration due to wear and tear. Obsolescence is occasioned by the availability of better processes or equipment. Equipment becomes obsolete for two basic reasons:
   (a) The user of the equipment may devise new processes making present facilities worthless, or a customer may demand a change in product of such nature that present facilities can no longer be used.
   (b) A producer of the type of equipment in use may offer new models, the economy of which prompts abandoning present facilities in favor of new ones, even though the mechanical condition of present equipment will permit further productive life. Here again, the material handling engineer should check on the accepted company method of handling depreciation.
2. *Interest on Investment*—it is often a question of policy whether interest on investment should be included in such an analysis. Some interest should probably be included on the investment in every procurement.
3. *Taxes*—property taxes on facilities being considered.

[6] Adapted from Brady, *op. cit.*

4. *Insurance*—to cover the proposed equipment.
5. *Supervision*—the costs of personnel required to manage and control the operation.
6. *Clerical*—the cost of personnel required to handle the necessary office duties related to the installation.
7. *Maintenance Personnel*—the cost of the persons required to provide inspection, maintenance, and repair work.
8. *Other*—any expenses not listed above which occur on a time basis.

The sum of the eight accounts listed above will give an estimate of the cost of making the equipment available for use, the standby charge or the fixed charges which can be pre-determined at the time the procurement is made.

VARIABLE CHARGES [7]

1. *Operating Personnel*—the cost of those persons actually assigned to operate the equipment, whose time is charged to this operation —but only when so assigned. This account should include the wages received as well as fringe benefits and other expenses involved in keeping an employee on the payroll. In a comparison of methods, this item will reflect personnel added or replaced by the proposed method(s).
2. *Power and/or Fuel Costs*—if the equipment is propelled by internal combustion engines this account will indicate the cost of fuel. If propelled by electric motors it will be based on the public utility charge. In the case of battery-operated equipment, the costs were considered under Investments (in the battery, etc.) except for electricity used in charging the batteries.
3. *Lubricants*—the cost of oil and grease used on the equipment.
4. *Maintenance Labor*—the cost of maintenance labor, which fluctuates with the use of the equipment, including the maintenance work on the equipment itself as well as the maintenance labor on the accessories required for use with the equipment. For example, any charges for repairing pallets might be considered a variable charge.
5. *Maintenance Parts and Materials*—the cost of repair parts to keep the equipment in operation as well as cost of equipment and materials to keep the supplies in usable condition. The discussion concerning accounting for maintenance labor also applies to this account.
6. *Other*—any variable costs not included in the previous accounts.

The sum of these six accounts will give the estimated cost of using the equipment.

---

[7] Adapted from Brady, *op. cit.*

The total of the above two general categories of cost—fixed and variable—will yield the annual operating cost. Procedures for determining these costs are discussed in Chapter 14.

Manpower. The other major category of direct costs is labor, i.e., that which has not been included in the above classifications but which is associated with the equipment operation. As previously noted, manpower costs allocated to the material handling activity may be:

1. Full-time, if such manpower is allocated 100 percent to the material handling activity under analysis.
2. Part-time, if the manpower is used only a portion of the time on the activity under analysis.

The "borderline" and "distribution" categories previously cited would be allocated in the same way—either full or part time. It should be remembered that manpower costs will normally include such items as:

1. Regular wages
2. Overtime wages
3. Premium pay (night shift, etc.)
4. Bonus or profit-sharing pay
5. Fringe benefits (social security, unemployment insurance, vacation pay, other insurance, etc.)

Labor costs should, of course, be determined for any or all of the categories (Fig. 13–1) applicable to the handling problem. Additional details on their calculation will be discussed in Chapter 15.

Indirect Costs

The second major type of material handling cost to be considered is the indirect category. *This group of costs consists primarily of those which are frequently included in overhead, overlooked in the analysis, or ignored because they are more difficult to identify and/or determine.* In fact, in many cases, the analyst may not even be aware of them as possible cost components. Nevertheless, they are nearly all reducible to dollars and should be evaluated with this in mind.

The *indirect* costs may be divided into two groups: (1) those which are related in some way to the *equipment* being considered or to the method of handling; and (2) those in which the degree of importance and therefore, the extent of their effect on the analysis, depends upon the effectiveness of the *management* of the plant, or on management policies.

Related to Equipment or Method. The following indirect cost factors are felt to be more closely oriented toward the equipment or method under consideration: [8]

1. *Space Occupied*—providing and maintaining space is costly, so it is necessary to evaluate the space required for the installation and operation of the equipment. However, management may place a different value on space under different situations. That is, when confronted with the necessity of acquiring additional storage facilities, economical utilization of space presently available is urgent. But, if space available is not being fully occupied and no other use appears for it, full utilization of that space takes on a different value. (This item may have been considered under fixed or other charges included in direct costs.)

2. *Effect on Taxes*—any saving resulting from the recommendation will increase the figure on the last line of the operating statement which in turn increases the taxes to be paid. Calculate the effect which such savings will have upon taxes and give thought to deducting the increase in taxes from the savings in operations which have been indicated.

3. *Inventory Value*—value of inventory is an important consideration to management. What effect will the method have upon cost of goods held in inventory, whether they are raw materials, goods in process, or finished goods?

4. *Value of Repair Parts*—in many cases, dollars tied up in necessary repair parts may represent a substantial investment and might be considered as an identifiable cost, rather than an expense item.

5. *Demurrage Charges*—such costs are to be avoided when practicable. In addition, good will of the respective carriers may be enhanced by prompt turn-arounds. Also, proposed methods which will speed up turn-around time could free valuable receiving and shipping dock space.

6. *Changes in Production Rate*—again, this item may have been included in relation to some other cost factor. If not, its cost consequences might be considered as an indirect cost factor.

7. *Downtime*—when alternative methods are being considered, some attempt should be made to evaluate and "cost out" the amount of downtime probable for each.

There are undoubtedly many other "equipment related" items belonging in the category of indirect cost factors. Any others identifiable should be isolated and evaluated.

Related to Management Effectiveness. In contrast to the items discussed above (equipment oriented), the following appear to be more closely identified with the effectiveness with which management carries

[8] Partially based on Brady, *op. cit.*

out its several functions. Although the line of demarcation may be "stretched," it is felt that this group is more closely controllable by management action or policy than by equipment characteristics or operation.

1. *Travel Expense Incurred in Investigation*—this may have been considered a portion of the investment cost. If not, include it as an indirect cost factor.
2. *Cost of Follow-Up Expediting*—in some cases, such a cost can be a sizable item in the procurement of an expensive installation.
3. *Re-layout Costs*—as incurred in relation to the proposed installation.
4. *Training of Personnel*—costs incurred in qualifying personnel to operate new equipment, and allowing for decreased production during the training period.
5. *Overtime*—required to make up for lost production prior to, during, or after installation.
6. *Volume of Work-In-Process*—effect of change in value as a result of installation and its cost consequences.
7. *Charges to Operation After Full Depreciation*—frequent accounting practice to be investigated and accounted for.
8. *Handling Returned Goods*—possibly an unorthodox item for this category, but again, a separately identifiable cost item, more than likely covered up in some other overhead account.

Other indirect cost factors may be identified as the analysis progresses. Any of consequence should be separated out and added to the list.

Chapter 14 will present a method for evaluating and "costing out" indirect cost factors so that they can be properly considered in the comparison of alternatives under consideration.

Indeterminate Costs

A third major category of cost factors is identified as *indeterminate*. This group consists of those items which are of a more debatable nature; which might be justifiably overlooked; which might be inadvertently neglected; and which are admittedly more difficult to evaluate in a quantitative manner. The indeterminate or imponderable factors may likewise be divided into equipment- and management-oriented groups, as follows:

Related to Equipment or Method
1. *Space Lost or Gained*—in addition to space *occupied* by the equipment or method under consideration, the space lost or gained by its installation may carry a value of significance.
2. *Overhead Changes*—direct costs may or may not have accounted for *changes* in overhead as a result of the equipment or method under consideration.

3. *Inventory Control*—the proposal may affect the cost of controlling the inventory, either making it easier or more difficult.
4. *Inventory Taking*—may be classified as a separate item, depending on how it is affected by the method under consideration.
5. *Production Control*—in a similar way (to inventory control), production control activity may be affected by the change.
6. *Changes in Product or Material Quality*—here, too, the alternatives being considered may have varying prospects of causing such changes. The changes might be for the better, or they could result in more scrap, rejects, damaged or wasted materials or products—even in combination with increased production or lower costs.
7. *Life-of Job-Using Equipment*—this may or may not be related to to the depreciation calculations included under operating costs. Specifically, the life of the job for which the equipment or method is being considered may be longer or shorter than that of the equipment. This factor is especially relevant if the equipment will outlast the use for which it is being installed.
8. *Reduction in Physical Effort*—would be affected in a way not easily measurable in time standards.

Related to Management Effectiveness

1. *Lost Production Due to Delay in Installation*—another cost factor easily overlooked or ignored, but which can be calculated in terms of sales or profits lost or sacrificed.
2. *Percent of Time Equipment Will Be Used*—may have been considered in determination of operating costs.
3. *Additional Labor Required for Increased Capacity*—even though future increased capacity is planned for from a proposed installation, the additional labor which may be required is easy to overlook.
4. *Turnover of Work In Process*—effect of rate of turnover, or reduction of cycle time by proposed installation and resulting costs.
5. *Change in Line Balances*—due to proposed installation, and their effect on the costs.
6. *Trends in Business Volume*—consideration should be given to the probable trend of business volume. First, what is the maximum probable tonnage to be handled and the cost under such conditions. Second, if business declines, what is the minimum production that can be expected? Then considering the pessimistic and optimistic estimates, what is the *best* estimate of the tonnage to be moved? Effects which each method of handling will have upon the overall cost should be determined.
7. *Trends for Equipment Cost*—must frequently be estimated by management.

8. *Improved Work Flow*—may be "visually" better than before, or even quantitatively better—but difficult to evaluate.
9. *Ease of Supervision*—may save a *portion* of a supervisor's time for other activities.
10. *Reduction in Paperwork*—possibility of affecting control activities and possibly resulting in a savings.
11. *Cooperation with Vendor/Customer*—the importance of this relationship has been emphasized many times, but the concern here is for the possible effect on cost or savings realized by the degree of cooperation in terms of shipping containers, methods, routes, rates, etc. For example, the container (vendor's or user's) can be designed:
    —to facilitate handling by the other party.
    —to promote sales by the customer.
    —for re-use in the inter- or intra-plant handling cycle.
    —as an inexpensive, expendable device and a saving to all parties involved.
    —to serve a second purpose, after its original use has been accomplished.

Intangible Factors

The fourth major category for consideration in analyzing material handling problems, is the group identified as *intangible factors*. These are *not* cost factors, but items which, in the ordinary sense, defy quantification, or the calculation of a dollar value for inclusion in the cost figures. Some of these factors will be identified in this chapter, and a proposed method of evaluation will be presented in Chapter 14.

Here, again, it may be helpful to subdivide the factors into "equipment" and "management" categories, since some of the intangible factors are equipment oriented, while the effect of others depends on management plans, policies or decisions for evaluation.

Related to Equipment and/or Manufacturer

1. Quality of equipment
2. Durability of equipment
3. Compatibility of equipment with present handling system
4. Standardization of equipment and/or components
5. Flexibility of equipment in terms of capacity, as volume changes
6. Adaptability of equipment to possible future applications
7. Complexity of equipment, both as to operation and maintenance
8. Safety hazards and/or safeguards
9. Rate of obsolescence
10. Manufacturer's reputation

11. Availability of equipment
12. Post-sale advice and/or service
13. Availability of service
14. Quality of service available
15. Availability of repair parts, etc.

Related to Management

1. Financial policies
2. Economic survival goals
3. Effect of future changes on utilization of equipment
4. Plans for expansion of plant and/or activity using equipment
5. Labor relations aspects of displaced personnel—labor savings vs. labor turnover
6. Effect on morale—positive, due to removal of "muscle work" and up-grading of employees; or negative, due to displacement of personnel or downgrading men to "button pushers"
7. Increased salability
8. Improved customer service
9. Pride in installation

This is the last category of material handling factors, and that which practically defies quantification or reduction to dollars and cents. Undoubtedly some of them can be assigned a quantitative value, by means of educated estimates, but the desirability of adding them into the real cost of the project being analyzed may be questionable. However, this does not justify their omission from consideration, nor does it minimize their usefulness in contributing to the required decision. They are extremely important, and in many cases may far outweigh or over-ride the more easily determined cost items. A method of evaluation, which will permit their importance to be judged in proper perspective to the more tangible aspects of the problem, will be presented in Chapter 14.

CONCLUSION

As an aid in interrelating the many factors previously identified, the following table (see Figure 13-2) lists them in parallel columns, and in abbreviated form. It will be seen that there are truly a large number of significant factors which *should* be considered in *any* equipment investment analysis.

It may be disparagingly concluded, at this point, that an unnecessarily large number of relatively insignificant factors has been uncovered or that they have been over-emphasized. However, the intent here is primarily to make the analyst aware of the many factors that are frequently hidden from easy view and, thereby, overlooked or ignored. One or a

1. Direct. Commonly associated with the operation of a piece of equipment, and including such items as:

Fixed Costs	Variable Costs
Depreciation	Operating personnel
Interest on investment	Fuel and power
Taxes	Lubrication
Insurance	Maintenance parts and supplies
Supervisory personnel	Outside maintenance labor
Plant maintenance personnel	

2. Indirect. Associated with the investment or operation, but not usually in a direct relationship. These will include such items as:

Equipment and Method Related Costs	Management Related Costs
Space occupied	Re-layout
Taxes	Personnel training
Inventory	Travel involved in investigation
Repair parts	Damaged equipment, etc.
Downtime	

3. Indeterminate. Cannot be precisely determined or fixed, or may be vague, or frequently not known in advance, or which do not lend themselves to the determination of a definite cost figure. This category might include some of the following frequently overlooked costs:

Equipment and Method Related Costs	Management Related Costs
Space lost or gained	Production lost due to delay in installation
Changes in overhead	Percent of time equipment is utilized
Inventory control savings	Turnover of work in process
Production control savings	Business volume
Changes in product or material quality	Equipment trends
	Paperwork

4. Intangible. In the ordinary sense, these defy quantification or calculation of a dollar value and therefore cannot be included as items in a cost comparison.

Equipment and/or Method Related Factors	Management Related Factors
Quality of equipment	Financial policy
Flexibility	Plans for expansion
Adaptability	Effect on morale
Safety	Improved customer service
Manufacturer's reputation	
Availability of equipment	
Availability of repair parts	
Quality of service	

Fig. 13–2. Factors for consideration in equipment investment analysis. (From *Production Handbook,* The Ronald Press Co., New York, 1972.)

combination of the above factors *might* be the "salvation" of the analyst —depending on whether or not it is covered in his investment cost determination. This chapter has identified those items that may affect the final cost figure in the investment decision. The next two chapters will suggest methods for evaluating and including these factors in investment and operating cost determinations.

14

Equipment Cost
Determination

This chapter is concerned with those aspects of the material handling cost problem which are related to equipment selection, ownership, and operation. The next chapter will deal with material handling *activity* cost—including owning and operating cost as a major component.

In review, Chapter 7 discussed preparing a justification of the material handling plan (Step X)—which, of course, includes determining all relevant costs. Chapter 13 covered a classification of the many types and categories of material handling factors. Finally, this chapter suggests the use of the Equipment Operating Cost Determination form as a part of the equipment selection procedure. The form will be covered in more detail in this chapter as one phase of a procedure for determining those costs involved in owning and operating material handling equipment, which are of significance in choosing between alternatives.

EVALUATION OF DIRECT COSTS

The direct costs discussed in Chapter 13 can best be accumulated with the aid of the Equipment Operating Cost Determination form, shown in Figure 14–1, which should be used as follows:

1. Fill in information identifying the several pieces of equipment under consideration, at the top of the sheet. (Use several sheets, side by side, if more than two alternatives are being compared, or devise a similar form to suit the specific type of equipment being compared.)

2. Enter specific cost data in the next three sections (investment, fixed, and variable). It should be evident that some costs *will* vary with oper-

ating hours and others will not. Therefore, where appropriate, a different figure should be entered in the 16- (or 24-) hour columns than in the 8-hour column. This will frequently depend on company policy and/or accounting procedures.

3. If applicable, enter the appropriate figure under "Other Overhead," as the percentage to be allocated to this equipment. For example, if the general overhead rate applied to the department where this equipment will be used is $5000, and it is estimated that 10% of it is applicable *to this* piece of equipment—enter the figures as 10 percent x $5000 and put $500 in the 8 hour column. If these figures vary with the number of shifts, enter appropriate figures in other columns. Be sure to check with Accounting on this matter!

A key item is the "Operating Hours Per Year," since this factor will be related to the company investment policies and procedures. It should be entered as 2000 hours (for one-shift operation), 4000, 6000, etc. The amount of time a specific piece of equipment is actually used on a certain job or *move* will be covered in Chapter 15, under the cost analysis procedure, after the actual operating time of the equipment has been determined for the move or job being "costed out."

4. Determine cost per hour of operation and enter on the last line of the form. This figure will be used in determining the cost of a particular move, as will be shown in Chapter 15.

After the cost calculations have been made, there remains the important task of comparing and evaluating the indeterminate and intangible aspects of the pieces of equipment under consideration. This is a most important phase of the selection process, and in many cases some of these factors may be of even greater significance than cost factors. This is especially true when cost figures are close, and several makes of equipment are being considered, any one of which might be acceptable from a functional *and* cost standpoint.

EVALUATION OF INDIRECT COSTS

Even though many of the more common types of indirect costs are included on the Equipment Operating Cost Determination form (Figure 14–1), it may be desirable to calculate a value for some of the more obscure items listed in the table at the end of Chapter 13.

If this is desired, it can be accomplished with the aid of the form shown in Figure 14–2. The columns are explained as follows:

1. *Factors.* From the list of indirect cost factors shown in the table at the end of Chapter 13, select those of significance to the project at hand. Include others as they may be appropriate to the project.

ITEM	ALTERNATIVE NO. 1		ALTERNATIVE NO. 2	
EQUIPMENT DATA				
Make	*Acme*		*Budget*	
Type	*direct*		*direct*	
Model	*46*		*B-3*	
Capacity	*5000/hr.*		*5200/hr.*	
Accessories	—		—	
Attachments	—		—	
Operating Characteristics	—		—	
INVESTMENT				
Invoice Price	*$39,000*		*$33,000*	
Installation charges	*4000*		*5000*	
Maintenance facilities	*1000*		*1500*	
Fueling &/or power facilities	*2800*		*2800*	
Alterations to present facilities	*6000*		*6000*	
Freight &/or transportation	*800*		*1000*	
Design Work	*1800*		*1400*	
Supplies	*1600*		*1800*	
Other charges *(travel & training)*	*3000*		*2500*	
Credits	—		—	
TOTAL INVESTMENT COST	*$60,000*		*$55,000*	
FIXED CHARGES	8 hours	16 hours	8 hours	16 hours
Depreciation *(5 yr. - st. line - 20%)*	*$12,000*		*$11,000*	
Interest on investment *(10%)*	*6,000*		*5,500*	
Taxes *(25%) at 30% assessment*	*500*		*420*	
Insurance *(5%) at 75% coverage*	*230*		*180*	
Supervision *(50%) × $5,000 wage)*	*2,500*		*2,500*	
Clerical *(25% × $4,000 wage)*	*1,000*		*1,000*	
Maintenance Personnel *(10% × 8,000 wage)*	*800*		*800*	
Other	*170*		*100*	
TOTAL FIXED COST	*$23,200*		*$21,500*	
VARIABLE CHARGES				
Operating Personnel (% × $ wage)	*$9,750* *(3 men)*		*$6,500* *(2 men)*	
Power &/or fuel costs	*250*		*200*	
Lubricants	*100*		*100*	
Maintenance parts & materials	*500*		*600*	
Maintenance labor	*6,200*		*5,100*	
Other	—		—	
TOTAL VARIABLE COST	*$16,800*		*$12,500*	
OTHER OVERHEAD (% × $)	—		—	
TOTAL ANNUAL COST	*$40,000*		*$34,000*	
OPERATING HOURS PER YEAR	*2,000*		*2,000*	
COST PER HOUR OF OPERATION	*$20.00*		*$17.00*	

Fig. 14-1. Equipment operating cost determination.

EVALUATION OF ☒ INDIRECT   COST FACTORS
             ☐ INDETERMINATE

Projects __Warehouse handling__   Alternative __No. 1__   Analysis by __A. M. J.__   Date __June 28__

| Factors | Probable Effect on Analysis | | Cost Basis (sq. ft., lbs., hrs., etc. in dollars/unit) | Evaluation Basis in No. of Units | Estimated Dollar Value of Factor | | Remarks |
	Adv. −	Disadv. +			Advant. −	Disadv. +	
Space occupied	√		$1.00/sq. ft. per year	5000 sq. ft.	$5000		less than previous method
Increased taxes		√		estimate		$3000	due to incr. in value of tot. facility
Repair parts inventory		√	$4000	25% carrying charge		1000	over & above previous inventory
Sub-totals					−$5000	+$4000	
Total evaluation of cost factors					−$1000		savings = negative cost

Fig. 14–2. Evaluation of indirect cost factors.

2. *Probable Effect.* This column provides for a consideration of the effect of the individual factor on the evaluation being considered. Care should be exercised here to be *sure* the factor is interpreted in the proper "direction," in terms of its effect. A factor which is considered advantageous to a project should be checked in the "Advantage," or minus (−) column, since it results in a saving, or *negative* cost. It should also be noted that a factor may move from the (+) to the (−) column, depending upon the point of view from which it is judged.
3. *Cost Basis.* This column should contain the *basis* upon which the cost evaluation is to be made for each factor, in terms of the unit to be used and the dollar value per unit (i.e., $5/sq ft; $10/hr, etc.)
4. *Evaluation Basis.* This column will show the number of "base units" (i.e., 1000 sq ft; 40 hrs, etc.)
5. *Estimated Value.* This column is the product of columns 3 and 4 and the value should be placed in the plus or minus subcolumn to correspond with the decision made in column 2, in terms of the effect of the factor on the evaluation.
6. *Remarks.* In this column may be entered a note to indicate the desired disposition of the factor and its resulting dollar value—i.e., *if* it will be included in the total (any factor may be deleted, if it is deemed proper or desirable).

The total of the indirect cost factors so evaluated is to be entered on the Recap of Comparative Costs form in Figure 14–5.

This "disposes" of all the direct and indirect cost items that can be easily reduced to dollars and cents. However, it still leaves an incomplete analysis, and the indeterminate cost factors will be considered next.

EVALUATION OF INDETERMINATE COST FACTORS

In general, the procedure outlined above may be used in evaluating the indeterminate factors, using the same form, as shown in Figure 14–3. In this case also, when the total is obtained it is entered on the Recap of Comparative Costs, as will be explained later.

EVALUATION OF INTANGIBLE FACTORS

This last category of factors, which practically defies quantification or reduction to dollars, is the most difficult to take into consideration in its proper relationship to the problem of investment evaluation. This is because the evaluation—by any means—is almost wholly subjective and therefore dependent on the judgment of the person or persons making the evaluation. Some can undoubtedly be assigned a quantitative value, by

☐ Indirect

☒ Indeterminate

Project _Warehouse handling_   Alternative _No. 1_   Analysis by _A.M.J._ Date _June 28_

| Factors | Probable Effect on Analysis | | Cost Basis (sq. ft., lbs., hrs., etc., in dollars/unit) | Evaluation Basis in No. of Units | Estimated Dollar Value of Factor | | Remarks |
	Adv. −	Dis-adv. +			Advant. −	Disadv. +	
Higher overhead		✓	$83/mo.	12 mo.		$1000	
Savings in taking inventory	✓		$4/hr.	500 hr.	$2000		
Reduced damage	✓		50% less	.50 x $2000	1000		based on last year
Reduced labor req'd.	✓		$1.50/hr.	10% x 8000 hr.	1200		increased productivity
Lost production due to delay in installation		✓	$2000/wh.	1 week		2000	
Additional labor req'd. for increased capacity		✓	5% = 1 man @$150/hr.	2000 hr.		3000	
Easier supervision	✓		$2.80/hr.	1000 hr. saved	2800		
Reduction in paperwork	✓		$2.00/hr.	250 hr.	500		
				Subtotals	$−7500	$+6000	
				Total Evaluation of Cost Factors	−$1500		

Fig. 14–3. Evaluation of indeterminate cost factors.

means of educated estimates, but none is likely to be accurate enough to justify "adding" it into the _real_ costs of the project being analyzed.

The following outline suggests a method of evaluation which will permit their importance to be judged in proper perspective to the more tangible aspects of the problem.[1]

1. Determine from the right-hand column of the list at the end of Chapter 13, all factors that affect any of the alternatives under consideration, adding any others which may be pertinent.

2. Review the factors selected and reword or restate them if necessary to be sure they are well defined and clear-cut; that is, none should imply another, nor should they be contradictory to each other, nor have a cumulative effect on each other. This may mean the elimination of some factors or the combination of two or more into a new, single, more clearly stated factor.

3. Determine the relative importance of each factor, from most important to least important. List them in this order in column 1 on the form shown in Figure 14–4 and check to be sure they are in their best order. This should most likely be done in co-operation with other persons acquainted with the project, before deciding on the final order.

[1] Adapted from Norman N. Barish, _Economic Analysis_, McGraw-Hill Book Co., New York, 1962, Chapter 27. This reference provides considerably more detail on such evaluation procedures.

4. Assign an importance value to each factor, using 100 for the most important and a lesser value for each of the others as agreed to by the collective opinion of the evaluator(s). The importance values should then be entered on the Intangible Factor Evaluation Sheet, Figure 14–4,[2] in column 2.

Project __Warehouse handling__

Evaluator(s) __A.M.J., M.E.M., J.J.J.__ Date __June 28__

Factors (in order of importance)	Importance Value	Adjusted Importance Value	Alternatives Under Consideration					
			Altern. 1		Altern. 2		Altern. 3	
			Eval-uation Rating	Weight-ed Eval. Rating	Eval. Rat-ing	Wgt'd. Eval. Rat'g.	Eval. Rating	Wgt'd. Eval. Rat'g.
1	2	3	4	5	4	5	4	5
Improved customer service	100	23	90	20.7	95	21.9	100	23.0
Quality of equipment	90	21	80	16.8	85	17.9	90	18.9
Availability of service	80	18	50	9.0	70	12.6	95	17.1
Availability of equipment	70	16	70	11.2	85	13.6	100	16.0
Effect on morale	50	11	80	8.8	90	9.9	95	10.5
Complexity	30	7	80	5.6	85	6.0	90	6.3
Flexibility	20	4	75	3.0	80	3.2	80	3.2
Totals	440	100	—	75	—	85	—	95

Fig. 14–4. Intangible factor evaluation sheet. (Adapted from Norman N. Barish, *Economic Analysis;* used with the permission of McGraw-Hill Book Co., New York, 1962, p. 424.)

5. If desired, adjust the values so that the total is 100, for convenience. This is done by totalling the unadjusted values, dividing *each* by the sum, and multiplying the result by 100. Enter these values in column 3.

6. Evaluate each factor for each alternative, in terms of its relative importance or *effect* on the project, on the basis of 100 for the greatest effect, most importance, etc. Enter these ratings in the columns numbered 4, for each alternative. Care must be taken in this evaluation to assure that the *best* or most *desirable* rating is at the high end of the 100 scale. That is, it is easy to become "mentally reversed" in evaluating some factors and assign a *low* value to the best rating because a low number is more compatible with the nature of the factor. For example, with "rate of obsolescence," the tendency might be to evaluate the *most* longevity with the *lowest* obsolescence, but a low obsolescence rate should be given a high value!

---

[2] Adapted from Barish, *loc. cit.*

7. Determine the weighted evaluation rating by multiplying column 3 by column 4 and enter result in column 5.

8. Total the weighted evaluations for each alternative at the bottom of each column 5.

EVALUATION OF INVESTMENT ALTERNATIVES

At this point, *all* factors—direct, indirect, indeterminate and intangible —will have been evaluated, and it is now possible to accumulate them as bases for the final decision on which alternative should be chosen. At this point, the analyst must make his decision on the basis of the information at hand. And, of course, there is always the likelihood that the evaluation of the intangible factors may be "counter" to the cost aspects of the problem. Here, the analyst must exercise *his* judgment in deciding whether or not the intangibles outweigh the cost factors and to what extent.

If it is desired, the analyst may "weigh" the cost results by the "value" of the intangible factors. At first glance, this may appear illogical, or even "illegal"—but due consideration will indicate the plausibility of such a procedure. If this is to be done, the calculation should be:

$$\frac{\text{Total of Cost Factors}}{\substack{\text{Weighted Evaluation of} \\ \text{Intangible Factors}}} = \substack{\text{Weighted Evaluation of} \\ \text{Cost Factors}}$$

The Re-cap of Comparative Costs form will guide the analyst in the thinking process described here, as shown in Figure 14–5. Careful ex-

	Alternative No. 1 ACME	Alternative No. 2 BUDGET	Alternative No. 3 DELUXE
1. Calculated value of direct cost factors	$ 40,000	$ 34,000	$ 41,000
2. Calculated value of indirect cost factors	1,000	+ 6,000 (disadvantage)	− 3,000
3. Estimated value of indeterminate cost factors	1,500	− 1,000	+ 2,000 (disadvantage)
4. Total of direct, indirect and indeterminate cost factors	$ 37,500	$ 39,000	$ 40,000
5. Weighted evaluation of intangible factors	75	85	95
6. Weighted evaluation of total of all cost factors	$ 50,000	$ 46,000	$ 42,000

Fig. 14–5. Re-cap of comparative costs.

amination will show some interesting interrelationships between the several "levels" of cost, as they are affected by the consideration of subsequent factors. For instance, on line 1, alternative no. 2 appears the best. Further examination will show that neither alternative no. 2 (lowest direct cost) nor alternative no. 1 (lowest total cost—line 4) comes out "best," *all* things considered. Alternative no. 3 (*highest* total *cost*) results in the lowest weighted evaluation of $42,000. It should also be noted that, if desired, the intangible factors can be given a proportional effect, by applying the weighted evaluations at less than full value. This can be accomplished as follows:

$$\begin{bmatrix} \text{Weighted} \\ \text{Evaluation} \\ \text{of all} \\ \text{Factors} \end{bmatrix} = k \begin{bmatrix} \text{Index of} \\ \text{Direct, Indi-} \\ \text{rect, and In-} \\ \text{determinate} \\ \text{Cost Factors} \end{bmatrix} + (1 - k) \begin{bmatrix} \text{Weighted} \\ \text{Evaluation} \\ \text{of Intangible} \\ \text{Factors} \end{bmatrix}$$

and applying the concept as in the following example:

Alternative	Cost + Indirect + Indeterminate	Weighted Evaluation of Intangibles	Index of Cost Factors
1	$37,500	.75	$\dfrac{\$37,500}{37,500} = 1.00$
2	39,000	.85	$\dfrac{\$37,500}{39,000} = .96$
3	40,000	.95	$\dfrac{\$37,500}{40,000} = .94$

The index of cost factors is established to insure that the "best" alternative will be represented by the largest number. Then, if intangible factors are determined to be four times as important as the cost factors:

1   .2(1.00) + .8(.75) = .800
2   .2(.96)   + .8(.85) = .862
3   .2(.94)   + .8(.95) = .948

and:

1   $37,500 ÷ .800 = $46,875
2   39,000 ÷ .862 =   45,244
3   40,000 ÷ .948 =   42,194

and, of course any other "ratio" could be established, as deemed appropriate.

While the above may not be totally "mathematically" acceptable, it *does* provide a unique way of considering the intangible factors in an investment analysis. Perhaps its greatest value may be in bringing out the serious effect such factors *could* have in the decision-making process—if one chose to view them this way. At the *most*, the approach could tip the scales in favor of a project. At the *least*, the analyst should feel secure in having "considered" *all* aspects of the problem.

CONCLUSION

This chapter has attempted to show that many factors must be given consideration in evaluating equipment investment alternatives. In addition to the more common direct and indirect costs, a large number of indeterminate cost and intangible factors have been identified. Techniques have been developed for evaluating the latter two categories and for taking them into consideration in arriving at an investment decision.

It is felt that more accurate results will be obtained by this method of analysis, and it may be found that in some cases the indeterminate cost factors and/or the intangible factors will alter the investment decision from that which might have been made without their due consideration.

The next chapter deals with the end uses of the cost concepts and procedures covered in Chapters 13 and 14. It will be concerned with determining the costs of material handling activities.

15

Activity Cost
Determination

Preceding chapters have dealt with material handling cost concepts and with determining the cost of owning and operating a piece of handling equipment. The next area of consideration is the development of the cost of carrying out a specific handling activity, a group of related activities, or the entire handling cost of a production facility.

This is primarily a problem of determining the costs for the various components of the activity and finding the total. Where alternatives exist, it is also necessary to make appropriate comparisons and consider related factors that may not be reducible to dollars, such as the intangible factors previously discussed.

The one major item of handling cost that has not been covered in the preceding chapters is the cost of manpower. This chapter will review the major sources of manpower cost data and techniques for determining these costs. Following that, the problem of accumulating total costs for a material handling activity will be discussed. A procedure will be outlined for accomplishing this, and several forms presented for accumulating costs and comparing alternative project costs.

DETERMINING MANPOWER COSTS

A large percentage of the people in any manufacturing or other business enterprise are performing many handling tasks. It is the job of the material handling engineer, along with accounting personnel, to isolate those tasks that *are* handling and assign appropriate costs to them. Previous chapters have covered the problem of isolating the handling tasks (moves) by means of various charting and analytical techniques. The next step is to assign costs to them, and this involves finding out how much *time* is spent on each move. There are many ways in which these costs can be obtained. Some of the well-known techniques or approaches are:

1. Time Cards—when a person's *full* time is applied to handling activities, as was described earlier, under Specialized Material Handling Activities.
2. Time Study [1]—when the handling aspect of the task may be a *portion* of the overall task, as previously discussed under Mixed Material Handling Activities.
3. Work Sampling [2]—in situations similar to the above.
4. Pre-determined Time Standards [3]—based on fundamental body motions, rather than on actual time studies of persons at work, and used in the same general way as standard data.
5. Standard Data [4]—based on time studies, work sampling, or pre-determined time standards, and permitting the synthesis of handling manpower time, based on studies of similar work previously done and then tabulated in convenient form.
6. Proportionate Time Allocation—where mixed or borderline activities include *some* material handling. That is, time worked can be allocated by estimate or work sampling, and a portion, say 30 percent, assigned to material handling.

The selection of the proper approach, tool, or technique will depend upon the situation at hand. Each move, as identified on a Process Chart, etc., must be examined to determine what classification of personnel is doing the handling activity. Then, the proper time data must be obtained by the appropriate means. Subsequent illustrations will point out the uses of the various sources of time and cost data.

EXAMPLES OF MANPOWER COST DETERMINATION

This section will illustrate briefly the more common methods of determining material handling manpower costs as described above.

Time Cards

In the simplest of the six approaches, it is assumed that a man's *full* time is spent on material handling activities. Then, his total time spent

---

[1] See any motion and time study text or industrial engineering handbook for details on these techniques.
[2] See footnote 1.
[3] See footnote 1.
[4] See footnote 1.

per week, say 40 hours, is multiplied by his hourly wage, say $2.00—and the cost of *his* activity per week is $80.00. Then, if the cost is desired per unit of product, material, weight, etc., it is necessary to divide the $80.00 by the units desired, as:

$$\frac{\$80.00}{800 \text{ drums}} = \$.10/\text{drum moved}$$

This cost is then applied at the appropriate place in the cost accumulation procedure, as will be explained later.

Time Study

If the time study technique is used, the handling operation under analysis would be studied and the cost per handling operation, per move, etc., determined from the time study. The results of a typical time study might appear as below:

Element	Allowed Time in Minutes
1. Push empty hand truck from drum storage into rail car	1.13
2. Pick up drum with hand truck	.10
3. Maneuver truck into clear	.20
4. Push truck (with drum) to storage area	1.52
5. Release drum from truck	.05
	3.00

The cost calculations are as follows:

$$\frac{60 \text{ min./hr.}}{3 \text{ min./drum}} = 20 \text{ drums/hr.}$$

$$\frac{\$2.00/\text{hr.}}{20 \text{ drums/hr.}} = \$.10/\text{drum moved}$$

Work Sampling

The work sampling technique is most commonly applied to determine the *percent* of a task that *is* handling. In this way, it can be applied to the "mixed" handling types of tasks described earlier, in which only a portion of a man's work consists of material handling.

Work sampling can also be used for *establishing* time standards, with results similar to those obtained by time study. The details of work sampling methods are beyond the scope of this text and the reader should investigate one of the several texts on work sampling for further instructions.

Pre-Determined Time Standards

Pre-determined time standards are time values for basic body motions. They are particularly useful when all or most of the handling activity is performed manually and are used in much the same manner as standard times, by tabulating the basic motions in the task, selecting time values from tables and charts available, and adding them up to obtain the total time. There are several well known "systems" of pre-determined time standards, such as Methods-Time-Measurement, Universal Standard Data, Work Factor Analysis, Basic Motion Times, etc. Texts and handbooks are available that explain them in sufficient detail for practical application. Figure 15–1 [5] illustrates an application of one such system, made up into a formula for banding palletized unit loads.

Standard Data

Standard data tabulates results of a large number of time studies taken over a period of time, or uses pre-determined motion times, covering an area of activity such as machining, assembly, car loading, stock picking, etc.

The accompanying example is based on work done by the Eaton, Yale and Towne Manufacturing Company.[6] In this example, it is desired to find the handling time for the fork lift truck operation shown in Figure 15–2. Drums stored on pallets are being loaded onto a tractor-trailer train. Time is to be determined for the fork lift truck, which in this case is the same as the operator's time. Loaded pallets weigh 200 lb, there is a good concrete running surface, and the work is performed indoors with normal temperatures.

The table in Figure 15–3 shows time values (standard data) for *basic* truck motions obtained from a large number of time studies. Next, appropriate *variables* are identified and tabulated from the data shown in Figures 15–4 and 15–5. Several of the variables are assigned allowance factors which were determined by time study, work sampling, or estimate.

---

[5] Donald E. Farr, "Applying Standards to Materials Handling Operations," a paper presented at an A.M.H.S. Regional Conference, Dallas, Texas, November 1962.
[6] Robert S. Rice, "How to Measure Fork Truck Performance," *Factory*, April 1954, pp. 84–93.
[7] *Ibid.*

K No.	Description	TMU	Occ.	Total
K1	Apply 1 band (long. or cross)	1747		
K2	Apply each add'l band (long. or cross)	1230		
K3	Add'l for double crimping (per band)	89		
K10	Apply vertical batten	804		
K11	Apply each add'l vertical batten	459		
K12	Prepare and position special horiz. band with 4 battens	3238		
K13	Bending reel, load, strip and cut off band (TMU per band from Table 1 below)	(Enter value below)		

Table 1

Pre-cut banding

Length of Band in Feet

Allowed TMU	8'	10'	12'	14'	16'	18'	20'		
One Band	229	270	312	353	395	436	477		
				No. Horizontal			X		
				No. Cross Bands			X		
				No. Longitudinal			X		

Total TMU Per Pallet   _____

Allowance_____%   _____

Allowed TMU Per Pallet   _____

Fig. 15–1. Formula application sheet for banding palletized unit load. (From Donald E. Farr, "Applying Standards to Material Handling Operations," *Proceedings, International Material Management Society Regional Conference,* Dallas, Texas, November 1962.)

The allowances shown below should be used to adjust the time values, for the factors indicated (Figure 15–4): [7]

10. Battery

Time Battery is in Actual Use	Allowance
1–5 hours	.00
6	.01
7	.08
8	.25

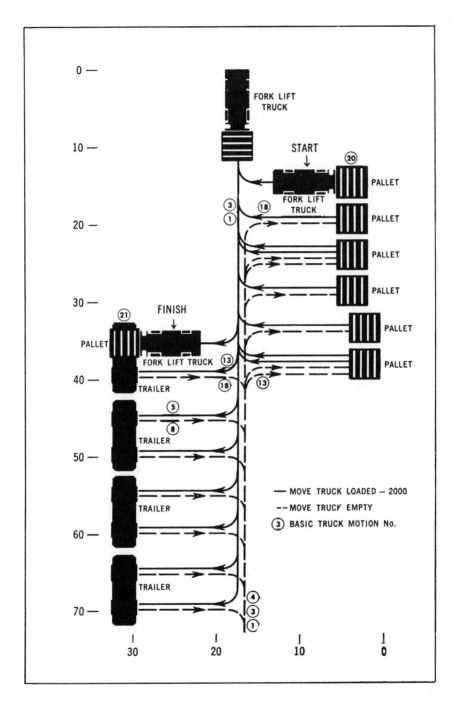

Fig. 15–2. Diagram of truck movements in loading tractor-trailer train. (From Robert S. Rice, "How to Measure Fork Truck Performance," *Factory*, April 1954, pp. 84–93.)

©1954 THE YALE & TOWNE MFG. CO.

	BASIC MOTIONS	DESCRIPTION	TRUCK. YALE K51 AT 40 TIME IN MINUTES				
			Empty	1,000 lbs.	2,000 lbs.	3,000 lbs.	4,000 lbs.
STRAIGHT RUNS	1. FORWARD Per Foot	Begins when the truck has reached full speed at the end of acceleration, ends when a truck begins to stop.	.0023	.0024	.0025	.0025	.0027
	2. REVERSE "		.0023	.0024	.0025	.0025	.0027
	3. ACCELERATE Per Occurrence	Occurs each time the truck moves from dead stop to full speed.	.030	.025	.025	.025	.025
	4. STOP "	Includes application of brakes to bring truck to dead stop from full speed.	.020	.033	.034	.035	.036
	5. RUN-IN, 1st LEVEL "	Covers moving the truck at slow speed from a dead stop to insert the forks into a pallet, or to place a pallet (after the forks have been raised). The time value includes starting and stopping. The horizontal distance through which the truck moves is approximately 4 feet, the length of the pallet. 1st level is ground level; 2nd level is 4 feet and 3rd is 8 feet above ground level.	.080	.080	.080	.070	.070
	6. RUN-IN, 2nd LEVEL "		.080	.090	.110	.100	.100
	7. RUN-IN, 3rd LEVEL "		.110	.120	.130	.120	.120
	8. RUN-OUT, 1st LEVEL "	Covers withdrawal of forks from a pallet or removing a pallet, includes starting and stopping. The truck moves backward approximately 4 feet when performing this motion. Levels are the same as for "run-in"	.060	.065	.065	.060	.060
	9. RUN-OUT, 2nd LEVEL "		.060	.065	.070	.060	.060
	10. RUN-OUT, 3rd LEVEL "		.060	.070	.070	.080	.080
TURNS	11. RIGHT, FORWARD "	A change of direction to the right, usually 90 degrees and in the minimum turning radius, while the truck is running forward (11) or backward (12).	.055	.055	.055	.055	.055
	12. RIGHT, REVERSE "		.055	.055	.055	.055	.055
	13. RIGHT AND STOP, FORWARD "	Same as motions 11 and 12, except that the truck comes to a dead stop at the end of the turn. This motion is usually followed by "hoist" or "run-in"	.070	.070	.070	.075	.075
	14. RIGHT AND STOP, REVERSE "		.065	.085	.080	.080	.080
	15. LEFT, FORWARD "	Same as motions 11 through 14, except turns are made to the left instead of right.	.055	.055	.055	.055	.055
	16. LEFT, REVERSE "		.055	.055	.055	.055	.055
	17. LEFT AND STOP, FORWARD "		.060	.060	.060	.060	.060
	18. LEFT AND STOP, REVERSE "		.065	.075	.075	.065	.070
STACKING	19. TILT "	Tilt the fork carriage forward or backward.	.025	.025	.025	.025	.025
	20. HOIST. UP Per Inch	Move the fork carriage up, while the truck is at rest.	.0028	.0029	.0030	.0032	.0033
	21. HOIST DOWN "	Reverse of motion 20.	.0030	.0018	.0018	.0018	.0018

Fig. 15-3. Table of time values for basic truck movements. (From Robert S. Rice, "How to Measure Fork Truck Performance," Factory, April 1954, pp. 84-92.)

14. Pavement

A. Asphalt, concrete road	.00
B. Brick, wood block, ice, snow, wood planking, good macadam, Tarvia, hard snow, poor concrete, granite blocks	.01
C. Soft snow, gravel, poor macadam	.02
D. Clay	.09
E. Sand road	.12
F. Loose sand (3″ deep) · · ·	.14

17. Lighting

Footcandles

5 or more	.00
4	.20
3	.40
2	.60
1 · · ·	.80

26. Angle of Tiering

Basic Motion Numbers	Storage Angle *			
	34°	45°	60°	90°
5 through 10	.31	.75	1.50	0.00
13, 14, 17 and 18	.66	.50	.33	0.00

* Angle is between front edge of pallet and aisle boundary line.

The time standards, variables, allowances, etc. are entered on the summary sheet shown in Figure 15–6 which shows how the calculations are made. The following description is from the source cited:

1. Forward straight runs—Truck covers 360 feet empty (0.0023 minute per foot from table in Figure 15–3) and 360 feet carrying a 2000 lb. load (0.0025 minute per foot) to load a train of 8 trailers. Total basic motion time for straight runs is 1.728 minutes (0.0023 × 360 + 0.0025 × 360).

3. Acceleration—There are 16 occurrences of acceleration: 8 empty at 0.030 minute per occurrence, and 8 loaded at 0.025 minute per occurrence. Total basic motion time for acceleration is 0.44 minute.

Other basic motions involving tabulation of number of occurrences and minutes per occurrence from the basic motion table include: Nos. 5 (run-in); 8 (run-out); 13 (right forward turn and stop); and 18 (left reverse turn and stop).

Total amount of hoist operation required to handle eight drums is 105 inches up at 0.0030 minute per inch, and 105 inches down at 0.0018 minute per inch.

Total basic motion time to pick up and load eight loaded pallets on the trailer train is approximately 7½ minutes (7.592). But that doesn't include the variables.

Values for the *variables* are shown in the summary sheet (Figure 15–6) to the right of the basic motion time summary. They are:

SUMMARY OF FORK TRUCK OPERATING VARIABLES

	VARIABLE FACTOR	REASON FOR TIME ALLOWANCE	HOW TO MEASURE THE ALLOWANCE
HUMAN	1. SKILL	Relative operator ability and effort in comparison with a normal operator.	Estimate per cent that your operator is above or below a normal operator in skill and effort.
	2. FATIGUE	Necessary rest and personal time for the operator.	Compare with plant fatigue allowances for similar work. Generally, it's about 10%, but local conditions may justify more or less.
	3. CARELESSNESS	Effectiveness of supervision of truck operators, including observation of safety rules.	Estimate or develop from time study percentage of time lost through the fault of supervision or safety rules.
	4. DISTANCE	Operation over distances too short to use truck's capacity speed.	Adjust running time by ratio of capacity to usable speed.
	5. TIER HEIGHT	Standard data (page 450) covers stacking to three levels. Higher stacking requires additional standards, or an extra time allowance to the third-level standards.	Apply percentage extra time allowance for run-in and run-out based on an estimate or time study
	6. FORK LOAD	Standard time tables cover loads from empty to 4000 pounds, in 1000-lb. increments.	Add new time values for other loads as required.
	7. DIRECTION	Different rates of speed in forward or reverse due to truck type.	Add basic motion time values to cover different equipment.

MECHANICAL	8. TRUCK CONDITION	Mechanical and electrical condition of a truck affects lost time due to breakdowns.	Develop percentage allowance from estimate, work sampling, or time study to cover lost time due to breakdowns.
	9. TRUCK TYPE	Make or model of truck other than that designated in the tables.	Set up separate tables of basic motion time values for different types and models.
	10. BATTERY	Power ebbs with use, generally slowing truck after five hours' constant operation.	Beyond maximum power time limit adjust time values according to battery specifications.
	11. MAINTENANCE	Truck outage time for preventive maintenance during operating shift.	Convert scheduled daily preventive maintenance time to percentage of basic motion time per day.
OPERATIONAL	12. TRAFFIC	Delays due to presence of pedestrians and other vehicles in truck operating area.	Find delay time to trucks by estimate, work sampling, or time study in relation to total time for basic motions performed by trucks.
	13. OBSTRUCTIONS	Low headroom, narrow passages, and similar layout obstacles that prevent free truck operation.	Total truck delay due to obstructions is delay time per occurrence – from estimate or time study – and frequency of occurrences. Convert to percentage of basic time.
	14. PAVEMENT	Type and condition of surfaces over which a truck operates.	Use data on page 451 to adjust basic motion time for travel over other than asphalt or concrete.

Fig. 15–4. Summary of fork truck operating variables—part I. (From Robert S. Rice, "How to Measure Fork Truck Performance," Factory, April 1954, pp. 84-93.)

SUMMARY OF FORK TRUCK OPERATING VARIABLES

VARIABLE FACTOR	REASON FOR TIME ALLOWANCE	HOW TO MEASURE THE ALLOWANCE
15. LOADING AREA CONDITIONS	Combination of several factors such as traffic, housekeeping, etc.	Apply adjustments to individual factors.
16. LOAD SIZE AND TYPE	Basic motion time values are based on a cubic load measuring 48 inches each way. Larger dimensions may affect time.	Set up a percentage adjustment for other size loads by estimate or time study — if required. Apply allowance only to basic motions affected.
17. LIGHTING	Basic motion time values apply only if there are at least 5 foot-candles.	Use the data on page 451 to adjust basic motion time when light is less than 5 foot-candles.
18. HOUSEKEEPING	Areas cluttered by poor housekeeping delay truck operation.	You may estimate this delay time. Better, use time study data of a day or more to find time trucks are slowed and held up in relation to necessary basic motion time.
19. SCHEDULING	Time lost by trucks waiting for loads or work instructions.	Estimate or find from work sampling study scheduling delays in proportion to basic motion time.
20. TEMPERATURE	If operating temperatures are outside a normal range of 32 to 90 degrees, extra time must be allowed above that in the tables.	Increase basic motion time by 10% (in addition to fatigue allowance) for operating in temperatures above 90 degrees or below 32 degrees.
21. WEATHER	Precipitation generally cuts truck performance out of doors.	Increase basic motion time by 10% for operating trucks on days when there's precipitation.

OPERATIONAL

22. AISLE WIDTH	Basic motion time values apply to aisles that are at least truck specification width plus one foot. Narrower aisles slow trucks.	Increase basic motion time affected by 43% for each foot, or fraction of a foot, that an aisle is narrower than specification width plus one foot.
23. ONE OR TWO-WAY TRAFFIC	Basic motion time values apply to one-way traffic, and to two-way traffic in aisles at least 18 inches in width, plus width of two passing trucks or loads.	Project team did not develop specific allowances. It suggests time study to find delay time per occurrence, work sampling to find frequency. Relate total time to basic motion time for percentage.
24. DOORWAYS	Some doorways cause no delay. Others require truck to slow or stop.	Find delay time per occurrence (time study) and frequency (work sampling) of delays for each type of doorway. Convert to percentage of basic motion time. Or you can estimate the effect.
25. INTERSECTIONS	Basic motion time for turns affected if one or both aisles are narrow. Some intersections require truck to stop.	Estimate or develop a percentage allowance as described for doorways.
26. ANGLE OF TIERING	Angle at which pallets are placed in relation to aisle boundary affects turn and stop, run in, and run out.	Use data on page 451 to adjust basic motion time for motions affected.
27. GRADES	Up grades reduce speed of electric trucks.	Increase straight run basic motion time by 8% for each per cent of grade (up grades only).

Fig. 15–5. Summary of fork truck operating variables—part II. (From Robert S. Rice, "How to Measure Fork Truck Performance," Factory, April 1954, pp. 84–93.)

LOCATION

DATE _Nov. 20_   TYPE TRUCK _Fork Lift_

	BASIC TRUCK MOTIONS	E	1000	2000	3000	4000		Skill 1	Fatigue 2	Carelessness 3
STRAIGHT RUNS	1. Forward—per ft.	360/0023		360/0025			1.728			
	2. Reverse—per ft.									
	3. Acceleration	8/030		8/025			.440			
	4. Stopping									
	RUN-IN 5. 1st Level Stacking	8/080		8/080			1.280			
	6. 2nd Level Stack'g									
	7. 3rd Level Stack'g									
	RUN-OUT 8. 1st Level Stacking	8/060		8/065			1.000			
	9. 2nd Level Stack'g									
	10. 3rd Level Stack'g									
TURNS	RIGHT 11. Forward									
	12. Reverse									
	RIGHT & STOP 13. Forward	8/070		8/070			1.120			
	14. Reverse									
	LEFT 15. Forward									
	16. Reverse									
	LEFT & STOP 17. Forward									
	18. Reverse	8/065		8/075			1.120			
STACKING	19. Tilt – Bkd. & Fwd.			16/025			.400			
	HOIST 20. Up—per in.			105/0030			.315			
	21. Down—per in.			105/0018			.189			
	22. TOTAL						7.592	.05	.10	

Fig. 15–6. Fork lift truck standard-time summary sheet. (From Robert S.

BY _T. L. F._

© 1954 THE YALE & TOWNE MFG. CO.

VARIABLE FACTORS																									**TOTAL**	**TOTAL TIME**
MECHANICAL								OPERATIONAL																		
Distance	Tier Height	Fork Load	Direction	Truck Condition	Truck Type	Battery	Maintenance	Traffic	Obstructions	Pavement	Loading Area	Load Types	Lighting	Housekeeping	Scheduling	Temperature	Weather	Aisle Width	1-2 Way Traffic	Doorways	Intersections	Tier Angle	Grades			
4	5	6	7	8	9	10	11	12	13	14	15	16	17	18	19	20	21	22	23	24	25	26	27			
				.03				.08							.05										1.31	9.95

Rice, "How to Measure Fork Truck Performance," *Factory*, April 1954, p. 84.)

1. Skill—To demonstrate the application of this variable we'll assume the purpose here is to determine how many trains per day could be loaded by a particular operator whose skill and effort is rated 95%. The basic motion time (based on 100%) must be increased 5%.

2. Fatigue—A 10% allowance is made for rest and personal time for the operator.

8. Truck condition—The amount of lost time due to breakdowns is estimated (or established by records or work sampling) at 3%—expressed as a decimal it's 0.03.

12. Traffic—By study it was determined that the average amount of time lost due to the presence of pedestrians and other vehicles in the area is 8%, or 0.08, of basic motion time.

19. Scheduling—Delays in making empty trailer trains available for loading run 5%, 0.05, of basic motion time. The value can be found by estimate, work sampling, or time study.

Total of all the factors is 0.31, so 31% must be added to the total basic motion time by mutliplying the total basic motion time by 1.31. Total standard time for the operation is 9.95 minutes (1.31 × 7.592), and the average operator should be able to load 6 trailer trains per hour (60 mins./9.95 mins.).

Note, that in this example all the variable allowances have been applied to the total basic motion time. In some cases an allowance might apply only to one basic motion. For example, if the truck had to travel over rough pavement during only a part of its straight-run distance, only basic motion number one need be adjusted.[8]

Frequently, charts and graphs are useful in the application of certain portions of standard data. Two such graphs are shown in Figure 15–7 [9] for truck travel distance and for raising or lowering forks. It should be noted that these graphs are for a *specific* truck, and should not be construed as being "standard" or "average." Such graphs are usually prepared by the people establishing the standard data, and are generally applicable only to specific types, makes, or models of equipment.

Proportional Time Allocation

Actually, this approach is a combination of the time card and a work sampling study, in which the portion of a man's total time spent in material handling is determined by work sampling. Then, the percentage so determined is applied to the total time spent or dollars paid. For example, if the man is paid $16.00/day and the work sampling study shows he spends 50% of his time in materials handling, then 50% × $16.00 = $8.00 should be included in the handling cost calculation for the activity under study. If he handles 80 drums during that 50% of his working day, then the cost calculation is:

$$\frac{\$8.00}{80 \text{ drums}} = \$.10/\text{drum moved}$$

[8] *Ibid.*

[9] David C. Prosser, "Standard Data Doubled Our Fork Truck Utilization," *Factory*, March 1954, pp. 90–92.

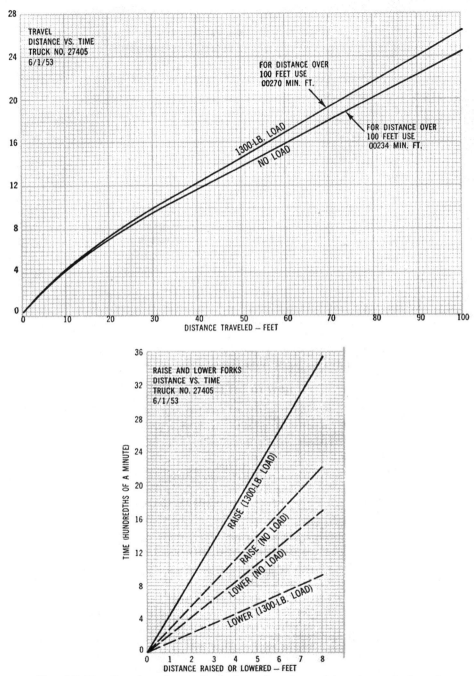

Fig. 15–7. Graphs of standard data for determining (*upper*) time for travel distance and (*lower*) raising or lowering forks. (From David C. Prosser, "Standard Data Doubled Our Fork Truck Utilization," *Factory*, March 1954, pp. 90–92.)

APPROACH TO MATERIAL HANDLING COST DETERMINATION

In previous discussions, it has been indicated that an eventual goal of material handling cost determination is the total material handling cost for an activity, a department, or an entire enterprise. The reasons for this have also been stated in considerable detail. However, no matter how commendable the goal, attaining it is more easily said than done. Such a task requires a prodigious amount of fact finding, analysis, detail work, correlating, evaluating, and summarizing. It cannot be done in one easy step, nor can it be done easily, at all. Nevertheless, no matter how "difficult" such a task may appear, it should now be apparent that it is definitely possible to accomplish it. Perhaps a review of the major aspects of the cost determination problem will aid in clarifying the situation.

If it is desired to know the cost of a material-handling activity, the overall task can be subdivided as follows:

1. Each and every move must be isolated and identified, and related moves combined if appropriate. Using the data from the tractor-trailer loading illustration (Figure 15–2) this would be:
   A. All *combined* moves for loading 8 pallets as depicted on the Flow Diagram.
2. All equipment used or to be used must be known.
   B. fork lift truck (pallets considered expendable)
3. Time required by all personnel and equipment must be calculated.
   C. fork lift truck = 9.95 min. (from Figure 15–6)
   D. truck operator = 9.95 min.
4. Hourly costs for operating equipment and for operators must be known.
   E. fork truck cost per hour = $3.00
   F. operator cost per hour   = $2.00
5. Equipment and manpower costs must be determined and summarized.

G. fork truck: $\dfrac{9.95 \text{ min}}{60 \text{ min/hr}} \times \$3.00 = \$.497$

H. operator: $\dfrac{9.95 \text{ min}}{60 \text{ min/hr}} \times \$2.00 = \underline{\$.332}$
$\$.829$ TOTAL

The result indicates that it will cost $.829 to load 8 pallets onto the 4 trailers. If it is assumed that 64 pallets are to be removed from the storage area, then the cost for the job is:

$$\frac{64 \text{ pallets/order}}{8 \text{ pallets/train}} = 8 \text{ trains/order} \times \$.829/\text{train} = \$6.632$$

For the complete job, it might be assumed that the tractor-trailer train hauls the pallets to a railway siding and that another lift truck removes the 64 pallets and loads them into the cars. Then, the related costs for these two operations would be calculated and added to the $6.632 to obtain the total cost of handling for the 64-pallet order.

The above procedure and example have shown how the handling cost for a selected activity can be determined. For a more complex situation, the problem involves somewhat the same procedure, except that many individual activities may have to be costed out and added together.

The major problem is the proper and complete identification of *all* of the move steps in an operation or process. There are no better tools for this purpose than the Process Chart, Flow Diagram, and Flow Process Chart. However, they *must* be made *accurately*, and this is where a primary difficulty arises. Entirely too many such charts are hastily made, omitting many handling steps, combining some with other steps in the process and in general, *omitting* the detail necessary for accurate cost determination. A previous chapter has described and illustrated the construction of Process Charts and Flow Diagrams. Suffice it to say that the analyst *must* make *accurate* charts and diagrams. Each move step *must* be identified and recorded.

COMPARISON OF ALTERNATIVES

The preceding pages have outlined methods by which handling costs can be determined—for either an existing situation, or for the synthesis of a proposed handling method. In many cases, the problem solution will require the determination of handling costs for two or more possible alternatives, one of which is to be selected and implemented.

The form used for accumulating the costs should probably be designed to fit the individualities of the specific plant, company, or even department. One such form is shown in Figure 15–8, as developed by a major U.S. manufacturer. It shows the present method of handling distribution transformer tanks. The bottom of the form is used to show the proposed method and its cost.

It will be noted that the form is designed to accomplish the goal of accumulating costs. The reader may find it worthwhile to study all of the form carefully and then design one to suit his particular needs. Care must be exercised to be sure *all* pertinent items are included.

Where alternatives are being compared, it is also important to include a consideration of the indirect and intangible factors. These were covered in detail in the preceding chapter. The forms suggested there (Figures 14–2 and 14–3) should be utilized to supplement the cost calculations covered in this chapter.

PROJECT NUMBER ___S-3164___

MATERIALS

DIVISION ___Tank___   WORKS ___Cleveland___   COMPILED BY _C. L. n._

BUILDING NUMBER ___8___   SECTION NUMBER ___B-30___   DATE COMPILED ___6/12/X2___

PROBLEM AND OBJECTIVES: Transportation of 188% increase in volume of steel tanks to assembly

HANDLING ACTIVITY

Operation Number	Starting Point (A)	Handling Operation (B)	Stopping Point (C)	Materials Handling Equipment (D)	Distance Moved (E)	Per Year (F) ÷	Per Oper. (G)
		HANDLING OPERATIONS		EQUIPMENT USED	DISTANCE	VOLUME OF	Quantity of Pieces
							EXISTING
1	Floor	Load trailers	Trailer	Trailer (12 pcs.)	30'	125,591	1
2	Bay F-20	Transpt. trailers	Bay A-90	2 trls., 1 tractor	1,630'	125,591	24
3	Buggy	Unload trailers	Pallet	Pallet (7 pieces)	5'	125,591	1
4	Floor	Stack pallets	6-7 high	Fork lift truck	50'	125,591	7
5	6-7 high	Unstack pallets	Floor	Fork lift truck	50'	125,591	7
6	Bay A-90	Transport pallets	Bay B-30	Fork lift truck	1,020'	125,591	14
7	Pallet	Unload pallets	Floor	None	10'	125,591	1
8	Bay A-90	Return trailers	Bay F-20	2 trls., 1 tractor	1,630'	125,591	24
		Actual Totals—Year, 19X1			4,425'	125,591	1
							FORECASTED
		Forecasted Totals—Year, 19X4			4,425'	362,400	1
							PROPOSED
1	Roller conv.	Load conveyor	Ovhd. conv.	Rope hoist	10'	362,400	1
2	Bay F-20	Transport pieces	Assy. stores	Ovhd. conveyor	600'	362,400	1
3	Ovhd. conv.	Unload conveyor	Pallet	Pallet (7 pieces)	10'	362,400	1
4	Floor	Stack pallets	6-7 high	Fork lift truck	50'	362,400	7
5.	6-7 high	Unstack pallets	Floor	Fork lift truck	50'	362,400	7
6	Assy. stores	Transport pieces	Bay B-30	Ovhd. conveyor	50'	362,400	1
7	Pallet	Load conveyor	Ovhd. conv.	None	6'	329,800	1
8	Bay F-20	Transport pallets	Bay A-32	Fork lift truck	300'	32,600	14
9	Palt. or con.	Unload pieces	Floor	Rope hoist	10'	362,400	1
10	Bay A-32	Return pallets	Assy. stores	Fork lift truck	300'	32,600	42
		Forecasted Totals—Year, 19X4			1,386'	362,400	1
						SAVING (')	MINUS (")
		Total Saving			3,039'		
		Percent Saving			69%		

Fig. 15–8. Material handing project-cost-determination sheet. (From Ronald Press Co.,

HANDLING PROJECT

REVISED BY   *D.C.*   APPROVED BY   *J.B.S.*

DATE REVISED   7/15/X2   DATE APPROVED   7/28/X2

OPERATIONS		LABOR COST				OPERATING COST			TOTAL COST
Number of Operations per Year = (H)	Operation Unit (K) ×	Labor Hours per Operation (M)	Labor Hours per Year = (N)	Wage Rate per Hour × (P)	Labor Cost per Year = (R)	Operating Hours per Year (S) ×	Operating Cost Per Hour (T)	Operating Cost Per Year = (U)	Total Handling Cost per Year (V)
METHOD (')						(N')			(R' + U')
125,591	Pieces	.018	2,261	$ .90	$ 2,035	None	None	None	$ 2,035
5,233	Trips	.460	2,407	.90	2,167	2,407	$ .37	$ 891	3,058
125,591	Pieces	.018	2,261	.90	2,035	None	None	None	2,035
17,942	Loads	.063	1,130	.90	1,017	1,130	.57	644	1,661
17,942	Loads	.063	1,130	.90	1,017	1,130	.57	644	1,661
8,971	Trips	.254	2,279	.90	2,051	2,279	.57	1,299	3,350
125,591	Pieces	.018	2,261	.90	2,035	None	None	None	2,035
5,233	Trips	.460	2,407	.90	2,167	2,407	.37	891	3,058
125,591	Pieces	(.1285)	16,136	$ .90	$14,524	9,353	($.467)	$4,369	$18,893
ACTIVITY (')						(.0745	Operating hours per piece)		
362,400	Pieces	(.1285)	46,568	$1.08	$50,293	26,999	($.467)	$12,609	$62,902
METHOD (")						(N")			(R" + U")
362,400	Pieces	.010	3,624	$1.08	$ 3,914	None	None	None	$ 3,914
362,400	Pieces	None	None	None	None	3,624	$1.01	$3,673	3,673
362,400	Pieces	.010	3,624	1.08	3,914	None	None	None	3,914
51,771	Loads	.063	3,262	1.08	3,523	3,262	.57	1,859	5,382
51,771	Loads	.063	3,262	1.08	3,523	3,262	.57	1,859	5,382
362,400	Pieces	None	None	None	None	737	1.01	744	744
329,800	Pieces	.004	1,319	1.08	1,425	None	None	None	1,425
2,329	Trips	.180	419	1.08	453	419	.57	239	692
362,400	Pieces	.008	2,899	1.08	3,130	None	None	None	3,130
776	Trips	.180	140	1.08	151	140	.57	80	231
362,400	Pieces	(.0512)	18,549	$1.08	$20.033	11,444	($.739)	$8,454	$28,487
IN PROPOSED METHOD									(W)
			28,019		$30,260	15,555		$4,155	$34,415
			60%		60%	58%		33%	55%

H. A. Bolz and G. Hagemann, *Materials Handling Handbook,* The New York, 1958.)

DETERMINING TOTAL HANDLING COST

For a more detailed example, using many of the techniques previously discussed, the plant shown in Figure 15–9 will be considered. This plant is designed to package an aerosol product (shaving cream, hair spray, etc.) and is somewhat simplified for the purpose of this illustration. The objective is to determine the *total* handling cost for the entire plant, for one year. The details for a portion of this cost are discussed.

Step 1. Identify the Moves

In this case, the handling of the wax (one of the ingredients) will be analyzed. It is known that 10,000 bags of wax are required per year. Figure 15–10 is a Process Chart for this activity, and shows 6 move steps. This same charting procedure would be carried out for (1) all 9 ingredients, (2) all other in-plant handling, and (3) all packing and shipping operations. This is partially shown on the Flow Process Chart in Figure 15–11, which identifies 53 moves.

Step 2. All Equipment Must Be Known

The Process Chart indicates that the methods to be used are (1) *hand,* and (2) *fork truck.* In addition, *pallets* are involved in the handling activity and there is a *bag dumper* which will be considered a piece of handling equipment.

Step 3. Time Required for All Personnel and Equipment Must Be Determined

These data are also shown on the Process Chart, as determined for the distances measured. For example, hand-carrying one bag 20 ft from the car to a pallet requires .01 hours. The 10,000 bags will require $10{,}000 \times .01$ hr $= 100$ hr/yr. No equipment is required in this step.

Step 4. Hourly Operating Costs for the Equipment and for Operators Must Be Known

If the operator is paid \$1.50/hr. for this task, the annual cost will be 100 hrs x \$1.50 = \$1500.

Step 5. Equipment and Manpower Cost Must Be Determined and Summarized

If the same procedure as above is carried out for all 6 moves on the Process Chart, the total annual cost for *this* portion of the plant activity

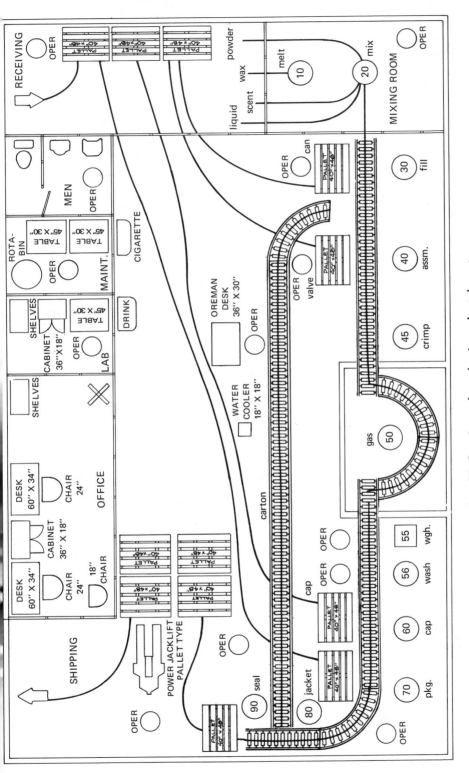

Fig. 15-9. Aerosol packaging plant layout.

PROCESS CHART

PART NAME　Item No. 10—Wax

PROCESS DESCRIPTION　Move wax from R.R. car to Melt

DEPARTMENT　Production

PLANT　Apple Aerosol Products Co.

RECORDED BY　A.M.J.　　DATE　9/20/—

SUMMARY	NO.
○ OPERATIONS	1
⇨ TRANSPORTATIONS	6
☐ INSPECTIONS	0
D DELAYS	0
▽ STORAGES	6
TOTAL STEPS	13
DISTANCE TRAVELED	96'

STEP	Operations Transport Inspect Delay Storage	DESCRIPTION OF PRESENT METHOD	Dist.	How Moved	Est. Hrs./ Load	Hrs. per Bag
1	○ ⇨ ☐ D ▽	in R.R. car—(10,000 100# bags)				
2	○ ⇨ ☐ D ▽	stack onto pallet (25/pallet)	20 ft.	hand	.01	.0100
3	○ ⇨ ☐ D ▽	on pallet at dock				
4	○ ⇨ ☐ D ▽	pallet from Dock to Receiving Stores (25 b./p.)	30'	F.T.	.08	.0032
5	○ ⇨ ☐ D ▽	in Receiving Stores on floor				
6	○ ⇨ ☐ D ▽	Pallet to Mixing Area (25 bags/pallet)	30'	F.T.	.10	.0040
7	○ ⇨ ☐ D ▽	On floor in Mixing Area				
8	○ ⇨ ☐ D ▽	Pallet to Mixing Level (25 bags/pallet)	10'	F.T.	.12	.0048
9	○ ⇨ ☐ D ▽	Pallets on floor at Mixing Level				
10	○ ⇨ ☐ D ▽	Lift bag from pallet to dumper (1 bag)	5'	hand	.08	.0800
11	○ ⇨ ☐ D ▽	Rest bag on dumper				
12	○ ⇨ ☐ D ▽	Dump bag into kettle (1 bag)	1'	hand	.05	.0500
13	○ ⇨ ☐ D ▽	Melt wax in kettle				
	○ ⇨ ☐ D ▽		96'			.1520
	○ ⇨ ☐ D ▽					hour/ bag

Fig. 15–10.　Process chart for one component (wax) of aerosol product.

will be known. The Cost Determination Sheet, shown in Figure 15–12, is used to re-cap all the necessary data. Each move step is entered on the Cost Determination Sheet from the Process Chart (Figure 15–10). Necessary information on yearly quantities, items/load, etc. are picked up from a Basic Data Required form, such as Figure 7–2.

Manpower requirements, i.e. the "time per load" column (D), are determined by one or a combination of the techniques previously dis-

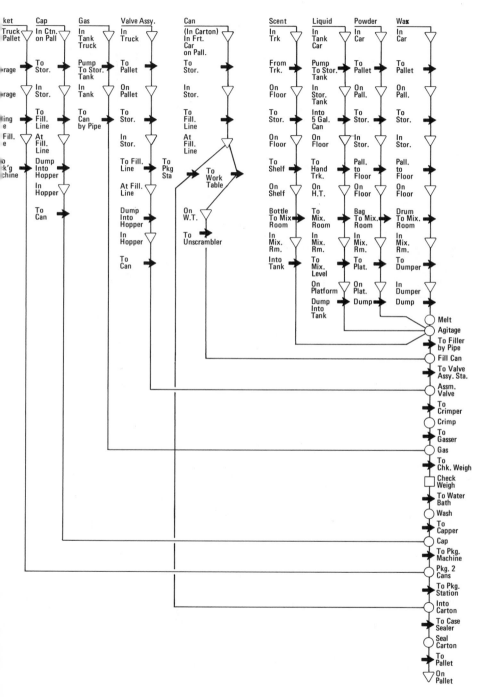

Fig. 15–11. Flow process chart for aerosol packaging plant.

COMPANY __APPCO__ PLANT __Filling__ DEPARTMENT __PRODUCTION__ PROJECT NO __1__ ANALYZED BY __AMJ__ DATE __9/25__

Move No.	MOVE IDENTIFICATION Move Description	Yearly Quan. A	Item per Load B	Loads per Year (A÷B) C	MANPOWER COST Time per Load Hrs. (C×D) D	Hrs. per Year E	Wage per Hour F	Cost per Year (E×F) G	HANDLING EQUIPMENT COST Equip. Identification	Time/Load in Hrs. H	Hrs. per Year (C×H) J	Cost per Hr. K	Cost per Yr. (J×K) L	AUXILIARY EQUIPMENT COST Equip. Ident.	No. Reqd. M	Cost per Item N	Amort. Rate P	% Used This Move Q	Cost per Yr. (MNPQ) R	TOTAL COST Man-pow. Cost/Yr. G	Equip. Cost per Yr. L	Aux. Cost per Yr. R	Total Cost per Yr. S
1	cart to pallet Bags	10,000	1	10,000	.010	100	1.50	150												150	–	–	150
2	Palletto rec.store	10,000	25	400	.080	32	2.50	80	fork truck	.08	32	1.50	48	pallet	40	5	25%	100%	50	80	48	50	178
3	rec.store to mixing area	400	1	400	.100	40	2.50	100	fork truck	.10	40	1.50	60							100	60	–	160
4	mix area mix to fill	400	1	400	.120	48	2.50	120	fork truck	.12	48	1.50	72							120	72	–	192
5	mix room to dumper	10,000	1	10,000	.080	800	2.00	1600												1600			1600
6	dump	10,000	1	10,000	.050	500	2.50	1250						dumper	1	2,000	20%	100%	400	1250	–	400	1650
																						TOTAL $	3930

Fig. 15–12. Cost determination sheet. (From *Production Handbook*, The Ronald Press Co., New York, 1972.)

cussed. The yearly manpower cost is an extension of the hours and wage columns and is entered in column G, as well as at the far right, also under G.

Handling *equipment* time requirements are determined in much the same way as manpower time, above. Equipment cost per hour is determined by using the Equipment Operating Cost Determination Sheet, Figure 14–1. Extensions in dollars are entered in column L and at far right, also in column I. Auxiliary equipment (containers, pallets, racks, etc.) are handled in a similar fashion, in columns M through R.

The total cost for *each* move is then entered in the far right-hand column. The "grand" total material handling cost for the entire operation is calculated at the bottom of the form, and is $3930.

Following this same procedure, for the other 8 ingredients, plus the filling, packing, and shipping operations, will result in the *total* annual handling cost for the entire plant. The result might appear as:

Handling Activity	Annual Cost	
Wax	$ 3930	(as calculated above)
Powder	3200	
Liquid	320	
Scent	100	
Cans	6245	
Valve assemblies	3750	determined by the
Gas	250	same general procedure
Caps	4500	
Jackets	1850	
Filling line	2700	
Packing	2180	
Shipping	1725	
Total Annual Handling Cost	$30,750	

If desired, the total handling cost can be prorated on the basis of annual production, say 1,000,000 cans. For this plant, the result will be a *handling* cost per can of $.03075.

Unfortunately, it is not common practice in many plants to determine material handling costs in the detail discussed here. However, if it were, a good many managers would immediately begin to *do* something about handling costs! Most of them would be *unpleasantly* surprised to find out exactly what material handling is costing each year, or per unit of product.

The diligent material handling engineer can do no less for his company than to point out the potential savings opportunities in material handling. And one of the best ways to do this is to find out how much the handling activities *now* cost. By conservative estimate, nearly any company can reduce handling costs by a *minimum* of 10%, through careful study. In the *small* plant discussed above, it would be $3075.00/year. This is not a tremendous sum at all, but "percentage-wise" it is certainly worthwhile. It is roughly the equivalent of one less operator in a plant employing only about 10—or a *10 percent* reduction in labor cost! This is a *rough* estimate of the untapped potential in material handling.

CONCLUSION

This chapter has outlined procedures for determining the handling cost for an activity, department, or plant. It has shown how to attack a problem which has been given far too little attention in the past—both in the literature and in practice. As previously pointed out, a "gold mine" exists in undiscovered savings in material handling. It is felt that only by determining accurate handling costs can proper attention be focused on this area. This chapter can serve as a guide toward that objective for the conscientious material handling engineer.

16

Storage and Warehousing

Within the overall production-distribution system, thousands of manufacturers are producing goods for millions of customers. One of the major problems is that of matching the production rates with the consumption rates. Customers do not often demand goods at the same rate as producers turn them out. To further complicate the problem, manufacturers want to produce at a uniform rate, for maximum economy, while the consumer wants an item when he wants it—not sooner nor later.

It is primarily because of these characteristics of the production-distribution system that the storage and warehousing functions exist, serving as stock-piles or cushions for holding goods until they are wanted. These functions add "time and place value" to goods, by making them available *when* and *where* they are wanted.

More specifically, *the storage-warehousing activity can be defined as that function which provides the proper space for the safekeeping of goods; provides a system to economically coordinate the necessary activities, facilities, and manpower; and provides for the overall control of the entire operation.* In order to carry out its overall objectives, the storage-warehousing function usually comprises the following activities.

1. Receiving
2. Identification and sorting
3. Dispatching to storage
4. Placing in storage
5. Storage
6. Order picking
7. Order accumulation
8. Packing
9. Loading and shipping
10. Record keeping

The above delineation of the warehousing function provides a basis for the discussion of the implementation of each activity—and more specifically, provides a basis for considering their mechanization or automation, which will be covered in Chapter 17.

As a means of interrelating these warehousing functions, Figure 16–1 depicts them in Process Chart form. It should be pointed out that the steps as recorded are realistic, in that they describe what occurs in the processing of a typical item through a typical warehouse. There is NO exaggeration intended in describing the activity, and yet the chart shows 33 steps which include *16 moves.* This is not at all atypical, and emphasizes the need for a careful study of the storage-warehousing activity to assure that it will operate in an efficient manner.

STORAGE OR WAREHOUSING

These two words are rather loosely used and often interchanged in common practice. In order to provide a rational basis for distinguishing between them, they will be used in this text as follows:

Storage: That activity which is primarily concerned with the orderly safekeeping of all materials in the plant, *prior* to their use; between production operations; and as finished parts awaiting dispatching to assembly operations.

Warehousing: That activity which is concerned with the orderly storage and issuing of finished goods or products, either within the plant proper, or at remote locations, whether operated by the manufacturer, or by one of the several "agents" in the distribution process, as shown in Figure 2–1, the Material Flow Cycle.

In either case, the overall function is pretty much the same, and commonly includes the ten activities listed above—or slight variations, as required by their particular role in the cycle. In order to simplify the reading of this chapter, the word *storage* will be used more frequently, and will be meant to imply the storage of *either* materials *or* finished products.

General Objectives of the Storage Function

In performing the activities indicated, the storage function attempts to carry out the following general objectives.

1. Maximum Use of Space.   The largest item of storage cost is very likely that which is allocated to providing storage space. Costs will commonly range from $.25 to $1. per sq ft per year. But too few people recognize that a unit of space costs a specific number of dollars, whether

PROCESS CHART

PART NAME _TYPICAL ITEM_

PROCESS DESCRIPTION _WAREHOUSING OPERATION_

DEPARTMENT _WAREHOUSE_

PLANT _ANY_

RECORDED BY _J.M.A_   DATE _Nov. 27_

SUMMARY

	NO.
○ OPERATIONS	1
⇨ TRANSPORTATIONS	16
☐ INSPECTIONS	1
D DELAYS	
▽ STORAGES	15
TOTAL STEPS	33
DISTANCE TRAVELED	

DESCRIPTION OF _TYPICAL_ METHOD

STEP	Description
1	in carrier at Receiving
2	UNLOAD carrier to pallet
3	on pallet
4	to receiving inspection
5	RECEIVE, IDENTIFY & SORT
6	to hand truck
7	on hand truck
8	DISPATCH to storage area
9	at storage area
10	to storage location
11	in STORAGE
12	PICK & place on truck
13	on truck
14	to ACCUMULATION area
15	at accumulation area
16	to order "spot"
17	at order "spot"
18	to packing area
19	at packing area
20	to packing bench
21	PACK item
22	item to hand truck
23	item on hand truck
24	hand trk to staging area
25	hand trk at staging area
26	hand truck to dock
27	hand truck on dock
28	hand truck into carrier
29	hand truck in carrier
30	LOAD items into carrier
31	items in carrier
32	SHIP to customer
33	at customer's dock

Fig. 16–1. Process chart of a typical warehousing procedure.

or not it is used. And many are not sufficiently aware of the importance of economizing on space by making proper use of every available cubic foot. Too often, their concern is for *square* feet and their most frequent complaint is that they are "out of space"—square feet, that is!

2. Effective Utilization of Labor and Equipment. It should be obvious that the economical use of these factors is as important in storage and warehousing as in any other phase of business activity. In fact, it should probably be considered *more* important—since the labor and equipment are actually being utilized in a function which is "non-productive" and which in theory might be considered less significant than production operations.

3. Ready Access to All Items. While it may not be apparent at first glance, accessibility for stock selection is the primary objective of the storage function. Storage, per se, is really secondary.

If an item cannot be found, it might as well not be there. And it can be easily found only if it can be identified accurately and located promptly.

Since storage adds time value to merchandise, the goods must be available immediately *when* requested. This implies a planned stock location system and good layout.

4. Efficient Movement of Goods. Most of the activity that goes on in a storage area is material handling. It is here that most of the manpower, as well as the equipment, is required in moving goods into and out of storage. Everything possible should be done to assure that the movement will be efficient, and that both manual and mechanized operations are economical and safe.

5. Maximum Protection of Items. Since the purpose of the storage function is to hold items until they are called for, they must be kept in good condition while they are in storage. No damage or deterioration should be allowed if they are to be delivered in the same condition as they were received.

6. Good Housekeeping. A key indicator in the effective operation of nearly any facility is evidence of good housekeeping. And certainly this is just as true in storage as in production. Clear aisles, clean floors, neat and orderly storage, and safe practices all indicate the concern of good management for those things which make for efficient working conditions and high morale in the work force.

Carrying out these objectives requires careful planning of the storage facilities and operations. The next portion of this chapter will outline the planning required for efficient warehouse design, as a basis for efficient operation.

STORAGE AND WAREHOUSE PLANNING AND DESIGN

This section will be concerned primarily with the planning and design of storage and warehousing operations. A certain amount of operating information will also be included—since it is often difficult to draw a line between planning procedures and operating procedures.

An efficient storage operation can only exist if there has been proper and sufficient preliminary planning for the facilities. This implies an orderly analysis of the several activity areas and the many factors and considerations necessary for the proper planning of the space and facilities needed for each. The following discussion will follow the sequence of the 10 functions previously listed.

Receiving

Receiving includes all those activities involved in accepting materials to be stored. Prompt and accurate processing of receipts is the primary objective of this function, which will usually involve:[1]

1. Prompt and accurate processing of receipts.
2. Control and scheduling of deliveries.
3. Procurement and processing of all due-in information, to check for:
   a. Special handling
   b. Re-location of existing stock
   c. Prompt handling of back-orders
   d. Consideration of first-in, first-out storage
   e. Shipments involving discounts
4. Analysis of documents for planning purposes
   a. Determine approximate date of arrival, type, and quantity of materials, from:
      (1) Copies of purchase orders
      (2) Shipping tickets
      (3) Bills of lading
      (4) Correspondence
      (5) Miscellaneous notices from shippers or carriers
   b. Mark records in some special way to call attention to unusual action to be taken
   c. Furnish carrier, or person controlling incoming traffic, with rail car or truck spotting information
   d. Pre-plan storage locations
   e. Processing of priority receipts
5. Scheduling and controlling
   a. Maintain balanced operation

[1] Adapted from *Warehouse Operations Handbook,* General Services Administration, U. S. Government Printing Office, 1958 printing, p. 16.

   b. Schedule deliveries from local vendors
   c. Assign unloading times to carriers
6. Spotting carriers
   a. Plan locations for rail cars and trucks to facilitate unloading and handling
   b. Avoid demurrage (charges made by railroad for holding a car for more than normal unloading period)[2]
7. Unloading carriers
   The physical work of unloading the carrier should be properly coordinated with the paperwork involved in checking and inspecting the goods. In general, the material handling method used in unloading will vary with the type of carrier, weight of goods, and type of unloading facilities available. For these reasons, each unloading operation will require both advanced and on-the-spot planning. However, there are certain basic principles common to nearly all unloading operations.
   a. Basic principles [3]
      1. Straight line flow, achieved by proper spotting of carrier to minimize number of turns to storage area
      2. Continuous flow, by maintaining proper balance of labor and equipment
      3. Concentration of operation, by localizing insofar as possible for ease of supervision, shorter hauls, and reduced equipment requirements
      4. Efficient handling, by handling containers only once, palletizing when applicable, and use of mechanical handling equipment
   b. Rail car unloading procedure
      1. General
         — Check seal for condition and serial number
         — Palletize or containerize materials in car as appropriate
      2. Rail cars at platform level [4]
         a. Distance from car to storage location *under 300 feet:* Use forklift truck, pallets, and bridge plate.
         b. Distance from car to storage *over 300 feet:* Use forklift truck, warehouse tractor, warehouse trailer trucks, pallets, bridge plate.
      3. Tracks *and* warehouse floor at ground level—use conveyors or pallet rollers placed on car floor, with loaded pallets rolled to car door for removal by forklift
      4. Refrigerated cars—usually prohibit entry of forklifts; use conveyor or pallet dollies

[2] For additional details, see *Storage and Materials Handling*, Dept. of the Army, TM 743–200, Sec. 3.1.1.3.
   [3] *Ibid.*; adapted from Sec. 3.1.4.1.
   [4] Adapted from *Warehouse Operations Handbook*, pp. 20–23.

      5. Carloads of mixed items—conveyorize items to outside of car, sort and then palletize if desired.

  c. Motor trucks
    1. Different from rail cars, because:
      a. Trucks utilized vary more than do rail cars
      b. Size of shipments vary
      c. Less notice of arrival
      d. Greater variations in truck bed heights
      e. May not permit use of forklifts
    2. May use pallet lift truck or conveyors

Identification and Sorting

The identification and sorting function is primarily concerned with determining what is received and deciding where it should be stored. This would commonly require the following activities: [5]

1. Initiate a Receiving Report or receipt document to notify those concerned that goods have been recieved.
2. Maintain an Inbound Shipment Register, to permit recording of basic control data.
3. Physically check merchandise against the delivery documents. Discrepancies should be noted on the appropriate document and verified by the agent of the carrier.
4. Check goods against a copy of the purchase order or other "due-in" document and the packing slip or delivery ticket.
5. Determine quantity actually received. Normally this requires an accounting for every item. However, if goods are received in full cartons, pallet loads, or other similar unit loads, the container count may be accepted. In large shipments, spot checks may be adequate.
6. Segregate goods received where there is any question of acceptance, such as shortages, overages, or damage. In such cases, it may be necessary to contact the carrier to determine responsibility and arrange a settlement.
   a. If inspection or testing is required before acceptance, the goods should be set aside to prevent issue before approval.
   b. Re-mark, re-label, or re-identify items if necessary, using appropriate "local" identification numbers, codes, etc.
   c. Pack or re-pack items, if necessary. This might be called for:
      (1) If a different pack is required for storage or issuing purposes
      (2) If contents are not known
   d. Palletize goods, if appropriate, and not done during unloading operations.

[5] *Ibid.* Adapted from pp. 17–19.

Dispatching to Storage

The dispatching activity as defined here is confined to the movement of goods to their desired or required areas. This will usually be a storage area, but not into a storage location—although it *could* be both. It could also be a movement to an inspection or testing area. In some situations, the dispatching may be done immediately upon unloading, provided the necessary record keeping, documentation, and sorting can be done quickly and on-the-spot.

This function is also separated out in this discussion because it is one that is frequently mechanized. Mechanization will be discussed in more detail in the following chapter.

Place in Storage

This phase of activity has also been singled out as a separate operation, for several reasons:

1. To emphasize the fact that in *most* cases, the previous operation (dispatching) has frequently resulted in a mere "dropping" of the goods in the general vicinity of the storage location.
2. It should point out the fact that the dispatching and placing operations *might* be accomplished in one move.
3. It is frequently mechanized in the mechanization or automation process.

Storage

The function of the storage activity is to hold, protect, and preserve merchandise until it is wanted for use or shipment. One of the keys to an efficient operation is the extent to which the storage area has been properly planned and laid out. This section will outline the concepts, procedures and practices useful in planning for efficient storage, which involves a careful consideration of the objectives of warehousing stated earlier. However, before considering the storage design procedure, it seems wise to identify some of the more important factors to be kept in mind.

1. **Commodity Factors.** It is generally agreed that the commodity factors governing storage location and space requirements are:
   a. *Similarity.* In general, materials are stored by classes. Those goods which are commonly associated with each other—ordered, shipped, received, and inventoried together—should be stored together.
   b. *Popularity.* Relative activity or turnover is another factor to be considered in selecting the storage location of a particular

item—fast movers near the front, slow movers in more distant locations. See Figure 16–2.

c. *Size.* Not only the size of the individual item but the size of the stored quantity will be important in determining storage location and space needs.

d. *Characteristics.* The characteristics of the material must also be given consideration, for instance:
—Hazardous commodities
—Items which may deteriorate
—High value items
—Perishable goods
—Sensitive materials

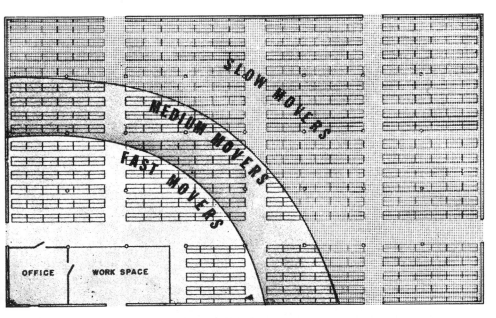

Fig. 16–2. Storage of stocks by popularity. (From *Storage and Materials Handling,* TM 743-200, Dept. of the Army, U. S. Gov't Printing Office, Washington, D. C., p. 22–2.)

Every commodity stored should be examined against these four factors and placed in a logical category as a basis for determining the proper location in which to store it.

2. Space Factors. In addition to the commodity factors, there are some characteristics of the space (available or being planned) which are of importance in determining where a given commodity can be stored. They are:

a. Size of space—volume
b. Nature of space—i.e. suitability for storage of a specific item
c. Location—in relation to other associated activities
d. Availability—at the time it is required
e. Building characteristics
   —Floor load capacity
   —Doors—number, location, size
   —Loading and unloading facilities
   —Column spacing, size, number
   —Clear stacking height
   —Elevators, ramps, etc.
f. Area required for auxiliary and service functions and activities
   —Handling equipment maintenance, repair and storage
   —Fueling or charging areas
   —Employee facilities—locker room, toilet, food service, smoking, etc.
   —Offices
   —Protection facilities—fire walls, fire extinguishers, water outlets, light switches, etc.
g. Space required for aisles—main, cross, picking, personnel access, fire

The above factors—both commodity and space—are representative of those which must be given consideration in storage planning and allocation.

Space Planning and Layout. This section will outline a general approach by which plans can be developed for the efficient utilization of storage space, keeping in mind the objectives of the storage function, as well as commodity and space factors.

1. *Factors in Determining Space Requirements.*[6] Before any intelligent space planning can be accomplished it will be necessary to accumulate a large amount of detailed data on the space (available or being planned). The data required will include:
   —Stock quantities—on hand, due in, and fluctuation
   —Inventory policies
   —Replenishment practices
   —Issue units
   —Issue volume (activity) per time period
   —Storage area type—available or being planned

—bulk	—racks
—reserve	—bins
—retail	—shelving
—security	—outdoor
—refrigerated, etc.	—etc.

[6] For additional details see *Storage and Materials Handling,* Chap. 2, p. 23–1f, and *Warehouse Operations Handbook,* pp. 10–11.

—Methods of handling—present or planned

—Equipment capabilities—available or proposed: type, size, capacity, turning radius, etc.

At the end of this chapter will be found a much more complete list of factors for consideration in storage and warehouse planning.

2. *The Warehouse Planning Work Sheet.*[7] In accumulating information such as indicated above, the Warehouse Planning Work Sheet (Figure 16–3) will prove helpful in organizing the data. One such form should be prepared for each stock class or group (items similar in nature) to permit the group to be handled as a separate lot, and so that its activity can be compared to that of other groups.

3. *Definition of Space Sizes.* Before proceeding with the space planning, it should be remembered that there are several kinds of space: bulk, reserve, retail, etc., and that for the retail or order-picking area, it is usually necessary to establish smaller units of space, such as shelves and bins, for the relatively smaller amounts stored there. The method of space subdivision will depend greatly on the items to be stored. A typical arrangement is shown in Figure 16–4, based on a "large" shelf box to fit *within* one-third of a shelf, or a box of less than 18″ L × 12″ W × 12″ H. Then, space sizes are designated as is shown, with the "X" indicating respective size, but *without* a box.[8]

4. *The Warehouse Planning Analysis Sheet.* After having filled in the work sheet and established space sizes, the Warehouse Planning Analysis Sheet [9] can be filled in to consolidate the data as in Figure 16–5.

5. *Space Layout.* In designing the space layout, there are a good many items to be given careful consideration. Among them are:

—Commodity size(s)

—Pallet size

—Mechanical equipment to be used—narrow aisle vs counter-balanced trucks

—Aisle width to pallet size ratio

—Pallet spacing on racks

—Pallet rack spacing, back to back

—Column spacing (bay size)

—Building size and shape

—Desired location of receiving and shipping

—Aisle location

—Required service areas and their desired location and size

---

[7] See *Storage and Materials Handling,* pp. 22–4 and 22–5, for instructions on filling in.

[8] For additional details, see *Storage and Materials Handling,* pp. 22–7f.

[9] See *Storage and Materials Handling,* pp. 22–5f for instructions on filling in.

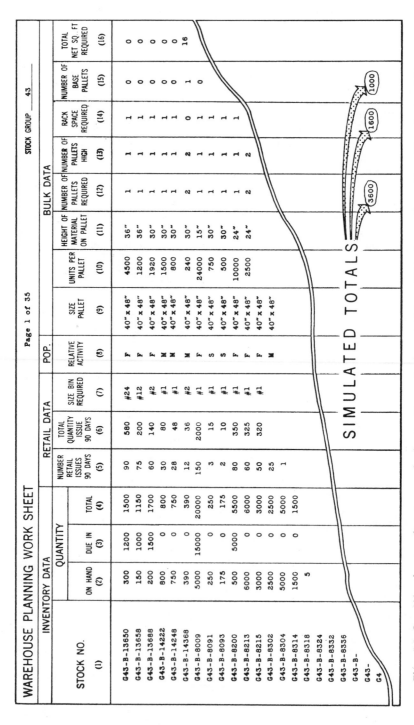

Fig. 16–3. Warehouse planning work sheet. (From Andrew J. Briggs, *Warehouse Operations Planning and Management*, by permission of John Wiley and Sons, Inc., 1960, p. 125.)

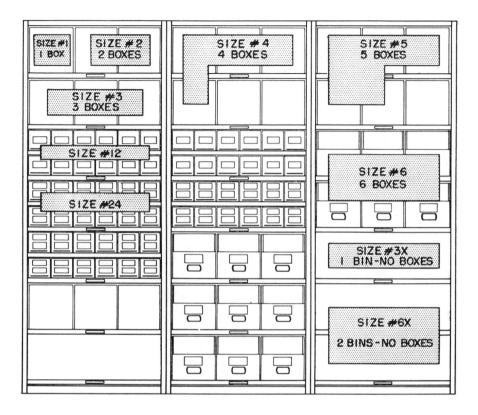

NOTE

THE SHELF BOX ARRANGEMENTS SHOWN ABOVE ARE EX-
AMPLES OF ONLY SOME OF THE LAYOUTS THAT CAN BE
USED. THE NUMBER OF SMALL OR LARGE BOXES OR
WHOLE SHELVES TO BE USED DEPENDS UPON THE PHYSI-
CAL CHARACTERISTICS AND VOLUME OF BIN STOCKS TO BE
STORED.

THE MAIN PRINCIPLES TO BE FOLLOWED ARE:

1. USE SHELF BOXES EXTENSIVELY FOR EASE OF IN-
   VENTORY AND STOCK RELOCATION.

2. SMALL LOTS IN THE CENTER SO THAT THE MAJORITY
   OF ITEMS ARE IN CHEST HIGH POSITION FOR EASY
   PICKING.

3. HEAVY, LARGE ITEMS TOWARD THE BOTTOM WITH
   MOST INACTIVE ON LOWEST SHELVES.

4. LIGHT, LARGE ITEMS TOWARD THE TOP WITH MOST
   INACTIVE ON HIGHEST SHELVES.

Fig. 16–4. Typical bin shelf box arrangements. (From *Storage and Materials Handling,* TM 743-200, Dept. of the Army, U. S. Gov't Printing Office, Washington, D. C., p. 22–7.)

WAREHOUSE PLANNING—ANALYSIS

Date

STOCK CLASS	CLASS DESCRIPTION		BUILDING	FLOOR	LOAD PER SQ. FT.	STORAGE HEIGHT	COLUMN CENTERS N/S	E/W
43	Bolts, Nuts, Rivets, Screws, Washers		42	2	450	7'-6"	20' 20'	20'

A. RETAIL BIN REQUIREMENTS (Equipment and Space)

1 SHELVING REQUIREMENTS

			2 SHELVES 36" x 18" x 12"		3 BOXES	
a.	No. 1	3350 + 10% x 0.333 =	1228	x	3	3684
b.	No. 2	350 + 10% x 0.666 =	257	x	3	771
c.	No. 3	0 + 10% =	0	x	3	0
d.	No. 3x	50 + 10% =	55			
e.	No. 4	0 + 10% x 1.333 =	0	x	3	0
f.	No. 5	0 + 10% x 1.666 =	0	x	3	0
g.	No. 6	0 + 10% x 2. =	0	x	3	0
h.	No. 6x	0 + 10% x 2. =	0			
i.	No. 12	1700 + 10% ÷ 12. =	156	x	12	1870
j.	No. 24	800 + 10% ÷ 24. =	37	x	12	444
k.	TOTALS		1733			1733

4. Total Line 1733 ÷ 7 or 8 = 217 TOTAL
   A. 1. k. Col. 2 18" x 36" x (87' or 99') shelf sections required
5. Total Lines A. 1. a. b. c. e. f. g. Col. 3 4455 QUANTITY
   large shelf boxes required
6. Quantity A. 1. i. Col. 3 1870 = TOTAL
   one compartment shelf boxes required.
7. Quantity A. 1. j. Col. 3 444 = TOTAL
   two compartment shelf boxes required
8. Total A. 1. i. and j. Col. 3 193 = NUMBER
   intermediate shelves required for small shelf boxes
   Answer A. 4 217 x 10.5 Sq. Ft. (Area occupied
9. by one section plus aisle requirements) = 2279 Gr. Sq. Ft.
   required for Retail Section

B. BULK REQUIREMENTS (Equipment and Space)

10. RACK REQUIREMENTS

a. Total Col. 14 (W.S.) 1600 ÷ 2 or 3 = 800 Total Racks Required
b. Total Racks Required 800 x 16 sq. ft. per Rack = 12,800 Net Rack Space Required

11. PALLET REQUIREMENTS

a. Total Col. 12 (W.S.) 3600 = Pallets Required
b. Total Col. 15 (W.S.) 16,000 Net Sq. Ft. Required x 16 Sq. Ft. per Pallet = Pallet Storage

12. SPACE REQUIREMENTS

a. B. 10. b. 12,800 + 16,000 + 10,000 (Operating space—ship'g. rec'g aisles, etc.) Total Gross Required for Bulk = 38,800
b. B. 12. a. A. 9.
   38,800 + 2279 = 41,079 Total Gross Space Required for Retail and Bulk Operations

NOTES:

11a – 1600 Pallets for racks
  2000 Pallets for bulk
  3600 Total pallets required

11b – 2000 Pallets of 11a for pallet storage
  2000 ÷ 2 (storage height)
  = 1000 base pallets x 16
  = 16,000 (net sq ft required for pallet storage)

RECAPITULATION

13. SPACE
Net 28,800
Gross 41,079

14. SHELVING
7 Ft. 0
8 Ft. 217

15. SHELF BOXES
Size	
1	4455
12	1870
24	444

16. RACKS
Level	
2	800
3	0

17. PALLETS
40" x 48" 3600
40" x 40" 0

18. OTHER

Fig. 16–5. Warehouse planning analysis. (From Andrew J. Briggs, *Warehouse Operations Planning and Management*, by permission of John Wiley and Sons, Inc., 1960, p. 128.)

Bay Size

Actually, the column spacing or bay size, is a function of several of the above items. While this distance is extremely critical in good warehouse design, it is at the same time difficult to determine. One of the most important factors is the pallet size, as discussed in Chapter 4.[10]

If pallets are to be used in any part of the storage activity, their size will determine the dimensions of the pallet racks (if any) and possibly the column spacing—to accommodate the racks. The reader should refer back to pages 80–81 for further consideration of dimensional interrelationships.

All of these factors, and their many interrelationships, must be studied in order to make optimum utilization of the space. An interesting relationship not often given proper consideration, is that between the pallet size selected and the aisle width (as determined by the handling equipment). Consider for example, the relationships shown in Figure 16–6. Also worthy of consideration in some cases, is the possibility of "angle-stacking" of pallets [11] when not on racks.

Building Size

Based on the Warehouse Planning Analysis sheet (Figure 16–5) and the above considerations, an approximation of total storage space can be made. Auxiliary service areas must be identified and their size estimated. Typical of such service areas are those listed at the beginning of the chapter, under "functions." And, incidentally, the *storage* space frequently used will be less than *half* of the total!

Stacking height has already been mentioned as a major factor in both warehouse design and warehouse efficiency. No more serious mistake can be made in warehouse design than failure to provide adequate height for efficient storage of goods. In general, available clear height should be as high as is practicable for the use to be made of the space under consideration. Some of the factors affecting required or permissible height are:

1. Type of goods
2. Turnover of goods
3. Weight of goods
4. Floor load capacity
5. Square feet available
6. Construction cost
7. Material handling methods

[10] For further details, see p. 85 or ANSI *Standard, Material Handling* 1.1–1965.
[11] For further details, see E. E. McVeigh, "There's an Angle to Increasing Existing Storage Space," *Flow*, Oct. 1952.

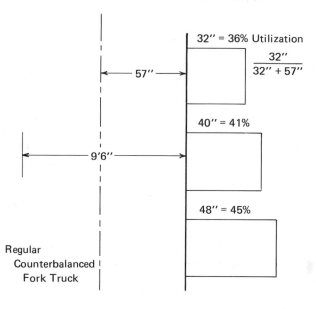

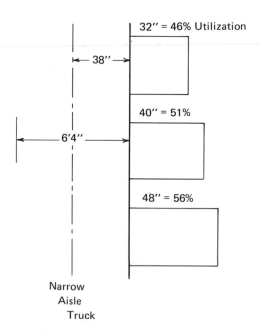

Fig. 16–6. Effect of aisle width, pallet size, and truck type on space utilization.

Warehouses are being built with upwards of 26 ft of clear stacking height for trucks and up to 65 ft for stacker cranes and storage-retrieval units. It should be obvious that sprinkler systems, utilities, etc. should be placed so as not to interfere with space utilization.

Location of Receiving and Shipping

The location of receiving and shipping activities will depend upon such things as:

—Existing roadways, railroad tracks, waterways
—Location of same in relation to building
—Size and shape of building
—Location of main aisles
—Orientation on plot

Due consideration should be given to selecting the location for these functions.

Aisles

The proper arrangement and sizing of aisles is one of the keys to the efficiency of the warehouse. They are the passageways between and within the storage areas and receiving and shipping. They should be located in order to provide proper access to stock, loading and unloading facilities and required service areas. Some of the factors affecting aisle location and width are:

—Type of aisle
—Handling equipment—type, size, capacity, turning radius
—Sizes of items stored
—Distance and accessibility to doors and unloading and loading areas.
—Lot sizes stored
—Location of fire walls
—Column spacing
—Location of service areas and facilities
—Floor load capacity
—Elevator and ramp locations
—Ease of accessibility desired

The common types of aisles are: [12]

1. Working aisles—from which material is placed in or removed from storage.
   a. Transportation aisles—run length of building, and permit 2-way traffic.

[12] For further details, see *Storage and Materials Handling*, pp. 25–16 to 25–18.

b. Cross aisles—run across the building, usually leading to opposite doors of warehouse.

2. Personnel aisles—used only for personnel for access to special or interior areas or to doors. Should be held to a minimum number.
3. Service aisles—provide access to interior of stacks for inventory or inspection. Should be eliminated if at all possible.
4. Bin aisles—only as required in number and width for stock selection and replenishment.
5. Elevator "aisles"—to provide access to elevators without blocking other aisles. Usually consist of an area at least the width of the elevator and extending 10–15 ft. to a cross or transportation aisle.
6. Miscellaneous aisles—as necessary for access to utility sources, fire fighting equipment, etc.

Aisle widths must of course be determined by their respective use. As a *general* guide, the following are suggested for 40 in. load *lengths:*

6000 lb. fork lift truck, counterbalanced	11 ft. 6 in.
4000 lb. fork lift truck, counterbalanced	10 ft. 6 in.
2000 lb. fork lift truck, counterbalanced	9 ft. 6 in.
3000 lb. fork lift truck, straddle	6 ft. 2 in.
4000 lb. pallet lift (walkie)	5 ft. 6 in.

Load *lengths* over 40 in. will require about 6 in. more aisle per 8 in. of load length, i.e., a 48 in. load length would add 6 in. to the above figures.

Past practice has resulted in some suggestions that will aid in proper aisle placement and sizing:

1. Aisles should be as straight as possible.
2. They should be unobstructed.
3. They should lead to doors when practicable.
4. Intersections should be minimized.
5. Width should be wide enough to permit efficient operation, but not wasteful of space.
6. Columns can frequently be used as boundary lines.
7. All goods stored should be conveniently accessible.
8. Aisles should be identified with 3 or 4 inch floor line markings.
9. All aisles need *not* handle 2-way traffic.

Floor Plan

After careful consideration of the above factors, a floor plan should be drawn up similar to those in Figures 16–7, 16–8, and 16–14, 16–15, and 16–16. The plan should be made for each area, to a convenient scale, and show all columns, stairs, elevators, offices, rest rooms, and other service features and areas.

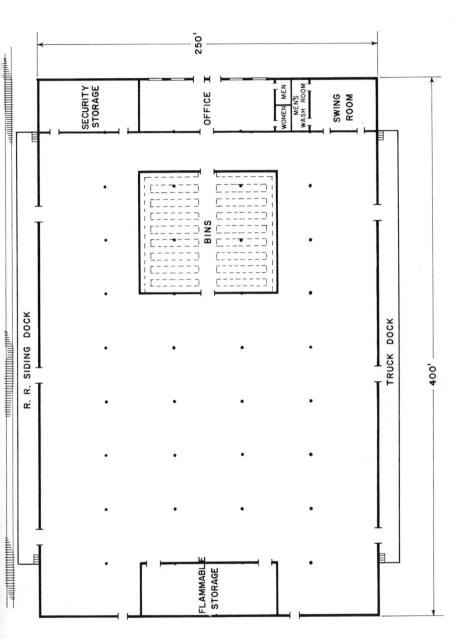

Fig. 16-7. Typical layout of a small warehouse. (From *Warehouse Operations*, General Services Administration, U. S. Gov't Printing Office, Washington, D. C., February 1969, p. 7.)

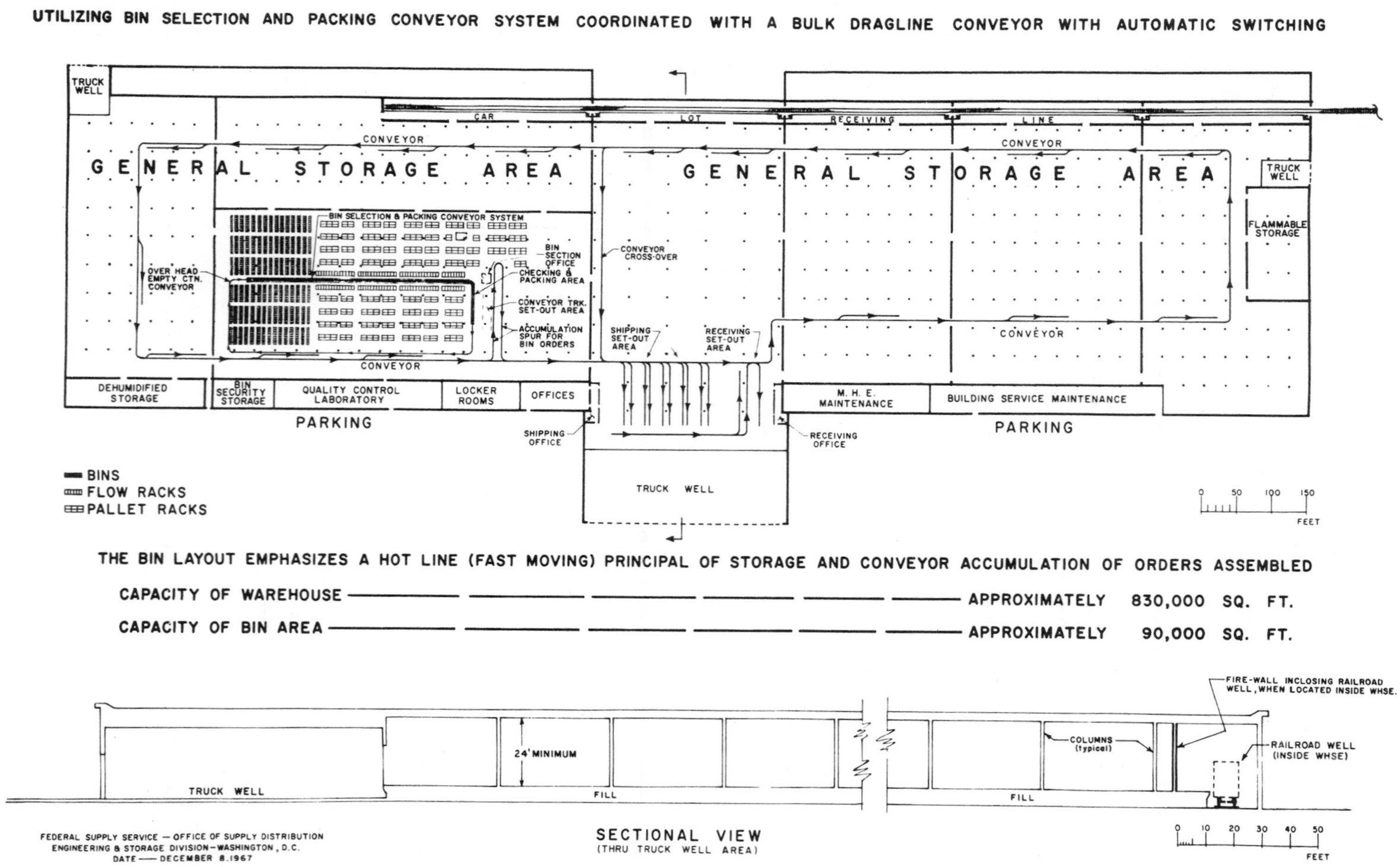
UTILIZING BIN SELECTION AND PACKING CONVEYOR SYSTEM COORDINATED WITH A BULK DRAGLINE CONVEYOR WITH AUTOMATIC SWITCHING
TRUCK WELL
CAR LOT RECEIVING LINE
CONVEYOR
GENERAL STORAGE AREA
GENERAL STORAGE AREA
TRUCK WELL
FLAMMABLE STORAGE
BIN SELECTION & PACKING CONVEYOR SYSTEM
BIN SECTION OFFICE
CHECKING & PACKING AREA
CONVEYOR TRK. SET-OUT AREA
ACCUMULATION SPUR FOR BIN ORDERS
OVER HEAD EMPTY CTN. CONVEYOR
CONVEYOR CROSS-OVER
SHIPPING SET-OUT AREA
RECEIVING SET-OUT AREA
CONVEYOR
DEHUMIDIFIED STORAGE
BIN SECURITY STORAGE
QUALITY CONTROL LABORATORY
LOCKER ROOMS
OFFICES
M. H. E. MAINTENANCE
BUILDING SERVICE MAINTENANCE
PARKING
PARKING
SHIPPING OFFICE
RECEIVING OFFICE
TRUCK WELL
BINS
FLOW RACKS
PALLET RACKS
0 50 100 150
FEET
THE BIN LAYOUT EMPHASIZES A HOT LINE (FAST MOVING) PRINCIPAL OF STORAGE AND CONVEYOR ACCUMULATION OF ORDERS ASSEMBLED
CAPACITY OF WAREHOUSE — APPROXIMATELY 830,000 SQ. FT.
CAPACITY OF BIN AREA — APPROXIMATELY 90,000 SQ. FT.
FIRE-WALL INCLOSING RAILROAD WELL, WHEN LOCATED INSIDE WHSE.
24' MINIMUM
COLUMNS (typical)
RAILROAD WELL (INSIDE WHSE)
TRUCK WELL
FILL
FILL
SECTIONAL VIEW
(THRU TRUCK WELL AREA)
0 10 20 30 40 50
FEET
FEDERAL SUPPLY SERVICE — OFFICE OF SUPPLY DISTRIBUTION
ENGINEERING & STORAGE DIVISION—WASHINGTON, D.C.
DATE — DECEMBER 8.1967

Fig. 16–8. Typical layout of a large warehouse. (From *Warehouse Operations*, General Services Administration, U. S. Gov't Printing Office, Washington, D.C., February 1969, p. 4.)

COMPUTERIZED WAREHOUSE PLANNING

It should be mentioned here that much of the calculation involved in the determination of storage space requirements can be done on a computer. In fact, several private concerns, as well as consultants, do use computer programs for such work. One series of programs is described as follows, in a consultant's news letter:

> SPACE I. Constructs loads of packages in optimum configurations to fit pallets, container systems, warehouse storage slots and racks, bins, shelves, etc. Can also be used as basis for improving consumer package and shipping carton design to increase efficiency of use of existing space.
> SPACE II. Determines which set of alternatives (aisles, floor or rack slots, handling methods, etc.) will result in least cost warehousing for a given product mix.
> SPACE III. Used to design actual warehouse layout on basis of forecast volumes and product mix.[13]

STOCK LOCATION

Having completed the layout, space may now be assigned to specific stock classes, commodities, and functional areas. The objectives specified earlier should be adhered to in selecting locations:

1. Maximum use of space
2. Effective utilization of labor and equipment
3. Ready access to all items
4. Efficient movement of goods
5. Maximum protection of items
6. Good housekeeping

In addition, in most cases it is desirable to plan for "first in, first out" stock rotation.

Generally speaking, commodity factors will determine the type of storage space for each item. Even though day-to-day problems may cause difficulties, the locations of the main groups of items should be planned and recorded on a copy of the layout. Of course some commodities such as hazardous items, security items, perishable items, etc. will rule them out of their logical areas.

Some suggestions on selecting stock locations are:

1. Store by commodity factors.
2. Use large areas for large lots and vice versa.

---

[13] From *SPACE I Progress Report,* circulated privately by Physical Distribution Information Services, Div. of Marketing Publications, Inc.

3. Use high area for goods that can be safely and efficiently stored at maximum heights available.
4. Store heavy, bulky items on strongest floor and nearest to shipping area.
5. Store light items on limited floor-load areas, mezzanines, etc.
6. Locate items as near as possible to identical or similar items already stored.
7. Use remote locations for inactive goods, or for small, light, easy to handle items.
8. Store slow movers farther from receiving and shipping and higher in warehouse.
9. Place fast movers near shipping and in lower locations.
10. Locate service activities in low-ceiling areas.
11. Use outdoor space for selected items.

In reviewing the concepts previously developed or suggested, stock location techniques can generally be classified somewhat as follows:

1. Fixed location
   a. Similarity
   b. Activity
   c. Random
   d. Divided into bulk (or reserve) and picking areas.
2. Random location
   a. For the entire storage area
   b. Divided into bulk and picking areas
   c. Semi-random (in conjunction with some of the other methods)

In addition to the problem of storing *items*, there is the somewhat different problem of storing *volume*. The volume parameter is commonly subdivided into: [14]

1. Large-lot or bulk storage—car load or truck load
2. Small- and medium-lot bulk storage—from less than one, up to three pallet stacks
3. Retail lot storage—amount required in picking area

Large lot bulk storage is done on pallets, from the wall out towards an aisle, in either row stacking or block stacking.

Row stacking is the stacking of supplies from the wall or from an imaginary line to the aisle, leaving sufficient space between the stacks so that any row of pallet stacks can be withdrawn without interference. When only a small number of pallet loads remain in long row spaces, they should be transferred to small-lot storage areas so the entire row space may be used for storage of larger lots.

---

[14] For additional details see *Storage and Materials Handling*, Chap. 2, Sec. V, p. 25–10f and *Warehouse Operations Handbook*, p. 43f, from which the following is adapted.

In large storage blocks, surrounded by aisles, the stack should start at an imaginary or floor-marked line running parallel to the longest dimension of the block. This arrangement provides for the storage of different commodities, in back-to-back pallet rows, and conserves aisle space, as only one end of each row requires accessibility. (See Figure 16–9.) The imaginary or floor-marked line need not be located in the center of the block.

Block stacking is the stacking of supplies in rows so that each row contacts another. In other words, there is no clearance or waste space between the rows. Block stacking conserves space but should be used only when storing large quantities of an item. Extreme care should be exercised in block stacking so as to avoid interlocking of pallets. Interlocked pallets create a hazard to operating personnel during stock withdrawal operations.

Honeycombing is a storage term that denotes the practice of storing and withdrawing supplies in such a manner that the empty space resulting from withdrawing is not usable for the storage of additional supply items. The "space-robbing" practice of honeycombing can be eliminated

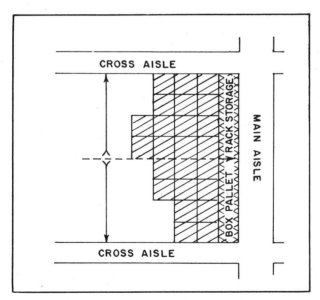

Fig. 16–9. Storing from an imaginary or floor-marked line. This arrangement provides for the storage in back-to-back pallet rows of different commodities, thereby conserving aisle space, since only one end of each row requires accessibility. (From *Warehouse Operations*, General Services Administration, U. S. Gov't Printing Office, Washington, D. C., February 1969, p. 50.)

by stacking in short rows and withdrawing supplies from one row at a time.

The term *small lot* is generally applied to a quantity of less than one individual tiered pallet stack (pallet column), stacked to maximum height. The problem involved in small-lot storage is to obtain maximum accessibility of stock without increasing aisle space. Small lots in bulk warehouse areas should be stored in pallet racks or box pallets placed at the end of large storage blocks.

A *medium lot* is generally defined as from one to three individual tiered pallet stacks (pallet columns), stacked to maximum height. Proper storage of medium lots may be effected by layout and utilization of four-pallet depth, starting from an imaginary center line, i.e., each row being two pallets in depth. The ends (short dimension) of large storage blocks can also be used for efficient storage of short lots in pallets rows of from one to three pallets in depth, without creating additional aisle space.

Figure 16–10 shows a possible floor layout for (a) large lot storage and (b) large *and* small lot storage.

Retail, loose-issue, bin or picking area is that space assigned to the bin or shelf storage of less than full package lots. It is usually from this area that orders are picked. However, in some situations, entire lots of goods may be stored here if the item is small and the total quantity does not occupy a large space.

The area generally includes space for related checking and packing activities and is often segregated from bulk storage areas for security and supervision purposes. For maximum space utilization it should be located in a low-ceiling area of the warehouse. Also, a fairly central location is recommended to facilitate bin replenishment, reduce internal hauling, and lessen the work of consolidating bin items which are processed for shipment with bulk quantities. Figure 16–11 shows a typical retail area layout. Figures 16–7 and 16–8 show such areas located within their related environment. Pages 503–8 deal in greater detail with the picking area.

Single rows of bins should be arranged back to back, and when practicable, along walls. Space along walls provides an excellent location for special type bin racks required for the storage of irregular-shaped and long-handled items which cannot be stored in standard type bins. Where possible "absorb" structural columns within the bin section.

Bins are frequently constructed of wood and may or may not have adjustable shelves and dividers. For maximum flexibility metal demountable or portable type bins are recommended. Readily adjustable steel bin shelves are also a means of providing maximum flexibility for various

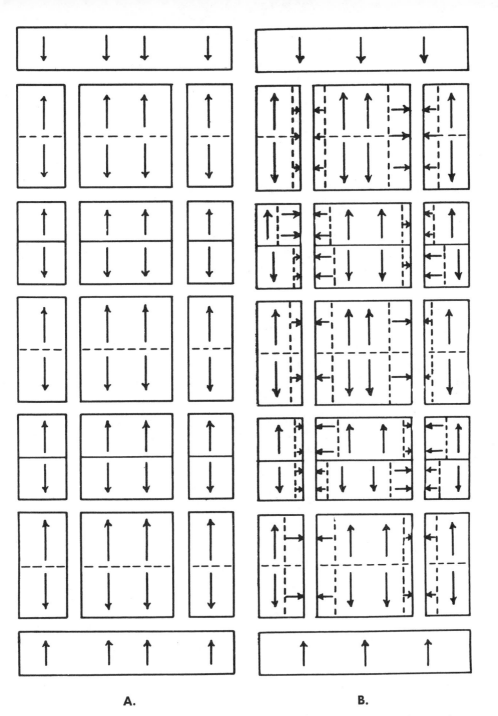

A.   **B.**

Fig. 16–10 A. Space layout for large lot storage. **B.** Space layout for large-lot and small-lot storage. (From *Storage and Materials Handling*, TM 843-200, Dept. of the Army, U. S. Gov't Printing Office, Washington, D. C., pp. 25–13 and 25–14.)

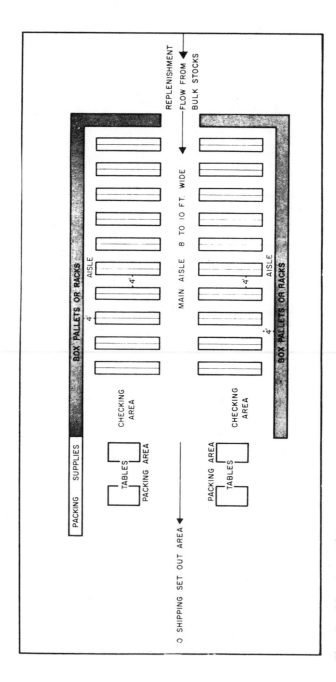

Fig. 16–11. Bin picking area. (From *Warehouse Operations*, General Services Administration, U. S. Gov't Printing Office, Washington, D. C., February 1969, p. 52.)

size compartments. The storing of various small loose items which, because of their shape, etc., are difficult to keep on shelves can be accomplished by use of several different types of drawers, boxes, or baskets placed within the bin. This type of arrangement was shown in Figure 16–4.

The use of portable steel bins represents an efficient method of storing hardware items and small quantities of pipe fittings and couplings. Most bins have a hopper front and are self-stacking for use with or without supporting racks. As each individual bin is removable, this equipment provides good flexibility for rearrangement of stock. For loose-issue storage of larger hardware items and also large quantities of small hardware items, bin type pallet boxes may be used. Wall space around bin areas may be used for the installation of "tailor-made" racks, for the storage of irregular and long-handled items issued in small quantities from loose-issue stocks.

When size permits, unit bulk packages (opened on one side) may be placed in bins and the items left in the original container. This reduces handling and renders added protection to the items.

Where practicable, the top of the bin sections can be utilized for storage of reserve supplies or bulk containers of fast-moving items. Placards on the shelves should indicate that reserve stock of that particular item is located on top of the bin. Items should not be mixed in a bin compartment or section unless they are properly segregated and easily identified.

Stock Location Systems

After carefully designing the storage area, a system must be established to permit the easy location of any desired item. In the past, the "memory system" has been used in many instances, and in fact is still in use. However, it has obvious shortcomings and should not be relied upon. Location by part, serial, code or other identifying number has also been tried, with items located in numerical sequence. This method has also proved inefficient and inflexible. What is needed, is a system which will more positively indicate where something is stored. In effect, each item must have an "address" where it can be found.

The "significant location symbol" system [15] has been found adequate for most warehousing situations. Basically, it establishes a symbol or number which accurately identifies any spot in the warehouse, for example: 324–112–123. These nine digits enable a stock picker to find

[15] For additional details, see Andrew J. Briggs, *Warehouse Operations Planning and Management*, John Wiley and Sons, Inc., N.Y., N.Y., Chap. 11.

any "piece of space" in the warehouse, within 2 or 3 feet. The symbol is interpreted as shown below

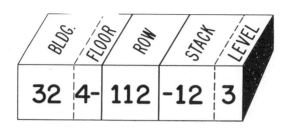

and applied as shown in Figure 16–12. The application of the row and stack numbers is shown in Figures 16–13, 16–14 and 16–15. It should be noted that numbers are assigned to *potential* row and stack locations in the event that aisles, etc. are re-located in the future. When applying the system to a floor plan layout, the lengthwise rows should be numbered up from the bottom of the layout and the short, or cross rows, from left to right. Usually, "long" rows will not exceed 50 in number, and the numbering of "short" rows can begin with 51. If several buildings contain storage areas, all should be numbered and arranged in a similar way, so that a person familiar with one, can find a location in any other.

The width of a stack as used here, is dependent upon the pallet size in use and is commonly 52 in., based on a 48 inch pallet width, plus 4 inches for overhang of the load and/or maneuvering space between pallets. The "width" marks shown in the accompanying figures represent a 52 inch grid pattern.

In situations where such small units of space need not be designated, a bay numbering system can be used. This would allow each bay to carry an identifying number, as shown in Figure 16–16. Or, letters could be used in one direction, as A-32, B-32, etc.

Flexibility

One last comment on floor plans and stock location should be made in regard to flexibility. Few, if any stock location plans will remain fixed for any length of time: stock levels change, amounts received do not always match expectations, advance planning data are altered, etc. These and other factors will require that layout changes be made frequently, and that the overall layout be flexible enough to accommodate such possibilities. The layout must be continuously adjusted in order to allow for such changes and to make the optimum use of available space.

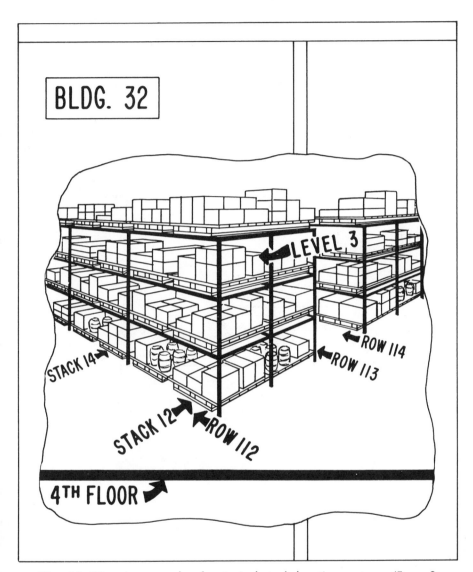

Fig. 16–12. An example of a typical stock location system. (From *Storage and Materials Handling*, TM 743-200, Dept. of the Army, U. S. Gov't Printing Office, Washington, D. C., p. 24–7.)

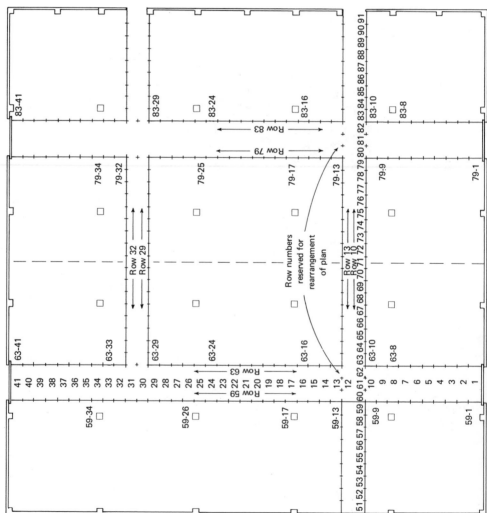

Fig. 16-13. Stock location layout for large-lot bulk storage. (From *Storage and Materials Handling,* TM 743-200, Dept. of the Army, U. S. Gov't Printing Office, Washington, D. C., p. 24–4.)

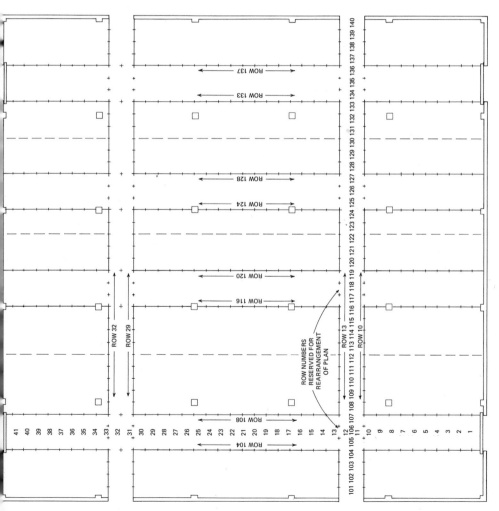

Fig. 16–14. Stock location layout for medium lot storage. (From *Storage and Materials Handling*, TM 743-200, Dept. of the Army, U. S. Gov't Printing Office, Washington, D. C., p. 24–5.)

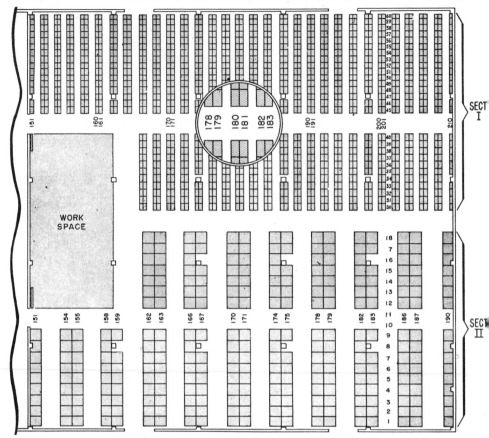

Fig. 16–15. Stock location layout for retail bin and small lot storage. (From *Storage and Materials Handling*, TM 743-200, Dept. of the Army, U. S. Gov't Printing Office, Washington, D. C., p. 24–6.)

Outdoor Storage

It should be remembered that many items, because of their nature, can be stored outdoors or in sheds. This practice lowers storage costs and at the same time frees indoor space for larger quantities of materials requiring greater protection. But efficient outdoor storage requires planning, too. Many of the steps previously discussed in regard to planning enclosed storage areas are just as applicable to outdoor storage areas.

Maintenance of the Floor Plan

An up-to-date drawing of the floor plan should be maintained for every storage area. Such layouts should show aisles, storage areas, bay boundary lines, direction of storage, etc. Other details will depend on intended use of the layout. Some of the reasons for keeping such layouts are:

1. Record of space assignments
2. Record of space available
3. Location of items or groups
4. Bases for control
5. Management information
6. Efficient space utilization

The plan should be kept up-to-date and should be distributed to key personnel for their information and guidance. Typical floor plans, in varying degrees of detail, are shown in Figures 16–7, 16–8, 16–13, 16–14, and 16–15.

Building Design and Construction

Now, and only now, are adequate data on hand to properly guide the design of the storage building. That is, *no* building should be designed or built until *after* the layout has been carefully designed as discussed above. All basic dimensions and space characteristics *must* be adhered to by the architects in designing the building and the contractors in constructing it. No alterations should be permitted without prior approval by those who have designed the layout. Additional data on buildings will be given later.

ORDER PICKING

The next major function of the storage activity is the withdrawal of items from storage—as called for—which is commonly referred to as order picking. And it will be remembered, that *this* is the most important function of the storage activity, i.e., quick and efficient order picking. All the activities and functions previously described are in preparation for efficient order picking, and while it may have been assumed that all items are "picked" from a bin, shelf, or rack, it must be recalled that some items do not lend themselves to such storage facilities. Therefore, order picking *may* consist of removing heavy items with an overhead crane; two-man lifting and moving operations; or loading a truck with lumber, concrete blocks, or gravel; etc. However, this section will deal with the more common types of order picking.

The Order Picking Area

In some warehousing situations, the entire warehouse is one big picking area, while in others, a separate area is set aside from which "broken

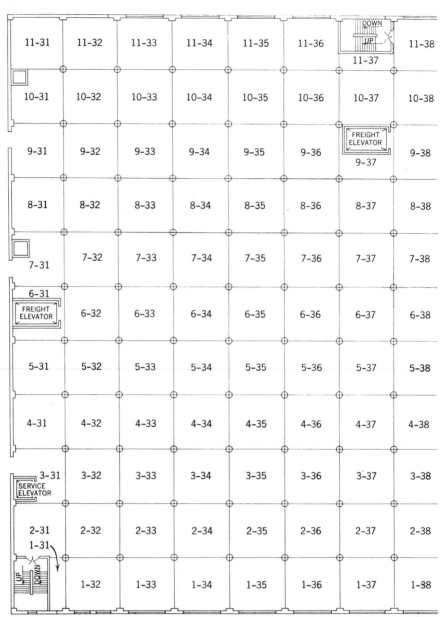

Fig. 16–16. Layout plan for bay system of location. (From Andrew permission of John Wiley and

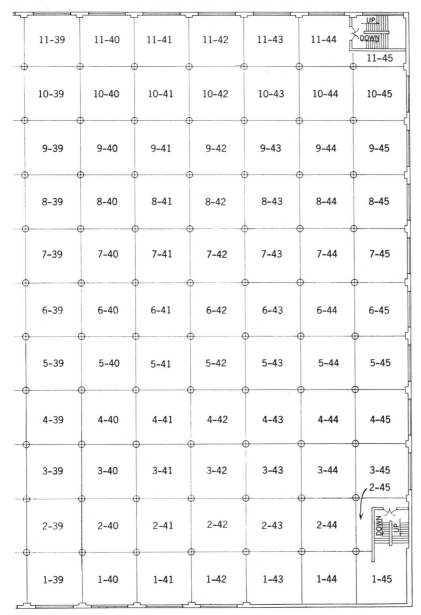

J. Briggs, *Warehouse Operations Planning and Management*, by
Sons, Inc., 1960, pp. 210–211.)

case" quantities are picked. Briggs [16] suggests the following criteria as indicators of a separate area:

1. Less than case lots are generally issued.
2. Full cases issued are few compared to total.
3. It is impractical to issue small quantities from bulk stock areas.
4. Counter or customer pick-up service is desired.
5. Items are fed to a production line.

Layouts showing such picking areas are seen in Figures 16–7, 16–8, 16–11 and 16–17. The layout of the order picking area and the location of stock within it should follow the procedures previously described.

Where it is difficult to resolve several criteria, a composite solution can frequently be worked out. Figure 16–18 shows a mixed arrangement of stock groups and popularity classifications.

The Picking Document

The stock picker usually receives his instructions on a "picking sheet" or from a group of "picking tickets." In either case, they amount to a list of items to be selected from the storage area, listed in an efficient *picking* sequence. The list will usually indicate the item identification, location, and quantity.

Picking Methods

Probably the most common type of order-picking arrangement consists of an area devoted to shelves and bins containing a large number of items in a variety of sizes and amounts. The stock picker circulates in and around the area, selects items called for on the picking sheet and deposits them on a stock picking cart. Stock picking carts should have a suitable number of shelves for order segregation, tray for carrying supplies, orders, etc., and a ladder attachment, if needed. See Figure 6–47.

When the area involved or the order to be picked is larger than one person can conveniently take care of, either the area *or* the order may be subdivided, and the separate portions of the order picked and subsequently accumulated. Figure 16–19 indicates several methods of storing goods and related picking methods.

A problem closely allied with order picking is that of replenishing the depleted stock. This activity must also be planned carefully, in order to assure that the proper reserve stocks are not only on hand, but in a logical and convenient location. Figure 16–20 indicates possible solutions to the replenishment problem, in relation to several common picking arrangements.

[16] Adapted from Briggs, *op. cit.*, p. 262.

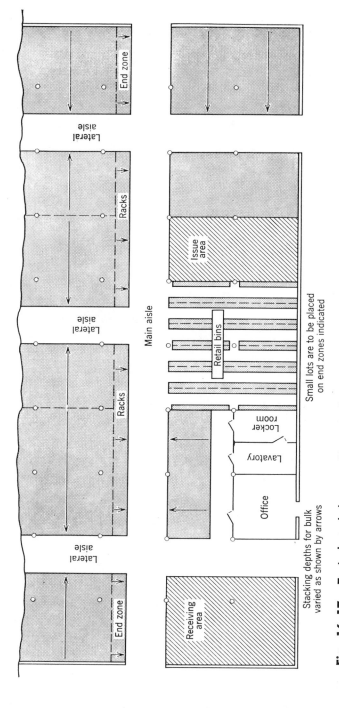

Fig. 16–17. Typical stock layout. (From Andrew J. Briggs, *Warehouse Operations Planning and Management,* by permission of John Wiley and Sons, Inc., 1960, p. 135.)

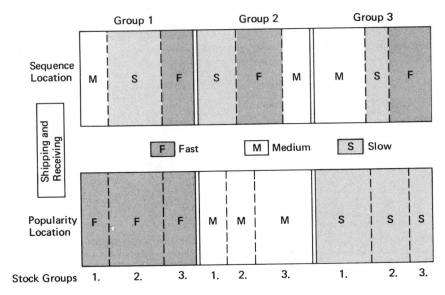

Fig. 16–18. Popularity location maintained while retaining group classification. (From Andrew J. Briggs, *Warehouse Operations Planning*, by permission of John Wiley and Sons, Inc., 1960.)

When issuing volume warrants, consideration should be given to the use of conveyers for order assembly and packing purposes. Such facilities should be located to continue a direct flow of issues from storage area to packing, on an assembly-line basis, as indicated under order accumulation.

The latest developments in this activity are mechanized and automated order picking. These methods are discussed in Chapter 17.

ORDER ACCUMULATION

The next function in the storage activity sequence is that of assembling or accumulating the items making up a specific order. As previously indicated, an order may consist of a large number and/or variety of items which are picked by different people or from different areas of the warehouse. All items for a specific customer or order must be gathered together to check them against the original order. The most common solution is for the picker to bring the items to a central order assembly area and then have someone physically collate them with other items for the customer.

In larger operations or more complex situations, the accumulation may be accomplished by mechanical means. Common methods are: [17]

[17] Many of these methods are equally useful in the dispatching function.

1. Conveyors running from picking area to packing area, and merely carrying items to a central location for sorting.
2. Manually loaded carts, marked to identify customer, and manually pushed to central location by picker.
3. Manually loaded carts pushed *only* to nearest tow-line conveyor, to which the cart is attached for delivery to packing area.
4. Same as above (3) except cart is mechanically or electronically coded before attaching to conveyor in order to predetermine spot for release from conveyor—in packing area.
5. Coded cartons or containers with symbols designating destination which are read electronically and then mechanically dispatched to predetermined locations.

Further details on mechanical operations will be found in Chapter 17.

PACKING [18]

After the order has been accumulated, it must be packed to provide protection during shipment. There are certain requirements, regulations, and practices governing packing, which vary in accordance with the type of carrier, type of commodity, etc. Such regulations and policies involve technical freight classification, tariffs, and ICC regulations, as well as traffic management policies and practices. Some of the factors to be considered are these:

1. Containers used should be as specified in applicable Freight Classification Tariff.
2. Use of the wrong container may result in higher transportation charges.
3. In some instances, bundles travel at a cheaper rate than containers of the *same* commodity.
4. Placing one "out of classification" item in a large container of a low rate class may result in a higher rate for the entire contents.
5. Items should be grouped for shipment in the most practical and economical manner, but those with the same freight rates should be packed together.

Containers, etc.

In selecting containers, consideration should be given to the following characteristics of the items to be packed:

Size	Degree of hazard
Weight	Monetary value
Shape	Perishability
Fragility	Tariff regulations

[18] For additional details, see *Warehouse Operations*, Chap. 10.

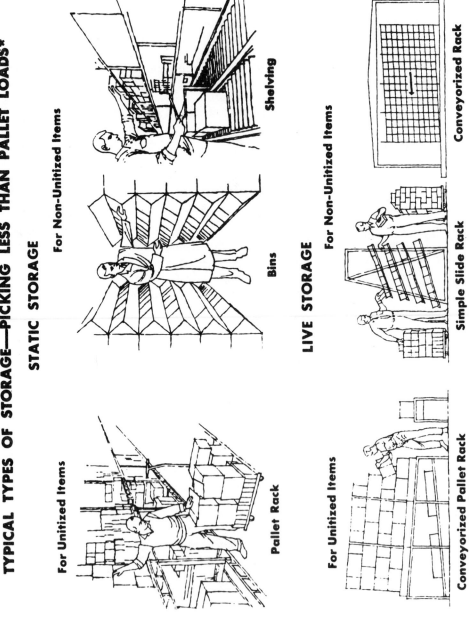

TYPICAL TYPES OF STORAGE—PICKING LESS THAN PALLET LOADS*

STATIC STORAGE

For Unitized Items

Pallet Rack

For Non-Unitized Items

Bins

Shelving

LIVE STORAGE

For Unitized Items

Conveyorized Pallet Rack

For Non-Unitized Items

Simple Slide Rack

Conveyorized Rack

* These illustrations show picking by straight manual methods. Mechanized methods of picking less than pallet loads include automatic release mechanisms for live storage racks. Also lift trucks where the operator rides on an order assembly platform secured to the forks, with both lift and travel controlled remotely by the operator on the platform. Also special devices for working in narrow aisles such as a remotely-controlled traveling carrier.

TYPICAL TYPES OF STORAGE—PICKING PALLET LOADS

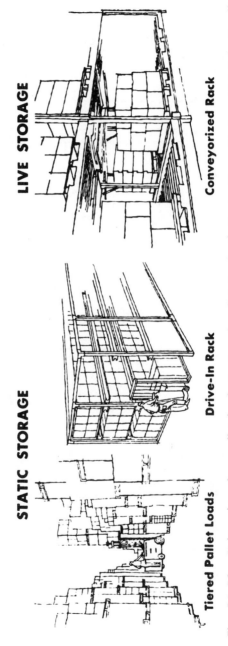

STATIC STORAGE

Tiered Pallet Loads   Drive-In Rack

LIVE STORAGE

Conveyorized Rack

Fig. 16–19. Picking less than pallet loads (top) and pallet loads (bottom). (From *Modern Materials Handling*, January 1960, p. 105.)

EXAMPLES OF ORDER PICKING ARRANGEMENTS

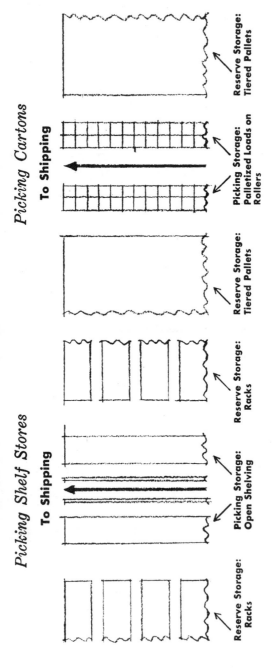

Picking Shelf Stores

To Shipping

Reserve Storage: Racks

Picking Storage: Open Shelving

Reserve Storage: Racks

Picking Cartons

To Shipping

Reserve Storage: Tiered Pallets

Picking Storage: Palletized Loads on Rollers

Reserve Storage: Tiered Pallets

Picking: Picker removes items by hand from picking storage and places in trays resting on bench along conveyor. When an order is completed, the trays are placed on the belt for delivery to shipping. Items for parcel post shipment are picked on one side, those for other shipment on the other side. A white line down center of the belt is used as a guide in keeping the trays on the proper side.

Replenishing: Open containers are moved by hand truck from reserve storage to picking storage. Shelving is open at both sides to give first-in, first-out control.

Picking: Pickers on each side of conveyor lift cartons from pallets and place them on conveyor for delivery to shipping. Conveyor has divider running down the middle lengthwise to keep items from each side separated. Or with large orders, lift trucks take palletized loads directly to carriers, bypassing the conveyor.

Replenishing: Lift trucks bring pallet loads from reserve storage to picking storage. Reserve storage consists of tiered pallets.

Picking Items From Cartons

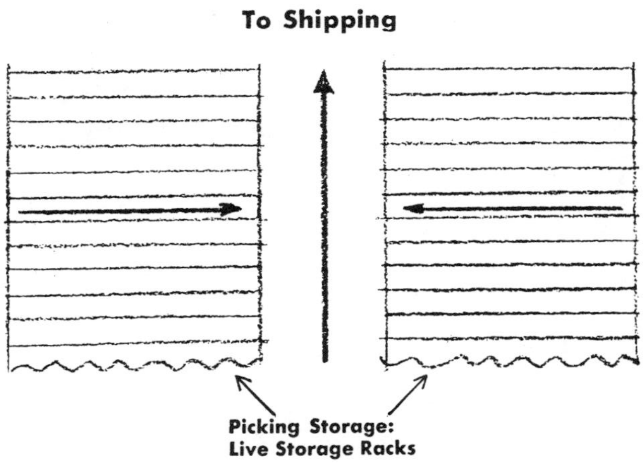

To Shipping

Picking Storage:
Live Storage Racks

Picking: Picker removes small items from cartons along picking face, then places them in boxes on hand truck for delivery to shipping.

Replenishing: Palletized carton loads are delivered directly from manufacturing to rear of live rack by lift truck. Cartons are placed by hand into appropriate slots. Excess for slots already filled is stored on top of rack.

Picking Pallet Loads And Partial Loads

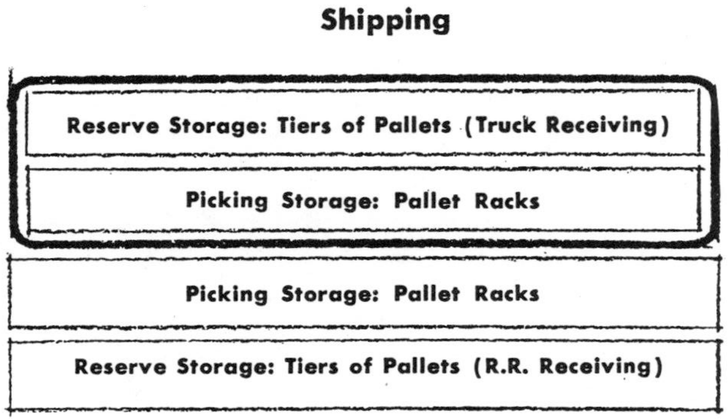

Shipping

Reserve Storage: Tiers of Pallets (Truck Receiving)

Picking Storage: Pallet Racks

Picking Storage: Pallet Racks

Reserve Storage: Tiers of Pallets (R.R. Receiving)

Picking: Pickers move through their own areas within picking storage with walkie tractors pulling tow conveyor carts. Single cartons are hand-loaded onto pallets. Full pallets are loaded onto carts by lift trucks assigned to serve the specific picking area. Tow carts are sent to shipping by engaging them into floor track of tow conveyor.

Replenishing: As picking supplies are depleted, fork lifts make quick run to reserve storage area bringing back pallet loads to picking storage. Reserve storage consists of tiered pallets.

Fig. 16–20. Examples of order-picking arrangements and replenishment suggestions. (From *Modern Materials Handling*, January 1960, p. 106.)

In addition, the relative costs of available containers should be known, and inasmuch as possible, as few sizes and varieties as practicable should be stocked. In order to reduce the range of sizes, large cartons can be cut down in size, and used cartons can be utilized. Steel, wire, plastic woven and paper tapes and strapping should be used as required. Cushioning materials of many kinds are available for protecting the contents of packages. When a shipment involves a number of small items, they may be individually protected by:

Cloth bags	Paper envelopes
Padded paper bags	Plastic bags
Corrugated paper	Plastic "bubble packs"

Packing Equipment

Packing operations may require specially designed tables, carton storage racks, scales, bins for cushioning materials, roll devices for paper and corrugated board, etc. With some of the later developments, packing machinery may also be required—for example, shrink-film packaging. Marking and labeling devices and equipment may also be necessary.

LOADING AND SHIPPING

After the goods have been packed for shipment, they must be set down in a marshalling area to await loading. This can consist of no more than spaces marked on the floor or by overhead signs designating customers, geographical areas, carriers, etc. and it may also contain racks for smaller size shipments. The floor areas may be used for stock picking trucks, pallet loads, or merely items placed on the floor. Figure 16–21 shows a layout for a marshalling area between packing operations and the shipping dock.

Upon removal of any item from the accumulation area, and prior to loading on a carrier, it must be checked in much the same way as were inbound goods. This is necessary to assure that the customer receives the correct item in the proper quantities, and that packing, addressing, etc. are adequate.

Loading operations will be influenced by such factors as personnel and equipment available, carrier equipment furnished, characteristics of the material to be loaded, and any time limitations on the activity. Whenever possible, such factors should be known in advance so that loading operations can be planned. Who actually does the loading may also depend on several factors; among them may be local customs of carriers, union regulations, relations between carrier and shipper, nature of the goods, etc. For example, if the load cannot be handled by the

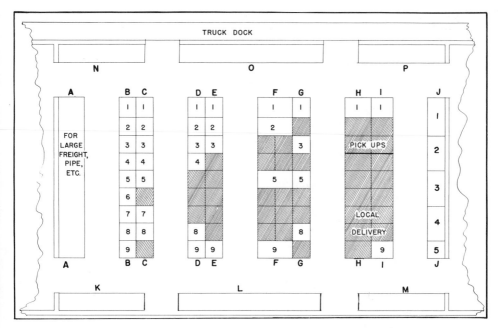

Fig. 16–21. Layout of shipping set-out area. (From *Warehouse Operations*, General Services Administration, U. S. Gov't Printing Office, Washington, D. C., p. 113.)

driver (and/or helper), the shipper will normally provide additional help or equipment.

The mode of transportation to be utilized should be specified by the traffic manager, based on whether the shipment:

—Is palletized or not
—Consists of high center of gravity items
—Is heavy, concentrated weight
—Consists of fragile or critical items
—Is contaminable, explosive, dangerous

It will also be determined by such other factors as:

—Destination
—Distance
—Rates
—Franchises

In choosing between railroad and highway modes of transportation, the following should also be investigated: [19]

[19] For additional details see *Storage and Materials Handling*, Chap. 4.

Carloading

1. Types of commodities
2. Types of cars
3. Shipper's loading responsibilities
4. Loading rules for rail carriers
5. Action of pressures on cargo
6. Use of floating loads
7. Special requirements of mixed loads
8. Bagged loads
9. Palletized loads
10. Cylindrical containers
11. Machinery and machine tools
12. Dangerous commodities
. . . and their specific characteristics and requirements.

Truck Loading

1. Importance of proper loading
2. Balanced loads
3. Load movement
4. Types of loading

Freight Loss and Damage

It is beyond the scope of this text to cover the implications of inadequate packing and loading. However, such practices can only result in unnecessary damage and costs. Reliable sources [20] should be investigated in determining responsibilities of the parties involved.

Shipping

The last phase of the storage cycle is the shipment of the goods to the customer, or the delivery to the plant point of use. Shipping is the last link in the chain between supplier and customer. All the activity that has preceded it may be of little value if the shipping operation is inefficient or uneconomical.

A major segment of the shipping activity is the actual transportation itself; however, this section will deal only with the "in-plant" portion of the overall shipping function. In planning for shipping operations, it is necessary to consider such things as:

—Total quantity to be shipped
—Total weight and/or cube to be shipped
—Number of shipping points

[20] An extensive presentation of the use of pneumatic dunnage is contained in *Storage and Materials Handling*, Sec. 4.5.19, p. 45–30 (31 July 1963).

—Distances involved
—Modes of transportation
—Dates required at destination
—Documentation

Actually, the shipping function is primarily one of documenting the loading activity, and calls for the preparation of the several shipping records. Since the systems of control vary with the type of carrier they will not be covered in detail. In general, each shipment requires a Bill of Lading, or other form, specifically listing the contents of a shipment. The amount of detail is partially defined by the carrier and partially by the shipment. Such data are required for tracing shipments if they should be delayed, or for establishing value, etc., in case of loss or damage during the shipping operation. Quick and easy identification also promotes prompt turn-around time of transportation equipment.

RECORD KEEPING

The final activity of the storage function is the paperwork or record keeping. An office should be provided as the center for such work to carry out all the activities of this nature related to the other 9 storage activities:

1. Receiving
2. Identification and sorting
3. Dispatching to storage
4. Placing in Storage
5. Storage
6. Order picking
7. Order accumulation
8. Packing
9. Loading and shipping

There is no need for repeating or re-listing the forms or procedures here. Suffice it is to say that there is a large amount of paperwork and record keeping required for the efficient operation of a warehouse. It will *not* get done without adequate planning.

WAREHOUSE EQUIPMENT

Throughout the above discussion, there have been many references to various kinds of equipment. In general, warehouse equipment may be divided into 3 categories:

1. Storage equipment
2. Handling equipment
3. Picking equipment

However, in many cases, it is difficult to place an equipment item in a distinct classification. Also, since equipment is covered in Chapter 6, the several types will only be identified in outline form, by functions, as shown in Figure 16–22. There are also several miscellaneous types of equipment useful to the storage function:

1. Fueling or charging facilities
2. Dock boards (separate or built-in)
3. Two-way radio
4. Weighing equipment
5. Marking equipment
6. Packing equipment
7. Stapling equipment
8. Strapping equipment
9. Sealing (taping)

Many of the equipment items are illustrated elsewhere in this chapter, or in Chapter 6. The selection of equipment is covered in Chapter 11; and a list of significant factors for particular attention in choosing storage equipment is shown in Table 16–1.

Table 16–1.   Factors for Consideration in Selecting Warehousing Equipment

A. *Material* Parameters
  1. Type
  2. Shape
  3. Dimensions
  4. Weight
  5. Crush resistance
  6. Receipt characteristics
  7. Order characteristics

B. *Move* Parameters
  1. Quantity
  2. Frequency
  3. Origin and destination
  4. Loading level
  5. Unloading level
  6. Distance
  7. Handlings/item
  8. Area covered
  9. Path
  10. Cross traffic
  11. Running surface
  12. Headroom

C. *Storage* Parameters
  1. Total volume
  2. Number of items
  3. Volume/item
  4. Fluctuation
  5. Size
  6. Weight
  7. Crush resistance
  8. Destination (from storage)

D. *Cost* Factors
  1. Investment required
  2. Start-up costs
  3. Operating costs
  4. Return on investment
  5. Space savings
  6. Cost of capital
  7. Depreciation policy

E. *Other* Factors
  1. Flexibility
  2. Adaptability
  3. Expansion
  4. Long range plans
  5. Maintenance
  6. Obsolescence
  7. Capacity
  8. Possibility of dual system
  9. Intangibles

Receiving	Identification & Sorting	Dispatch to Storage	Place in Storage	Storage	Order Picking	Order Accumulation	Packing	Loading	Records and Controls
Manual carts	Manual	Manual	Manual	Floor	Manual	Manual	Manual	Manual	Manual
Trucks	Mechanical	Conveyor	Conveyor	Shelf	Lift truck	Conveyor	Mechanical	Conveyor	Mechanized
Conveyors	Electr.	Hand truck	Hand truck	Bin	Conveyor	Hand truck		Hand truck	Card
		Power truck	Power truck	Conveyor	Crane	Power truck		Power truck	Tape
		Lift truck	Lift truck	Rack fixed flow	Hoist	Tow-line		Lift truck	Automated
		Tow-line	Crane		Stacker crane	Tractor-trailer train		Crane	On-line
		Trac.-tlr. train	Hoist	Pallet floor rack fixed flow	Retriever	Crane		Hoist	
		Crane	Stacker crane		TO	Hoist Stacker crane		Stacker crane	
		Hoist	Stacker unit		Shipping Stacker crane	Retriever		Special device	
					Conveyor				
					Hand truck				
					Power truck				
					Tractor-trailer train				
					Tow-line				
					Lift truck				
					Pick up station				

Fig. 16–22. Basic warehousing functions and equipment types commonly used in implementing them.

519

WAREHOUSE BUILDINGS

Generally speaking, the warehouse building is merely a means of protecting the goods from the weather. However, this must be done in an efficient and economical manner. In planning the warehouse building, the following factors are among those which should be given consideration:

1. Location
2. Plot size
3. Building size
4. Layout
5. Flexibility: growth, and expansion
6. Material handling methods
7. Aisles
8. Service area location
9. Column spacing
10. Clear stacking height
11. Floors: number, type, capacity, elevation
12. Doors
13. Docks
14. Construction methods
15. Lighting
16. Ramps and elevators

A number of these have been considered earlier in this chapter and will therefore be omitted here. Others are discussed briefly below.

Plot Size

Very seldom does one hear complaints from anyone having too large a piece of property! For future protection, the land space required for present needs should be determined—then multiplied by at least four or five. One industrial contractor recommends *ten* times—for manufacturing facilities!

Building Size

Building size has been partially covered previously, as it is primarily determined by the layout. However, one more plea should be entered for expansion allowances and for flexibility. Building size may of course be partially governed by funds available. A related factor is building shape. A square building not only has lesser amount of wall, but is also a very efficient shape, since it minimizes the average travel distances. However, it should be remembered that the building dimensions are interrelated with the dimensions of several other physical aspects of the material flow cycle. (See Figure 4–5.) For example, if a building is to be square, it might be wise to base the bay size on the pallet size—and have columns on a rectangular pattern, to match the pallets and/or racks.

Service Activity Location

Service activities have also been mentioned previously, but some related items were not, such as: electrical power, water, compressed air and gas, sanitary and storm drains, sprinklers, fire doors, lighting, timeclocks, telephones, intercom system, battery chargers, maintenance area, etc. These, plus the service activities should all be located at appropriate places. As an aid in their location, the Activity Relationship Chart[21] and Diagram may be employed.

Clear Stacking Height

It is frequently forgotten that cubic feet cost less than square feet, i.e. a warehouse cost of $6.00 a *square* foot, with a 15 ft. height costs $.40 per cu. ft. However, if the height were 20 ft., the additional 5 ft. of wall height will reduce the cubic foot cost to a little over $.30. But there are other costs to be considered. One study[22] includes: (1) the racks, (2) the vehicles, (3) the building, (4) the system and the inter-relationships of the four factors. The study used a space module 4 ft × 5 ft and determined the costs and inter-relationships as shown in Figure 16–23. The resulting "best height" is shown in Figure 16–23d as 22 ft. Similar studies for other conditions would of course lead to different conclusions.

Footlik[23] states that for every two-foot increase (over 16 ft) there is only 4 percent increase in the building cost. His experience suggests 18–22 ft clear heights. One additional argument for the higher building is the possibility of including a mezzanine or balcony for a relatively low additional cost per foot.

Floors

Floors should be built on a solid base and thoroughly compacted. The use of sufficient reinforcing rods and an adequate number of joints will help make a satisfactory floor. Planned joints will regulate the cracks which will inevitably occur. Frequently a surface hardener and/or a dust preventing sealer is advisable.

---

[21] See J. M. Apple, *Plant Layout and Materials Handling,* The Ronald Press Co., 2nd ed., 1963, Chapter 8 and pp. 172–176.

[22] E. H. Kidera, "How High Is Up?", *Handling and Shipping,* Oct. 1965, pp. 41–42.

[23] I. M. Footlik, "Sizing the Building," *Supply House Times,* Feb. 1966, p. 71.

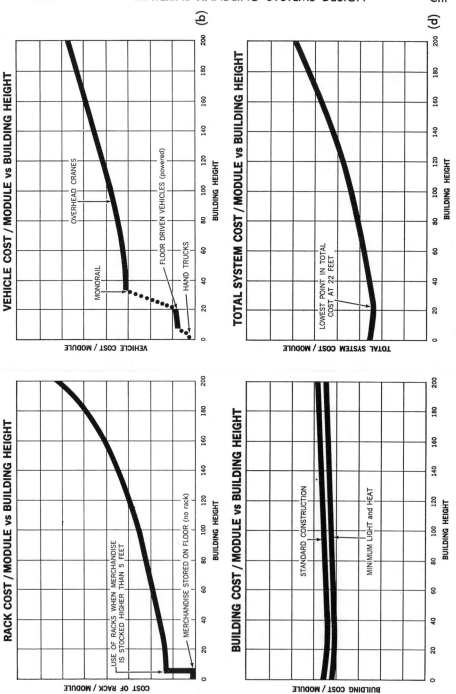

Fig. 16-23. Relationships between building height and rack cost, vehicle cost, building cost, and the total system cost. (From E. H. Kidera, "How High Is Up?", *Handling and Shipping*, October 1965, p. 41.)

Floor load capacity should be carefully predetermined. Footlik [24] suggests that a gasoline lift truck will weigh roughly twice its capacity and an electric lift truck four times its capacity.

Floor elevation is another factor of importance. Trailer bed heights will vary from 44 to 54 inches. Probably a height of 52 in. is a satisfactory compromise. If a mechanical dockboard (leveler) is used, 50 in. is satisfactory. See Figures 6–74 and 6–75.

Doors

Exterior as well as interior doors should be 9 ft × 9 ft to permit (1) easy unloading of unit loads from highway trailers and (2) safe passage of vehicles and personnel. Overhead doors should be installed with door rails or tracks straight up from the door, and then out at ceiling height. If extended out from door height, they will surely be damaged by lift truck masts, as well as creating a safety hazard. In general, interior (and sometimes exterior) doors should be of flexible plastic or rubber, so that vehicles can merely *push* their way through. An alternative is a power-operated door, with a control switch located conveniently (radio, pendant, etc.) for the driver to operate *from* his vehicle, while on the move.

Building Construction Methods

Single story buildings are usually best for warehousing purposes if: [25]

1. A site is available at reasonable cost, with room for expansion in two directions, as well as up.
2. The resulting building will not become too big, requiring stock pickers to cover too large an area, i.e., travel over 600–800 ft to pick orders.
3. Stock is homogeneous and does not easily sub-divide itself into logical groupings (that is, if it *does*, a multi-story building would provide logical space divisions for the groupings.)

A multi-story building *can* shorten distances and reduce handling costs. Also, gravity is the cheapest type of motion. Ramps, tow-line conveyors, elevators, and even lift trucks can be used to elevate or lower merchandise. Or, vertical lifts can be used in place of elevators, and can be either automatic or semi-automatic.

Common methods of constructing warehouse buildings are:

1. Concrete block and brick
2. "Thin wall" brick (4 in.)

[24] *Ibid.*, p. 70.
[25] Adapted from Footlik, *loc. cit.*, p. 104.

3. Tilt-up concrete slab
4. Concrete panels (smaller than slabs)
5. Metal (pre-engineered or curtain wall)

Translucent panels are commonly used as a continuous course on the upper wall, or as "skylights" in the roof. The panels yield an abundance of light at a low cost—about 1/3 the cost of other wall materials.

Two unique types of lower cost buildings are the "pole building" and the "inflatable" building. Each can be erected for about $2.00–3.00 per sq ft. The pole building is built around treated wood poles, set in the ground. Inflatable buildings are just that! Most are a half-cylinder shape with quarter-sphere ends, are made of a durable fabric, and are inflated with low-pressure air. See Figures 16–24a and 16–24b.

Detailed discussion of construction types is beyond the scope of this text, but several alternative methods should definitely be analyzed and compared.

WAREHOUSE LOCATION

While a detailed discussion of warehouse location is also beyond the scope of this book, it should nevertheless be given proper consideration. Major factors are distances to important customers and quantities they purchase in a year. A ton-mile cost of movement can be determined, and the location selected by cost, plotting techniques, or linear programming methods. Figure 16–25 shows a graphical solution intended to select prospective locations. Costs can then be determined for the most promising or logical locations for more detailed study. Figure 16–26 is such a cost tabulation. See also pp. 625–630.

WAREHOUSE TRENDS

Having outlined in detail the various aspects of warehouse planning and design, it seems appropriate to indicate apparent trends in the overall field of storage and warehousing. When practicable, these trends should be given proper recognition during the design process. Among the trends observed in recent years are:

1. Locations changing from center-city railroad areas to outlying locations with access to airports and freeways.
2. Selection of locations by more sophisticated techniques.
3. Customer service areas defined by market areas, delivery times and customer, rather than by states or other geographical boundaries.
4. Warehouse stock lists are becoming smaller, as slow moving items are shipped from factories—often with expedited delivery

Fig. 16–24 a. Exterior view of air-supported warehouses (each 100 ft ✕ 500 ft) for storing automobile parts. Note: (1) bottom is held down by anchored cables; (2) blowers are seen next to buildings; (3) double doors serve as air locks. (Courtesy of Cidair Structures Co.)

Fig. 16–24 b. Interior view of air-supported warehouse. (Courtesy of Cidair Structures Co.)

This Procedure Will Rapidly Narrow The Field Of Choice As To Potential Locations Of Finished Goods Warehouses

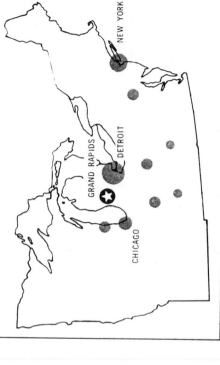

1. PLACE CIRCLES ON MAP at the geographical center of each sales region. Areas of the circles represent the respective volumes at each location for the particular product. The circle at Grand Rapids indicates the plant location.

2. DRAW AXES at bottom and left sides of map about the area in which customers are located: in this case, east of the western borders of Minnesota, Iowa, Missouri, and north of the southern borders of Missouri, Kentucky, Virginia.

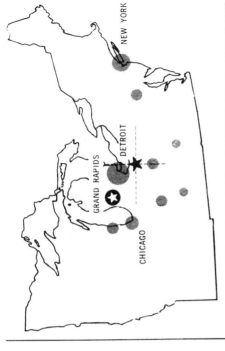

3. DRAW LINES from each sales circle to each axis. Multiply each area by its distance to the vertical axis to get the moments about this axis. Add these moments to get the total moments about this axis. Do the same for the horizontal axis.

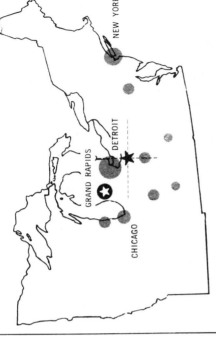

4. LOCATE WEIGHTED CENTER of distribution (star) by dividing the total moments about each axis by the total volume. Draw lines representing the resulting distances parallel to each axis. The intersection is the weighted center (see text).

Fig. 16–25. Graphical method of determining number of warehouses by weighting center of distribution. (From R. J. Sweeney, "How to Determine the Number and Location of Warehouses," *Modern Materials Handling*, January 1962, p. 76.)

Cost Element	Base Case (One Warehouse in New York)	Alternate 1 (One Warehouse In Detroit)	Alternate 2 (Warehouses In New York & Detroit)	Alternate 3 (Warehouses In N.Y., Det. & Chi.)
Production Cost—Stock Items	$100,000	$100,000	$110,000	$120,000
Transportation From Plant to Warehouse	12,000	5,000	10,000	15,000
Warehousing Cost (Annual)				
Building	20,000	18,000	30,000	40,000
Labor	20,000	20,000	25,000	30,000
Overhead	18,000	18,000	23,000	27,000
Transportation From Warehouse to Customers	31,000	21,000	20,000	19,000
Inventory Cost	6,000	6,000	9,000	12,000
Total Cost	$207,000	$188,000	$227,000	$263,000

Fig. 16–26. Comparative warehouse costs (design year). (From R. J. Sweeney, "How to Determine the Number and Location of Warehouses," *Modern Materials Handling*, January 1962, p. 79.)

—rather than carry them in small quantities at several remote locations.

5. Elimination of warehousing by means of tighter inventory control and use of air freight.
6. Higher stacking heights, for economy of space utilization and because of improved handling equipment.
7. Narrower aisles and use of stock picking equipment that can operate in 6 ft. (or less) aisles.
8. Buildings constructed with expansion in mind (present outer wall a future fire wall)
9. More judicious selection of pallet (or unit load) sizes and column spacing.
10. Panel construction to speed erection and facilitate expansion.
11. Use of mezzanines and balconies.
12. Overhead obstructions (heaters, etc.) located *over* main aisles instead of over storage areas.
13. Consolidation of warehouses into a smaller total number.
14. Increased use of outdoor storage.
15. Elimination of pallets.
16. Greater attention to planning and design.
17. Increased mechanization.
18. Automation, where feasible.
19. Use of public warehouses to furnish supplemental stocks at selected locations.

Each of the above items should be considered during the planning and design process and those deemed appropriate should be worked into the plans.

CONCLUSION

This chapter has attempted to present the storage/warehousing function as an important link between the producer and the customer, and has suggested a general procedure for planning and designing facilities for carrying out the functions.

As a partial review of the many aspects of the storage/warehousing problem, Table 16–2 presents a composite list of many of the factors pointed out in this chapter. It should be supplemented and adapted to suit the needs of a particular planning situation.

Table 16–2. Factors for Consideration in Storage and Warehouse Planning

I. *Material*

  A. Item

    1. Physical
      —Type(s)
      —Dimensions
      —Shape
      —Weight
      —Receipt characteristics
      —Order characteristics (See No. II)
      —Machine handlable
      —Palletizable
      —Crush resistance
      —Perishable
      —Unusual characteristics

    2. Quantity
      —No. of stock keeping units
      —Totals (max./min.)
      —Turnover
      —Seasonality
      —Trends
      —Fluctuation

  B. Storage unit
    1. Type
    2. No. of units
    3. Dimensions
    4. Shape
    5. Weight
    6. Receipt characteristics
    7. Machine handlable
    8. Stackable
    9. Unusual characteristics

II. *Order*

  A. Number of customers
  B. Orders/day
  C. Stock keeping units/order
  D. Quantity/stock keeping unit
  E. Popularity
  F. Order mix
  G. Issue units
  H. Issue volumes
  I. Need for re-packing
  J. Order reading time
  K. Order filling time

III. *Space*

  A. Storage
    1. Material (See No. I)

      2. Stock quantities
      3. Inventory policies
      4. Replenishment practices
      5. Space type(s)
      6. Order characteristics (See No. II)
      7. Equipment requirements (See No. V)
      8. Availability
   B. Services
      1. Activities
      2. Interrelationships
      3. Space requirements of each

IV. *Space Layout*
   A. Space requirements (See No. IIIA)
   B. Required services (See No. IIIB)
   C. Equipment requirements (See No. V)
   D. Building factors (See No. VI)
   E. Pallet spacing on racks
   F. Pallet rack spacing
   G. Desired location of interrelated activities
   H. Aisle location

V. *Equipment*
   A. Handling and movement

1. Quantity	7. Unit handled
2. Frequency	8. Area covered (scope)
3. Origin and destination	9. Path
4. Loading level	10. Cross traffic
5. Unloading level	11. Running surface
6. Distance	12. Clear height

   B. Storage
      1. Material characteristic (See No. IA1)
      2. Quantity characteristics (See No. IA2)
      3. Storage unit characteristics (See No. IB)

   C. Picking

1. Issue unit characteristics	4. Item destination
2. Order characteristics	5. Order documentation
3. Storage method	

   D. General

1. Functions to be mechanized	5. Intangibles
2. Potential equipment types	6. Pay-off policies
3. Investment costs	7. Savings
4. Operating costs	

VI. *Building*

A. Space available/required (See No. III)	L. Elevators, ramps
B. Dimensions	M. Door—no., size, location
C. Clear height	N. Dock—no. openings, size, location, height
D. Structural design	O. Lighting
E. Construction	P. Column spacing
F. Floor load capacity	Q. Aisle requirements—no., type, location, width
G. Overhead load capacity	R. Loading and unloading facilities
H. Handling methods	
I. Number of floors	
J. Floor condition	
K. Environment	

VII. *Operations*
   A. Stock location system
   B. Order picking method
   C. Communications system
   D. Record keeping system
   E. Information system
   F. Training requirements

VIII. *Shipping and Receiving*
   A. Receipts and shipments/day
   B. Frequency distribution
   C. Sizes of receipts and shipments
   D. Schedules
   E. Shipping and receiving methods
   F. Carrier characteristics
   G. Vendor/customer restrictions

IX. *Costs*
   A. Investment required
   B. Start-up costs
   C. Operating costs
   D. Return on investment
   E. Space savings
   F. Cost of capital
   G. Depreciation policy
   I. Indeterminate costs

X. *Other Factors*
   A. Flexibility
   B. Adaptability
   C. Expansion
   D. Long range plans
   E. Maintenance
   F. Obsolescence
   G. Capacity
   H. Possibility of dual system
   I. Intangibles
   J. Manpower requirements

The following chapter will be concerned with the mechanization and automation of storage and related problems involved in the several storage and warehousing functions.

17

Automated Warehousing

INTRODUCTION

The previous chapter has outlined common practice in warehouse planning and design, with operations being carried out in much the same way as they have been for many, many years. However, it is only reasonable to assume that with the growing emphasis on the mechanization and automation of production, the concept should also be applied to the warehousing functions. In fact, when one considers the major warehousing functions, it appears considerably easier to mechanize or automate some of *them*, than many of the production functions. And, in general, it is. But there are many factors to be considered and characteristics to be evaluated before serious thought can be given to warehouse automation.

To begin with it may be helpful to distinguish between "mechanizing" and "automating," since these two terms have been given a wide variety of definitions and interpretations. For the purpose of this chapter the term *mechanizing* will imply the application of mechanized equipment to the warehousing functions. Some examples of this would be: belt conveyors from or to common carriers; a tow line moving carts into, through, and out of the stock picking area; lift trucks loading or unloading carts; or overhead conveyors transporting goods from one section of the warehouse to another.

On the other hand, *automation,* as used in this chapter—in its ultimate application—implies the maximum amount of practicable mechanization, *plus* total, self-regulating control of the function. This would imply control not only of the mechanized handling operations, but also the information aspects of the warehouse operation, including feedback and self-regulation of the stock level–purchase order process.

From the above it can be seen that there are several "levels" of warehousing automation, which might be classified as follows:

1. *Theoretical.* Complete automation and control of the entire cycle of warehousing activities, without human intervention.
2. *Practical.* The mechanization and/or automation of as much as the cycle of activities as is practicable.
3. *Actual practice.* The most sophisticated installations in operation are an attempt to identify and sort, dispatch, store, pick, consolidate orders, and keep records. Usually omitted are receiving, packing, loading, and shipping. In fact, examination of many of the most widely publicized installations will show that they are merely the mechanization of the order picking activity, the consolidation of orders, frequently involving a computer tie-in for the control of the picking function and/or the inventory function.

If one were to envision the totally automated warehouse of the future, it would involve the complete mechanization and automatic control of the entire warehousing cycle, including:

1. Automated *receiving* and *unloading* of goods.
2. Automated *identification, sorting,* and *inspection* of all goods received.
3. Automated *dispatching* of goods to their respective storage locations.
4. Automated *placement* of goods into storage locations.
5. Automated *picking* of items as required by customer orders.
6. Automated *order accumulation,* by orders and/or customers.
7. Automated checking and *packing* of each order.
8. Automated *loading* of carriers.
9. (*Shipping* most likely would be carried out by conventional means of transportation. However, delivery by magnetic or electronically coded common carriers, or even automatic guided missiles, directly to customer locations, is coming closer to reality.)
10. A completely integrated information and order-processing system for *record* keeping.

It can be seen that implementing the total warehousing function, as implied above, would not only be highly complex, but at this stage in the state-of-the-art, impractical, expensive, and very unlikely. Nevertheless it should be pointed out that the total automated cycle described above might well be used as a goal in the consideration of any automated warehousing plans, and with the above potentials in mind.

In order to visualize the activities outlined above, as they would be tied together in a totally automated warehouse, Figure 17–1 represents the situation in diagrammatic form with each of the basic warehousing functions shown in its approximate location in the overall sequence. The

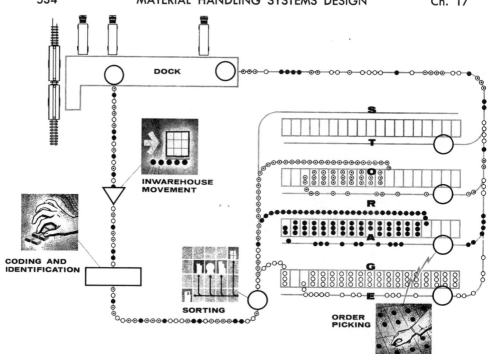

Fig. 17–1. The mechanized warehousing concept. (Courtesy of FMC Corp.)

implication is, of course, that merchandise would be automatically un-loaded from a delivering carrier, and routed throughout the entire ware-housing function with the picked orders being automatically loaded into an outgoing carrier—all without human intervention.

G. I. Ross [1] has said that "The automated installation seeks to pick up where prevailing equipment and techniques leave off. It seeks to achieve its increment of efficiency by eliminating the man altogether, where eco-nomically advantageous to do so, or, in the alternative, by minimizing his tasks so that he can accomplish more." He goes on to point out that these objectives are commonly approached in the following ways:

1. Through the use of punched cards or tapes, computers, memory equipment or other data processing equipment, to provide simpli-fied time saving and space saving automatic machines or devices.
2. Use of identifying labels, tags, and marks on packages—or signals on carriers—which may be recognized by electrical, electronic, mag-

---

[1] G. I. Ross, "Automatic Warehousing—The Concept," *Automation*, November, 1959, p. 86.

netic, or mechanical devices to actuate switches, deflectors, brakes, meters, recorders, etc.

3. Design and development of mechanical or electrical devices and equipment to pick up, move, rearrange and put aside packages and loads of various kinds. Such equipment to be set in motion manually, or by machine instruction.

And, another source continues, as follows:

When we refer to the truly automatic warehouse, we describe a mechanical storage system programmed by punch card, tape or push button. Order selection and delivery to shipping are mechanized. Product input is preferably mechanized, too.

Understand, we're discussing total system. Portions of these systems are seen in great numbers. You can find thousands of automatic systems for breaking down incoming loads and dispatching them to storage. You can find thousands more which consolidate and deliver the orders, but somewhere—usually in order picking—there's some manual handling that "undoes" them as truly automatic warehouses.

Not surprisingly, most truly automatic warehouses are production warehouses, since they sit at the end of the production line. The controllable product and limited number of line items can easily justify automatic equipment. On the other hand, the multi-product distribution warehouse probably needs automatic equipment just as much, if not more. But the distribution warehouse has much less control over size, weight and quantity of product, thus finds automatic equipment a greater risk.[2]

REASONS FOR CONSIDERING AUTOMATED WAREHOUSING

As complex and expensive as automated warehousing may be, there are a large number of reasons and advantages for its consideration. Among the business considerations and factors causing management to look more closely at the possibilities of warehouse automation are the following:

1. Demand for Better Customer Service. In many automated warehouse installations, the primary objective is to provide faster, more accurate service to customers. In other situations, it turns out to be a bonus realized *after* other basic advantages had been gained. The ability to give customers quicker service on orders can become a vicious circle. If one aggressive supplier—through automation—can provide this fast service, competing suppliers must match this service or lose orders. Better customer service and lower transportation costs previously possible with *de*centralization are often partially or completely offset by the faster order-filling time possible with modern data processing equipment in the

[2] "The Automatic Warehouse—Three Years Later," *Material Handling Engineering,* October, 1964, p. 101.

centralized automated warehouse. Other factors contributing to improved service are:

    a. Reduced errors and damage due to less handling
    b. Lower shipping charges due to better correlation of orders and better utilization of transportation facilities.
    c. Fewer stock-outs and back-orders, since re-order routine is built into the system.
    d. Shorter waiting time between order placement and receipt
    e. Fewer complaints, due to above

2. Impact of Data Processing. Management has already seen the results of the automation of paperwork in other business functions which has increased their interest in carrying the data processing function into the handling and distribution of merchandise. Some of the ways in which the data processing and communications systems work together, integrating the distribution and material handling include the following.

    a. Order picking papers or instructions are prepared on punched cards, tape or print-out sheets
    b. Inventory records are updated instantaneously
    c. Stock-outs can be identified immediately
    d. Purchase orders can be automatically prepared when inventory stock falls below the order point
    e. Demand can be recorded continuously, to permit adjusting production schedules
    f. In order filling, cartons can be weighed as they move along the conveyor. The computer can accumulate total weight, determine method of shipment, select carrier, and establish routings.
    g. An on-line computer can provide information directly to the office, making it possible to:
      —confirm a customer order while it is being placed
      —analyze orders as a basis for better sales planning
      —improve sales forecasting
      —facilitate work scheduling
      —expedite accounting functions

In addition to the above general factors causing management to look closely at automated warehousing, there are the following more specific benefits to be gained:

1. *Direct Benefits*
    a. Reduced labor costs, primarily in sorting, dispatching to storage, order picking and office operations.
    b. Reduced investment in storage space due to better utilization of aisle space and more efficient use of overhead space.
    c. Reduced spoilage and pilferage as a result of less handling, fewer employees, and less access to merchandise.

    d. Lower transportation costs.

    e. Reduced overhead resulting from less manpower.

    f. Reduced inventory levels since production and demand are better coordinated.

    g. Lower production costs due to better production and inventory control, therefore smoothing out fluctuations in the operating cycle.

    h. Mechanization of slow-moving items is often possible, since the expensive components have been justified by the fast movers.

  2. *Indirect Benefits*

    a. More stable employment and more positive control of work force, since pace of operation is established by equipment.

    b. Public relations value of installation.

    c. Quicker identification of problem situations and more rapid response to emergencies.

    d. Some costs may be changed from variable to fixed.

    e. Closer coordination of information flow between related departments.

    f. Tighter overall management control.

It can be seen that there are many reasons and potential benefits to be gained from mechanized or automated warehousing, and each should be carefully identified, investigated, and evaluated. A graphical review of some of the benefits is shown in Figure 17–2, indicating some of the ways in which warehouse automation can deliver those things that customers, retailers, manufacturers and management desire of such an installation. Chapter 18 (pp. 602 to 610) outlines some of the changes in the physical distribution field which may also influence the decision on mechanizing or automating warehousing functions.

POTENTIAL DIFFICULTIES OR PROBLEM AREAS

Although the above might indicate that there is nothing *against* automated warehousing, Burr W. Hupp suggests the following difficulties which may be encountered.[3]

1. The development of such complex systems takes time.
2. Management acceptance of complex systems and large investments requires thorough consideration.
3. There is a great need for additional research and development work.
4. There is a need for better coordination between the mechanical and electrical suppliers.

---

[3] Numbers 1 to 9 adapted from Burr W. Hupp, "Automatic Warehousing," an outline for a presentation given at the Materials Handling Management Course, Lake Placid Club, New York.

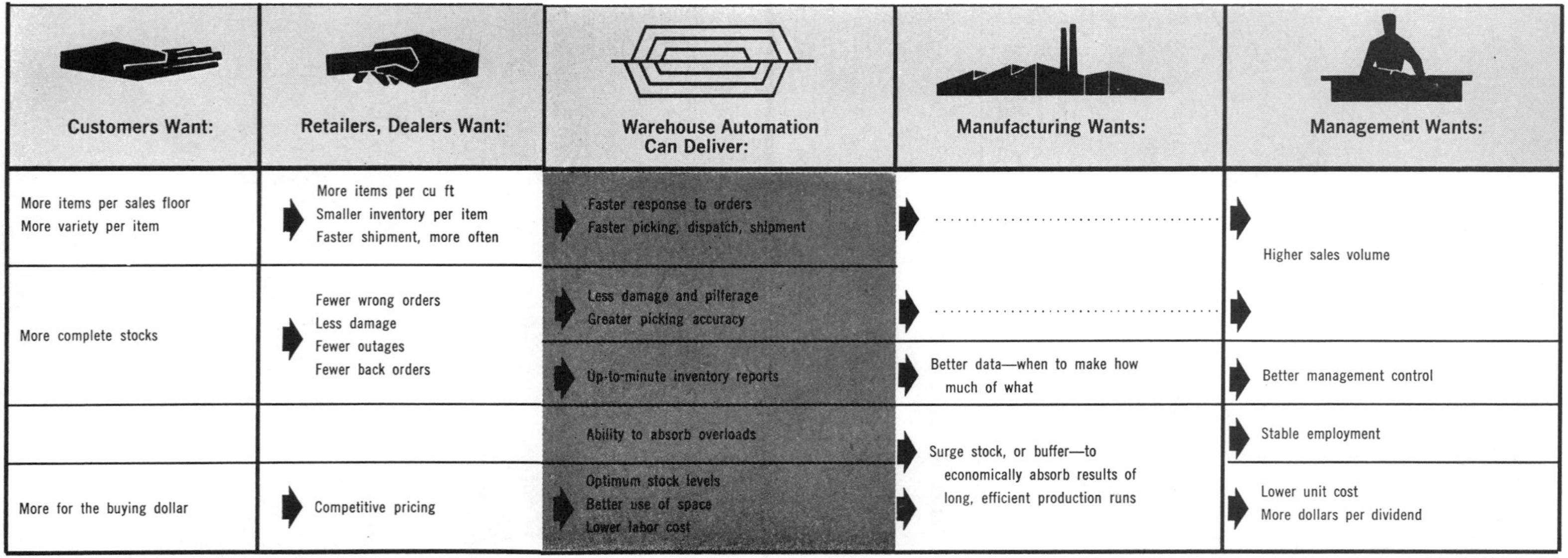

Customers Want:	Retailers, Dealers Want:	Warehouse Automation Can Deliver:	Manufacturing Wants:	Management Wants:
More items per sales floor More variety per item	More items per cu ft Smaller inventory per item Faster shipment, more often	Faster response to orders Faster picking, dispatch, shipment		Higher sales volume
More complete stocks	Fewer wrong orders Less damage Fewer outages Fewer back orders	Less damage and pilferage Greater picking accuracy		
		Up-to-minute inventory reports	Better data—when to make how much of what	Better management control
		Ability to absorb overloads	Surge stock, or buffer—to economically absorb results of long, efficient production runs	Stable employment
More for the buying dollar	Competitive pricing	Optimum stock levels Better use of space Lower labor cost		Lower unit cost More dollars per dividend

Fig. 17-2. How the automated warehouse satisfies distribution needs. (From *Modern Materials Handling*, January 1963, p. 42-3.)

5. The cost of components must be reduced (some of the high cost is undoubtedly due to over-engineering in the earlier units).
6. There is a need for standardization in order to spread the engineering costs of complex components.
7. Competition is growing from good, non-automated warehousing systems.
8. Some authorities still question the trend toward centralized warehousing.
9. There are still problems involving mental attitudes or automated warehousing philosophies, such as:
   a. Over-optimism, implying that "automation is just around the corner"
   b. Disillusionment, which suggests that "automation is too expensive"
   c. The "no compromise" attitude, suggesting the "all or nothing" approach versus the "half a loaf" point of view
10. Cost vs. potential labor savings [4]
11. Replenishing merchandise in the storage unit
12. Potential changes in product size
13. Equipment flexibility in relation the changes in product size
14. Increasing numbers of items to store
15. Downtime
16. Dependability of installation
17. Surge areas
18. Equalization of delivery loading time
19. Compatibility of palletizing and depalletizing equipment
20. Application of codes to containers, packages, etc.
21. Accuracy of sensing devices in recognizing the codes

As implied by the above there are both benefits to be derived and difficulties to be overcome before embarking on an automated warehousing project. Nevertheless, automated warehousing is growing in acceptance and new installations are being made at a rapidly increasing rate. Probably this is due to one or more of the following reasons:

1. Systems which automate portions of the warehouse function are now available.
2. Small, inexpensive computers can handle most of the information requirements.
3. Increased number of available, qualified personnel.
4. Management realization of importance of warehousing costs.
5. Installations often have a high public relations value.
6. Relative ease of building in potential for extra capacity to handle fluctuations in volume.
7. Technological break-throughs are reducing investment required.

[4] Numbers 10 to 18 from Dick Dietz, "New Excitement in the Automated Warehouse," *Material Handling Engineering*, April 1961, p. 67.

1. Volume
   a. Number of line items stocked
   b. Line items per day
   c. Turnover
   d. Fluctuation—peak, ave., min.
   e. Continuity of production
   f. Storage amount—max., min.
   g. Trends
2. Item Characteristics
   a. Dimensions (uniformity)
   b. Shape
   c. Weight
   d. Storage unit characteristics
   e. Machine handleable?
   f. Palletizable?
   g. Resistance to damage
   h. Special handling
   i. Turnover (in items)
   j. Handling characteristics
   k. Volume per item
   l. Ease of delivery: factory to warehouse
   m. Trends
3. Customer Characteristics
   a. Number of Customers
   b. Size of customers
   c. Type—warehouse, retail, consumer
   d. Number of delivery areas
   e. Distances from warehouse
   f. Customer handling capabilities
4. Order Characteristics
   a. Orders per day
   b. Mix, and possibility of changes
   c. Composition of order
      1) Line items per order
      2) Quantity per line item
      3) Packages per order
      4) Size of order
         —cases
         —less than case
         —pallet
         —less than pallet
         —other
      5) Need for re-packing
   d. Accuracy required/desired
   e. Interpretation time

f. Filling time
g. Number of special requests
h. Seasonality
i. Trends

5. Labor
   a. Number of persons picking
   b. Labor restraints
   c. Efficiency
   d. Cost
6. Shipping
   a. Frequency distribution
   b. Shipments per day
   c. Shipment size
   d. Shipment accumulation time
   e. Shipping methods
7. Carrier Characteristics
   a. Availability
   b. Dependability
   c. Capability
8. Delivery Time and Effect on Service
9. Competition
   a. Number of automated installations
   b. Number of automation plans
10. Receipts
    a. Volume
    b. Pattern/Mix
       1) line items per receipt
       2) quantity per line item
       3) composition of receipt
          —packages per order
          —no. of cases
          —less than case
          —no. of pallets
          —less than pallet
          —other
    c. Lot sizes
    d. Frequency of receipt
    e. Marking code
11. Attitude Toward Centralization
12. Long Range Plans
13. Automation Readiness
14. Pay-off Policy

Fig. 17–3. Factors for consideration in warehouse automation.

15. Secondary Motives
    a. Tangible factors
    b. Indirect factors
    c. Intangible factors

16. Building Characteristics
    a. net usable—ft.^{2}, ft.^{3}
    b. Remodeling necessary

17. Potential Equipment
    a. Functions to be mechanized
    b. Types
    c. Investment costs
    d. Start-up costs
    e. Operating costs
    f. Pay-off policy
       1) capital charges
       2) amortization period
       3) return on investment desired
    g. Savings

Fig. 17–3. *(Continued)*

8. Portions of the system can be automated, with additional elements installed later.
9. Management awareness of the potential of automated warehousing.
10. Success of the pioneers is encouraging.
11. Growing number of equipment producers, making for lower prices and a wider selection.
12. Equipment is more reliable than in the past.
13. Expected future volume will demand mechanized or automated handling.

The above advantages, disadvantages, benefits, and trends greatly emphasize the need for the analyst to be aware of the "weight" of facts as well as the "force" of intangible factors in analyzing automated warehousing possibilities. He must carefully consider all aspects of the problem to be sure his analysis is both factual and accurate.

FACTORS FOR CONSIDERATION IN WAREHOUSE AUTOMATION

In assuring that the analysis *is* both factual and accurate, the engineer will find it necessary to make an exhaustive investigation of the factors bearing on the problem, and particularly those which interrelate the storage operation itself with the automation aspects as they effect the overall operations. The list in Figure 17–3 indicates some of the factors which must be taken into consideration.[5]

While the above list may seem rather exhaustive, it should be evident

[5] This list was compiled from the following sources: (1) H. H. Bixler, "Keys to Successful Automation," *Automation*, August, 1964, p. 76; (2) I. M. Footlik, "Should You Go To An Automatic Warehouse?," *Modern Materials Handling*, August, 1957, p. 116; (3) R. J. Sweeney, "Warehouse Automation—How Much Is Justified?," *Modern Materials Handling*, January, 1963; (4) "Quick Test—Is Automation For You?," *Modern Materials Handling*, January, 1963, p. 44.

that undertaking anything as complex as the automation of a warehouse activity requires a thorough, in-depth study of as many factors as it is possible to identify, and isolate. In fact, it should be emphasized that some of the early automated warehousing failures can be traced directly to an incomplete analysis of the *total* situation, or the fact that a key item was overlooked during the analysis.

INDICATORS OF AUTOMATION FEASIBILITY

If the above list of factors is to be considered meaningful, then there must be *some* characteristics of a situation which will be helpful in indicating the advisability or feasibility of considering automation. One authority [6] suggests the following indicators of automation feasibility (all, of course, subject to qualification and exceptions):

1. High labor cost per unit or per move
2. Excessive travel time
3. Excessive order reading and searching (locating) time
4. Large fluctuations in volume; seasonality
5. Problems of space
6. Problems of balance
7. Problems of assembling or coordinating shipments
8. High volume items and movements
9. Dual systems (automated and non-automated)
10. Fast turnover (large lots in storage and automatic handling of palletized or unit loads)
11. Limited number of travel paths
12. Limited space
13. Length of travel
14. Uniformity of package or load size
15. Randomness

Even though this list is not all-inclusive, it should prove helpful in evaluating the feasibility of automation. While it would be desirable if there were quantitative values for a number of significant factors that would either prove or disprove automation feasibility, no such definitive list has been developed. This is no doubt due to the range of factors to be considered, the relative points of view on automated warehousing, the subjective nature of many of the factors, the inability to quantitatively evaluate many of the factors, and the near impossibility of reducing the whole to a compact "mathematical" package.

Based on information available, Figure 17–4 attempts to identify those characteristics or selected factors which might tend to indicate the feasibility of manual operation, mechanization, or automation.

[6] B. W. Hupp, *op. cit.*

	Manual	Mechanized	Automated
1. What is the volume (cases/day)?	1000±	1500–3500	4000 or more
2. How many line items in stock?	Many	Many	Few
3. Is the turnover . . .	Low	Moderate or high	Very high
4. Any limits on size of units stored?	Capacity of man	No limits	Not too large
5. Any weight limits on units stored?	Capacity of man	No limits	Not too heavy
6. Are the dimensions of units stored?	Irregular	Regular	Regular
7. Any restrictions on shape of units?	No limits	Best if standard	Limited number, regular
8. What is the storage unit?	Mostly loose items	Cartons, Cases, pallets	Items, cartons, cases, pallets
9. Any special characteristics?	Fragile items	—	Sensitive to heat, light, etc.
10. How many customers?	Relatively few	—	Many
11. How many items/order?	Few items	—	Many items
12. What is desirable order accuracy?	Some errors OK	Few errors OK	Fewer errors OK
13. How many men picking orders?	6 or less	7 to 9	10 or more
14. Order reading time	Slow	Medium; Fast	Fast
15. Are there any labor restraints?	No	Some	Yes
16. What is the carrier availability?	Poor	Average	Good
17. What about competitors warehouses?	None automated	Some automated	Many automated
18. Is industry trend toward warehouse centralization?	No	Undecided	Yes
19. Is management ready for automation?	No	So-So	Yes
20. Do marketing plans favor automation?	No	Undecided	Yes
21. What is the reliability of sources?	Poor	Average	Good
22. What degree of flexibility is possible?	High	Medium	Low

Fig. 17–4. Guide to selecting warehousing method.

While the table is not complete, nor applicable to all situations, it will give some idea of the characteristics more desirable for mechanized and automated operations.

At least an initial insight into the potential of mechanization can be gained from the figure by "answering" the questions in terms of the situation under analysis. The column containing the largest number of compatible characteristics suggests the level to be further investigated.

WHICH FUNCTIONS TO MECHANIZE/AUTOMATE?

If the analysis to this point has encouraged further investigation into mechanization and/or automation potential, then some decisions must be made as to which functions are the most likely candidates. In review, the major activities of the warehousing function are:

1. Receiving
2. Identification and sorting
3. Dispatching to storage area
4. Placing into storage location
5. Storing
6. Picking
7. Accumulating order
8. Packing
9. Loading and shipping
10. Records and controls

However, few—if any—installations could justify *total* automation, although some of the less complicated, in-process storage devices, where some functions are absent or abbreviated, *do* approach complete automation.

Then it is implied that an approach should be taken which would apply the more sophisticated degrees of automation to those functions which lend themselves more readily to such treatment. Although it is difficult to generalize, due to the variations in many of the factors previously cited, it may be fairly assumed that mechanization and/or automation is easier to implement and less difficult to justify in:

1. Order picking (highest labor content)
2. Dispatching to storage area
3. Order accumulation

In the "grey area" of feasibility are such functions as:

1. Identification and sorting
2. Packing
3. Record keeping

Those functions probably more difficult to implement and/or justify may be:

1. Receiving
2. Placing into storage location
3. Loading

It will be noted that storage has been omitted. This is because storage, per se, is not automated—it is the *putting in* and *taking out* that is mechanized!

It should be emphasized that the "ranking" of any function will change with technological developments, as well as characteristics of the operation under analysis. This lends even greater importance to the careful analysis of the actual functions themselves, as well as to the characteristics of the problem situation. These have both been covered earlier in this chapter, and in the previous chapter.

In recapping and suggesting guidelines for pointing out which functions to mechanize or automate, the following are offered:

1. Most "susceptible" functions first, such as order picking, dispatching to storage, and order accumulation—i.e., high labor content
2. Least expensive to automate, such as dispatching and accumulation
3. Easiest to accomplish
4. Easiest to justify
5. Greatest potential savings

Rather obviously, many facts will be needed, much data gathered and many calculations made before a defendable conclusion can be reached. Later sections of this chapter are devoted to some of these aspects of the problem.

WHEN TO AUTOMATE?

Becoming more specific, one authority suggests automating the *picking* of that 10 percent of the line items that make up 85 percent of the volume —and the balance if economically justifiable—i.e., the 90 percent may account for less picking labor than the 10 percent! One government agency has charted this relationship, as shown in Figure 17–5.

Unfortunately, there is no infallible rule or guide that says exactly when to mechanize or automate each of the several warehousing functions. Every individual case will require a detailed feasibility study and a subsequent engineering economic analysis, before a decision can be reached. And, very likely, this must be done for *each* function (or subfunction) as it comes up for consideration.

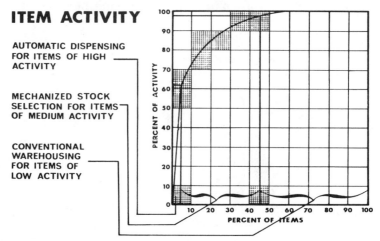

Fig. 17–5. Relationship between item activity and method of order selection. (From *Semi-Automated Warehouse*, Hill Air Force Base, Bulletin AF/OPSU, Jan. 66/500.)

In a specific example, Shenton [7] suggests:

There are three major factors to consider in the engineering analysis:

1. The total volume.
2. The number of different items to be handled within that volume.
3. The distribution of the volume over the different items.

The number of orders filled per day; the maximum, average and maximum number of items per order; the number of customers served; and the number of shipping destinations are also considerations. But they only determine the details of mechanical and electrical construction, *not the basic decision* to use, or not to use, an automated system.

For an example, Shenton selected the typical system shown in Figure 17–6. Shenton continues as follows:

Case goods are received on pallets and stored in a buffer pallet storage area.
Pallets then go to the pallet unloading rack. Here, replenishers take cases from pallets and insert them in the rear of the manual and automatic racks and they flow forward in each lane.
Manually picked goods are then picked from the rack and placed on assembly conveyors. Automatically picked goods are picked from their lanes by the control which opens the gates. They then merge with the manual goods from the assembly lanes on the take-away conveyor. From there, each order goes to the dispatch conveyor and on to the trucks.

[7] Adapted from D. W. Shenton, "Is Automatic Order Picking for You?," *Modern Materials Handling*, March, 1961, pp. 106f.

To come up with the needed answers, the following data must be collected:

1. The number of case goods items handled, average and peak daily or weekly total volume handled, most frequently handled items, and the volume of each.
2. Number of employees now in order picking.
3. Average annual wages with fringe benefits.
4. Depreciation life, in years, of automatic equipment.
5. Cost of investment capital expressed as a percentage or interest rate.
6. Estimated average maintenance costs on conveyors and electrical equipment.

Disregarding those goods shipped by pallet loads or broken case lots, you rank the items in your inventory according to their volume shipped. These are listed as in Fig. 17–7 in decreasing importance with the volume, cumulative volume and cumulative percent for each.

The volume by items can also be expressed as a curve as in Fig. 17–8, which helps to analyze the operation. But it is more meaningful for purposes of this analysis to plot your cumulative volume distribution (Fig. 17–9) from Fig. 17–7.

HOW TO MAKE CALCULATIONS

The next step is to pinpoint the costs that can be cut through automaticity. The total of these can be called the gross dollar savings. Once they have been determined, you then find the cost of the equipment needed to get these savings. The difference between the gross dollar savings and the cost will give the net dollar savings to be realized.

Gross Dollar Savings. The gross savings from a system of this kind will come largely from reduction of the order picking labor. In this example, we are considering replacing a manual system which uses ten order pickers who get $5000 per year plus $1000 in fringe benefits. In ten years, this cost can be expected to rise to $9000 per year. The average total labor cost, over ten years, can be called $7500 per man per year, or $75,000 per year.

There will be other savings, however, whose dollar value will vary widely in each application, such as those listed earlier in this chapter.

The gross savings will be very nearly proportional to the percentage of the daily or weekly volume which is handled automatically.

Because of this proportional relationship, you can plot gross savings on the same curve as Fig. 17–9. The vertical scale can be established by fixing one point. The easiest point to determine is the savings for 100 percent of the items in automatic racks. This point will correspond with the same point that represents 100 percent of total volume in Fig. 17–9.

In this example, the total equals $75,000, based on order picking labor alone.

From Fig. 17–10 we can then see the gross savings resulting from 100 percent automation or the automating of a specific number of items less than the total but still a large percentage of the daily volume.

Cost of Automation. The initial cost of an installed system of this kind is essentially equal to a fixed amount plus an amount proportional to the number

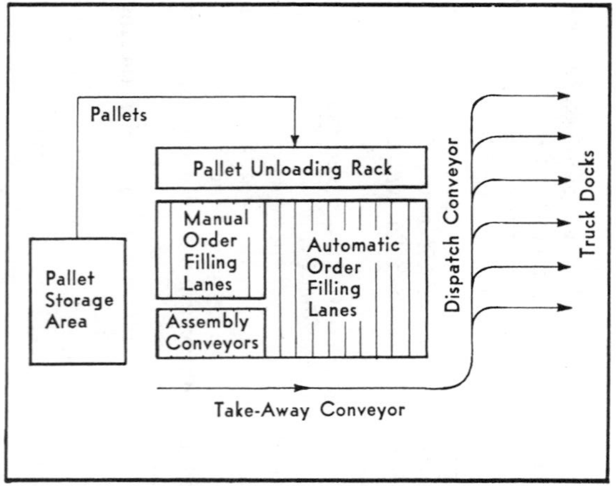

Item No.	Cases Per Day	Cumulative Volume	Cumulative Percent
1	641	641	6.4
2	512	1153	11.5
3	424	1577	15.8
4	364	1941	19.4
5	307	2248	22.5
6	264	2512	25.1
7	234	2746	27.5
8	204	2950	29.5
9	183	3133	31.3
10	167	3300	33.0
Others			
Total	10,000	10,000	100.0

First determination to be made is what case goods items are shipped in the greatest volume. We list these items and the daily or weekly volume for each—in the order of decreasing volume. We continue until we have listed the items which account for most of the daily or weekly volume. The information is often plotted as a distribution curve (see Fig. 17-8).

Fig. 17-7. Distribution breakdown.

The typical system used for this example involves case goods. It is controlled by an operator at a console. When he receives word that the manually picked portion of an order is ready, he will set up the automatically picked portion. He puts information into the console in the form of punched cards, punched tape, or by pressing buttons on a keyboard.

Fig. 17-6. Nature of system.

(From D. W. Shenton, "Is Automatic Order Picking for You?" *Modern Materials Handling,* March 1961, p. 108.)

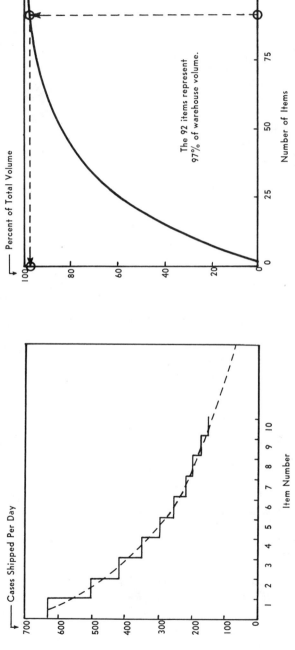

The 92 items represent 97% of warehouse volume.

The information in Fig. 17-7 is often plotted as a volume distribution curve. Here in Fig. 17-8 we have plotted the volume for each item versus the item number. While Fig. 17-8 is helpful in analyzing the operation, it is more meaningful for purposes of analysis to plot the cumulative percent data from Fig. 17-7. This curve has the general form of Fig. 17-9.

Fig. 17-8. Distribution curve.

(From D. W. Shenton, "Is Automatic Order Picking for You?" *Modern Materials Handling,* March 1961, p. 108.)

A plot of the cumulative percent data taken from Fig. 17-7. From Fig. 17-9, we can readily see the number of different items which account for any desired percentage of the total daily, weekly, or monthly volume. In the case of the 92 items determined on the next figure to be the number to be picked automatically, the percent of total volume is 97.

Fig. 17-9. Cumulative distribution curve.

of items in the automatic rack lanes, as shown in the top curve in Fig. 17–11. The fixed amount takes into consideration:

1. Multiple automatic lanes for fast movers and slow movers.
2. The manually picked racks.
3. Cost of the controls.

The total fixed cost of the initial installation can be said to equal 1800 k, where k is the smallest number of items that represents 75 percent of the total volume. You select k at 75 percent because the significant effect of all three factors above takes place with the automation of the fast movers making up this volume.

To find k, look at Fig. 17–7 for the number of items for which the cumulative percent reaches 75.

The variable amount is roughly $2500 per item handled automatically. This can be shown as equal to $2500n$, where n is the number of items in automatic lanes.

This gives us the formula:

$$\text{Initial cost of installation} = 1800k + 2500n$$

This can be plotted as in Fig. 17–11, giving initial cost versus number of automatic items.

You can consider the annual cost of the system as a percent of the initial cost. Depreciation, capital charge and maintenance are the three factors.

In the example shown, depreciation costs 10 percent, capital charge 3 percent and maintenance 2 percent per year.

The three values are added together and plotted as in Fig. 17–11 to complete the picture of initial cost.

Net Annual Dollar Savings. The net annual dollar savings before taxes can be obtained by subtracting the annual cost (Fig. 17–11) from the gross annual dollar savings (Fig. 17–10). This should be plotted as in Fig. 17–12.

Return Average Investment After Taxes. This can be plotted to show the percent of return on the average investment after taxes versus the number of items in automatic racks, as in Fig. 17–13.

Percent of return on average investment is equal to the net dollar savings after taxes, divided by the average investment, multiplied by 100. Net dollar savings after taxes are approximately equal to the net dollar savings divided by two, since the corporate tax is 52 percent. Average investment is equal to the initial investment divided by two (Fig. 17–11).

Return investment can easily be calculated for any number of items in automatic racks. In our example, a 10 percent return is obtained by putting 92 items in automatic lanes. The initial investment (Fig. 17–11) is $290,000 and the gross annual savings (Fig. 17–10) is $73,000. Dividing 290,000 by 73,000 thus gives us a payback of approximately four years.

Similar and/or more detailed calculations will normally be required for justifying the *other* warehousing functions. And—although the above example does not *tell* when to automate—it implies the type of analysis required in making such decisions.

RELATIONSHIPS BETWEEN WAREHOUSING FUNCTIONS AND WAREHOUSING EQUIPMENT

Before becoming involved in the specifics of warehousing equipment, it seems wise to recall the basic warehousing functions (page 544) and relate them to potential equipment categories. Figure 17–14 is an attempt to identify commonly used equipment with those warehousing functions with which it is usually associated. It will be noticed that there is a wide range of equipment possibilities applicable to *each* function. Many of these are "standard" material handling devices, and are dealt with in previous chapters. This chapter is primarily concerned with the more sophisticated forms of mechanized and/or automated equipment. It can also be seen that in many cases Figure 17–14 shows only a *type* of equipment, such as "conveyor"—of which there are about 150 varieties! (See Chapter 6.)

Rather obviously, the final selection of specific equipment type will still depend on a careful analysis of each *material* and *move*—as discussed in previous chapters. The concern here is for a basic understanding of the interrelationships between the types of equipment and their application to the several warehousing functions. While Figure 17–14 will not solve any equipment selection problems, it does present an array of the possibilities, for ease of review and further evaluation.

LEVELS OF MECHANIZATION

Figure 17–14 indicates three "levels" of implementation, in terms of the types of equipment utilized in carrying out the several warehousing functions. They might be defined as:

1. *Manual*—in which all operations are performed by hand, with the possible use of such elementary equipment as 2- or 4-wheel hand trucks.
2. *Mechanized*—where human effort is assisted by such equipment as lift trucks and conveyors. This generally permits higher stacking and larger handling units. It may also involve rather sophisticated equipment, such as stacker—retriever units and mechanized stock-picking trucks—but all under manual control (hand, card, tape, etc.).
3. *Automated*—where equipment *does* the work of the operator(s) and all activity is self-regulating and controlled—usually by an on-line computer.

Although the above brief distinctions do not describe the many possible variations and adaptations of each, they do suggest a general frame

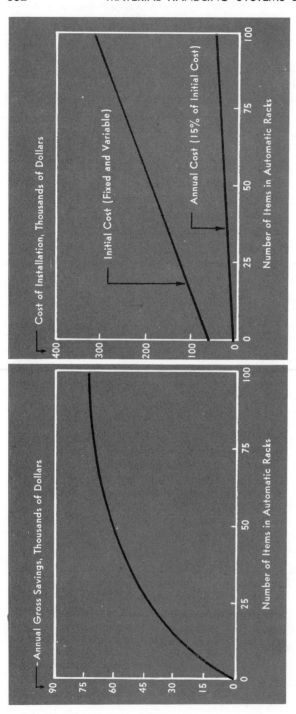

Fig. 17-11. Cost of installation.

Initial cost includes a portion which is variable depending on the number of items in automatic racks. Annual cost includes depreciation, capital charge, and maintenance—and is approximately 15% of initial cost.

Fig. 17-10. Annual gross savings.

If we assume that gross savings will be very nearly proportional to percentage of volume handled automatically, this curve can have the same shape as the Fig. 17-9 curve. Gross savings at 100% volume are $75,000.

(From D. W. Shenton, "Is Automatic Order Picking for You?" *Modern Materials Handling,* March 1961, p. 109.)

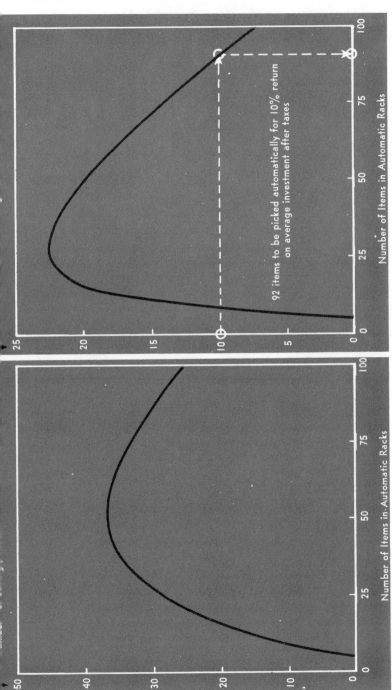

The difference between the gross annual savings (Fig. 17–10) and the annual cost of the automated installation (Fig. 17–11, lower curve) represents the net annual savings shown here. This curve peaks at around 50 items in automatic racks.

Fig. 17–12. Annual net saving.

Dollar savings are relatively meaningless until we look at them with respect to the investment needed to make these savings. In the example, this curve shows that 92 items should be picked automatically.

Fig. 17–13. Percent return on average investment after taxes.

(From D. W. Shenton, "Is Automatic Order Picking for You?" *Modern Materials Handling,* March 1961, p. 109.)

	1. Receive	2. Sort	3. Dispatch	4. Place in Storage	5. Store

Function	—check documents
	—schedule deliv.
	—spot carriers
	—unload
		—identify
		—sort
		—ck. vs. record
		  (item, amount,
		  cond.)
		—segregate
			—move goods to
			  storage area
				—actually place
				  items *in* specific
				  storage locations
					—hold and
					safeguard
					until
					required

Manual	—manual —dock board —dock leveler —truck leveler —hand truck —hand cart —dolly	—manual —visual	—manual —hand truck —hand cart —dolly	—manual —portable lift	—floor —shelf —bin —drawer —rack —fixed —flow —slot

Mechanized	—gravity conv.
	—power conv.
	 —belt, roller
	—power truck
	 —pallet
	 —skid
	 —palletizer
	 —de-palletizer
	—trac.-tlr. train
	—tow line
	—O.Hd. trav. crane
	—monorail hoist
	—stacker crane
	—straddle carrier
	—roller-floor
	—air-in-floor
		—sense
		 —visual
		 —mechanical
		  —scale
		  —meas. dev.
		 —electrical
		  —lim. switch
		  —magnetic
		  —prox. switch
		  —photo elec.
		  —dielectric
		  —X-ray
		  —radio activ.
		  —elect. device
		—code
		 —item
		 —carrier
		 —belt
		 —conveyor
		—divert
		 —air cylinder
		 —hydr. cylinder
		 —mech. device
		 —elect. device
			—gravity conv.
			—power conveyor
			 —belt
			 —roller
			 —trolley
			 —tilt-tray
			 —carousel
			 —slat
			—power truck
			 —walkie
			 —rider
			 —special
			—trac.-tlr. train
			—tow-line
			—O.H. Trav. crane
			—monorail hoist
			—stacker crane
			—straddle carr.
			—storage mach.
			—combination
				—gravity conveyor
				—power conv.
				—O.H. trav. crane
				—monorail hoist
				—stacker crane
				—straddle carrier
				—storage machine
					—slides
					—grav. conv.
					—power conv.
					—pallet
					—skid

Automated	—car "dump" —truck "dump" —car tilt —truck tilt —roller-floor —air-in-floor —palletizer (unitizer) —depalletizer	(as above, but with automatic control)	—gravity conv. —power conv. —stacker crane —storage mach. —tow-line	—gravity conv. —power conv. —stacker crane —storage machine	(as above)

(This Area Implies Self-Regulating, Automatic Control of All Functions)

Fig. 17—14. Basic warehousing functions

6. Pick	7. Deliver	8. Pack	9. Load	10. Record
—select & take item from storage location to means of deliv. to pack	—move goods away from stor. loca. and deliver to packing area.	—package and/or pack for shipment	—place on or into carrier	—order entry —inventory cont. —order-pt. contr. —data processing —invoicing —records & reports
—manual —portable lift	—manual —hand truck —hand cart —dolly	—manual	—manual —dock board —dock leveler —truck leveler —hand truck —hand cart —dolly	—manual —form —card

—chute
—conveyor drop
—power truck
  —lift
  —platform
  —order picker
    —manual
    —mechanical
    —electronic
—O.H. trav. crane
—stacker crane
—stor. machine
(above may be electronically guided)
	—gravity conv.
	—power conv.
	—power truck
	—tractor-trailer
	—tow-line
	—O.H. trav. crane
	—monorail hoist
	—stacker crane
	—straddle crane
	—storage machine
		—packaging mach.
		—cartoning mach.
		—labeler
		—tying machine
		—taping equip.
		—sealing equip.
		—strapping equip.
		—palletizer
		
		NOTE: in using this chart, read DOWN, as method or equipment previously listed may apply at higher levels of mechanization or automation.
			—gravity conv.
			—power conv.
			—power truck
			—trac.-trailer
			—tow-line
			—O.H. trav. crane
			—monorail hoist
			—stacker crane
			—straddle carrier
			—storage machine
				(above, plus manual, mechanized, electr. accounting machine or computer calculation and recording)

—drop —order picker —stacker crane —stor. machine (all above electronically controlled)	—gravity conv. —power conv. —tow line —stacker crane —storage mach.	(as above)	(as above)	(above plus computer control)

and methods of implementation.

of reference for considering mechanization possibilities. The concepts implied above are referred to in this chapter, while additional details were covered in Chapter 11.

Further guidance is offered by the tabulation [8] in Figure 17–15. It presents 6 levels of mechanization, in contrast with Bright's 17, and Bazaraa's 10, in Figures 11–2 and 11–3. Obviously the term "turnover rate" on the tabulation depends on what is being handled, and can be estimated by dividing total quantity handled over a period of time by the average inventory.

COMMONLY MECHANIZED FUNCTIONS

Examination of current "automated" warehouses suggests that only a few of the 10 basic warehousing functions are actually implemented by the equipment which has been installed. In most cases, the "mechanization" is limited to

Dispatching *to* storage area
Placing *into* storage location
Picking *from* storage
Order *accumulation*

and frequently some portion of the record keeping and/or control aspect of the installation.

So, warehouse *handling* equipment can really be classified into only 2 types:

Getting *into* storage
Getting *out* of storage

Therefore, in a general way, a "typical" automated warehouse would probably utilize some of the following, relatively small, equipment list:

A. Getting *into* storage
  1. Dispatching *to* storage area
    a. Conveyors
      (1) Roller, wheel, belt.
      (2) Trolley
      (3) Tilt-tray
    b. Stacker crane
    c. Storage machine [9]
    d. Tow-line
  2. Placing *into* storage location
    a. Conveyors
      (1) Roller, wheel, belt

---

[8] "Levels of Mechanization for Storage Systems," *Modern Materials Handling*, p. 59.

[9] Actually in nearly all cases, the *unit* is both a stacker and picker.

      (2) Trolley

      (3) Tilt-tray

    b. "Cranes"

      (1) Overhead crane with suction attachment

      (2) Stacker crane

      (3) Storage machine

  B. Getting *out* of storage location

    1. Removal from storage location

      a. Conveyor release—drop mechanism

      b. "Crane"

        (1) Overhead crane

        (2) Stacker crane

        (3) Storage machine

    2. Order accumulation

      a. Conveyors

      b. Tow-line

The control aspect is frequently handled by a computer, and may merely keep track of items stored and picked (inventory)—or the computer may control the operation of the mechanisms and movement of goods.

BASIC AUTOMATED WAREHOUSING "SYSTEMS"

It might be said that there are 3 basic automated warehousing "systems":

1. *Rack or slide and conveyor,* in which individual items, cartons or case goods are stored and dispensed from gravity racks, lanes, or chutes, onto conveyors.
2. *Pallet rack with stacker crane or storage machine*—where items are stored on pallets (or equivalent) and *in* a rack structure. Placement and retrieval are by means of a six-directional handling unit, usually moving back and forth between 2 rows of racks; up and down to various rack levels; and side to side into the racks on either side of the row.
3. *Overhead crane/suction retriever,* in which goods are usually handled in unit loads or layers from high stacks, without racks.

The first is possibly the most common, as well as the earliest on the scene. The second method (especially the storage machine) is growing in popularity, with new variations being introduced constantly. However, it is usually limited to applications where the handling and/or picking unit is pallet loads, layers, or large containers—while the rack or slide type can handle smaller, carton, and consumer-sized items.

The term "systems," as used here, is somewhat misleading, since the major function of the above devices is primarily storage and order picking. And it should be pointed out that much of the equipment which

Level of Mechanization	Equipment and Methods		Control	Motive Power	Picking Unit		First-In First-Out	Turnover Rate
	Lifting, Traveling	Storing			Pallet-load	Case Lot		
Non-mechanized	All manual	Floor loading, no pallets	Manual	Man	No	Yes	No	Low
	All manual	Shelves	Manual	Man	No	Yes	No	Low
Non-powered equipment	Hand pallet trucks	Pallets on floor	Manual	Man	Yes	Yes	No	Low
	Hand pallet trucks, platform trucks, and portable stackers	Racks	Manual	Man	Yes	No	Yes	Low
	Hand pallet trucks	Gravity flow lanes in racks, manually loaded and picked at floor level	Manual	Man	No	Yes	Yes	Average
Powered equipment	Lift trucks and cranes controlled from driver position	Floor-stacked palletloads	Manual	Electric or internal combustion	Yes	No	No	Average
	Lift trucks and cranes controlled from driver position	Racks: pigeonhole or lane	Manual	Electric or internal combustion	Yes	No	Yes	Average
	Stockpicking trucks and cranes whose operator rises and travels with the load	Racks	Manual	Electric	Yes	Yes	Yes	Average to high
	Stockpicking trucks and portable elevators	Gravity flow lanes in racks, manually loaded and picked by operator on portable elevator or stockpicking truck	Manual	Electric or internal combustion, gravity	No	Yes	Yes	Average to high

Category	Description	Storage	Control	Power				Cost
Remote control, pushbuttons	Stacker cranes or retrieval units operated from a console by pushbuttons	Racks: pigeonhole or lane	Manual remote	Electric	Yes	No	Yes	High
	Palletloads delivered by lift trucks to racks for manual case-by-case loading	Gravity flow lanes in racks, manually loaded but picked mechanically under control of pushbutton console	Manual remote	Electric or internal combustion, gravity	No	Yes	Yes	High
Remote control, cards or tape	Stacker cranes or retrieval units operated from a console by punched cards or tape	Racks: pigeonhole or lane	Remote via cards or tape	Electric	Yes	No	Yes	Very high
	Palletloads delivered by lift trucks to racks for manual case-by-case loading	Gravity flow lanes in racks, manually loaded but picked mechanically under control of cards or tape at console	Remote via cards or tape	Electric or internal combustion, gravity	No	Yes	Yes	Very high
Remote control, computer	Stacker cranes or retrieval units operated directly by central computer or indirectly by the computer through a local logic circuit	Racks: pigeonhole or lane	Remote via computer	Electric	Yes	No	Yes	Very high
	Palletloads delivered by lift trucks to racks for manual case-by-case loading	Gravity flow lanes in racks, manually loaded but picked mechanically under direct control of computer	Remote via computer	Electric or internal combustion, gravity	No	Yes	Yes	Very high

Fig. 17–15. Levels of mechanization for storage systems. (From "Levels of Mechanization for Storage Systems," Modern Materials Handling, December 1969, p. 59.)

mechanizes many warehouses is not at all concerned with the storage/ order-picking functions mentioned above. Indeed—a large investment is frequently made in a mechanized warehouse, in which the placement of goods into storage, as well as picking them out, is still done 100 percent by manual methods! The *mechanization* is in the dispatching of goods *to* the storage area and the delivery of goods *from* the storage area to the order accumulation point. For example, one rather sophisticated system consists of a stock-picking truck, whose route and movement are computer controlled. The truck is guided to the appropriate warehouse location, stopped at the proper spot, while a visual display console presents a read-out of the item number and quantity, and an arrow points to the proper side of the narrow aisle. Then a stock picker takes the item from the bin, presses a button, and the truck proceeds to the location of the next item on the order. The computer also up-dates the inventory.

The logical extension of this concept will replace the manual handling with pallet forks, mechanical arms, or other devices, thereby extending the mechanization to at least *two* more functions:

1. Placing *into* storage
2. Picking *from* storage

—and becoming more of a "system."

By way of review and orientation, the most common approach to the mechanization of warehousing, aside from the mere movement of goods, is through the provision of a storage facility, integrated with a mechanized order-picking device. Methods commonly in use may be classified as:

    I. Manual. Hand truck; hand pick
   II. Mechanized
       A. Stock-picking truck, rider controlled; and manual pick
       B. Guided truck
          1. Rail
          2. Electronic }
          3. Computer } hand pick
  III. Automated
       A. Truck—computer controlled; mechanical pick
       B. Conveyor—flow rack with automatic drop and take-away conveyor
          1. Slide
          2. Wheel }
          3. Roller } also with storage machine on flow-through racks
       C. "Crane" or storage machine
          1. Stacker crane with cantilever racks (the original concept)
          2. Stacker-rider mounted on rack
          3. Storage machine between racks
             a. Top mounted (possibly floor stabilized)

b. Floor mounted (possibly top stabilized)
   (1) Operating *in* row only
   (2) Transfer-type
       —Self-standing
       —Overhead supported
   4. Floor stacks, with overhead crane and suction (or similar) device
D. Other
   1. Rotary (ferris-wheel style)
   2. Vending machine type

Some of these are illustrated in Chapter 6, while others are shown in Figures 17–16 through 17–21.

As pointed out elsewhere in this chapter, control may be manual, by card or tape, or by on-line computer. One authority estimates there were only about *10* on-line, computer-controlled warehouse installations in existence in 1970. He estimates there will be *200* by 1975.

Fig. 17–16. Order picking truck. Operator has truck controls on platform. Travel is guided by rails on racks and outriggers with guide wheels. (Courtesy of Clark Equipment Company.)

Fig. 17–17. Order-picking truck with rack for picking 6 orders at one time. (Courtesy of Barrett-Cravens Company.)

An interesting sidelight to the automated warehousing story is the fact that in a large, rack-based installation, the rack *can* be the building structure, a roof can be placed on top of the racks, and wall sections "hung" on the sides. However, this poses an interesting question from an accounting angle. Is the rack a piece of equipment, with a 5-year write-off? Or is it a part of the building, with a 20–25 year write-off? The engineer should check with his accounting department and their tax experts before reaching any pay-off conclusions.

THE MEANS FOR MECHANIZATION [10]

Based upon an understanding of the concepts previously discussed, this section will briefly describe a composite of the many types of equipment in use, classified by the functions for which they are utilized.

[10] Note: this section is adapted and/or quoted from a number of periodical sources, which are listed at the end of this chapter.

Fig. 17-18. A unique order-picking (and stock replenishment) operation from vehicle-mounted storage module, automatically operated and controlled by a computer-prepared picking list. Stock location is entered by operator on vehicle keyboard, or by means of a "deck" of punched cards. An alternate version is on-line, computer controlled—with data transmission by radio, to a digital read-out device displaying the item number and quantity to pick as well as which side of the aisle it is on. Vehicle guidance is via an under-floor cable which (1) starts and stops vehicle, (2) at pre-determined locations, and (3) initiates the next action by pressing a "go" button. (Courtesy of Mobility Systems, Inc.)

Fig. 17–19. Gravity conveyor-rack type of mechanized warehousing. Carton release to belt conveyor is by means of console at lower right. (Courtesy of Mathews Conveyor Division, Rex Chainbelt, Inc.)

RECEIVING

Receiving and putting away stock in a warehouse offer the poorest possibilities for the overall application of automated techniques. There have been some successful cases in these areas, and hardware does exist for the purpose. Automatic palletizers and depalletizers are the most obvious example.

From the warehousing viewpoint, packages may be received as individual units from nearby manufacturing areas or in large lots from remote manufacturing areas. In the first case, the packages usually arrive at the warehouse in single file on a conveyor line. Large lot shipments are typically received on pallets or in "cubes" (assemblies of packages into unit loads that can be easily transported). The general problem of automatic warehousing at this receiving stage is determined by the intended technique of storage within the warehouse.

Where packages are to be stored as units on live conveyor lines, the individually received packages on conveyors can be directed to the storage conveyor lines or bulk storage areas. Packages that have been received on pallets or in cubes must be separated at the receiving point. Automatic pallet unloaders dismantle pallet loads and place individual packages in single file on a conveyor line.

Where packages are to be stored in pallet loads, those received in palletized form can be directed to live conveyor lines capable of handling complete

Fig. 17–20. Stacker crane type of mechanized warehousing (see also Fig. 6–33). Can be manual, card, or computer controlled. *This* type is the predecessor of the stacker-retriever type of storage machine. (Courtesy of Shepard-Niles Crane and Hoist Corp.)

pallet loads. Individual packages received direct from the production line must first be placed onto pallets before storage.

The advent of equipment such as card- or tape-controlled trucks and cranes has substantially altered this picture.

Nevertheless, receiving and putting stock away is a less fertile field for automation, than some of the other functions. However, when receiving is not involved, as when goods come directly from production into the warehouse, the potential for automating the input to storage is considerably enhanced.

IDENTIFICATION

Manual identification involves an operator who visually recognizes different types, colors, sizes, addresses, or whatever identity is necessary and who either puts this information into a control memory system or "tags" the items or a carrier. The input to the control memory usually is in the form of keyboards, dials, or push buttons. Tags usually take the form of matrix codes for readers using photoelectric, magnetic, or contact making principles.

Automatic identification does not require an operator but identifies items by recognizing significant physical characteristics such as size, weight, chemical composition, or symbols printed on the item. The input to the control

Fig. 17–21 A. Stacker-retriever type of storage machine, supported on rails at top and bottom. Notice that narrow "aisle" required is only inches wider than load. See also Fig. 6–34 for overall view of a similar device. (Courtesy of Triax Company.)

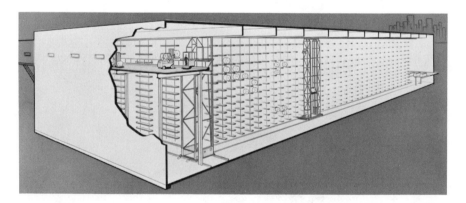

Fig. 17–21 B. Transfer car plus stacker-retriever unit type of storage mechanization. Car travels up and down aisles, as shown at right. Transfer car moves unit from aisle to aisle. (See also Figs. 17–21 C and D.) (Courtesy of Clark Equipment Co.)

Fig. 17–21 C. Stacker-retriever unit in the aisle. Unit is punch card controlled. (See also Fig. 17–21 B.) (Courtesy of Interlake, Inc.)

Fig. 17–21 D. Transfer car at left with stacker-retriever unit at "home" location. Also: manually operated picking unit on outer aisle, at right. (See also Figs. 17–21 B and C.) (Courtesy of Interlake, Inc.)

memory may originate with limit switches, load cells, or composition or symbol detectors. For example, the lumber industry makes use of limit switches to sort mixed lengths of lumber on a conveyor. This is done simply by arranging the limit switches (mechanical or photoelectric) to determine the length of a board by counting the number of switches that the board actuates simultaneously. The same principles could be applied to identify different-size packages.

SORTING

One of the more common methods of "automated" sorting of items is by way of optical or magnetic coding on the item, a belt, or the conveyor itself.

Simply explained, belt coding puts the package destination address *in* the conveyor belting. Thus, the destination information travels with the package. The belt becomes its own memory.

With coded item, coded carrier, or coded conveyor dispatching methods, the destination also travels with the package. However, the code is not carried in the belt of a belt conveyor. Rather, the address code is affixed to a tote box or tray in which the package to be sorted is placed (coded carrier), or it is placed on the hanger of a chain-driven trolley conveyor or on the tray of a carousel conveyor (coded conveyor). For each of these methods, including belt coding, a read device with a matching code at each exit actuates a diverting device or release mechanism.

Figures 17–22 and 17–23 indicate this method applied to a belt conveyor and four kinds of tasks which can be accomplished through the use of magnetic belt coding.

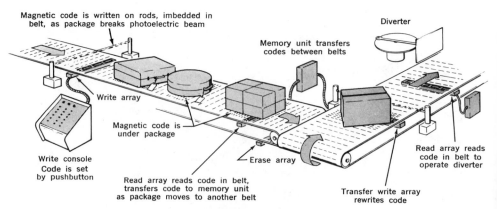

Fig. 17–22. Magnetic belt dispatching system with belt transfer. (From *Modern Materials Handling*, April 1963, p. 53.)

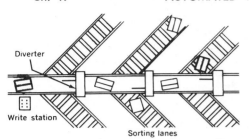

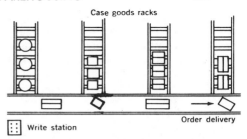

SINGLE-BELT SORTING: Matching pre-set code at read station closes relay which, in turn, actuates diverter.

ORDER SELECTING: Code trips correct case goods rack as belt passes read station. Order is automatically picked.

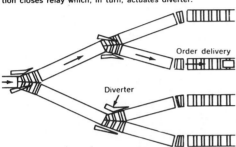

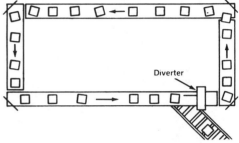

MULTIPLE-BELT SORTING: Code stays with package, is transferred from belt to belt as package is transferred.

PACKAGE SELECTING: Code is transferred from belt to belt. Package selecting is made in any desired sequence.

Fig. 17–23. Four common types of jobs belt coding can do. (From *Modern Materials Handling*, April 1963, p. 54.)

DISPATCHING

The complicating factors in this phase of warehousing are the variety of classifications of packages to be stored and the time relationship of the receipts of the various classifications at the warehouse.

If large lots of similar packages are received and are to be directed to a given location, the dispatching function lends itself to manual selection of locations. Identification in such cases is simplified since a single identifying code is used to identify a lot containing many individual packages.

Where it is necessary to examine each package, as when packages are received in mixed lots, they can be identified either manually or automatically. With some classifications of packages it is feasible to route individual units directly to storage locations. Automatic systems provide for sensing the identification code, spacing out succeeding units on a conveyor, and diverting the package at a desired point in the system.

Dispatching can be accomplished in one of two basic ways. It is possible to either read the identity of the item at each conveyor exit, or identify the item at one point and remember the identity and location of the item as it passes through the conveyor exit areas. When the exit code and the item code match, the object is discharged.

Read identification dispatching involves reading the identification of each item at each storage exit and either diverting it or letting it pass by. The item's identity may have been previously established either manually or automatically. For instance, the item may have been identified previously by weight and have had a code stamped on it that can be read photoelectrically. At each storage exit a photoelectric decoder would read the code and control the diverting gate. On the other hand, the item's identity may not have been established prior to the time it was dispatched. Then each storage exit must identify the object and control its dispatching to storage, all in one operation.

The decoders may work on any number of basic principles. Some of the more popular types include those made up of limit switches, electrical contacts, magnetic pickups and photoelectric relays. Many systems in operation consist of fingers or dogs that protrude from carriers. The dispatcher sets up the dogs according to the destination desired and, at the destination, a limit switch senses that the dogs are up and the carrier is diverted. This type of dispatching system has been used for many years.

Remember identification dispatching is basically remembering the position of an identified item and, when it arrives at the proper storage area, giving a signal to divert it. The previous stage of identification could have been manual or automatic. Logic circuitry determines the destination for identified items. The destination and position of the items is kept track of in a memory portion of the control. Logic circuitry again comes into play to actuate the diverting mechanism when the item's position corresponds to its destination.

In some cases it is more practical to have an accumulation area between the receiving and storage areas. Such an arrangement permits individual packages to be identified and directed to an accumulator station where like packages can be gathered into lots. The accumulators are conveyor lines that discharge into a common conveyor line leading to the storage area. In operation, packages are fed into the accumulating lines and then in a programmed sequence, the accumulating lines deliver their groups of packages to the common line. The discharge of lines is controlled electrically to prevent two lines discharging simultaneously, causing interference or mixing of packages on the common line. As an additional control technique, each line starting to discharge its lot of packages can register on a memory system which in turn creates signals that actuate diverters or deflectors at a time that coincides with the arrival of the lot at the proper storage point.

Memory systems for these applications can be developed around magnetic tape, punched tape, or any mechanical device synchronized with the conveying system such that a pin, lever, or other element operates an electrical circuit at the instant a deflecting point is reached.

Multi-story warehouses present no problem in these automatic operations. The well publicized inefficiencies of multi-story buildings have been overcome by modern equipment.

STORE

Storage represents a buffer between flow rates into and out of the system. Items are generally stored in one of two ways: By classification, or at random. For example, a luggage manufacturer may want to store luggage by types and colors, but an airline passenger baggage handling system must use a random storage from which specific luggage can be recalled for delivery to individuals. An auto manufacturer would desire to store by type, color, and style, but a parking garage must have a random serial storage to be able to recall a particular auto.

Activity within the storage area is limited to accepting dispatched items, giving up recalled items, counting in and out for inventory data, and moving items within the storage lines to facilitate random access where needed.

The various types of gravity racks are excellent examples of improved storage equipment that have been developed. The several forms are: 1. Simple slide consisting of inclined pans or angle shaped sides that permit packages to slide or roll down toward the discharge point as successive packages are removed. 2. Inclined side rails equipped with wheels that support the packages. In this type of rack the packages are supported only along their edges. 3. Inclined wheel conveyor racks. Here the racks consist of a multiplicity of wheels and the packages are supported at various points. 4. Inclined roller conveyor racks in which the packages are supported by rollers making numerous line contacts across the base of the package.

In automatic systems, packages are placed in the racks by a conveying unit. In other systems, packages arriving in the storage area are manually transferred to the storage racks or, in some cases, to a bulk storage area for later transfer to the storage racks as requirements demand.

Where control of speed of travel is essential, as in the handling of fragile or heavy loads, a powered rack is usually specified in place of the gravity type of rack. A powered rack can be constructed from many types of power conveyors. With this more expensive rack design, the loading end can be at the same elevation or even lower than the discharge end.

The other basic types of storage methods are the rack, stacker crane or storage machine, and floor storage, with crane and lifting unit.

PICKING

Since the prime purpose of finished goods warehousing is fulfilling customer requirements, the heart of the operation is order picking. This work usually consumes the majority of warehousing labor. For these reasons, it usually is considered to be the prime target for automation studies.

In general, there are two common systems of mechanizing order picking, as previously indicated:

1. Flow rack units—where electrically controlled escapements permit individual items to drop from the racks onto conveyors. This system is usually used when high flow rates per item are required.
2. Stacker crane—where a crane or truck-like device, or storage machine, selects items stored in individual rack locations. This system is most commonly applied when items are large, bulky or palletized.

It should be noted, however, that manual order picking still has a place in the "automated" warehouse, and is frequently used for the slow moving items on an order, which must be consolidated with the items automatically picked.

With the flow rack type of installation, orders are picked in one of three ways:

1. One item at a time. This simply involves opening a "gate" and counting out of the correct storage line the quantity of the item desired.

2. One order at a time. This involves counting out the desired quantity of items from each of several different storage lines, sequentially or simultaneously, and collecting the order on one conveyor.

3. Several orders at a time. This requires a much more complicated recall system since the control must now remember to which order each of the recalled items belongs so it can be delivered to the particular shipping dock collecting the order.

While recall may be accomplished manually by selecting items by pushbuttons, it will frequently require more sophisticated direction such as tape or card inputs for order picking.

There are three basic techniques for controlling flow rack systems. They are:

Simultaneous recall. With simultaneous recall, items may be released from a number of live storage lanes simultaneously. No attempt is made to program these releases to prevent collision from occurring on the conveyor.

The simultaneous-recall principle has generally been restricted to broken-case-lot picking where individually cans, for example, are being released. Punched cards for an entire order may be read through the card reader and the items released from the gravity racks as fast as the escapements can be operated.

The entire order is released onto take-away conveyors in a very short time. But clearing time must be allowed to clear the order out of picking and to get it on its way to packing and shipping before picking can start on the next order. Otherwise, items for several orders would be intermingled.

Sequential recall. With casegoods order picking, operation of the escapements on each lane of the live storage rack is generally programmed to avoid collisions on the conveyor, such as would occur if a case were released onto the take-away conveyor just as another case came by.

A simple way to avoid collisions is to arrange the picking sequence to pick upstream. If lane 1 is nearest the discharge end of the take-away conveyor, then for each order, items from lane 1 are released first, followed by items from lanes 2, 3, 4 and so on, in upstream sequence.

This is a simple straight-forward approach, but it has certain limitations which result in lower productivity than the synchronous systems to be described later. If the punched cards for order picking have not been pre-sorted, then all cards for each order must be read into a memory and the memory then scanned, to operate the gates in sequence. The expense of this full-order memory can be saved by pre-sorting the cards for each order. However, this tends to limit flexibility to put any product in any storage lanes. Shifting a product from one lane to another changes the order in which cards must be arranged.

A further limitation of the sequential-recall system is runout time. The last item released for each order will be farthest from the discharge end of the take-away conveyor. In a 20-lane rack, the last item may be released from lane 20. Picking of the next order must be delayed until the case from lane 20 has traveled the full length of the take-away conveyor, because the first case in the next order may be released from lane 1.

With multi-deck live storage racks, the sequential-recall system requires accumulation conveyors. With a three-deck rack (Figure 17–24), approximately one-third of an order will be picked on the average from each of the three decks. The order will come out on the three separate take-away conveyor belts A, B, and C. Next, items from A1, then B1, and then C1, will be released onto a single conveyor D for dispatching to shipping. In the meantime, the next order is being picked and is being accumulated on conveyors A2, B2, and C2.

Another approach permits operating with one accumulation line per deck. One card is used to release a signal item for each order on each deck. This signal item leads the remaining items of the order to an accumulation line. It also controls the merging of items from the accumulation line for each deck. This cuts waiting time when an unbalanced condition occurs and a large number of items are picked on one deck and a smaller number on other decks.

Synchronous recall. The principle of synchronous recall is this: for each case to be released from the racks, the control reserves a definite spot on the take-away conveyor. The punched cards for an order can be fed into the card reader in any order. The items will be picked in the sequence in which the cards are read. There is no problem of collisions because, as each card is read, the control immediately reserves a spot on the conveyor for that item.

For example, assume the items to be picked are read into the card reader as 6,6,1,4,5,3,7. Then, just before the release of carton 1, the take-away conveyor will appear as shown in Figure 17–25. Carton 1 will drop between

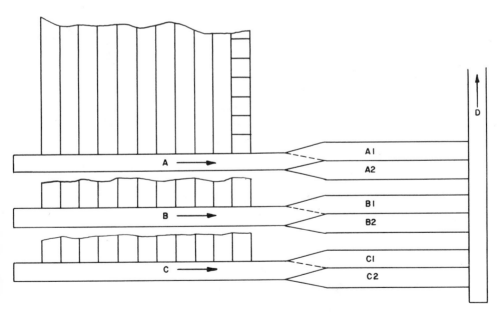

Fig. 17–24. Sketch illustrating package flow from 3-deck rack, with sequential recall. (From J. M. Delfs, *Automatic Warehousing—Why, Where, How;* unpublished notes privately circulated.)

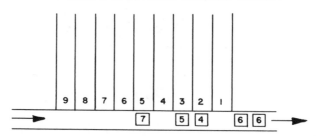

Fig. 17—25. Sketch illustrating principle of synchronous recall. (From J. M. Delfs, *Automatic Warehousing—Why, Where, How;* unpublished notes privately circulated.)

cartons 6 and 4, and a moment later carton 3 will drop between cartons 5 and 7 as the space reserved for it comes by.

With the synchronous-recall system, the machine can start picking the second order immediately after the first. Therefore, no run-out time is required. Also, with a multi-deck rack, no accumulation conveyors are needed. Automatic merging is provided as shown in Figure 17–26.

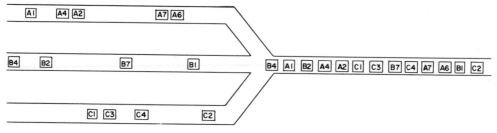

Fig. 17—26. Sketch illustrating merging of items with synchronous recall systems with a multi-deck installation. (From J. M. Delfs, Automatic *Warehousing—Why, Where, How;* unpublished notes privately circulated.)

Figure 17–27 is a tabulation of order picking methods at so-called "automatic" warehouses. It can be seen in the columns titled—

Replenishment of storage
Picking instructions
How picked

that about *two-thirds* of the entries are "manual" or "visual"!

The other basic automated warehousing technique—based on the stacker-crane/storage machine—is referred to as *random recall.*

This is the control method for the retrieval—or automatic-parking-garage—approach. Each item is stored in separate pigeon-hole racks. They permit major space savings by working in narrow aisles and providing high stacking.

Both stocking and picking operations are performed by equipment that may operate unattended once it receives instructions.

Items are picked one at a time in the order in which the information is fed into the control. Generally, the first item picked must be cleared from the system before it will accept another command to handle the next item. Controls, however, may permit a stocking and a picking operation on one command cycle.

The random-recall principle can be applied to live storage systems but is generally too slow to be used with high-volume order picking of the type employing gravity racks and automatic release mechanisms.

Another view of the order picking process is displayed in Figure 17–28, which compares order picking "systems" for packaged, cartoned, or cased goods.

CONSOLIDATION

The gathering of picked items and their delivery to specific production or shipping areas is similar to the dispatching function, but it is a separate system problem and usually unlike the dispatch problem in the same system. Usually the identity of an item is remembered until it has been delivered to the proper area, once it has been recalled. Identification of an order which has been recalled and loaded on a pallet may be made by tagging the pallet and then reading item identity. In this case the pallet could also have been identified manually and its identity remembered as it was sent to the shipping area.

With automated recall from flow racks or escapements, accumulation is built into the order-picking operation, since the various items for each order are all released simultaneously or in sequence. Consolidation is then used merely to send the order to packing or shipping.

In spite of the similarity to the dispatching problem previously described, careful study and planning are required to avoid bottlenecks in the flow. Normally the orders will flow along a conveyor and each will be automatically diverted onto an accumulation conveyor at each truck loading dock.

CONTROL

Once a system has been designed to accomplish the desired basic material handling control functions, information becomes readily available which may be used to advantage in other parts of the business. Frequently the use of data processing equipment will make possible significant improvement in operations and business procedures of portions of the business responsible for inventory, production, and billing. Thus, the three basic data processing functions of automated material control systems (inventory control, production

PICKING UNIT	UNITS OUTPUT PER HOUR	REPRESENTATIVE TYPE OF WAREHOUSE	NO. OF ITEMS STOCKED	STORAGE UNIT	REPLENISHMENT OF STORAGE	PICKING INSTRUCTIONS	HOW PICKED	ROUTING INSTRUCTIONS	CONTROL OF ROUTING — SORTING — ORDER ASSEMBLY
PALLET LOADS	300	1 Brewery	6	Pallet Conveyor	By Conveyor From Production Lines	Machine Read Tape	Automatic Release From Conveyors	NA	NA
	75	2 Electric Motor Mfg.	500	Pallet Rack	Auto. Controlled Stacker Crane	Machine Read Punchcards	Auto. Controlled Stacker Crane	NA	NA
	60	3 Metal Materials Distributor	1,000	Pallet Rack	Keyboard Contrl. Stacker Crane	Manually Operated Keyboard	Keyboard Contr. Crane & Singulator	Manually Operated Keyboard	Keyboard Operated Control Console
TIERS OF CASES	540	4 Frozen Food Mfg.	8,600	Pallet Rack	Auto. Controlled Stacker Crane	Machine Read Tape	Auto. Suction Pickup by Bridge Crane	Machine Read Tape	Computer
	1,200	5 Major Appliance Manufacturer	140	Case Flow Conveyor	By Conveyor From Production Lines	Machine Read Tape	Automatic Release From Conveyors	Escort Code Imprinted on Case	Computer
	1,500	6 Egg Processing Plant	72	Case Flow Conveyor	By Automatic Restocking Vehicle	Manually Operated Keyboard	Automatic Release From Conveyors	NA	NA
	2,000	7 Air Force Supply Depot	150	Case Flow Conveyor	Pallet Truck Contrl. Fm. Mast	Machine Read Punchcards	Automatic Release From Conveyors	NA	NA
CASES	2,000	8 Drugstore Supply	600	Pallet Flow Rack	Manually Operated Stacker Crane	Visually Read From Display Unit	Manually From Pallet to Vehicle	Machine Read Tape	Computer
	2,500	9 Institutional Food Supply Distributor	2,000	Pallet Rack	Fork Truck	Visually Read Punchcards	Manually From Pallet to Vehicle	Punchcards Manually Fixed To Cases	Keyboard Operated Control Console
	3,000	10 Dry Grocery Distributor	3,000	Pallet Rack	Fork Truck	Visually Read Picking List	Manually From Pallet to Take-away Conveyor	NA	Assembly Keyboard Controlled From a Console
UNIFORM SIZE & SHAPE OBJECTS	1,500	7 Air Force Supply (Parts in Envelopes)	150	Envelope Dispenser	Manual	Machine Read Punchcards	Automatic Release of Envelopes From Dispensers	NA	NA
	3,500	11 Department Store Chain (Garments on Hangers)	*	Hanger Flow Rod	Manual	Machine Read Punchcards	Automatic Release of Hung Garments From Flow Rods	Manually Encoded Escort Code on Monorail Carrier	Automatic Escort Code Readers
	1,000	12 Shirt Distributor (Shirts in Poly-Bags)	2,000	Carton Flow Rack	Manual	Visually Read Picking List	Manually From Conveyor to Vehicle	NA	NA

Fig. 17-27. Order selection at automatic warehouses.

			Case Flow Rack	Pallet Truck Contrl. Fm. Mast	Visually Read Picking List	Manually From Case to Towline Cart	Punchcard on Box Applied at Production Line	Computer and Automatic Punchcard Reader
12,000	13 Shoe Manufacturer (Shoes in Boxes)	50,000	Slide	Manual	Manually Operated Keyboard	Automatic Release of Items From Slides	NA	NA
2,000	14 Drug & Medical Supplies	90	Bin	Manual	Visually Read Picking List	Manually From Carrousel to Conveyor	NA	NA
800	15 Defense Supply Depot	2,000	Bin	Manual	Visually Read Picking List			
1,200	16 Auto Parts Distributor	20,000	Bin	Manual	Visually Read From Display Unit	Manually From Bin to Automatic Control Cart	Tape Programed Cart	Routing Control Units on Carts
1,500	8 Drugstore Supply	1,800	Shelf & Tray in Rack	Manually Operated Stacker Crane	Visually Read Picking List	Manually From Rack to Gather Shelf to Tray	Manually Read Invoices	Keyboard Operated Control Console
1,000		600	Bin	Manual	Visually Read From Display Unit	Manually From Bin to Gather Shelf to Tray		
2,500	17 Air Force Supply Depot	200,000	Bin	Manual	Visually Read Picking List	Manually From Bin to Tray	Manually Encoded Escort Code on Monorail Carrier	Automatic Escort Code Readers
10,000	18 Book Publisher	500,000	Shelf	Manual	Visually Read Picking List	Manually From Shelf to Tray	Manually Set Escort Codes on Trays	Automatic Escort Code Readers
50,000	19 Mail Order	500,000	Bin	Manual	Visually Read Label	Manually From Bin to Pushcart	Manually Applied Label on Item	Some Keyboard Control Sort and Assembly; Balance Manual

DIFFERENT SIZE & SHAPE OBJECTS

*Dresses allocated to stores immediately following receipt at warehouse — not held in stock.

NA - Not Applicable because orders are picked sequentially, one at a time, thereby avoiding problems of simultaneous multi-order picking.

Fig. 17-27. Order selection at automatic warehouses. (Reprinted by permission of the publisher from Order Selection, American Management Association, Management Bulletin No. 112, © 1968 by the American Management Association, p. 6.)

Basic Picking Method	Definition	Types of Stock Arrangement
Manual	Where warehousemen travel to picking locations, pick, and move items to the packing or shipping area. These operations are basically manual, although such simple devices as picking carts may be used. Manual picking may be combined with other warehouse functions to eliminate separate operations: 1. Picking may be combined with filling to eliminate separate checking. 2. Picking may be combined with packing to eliminate separate checking and packing. 3. Picking may be combined with labeling, when picked items are in shippable containers, to eliminate separate checking and overpacking.	Stock may be arranged according t stock (or item) number, popularit or at random. When according to popularity, stoc is arranged with the most popula items near the aisle and at the bes picking elevation. This may be moc fied to popularity by line or zone.
Mechanized	The introduction of mechanical devices to reduce the manual picking effort involved in any or all of the following: 1. Assisting pickers by bringing stock to them (as with gravity and powered storage). 2. Assisting pickers in the actual picking (as with portable elevators, powered picking trucks, cranes, etc.). 3. Assisting pickers in moving items to the packing or shipping area (as with electronically-controlled tractors, powered conveyor lines, etc.).	Most useful with popularity or moc fied popularity storage (see defir tions above) to minimize time p pick.
Automated	Whereas mechanized picking involves providing mechanical assistance to pickers, automated picking is the substitution of machinery ror pickers. Controls for recalling items from storage may be manually operated with automated order picking.	Automated picking usually is re served for most popular item Others may be arranged in any su able fashion.

Fig. 17–28. How manual, mechanized, and automated order–picking
Materials Handling,

Picking Techniques		
Type	Overall Description	Order Assembly Phase
Area	Pickers take each order, move through the warehouse, pick the customer requirement, and deposit the finished order in (or send it to) the packaging or shipping area. The stock can be arranged by stock (or item) number, by popularity, or at random. The arrangement is uniform throughout the warehouse. Area picking is used where there is low volume, few items, and small area.	Order assembly is built into the actual picking procedure. Orders as deposited at the packing or shipping area are already assembled.
Modified Area	Represented by a forward picking line combined with a bulk reserve stock area (often palletized).	Bulk picks from reserve, if any, must be combined to complete the order at the packing or shipping area.
Zone	Each picker is confined to one portion of the warehouse. Each picker picks part of an order. As soon as he deposits his part of an order in (or sends it to) the packing or shipping area, he starts on another order. Thus more than one order is worked on at a time in different zones, and each of the components of an order must be identified clearly to permit order assembly. Being limited to a zone, a picker becomes more familiar with the stock arrangement than with area picking.	Pickers deposit items at the packing or shipping area so as not to mix orders. Or, if conveyors are used to move items to the packing or shipping area, the items may be directed to different spots while en route to avoid mixing orders.
Modified Zone (Assembly Line Type)	Each picker is confined to one portion of the warehouse. Each picker picks part of an order. When his portion is completed, he sends it to the next zone, where the process is repeated. The next order is begun immediately after the first has cleared the first zone. Some picking delays may be introduced because of waiting for orders.	Order assembly is simplified as all containers on an order move to the packing or shipping area together.
Modified Zone (Roving Work Force)	Here pickers start in one zone, and pick requirements for an order from that zone. Then they move to a second zone, and repeat the process until the order is completed. This method is used when there is a low volume of orders in a warehouse set up for zone picking.	Order assembly is built into the actual picking procedure.
Multiple Order (Or Bulk)	Here a group of orders is collected and sorted by item and stock location. A cover sheet is prepared, listing total requirements for each item in picking sequence. This technique is adaptable to any type of stock arrangement. It can be used with both area and zone picking techniques. Each batch of orders is cleared from the picking area before the next batch is introduced. The method is particularly useful where individual orders are small, contain few line items, and have repetitive demand.	Each batch of picked stock is broken down into individual orders in a large order assembly area.
Area	The above basic picking techniques as described apply to manual and mechanized order picking. However, automated order picking incorporates the basic elements of the area picking technique, in that only one or a few orders are picked at a time from the entire area devoted to automated picking.	Order assembly with automated order picking involves merging parts of the same order and combining them at the packing or shipping area with any other portion of the order which may be picked from areas set aside for manual or mechanized picking.

systems compare for packaged, cartoned, or cased goods. (From *Modern* January 1963, pp. 48–49.)

control, and billing control) are concerned with the control and flow of information through useful channels.

Inventory control in a warehouse or production area by manual methods is time consuming and often unreliable, and it is difficult to continually have up-to-date figures available. Inventory control involves sensing, remembering and displaying counts of items. It may include items in storage, in process, in transit, or all three. The display may be continual, such as a mechanical counter displaying a running count of the number of each type of item in storage, or it may be typed out or visually presented on demand or periodically in which case the information is stored in some type of memory prior to presentation.

The subfunctions of inventory control are data presenting, data accumulating, and calculating. Data presenting can be accomplished with mechanical counters, electrically pulsed, that can count up or down; numerical indicating lights; decade counting tubes; or typewriters. Data accumulating can be accomplished with mechanical counters, two way stepping switches, static counters, or magnetic drums or tape. Calculating (add, subtract, multiply, and divide) can be carried out with arithmetic units built to accomplish specific operations, or by a general purpose industrial type computer, where it can be applied to the complete system.

When inventory control is to be used in a system incorporating any of the material handling control functions, some portion of the equipment to do this job may be present. For example, a manufacturer automatically dispatching his products to a number of storage areas may need to count them in and out of the storage areas to prevent jam-ups. Adding inventory control then requires only the addition of appropriate display equipment.

The data processing function of *billing control* is most closely associated with systems incorporating order picking. Information is readily available in the control system detailing the order and the actual items shipped (the order, less stock shortages). By adding equipment to type out this information, lists can be automatically made of items ordered, order shortages and items shipped. With the addition of computing equipment, or further programming of a computer already in use, the entire invoice can be typed out including the unit prices and the total.

Production control is a further extension of the inventory control and makes use of inventory figures to control or schedule production. The simplest type of production control is low-level indication. This control can be accomplished by one limit switch in each storage line operating a remote indicating light, or by receiving signals from counters associated with each line.

A more elaborate system of production control may use inventory figures read out on demand, or a complete inventory readout at the end of each day. The most elaborate approach would be a system with a computer combining inventory data with orders-received data to compute production schedules. This same computer could be the heart of the control system that would be needed to automatically dispatch, store and pick orders.

All of these data processing functions are partially accomplished by the control equipment needed to control the material flow. In most cases, the addition of some type of readout equipment will be all that is necessary to upgrade the system and provide the added function.

It is recognized that such descriptions as the above can never be up-to-date in a textbook. The information given here is intended primarily to give the reader an idea of what has been done, and provide a background for conceptualizing potential future systems for accomplishing similar purposes.

RELATIONSHIPS BETWEEN MATERIAL AND INFORMATION HANDLING

The interrelationships between the physical (handling) and information (control) aspects are shown in Figure 17–29, which is described by T. A. Keenan as follows:

. . . we look at the warehouse as having two separate but integrated systems, not one: accounting and handling.

The *accounting* functions include: (1) inventory control, (2) reorder point control, (3) order entry, (4) data logging, (5) data processing, (6) invoicing and billing, and (7) reports.

The physical or *handling* functions include: (1) receiving and identification, (2) sorting and routing, (3) storage, (4) order picking, (5) order accumulation, and (6) final loading and shipping.

These accounting and handling functions are basic building blocks of a completely automated warehouse.

Let's assume now that these building blocks are controlled by a central computer.

Receiving and identification: In these steps we have products accepted into the warehouse. We identify them as to style, size, code and quantity. This information goes to inventory control.

Inventory and replenishment control: Here are the keys to optimum inventory size, reduced back-orders, lower holding costs, and short order-picking time. As product is identified in receiving, the computer's memory is updated. The product is assigned a location and is then sent to the sorting and routing block.

The computer thus can know currently what is coming in, how much of what is on hand, and where, and when to re-order how much.

Sorting and dispatching: The mix of incoming products is accumulated in batches for economical movement to storage. When pre-determined batch sizes are reached, they move to the computer-assigned storage locations.

Storage: Two things happen in the storage block. Either the computer notes that an incoming product is on-order for that day's shipment and directs it to an on-order area to avoid double handling, or it notes that the product is not on order and directs it to be put into stock. Order entry tells the computer which is which.

Order entry: This block feeds data to many points in the system. The computer searches inventory to see if the order can be filled. If so, the order goes to billing and invoicing while, at the same time, the warehouse gets instructions for filling the order. If the order can't be filled, this fact is printed-out so a decision can be made as to whether or not to ship a partial order.

When an order is entered, of course, the product on it is removed from the inventory available category.

Order picking: While billing and invoicing process the paperwork the warehouse picks and moves the product.

Order accumulation: This block receives the product, sorts it into specific customer orders, and releases it to final loading and shipping. At the release

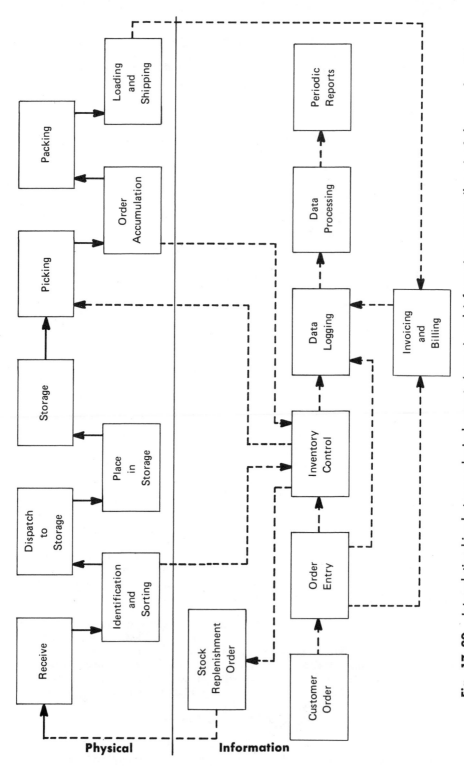

Fig. 17-29. Interrelationships between physical aspects (*upper*) and information aspects (*lower*) of the warehousing function.

point, the amounts of products are deleted from the computer's memory as having left the warehouse.

Invoice and billing: As each order is picked, its paperwork is prepared in time to meet the order at the dock.

Final loading and shipment: In this block, computer control is not essential. It can range from manual to automatic. If it were under computer control, however, the computer could direct the order to the loading area, and could issue the loading logic needed.

Data logging and processing: To combine information into useful figures for management use, these blocks take all accounting data from all generating blocks, log it into the computer and then process it.

Daily, weekly, and monthly reports: Thanks to the computer's ability to sift quickly through mountains of data, complete and current reports can be issued whenever management needs to see the entire operation in detail.

But it should by no means be inferred that these building blocks can form only a computerized system. A facility can range from a brute-force, manual operation to a highly sophisticated one, using the same building blocks.[11]

If a warehouse installation were to be *completely* automated, all of the functions and activities implied in Figure 17–29 would be performed by self-regulating mechanisms and controls in such a way that *no* human intervention would be necessary—from receipt and unloading of goods, through the loading of customer orders, including *all* aspects of information flow and record keeping.

SELECTING APPROPRIATE EQUIPMENT

With the bewildering array of equipment possibilities facing the engineer, the task of selecting the *right* equipment for a specific situation can become an awesome task. Chapter 11 has previously dealt with the selection of material handling equipment and suggested that the selection should be based on a comparison of *move* requirements with *equipment* capabilities, by considering certain factors.

A more complete list of factors for the automated warehousing equipment selection problem is shown in Fig. 17–30, collected from throughout the text. The task of the analyst is to evaluate the more significant factors in terms of the feasibility of implementing the mechanization and/or automation of the segment of the warehousing system under consideration.

DESIGN PROCEDURE

Once it has been determined that warehouse automation appears worthy of more than casual interest, it is wise to begin the feasibility study portion of the overall design procedure. This might well begin

---

[11] Adapted from T. A. Keenan, "The Building Blocks of Automated Warehousing," *Modern Materials Handling*, Dec., 1964, p. 38.

A. *Material* or *Handling* Unit Parameters
   1. type
   2. shape
   3. dimensions
   4. weight
   5. items/handling unit
   6. handl. units/tot. quantity
   7. crush resistance
   8. total volume
   9. no. of items
  10. volume/item
  11. fluctuation
  12. receipt characteristics
  13. order characteristics
  14. machine handleable
  15. palletizable

B. *Move* Parameters
   1. quantity
   2. frequency
   3. origin and destination
   4. loading level
   5. unloading level
   6. distance
   7. handlings/item
   8. area covered
   9. path
  10. cross traffic
  11. running surface
  12. headroom

C. *Storage Space* Parameters
   1. method
   2. clear height
   3. floor load capacity
   4. floor characteristics
   5. overhead load capacity
   6. ramp or elevator
   7. environment
   8. column spacing

D. *Cost* Factors
   1. investment required
   2. start-up costs
   3. operating costs
   4. return on investment
   5. space savings
   6. cost of capital
   7. depreciation policy

E. *Other* Factors
   1. flexibility
   2. adaptability
   3. expansion
   4. long range plans
   5. maintenance
   6. obsolescence
   7. capacity
   8. possibility of dual system

Fig. 17–30. Factors for consideration in selecting automated warehousing equipment.

with a reconsideration of the desired goals to be met by the potential system. The overall objective might be stated as:

> the mechanization of that portion of the overall warehousing activity which will economically accomplish the most important of the benefits which it is hoped will be realized.

Such a feasibility study might then proceed somewhat as follows:

1. Conceptualize the entire physical distribution system of which the warehousing activity under consideration is only a part.
2. Establish functional relationships between warehouse activity and the overall system.

3. Identify and delimit individual warehousing functions (as on page 544 of this chapter).
4. Review "factors", etc. indicated throughout the chapter.
5. Determine areas of excess cost, or cost reduction targets.
6. Establish cost of each.
7. Conduct a preliminary investigation of the mechanization potential of the functions selected for consideration.
8. Review (visit, look up, etc.) examples of existing mechanization of similar functions—through vendors, associates, friends, etc.
9. Gather data necessary for subsequent stages of the project.

One way of carrying out an evaluation of areas open to improvement through mechanization might be to develop a list of expected benefits from the proposed installations, such as:

1. Improved customer service
2. Reduced warehousing cost
3. Centralized warehousing function
4. Reduction in damage, spoilage, pilferage
5. Smaller inventory
6. Better inventory control
7. Integration of warehousing function with E.D.P. system
8. Adaptability to future products
9. Ease of expansion

and others, as appropriate. Each of the above would then be evaluated against the possible methods of accomplishment and the expected cost of implementation.

For example, the analyst might adapt the procedures outlined in Chapter 14, and/or he might develop an approach similar to that suggested in Fig. 17–31.

Having determined some measure of the value to be derived from an automated warehousing installation, a decision can be made as to whether or not to proceed further with the investigation. If the decision is positive, a thorough systems-type project design procedure should be initiated, as outlined in Chapter 9.

DESIGN GUIDE LINES

In developing the automated warehousing system, the designer should pay careful attention to such general guide lines as: [12]

1. Design for *flow*, not storage: An automated warehouse is primarily an order servicing facility and not a stockpile.

[12] Numbers 1, 2 and 7 adapted from J. M. Delfs, *op. cit.* Numbers 3 to 6 adapted from J. C. Wolff, privately circulated notes on "Automated Warehousing Concepts."

Objectives to be Realized, in order of importance	Potential Methods of Accomplishing Objectives	Bases for Evaluation of Accomplishment	Economics of Accomplishment	
			Cost factors to be investigated	Potential Savings from Installation
1. Improved customer service	—faster and more accurate order picking	—time/order; reduced complaints; number of errors	—orders/hour; cost/complaint; cost/error	—goodwill; "saved" customers; reduced cost of handling complaints and errors
2. Reduced manpower	—mechanized dispatching to storage; placing in storage; order picking; order accumulation	—number of men (10) now used vs. (1) trouble shooter and mechanic	—manpower cost	—9 men X $7000/yr. = $63,000/yr.

Fig. 17–31. Preliminary analysis of automated warehousing feasibility.

2. Design for balanced flow: All planning and equipment should be aimed at eliminating bottlenecks and assuring rapid flow of goods through the system.

3. Plan to batch orders for more efficient order picking of larger quantities of specific line items.

4. Design system to bring work to the man, rather than vice versa. Men walking cost more than goods moving.

5. Design manual effort out of the system—in walking, stocking and order picking.

6. Design to permit combining functions—such as identification, inspection, sorting, etc., merchandise *during* a move.

7. *Don't* try to copy someone else's warehouse design. No two problems are alike in their details, and a project of the scope implied here deserves a "custom" treatment. However, it *is* wise to incorporate the experience of others—in terms of segments of other systems appropriate to the project at hand.

8. Retain as much flexibility as possible. An initial investment in an automated system may be the beginning of a long-range program —overlapping periods of change in lines, products, distribution methods, etc.

9. Don't strangle vendors with tight specifications. Leave them room for creativity and innovation.
10. Don't overlook the possibility of a dual system, part automated and part only mechanized.
11. Don't mechanize everything. Some items, in nearly every situation, will not warrant mechanization. They can best be handled manually.
12. Don't mechanize for the sake of mechanization! Some functions may not justify mechanization and should be carried out in the least costly manner.
13. Plan for progressive mechanization. A long-range plan, partially implemented, then subsequently developed through pre-planned stages, may be the best way to get started.

A careful review of this chapter—as well as of others—will suggest additional guidelines applicable to specific problem situations.

EVOLUTIONARY PHASES OF WAREHOUSE MECHANIZATION

As suggested above, it may be wise to formulate a long-range plan, and then proceed, step by step, to implement it. For example, the phases might be somewhat as follows: [13]

1. Individual order—lowest volume, highest unit cost
   a. Individual handling
   b. Individual stock picking
   c. Individual packing and loading
2. Departmentalized—moderate volume, high unit cost
   a. Individual handling
   b. Stock picking by department
   c. Semi-automatic machines
   d. Handpicking and loading
3. Progressive—medium volume, medium unit cost
   a. Individual handling
   b. Semi-automatic and automatic machines
   c. Partial straight-line stock picking and packaging
   d. Hand loading
4. Conveyorized—high volume, moderate unit cost
   a. Conveyor handling of items between processing points
   b. Straight-line stock picking and packing
   c. Hand loading
5. Automation—highest volume, lowest unit cost
   a. Automatic straight-line stock picking and packing
   b. Automatic handling of items

[13] Yale Brozen, "Putting Economics and Automation in Perspective," *Automation*, April 1964, p. 30.

c. Automatic control
d. Continuous flow
e. Mechanized loading

Again it can be seen how a different approach can give an entirely different impression. The above list also illustrates the point that there are really no *distinct* levels of warehouse automation. Each level is actually a combination of levels, as is the general case in the installation examples found in this chapter.

COST ASPECTS OF AUTOMATED WAREHOUSING

If there is one outstanding feature of automated warehousing, it is the expense involved including the risk-investment relationships. And, although the somewhat staggering amounts of money often needed may be a psychological barrier, a relatively small expense can reduce the risk element very substantially. Joel C. Wolff [14] suggests the relationships shown in Figure 17–32, which indicates that a small amount of money, invested in a careful preliminary analysis, can greatly reduce the risk involved in proceeding with further development of the system.

One of the more common ways of evaluating warehouse savings is in terms of space utilization. One aspect of space utilization is the cost per opening (in a rack-based system), as shown on the graph in Figure 17–33.

A Case History

In order to give some idea of the method of approach and the type of data required, the following example is presented: [15]

To develop and evaluate alternate methods for meeting requirements, a warehousing operation was divided into the following eight suboperations:

1. Receive packaging materials.
2. Move materials from receiving to storage.
3. Store materials.
4. Move materials from storage to packaging lines.
5. Handle materials on packaging lines.
6. Move finished goods from packaging to storage.
7. Store finished goods.
8. Move finished goods to order filling area.

[14] Wolff, *op. cit.*
[15] Drake Sheahan/Stewart Dougall, "Management of Materials Handling Automation," Memorandum 137, privately circulated.

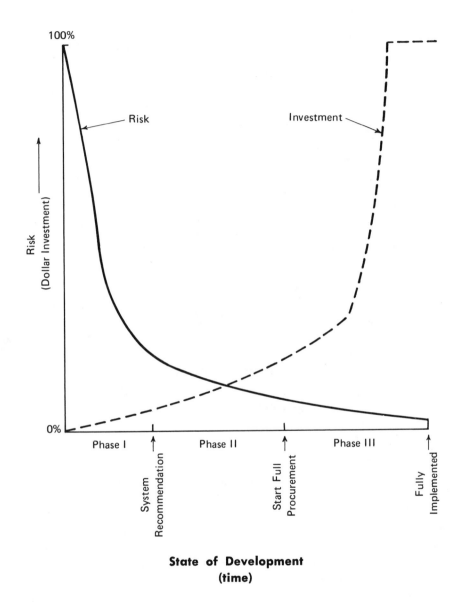

Fig. 17–32. Risk-investment relationship. (From J. C. Wolff, *Automated Warehousing Concepts,* notes circulated privately.)

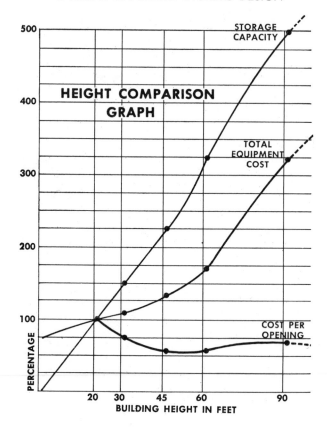

Fig. 17–33. Economical height of stacker system in relation to costs. (From D. Bowman, "The Future of Material Handling," *Plant Engineering,* October 17, 1968.)

From each suboperation, a series of subsystems was developed. For example, for item 3, "Store materials," four subsystems were worked out. One was conventional (fork lift trucks, pallets, and pallet racks). Three were fully or partly automatic (stacker cranes, live-pallet conveyors, and live-container conveyors). Costs were estimated for the equipment, space, and labor for each subsystem, as shown on page 591.

Storage and handling cost estimates per pallet load (or equivalent) for the four subsystems are tabulated and plotted on Figures 17–34 and 17–35, and show that handling costs tend to be higher for non-automated systems, that is, systems which are less mechanized and therefore require more labor. Storage costs per day, however, are higher for automated systems. In other words, automated systems are best when stock turns

Equipment

		Cost
1. *Conventional floor and pallet rack.*		
1,150 pallet rack openings		$ 11,500
[2] 2,000-pound fork lift trucks		16,000
11,200 pallets		40,500
		$ 68,000
2. *Stacker cranes.*		
10,000 stacker crane pallet openings and required cranes		715,500
1 fork lift truck		8,000
11,200 pallets		40,500
		$ 764,000
3. *Live pallet.*		
10,000 live rack spots and		
11,200 pallets		$ 600,000
1 fork lift truck		8,000
		$ 608,000
4. *Live container.*		
330,000 container spots (equivalent to 10,000 palletloads)		$1,065,000
1 fork lift truck		8,000
		$1,073,000

Space

	Square feet
1. *Conventional floor and pallet rack.*	
1,150 pallets in racks	12,000
8,850 floor spots	69,500
Main and cross aisles	20,500
	102,000
2. *Stacker crane.*	
10,000 stacker crane spots and service aisles	48,000
Main and cross aisles	12,000
	60,000
3. *Live pallet.*	
10,000 live pallet spots and service aisles	88,000
Main and cross aisles	22,000
	110,000
4. *Live container.*	
330,000 containers (10,000 pallets)	48,000
Main and cross aisle	12,000
	60,000

Labor

	Conventional	Stacker cranes	Live pallet	Live container
Assistant stock locator	2	1	1	4
Fork truck driver	2	1	1	1
Laboratory pool leadman	1	1	1	1
Closeout leadman	1	1	1	1
Total	6	4	4	7

Fig. 17–34. Cost estimates for the equipment required for each subsystem. (Courtesy of Drake Sheahan/Stewart Dougall.)

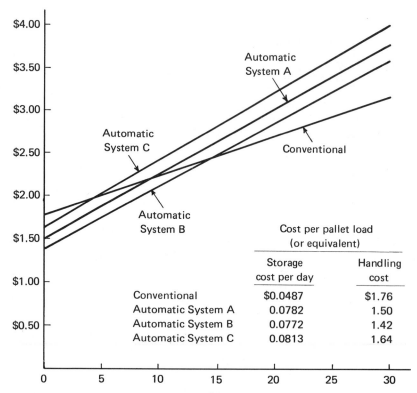

Fig. 17–35. Graphical representation of the costs of each subsystem. (Courtesy of Drake Sheahan/Stewart Dougall.)

over rapidly and when the expensive automatic equipment is being used frequently.

Finally, the various subsystems were put together into 20 different complete systems. Cost estimates are shown for the system that was found to be best and was therefore recommended (Figure 17–36) and for the fully automated system (Figure 17–37).

TRENDS IN WAREHOUSE MECHANIZATION

Although the mechanization and/or automation of storage and warehousing activities is growing rapidly, it will probably never be practicable in many, many situations. Nevertheless, the alert warehouseman should keep up with the trend towards mechanization and make his long-range plans in such a way that he can accommodate the next level of mechani-

Suboperations	Equipment (initial cost)	Space (square feet)	Labor	Total annual cost
1. Receive packaging materials. Palletize at truck dock	$ 8,000		8	$ 65,600
2. Move materials from receiving to storage by electronic, driverless tractor-trailer.	23,000		1	12,600
3. Store palletloads on floor and in pallet racks.	68,000	102,000	6	163,600
4. Move palletloads from storage, and place in live-pallet picking section. Pick containers manually, and place on conveyors to packaging lines.	129,000	2,500	5	68,300
5. Handle materials on packaging lines as at present.			12	96,000
6. Move finished goods from packaging to storage by conveyor. Palletize by automatic palletizing equipment.	89,000		2	33,800
7. Store palletloads of finished goods in floor storage.	7,600	41,000	5½	86,500
8. Move palletloads of finished goods to pallet racks near order-assembly lines. Manually pick containers onto pallets for peddling to order-assembly bins.	32,000		4	38,400
Total	$356,600	145,500	43½	$564,800

Fig. 17–36. Cost estimate for the recommended system. (Courtesy of Drake Sheahan/Stewart Dougall.)

Suboperations	Equipment (initial cost)	Space (square feet)	Labor	Total annual cost
1. Receive packaging materials. Palletize at truck dock.	$ 8,000		8	$ 65,600
2. Move materials from receiving to storage by electronic, driverless tractor-trailer.	23,000		1	12,600
3. Store palletloads on floor and in pallet racks.	68,000	102,000	6	163,600
4. Move palletloads from storage, and place in live-pallet picking section. Pick containers manually, and place on conveyors to packaging lines.	129,000	2,500	5	68,300
5. Handle materials on packaging lines as at present			12	96,000
6. Move finished goods from packaging to storage by conveyor.	110,000		3	46,000
7. Store containers of finished goods in live-container racks.	416,000	30,000	5½	157,200
8. Manually pick containers from live-container racks, and place on pallets for peddling to order-assembly bins.	32,000		4	38,400
Total	$786,000	134,500	44½	$647,700

Fig. 17–37. Cost estimate for the automated finished goods system. (Courtesy of Drake Sheahan/Stewart Dougall.)

zation when it *does* become feasible for his own operation. Listed here are some of the trends he should keep a close watch on:

a. The *high-lift fork truck,* storing (with or without racks) up to 30 feet.

b. The *narrow aisle truck,* cutting aisle space about in half and increasing warehouse space utilization.

c. The *remote-control order-picking lift truck,* greatly speeding order picking in dense, high stacks of materials.

d. *Remote or radio control* of tractor-trailer trains, lift trucks, stacker cranes and conveyors.
e. Development of *automatically dispatched truck-tow conveyors,* enabling platform trucks to be dispatched and discharged automatically throughout a large warehouse.
f. The *stacker crane,* offering storage heights of 60 ft in minimum aisles (3–5 in. wider than the load).
g. The development of *gravity flow racks,* providing continuous availability of items to an order picking line.
h. *Automated order picking,* linking the flow rack, stacker crane, etc. to a take-away conveyor as triggered by an order card or a computer.
i. *Automatic palletizers,* linking the factory to the warehouse.
j. *Mechanization of packing* and strapping.
k. *Conveyorized order assembly,* and automatic dispatch of shipments to carrier locations.
l. *Order processing by computer* and its application to picking, packing, and shipment activities, is eliminating delays once caused by preparation of paper work.
m. The *rise of automation in the production process,* resulting in systems producing so fast that the warehousing and shipping systems *must* be mechanized to accommodate the high flow of goods.

These developments in mechanization have led to explicit, aggressive efforts to create "automatic warehouses." While critical examination shows that only a few of these truly justify their title, there is no question but that these pioneering efforts have inspired and warned the rest of industry to advance their distribution system mechanization.

THE FUTURE OF AUTOMATED WAREHOUSING

Automated warehousing is not a panacea for all physical-distribution, warehousing, or customer-service ills. Nevertheless, it opens up wide vistas of cost reduction, increased efficiency, and imagination. For example, there is no *technological* reason why an entire warehousing-distribution system could not be totally automated somewhat as follows:

Warehouse of the Future

A customer in the men's department of a large department store selects a white shirt: oxford weave, button-down collar, size 15 neck, 34 inch sleeve. Upon presenting the item to the clerk, a tag is removed and inserted into the men's department bookkeeping machine along with the customer's universal credit card. At one and the same time the customer's bank account is automatically debited for the value of the shirt and the department store account is credited for the same amount (no cash changes hands, no billing is involved). Meanwhile, in the department store's central computer, the shirt inventory is reduced by 1, and the data is transmitted to the warehouse some distance away to be added to a continually accumulating shortage list of items in the men's department. At the exact moment when the computer has calculated that there is either a sufficient shortage of a reasonable number of items, or a "standard unit load" of items needed in the men's department, the computer triggers the picking of the entire order and/or unit load. The items picked are automatically subtracted from the warehouse inventory, and at the same time, proper information is transmitted to the supplier's factories so that their computers are accumulating orders either for picking from their stock or for initiating production orders.

Back at the department store warehouse, conveyors consolidate the order for the men's department in the packing area where an automatic "unitizer" constructs a unit load for delivery to the men's department. The unit load order is dispatched to a staging area awaiting the accumulation of one trailer load for the department store. Upon arrival of the last unit load, which will fill the truck trailer, a trailer which has been parked in the adjacent yard is triggered to back up to the warehouse door, following an electronic path, and requiring no driver. Upon approaching the warehouse door, proximity switches actuate the doors of both the warehouse and the trailer. When the trailer makes contact, it releases into the trailer the group of unit loads destined for the store. When the trailer is loaded, doors close and the trailer is dispatched to the department store dock following another electronic path through the city—still without a driver. Upon reaching the department store, the sequence of events is reversed and the trailer is unloaded. Individual unit load orders are dispatched directly to the departments concerned by means of a built-in handling system. In the men's department, the unit load is disassembled by sales personnel (alas, people *are* necessary!) and the "replacement" white shirt is put on the shelf ready for another customer.

As suggested earlier, there is nothing implied in the preceding illustration which is not feasible. In fact every concept implied is in operation at some location as a part of an existing system. The primary reason no department store has implemented such a system is the cost! When each of the individual segments of the system envisioned is in great enough demand, the price will be low enough so that all of the segments can be economically combined.

Even though such systems may not be available in the immediate future, very worthwhile cost savings, better customer service, better inventory control, and many other advantages are still obtainable through warehouse mechanization and automation. As Delfs has stated: [16] "They are available to all who are willing to make the necessary investment in analysis of their problem and planning for their solution."

CONCLUSION

In conclusion, a few general statements can be made, more or less summarizing the automated warehousing situation, as it exists today, some of which are "borrowed" from Chapter 9, on the systems concept.

1. A project of the magnitude implied by automated warehousing requires much—and early—planning.
2. Plan for a total system, but with the possibility of implementation by stages.
3. There will still be "gray" areas of fact, feasibility, and costs.
4. Much of the equipment needed is currently on the market.
5. New developments will continue to be made in the "hardware" of individual functions.
6. Many of today's warehouses were built for "manual" operation, and may not be adaptable to automation.
7. Carefully consider lesser improvements in the present warehouse —but from the systems point of view.
8. People acceptance is an extremely important factor in successful operation.

REFERENCES

The information contained in the section of this chapter on "The Means of Mechanization" (p. 562) was adapted and/or quoted from the following sources:

Automation
    "Automatic Warehousing—The Means," H. C. Keller, December 1959
    "Automated Material Control," D. W. Shenton and H. Gleixner, January 1961
General Electric Co. bulletins
    "Automated Warehousing," D. W. Shenton and H. Gleixner
    "Automatic Warehousing—Why, Where, and How?" unpublished notes by J. M. Delfs
Modern Materials Handling
    "Warehouse Automation—How Much is Justified?," R. J. Sweeney, January 1963
    "How Automated Warehousing Systems Work," January 1963
    "Magnetic Belt Coding," April 1963

[16] Delfs, *op. cit.*

Other articles, not directly quoted, but covering similar material are:

"Controlling Order Picking Systems," D. W. Shenton, *Automation*, May 1962

"Automatic Controls for Material Handling," in *Materials Handling Engineering Handbook and Directory*, 1967–68 edition, pp. 132–143

"The Building Blocks of Automated Warehousing," T. A. Keenan, *Modern Materials Handling*, December 1964

"Photo Electric Code Readers," C. S. Vincent, Jr., *Modern Materials Handling*, March 1966.

18

Physical Distribution

When the sales department receives an order, it triggers a chain of events aimed at fulfilling that order. Three kinds of classic economic events must take place to satisfy the customer's desire.

First, materials must be given the characteristics ordered. Form, shape, and physical nature must be modified by the factory, i.e., the materials are given *form utility* through the manufacturing process.

Second, the product must be moved from the factory into the customer's hands. This change of location provides another basic value: *place utility.*

Third, the above events must occur quickly enough to satisfy the customer (or even to create, in the first place, conditions that encourage the sale). Thus *time utility* becomes an essential goal of the satisfaction process.

To improve time and place utility, to provide sales assistance, and to reduce manufacturing costs, many firms anticipate and plan elements of this sequence. Therefore, they manufacture large lots in advance of actual orders; and they may move these goods from factory premises to regional warehouses or to a nationwide store system in order to enhance time and place utility. This anticipation of the location and timing of demand usually involves shipments of large quantities to reduce transportation and handling costs; but this action then results in inventory levels that may require weeks or months to consume. And so inventory costs rise. Here we see the beginnings of the dilemmas of physical distribution. Contrast, for the moment, physical distribution and manufacturing.

Manufacturing is a complex affair involving many activities. To optimize these activities, manufacturing is largely integrated under a single authority and a single roof. The creation of form utility—manufacturing

—commonly is closely planned, controlled, and interrelated to provide necessary results at minimum cost. Manufacturing locations are chosen to optimize contributing costs such as transportation, labor, taxes, and power. There is one manager responsible for the total activity.

What about the creation of time and place utility—distribution? Are these economic functions under a single authority? Are their component activities integrated? Are they performed in a manner that optimizes customer satisfaction and vendor cost? The answer is painfully obvious for most firms . . . and oddly enough, for apparently logical reasons.

Since the distance between factory, warehouse, and customer's premises is measured in miles (or even continents) it cannot take place under one roof. Material movement to customers usually radiates in many directions from the factory; hence it is diffused geographically, and management authority becomes even more fragmented because of technical reasons. Physical distribution involves different technical activities which must be performed by specialists with the necessary functional skills. These functions may include:

1. Distribution planning
2. Requirements forecasting
3. Materials control
4. Materials storage (incoming materials and supplies)
5. Production scheduling
6. Transportation planning
7. Inventory planning and control
8. Consumer packaging
9. Order processing
10. Warehousing (finished goods, in-plant and in the field)
    —Receiving
    —Identification and sorting
    —Dispatching to storage
    —Placing in storage
    —Storage
    —Order picking
    —Order accumulation
    —Protective packing
    —Loading and shipping
    —Record keeping
11. Communications system
12. Facilities location and planning
    —Plants
    —Warehouses
    —Distribution centers
13. Raw materials and finished goods handling methods
14. Traffic
15. Customer service
16. Raw materials and finished goods transportation

These functions, collectively termed physical distribution management, are defined by the National Council on Physical Distribution Management as follows: ". . . the broad range of activities concerned with the efficient movement of finished products from the end of the production line to the consumer, and in some cases includes the movement of raw materials from the source of supply to the beginning of the production line."

Since the whole area of physical distribution management is relatively new as an academic discipline, it will be found that the function—or variations of it—will be referred to as:

1. Business logistics
2. Physical supply
3. Materials management
4. Market supply
5. Distribution logistics
6. Total distribution
7. Rhocrematics

The entire physical distribution process might be visualized as was shown in Figure 2–1, which depicts the overall material flow cycle—from source of raw materials, through manufacturing and distribution to the customer, including the "feedback" of waste, scrap, etc., into the cycle again. More specific interrelationships among the individual aspects of physical distribution are shown in Figure 18–1, the total physical distribution system.

Unfortunately, the activities traditionally included in physical distribution report to different functions of the firm, whose objectives are frequently at odds with each other, as Figure 18–2 indicates. Furthermore, the traditional accounting system frequently aggravates the problem by collecting costs related to the functions previously listed and assigning them to *several* managers, while burying some costs in overhead. This can be seen by taking the typical organization structure of a manufacturing enterprise and "distributing" the physical distribution activities among its functions, where they might be commonly found, as shown in Figure 18–3.

It is interesting to note that "Management had earlier rationalized its production problem, and gained control of efficiency in its factories, through the application of . . . scientific management . . . (and that) even today . . . management exercises no equivalent control over physical distribution." [1] However, today's efforts in the area of physical distribution management *are* seeking to place this heterogeneous and diffused activity, with its divided responsibilities, under one authority, and to

[1] J. F. Spencer in "The Inevitable New Structure of Management," in Presidential Issue, *Handling and Shipping*, Fall 1968, p. 7.

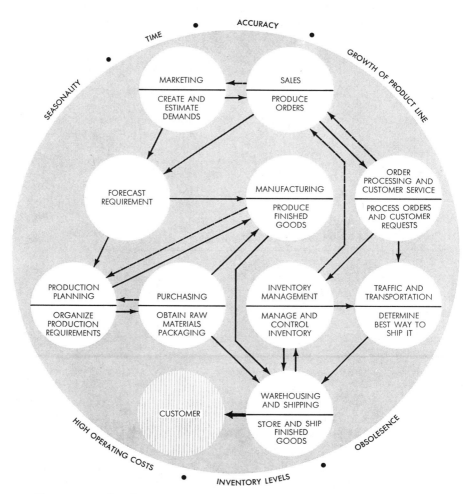

Fig. 18–1. Total physical distribution system. (From Alfred Opengart, "The Challenge of Physical Distribution," *Journal of Industrial Engineering,* January 1968.)

plan and operate them so as to provide adequate satisfaction at minimum cost.

WHY THE PHYSICAL DISTRIBUTION MANAGEMENT CONCEPT IS GROWING

Distribution is becoming more important because of its great economic significance and its competitive importance to firms with high-volume, multi-product, multi-customer activities. At the same time, there are a

Production	Transportation	Sales	Control & Finance
—Prompt removal of finished goods	—High-volume shipments	—Product availability	—Minimum inventories in process and finished goods
—Long runs	—Full carrier loads	—Fast shipment of any order	—Fast billing
—Few setup changes	—Lowest freight rates	—Production responsive to orders of any size	—Minimum cost in each department
—Uniform production rates		—All product variations immediately produced on demand	—Accurate and timely data
—Adequate lead time		—Fast order processing	
		—Minimum damage	

Fig. 18–2. Varying objectives of organizational functions commonly involved in physical distribution.

number of factors in the economic and technical environments that are changing distribution practices, or are altering elements of the distribution activities. Some of the major influences are discussed in the paragraphs that follow.

1. Physical Distribution Costs

As manufacturing costs have dropped through managerial concern and technical progress (such as simplified product design, lower material costs, automation, and improved methods) distribution costs appear to be a relatively more significant factor in total product cost. It has been estimated that the annual cost of physical distribution activity in the United States amounts to over 150 billion dollars. However, the cost of physical distribution varies with industries, products, and volumes, as well as by geographical areas and countries. The U.S. Department of Commerce has reported that, in the United States, each dollar the customer spent had a distribution cost component as follows:

Out of $1.00 Spent for	Total Distribution Percentage, Including Advertising
Food	18½%
Auto parts	27
Department store (chains)	43
Variety store (chains)	49

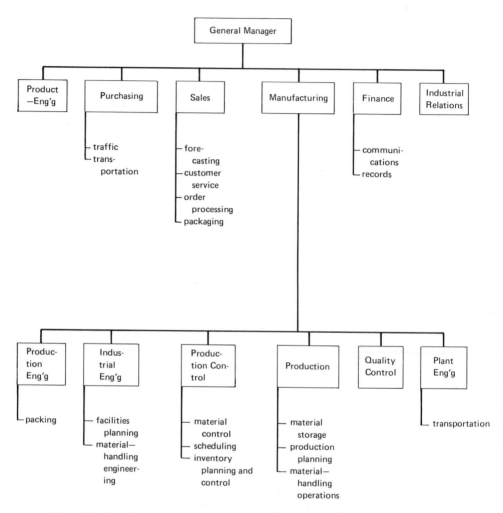

Fig. 18–3. Scattered organizational locations of physical distribution functions.

The Wall Street Journal reported that among food, clothing, and consumer products the total distribution cost was 20 to 50 percent of the sales dollar (including advertising). For appliances, 20 percent went for transportation and warehousing alone!

Distribution Age magazine surveyed physical distribution costs in 10,000 firms in six major industry groups and found that the sum of transportation, warehousing, materials handling, and shipping room expenses (far from a complete list of distribution costs) averaged over three years as follows:

Industry	Physical Distribution Cost as Percent of Manufacturer's Selling Price
Machinery	9.8%
Wood products and furniture	16.1
Paper and paper products	16.7
Chemicals, petroleum, rubber products	23.1
Primary and fabricated metals	26.4
Food and food products	29.6

The significance of these figures increases in their relationship to profit. Consider the food industry with a transportation and warehousing cost of 2 percent of the sales dollar. Profits in this industry run about 1½ percent of gross sales. Thus if transportation and warehousing costs can be cut 25 percent, it amounts to a 33 percent increase in profits! Or consider a firm with total distribution costs of 100 million dollars making 5 percent savings on distribution. This savings will equal the profit on perhaps $50 million dollars additional sales! Many firms are just beginning to realize the sizable costs of moving their product to the customer—and the opportunities for savings.

2. Changing Patterns of Distribution

Distribution patterns are changing, due to pressures from social, economic and technical sources. These trends are complex and interrelated, but some stand out as having major effects on distribution activities.

Consumer Demand for Product Variation. Years ago appliances came in one color—white. Today they are available in a dozen colors and special trims. Similarly, soap, toilet tissue, light bulbs, bathroom fixtures, kitchen sinks, and many other consumer products are available in different decorative motifs. Color, alone, has multiplied many product lines six-fold. The numbers of product sizes, styles, capacities, and features of traditional products have multiplied. Auto manufacturers report that tens of thousands of different models are possible by combinations of *standard* components, colors, and accessories.

The flavors of foods and beverages, the sizes and quantities of packaged goods and the growth of numbers of products due to manufacture from new materials has added to product variety. Thus the chain store grocery warehouse of a dozen years ago, which carried about 3,500–4,000 items, must stock over 8,000 items today. Improved transportation and preservation techniques add even more regional and seasonal specialties to many grocery store product lines. And a mail order catalog may require the warehousing of 100,000 items!

The numbers of new durable products in the home and the factory have multiplied. In 1940 the refrigerator, vacuum cleaner, stove, washing machine and radio were the common appliances. The same home today is likely to have added a freezer, dryer, dishwasher, ironer, TV set, as well as powered toothbrushes, carving knives, lawn mowers, snow blowers, razors, home workshop tools, hair dryers, clock-radios, and similar items.

This explosion of product lines has had profound effects on distribution:

  a. A vast increase in stock items to be supplied and stored.
  b. Hence, fewer numbers (or relatively fewer) of many individual items are needed. Shipping volumes of each item are lower.
  c. For any given volume of goods, order picking becomes a bigger part of order filling. The associated clerical work expands.
  d. A rise in inventory levels required to satisfy the same sales volume automatically occurs. John Magee of Arthur D. Little, Inc., cites a striking example: [2] Consider three items—B, C, D, substituted as variations of item A with the same total sales volume distributed as 60 percent B, 30 percent C, and 10 percent D. Experience shows that field inventory requirements probably will rise about 60 percent! If sales volume increases 50 percent, then inventory requirements tend to double. If it costs 20 percent per year to carry inventory, the inventory cost per unit sold would increase 30 percent. And much of the cost is due to field inventories of the small-volume items.
  e. Production runs may be shorter, with attendant changeover costs.

Changes in Retail Outlets. With the growth of supermarkets and the decline of the corner grocery store, the number of retail stores is decreasing. For example, in 1955 Pillsbury supplied 5000 customer stores; by 1965 these had declined to some 2300 outlets. Also, the explosive growth of the "discount" store has had its impact on the retailing field. But as today's retail outlets are larger and move as much volume as regional distributors once did, there is a tendency to ship from factory to retailer, and to bypass the distributor and his warehouse. It follows that order filling on a far more detailed, larger scale is required of the manufacturer. Order filling is pushed back toward the factory, and may even become a part of factory cost.

Changes in Inventory Policy. There is increasing cost consciousness in retailing as well as in industry, and labor cost is no longer the only or major cost target. Materials, including the cost of carrying inventory,

[2] John Magee, "The Logistics of Distribution," *Harvard Business Review*, July–August, 1960, pp. 90–91.

have now become a serious management concern. Everyone—manufacturer, distributor, retailer, and customer—is seeking to cut inventory levels and still have adequate supplies on hand. Coupled with the technical progress to be discussed shortly, this means a demand for more frequent and faster small-lot shipments.

Competition Through Customer Service. The intensity of competition and cost consciousness have led to demands for better customer service. Shorter order filling time is expected by both industrial and domestic customers. Furthermore, any supplier who does not come reasonably close to matching his fastest competitor on order filling service is bound to lose out.

Reduced Flexibility in Pricing. New legislation, consumer pressures, and court decisions all contribute to the confusion of pricing practices and policies. Each, in turn, has its effect on physical distribution activities.

3. Technical Progress

Technological progress has compounded the pressures for change in the distribution system. Data processing has been a prime mover in change. Since the late 1950's the computer and its communication networks have tied the information function of distribution into an integrated system. With almost instantaneous responsiveness as to the status of stocks, their location and demand, the computer reveals needs, enables faster movement directives, and hence changes stocking practices. As a result physical goods are stored and moved in different patterns and time schedules than in the past.

The computer has also facilitated the solving of complex problems.[3] Distribution problems such as the optimum numbers and locations of warehouses, the best combinations of transportation systems to satisfy time and cost standards of delivery service, the levels of inventory stocks, and the effects of different delivery schedules, production schedules and similar logistic decisions can be rapidly modeled, computed and evaluated. Indeed, the whole concept of *simulation* (i.e., of modeling distribution systems and of simulating changes in schedules, inventory policies, stock levels, locations, quantities and similar parameters) is leading to new understanding of distribution systems, their development and operation.

The speed and thoroughness of information flow have dramatized the weaknesses in physical movement of goods. The supporting movement of goods lags the information flow and thus has attracted the attention of engineers as well as top management. Automation of physical movement,

---

[3] Adapted from Harvey N. Shycon and Richard B. Maffei, "Simulation—Tool for Better Distribution," Harvard Business Review, November–December, 1960.

including order picking, packing, and the loading of carriers, commands keen attention today.

Transportation Progress.   Improvement in transportation systems has shortened delivery time (and often cut down packaging requirements) and so affected stock location and stock levels. The jet airplane has made overnight shipments practical between almost any points in the United States. Routine air shipment of perishable and fragile products is growing, and has altered markets and competition concepts by literally wiping out distance as a barrier to marketing. It changes concepts of spare parts supply and emergency service.

The California strawberry crop moves largely by air, to every point in the eastern United States. Air freight costs are dropping from over 20¢ per ton mile to 18¢. With the growing use of the C-41 jet freighter of 100 tons plus capacity, rates of 10¢ per ton-mile look likely, and with the commercial versions of the 747 and C-5A, even lower.

The integrated shipping container system—whether the piggyback trailer-train, or the container system for ship, plane, or truck, or the large special bulk container or rack that serves the production line and moves between vendor and buyer's production machines in a captive system—has reduced the loading and discharge time for common carriers and has thus shortened the delivery cycle. The shipping container often performs a warehousing-packing role, enabling goods to move to the consignee with minimal packing and without rehandling at terminals or for storage. In some instances, the container even feeds the production line or machine directly.

The interstate highway system, the supersize (100-ton) or the special railroad car, the piggyback railroad movement of trailers, and the improved freight train service have all cut transportation time and cost, and hence affected warehouse location.

It is not widely appreciated how low-cost water transportation has progressed. *Business Week* of August 1, 1964 reports that a modern inland waterway tow-tug system can produce 4 million ton miles per day upstream and 10 million downstream at less than one-half cent per ton mile.

Warehouse Mechanization.   Progress in mechanical aids to warehousing (and carrier unloading) have improved warehouse cost and service. Many of these have been covered in previous chapters, especially Chapter 17.

4. New Organization Concepts—The Distribution Center

Finally, there must be recognized the influence of the "distribution center" concept, regardless of the amount of mechanization employed.

As the size and number of production lines, customers, and products have risen, it has become increasingly logical to divorce the finished goods storage and shipping activity from the factory. It is not efficient for a number of production facilities each to maintain storage and shipping facilities, and to make virtually simultaneous shipments to identical customers. The distribution center concept concentrates warehouse stocks in a few large warehouses, with custor·:er orders filled from these central distribution centers. It involves shipping from the factories in bulk quantities to regional distribution centers where orders are filled from a location closer to the customer. The trend toward centralization may be for one or more of the following reasons, as well as others listed on these pages:

1. Modern communication systems minimize the distance factor in getting the customer order to the warehouse.
2. Transportation costs and time are reduced by order consolidation, minimizing the number of packages handled and shipped, packaging materials used, etc. Faster transportation is obtained by direct truck delivery over interstate highways or by air express.
3. Large, centralized warehouses can more easily justify investment or expense required by modern data processing equipment.
4. The concentration of stock permits a better matching of the production schedule to customer demand, minimizing setup costs necessary to fill shortages.
5. The centralized warehouse eliminates the duplication of certain warehouse personnel.
6. Reduction in total floor space and costs. In most cases, warehouse costs per square foot are lower in one large distribution center than if the same amount of floor space were placed in several locations and buildings.
7. With stock and order filling activities centralized, inventory control is easier to achieve by elimination of time delays and immediate knowledge of inventory status through data processing.

The obvious efficiency of consolidating the paperwork, storage, order-filling–shipping functions has led to the rise of the distribution center to serve the multi-product, multiwarehouse firm. For example:

1. Coleman Company's distribution manager claims to have saved 3 percent of sales in 18 months by cutting 40 warehouses to 17.
2. General Foods replaced over 100 warehouses with 16 regional distribution centers.
3. Borden Company, by 1962, used 15 distribution centers to replace 136 warehouses.

Should such a center be under the direction of the factory because it receives finished goods? Or the sales department because it responds to customer orders? Or under some other authority?

The distribution center is a physical embodiment of the distribution function. It is seed for the growth of a single management for the whole complex of physical distribution activities from factory to customer. The coming trend seems to be to regard this as a single management function, but still with some question as to whom it shall report.

In 1963, *Transportation and Distribution Management* magazine surveyed 219 companies and reported that 44 percent had created integrated physical distribution (PD) departments. These departments were not always formally responsible for all the functions involved, but they definitely were participating in transportation, warehousing, order processing, and plant and warehouse location, and, to a lesser extent, inventory control, protective packaging, material handling, market forecasting, and production planning.

The center of the authority varied widely. No fixed pattern has emerged although advocates are found for assigning PD management to traffic, to production, to marketing, and to a separate executive in top management.

Kodak's Assistant Vice-President, Distribution, Thomas McGrath says:

. . . One responsibility of the Kodak Distribution Center is control of finished goods inventory. This is a general management function; it is not a marketing responsibility.

. . . The marketing people should devote their time to the job of producing sales and satisfying customers, not to problems of physical distribution.

And by way of contrast, Anthony Cascino, Vice-President, International Minerals and Chemicals, says:

. . . Concurrent with the establishment of complete centralization of all elements of physical distribution within a single area was another most important recognition . . . the inseparability between the acquisition of an order and its fulfillment. . . . As a result, IMC's newly created department of distribution became an integral part of the company's marketing division.

This division of opinion only strengthens the basic point that distribution is a function that must be concentrated under one authority. To whom it reports can vary with the industry, the company, and the personalities involved.

5. Competition

As implied in several of the above "pressures" on physical distribution, competition in all its aspects is having its influence on physical distribution policies and practices. Pressure on profits will always turn management heads in the direction of previously overlooked sources of cost improvement.

THE NEED FOR COORDINATION

With the broad range of physical distribution activities, the varying objectives of interrelated organizational functions and the increasing pressures for improving the effectiveness of the Physical Distribution function, it would seem reasonable to argue for centralized control of the overall activity. In addition to the factors discussed above, the following offer further justification for a unified approach:

1. Increased foreign competition
2. Increasingly smaller savings possible in other areas
3. Improved management control
4. Improvement opportunities *inherent* in physical distribution
5. Need for an overall systems approach
6. Need for increased market share
7. Difficulties in bridging present company organizational boundaries
8. Difficulties in coordinating inter-organizational aspects in relationships with outside contacts.
9. Complex interrelationships between phases of the physical distribution process
10. Problems in reconciling apparent conflicts between presently scattered organizational units

Based on the physical distribution activities listed earlier in the chapter, the organizational interrelationships previously discussed, and the obvious need for the coordination of the overall function, a possible physical distribution organization structure is shown in Figure 18–4.

MATERIAL HANDLING vs. MATERIAL MANAGEMENT vs. PHYSICAL DISTRIBUTION MANAGEMENT

It goes without saying that the rapid growth of a "new" organizational function would cause some disruption in an existing organizational hierarchy. And it has, in regard to physical distribution, with the other two "combatants" being *material handling* and *material management*. For the present purposes, let the problem be resolved by suggesting the following distinction among the three:

1. Material *handling*—traditionally, production or *handling* oriented.
2. Material *management*—assumes responsibility for "all" activities dealing with materials.
3. Physical *distribution* management—oriented more towards *finished* goods warehousing and transportation, plus related functions, and often raw materials management.

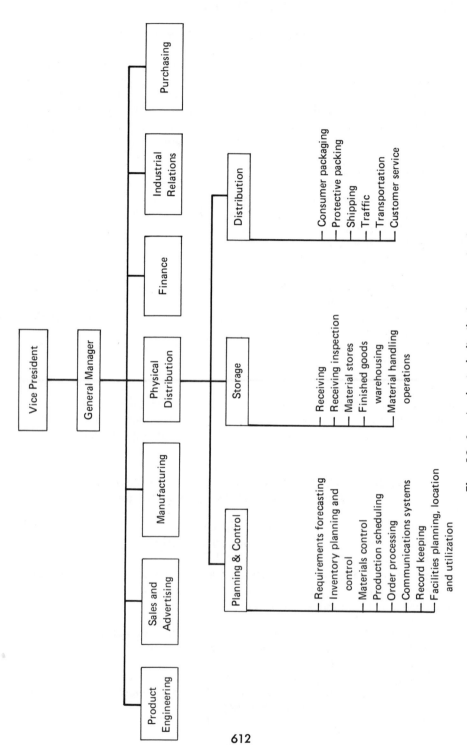

Fig. 18-4. A physical distribution organization.

However, the "border lines" are *far* from distinct, nor are they commonly agreed upon. Some groups lean one way, some the other. Probably the individual company's point of view is the most important factor in aligning related functions into an organization unit.

Some of the factors for consideration in locating the physical distribution function *in* the organization structure are:

1. Type of company
2. Value of product
3. Cost of physical distribution activity
4. Size of company
5. Relative importance of physical distribution

Organizational types or concepts for consideration might be:

1. Line responsibility
2. Staff service
3. Specialists, working out of company or corporation central office
4. Plant, company or corporation-wide committee
5. Combination of the above

If the physical distribution function is set up as a corporate staff, Arbury suggests the following basic responsibilities: [4]

1. To implement changes recommended by the planning group.
2. To work with and gain the cooperation of other corporate departments in resolving disputes and in determining actions to be taken to balance the needs of several functions.
3. To set new physical distribution policies and guidelines in response to changes in corporate resources, competitive actions technological advances, and other factors.
4. To coordinate the physical distribution activities of the divisions.
5. To provide advice and guidance to the divisions.
6. To perform certain distribution functions that are a service to the various divisions.

PHYSICAL DISTRIBUTION COST CONCEPTS

One of the first tasks in achieving control of the physical distribution function is a delineation of PD costs. The following is probably a more extensive list than is commonly found—but it is intended to be more complete, to reflect *all* physical distribution and related costs:

1. Receiving
2. Storage

---

[4] James N. Arbury *et al.*, reprinted by permission of the publisher, from *A New Approach to Physical Distribution,* American Management Association, Inc., New York, © 1967, p. 103.

3. Transportation (inbound)
4. Material handling (related to other functions listed *here*)
5. Inventory carrying cost
6. Inventory obsolescence cost
7. Over, short and damaged goods
8. Warehousing
9. Distribution (outbound)
10. Transportation and distribution facilities
11. Transportation and distribution equipment operation
12. Traffic operations
13. Selected administrative costs
    a. Material control
    b. Inventory control
    c. Scheduling
    d. Order processing
    e. Customer service
    f. Communications system

A more detailed cost breakdown, including most of the above items, plus details of several, is shown in Figure 18–5. The division between "direct" and "indirect" is an approach to better control of Physical Distribution costs. The separation is open to re-alignment, as deemed desirable by those applying the cost categories.

A less extensive, though more common cost breakdown is shown in Figure 18–6. It can be seen that *complete* control of physical distribution costs would be questionable with the more abbreviated listing. That is, those who "claim" the total list of physical distribution functions, as listed at the beginning of the chapter, should be held accountable for *all* physical distribution costs—not merely the traditional ones.

Based on the cost elements indicated in Figure 18–6, *Distribution Age* magazine has presented the industry averages shown in Figure 18–7 as bases for comparison. Such data are helpful in evaluating one's physical distribution costs against those of comparable enterprises. In a similar manner, Figure 18–8 charts comparative physical distribution costs for selected years.

INTERDEPENDENCE OF PHYSICAL DISTRIBUTION COST COMPONENTS

One of the obvious conclusions to be drawn from the above discussion, is that management is interested in *total* physical distribution cost —*not* the reduction of any specific cost component at the expense of the total. However, it should be recognized, that in many cases, a reduction in one, *may* increase another, or others—but the net result

Direct	Indirect
Warehousing	

Direct	Indirect
Labor —Unloading Receiving Identify and sort Dispatch to storage Place in storage Order picking Order consolidation Protective packaging Loading Order processing	*Labor* —Supervision Inspection Inventory clerks Housekeeping Salvage labor Plant protection General clerical Customer service Order processing
Space —Rent (or depreciation) Utilities Maintenance Repairs Taxes Insurance	*Space* —(for above) (same as at left)
Equipment —Depreciation Maintenance Repairs Supplies	
Supplies —Packing Misc.	
Other —Shift premium Overtime	*Other* —Damaged goods Unabsorbed labor
Transportation	
Freight, etc. —as billed	
Labor —Drivers } full or —Helpers } part time	*Labor* —Dispatching
	Space —Garage rent (or depreciation) Maintenance Repairs
Equipment —Depreciation Maintenance Repair Supplies License fees	*Equipment* —Leasing costs Rentals

Fig. 18–5. Physical distribution cost components. (Adapted from Robert M. Sutton, "Physical Distribution for Profit . . . or Loss," *Transportation and Distribution Management*, August 1965.)

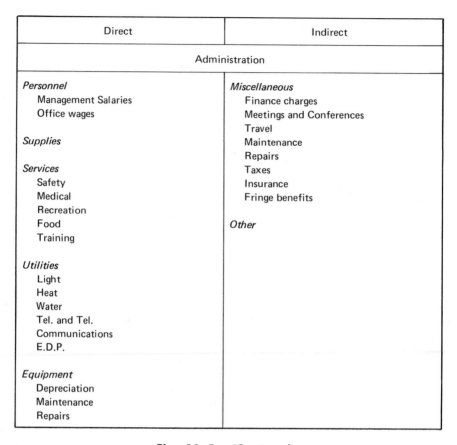

Direct	Indirect
Administration	

Personnel
    Management Salaries
    Office wages
 	
 Supplies
 	
 Services
    Safety
    Medical
    Recreation
    Food
    Training
 	
 Utilities
    Light
    Heat
    Water
    Tel. and Tel.
    Communications
    E.D.P.
 	
 Equipment
    Depreciation
    Maintenance
    Repairs
	Miscellaneous
	    Finance charges
	    Meetings and Conferences
	    Travel
	    Maintenance
	    Repairs
	    Taxes
	    Insurance
	    Fringe benefits
	
	 Other

Fig. 18–5. *(Continued)*

should be a lower total cost. This concept is graphically depicted in Figure 18–9, which shows *some* of the many physical distribution cost components and their effect on the total—as related to the number of warehouses.

Other interrelationships between cost factors are shown in Figure 18–10. A careful examination of such relationships only emphasizes the need for attention to each component as *it* influences total physical distribution costs. It also points out the almost hopeless task of achieving the lowest total by haphazard means. Only a "systems" approach can accurately interrelate so many cost categories, varying in such elusive ways as to make their integration extremely difficult.

THE SYSTEMS APPROACH TO PHYSICAL DISTRIBUTION

The systems approach, in the general situation, was discussed in detail in Chapter 9. The reader may find it advisable to review the systems "procedure" in that chapter, and contemplate its application to the physical distribution function. Interpreting the systems concept in relation to the physical distribution function, it can be concluded that the overall objective is to determine that mix of the physical distribution activity cost components that will result in the lowest net cost for the *total* function. The overall approach is that of examining the individual cost components and their interrelationships, with the idea of determining or predicting the effect of a change in one or more factors on each of the other factors, as well as on the entire physical distribution system. Terms frequently used to describe this approach are:

Total logistics concept
Distribution profitability analysis
Total cost distribution analysis

Although the complexity of the physical distribution function is "crying" for the type of analysis implied here, it cannot succeed without proper support from the rest of the organization. Harvey [5] and Neuschel [6] suggest the following areas of support to assure the success of the systems approach to physical distribution:

1. A management committed to make a major breakthrough in dealing with important problems
2. A management environment favorable to objective and hard-nosed decision-making
3. A management prepared to support the development of the kind of information that the approach requires
4. A management that is prepared to follow through to the implementation of the solution
5. A willingness to identify and deal with important human considerations
6. Executives both willing and able to deal with distribution activities from a corporate rather than a functional viewpoint
7. Transportation personnel free from the functional parochialism found in many traffic departments
8. Adequate emphasis on obtaining timely cost information

[5] Numbers 1–5, from Allan Harvey, "The Systems Approach in Distribution Engineering—the State of the Art," *Proceedings of American Institute of Industrial Engineers,* 18th Annual Conference, 1967.

[6] Numbers 6–8 from Robert P. Neuschel, "Physical Distribution—Forgotten Frontier," *Harvard Business Review,* March–April 1967, p. 133.

USE THIS WORK SHEET FOR COMPARING YOUR COMPANY'S 19X0-19X1 P-D COST RATIOS WITH THE AVERAGES FOR YOUR INDUSTRY.

	(1) Your Co's. 2-Year Net Sales & P-D Cost $ Figures	(2) Your Co's. 2-Year P-D Cost Ratios to Net Sales (N.S. = 100.00)	(3) Your Industry's 2-Year Avg. P-D Cost Ratios	(4) No. of Ratio Points Your Co. was High (+) or Low (−)
Total Net Sales	$____	100.00%	100.00%	____
Total P-D Costs	$____	____%	____%	____
Common Carrier Expense—Total	$____	____%	____%	____
Rail shipping expense	____	____	____	____
Truck shipping expense	____	____	____	____
Water transportation	____	____	____	____
Air transportation expense	____			____
Private Trucking Expense—Total	$____	____%	____%	____
Truck driver's pay	____	____	____	____
Equipment leasing charges	____	____	____	____
Depreciation of equipment	____	____	____	____
Truck maintenance and supplies (including license fees, insurance and taxes)	____			____
Public Warehousing Expense (including accessorial charges)	$____	____%	____%	____

Private Warehouse Costs—Total	$ _____	_____ %	_____ %
At distribution and sales centers	_____	_____	_____
Depreciation	_____	_____	_____
Total overhead, including payroll and maintenance	_____	_____	_____
Materials Handling Expense—Total	$ _____	_____ %	_____ %
Freight handlers' pay	_____	_____	_____
Material handling equipment depreciation	_____	_____	_____
Material handling equipment maintenance and supplies	_____	_____	_____
Shipping Room Costs—Total	$ _____	_____ %	_____ %
Payroll	_____	_____	_____
Supplies (including cartons, strapping, etc.)	_____	_____	_____
Overhead	_____	_____	_____
Over-Short and Damaged Goods	$ _____	_____ %	_____ %
(Warehousing and Transportation)			
Selected Administrative Expenses Related to			
Distribution Costs—Total	$ _____	_____ %	_____ %
Management: Vice President of Traffic	_____	_____	_____
Department Heads	_____	_____	_____
Clerical	_____	_____	_____
Other	_____	_____	_____

Fig. 18–6. Typical physical distribution cost breakdown—smaller scope. (From R. E. Snyder, "Physical Distribution Costs—A Two Year Analysis," *Distribution Age*, January 1963, p. 44.)

Expense Element	Food & Food Products Industry			Machinery (Elec. & Non-Elec.) Industry			Chemicals, Petroleum & Rubber Products Industry			Paper & Paper Products Industry		
	1960	1961	2-Year Avg.	1960	1961	2-Year Avg.	1960	1961	2-Year Avg.	1960	1961	2-Year Avg.
TOTAL PHYSICAL DISTRIBUTION EXPENSE RATIO TO NET SALES (X)	34.42	29.60	32.01	11.40	8.83	10.02	25.95	21.72	23.80	19.93	16.60	18.13
Common Carrier Expense	10.18	9.63	9.91	8.15	5.29	6.72	10.32	9.31	9.81	4.56	5.60	4.98
Private Trucking Expense	7.50	5.95	6.73	1.22	.84	1.03	4.51	3.47	3.99	4.39	2.54	3.45
Public Warehousing Expense*	2.37	1.89	2.13	.29	.35	.32	1.55	1.09	1.32	2.44	1.40	1.92
Private Warehouse Expense	5.70	4.02	4.87	.51	.53	.52	3.91	2.88	3.39	2.85	2.01	2.43
Materials Handling Expense	2.59	2.34	2.46	.42	.36	.39	1.43	1.41	1.42	1.41	1.27	1.34
Shipping Room Expense	3.98	3.88	3.93	.58	.95	.76	2.61	2.41	2.51	3.55	3.01	3.28
Over-Short & Damage	.33	.27	.30	.12	.02	.07	.26	.19	.23	.21	.20	.20
Selected Administrative Expense	1.77	1.62	1.68	.11	.49	.21	1.36	.96	1.13	.52	.57	.53

Expense Element	Primary & Fabricated Metals Industry			Wood Products (Including Furniture) Industry			Textiles Industry			Transportation Equipment Industry		
	1960	1961	2-Year Avg.	1960	1961	2-Year Avg.	1960	1961	2-Year Avg.	1960	1961	2-Year Avg.
TOTAL PHYSICAL DISTRIBUTION EXPENSE RATIO TO NET SALES (X)	33.14	26.43	29.23	17.27(R)	15.81	15.99	16.15	NA	NA	NA	10.22	NA
Common Carrier Expense	5.51	5.14	5.32	9.15	8.81	8.46	5.42	NA	NA	NA	5.27	NA
Private Trucking Expense	5.87	3.53	4.70	2.82	2.46	2.64	.10	NA	NA	NA	1.83	NA
Public Warehousing Expense*	—	.58	—	.10	.10	.10	1.00	NA	NA	NA	—	NA
Private Warehouse Expense	11.30	9.53	10.42	.70(R)	1.00	.85	5.74	NA	NA	NA	.74	NA
Materials Handling Expense	1.61	1.51	1.56	1.08	1.09	1.09	1.00	NA	NA	NA	.80	NA
Shipping Room Expense	3.33	2.49	2.91	1.75	1.43	1.59	2.17	NA	NA	NA	1.12	NA
Over-Short & Damage	.02	.02	.02	.22	.13	.17	.01	NA	NA	NA	.01	NA
Selected Administrative Expense	5.50	3.63	4.30	1.45	.79	1.09	.71	NA	NA	NA	.45	NA

* Public **Warehousing** ratios for 1960 included the effect of local distribution charges. The 1961 ratios exclude such charges. NA Not available. (R) Revised.
(X) All totals relating to 2-year average figures are additive.

Fig. 18–7. Ratios of net sales for selected physical distribution costs. (From R. E. Snyder, "Physical Distribution Costs —A Two Year Analysis," *Distribution Age,* January 1963, pp. 46–47.)

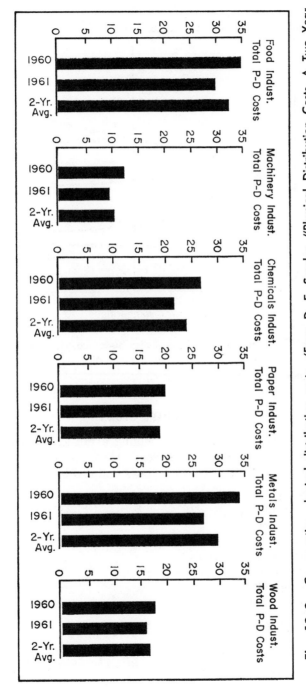

Fig. 18–8. Comparative physical distribution costs. (From D. E. Snyder, "Physical Distribution Costs—A Two Year Analysis," *Distribution Age*, January 1963, p. 48.)

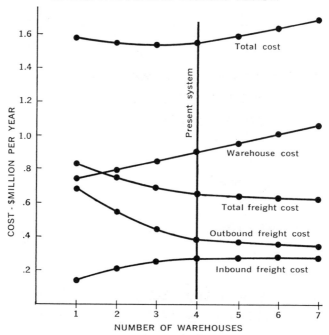

Fig. 18–9. Effect of selected physical distribution costs on number of warehouses. (From J. C. Jessen, "How duPont Attacks Distribution Costs," *Modern Materials Handling*, September 1964, p. 7.)

THE FEASIBILITY STUDY

In evaluating the desirability of mounting a full-scale systems study of the physical distribution function, Booz, Allen, and Hamilton suggest a feasibility study somewhat along the lines outlined below: [7]

1. Analyze and describe existing system.
    a. Characteristics
    b. Volume flows
    c. Costs
2. Identify relevant variables.[8]
    a. Products or product lines
    b. Warehousing
    c. Geographical areas
    d. Order size or category
    e. Individual customer

---

[7] Adapted from Booz, Allen, and Hamilton, Inc., *The Effective Management of Total Distribution Costs*, p. 18.

[8] Sutton, *op. cit.*

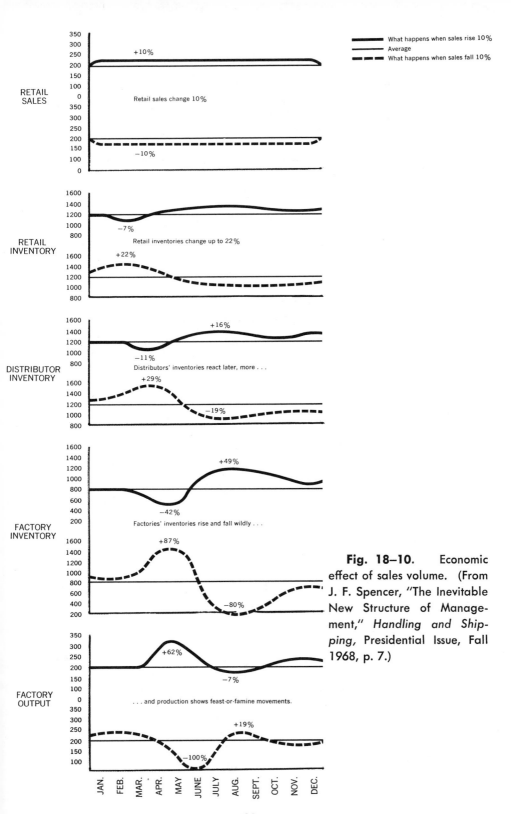

Fig. 18–10. Economic effect of sales volume. (From J. F. Spencer, "The Inevitable New Structure of Management," *Handling and Shipping*, Presidential Issue, Fall 1968, p. 7.)

623

3. Determine availability of data required to quantify the variables.
4. Establish method, time, and cost required to convert these data into forms suitable for further computation.
5. Determine range and kinds of alternatives that should be taken into consideration.
6. Estimate the need for and/or the nature, size, and complexity of mathematical models and computer programs that would be required to develop optimum solutions from among the alternatives available.
7. Determine whether sufficient profit improvement potential is available to warrant further investigation.

TOTAL COST DISTRIBUTION ANALYSIS

Having determined the feasibility of a potential physical distribution cost study, the analysis might proceed as follows: [9]

1. Quantify variables . . . as necessary to supplement available data.
2. Construct mathematical models or calculation procedures.
   a. Trace all interactions.
   b. Test correlations.
3. Test the models.
   a. Run known results of previous years to check actual experience against predicted results.
   b. Usually requires computer.
4. Test all alternatives to find optimum solutions, running models repeatedly, while varying data representing the different alternatives.
5. Evaluate optimum solution as a business proposition.
   a. Organizational requirements.
   b. Return on investment.
   c. Competitive implications.
   d. Practicality of time schedule.

Having made the study, the task of implementation involves the following steps:

1. Clarify assignments of responsibilities and duties of the distribution function.
2. Develop reporting systems that regularly identify total distribution cost and provide a means of evaluating performance.
3. Adopt data-gathering techniques to develop data needed as inputs to total cost distribution analytical and reporting systems.
4. Establish capability to measure competitive customer service levels periodically, for comparison with own.

[9] Adapted from Booz, Allen, and Hamilton, *op. cit.*, p. 19.

Examples of Physical Distribution Studies

The following case histories illustrate how specific problems can be approached in different degrees of breadth and depth.

PROBLEM 1
Public Warehouse Location Study [10]

A firm manufacturing a broad line of household detergents at two plants used 55 public warehouses from which to serve several thousand customers. It was believed that there were too many warehouses, which meant:

Higher rates at each warehouse
Extra costs of paper work and communications for each warehouse
Probable higher transportation costs per unit due to shipment sizes
Higher inventory costs in order to maintain stock at more locations.

Desired customer service was established as 48-hour maximum transit time. It was decided that shipments would be cheapest, yet not involve excessive inventories, if rail carload sizes were the unit of shipment from plant to warehouse.

ANALYSIS

Step 1. By comparing the rate of shipments out of each warehouse to *its* customers, it was found that the "weeks between replenishment" gave the chart in Figure 18–11. In other words, using the selected shipment unit

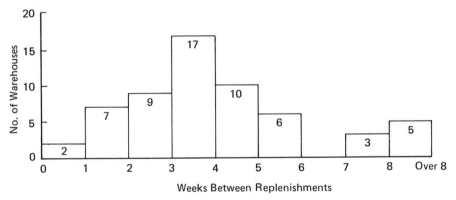

Fig. 18–11. Warehouse replenishment frequency: plant—direct volume shipments. (Courtesy of Drake Sheahan/Stewart Dougall.)

(railroad carload), two warehouses would require weekly replenishment, while five would require more than 8 weeks to exhaust a carload size shipment. Obviously, these latter five were doing very little business. One could arbitrarily guess that between 20 and 30 warehouses could be selected to serve

[10] By permission, from the files of Drake Sheahan/Stewart Dougall, New York.

the customers by receiving carload shipments and exhausting them in three weeks or less.

Step 2. How many warehouses were doing how much of the business? The chart in Figure 18–12 was prepared by plotting an average month's volume starting with the largest volume warehouse and concluding with the smallest. It is immediately apparent that 12 warehouses do 50 percent of the volume, and the last 25 warehouses do only 25 percent of the volume. Another rough guess suggests that less than 30 warehouses could do the job. But just how many are needed and at what cities?

Fig. 18–12. Shipments to warehouses in an average month of 1965. (Courtesy of Drake Sheahan/Stewart Dougall.)

Step 3. A computer was employed to:

Perform calculations on many configurations of warehouse numbers and locations.
To test the effect of changes in transportation rates and warehouse sizes.
To find eventual basis for cost control of the selected system.
To test for sensitivity in alternative arrangements.
To gain confidence in the results.

Notice the characteristics of this analysis. It is heuristic rather than optimal. It is a simple mathematical approach of comparing the cost of many arrangements and using some simplifying rules, such as:

1. Assume a number of "average customer" locations. That is, there are a number of marketing areas, such as Boston. Each area has an average of X size which is located Y miles from the logical warehousing point in that marketing area. For this company, 110 "customer locations" were developed.
2. Data were then developed for these factors:
   —Warehouse to "average customer" rate.
   —Plant to warehouse rate.
   —Customer demand.

—Warehouse fixed cost.

—Warehouse variable cost.

The above data were then modified on later computer runs by assuming that the warehouse shifted to another nearby marketing area, yet continued to serve the "average customer" in the first marketing area.

Computer Analysis. Four computer runs took less than 10 minutes at a cost of $100. Preparation costs were mostly data collection. The program modification cost $750. Four computer runs were made:

First—Start with eight basic area warehouses and add those needed to reach minimum cost. Then use "bump" and "shift" routines to test various locations.

Second—Start with 54 warehouses and work down to minimum cost. Compare results with first run.

Third—Start with result of runs 1 and 2 and modify warehousing and transportation rates.

Fourth—Repeat run 3 with increased demand.

These run results are shown in Figure 18–13. The recommendations were made with due allowance for special conditions such as availability of warehousing, transportation, quality of service and even some personal preferences of local marketing management.

RESULTS—Savings accrued from:

1. Paperwork eliminated with 31 warehouses. Fixed cost of operating at 31 warehouses also eliminated.
2. Reduced inventory.
3. Lower warehousing costs per unit of product because of increased volume at each warehouse.
4. Lower transportation unit cost because rate negotiations for heavier car loading, better car utilization, higher volume with consistent shipments from point-to-point, similar reduced rates for similar products.

PROBLEM 2
Basic Distribution System Design Study [11]

A manufacturer of food products with $100 million annual sales and 10 factories decided to re-examine its distribution system of 35 warehouses.

ANALYSIS

Step 1. Using assumed locations and "average customer" volumes, the breakdown of cost was developed as shown in Figure 18–14. The warehousing cost assumes that a minimum fixed cost of $25,000 is required to operate a warehouse; thereafter warehousing cost is proportional to volume.

Apparently, these costs are minimized at about 40 warehouses. Note that the costs are relatively insensitive to the higher number of warehouses.

Step 2. Consider inventory costs. Each additional warehouse raises the

---

[11] From Harvey Shycon, *Notes on Simulation in Physical Distribution,* privately circulated.

Location	Run 1	Run 2	Run 3	Run 4	Recommendation
Boston	X	X	X		X
Hartford				X	
Albany				X	
Syracuse	X	X			X
Buffalo					
New York					
Philadelphia	X	X	X		X
Harrisburg					
Altoona		X	X	X	X
Baltimore					
Washington, D.C.	X	X	X	X	X
Richmond	X	X		X	
Charlotte					X
Atlanta	X	X	X		X
Nashville					
Birmingham				X	
Jacksonville				X	
Tampa			X	X	
Miami					X*
Pittsburgh					
Cleveland			X	X	
Detroit			X	X	X
Grand Rapids	X	X			
Columbus	X	X			
Cincinnati					
Indianapolis					
Louisville					
Chicago	X	X			
Milwaukee					
Peoria					
St. Louis	X	X	X	X	X
Des Moines					
Minneapolis	X	X	X	X	X
Fargo					
Omaha	X	X	X	X	X
Kansas City					
Oklahoma City	X	X	X	X	X
Memphis					
New Orleans	X	X	X	X	X
Houston	X	X	X	X	X
Arlington					
Lubbock					
San Antonio					
El Paso					
Denver	X	X	X	X	X
Salt Lake City	X	X	X	X	X
Phoenix	X	X	X	X	X
Los Angeles	X	X	X	X	
San Diego				X	
San Francisco	X	X	X	X	X
Seattle	X	X	X	X	X
Portland					
Great Falls	X	X	X	X	X
Spokane	X	X	X	X	X
Providence					
No of warehouses	22	23	19	24	24

*Poor facilities in Tampa, Miami local management preference.

Fig. 18–13. Summary of computer runs on warehouse locations. (Courtesy of Drake Sheahan/Stewart Dougall.)

Number of warehouses	10	20	30	40	50
Transportation cost plants to warehouses	5.2	5.4	5.6	5.8	6.0
Delivery cost warehouses to customers	6.7	4.0	2.9	2.2	1.8
Warehousing ($25,000 fixed cost)	.25	.5	.75	1.0	1.25
Sub total	12.15	9.9	9.25	9.0	9.05

Fig. 18–14. Total costs in millions of dollars annually for various numbers of warehouses. (From "Notes on Simulation in Physical Distribution," privately circulated by Harvey N. Shycon.)

amount of inventory that must be carried. The cost of carrying inventory is not available in many accounting records. It includes capital cost, obsolescence of inventory, deterioration, damage and other losses to inventory, additional paperwork, increased unit shipping costs because of smaller volume shipments, space requirements cost (exclusive of handling), taxes and insurance. Figures cited vary with the product, location, etc. and range from 6% to 40% per year of the value of the inventory held. Figures from 15 to 25% are most commonly cited in the United States. This firm estimated 25% per year.

Adding the cost of carrying inventory, distribution costs build up as shown in Figure 18–15. It should not be forgotten that out-of-stock conditions also have costs, such as loss of profits on lost sales, loss of customers, excess costs of expediting, and loss of management time diverted to emergencies.

Number of warehouses	10	20	30	40	50
Inventory carrying cost at 25% per year	6.5	7.53	8.65	9.60	10.45
Sub total	18.65	17.43	17.90	18.60	19.50

Fig. 18–15. Inventory cost additions. (From "Notes on Simulation in Physical Distribution," privately circulated by Harvey N. Shycon.)

It now looks as though 18 or 19 warehouses would provide the cheapest solution.

Step 3. The next step is a complex mathematical one using linear programming to select the 19 apparently best locations.

Visualize a map of the United States with 2000 red pins on it, representing the customers. Add 10 black pins representing the factories, then add 19 yellow pins representing the warehouses. By the use of simulation techniques, the analyst assigned each point a volume, activity costs, and relative time scale, thus forming a model of the distribution system. By manipulating this model—changing volumes, times, locations, costs, etc., which management believed possible or of potential significance—the distribution "model" was tested.

Thus management determined the effect of likely or possible changes on the total system and determined the sensitivity of the proposed system while identifying critical factors. Obviously, this step requires an operations research skill and a computer. But through this "optimizing" of a systems design, one can presumably create the "best" distribution system and identify sensitive parameters. However, such solutions frequently show a very "flat" characteristic in the middle range, with the conclusion that there is considerable latitude in the number of warehouses used.

The analyst will realize that the results of such a study are no better than the assumptions made in developing the model and the reality of the conditions tested.

DISTRIBUTION PROFITABILITY ANALYSIS [12]

Another fruitful area of distribution cost study is profitability analysis. Normally, manufacturing costs are determined and assigned to each product and production event, but distribution costs are rarely analyzed in the same spirit. Progressive firms are beginning to analyze distribution profitability. The concept is to establish a distribution cost, as in Figure 18–5, and then:

1. Cost the order "as processed."
2. Compare cost to a standard.
3. Determine the variance.
4. Establish procedures and policies to maximize profits by minimizing variances or changing the system.

Some examples of distribution profitability analysis (DPA) follow, but first it is necessary to establish a proper costing system, including such items as were listed in Figure 18–5.

Such costs are generally scattered through the accounting records, and thus must be collected for DPA purposes. Actually, for physical distribution activity, some of these costs are fixed, while others are variable with volume, type of product, type of order, etc. The goal is to discover these true cost figures and deal accordingly with the sales activity. Figure 18–5 showed such an assignment of fixed and variable costs, which will of course vary with individual firms.

The job now is to isolate these costs. In doing so, it will become apparent that the costs of physical distribution vary widely by type of product, size of order, volume of the shipment, method of transportation, packaging and similar factors.

Analysis of profitability thus becomes the tool by which the distribution manager can support and improve the marketing profit goals. The technique is to separate the activities, isolate and identify their costs, and then look for variables. Avoid the use of average figures.

[12] A procedure developed by Drake Sheahan/Stewart Dougall, New York.

Experience of one leading consulting firm has shown that significant variables creating cost differences often lie in such fields as:

1. *Products and product lines,* which are affected by volume, packaging requirements, the timing and location of demand, and inventory levels.

2. *Warehousing,* in numbers, efficiency, overhead, and location.

3. *Orders,* by size, seasonality, location of stock, and method of servicing.

4. *Transportation,* by rate per volume shipped, packaging required, associated handling, speed of delivery, and its influence on inventory levels and their location.

5. *Inventories,* their levels, replenishment, location, warehousing requirements, and carrying cost.

Some typical examples are shown in the following pages. Figure 18–16 shows a study of cost variation by size of order. It reveals that margin is badly eroded by the distribution cost on small orders.

| | Dollars | |
	20 Piece Order	200 Piece Order
Sales income	$21.00	$210.00
Cost of goods sold	10.00	101.00
Gross profit	$11.00	$109.00
Direct Costs—Branch Warehouse		
Order processing—clerical	0.75	0.75
Order picking, assembly	0.30	0.80
Check order	0.25	0.40
Pack order, ship	0.40	0.65
Packing material	0.25	0.45
Total Warehouse Costs	$ 1.95	$ 3.05
Transportation*	$ 2.25	$ 2.25
Total direct cost	4.20	5.30
Margin	$ 6.80	$103.70
Margin as % of sales	33%	50%
Direct distribution cost as of % of sales	20%	2.5%

*Both are in "minimum" shipment category.

Fig. 18–16. Cost variation—large vs. small order. (From Robert M. Sutton, "Physical Distribution for Profit . . . or Loss," *Transportation and Distribution Management,* August 1965, p. 22.)

Figure 18–17 suggests that orders are more profitable if processed directly rather than through the warehouse. Figure 18–18 shows the result of a profitability analysis by customers, and reveals some interesting and disturbing things. For instance, apparently profitable sales are actually losing money. Infrequent shipments in small lots are loss producers. There are very large distribution costs with customer D, which turn his relatively large orders into losses.

Schedule 1, Handling Cost

Includes cost to receive, put in reserve storage, replenish picking stock, pick order, check, pack, accumulate, and ship. Total cost = fixed order + variable unit cost.

A. Direct Order (Filled by the factory)

Product Group	$ Per Order +	$ Per Unit
A	0.85	0.025
B	0.70	0.020
C	0.50	0.015

B. Warehouse Order (Filled by the regional warehouse).

Product Group	$ Per Order +	$ Per Unit
A	1.35	0.040
B	1.10	0.032
C	0.80	0.012

Schedule 2, Order Processing Cost

Includes cost to edit, credit check, prepare invoice, shipping documents, deduct inventory.

	$ Per Order
Direct order	0.75
Warehouse order	0.95

Fig. 18–17. Direct cost factors. (From Robert M. Sutton, "Physical Distribution for Profit . . . or Loss," *Transportation and Distribution Management,* August 1965, p. 29.)

All these cost producing factors now can be subjected to review. Consideration should be given to whether changes in distribution methods, in sales policy, pricing of various products, shipments, or packs should be changed. Inventory policy, product line policy and similar considerations can be explored. Working with certain customers might improve profitability.

Customer	Location—Type Orders Code	Shipments	Sales	Cost of Goods Sold	Selling Expense	Physical Distribution Cost	Margin	Profitability Index
A	D4	5/5	25,120	13,300	2,510	3,760	5,550	78
B	A3	2/2	22,100	10,450	2,200	2,640	6,810	69
C	A4	9/12	15,200	8,350	1,510	2,800	2,540	70
D	A9	6/18	15,100	8,910	1,500	5,200	−510	103*
—								
—								
—								
K	D2	9/9	1,310	750	130	420	10	99
L	E1	4/10	980	480	100	530	−130	113*
M	E4	4/4	970	450	100	235	115	81

*These sales handled at a loss.

Fig. 18–18. Customer profitability summary. (From Robert M. Sutton, "Physical Distribution for Profit . . . or Loss," *Transportation and Distribution Management*, August 1965, p. 24.)

INFORMATION REQUIREMENTS IN PHYSICAL DISTRIBUTION

If the systems concept is to be applied to the physical distribution function, and if realistic costs are to be determined, then complete and accurate data are required. However, it is very likely that the most common excuse for inadequate physical distribution costs is the *lack* of sufficient data. And—the excuse for a lack of data is the "difficulty" of obtaining it. Both of these *are* excuses! Neither *has* to be valid if the analyst really *wants* good data, and accurate costs. Steps 9, 11, and 12 in Chapter 9 outline a general approach to identifying data requirements, collecting data, and evaluating data. In the present instance, it might also be suggested that, in general, the data requirements should be based on those quantifiable characteristics of basic physical distribution activities which have a distinct relationship to costs. As a guide for the analyst, the following list is presented, subdivided into those types of data useful to (1) operating departments, and (2) management:

A. Information Required by Physical Distribution Operating Departments [13]
   1. Daily
      a. Sales
      b. Unfilled and back orders
      c. Anticipated stockouts

[13] Arbury *et al., op. cit.,* p. 116.

    d. Warehouse shipments and replenishments
    e. Expediting information
  2. Weekly
    f. Inventory status
    g. Order and customer profiles
  3. Monthly
    h. Sales forecasts by:
      —sales territory
      —product line
      —customer class
    i. Present and future production outputs and capacities
    j. Actual distribution costs vs. planned costs
  4. When appropriate
    k. Planned new product introductions
    l. Sales promotions and advertising campaigns
    m. Competitive information—past, present, future
    n. Transportation rates and services
B. Information Required by Management [14]
  1. Transportation costs
    a. Total by company and operating division (or major product
      groups)
      —rail
      —truck—common carrier
      —comparison of above costs to sales, this year vs. last
    b. Total plant to warehouses
      —to individual warehouses
      —each as percent of sales, this year vs. last
    c. Total warehouse to customers
      —by areas
      —each as percent of sales, this year vs. last
    d. In-bound freight
      —major material categories
      —cost per dollar of material
    e. Penalty costs
      —for partial shipments
      —for other than lowest method of transportation
  2. Warehousing costs
    f. Total cost (per division)
    g. Public warehouse cost
      —per square foot
      —per dollar of product handling
    h. Company-operated (by plant and in field)
      —total operating cost
      —per square foot
      —per dollar of product handled

[14] Neuschel, op. cit., pp. 128–129.

　　3. Inventory performance
　　　　i. Actual vs. planned
　　　　　　—by major category
　　　　　　—by location
　　　　j. Inventory vs. sales
　　　　　　—by major item
　　　　　　—as a group for low-volume items
　　　　k. Cost of carrying inventories
　　4. Quality of service
　　　　l. On-time order performance
　　　　　　—percent of orders shipped on time
　　　　m. Severity of late orders
　　　　　　—customer problems
　　　　n. Comparison with competitive service
　　　　　　—reliability
　　　　　　—speed
　　　　　　—timed delivery

Rather obviously, the situation at hand will determine whether *all* of the above, *less* than the above, or *additional data* will be required. A careful examination of the operation will suggest which—and will serve as a basis for developing a data list to suit the situation being studied.

Once data are collected, the task is one of classifying and organizing them—and then, interrelating the various characteristics to achieve the cost parameters or other measures desired.

Some idea of the complexity of the relationships between information and product flow can be obtained from a study of Figures 18–19 and 18–20.[15]

THE ROLE OF SIMULATION IN PHYSICAL DISTRIBUTION SYSTEMS

Inevitably, the effective utilization of the range and depth of data suggested above will cause great difficulty in interrelating the data and making decisions based on it. As suggested in Chapter 10, simulation can be a valuable approach to such a perplexing situation. It will be remembered that the systems approach (including simulation, when necessary) attempts to examine each cost component, with the aim of determining or predicting the effect of a change in one or more factors on each of the other factors, as well as on the entire physical distribution system.

Some of the reasons for using simulation are:

　　1. To assure proper interaction of all relevant costs to each part of the system

[15] W. M. Kordsiemon, "Communications: Link Between Time and Money," in Presidential Issue, *Handling and Shipping*, 1968.

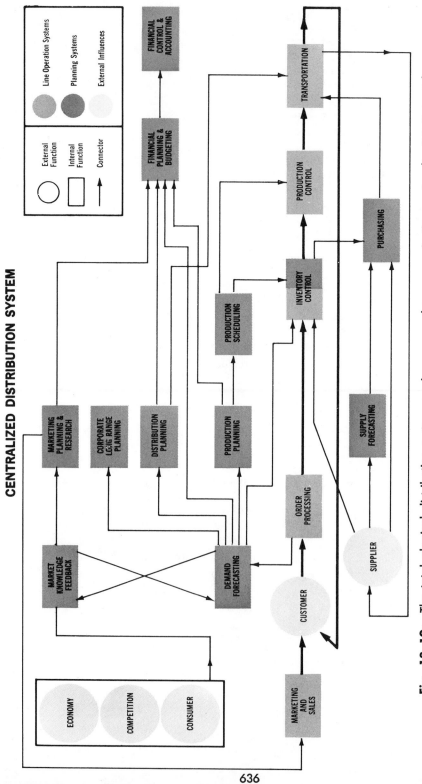

CENTRALIZED DISTRIBUTION SYSTEM

External Function	◯
Internal Function	▭
Connector	→

Line Operation Systems	⬤
Planning Systems	⬤
External Influences	⬤

Fig. 18–19. The total physical distribution system requires a complex communications network. But it must be rational and workable, and permit a rapid transfer of information, which will parallel both the product and information flow lines. (From W. M. Kordsiemon, "Communications: Link Between Time and Money," *Handling and Shipping,* Presidential Issue, 1968, p. 20.)

2. To develop a system to permit each part (subsystem) to be developed in proper relationship to all others.
3. To provide the capability of testing a large number of combinations in order to find the lowest cost combination
4. To avoid suboptimization
5. To make the comparisons in a short period of time—before factors change (i.e., while all *are* comparable)

If simulation is the chosen approach, Arbury suggests the following decision steps for designing and operating a physical distribution model: [16]

1. Set limits on order cycle time
2. Select warehouse patterns
3. Choose eligible warehouse-customer combinations
4. Determine order cycle methods
5. Specify service policies
6. Group customers by service policy
7. Examine warehouse-customer configurations
8. Calculate demand
9. Consider plant-warehouse configurations
10. Estimate the stock-out cost
11. Calculate the reorder level and quantity to reorder
12. Choose size of warehouse
13. Determine the residual income
14. Derive information from the model

Again it should be noted that the situations under analysis may very possibly require some alteration or variation of the above general procedure.

And, as a final "warning," Shycon and Maffei suggest the following limitations of simulation: [17]

1. Resources can only be stretched so far, some compromises must be made.
2. The technical characteristics of computer equipment establish boundaries.
3. The accuracy and adequacy of input information impose limits on the program.

A proper understanding of the above, along with a knowledge of the simulation process, will be helpful in assuring an intelligent and useful application of the technique to the complex Physical Distribution problem.

---

[16] Arbury, *op. cit.*, pp. 75 f.
[17] H. N. Shycon and R. B. Maffei, "Simulation—Tool for Better Distribution," *Harvard Business Review*, Nov.–Dec., 1960, p. 75.

COMPREHENSIVE ORDER PROCESSING SYSTEM

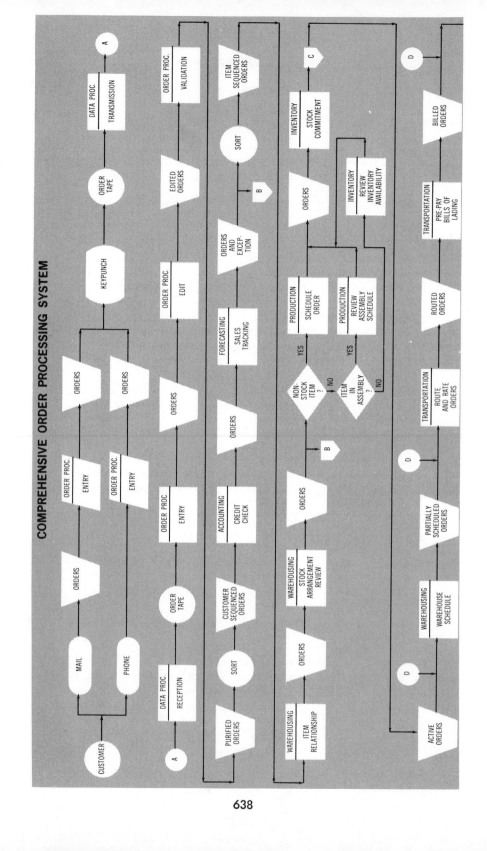

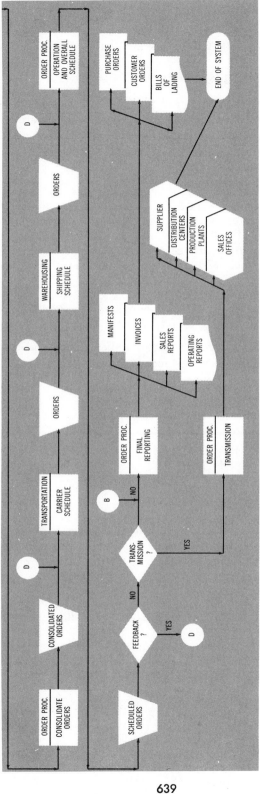

Fig. 18-20. Example of a comprehensive order processing and communication system making use of order information to influence sales forecasting and allowing for prompt reporting to management (B) and providing important feedbacks integrating transportation and production operations (D). (From W. M. Kordsiemon, "Communications: Link Between Time and Money," *Handling and Shipping*, Presidential Issue, 1968, p. 22.)

IMPROVING PHYSICAL DISTRIBUTION OPERATIONS

Having seen the complexity of the overall physical distribution function, and with an appreciation of the tremendous cost of such operations, it is apparent that there is frequently much room for cost improvement, as was pointed out earlier in the chapter. Magee suggests the following overall approach: [18]

1. Taking a fresh look at the responsibilities, capabilities, and organizational positions of executives in traffic, warehouse management, inventory control, and other functions which make up the overall system.
2. Re-examining the company's physical plant and distribution procedures in the light of technical advances in such areas as transportation, data processing, and materials handling.
3. Thinking of the physical distribution process as a *system* in which, just as in a good hi-fi system, all the components and functions must be properly balanced.

One consulting firm, having analyzed a large number of physical distribution organizations, concludes that the more common steps usually taken to improve distribution efficiency are as follows: [19]

1. Revise channels of distribution.
2. Alter number and location of plants or warehouses.
3. Alter transportation concepts.
4. Automate warehouses or plants.
5. Change inventory management practices.
6. Reallocate territories among plants or warehouses.
7. Reorganize distribution responsibilities.
8. Change customer service policies.

Since the concept of a distribution *system* leads to the expression "Total Distribution Costs," and given the target of reducing physical distribution costs, where should efforts be directed? Functionally, there are four goals:

a. To *improve service* to customers (or one's own plant) by reducing response time to an order, inventories, and order-filling errors.
b. To *reduce costs*.
c. To *improve* managerial *controls* of inventory and other costs.
d. To *improve* product *quality* by protection and by promptness of deliveries.

The goals are achieved by making improvements in the several parts of the distribution system.

[18] Magee, op. cit., p. 89.
[19] Booz, Allen and Hamilton, op. cit., pp. 9–11.

One consulting firm divides the physical distribution function into 18 major subdivisions, and suggests the following more specific areas for evaluation, analysis and possible improvement: [20]

A. DISTRIBUTION SERVICES

1. Distribution Policies and Planning
   a. Corporate strategy on support of marketing plans and sales effort.
   b. Market analysis and research as a basis for distribution policies.
   c. Defining objectives for customer service.
   d. Long-range planning for growth of distribution operations.
   e. Setting goals for distribution.
   f. Forecasting.
2. Distribution Systems
   a. Coordination of production, packing, warehousing, and transportation.
   b. Setting up a network of plants and distribution centers.
   c. Assigning responsibilities of each distribution point—items and stock levels to be carried, areas to be served, standards of service to be maintained.
   d. Use of company and public warehouses—selection of warehouses, establishment of supply points to improve service to customers.
   e. Determining trade-off points, transportation costs and inventory costs and inventory-carrying cost; employment of air and other premium methods of transportation to reduce need for carrying stock in the field.
3. Operations Research, Statistical Analysis, Economic and Feasibility Studies
   a. Application of mathematical programming—simulation, queueing theory, modeling, and similar applied mathematical techniques for better understanding of complex operational relationships, for problem solving.
   b. Feasibility analysis—recommendation of economical and practical courses of action; decision rules; trade-off and break-even points.
   c. Statistical testing of proposed alternatives; statistical representations of operations; sampling.
   d. Sales forecasting—projection of requirements; time-series analysis; growth and seasonal patterns.
   e. Capital expenditures projections, programs, controls.

---

[20] "Areas for Study and Improvement in Physical Distribution," a check list privately circulated, by Drake Sheahan/Stewart Dougall.

B. FACILITIES

4. Site Selection, Plants and Warehouses
   a. Studies of market needs—trends, centralization vs. decentralization, determination of optimum number and locations for plants and warehouses, long-range planning.
   b. Selection of site—studies of labor supply, transportation costs, water, utilities, service, building costs, proximity to supply source and markets.
5. Facilities Planning, Layout, and Space Utilization
   a. Estimating requirements for plants, warehouses, terminals—amount and type of space needed.
   b. Integration of the structure with the operation it will house: liaison with architects and contractors.
   c. Planning the building—size and shape of structure, single or multistoried, placement on site, column spacing and bay sizes, ceiling and clear stacking heights, floor loads, dock sizes and location, lighting, heating.
   d. Layout and arrangement of space—material flow patterns, storage and stacking methods, aisle widths, storage depths and racks to assure full use of cube.

C. MATERIAL HANDLING

6. Material Handling
   a. Handling into, through, and out of plants, warehouse, terminals, and distribution centers.
   b. Handling to and from production, and between production processes.
   c. Functional specifications, selection, use, and maintenance of material handling equipment.
   d. Coordination of lift trucks, conveyors, tractors, and other handling equipment.
   e. Receiving and shipping; unloading and loading.
   f. Stock-picking, order assembly, sorting, marking.
7. Warehousing, Storage, Freight Terminal Operations
   a. Storage of raw materials, components, in-process stock, finished goods.
   b. Site location, functional design, and layout of warehouses and terminals.
   c. Operating procedures—space, equipment, and manpower requirements.
   d. Bins, racks, and other storage aids.
   e. Order-filling operations; picking lines; forward and reserve stock; replenishment.
8. Packaging, Packing, Unit Loads, Containerization

    a. Protective packaging; corrosion and damage prevention; cushioning materials.

    b. Design and standardization of shipping containers; cost-reduction programs for packing materials.

    c. Productivity of packaging labor; production-line techniques; line balancing; layout of packing areas.

    d. Mechanization of packaging, bottling, and filling.

    e. Unit-load design; palletization; pallet specifications; clamp and vacuum handling.

9. Equipment Planning, Maintenance, and Utilization

    a. Concepts and functional specifications for production packaging and handling equipment.

    b. Equipment requirements—number, type, speed; projection of future needs; purchase vs. lease; replacement programs.

    c. Preventive maintenance programs—organization and responsibilities; schedules; shop operations.

    d. Improving utilization of equipment.

D. AUTOMATION

10. Automation, Advanced Mechanization

    a. Basic automation philosophy—concept engineering; planning of automatic systems; applications of new types of controls and equipment.

    b. Feasibility studies—technical and economic; identification of operations and areas where automation will pay.

    c. Functional specifications—volumes and rates; determining what the system must be able to do.

    d. Liaison with designers and manufacturers of automatic equipment and controls.

    e. Bid evaluation—implementation; preventive maintenance; procedure manuals and detailed operating plans.

E. TRANSPORTATION

11. Transportation

    a. Coordination of traffic functions; traffic organization and management.

    b. Working with common and contract carriers to reduce transportation cost; negotiation of new transportation arrangements and rates.

    c. Scheduling of carriers to tie in with receiving, warehousing, and shipping; selection of carriers; routing; use of common contract and private carriages; use of rail, highway, air waterway, and ocean transport.

    d. Unloading and loading cars, trucks, ships, barges, planes; stowage procedures—bracing, blocking, tie-downs.

12. Carrier and Vehicle-Fleet Operations
   a. Planning, designing, and operating terminals and docks.
   b. Setting up and managing a company-operated fleet of vehicles; ownership versus leasing; equipment specifications; number and types of vehicles required.
   c. Vehicle maintenance; number and types of vehicles required.
   d. Pick-up, delivery, and over-the-road routes and schedules; sorting, routing, and handling freight.
   e. Driver productivity; cost finding and control.
   f. Documentation; rating; office procedures.

F. SYSTEM AND PROCEDURES

13. Electronic Data Processing
   a. Application of EDP to production and physical distribution; computer feasibility studies; justification on economic and "intangible" factors.
   b. Functional specification for systems; determining objectives and requirements.
   c. Systems development—flow charts and conceptual diagrams; liaison and guidance for programming staffs.
   d. Data transmission; computer networks, teleprocessing, control of branch and similar operations at distant points.
   e. Tying together EDP with manual and other less sophisticated data processing systems.
14. Planning and Control of Inventories, Production, and Purchasing
   a. Sales forecasting—estimating future requirements to guide purchasing and production; measuring growth trends, seasonal variations, and other fluctuations.
   b. Economic lots; inventory carrying costs; trade-offs on risks of excess stock versus running out.
   c. Order points and quantities; safety stocks for surges in demand; inventory turnover; cataloging and classification of items; production and inventory record systems.
   d. Production planning, routing, scheduling, dispatching, expediting; establishment and control of banks of material between production processes.
15. Order Processing, Paperwork, and Office Procedures
   a. Manual, mechanized, electronic systems for handling documents and data in production and distribution.
   b. Order processing systems—control of flow of orders; redesign and rearrangement of order processing to minimize time lag and errors.
   c. By-product information from orders—integration of order processing with invoicing, credit, accounts receivable, and inventory control.

    d. Production, inventory, and distribution recordkeeping; verification of record and actual balances.

    e. Office layout and space requirements; office procedures; document flow charts; design and control of forms.

G. CONTROLS

16. Management Controls, Supervision, Organization
    a. Organization charts and manuals—defining authority and responsibility.
    b. First-line supervision—number and type of supervisors needed, job descriptions, assignments; supervisory training; evaluation of needs; setting up courses.
    c. Productivity standards for planning, scheduling, improving performance of men, and signaling potential problems; cost, time and volume reports for control.
    d. Work simplification; standard operating procedures, manuals, flow charts; techniques for balancing men, equipment, facilities and workloads.
17. Manpower, Cost and Productivity Controls
    a. Manning tables for production and physical distribution operations at various levels of activity; job descriptions.
    b. Estimating manpower requirements from sales forecast to avoid excessive hiring and later layoffs.
    c. Leveling workload peaks; policies on overtime and part-time labor.
    d. Standards of performance—work-measurement records and reports; control of labor costs.
    e. Reassignment of men as workload fluctuates—labor pools; "well of work" projects for slack periods.

H. PROJECT MANAGEMENT

18. Implementation and Training
    a. Setting up organization to carry out project—development of implementation schedule, supervision and control of progress, application of PERT, CPM, other techniques when required.
    b. Review and evaluation of architectural plans, bids for equipment, construction.
    c. Preparation and review of progress reports and performance reports.
    d. Employee training programs; management orientation programs regarding new systems and facilities.

PHYSICAL DISTRIBUTION SYSTEMS ANALYSIS

As an alternative to tackling individual aspects of the physical distribution system, like those listed above, it may be desired to make a thorough study of the entire function. If so, the following outline will provide a general procedure for the analysis: [21]

A Procedure for Physical Distribution Systems Analysis

1. Overall assessment of present operation
   a. Establish objectives
      —service desired
      —production level
      —etc.
   b. Determine production capabilities at each plant (source)
   c. Investigate marketing and customer relations
   d. Obtain product data [22]

      —number of lines
      —number of items
      —rate of introduction of new products
      —expected growth
   e. Procure data on volume
      —present
      —deviations from forecast
      —expected rate of growth; trends
      —seasonal fluctuation
      —quantity/item
      —re-order points
      —irregular fluctuation
   f. Get information on E.D.P.
      —present uses
      —potential applications
   g. Regarding orders, find out:
      —frequency
      —sources
      —processing methods
      —types
      —stock-outs
      —back orders

---

[21] The following list is a composite of materials adapted from: H. W. Davis, "Opportunities for Improvement in Physical Distribution," p. 7, privately circulated, Drake, Sheahan/Stewart Dougall; F. R. Denham, "Making the Distribution Management Concept Pay Off," *Proceedings of A.I.I.E. National Conference,* 1967; Ashdown, *op. cit.*

[22] *Note:* In addition to the data listed in "d" through "n," the analyst should check the items on the "Information Required" list on pp. 633–635.

    —order size

    —line items/order

  h. Regarding shipments, obtain:

    —number of shipments

    —shipments/item

    —number orders vs. number shipments

    —weight/shipment

  i. Transportation methods, determine:

    —types used

    —potential types

  j. Channels of distribution

  k. Methods of distribution

  l. Service levels, by:

    —product group

    —customer classification

    —geographic classification

  m. Important competitive aspects

  n. *Costs*—on each component of the present method

2. Isolate and examine in greater depth any unusual factors peculiar to the present system.

3. Examine inventory function in relation to overall system.

4. Determine possible alternative methods of distribution.

  a. present system is first alternative

  b. an "improved" present system should be the second alternative

    —make the best use of what is available

    —work toward improvement of any phase of present system that may become a part of the new one

    —improving present system is easier, quicker, and maybe better than a questionable new one.

5. Determine which alternatives are operationally practicable, by comparing such factors as:

  a. service level

  b. other requirements; specifications

  c. investment

  d. effect on production

  e. relationships to transportation

  f. effect on packaging

  g. order processing

  h. E.D.P. requirements

  i. costs

  j. intangible factors

6. Simulate costs of each alternative method for comparison with base data of present method.

7. Determine least cost method commensurate with equal or better service than present method.

8. Evaluate return on investment.

CONCLUSION

This chapter has attempted to provide a basic understanding of the physical distribution function in order that the reader can better comprehend the interrelationships between it and the material handling function. It can be seen that there are a number of interfaces offering opportunities for cooperation as well as significant savings. The alert and progressive material handling engineer will promote such efforts as will be beneficial to the overall organization, not only with the physical distribution "function"—but with all other related functions, with which he has common interests in achieving profit improvement.

Index

✧ W9-BMW-311

AVERY'S LAW

Ben wandered out to the barn. Avery and Clay were playing cards by the light of a single lantern.

"I suppose you'll be heading out tomorrow," Ben said, settling in between them.

"Likely," Clay admitted.

"Ever consider going by way of Buffalo Springs?"

"That where you figure the riders went?" Avery asked.

"They wouldn't go to Jacksboro," Ben declared. "Not with a cavalry post half a mile from town. Buffalo Springs is a wild place. There's little law, and even that's got a nose for minding its own business."

"So have I," Avery said, "but I don't suppose it would hurt to swing out that way and have a look. Clay?"

The younger man nodded, and Ben mumbled. "Good. I'm going with you."

"You got family to tend," Clay reminded him.

"I've got something else to settle first," Ben objected. "If a man hurts me, I have to hurt him back. Right, Captain?"

"That's the law I live by," Avery said. "We ride at daybreak, Ben."

REVENGE . . . AND A SCORE TO SETTLE

AVERY'S LAW

G. CLIFTON WISLER

PaperJacks LTD.

TORONTO   NEW YORK

AN ORIGINAL

PaperJacks

AVERY'S LAW

PaperJacks LTD

330 STEELCASE RD. E., MARKHAM, ONT. L3R 2M1
210 FIFTH AVE., NEW YORK, N.Y. 10010

First edition published March 1988

This is a work of fiction in its entirety. Any resemblance to actual people, places or events is purely coincidental.

This original PaperJacks edition is printed from brand-new plates made from newly set, clear, easy-to-read type. No part of this book may be reproduced or transmitted in any form or by any means, electronic or mechanical, including photography, recording, or any information storage or retrieval system, without permission in writing from the publisher.

ISBN 0-7701-0705-2
Copyright © 1988 by G. Clifton Wisler
All rights reserved
Printed in the USA

*for my grandad, C. S. Higgins,
who shared so much of his West*

Chapter 1

It was a bright morning, even for spring. The skies were clear and blue, and only a light dew on the ground reminded Ben of the heavy rains that had been his constant companion since the end of April. Those rains had given the garden life, had filled the hillsides with wildflowers, and had brought the creek flowing over its banks in a dozen places.

"Wettest May in twenty years," old Mrs. Berry had told Ben's mother the week before at Sunday meeting. Ben had taken her word for it since he hadn't been around five of those years and didn't remember much about some of the others.

Spring rains were good for the farm. They softened the earth and made late planting of summer corn easier. They brought the pasture grass halfway to Ben's knees, made it green and soft so the cows ate themselves plump and heavy. When the water in the creek rose, the little well he and his father had dug before the war would fill with good clean water, saving him and his brother Michael the long trip upstream with the cumbersome water barrels. One less chore meant more time for swimming and plowing, mostly the latter.

"Your father always intended to open up that west pasture to the plow, Ben," his mother had said to him only the day before. "Next year I believe you'll be planting corn there."

"Yes, ma'am," Ben had said, knowing full well it would take a new team of mules to break that ground. There would never be money for buying livestock.

As Ben joined his brothers and sisters around the hard oaken table, he couldn't help frowning. Money for mules? Michael and Matthew had worn through the knees of their britches and the elbows of their shirts, and Martha was close to threadbare. Ben had to roll up the sleeves of one of his father's old shirts so they didn't overlap his fingers. Even so, the shirt nearly swallowed his chest. The lot of them looked to be shaggy yellow-haired vagabonds just wandered in off the range. Only Catherine had anything close to respectable clothes, and that was because their mother had sewn her a simple dress from some gingham cloth left over from Mrs. Berry's new curtains.

"A girl's entitled to a new dress when she turns thirteen," their mother had argued. Little Martha hadn't complained. The dress would pass down to her sooner or later.

Well, times were hard, people said. Nobody much cared when Jack County boys went about in fathers' shirts, barefoot and a bit ragged. Ben took it hard that his mother didn't have a new dress for Sundays, though. Willa Haskell did love a bit of lace and a hair ribbon.

She never complained. Instead, she slaved away like the dickens, cooking and cleaning and getting her children schooled in all she deemed most important. As they ate, Ben couldn't help admiring the way she stretched a slab of bacon and some cornmeal into breakfast for five. It troubled him, though, to note how seldom she smiled, that her bright blue eyes so rarely lit up with their old sparkle.

"Your sister Carrie's with child again, Catherine," Ben's mother said when the last bite was eaten. She looked to Catherine as if the girl would be the only one interested. "We ought to make a journey down to see her once the corn's brought in. It's been a time since we've been to Austin."

"A year and a half," Ben mumbled. "And she was up here last Christmas."

"Well, there's a new child to be seen," his mother declared as she cleared the plates. "Besides that, Ben Haskell, a woman never sees her girl children as often as she'd like!"

"I suppose that means you can go awhile without seeing the boys, eh, Ma?" Ben asked, nudging Michael.

"Well, as it happens, that's true enough," the woman said, taking a broom and sweeping the two of them out the door. "Boys the likes of you two I can do without."

Ben leaped off the porch and stood beside Michael in the empty farmyard. Their mother stood in the doorway, laughing. The boys knew all too well she hadn't meant those words. It was only that Haskell boys had a way of getting off on their own. The older ones were running a freight business off near Tyler on the other side of the state, and even a letter was a rarity.

"You two best get to work," Catherine ordered as she took the broom and began sweeping the porch. "I can't do everything myself."

"Just listen to her," Michael grumbled, shaking his head. "You'd think she was the biggest one with all that high talk."

"She's bigger'n you," Ben said, starting for the barn. "And she's bossier'n me. You get the hogs tended to. I'll feed the chickens."

Michael didn't bother answering. He simply headed for the back of the house where his mother kept the slop bucket. By the time Ben was spreading feed for the chickens, he could hear Michael and the hogs grunting at one another over at the pen.

Ben couldn't help sneaking a glance. Michael put on his best hog face, then called the animals every foul name an eleven-year-old could think of. One or two new ones cropped up now and again, and Ben knew Michael had spent an afternoon up the creek with Henry Berry when work should have been done.

Boys and hogs just naturally went together, Ben decided as he turned back to the chickens. Half the time one couldn't be sure which smelled better. Fortunately, boys outgrew the hog stage. Otherwise, Ben figured the human species would stop right there, for his mother often remarked that no woman would take anything that smelled like a hog inside her house.

Michael would outgrow that pretty soon. Ben was mostly civilized by the time he'd turned twelve. Another year, maybe a year and a half, would do it. By then little Matthew would be at the hog stage.

"I wonder why girls don't go through all that," Ben said to the cranky old gray rooster as he gave the bird a good kick away from the barn. The hens all scurried around, and Ben shrugged it off as the way things were. Girls were more refined, at least the way his mother raised them. Catherine was learning to play the pianoforte before the thing had to be sold to pay taxes. Even little Martha had taken to wearing a bit of ribbon in her hair, and she was but eight. Or was it nine? Sometimes it was hard to keep track.

As Ben tossed out the last of the feed, he recalled the fine white dress Carrie had worn at her wedding in

Jacksboro. No one ever looked prettier than Carrie, not ever. That man of hers, Tom Plummer, had been decked out in his gray uniform with the yellow cuffs. They'd been as smart-looking a pair as ever graced the meeting house, that was for sure.

That was the last time they were all together. Bob and Ed had joined their father up in Tennessee that next summer, and Carrie had gone to live with her in-laws in Austin until the war was won. Nobody had expected to lose in those days. It was all so far away, back East, where nobody ever went.

Even when the men started straggling back with the bad news, things didn't change much. Only when the Yanks built their new fort at Buffalo Springs, then moved it right up on top of Jacksboro, did it all become clear. Now the bluecoats were mostly occupied chasing Comanches, and that suited Ben just fine.

If he hadn't been so busy daydreaming about Carrie's wedding and the war and all, Ben might have noticed the dust swirls appearing on the Buffalo Springs road. It wasn't as big a cloud as usual. The road was still damp from the rain. Still, it marked the arrival of visitors. Only when the sound of hooves approaching the house reached his ears did Ben investigate.

Michael had noticed them earlier. The boy was standing near the hog pen, taking the reins of a tall brown mare. The horse's rider and three companions stood close by, all dressed in worn cotton shirts and ragged trousers. Ben judged them ranch hands, probably some new men brought in by Mr. Cyrus Handley over at the Bar H. There was talk of taking cattle up the Chisholm Trail to Kansas. If Ben hadn't had the farm to manage, he would have signed on himself.

"Howdy," Ben said to the men as he approached. "Can I do something for you?"

"You must be Ben Haskell," a tall man with narrow gray eyes said, stepping out from the others and extending a hand. "My name's Caldwell, Zach Caldwell. I was told you might have a horse or two to sell."

"No, no horses to spare," Ben said, gazing at the four sturdy animals Michael was leading to the water trough. "Yours don't look to need replacing, though."

"Oh, they aren't for us," Caldwell explained. "I'm scouting the county, buying mounts for my outfit. We're fixing to drive a herd of cattle up to Kansas."

"Then you must be working for Mr. Handley," Ben said.

"That's right," Caldwell said, shaking Ben's hand now that it was finally offered. "No horses, you say?"

"None to spare, and what we've got wouldn't get a man to Kansas," Ben grumbled, pointing to the lone saddle horse that remained in the corral. "Pa took the good ones with him to Tennessee."

"It's the same story all over," Caldwell remarked, shaking his head sadly. "Your pa didn't make it back, I take it."

"Fell back in Alabama," Ben told them.

"He rode with General Forrest!" Michael boasted.

"Got himself shot in the head," Ben added, staring at his toes. "My brothers buried him there."

"Many a fine man rode and died fighting with Bedford Forrest," Caldwell declared. The other men nodded, mumbling their agreement as they followed Ben toward the porch.

"My, I wasn't expecting company the day before Sunday meeting!" Mrs. Haskell exclaimed when she appeared in the doorway. "Ben, who are these gentlemen?"

"Horse buyers," Ben told her. "I let 'em know we don't have any stock to spare."

"You might try Frank Simpson's place across the creek," she suggested, pointing the way. "He rounds up range mustangs each spring, breaks 'em to the saddle."

"They make fine cow ponies," Ben added. "I don't think he's driven them to market as of yet."

"We'll have to try the man," Caldwell replied, turning to his companions. They seemed in agreement. "Ma'am," Caldwell then said, making a slow half circle around Ben, "if it wouldn't be too much to ask, do you suppose we might have something cool to drink? My boys and I have been riding most of the morning, and we're parched."

"Well, I suppose I can find you some bark tea," Mrs. Haskell said somewhat reluctantly. "Would that suit you?"

"Just perfect, ma'am," Caldwell said, grinning.

"Anything, ma'am," one of the others said.

"Ben, would you fetch some well water?" Mrs. Haskell asked as she motioned the men toward the porch. "You might also see that Catherine has the little ones seen to."

"Yes, ma'am," Ben said, setting off as ordered.

He trudged around the side of the house, shaking his head. There was a whole bucket of cold water in the kitchen. He'd set it there just before breakfast, not even an hour ago. And Catherine! She never let the little ones out of her sight, not even for a minute. She hardly gave Ben or Michael a minute's peace, and she never let up on Martha or Matthew.

Ben filled the well bucket and went back toward the house. As he started up the back steps, Catherine appeared in the doorway.

"Listen," she whispered.

Loud voices filled the house, and Ben frowned. Caldwell was yelling — screaming — at Ben's mother. Mrs. Caldwell's voice was different. There was a new tone. She was frightened. Ben felt his skin grow cold.

"Catherine, take the little ones to the smokehouse," he said, trembling.

"Ben, who are those men?" she asked.

"I don't know, but they don't act like anybody I ever saw come to look at horses," he told her. "You keep those little ones in the smokehouse till I come get you. Understand?"

"I'm not stupid," she reminded him. "What about Michael? You want me to look for him?"

"Only if you see him straightaway. Whatever, don't let those fellows see you."

"You think those men are trouble?"

"I don't know, but I won't have anybody yelling at Ma. She always says it pays to give danger a fair amount of leeway."

"Yeah," Catherine said, smiling nervously. "Be careful, Ben."

"I'm not exactly stupid myself," he told her as he stepped past her with the bucket. He waited for Catherine to escort Martha and Matthew on toward the smokehouse before continuing to the kitchen.

"I got a bucket of cold water right here!" Ben announced as he marched on to the parlor. "Ma, you want to fix up that tea now?"

"Set the bucket down, boy. Then sit yourself on the floor. We've got a discussion going on here with your ma," Caldwell explained as he pointed the long barrel of a Colt revolver at Ben's stomach.

"I tell you we have no money," Mrs. Haskell said. "I had to sell furniture to pay this year's taxes. Do you think I'd have my children dress in rags if I had money?"

"Everybody's got a little cash put aside, Zach," said a tall man with a scar across his chin. "People have to buy feed, purchase seed corn."

"We barter for what we don't raise ourselves," Ben argued, stepping away from Caldwell's pistol and joining his mother. Ben gripped her hand tightly, then continued. "We have some cattle, a few hogs, and chickens. We sell an animal sometimes. Harvest last year was poor. I wasn't big enough to plant enough corn, and the rains were scant."

"Come on, boy," said the man with the scar, reaching over and grabbing Ben by the shirt. "You got this big house. You're bound to have money somewhere! Where is it, boy?"

"I'll tell you," Ben's mother said, laughing sourly. "Here. It's right here in this box."

Ben scowled as his mother opened a drawer on the side of a small table and drew out a small metal box. Caldwell took it, opened the lid, then tossed it angrily against the wall.

"What kind of joke is this?" asked the man with the scar, snatching a pair of notes from the floor. "It's all Confederate! Government bonds! Treasury notes! Worthless!"

"The government might come back," Mrs. Haskell said grimly. "Look, my husband gave his life for the cause. We sent all our horses and most of our stock to the commissary. We put every ounce of hard money into bonds. We're dirt-poor now. You can't bleed money out of cactus and buffalo grass!"

"You can get it out of stubborn women and their kids, though," Caldwell declared, motioning to one of the others, a thin-faced man with rusty-red hair. The red-haired cowboy drew out a knife and started toward Ben's mother.

"She's telling you the truth!" Ben shouted, sliding over to block the redhead's path. At the same time Mrs. Haskell reached down and took a pistol from the open drawer.

"She's got a gun, Zach!" the scarred man yelled as Ben's mother cocked the hammer and fired at Caldwell's smiling face. Before Ben knew what had happened, Caldwell's shoulder exploded. The redhead then charged toward Ben like a bull buffalo.

"Ma?" Ben cried as the man slammed him against the wall and kicked him hard in the ribs.

"Run, Ben!" his mother screamed as she fired the pistol a second time.

Ben felt his chest catch fire as he struggled for air. His left arm suddenly erupted with pain, and something shattered over his head. He couldn't see what was happening, but he groped for his mother.

"Ma?" he called again, reaching out in desperation. His fingers crawled along the cold wooden floor until they reached something warm and soft. He blinked away the confusion clouding his vision. He located his mother's face. A brown, sticky ink stained the front of her dress. "My God!" Ben screamed as her eyes fixed in a terrible final stare. "Why?"

There was no one to answer. He heard the clatter of boots and the jingle of spurs on the floorboards as the killers made their escape. Moments later the sound of horses drew his attention as they raced off toward Buffalo Springs.

"Ma, please, Ma," Ben mumbled, stroking her soft hair, hoping that somehow his fingers might restore life to her cold blue eyes. She never spoke — couldn't. He rested her head gently on the floor beside him and closed her eyelids.

"If Pa was here, they never could've done this," Ben whispered, holding his aching arm carefully as he struggled to his feet. "If I'd been a man, they'd be the ones dead, and Ma'd still be alive."

He stumbled over to a chair and sat down. Tears streamed down his cheeks, but he blinked them away. The pain in his arm grew worse, and his head clouded.

"Why?" Ben cried as he slumped against the wall. "Haven't we suffered enough?"

But his voice was little more than a whimper. Nobody heard.

Chapter 2

Ben didn't know how long he lay in the chair unconscious. It must have been hours because the sun had crossed half the sky when he finally opened his eyes. He managed to rise, but the aching in his arm had turned to sharp pain, and he got no farther than the door before halting.

"It's broken," he mumbled, running his fingers along the bone to where the flesh was purple and swollen. He'd broken the other arm a few years before. It was the same as then, only an inch or so closer to the elbow.

Ben rubbed his eyes dry, then stared at the bloodstains on the floorboards. His mother was gone. Maybe she hadn't been hurt as badly as he'd thought. He heard someone moving about in the kitchen. A pot boiled on the stove. He stumbled toward the door, but the slightest movement sent waves of pain rolling up his arm. He sat down on the floor instead and fought the urge to shout.

After a few minutes, Ben heard footsteps. He muffled a cry, and voices whispered fearfully. Then Catherine's face appeared in the doorway. Her normally rosy face was now painted a peculiar shade of pale white.

"I'm sorry, Ben," she said, kneeling beside him. "I heard the men go, so I brought everybody back to the house."

"Where's Ma?" he asked, gazing hurriedly down the hall.

"They killed her, Ben," Catherine said, tears welling up in her eyes. "Michael and I took her out to that hill where we set the stone for Pa. She wasn't very heavy, you know. We dug pretty far. Michael could stand up in the hole and not see over the top. That seemed deep enough."

"Sure." Ben nodded his agreement.

"We never buried anybody before."

"I know. Is everybody else all right?"

"Yeah, but I don't think Matt and Martha really understand."

"Neither do I," he mumbled. "Help me up?"

Ben gave her his good right hand, then fought to hold the left one as still as possible. He couldn't, and he winced as Catherine helped him rise.

"Is it broken?" she asked when Ben pressed the arm to his belly.

"I think so. You suppose you can tear some strips of an old sheet so I can bind it?"

"We'll need splints, too," Catherine said, turning to go. "I do know how to tend a fracture, Ben. Who do you think splinted the last one?"

Ben made his way to the heavy oak table he'd helped his father craft the year Matthew was born. Catherine soon returned and set to work. After straightening his arm, she bound it tightly.

The smaller children soon appeared. Martha held on to Matthew's hand. She was at the age when some of the mysteries of life began to fade, and facts became necessary. Matthew was young enough to rely on things and people, smiling and laughing and playing his way through life.

Who will he rely on now? Ben asked himself.

He wished he was strong like his mother. Catherine had her grit. Here she was, just thirteen and taking charge. That was Ben's job. Why wasn't he able to do it?

Instead, his mind filled with Zach Caldwell's grinning face, those cold gray eyes that had been all too ready to order pain and death. Ben saw the blood on the floor and remembered his mother's empty eyes. He wasn't thinking of his brothers and sisters, and he should have been.

"Where's Michael?" he asked finally, glancing around the room for some sign of the boy.

"I sent him to fetch Dr. Mitchell, or at least Mrs. Berry. Somebody. I didn't know how bad you were hurt. You have an awful bump on your head. Besides, I thought we ought to warn everybody about those men."

"That was a good idea, Catherine," he said as she tightened the bindings. He wanted to scream, but instead he gripped the side of the table and ground his teeth.

"Does it feel tight enough?" she asked as she tied off the ends of the bandages.

"Feels like an old mule's stomped it!" he cried. "It's fine. You did a fair job of it."

"Did my best anyway," Catherine said, stepping away. "I suspect Doc will want to do it over. He'll say you didn't scream loud enough for it to be done proper."

She tried to smile, and Ben added, "Probably cut it off." He then slipped his broken arm behind the tabletop and pretended to be a one-armed cowboy. The little ones laughed.

"You feel like watching 'em a bit?" Catherine asked as the children dragged chairs closer to Ben. "I want to scrub the floor. You know. I want to get rid of the . . ."

"Sure," Ben told her. "Go on, Catherine, do it."

"I thought we might have a chicken for supper," she called from the hall. "Maybe a good meal will make us all feel better."

"I don't think I could eat anything," he mumbled.

"What about you two?" she asked. "Think you could eat some roast chicken? With boiled potatoes and maybe some carrots?"

"No carrots for me," Martha whined.

"I'll eat yours," Ben offered, pulling Martha over onto his lap. "I love carrots."

Catherine glanced through the doorway and laughed. Ben read traces of strain on her face, though. Jack County girls were grown at fourteen, and Catherine was well on her way. Boys took longer, he told himself.

Matthew hopped up and nestled in on Ben's right knee, and Martha scooted over onto the other. It warmed him, feeling them so close. Ben's insides remained hollow, frozen by terror and loss. He remembered the times his mother had held him or helped him or passed along some secret of the universe. A tremor wound itself through him.

"You sick, Ben?" Matthew asked. "Does your arm hurt bad?"

Ben shook his head and reached his good arm around the little ones. He hoped somehow the closeness would fend off the heavier questions, erase the darker faces that would come with understanding.

He couldn't explain how he felt, how it wasn't a physical thing gnawing at him, that if he had been stronger or smarter the whole thing might have turned out differently. A fool should have seen they were thieves! Michael could have run for help while Ben and his mother held off the strangers with rifles.

What does it matter now? he asked himself as Catherine grabbed a hatchet and started for the chicken coop.

"Get that old gray hen, the one with the speckled beak," Martha called, hopping off Ben's knee. "That's the one always pecks at us."

"Can't have that, can we, Ben?" Catherine asked, hugging little Martha when the girl reached her side. "One gray hen for supper."

Matthew squirmed, and Ben helped him to the floor. The two children started outside, but Catherine pointed them back to the table.

"You stay inside," she said. "Ma never let you watch."

"Ah, Cate," Matthew complained.

"Mind your sister," Ben said, standing.

The little ones returned to their chairs, and Ben watched Catherine nod silently before continuing to the coop.

"Ben, is Ma coming back for dinner?" Matthew asked.

"She's dead," Martha said, suddenly growing confused. "Dead people don't come to dinner, do they, Ben?"

"No," he told them, leaning on the wall for support. "You remember how it was when Pa died."

"I don't even remember Pa," Matthew explained with a heavy sigh.

"They don't ever come back," Ben said solemnly. "Now, look. There's all sorts of work to be done around here. Martha, you go fetch the potato sack. You know how to cut them up. Pick out three good ones and start at 'em. You can cut 'em in halves. Then put the pieces in Ma's stew pot. Okay?"

"Yes," Martha said, reluctantly heading for the potatoes.

"And you, Matthew — get out the plates and glasses. All right?"

Matthew shrugged his shoulders, then stumbled to the cupboard.

Ben left them to their duties. He walked through the front of the house, picking discarded bonds and upset odds and ends from the floor. He emptied the cartridges from the old pistol on the floor, then set the gun atop a cabinet in the hall so it would be out of reach of the young ones. He smiled as he noticed Catherine had erased the bloodstains from the floor, then started back to the kitchen to oversee the dinner preparations.

He was striding through the door when he heard horses outside. Moments later Catherine shouted an alarm.

Ben surprised himself. For the first time he forgot all about what had happened earlier. He reached up and grabbed the Colt. Quickly he loaded fresh cartridges and fixed the percussion caps in place. Then he took the heavy revolver in his right hand and stepped out onto the porch.

Ben expected to discover Michael and maybe one of the Berry boys. It couldn't be the doctor. He rode around in a small carriage. Mrs. Berry would have brought a wagon. The two figures sitting atop horses opposite the porch were strangers.

"What do you want?" Ben asked warily, aiming the gun at the nearest one, a dark-browed man with wavy black hair. He appeared to be aged around forty and was wearing a gray cavalry hat and faded cape.

"No harm to you, boy," the man said, dropping his reins and holding his empty hands skyward. "That's for certain."

"Nor me, either," the other added, raising his hands in like manner.

Ben stared hard at the riders. The second one flashed a youthful grin. Intense chestnut eyes gazed out from beneath a forehead overgrown with unruly strawberry-blond hair. He couldn't have been much older than Ben himself, eighteen or nineteen at the outside. More likely sixteen or seventeen. Both riders wore black cavalry boots and homespun gray trousers. Their accents came from the Deep South — Alabama, maybe Georgia.

"Mind if we step down?" the older man asked. "We've been in the saddle most of the past two days."

"You stay where you are!" Ben ordered. "We've had enough of strangers this day."

"If you've had trouble, we might help," the younger one said. "My name's Clayton Hamilton, late of Putnam County, Georgia. This here's Captain Avery. We been riding west ever since Yanks burned us out."

"Keep those hands up!" Ben shouted as young Hamilton's wrists began to drop.

"Look, son, we're tired, and we mean you no harm," the captain told Ben. "Why don't you let us set our guns down and walk on over? All I ask is a cool drink of water."

Ben stared angrily at the men as the words tore through him. But there wasn't a hint of violence in either of the strangers' eyes. The uniforms ate away at Ben's suspicions. His father had worn a uniform like that, homespun gray trousers and butternut-brown tunic.

"Okay," Ben relented. "You step on down. Leave your pistols, though. Hang the gunbelts on your saddle horns. I won't have anybody else in my family shot!"

Catherine wandered over. She led the horses to a trough and left them to drink. The gunbelts she took into the barn.

"What's been going on here?" young Hamilton asked, pointing to the earth torn by frenzied hoofprints. "What manner of trouble you have here?"

"Four strangers," Ben mumbled, lowering the pistol at last. "They killed my mother."

"Looks like you had a touch of bad luck yourself," the captain noted, pointing to Ben's arm. "Broke?"

Ben nodded. "I should have suspected something," he muttered. "Times've been bad lately, what with the occupation and all. We get a lot of drifters riding through."

"Like us?" Hamilton asked, laughing. "Guess we might look a little ragged at that."

"These four looked like ranch hands," Ben explained. "They said they wanted to buy horses. If I'd just been more careful, Ma would still be . . ."

"A man does his best," the captain declared as he examined the tracks. "Ole Clay and me, we rode right into a Yank ambush outside Milledgeville. Looking back, there were a thousand signs it was coming. We didn't take note of a single one, though. There's blood on the road there. You hit one of 'em?"

"Ma did. I figured he'd die straightaway. Was a pretty big hole she put in him."

"With that dragoon Colt?" Hamilton asked. "That cannon ought to've put him in his grave by now."

"Grave?" Ben scowled. "I'd feed the whole lot of 'em to the buzzards! I'd kill every one of 'em."

"That's how it should happen," the captain declared.

"But how do you get four grown men when you're just fifteen years old?" Ben asked, frowning at the thought. "Mister, tell me and I'll do it."

"What's your name, son?" the captain asked as he walked to Ben's side.

"Ben Haskell. And I'm not anybody's son. Not anymore."

"Well, Ben, they call me Clint Avery. Clay here, he calls me Captain since I held the rank in the Georgia militia during the late war. I wasn't much for fighting early on. Never owned a slave, you see, and I never had much to do with a government — Yank or reb, either one. Then this bunch of bluecoats rode onto my farm, shot up all my horses and pigs and cows, burned the crops in the field, and shot down friends of mine. When

I went to town to get help rebuilding my house, those same Yanks came back and killed my Mary, left my boys with bullets in their heads. Well, I got only one law to live by, Ben Haskell. I need no government or sheriff or army. If a man hurts me or mine, he'll get hurt in return. And people know me by that law."

"The captain, he tracked down those fellows," Clay explained. "He gathered up a few of us along the way who also got burned out. We found those Yanks roasting a pig down on the south bank of Snyder's Creek. Was close to twenty of 'em, and they were hauling two whole wagons full of fine china and silver stolen off honest folk. Those skunks weren't fighting, Ben, just scavenging after the real army was through."

"We made short work of them renegades," Avery boasted with eyes full of rage. "I saw to it not a one of them walked away."

"We don't like scavengers much, Ben," Clay said, staring past the road toward Buffalo Springs. "Maybe we ought to catch up with these riders of yours and have a little talk with 'em."

"Might be a fair notion," Avery agreed.

Ben heard someone coming up the road then, and he swung his pistol in that direction and took aim. Avery dodged out of the way, and Clay took shelter on the porch. Ben relaxed, though, when he spotted Michael leading the way for Dr. Mitchell's buggy.

"Catherine!" Ben shouted.

His sister raced to the porch, but he waved off her concern.

"Michael's back," he announced. "Best put a second chicken in the oven. Would you men care to stay for supper?"

"For baked chicken I'd fight a Yank brigade," Clay said, grinning. "Mind if I tend the horses and get our guns? I feel a little naked without mine."

Ben felt uneasy. He glanced at Catherine, and she

nodded. Ben nodded his approval. By then the doctor had driven the carriage up to the porch.

"Well, Ben, it appears you have all sorts of company," Dr. Mitchell said, glancing warily at Captain Avery. "Shall we go have a look at that arm of yours?"

Ben nodded, then followed the doctor inside. Dr. Mitchell examined the bindings, then opened his medical bag.

"A fine job, Catherine," he pronounced. "Just let me dab that slice on your head now, Ben Haskell, and I'll be on my way back to town."

"Won't you stay to dinner?" Catherine asked. "We can't pay you any money, but you're welcome to a chicken leg."

"Thanks, dear," the doctor said, smiling. "I'll catch a world of trouble from my Judith if I'm not home on time."

Catherine conducted the doctor to the door. Ben, meanwhile, put Matthew and Martha to work setting the table.

While Catherine prepared supper, Clay Hamilton recounted various adventures he and the captain had shared during the war. To hear Clay tell it, Clint Avery was the bravest, most clever man alive. In truth, though, there was something about Avery that inspired confidence. He didn't say much, but what he did say could be taken to heart.

Ben appreciated how Clay and the captain ate sparingly. Another man might have taken more than a fair portion of the meager meal. As it was, Clay took only a slice or two of chicken and a potato. Avery took nothing at all until he was satisfied Matthew and Martha had taken a turn.

Following supper, Michael led the way to the little knoll where he and Catherine had buried their mother. Catherine read a favorite Bible verse, and they joined in a hymn. Then Avery sighed and picked up a small clod of dirt.

"We leave this good woman to the rich, warm earth." He spoke in words that seemed to resound across the hills. "Our trust is in the Lord, that He will raise up His sword and lay low those who have committed this outrage. We pray for the safety of these innocents. May they be watched over and cared for."

"Amen," Clay added.

"Amen," the others echoed.

Mrs. Berry appeared a half hour later. She sat with the little ones a few minutes, then took Ben aside.

"What will you do now?" she asked. "You can't hope to run this place all by yourself."

"I'll send word to my brothers," Ben explained. "They'll be sure to want the farm."

"And yourselves — you and the children?"

"I thought maybe they could stay with you awhile, Miz Berry. We'll wire Carrie. I'll bet she'll take Martha and Catherine in with her. Maybe Matthew, too. Cate's practically grown, and the little ones aren't much trouble. I figure Michael will want to stay on the farm with Bob and Ed."

"What of you?" the woman asked.

"I have something to do," he told her, staring out toward the road.

"You leave such thoughts where they lay, Ben Haskell," Mrs. Berry warned. "You shouldn't even sit a horse with that arm as it is. We'll inform the cavalry at Fort Richardson. They're good at tracking renegades."

"Since when?" Ben asked. "They can't even catch a few dozen Comanches. They're best at putting poor folks off their land on account of taxes due. By the time the bluecoats get around to riding to Buffalo Springs, those killers'll be north of the Red River, up in the Nations and out of reach of the law."

"Ben, you'll get yourself killed for sure."

"Maybe it should've been me in the first place," he mumbled, gazing back toward the knoll and its two lonely stones. "If I'd been more of a man, they'd never have killed Ma."

"Now how were you to hold off four grown men? Use your head, Ben. You never had one chance against such odds. Nor do you now."

"I'll never know that, Miz Berry, not for sure," he cried, stepping away and rubbing his eyes. "That's why I have to ride to Buffalo Springs and find out."

"No!" Mrs. Berry objected. "No!"

"Yes," Ben whispered. Then he led her back to the house.

That night when Catherine had put the little ones to bed, Ben wandered out to the barn. Avery and Clay were playing cards by the light of a single lantern.

"I suppose you'll be heading out tomorrow," Ben said, settling in between them.

"Likely," Clay admitted.

"Ever consider going by way of Buffalo Springs?"

"That where you figure the riders went?" Avery asked.

"They wouldn't go to Jacksboro," Ben declared. "Not with a cavalry post half a mile from town. Buffalo Springs is a wild place. There's little law, and even that's got a nose for minding its own business."

"So have I," Avery said, "but I don't suppose it would hurt to swing out that way and have a look. Clay?"

The younger man nodded, and Ben mumbled, "Good. I'm going with you."

"You got family to tend," Clay reminded him.

"I've got something else to settle first," Ben objected. "If a man hurts me, I have to hurt him back. Right, Captain?"

"That's the law I live by," Avery said. "We ride at daybreak, Ben."

Ben rose slowly, nodded grimly, then headed back toward the house. He paused long enough to gaze at the cloudy sky overhead. He hoped it wouldn't storm. That would make the trail difficult to follow. After sharing his plans with Catherine, he entered the small room he shared with Michael and Matthew.

"You be careful, Ben," Michael urged after Ben shared his plans.

"Keep an eye out for the little ones," Ben replied. "I'll be back before long."

But as they let sleep whisk them away to a better place, neither of them much believed that. Those words had been spoken often by Haskell men during the past eight years. Many had left. None had come back.

Chapter 3

By noon the next day Ben was riding with Captain Avery and Clay Hamilton down the dusty road to Buffalo Springs. As Ben urged his spotted mustang pony along, he kept a lookout for signs of the riders who had killed his mother. Sometimes the captain's keen eyes detected leaves spotted with blood. Other times the loose sand revealed the tracks of horses ridden hurriedly down the road not long before.

Ben left the tracking to his companions. They were good at it, and he suspected they'd had practice during their militia days. As for himself, he struggled to keep pace and fight off the throbbing of his arm and the ringing inside his head. There weren't many who could have stayed atop a horse, but Ben had sat a horse before he could walk. Sometimes he felt he'd been born in the saddle.

Even so, if he'd ridden a bigger horse, one that didn't recognize the gentle nudge of Ben's knees in its ribs or the soft touch of his fingers as he stroked the tough length of the mustang's neck, he might have been in real trouble. As it was, the pony sensed the urgency in Ben's heart, and it kept pace with the big black stallion ridden by the captain and the sorrel Clay kept carefully at Ben's right hand.

The past thirty hours had taken a toll on Ben. His normally crystal-blue eyes were streaked with red, and he wiped cold sweat from his forehead. Fatigue cast his face in pale tints, and his cheeks seemed hauntingly hollow.

Mainly it was from lack of sleep. Most of the night he'd tossed and turned, any hint of rest stolen away by nightmare and recollection, fragments of reality interwoven with terrifying images of what might occur when Ben stood at last face to face with the four killers.

Long before dawn he'd started packing up clothing and linens, boxing the silver candlesticks and his mother's jewelry box — the sole surviving valuables after spring taxes had been paid. He and Michael had carried the cedar chest that contained Grandmother Handley's wedding dress and their father's polished saber out to the wagon. Matthew had dragged along a prized Kentucky rifle used by some ancestor when Andy Jackson beat back the British from the gates of New Orleans.

Catherine and Martha brought along other possessions — a few plates and cups, old clothes, some rag dolls, and a few toys passed through the family from child to child. Ben then led out the two plow horses, and Clay helped Michael harness the animals to the wagon. After devouring a hearty breakfast of smoked bacon and fresh eggs, Michael fed the animals. Then they all started down the road.

The wagon rumbled along only as far as the Berrys' farm. Ben knew Mrs. Berry would see the necessary wires were sent, would ensure that Catherine, Martha, and Matthew got aboard a coach headed south. Michael could stay with the Berrys and look after the Haskell hogs and chickens until his older brothers arrived from east Texas.

Ben waved his family a sad and silent farewell, then accompanied Clay and the captain northward.

"Seems like old times, doesn't it, Clay?" Avery had asked when they'd located the first traces of blood on the road.

"Yeah, we've been down this trail a time or two, all right," Clay had replied. Ben had noticed Clay's face shared none of Avery's eagerness.

Soon they reached the Trinity. The road, such as it was, came to a halt there. A few homesteads clung to the north bank of the river before the war, but bands of Comanches prowled the region now, and the families had fled. In truth, there were scarcely any people to speak of between Jacksboro and Buffalo Springs. North of the springs the country was wild, buffalo prairie broken by spotted hills and jagged ravines. Only a few isolated settlements appeared between the springs and Red River Station, seventy miles to the north.

Up to that point, Ben had been content to ride alongside Clay, letting Captain Avery take the lead. Now the youngster urged his mustang on past the others as he sought out the Trinity crossing.

"You know this country, Ben?" Clay asked as they inched closer to the river.

"I've been up here some," Ben explained as he studied the currents. "The Trinity twists and turns a lot, and the channel can trick you."

"You recognize the ford?" Avery asked.

"There isn't a true ford along here," Ben answered. "The crossing changes by seasons. See here," he added, pointing to a churned-up section of the bank. "Our riders tried to cross here, but it was too swift. The best place is downstream, I'd guess, maybe another quarter mile or so."

"Could be they've laid a nice little trap hereabouts," Avery warned as he scanned the far bank. "This'd be the place for a bushwhack."

"I thought about that," Ben confessed. "You have to cross somewhere, though, and I can't see 'em figuring anybody from our place would follow. Only one they saw 'sides me and Ma was Michael. Who'd figure him to trail along?"

"They couldn't know we'd happen along," Clay said, gazing sourly across the river at the seemingly deserted far bank. "Let's find Ben's crossing and get on along."

"Lead away, Ben," Avery instructed. "But keep your eyes and ears open. I've noticed there's a lot of blood on the trail now. Somebody's getting mighty weak."

"You figure them to hold up and let him get his strength back?" Ben asked.

"Not these four," Avery said, spitting. "They'd kill their own ma rather'n let her slow 'em down."

Ben frowned. It wasn't a pleasant thought, and he reminded himself to stay alert. But as he splashed into the river and started the crossing, he found no sign of anyone waiting on the far side. Fresh tracks greeted them on the north bank, and they stepped up their pace.

"Look over here," Clay called as they threaded their way up a hillside cluttered with black locusts and post oaks. Over to the right was a clearing marked by the black scar of an extinguished campfire.

"They were here," Avery said, spurring his horse onward. "We're closing in. See? The trail's fresh."

Ben saw the tracks were deeper, easier to follow. That was good. The killers had grown careless. They were tiring, and their pace reflected it.

"Any of this look familiar, Ben?" Avery asked, pulling his big stallion up alongside Ben's spry pony.

"I've been up here once or twice," Ben said, "but it's been a good while."

"Well, ease the pace whenever you're unsure as to what's ahead. And keep that cannon of a pistol handy."

"You see something, Captain?" Clay asked.

"Over there," Avery said, pointing to a nearby mound of prickly pear.

Ben pulled up his horse and stared hard at the ground. He spotted saddlebags and what appeared to be a tin of biscuits.

"I don't understand," Ben said, nudging the horse back into motion.

"Your man must be getting pretty near his end," Avery remarked. "He's lightening his load. I expect the others may have left him behind. Be ready. We could stumble on him any time now."

Ben wiped his forehead and fell back behind Clay.

"Don't you worry, Ben," Clay said, ducking under a low locust branch. "We'll have those men in no time at all."

But it was another two or three miles before they came across anything out of the ordinary.

"Over on the left, Captain!" Clay shouted.

Ben turned that way instantly. He drew his pistol when he spotted a riderless horse wandering in the trees up ahead. As Avery moved in that direction, the horse darted away.

"You boys stay put," Avery commanded as he climbed down from his horse and drew a long-barreled rifle from a saddle scabbard.

"Best to do as he says," Clay advised. "Might do well to get off these horses, too. A man in the saddle makes a fair target."

Ben didn't argue. He slid off his horse and led the animal to a stand of locusts. Clay was tying his horse's reins to a low limb when Avery called for them to rejoin him.

"Well, there's just three now," the captain said, pointing to a dark shape half buried by the foot-high buffalo grass.

Ben dropped the reins of his horse and stumbled to the body. It was Caldwell, all right — what was left of him, anyway. The man's entire shirt was soaked in blood, and his eyes stared blankly skyward.

"You won't be killing anyone again, will you?" Ben asked, his lower lip quivering as he stared hard at the man's face. For a moment Ben considered firing his pistol at the corpse to release some of his anger. Something held him back. Already the flies were gathering. The body was stiff and smelled vile.

"It's time we headed on," Clay whispered, pulling Ben away. "The others are probably up at Buffalo Springs."

"Come on, boys," Avery called. "Don't plan to bury him or say prayers, do you?"

"Let the buzzards have him," Ben growled.

"You're pretty cold to be so new at this," Clay said as they mounted their horses. "Usually takes a while."

"Even when you see your ma shot down in front of your own eyes?"

"Yes, even then," Clay answered with a darkening brow.

Avery eased the pace more and more as they approached Buffalo Springs. The rocky ground hid the killers' trail now, and Ben worried that the riders might successfully make their escape. Deep down Ben knew it wouldn't happen. Men who would rob a poor farm family, shoot down a woman, and leave children parentless and alone wouldn't scatter into Comanche country. No, they'd ride to the springs. They'd be waiting.

The miles began taking their toll on Ben. There was no

hope of relaxing, no chance to let down his guard. Every bend in the trail offered an ambush. But as the sun began to sink into the western hills, they found no sign of the riders.

"We'll pitch camp along here," Avery announced, waving at a break in the trees just ahead.

"We're almost there," Ben complained.

"Maybe so, but I'd as soon not happen across those boys in the dark. I'm bone-tired, and Ben, you look like a walking ghost."

Ben tried to return Avery's grin. Exhaustion had set in, though, and Ben's lips barely moved. His face was white as a midsummer moon, and his eyes were a washed-out blue. His left arm hung limp and heavy as cast iron. His feet ached, and his head throbbed.

"I'll get a fire built," Clay whispered as he helped Ben off the mustang. "You get yourself some rest."

But as Ben tied the horses to a small willow and sat down on a nearby boulder, Avery strode over and ordered Ben up.

"There's work to be done," the captain grumbled. "Tend the animals and help Clay round up some wood."

"Can't you see he's worn through, Captain?" Clay called out from the brush.

"A man takes to the trail with me, he pulls his own weight," Avery declared. "You know that, Clay."

"He's got a broken arm, and he's ridden twenty miles since morning," Clay argued. "He can't very well strip the saddles. I'll take care of the mounts after I get the fire built."

"Nobody ever had to do my work for me," Ben said, struggling to his feet. "I'll do it."

Avery smiled in triumph, then grabbed a can of beans and a slab of salt pork from a provision bag Catherine had given them that morning. He pulled a skillet out of one of his saddlebags and walked to where Clay piled kindling for the fire. The captain took his knife and began slicing the pork while Clay built the fire. Meanwhile, Ben staggered over to the horses and began loosening the cinches.

By the time Ben managed to drag the saddles from the animals and fold the saddle blankets, Clay had a fine fire burning. Ben bit his lip to stave off the ache from his arm and slipped the bit from the big black's mouth.

"Let me help," Clay whispered, appearing quietly at Ben's elbow. "Tough to do with only one arm."

"Yeah," Ben admitted as he leaned against the trunk of a nearby oak.

"He's a hard man," Clay told Ben, tossing the bridle atop Avery's saddle. "Don't take it to heart. He's never known an easy day in all the time I've ridden with him."

"How long's that?" Ben asked.

"Four years now. Since '64. The captain's boys and I were at cadet school together. Thomas and Rustin — those were their names. Strange thing is they left school 'cause word was the Yanks were burning academies and shooting the cadets. I wound up in the militia, and they ended up dead."

"I guess Avery took it pretty hard, huh?"

"I couldn't say. He's never said much about it. He cut down those Yanks, though, every last one of them."

That night as they ate their meager dinner, Ben found himself watching Avery's every move, struggling to solve the riddle of the man. But Avery had a way of masking his emotions, and the captain's eyes gazed right past his companions and on into the night. There was an absence of emotion on Avery's face, but an angry darkness clouded the man's eyes.

Ben found himself reassured by Avery's cold, heartless look. The man would be up to the task of avenging Ben's mother's murder. Ben was afraid as well, though.

Avery was the kind who must be watched carefully.

After eating, the captain carried his blankets off into the brush and spread them there. Ben made his bed close to the fire, near Clay and the horses.

"Does he always go off like that, away from everyone?" Ben asked.

"Only when we're on the trail," Clay explained. "He sleeps light, and he knows what to do when there's trouble. Ben, you stop worrying about him and get some rest. Tomorrow morning we're likely to find those other riders. You'll need a clear head."

Ben nodded and crawled into his blankets. He lay still, staring up at the sky.

"What're you thinking on?" Clay whispered.

"Home. Or what used to be home," Ben mumbled. "You ever think about Georgia?"

"Not much. Sometimes I remember my mama and papa. Sometimes my sister. It's a waste of time, though."

"Don't you ever figure to go back?"

"Can't."

"You can't go back to Georgia? Why not?"

"Wouldn't want to. Look, Ben, you should've stayed with your brothers and sisters. You had somebody. Me, my father fell at Manassas. He wasn't a military man. He painted portraits of the governors and their wives. But he rode off with his regiment and got killed just the same.

"I suppose that's part of life, losing your papa. I worked harder on my studies. I did fair, especially painting. Then Sherman started down from Atlanta. Milledgeville, being the state capital, was right there in his way. The same bunch that got Captain Avery's family killed my mama and sister. Ben, I was fourteen the day my company rode up to my house. I found 'em myself,

Mama and Clem. Those scavengers even shot the dogs! When a boy comes upon his family slaughtered, his home in ruins, he grows up mighty fast.''

"I know," Ben said, closing his eyes and fighting off the memory of his mother's frozen eyes.

"Sometimes when the captain's off looking things over and I'm all alone, I do a little sketching. But I am what I am now. There's no going back.''

"Why?"

"Look, Ben, we didn't stop with those raiders. The captain said there was a general responsible for all the murdering. We meant to have our revenge on him, too. The captain, a few of his neighbors, and half my company found the Yanks' camp. We hit 'em hard, Ben. There were two generals there, and we hung the both of 'em. The Yanks posted notices. They offered a bounty for our heads.''

"That was Avery, Clay."

"No, Ben, it was me. I was there. Shoot! I was the one tied the nooses. Those weren't the last ones I killed, either. I don't even know how many anymore. I ride with the captain 'cause we're two of a kind. Killing changes a man. You'll see tomorrow. It makes a difference. If you know what's good for you, you'll head back home.''

Ben shook off his sadness and gazed across at Clay Hamilton. The Georgian's words rang through Ben's mind, but he already felt different. He knew no matter what took place in the morning, he'd never again be a simple farm boy. Zach Caldwell and the others had seen to that.

Chapter 4

Two hours after dawn Ben followed Clay Hamilton and Captain Avery into Buffalo Springs. It would have been an exaggeration to call the place a town. For the most part it was an odd collection of wooden shacks strung together along a dusty road. The federal troops had stationed a garrison there for a time, but the location proved unsuitable. The previous autumn the troops had relocated their post south of Jacksboro on Lost Creek.

Nothing was stirring that early. An old Mexican was sleeping in the doorway of a ramshackle stable, and the aroma of eggs frying in a shack down the road drifted through the air. Captain Avery led the way toward a red adobe hut at the far end of town.

"Saloon," Clay said, sniffing the air, then pointing out a small sign beside the door. "Could be your friends'll be there."

"They're no friends of mine," Ben barked as they dismounted. "I guess we'd better get it done, though."

"Hold up there, boy," Avery said, grabbing Ben's shoulder and holding him in place. "You don't even know who you're after. For my part, I'd as soon get the right ones. I'd also like to keep my hide free of bullet holes."

"Come on, Ben," Clay said, motioning toward a side window. "Let's have a look."

It proved impossible to see anything through the layers of accumulated dust and smoke coating the window. Avery finally joined them.

"Ben, you sure you can recognize these fellows?" the captain asked.

"Wouldn't you if they killed your mother?" Ben answered sharply. He glared at Avery with cold eyes.

"You have to be sure," Avery went on to say. "Men's lives are at stake. This won't be easy. There are bound to be at least a dozen or so men in there. And Ben, don't you let on you notice anything! Keep your thoughts to yourself. Just watch and listen. We'll come back out here, talk it out, make our plans. Got it?"

"I understand," Ben assured the captain.

"Look, take my hat and pull it down so that it covers your forehead. Slip your arm down under the tabletop so they won't notice the splints. Then you pay attention to everything. If trouble breaks out, get that dragoon Colt of yours and fire quick as you can. Just don't hit ole Clay here or me. We'd take offense at that, I'm afraid."

Clay laughed, and Ben cracked a faint smile. It passed quickly, though. His insides were cold and dark, and he was prepared to do murder.

Ben followed Clay and Avery inside the saloon. There was a wooden bar in the back of the place, with kegs of spirits and a few bottles sitting on a nearby shelf. Makeshift tables and chairs cluttered the rest of the room. Avery pointed out three chairs and an empty table in the shadows to the left.

"I'll get a bottle," Avery told them.

Clay ushered Ben to a chair beside the wall, then sat down across the table. They stared out at the eight or nine others scattered around the room. Ben slid his left arm beneath the table and allowed the rim of the captain's hat to shield his face from view.

"Recognize anybody?" Clay whispered.

"I think that one at the bar with the Mexican spurs is one of them," Ben said, coughing. "There's something familiar about the tall one at the table on the right, too."

"That's not enough to kill a man for," Clay said, a frown spreading across his face. "You've got to be sure. We can't just go kill some cowboy who stopped by your place for a dipper of well water."

"I know," Ben said. "I'll be able to spot their voices for sure."

"I hope so. You be sure to keep yourself in the shadows, too. If they spot you, that'll be the end of the three of us."

"I will," Ben pledged.

Avery returned with a bottle of trade whiskey and three glasses. Ben drank none of his, though. His mother had been powerfully against spirits, and he wasn't ready to start making his own rules for living just yet.

"Sip a hair of it, Ben," Avery advised. "It'll settle your nerves."

Ben felt his fingers tremble, but he ignored the liquor.

"I'll be steady enough when the time comes," Ben assured them.

"Have you spotted the three that did it yet?" Avery asked.

Ben shook his head.

"He thinks he can recognize their voices," Clay said.

"I'd hope so. Don't like to think I rode all the way up here for nothing. You boys wait here. I have a thought."

Avery took the bottle over to the right-hand table and

set it down. He also drew out a pack of worn playing cards and waved them in front of the men sitting there.

"Anyone for a little morning amusement?" the captain asked.

"Well, we got some new blood in town," the man with the Mexican spurs said from the bar. "Sit on down, friend. I'll be right over."

"Don't mind if I do," Avery said, grinning broadly as he joined the others. He then flashed a hard glance at Ben. "What do you play hereabouts? A little stud poker?"

"Draw," the man with the Mexican spurs called as he sat down. "Jacks or better to open."

Ben felt something rattle in his head. He knew those voices. But there was a third man. Where was he?

"Those the two?" Clay whispered.

"They were there," Ben grumbled. "There was another man, too. He was the one who used his knife on Ma and broke my arm."

"See him around anywhere?"

"Not in here," Ben said, glancing around. "I'd remember that man's eyes. They were green, and he had a small scar on his chin."

"Now we're getting somewhere. Maybe we ought to look around outside some," Clay suggested.

"I don't know," Ben said, sighing. "Might be better if we just waited. He might come in here, or one of these fellows could lead us to him. Either way'd be safer than looking for somebody in a town this size. People notice things, especially from strangers."

"You're right. Well, best relax and leave things to the captain. He'll figure it all out."

Ben worried more and more as time passed, though. There was no trace of the green-eyed man, and Avery seemed more concerned with winning at cards than doing anything about the two killers sitting at the table with him. Around noon a Mexican boy came around with food from an adjacent cantina. Clay handed the boy a dollar, then took a plate of tamales and passed a second one to Ben.

The food took Ben's mind from his troubles. For a few minutes he gobbled tamales and listened to the chatter at the nearby table. Then the saloon door swung open, and three men strode inside.

"Three more," Clay said, pointing to the Mexican spurs jingling as the dusty men made their way to the bar. They downed a quick drink at the bar, then joined the card players. Ben tried to catch a glimpse of the newcomers' faces, but they were turned away from him. He knew no subtle way of walking over without revealing his splinted arm and, with it, his identity.

The game heated up. The new arrivals seemed to possess an excess of fresh banknotes, and they didn't mind betting them freely on the chance of winning a large pot. A sizable portion of the wagered currency wound up between Avery's protective elbows.

He's going to take their money and let them go, Ben told himself. *He doesn't care if they stabbed my mother!*

But Avery was only biding his time. In the middle of the afternoon he excused himself from the table, saying he needed to check on his horse. Ben and Clay followed the captain outside. They made their way down the street to a deserted clapboard hovel. Avery frowned, then spoke.

"Well, our little party grew some," the captain pointed out. "These others seem to be part of the same company. Likely they had someone watch the road in both directions while they went about their business."

"Could be," Ben admitted. "Did one of those three that came in happen to have green eyes and a small scar on his chin?"

"I'm not much for noticing a man's eyes," Avery said, "but a scar I would have seen. There's nobody like that among this outfit."

"Then there's still one more," Ben grumbled. "The one that killed Ma and broke my arm had a scar on his chin. I seem to remember he carried a knife in his boot, too."

"Well, that beats all!" Avery cried, kicking up dust with his boot. "Six men it is now. Boy, you do like long odds, don't you?"

"You want out?" Ben asked nervously. "I wouldn't blame you."

"Didn't say that, did I?" Avery growled. Wrinkles appeared on his forehead as he glanced back at the saloon. He scratched his head and paced back and forth a few minutes. "Look," he finally said, "we'll wait for old scarface. When he gets here, I'll talk him into joining the game."

"Then what?" Ben asked.

"If you'd keep quiet and listen, you'd find out," Clay complained. "Pay attention, too. All our lives depend on it."

"Good advice," Avery declared. "Ben, you watch me good. When I pull back from the table, you draw that cannon of yours and start shooting."

"Shooting?" Ben asked. "At what?"

"The ceiling, those men — I really don't much care. Make some noise, and add to the confusion. Clay, you handle the one in the yellow shirt over on my left. Kill him sure before you turn to anybody else. He's got the sights filed off his pistol, so he's a man to take into account when the shooting's close and fast. After he's finished, work on the rest of 'em from left to right. Likely they'll scatter. Keep 'em away from the door."

"What about me?" Ben asked.

"Once it starts, keep your eyes on anybody breaking for the right. They'd be behind me, and I don't do too well with my back shot up. See you don't hit me or Clay, though. We're on your side, remember? Just take your time. Cock the hammer and squeeze off each shot slow and careful. One shot that hits is worth twenty that miss."

Ben nodded and stuffed his trembling fingers into his pockets.

"Clay, I'll start with the two on my left," Avery continued. "Then I'll work to the center, just as you do. Got it?"

"Sure," Clay muttered as he began loading the last empty cylinder of his pistol. "I'll wait for your move."

"You do the same, Ben," Avery cautioned. "I know it's eating at you some, those fellows laughing and playing cards. You do as I say, though. This way we'll be rid of the whole batch and still ride off in one piece. Got to do it quick and certain, before they catch on."

"I'll do my part," Ben promised. "Don't you worry. I'll kill my man."

"You don't have to," Clay added, staring grimly at the saloon. "Just keep 'em distracted some."

Avery then led the way back down the street. Avery went in first. When the captain had rejoined the game, Clay led Ben back to the table. They sat in the shadows, and Ben ran over and over in his mind the deadly plan Captain Avery had drawn for the execution of the five card players.

Time passed, and Ben's nervousness eased. He began to relax. His eyes closed once or twice, but a nudge from Clay's boot always restored vigilance.

Even in a state of weariness, Ben would have reacted to the entry of the green-eyed man. He was much larger than Ben had recalled, six and half feet tall and well over two hundred pounds. The group at the poker table called out at once, and the heavyset newcomer turned their way.

Ben let Avery's hat fall across his face, and he made

sure his splinted arm was concealed. Then he concentrated on the captain.

The conversation at the card table was loud and somewhat heated. Ben couldn't catch all the words. The saloon had filled with an odd assortment of drifters: cowboys between jobs, halfbreed Tonkawa and Wichita Indians, veterans or ranchers who'd lost their homes to the new heavy taxes imposed by unsympathetic carpetbagger politicians supported by federal occupation troops. Two squaws sat in the doorway, and anyone entering or leaving had to stumble over them. The crowd worried Ben, but many of the drifters were unarmed, and the majority were drunk.

Two of the card players slid their chairs over so that their tall friend with the scarred chin could join in. It grew quieter. Ben fixed his eyes on the back of Captain Avery's chair and waited for the signal. When the captain finally stirred, though, Ben froze. The pistol seemed suddenly heavy. His knees locked. His fingers seemed unable to grip the handle.

"What's your hurry, friend?" the big green-eyed newcomer asked, rising also. "Sit back down. Say, I've got a trinket I'll bet you'd enjoy eyeing."

The big man pulled out a small locket and opened it up. The tintype inside was of Ben's mother. Ben recognized it at once. His insides boiled with rage.

"Pretty, ain't she?" the scar-faced killer asked. "Just got it from a little gal down on the Trinity. Pretty, she was."

"You!" Ben screamed, lifting the cumbersome pistol and swinging it to bear on the hulking man. "Murderer!"

Men scattered as Ben rammed the hammer back with his thumb and pulled the trigger. The resulting explosion sent a heavy ball slamming into the green-eyed man's chest. He instantly slumped back against his chair. One hand fumbled with his holster while the other gripped the edge of the table. Ben fired a second time, and the big man's head snapped back. The ball struck just above his nose and tore through the skull. Even as the dead raider toppled to the floor, stunned onlookers tossed cards aside and reached for pistols.

Clay quickly dropped the two on the left, and Avery opened up on the others. The table was like the unfortunate target at an October turkey shoot, and splinters whined through the air almost as fast as bullets tore through the surprised raiders.

Ben took shelter behind a cupboard and repeated the difficult procedure of cocking the hammer and firing the huge pistol. Each chamber went off in turn, blowing holes in the table, in the wall, finally in one of the killers who tried to circle to Avery's right. Quickly the six men who moments before had sat quietly playing cards were converted to moaning, bleeding bodies gasping out their lives. The other occupants of the saloon dodged for cover or stampeded over the squaws and out into the street.

When the powder smoke began to clear, Ben stared in horror at the scene before him. Avery collected coins and those bills not sliced to pieces on the bloodstained table and floor. Clay made his way from raider to raider, making certain all were dead. Ben let the heavy Colt drop from his fingers onto the hard wooden floorboards. His head pounded, and his stomach turned over. He refused to be sick, though. There was too much hatred surging through his heart for anything akin to sympathy to seep in. His fingers trembled, though, and he tore open the collar of his shirt as the smoke choked him.

"Come on, Ben, let's get some air," Clay urged as he picked up the discarded pistol and stuffed it into Ben's belt. "There's nothing left for you here."

Ben resisted Clay's outstretched hand, but the sadness in the young Georgian's eyes penetrated Ben's anger.

"Just one thing," Ben whispered as Clay led the way toward the door. Ben bent over and pried the locket from the green-eyed man's grasp. Blood spotted the frame, and the back was dented. The gentle face and loving eyes, though, were a sharp contrast to the sounds of terrified women sobbing outside or the curses of the saloon owner.

"Here, this should pay any damages!" Avery shouted as he tossed a few bills on the bar.

"What about buryin' these fellows?" the owner demanded.

"I don't much care if you feed 'em to the hogs," Avery replied. "Two days back they rode in on that youngster's farm and killed the boy's ma. Broke his arm when he tried to stop 'em! Now, you figure if we're lacking in respect, friend. I figure they're lucky we shot 'em quick."

Ben watched as Avery's long finger pointed the way out the door. Clay grasped Ben's right wrist and pulled him along. Ben stumbled along as his two companions headed toward where the horses stood tied to a hitching post.

"Doesn't it bother you, Clay?" Ben cried as they mounted up. "The killing and all?"

"Not for a long time," Clay muttered. The young man's eyes told a different story.

"No different than shooting a wolf on the prowl, Ben," Avery declared.

"No different?" Ben cried.

"One animal's the same as another," Clay added. "No *man* kills women and robs honest folk."

Ben let the words work on the dark pall of guilt that was beginning to descend on him. He couldn't help remembering the cold, lifeless green eyes of his mother's murderer, though. By the time they passed the last of the shanties that housed the residents of Buffalo

Springs, Ben shivered from the chill realization that now he, too, was a killer of men.

"So what do we do now?" he asked Clay.

"That's up to you, Ben," his young companion told him. "You can ride back down that road and return to your brothers and sisters."

"Or?"

"Come along with us," Clay added sadly. "We'll probably wander west a bit more. It's what we always do."

"I can't go back," Ben mumbled, feeling the still-warm barrel of the pistol against his belly. "How could I tell them what I did?"

"Yeah," Clay said, sighing. "I remember."

"Is this how it always is for you, Clay?" Ben asked, clutching the reins with trembling fingers. "Ride through, shoot a few men, then ride somewhere else?"

Clay didn't answer. Instead, he tapped his horse's shoulder and closed the gap between himself and the briskly trotting Clint Avery. They left the timeworn road to Red River Station and turned westward toward the late-afternoon sun.

"It's not always like this," Clay said when they'd left Buffalo Springs five or six miles behind. "We rode a long ways after the militia disbanded. Then we worked our way across Tennessee and Arkansas, tending stock or harvesting crops. Sometimes we'd do some carpentry. We wintered in Memphis in '65 building cabinets or putting up sheds. The captain's got a fine touch with a hammer."

"You never settled anywhere?"

"Captain gets itchy. We've been cautious of towns, especially ones with a garrison about. Never can tell when some Yank officer who was down in Georgia might pop up. It was safer to keep moving. We've ridden close to six months around Texas, though. It's been quiet enough. Nobody's bothered a couple of old broken-down rebs.''

''Until now.''

''There won't be any trouble about this, Ben,'' Clay assured him. ''People in towns like that don't cry over a few drifters. It's clear there's no honest living to be made in Buffalo Springs, though. If you've an itch for robbing the mail or stealing horses, maybe, but I never took to those lines myself.''

Clay grinned for the first time that afternoon, and Ben breathed a trifle easier.

''There's a lot of ranch work out here,'' Ben declared. ''Out past Jacksboro, especially. People are starting to go back to the places they left in '64 and '65. There's a cattle trail up to Kansas, and I heard several outfits down in Young County are hiring hands.''

''Might be worth a try. We'll tell the captain. I always did like horses, you know. Riding the range might be a fair kind of life.''

Ben could have argued that, but he didn't. It was good to have a horizon to look forward to, even if it proved to be a disappointment.

Avery soon halted the conversation anyway. They were heading into hostile country now. Only weeks before the bluecoat cavalry had tangled with Comanches thereabouts, and the captain had turned cautious.

Ben appreciated the slower pace. A fresh spring breeze struck his face, and his eyes began to rid themselves of the sting of powder smoke. Around him the trees filled with songbirds, and squirrels scurried about branches. A hawk soared high overhead.

He realized it was good to be alive.

A man has to leave home sometime, he told himself. His brother Ed rode to war at seventeen, and Ben was only a year and some odd months younger. Recalling Ed's shiny buttons, the yellow trim their mother had sewn on each sleeve, brought back to Ben the memory of his family, though. His smile faded, and he remembered the mixed sense of terror and hatred that had filled him as he shot the big green-eyed murderer in the saloon.

"You'll grow accustomed to the wayfaring kind of life," Avery said, humming an old camp song as they rode up a hill, carefully ducking beneath the jagged thorns reaching out from locust trees to tear at the intruders.

"I suppose," Ben said as he pulled his pony alongside the captain's huge black. Ben then took the weathered gray felt hat from his head and passed it back to Avery.

"It's a good habit, returning things," Avery observed. "You'll make a fair man, Ben Haskell."

But as they rode along, Ben wondered. He constantly urged his horse along to keep pace with the others, but he wasn't at all sure he'd ever grow accustomed to living on horseback.

Chapter 5

Ben Haskell soon grew accustomed to sleeping under the open and often stormy Texas sky. The weeks spent camped along the winding creeks and flood-swollen rivers of north central Texas provided a chance to mend, to cast off the nightmares that plagued his troubled soul, and to rediscover the wonderful closeness he had once enjoyed with the land.

Avery was a wanderer, and the three floated across the countryside like a band of gypsies, never staying anywhere more than a few days. They got their living shooting an occasional deer, pulling catfish from a stream, or else bagging a pair of rabbits in a small snare. It was a bountiful country, Ben told himself, and it yielded everything a man needed to survive. Except, perhaps, true peace.

By early May they reached the wild, abandoned hills of northern Young County. Before the war, close to a thousand souls had farmed and ranched that region.

Comanche deprivations had erased most of the buildings and sent their residents scurrying for safety. Ben recalled two wagons of Young County refugees passing through Jacksboro after the fierce Elm Creek raid of '64. Pitiful, distraught faces of widows and orphans had stared out from the plodding wagons. He'd wondered what could empty those eyes, could chase the life from a six-year-old's face. He knew now.

"This is Comanche country here," Ben told his companions as they camped along the Brazos in the northwestern section of the county. "Old Fort Belknap's down south, and the new Yankee fort on the Clear Fork is well to the west. We'd best be careful."

"Always am," Avery declared. "How's that arm coming, Ben? You about ready to leave those splints behind you?"

"I'm ready," Ben confirmed. "Not sure the arm is, though."

Clay trotted over and examined the arm. Even with the splints still in place, a bump of sorts could be spotted where the break had been.

"Looks to me like another week, Captain," Clay announced.

"Take it off and let's see," Avery commanded.

Clay shrugged his shoulders, took out a knife, and cut loose the bindings. As the pressure holding the splints in place was eased, a sharp pain ran up the length of Ben's arm. Avery scowled, then turned the injured arm over and over in his weathered hands.

"Bone's knitted," Avery announced. "Now it's time to ease it into use."

Ben gazed at Clay, who was clearly less certain.

"Captain, another week might be surer," Clay suggested finally.

"Make it stiff, keep it from healing proper," the captain grumbled. "It's time Ben was a two-armed man again. He might come to have use of those arms before long. What do you say, Ben? Ready to give it a try?"

Ben bit his lip and nodded. The arm was sore, true, but as he worked the elbow and flexed his fingers, the pain seemed to fade. Later that night it returned.

"I thought it a little early," Clay complained.

"It's no such thing," Avery argued. "Man's bound to suffer some. Pain's something you get used to, just like hunger and cold."

Ben nodded, though he was unconvinced. And as the arm continued to ache, he regretted he hadn't made a stand. The captain always spoke with a commanding voice, though, issued orders even when he seemed to be asking favors. Ben always complied.

Clint Avery was a puzzle Ben couldn't solve, but he spent little time worrying about it. After all, Avery kept to himself, and he did seem to know what he was doing. Not once did the three riders stray into the midst of Comanche raiding parties. Avery also avoided renegade whites like the bunch they'd tangled with at Buffalo Springs. Ben was grateful, and he kept his doubts to himself.

So did Clay. As Ben grew to know and rely on the young Georgian, a strong bond was formed. Maybe it was the loss of family that drew them together. Or maybe it was Avery's habit of remaining distant. For whatever reason, the two teen-aged vagabonds swam and fished and hunted away those last weeks of spring. More than once they swapped outrageous tales or played pranks upon each other or their leader.

"Infernal boys!" Avery growled each time he was victimized. A storm of curses and several descriptive phrases would usually follow. Ben and Clay then made a rapid escape, returning only hours later when the sting of injured pride had passed.

Those days spent on the banks of the Brazos breathed

fresh life into Ben's weary chest. For six years he'd been the eldest son in a fatherless family. The responsibilities had weighed him down. Now he felt light, liberated. His legs regained their old spring, and he bounced along on horseback, his eyes quick to catch a glimpse of anything out of the ordinary, whether maverick longhorn, lazy jackrabbit, or prowling cougar.

Animals, even mountain cats, were of little concern. But when Ben spotted a half dozen riders splashing their way through the shallows a hundred yards away, he instantly pulled out of line and silently waved for Avery to halt.

The captain drew in his rein, then followed Ben's gesturing hand to where the riders approached from the right flank. Avery pulled a rifle from his saddle scabbard and turned his horse to face the oncoming horsemen. By that time Ben could already see clearly that the riders wore the leather chaps, homespun cotton shirts, and broad-brimmed hats of range cowboys.

"A ranch crew," Ben whispered.

"Yeah?" Avery asked. "Those boys who raided your place were dressed like cowboys, too, remember?"

Ben frowned and steadied his nerves. He felt the big Colt in his belt and hoped it wouldn't be needed. Clay had already rested a long rifle across one knee. By now the lead cowboy had noticed the three strangers on his left and formed his companions into a crescent twenty yards long. The cowboys drew pistols, and their leader shouted, "All right, boys, let's show them how we treat rustlers in Young County!"

Ben felt an icy fist grip his insides, and he cried out, "Hold up, there! We're no thieves. We mean you fellows no harm."

"Oh?" the leader asked. "You just restin' those rifles on your knees for the feel of it, I guess?"

Avery's eyes concentrated on the opposing riders, and Clay backed his way toward a large boulder. Ben, though, raised his right hand and held the reins in his left. He then edged his way toward the cowboys.

"That's close enough, boy!" the leader called.

"Close enough to tell I'm no cattle thief?" Ben asked. "My name's Ben Haskell. I'm from Jack County, and I can't see why anybody in his right mind would steal another man's beef when the whole of northern Texas is running with mavericks!"

For the first time the anger in the cowboys' eyes abated. Their leader cracked a smile and pushed his oversized hat back from his forehead, revealing thick curls of oily black hair.

"How old are you, boy?" the dark-haired man asked.

"Fifteen," Ben replied. His nerves settled as the cowboys replaced their pistols in holsters. Some bit off plugs of tobacco. Their eyes kept a vigilant watch on Clay and Avery, though.

"Well, Ben Haskell of Jack County, just what are you and your friends doin' on my range? I'd agree with you there are maverick longhorns about, but the truth is that a few men would always rather steal than work."

"Maybe," Ben agreed. "But you can see for yourself that we're hardly driving any cattle. As to it being your range, how were we to know? Last time I was out here, this whole county was crawling with Comanches."

"And when was that?" the rancher asked. "Boy, you're hardly as tall as a good-sized goat as it is, and you say you rode through here when the Comanches were raidin'?"

"Tell you what," Ben said, warming to the dark-haired man's smiling eyes. "Let's make ourselves a camp and I'll tell you all about it, Mr. . . ."

"Adams," the rancher said. "Tom Adams."

"Well, Mr. Adams, I'd have you meet Captain Avery and my good friend Clay Hamilton."

Adams waved the two gray-coated riders toward him, then dismounted. The cowboys followed suit, and soon ten men congregated on the north bank of the Brazos.

"I'm afraid we don't have much in the way of food to offer you," Avery said, passing his reins to Ben and taking command. "You cut our afternoon's hunting a bit short."

"Well, we've got beef and beans," one of the cowboys said. "And Henry over there knows how to make it into a fair feast."

A thin-faced old-timer tipped his hat, and in that instant, the fear and suspicion seemed to pass.

Old Henry clearly knew his way around a campfire. The old-timer sliced green peppers and mixed in a bit of this and that. As strips of beef sizzled in a pair of skillets, a kettle of beans bubbled nearby. The cook also baked biscuits in two Dutch ovens. To Ben, who had grown accustomed to Clay's broiled rabbits or fried catfish, the aroma that enticed his nostrils was irresistible.

"Been a time since you ate good, huh?" Adams asked Ben.

"Oh, we do all right," Ben replied. "Not much taste to it, though."

"You ought to come along home with me for a time. My Eliza's biscuits melt a man's heart."

"Thanks, but I'm kind of tied to Clay and the captain," Ben said, nodding to the two ex-Confederates. "They helped me out a while back, and I owe 'em."

"Well, you do as you think best," the rancher muttered.

Ben nodded, then sat beside Clay and watched old Henry cook.

An hour later all the men gobbled down the wondrous meal and listened as Tom Adams described how a band of cattle rustlers had plagued his ranch that spring.

"They're ghosts!" Adams cried in disgust. "We've been close to 'em a dozen times, but they run the stock into the river and vanish."

"Isn't right a thief should have such a run of luck," Clay grumbled.

"No, and I'll see it ended soon," Adams declared.

"Won't be easy this late into spring, though," Ben said, scratching his head. "Be time to trail your beeves to market soon, won't it? If I was a rustler, I'd lay low, then ride in once your outfit heads out."

"I was thinking the same thing, boss," one of the cowboys said. "That bunch is too clever by half for us to trap 'em and still organize roundup."

"Why don't you leave these thieves to us, Mr. Adams?" Avery asked then.

"What?" the rancher responded.

"Clay and I've done bounty work before, back in Fannin and Dallas counties," Avery explained. "Trust us to tend to it. We're fair trackers, you see, and we don't have a ranch to run."

"And young Ben?" Adams asked. "Does he hunt posted men as well?"

"I do what I have to," Ben answered.

"Includin' killin'?"

"Yes, sir," Ben said with dark, sullen eyes. "If it's thieves and murderers."

"I don't know," Adams said, shaking his head.

"I do." Avery spoke in a commanding voice. "Truth is, we need work, and you need to be rid of these snakes. A dozen men's too many to do what's needed. Three's enough to do the job without being too many to keep out of sight."

Adams stared at Ben with solemn eyes, then nodded. It was settled.

Early the next morning the two bands of riders went their separate ways. Clint Avery pocketed two fifty-dollar bank notes, wages for the three of them. Another hundred was pledged if the rustlers were caught or shot.

"That means shot," Clay whispered as he and Ben

saddled the horses. "The captain won't mess with prisoners, especially when they'll only get hung later on."

Still, a man couldn't be shot until he was found, and for the next half week Avery and his two young companions scoured the northern half of Young County in search of the cattle thieves. Twice they located riders, only to discover they were rounding up strays for some other Young County outfit.

"How will we recognize the rustlers?" Ben asked after Avery let a pair of young drovers go.

"You won't have to," the captain explained. "I'll know."

It troubled Ben considerably that a desperate Avery might swoop down on the first batch of idlers who, like themselves, wandered onto the Adams ranch. Clay dismissed the possibility out of hand, though.

"The captain knows what he's about," the young Georgian assured Ben. "Me, too. We've done this before, and we're good at it."

In the end, though, it was Ben who located the elusive outlaws.

There were four of them, all foul-smelling drifters with unkempt beards dressed in dark buffalo hides and wide sombreros. They talked loudly, drank freely, and seemed little concerned that anyone should hear them.

Ben assumed they were harmless, but when he hid his horse in a thicket and crept closer for a better look, he discovered they rode cavalry ponies that even now bore the distinctive U.S. brand. Moreover, he spotted a pair of running irons in the back of a wagon hidden nearby.

He retraced his steps and rode off to locate Clay and Captain Avery. They were washing the day's sweat off down at the river. Ben said little. The worried gaze in his eyes told the story.

"Lead the way, boy," Avery urged once he'd pulled

on his pants and buttoned his shirt. "Let's finish these skunks and head on along."

Ben led the way quietly to the rustlers' camp. The four men had now been joined by a pair of women — one of rather generous proportions, and the second no older than Ben. The six of them seemed to be a family of sorts, and it ate at Ben that they should show affection, exhibit feelings.

"Ben, you follow Clay around to the right," Avery instructed. "I'll take the left."

"Aren't we going to offer 'em a chance to give up?" Ben asked. "There are women down there."

"No, just rustlers," Avery said, grabbing Ben's wrist and shaking him. "Don't you feel sorry for them, Ben. They'll kill you without blinking, and if you don't do your job, it's likely Clay there or I could get ourselves killed by the man you should have tended. Understand?"

Ben nodded grimly.

After Avery left, though, Ben turned to Clay.

"I know it's hard," Clay confessed as they closed in on the raiders' camp. "It's how it's done, though."

"Even when there's a woman?"

"If you don't think a woman can kill, you're wrong," Clay whispered. "I've seen it. Now quiet yourself and do as I show you."

It was easy, Ben thought as he followed Clay past the wagon. In a matter of minutes the two youngsters held their pistols cocked and ready. The backs of three of the rustlers were less than fifteen feet away. It was impossible to miss. As soon as Avery opened fire, those three would die.

Avery's rifle barrel protruded from a tangle of underbrush maybe twenty yards distant. The rustlers gathered around their campfire. They sat in a perfect trap.

Ben's hands shook as he aimed the enormous pistol squarely at the sombrero on the right. When Avery's rifle spit out a yellow tongue of flame, Ben pulled his trigger. Clay fired, too, and instantly the air exploded. Ben rammed the hammer of his Colt back and fired again, and again. Clay shouted and raced toward the fire, blasting away at anything that moved. The fat woman grabbed a shotgun, then fell sideways as Avery's rifle sent her to an early grave. The younger woman was killed trying to reach the last of the men, a thin, youthful-looking man dressed in a bright serape.

"I give up!" the young man cried as he cradled the head of the girl in his hands. "Please, don't shoot!"

Avery coldly cut the rustler down with the rifle at close range.

Ben gaped in horror at the carnage they had wrought. Bodies had been torn apart, shot to pieces. He'd swallowed his nausea at the saloon, but now his stomach revolted, and he vomited violently.

"Ben, you all right?" Clay called.

"Are you?" Ben gasped as he collapsed to his knees. "How can anybody or anything be all right ever again?"

"I told you," Clay said, helping Ben back to his feet. "It's what's done! They'd have shot us the same way, my friend, and never thought twice."

"I'm not that way, Clay," Ben explained. "I can't kill a man and then turn aside as if I'd picked an apple from an orchard or planted a garden."

"Then you'd best learn," Clay warned with somber eyes, "because, Ben, it's the way you survive. The only way."

Chapter 6

Tom Adams owned some five thousand acres of rolling hills and buffalo prairie nestled along the north bank of the Brazos River. He ran longhorns over that range and most of the open ground north and west of his holdings. Thousands of cattle wandered those acres, and most bore the TA brand. He proved as grateful and generous to Clint Avery and the captain's two young companions as he'd been cold and relentless where the rustlers were concerned.

Adams assembled two thousand head in June and drove them across the Red River and the hostile lands north to Kansas railheads. In his absence, Avery, Clay, and Ben patrolled the range. For Ben's part, he would rather have ridden north, shared the perils and the excitement of the journey. Riding the range proved tiresome and uneventful.

"Don't complain, Ben," Clay warned. "The money's fair, and the food's good."

Ben had to admit that was true. Eliza Adams was even a better cook than Henry Sykes, and the touch of mothering she lent Ben was more than a little welcome. Though the Adamses had seven children of their own, the oldest only ten, both Tom and Eliza seemed prone to adopt the worries of the young ranch hands as well.

"Tom says your family still lives in Jack County," Eliza told Ben one morning when the young man brought kindling for the stove. "It seems strange to me you don't write them, or, better yet, ride over there and have a visit. A family's a fine thing to have, Ben. It's a kind of anchor of sorts."

"My ma and pa are dead," Ben explained. "The farm's not big enough to support another brother, and by now my sisters are all likely in Austin. I'm best forgotten, ma'am. I'd be a stranger to 'em now."

"Because of the killing?"

Ben looked up into her eyes with surprise. Did it show that much? He nodded, then went back outside to split another log.

By the time Tom Adams and his outfit returned from Kansas, Ben knew the ranch from one end to the other. The June sunshine had restored his arm to health and his spirits to life. He enjoyed racing Clay across the open country, and both of them flew with the wind.

Ben always prided himself as a rider, but he had to confess Clay outclassed him. Maybe it was something learned back in Georgia at the academy Clay so rarely spoke of. Captain Avery sat a horse like some kind of general, and his movements were always sharp, sudden, even startling. Clay was so much a part of his horse that Ben could never determine exactly where one left off and the other began.

For his part, Ben had the edge working stock. He'd grown up around the stubborn longhorns, and he knew when to administer a bit of rope's end and when to give the dangerous creatures room.

"You've got the cattleman's touch," Adams told Ben more than once. "That and the cowboy's instincts. That can't entirely be taught, you know."

"It can't?" Ben asked.

"No. It comes with feeling you're part of the land. These newcomers, like your Captain Avery, will never tumble to that, Ben. They look to take what they need and ride on. You understand that to grow, you have to nurture the range, grow with her."

"I don't think I ever thought anything like that."

"Yes, you did," Adams said, grinning. "You just haven't realized it yet."

It startled Ben that Clint Avery remained at the TA Ranch. For a man who liked to roam, Avery seemed oddly content with his job patroling the far stretches of isolated prairie. The captain twice tended to troublesome raiders, but he clearly was no stockman and had not the slightest interest in becoming one.

Clay and Ben, on the other hand, had become dependable cowhands. They found in the camaraderie of the other cowboys a kind of brotherhood of the homeless and forsaken. And more and more, Tom and Eliza Adams became second parents, and the children came to be little brothers and sisters.

The TA Ranch was a big family, Ben concluded, and when first autumn and later winter painted dark shadows across the heavens and shut out the brightness of the stars overhead, some of the gloom was fended off by the warmth of Eliza's smiles, the sweet taste of her peach preserves, and the approving nods of big Tom.

Winter whispered an eerie, lonely song across the range. As the wind grew shrill and snow peppered the December landscape, Ben found himself passing more and more of the evening in a corner of the bunkhouse, staring at his mother's face in the dented locket and searching his memory for a better, warmer time. He'd never spent Christmas away from his family, and the notion plagued him, tore at his heart like the talons of an angry eagle.

"Ma, I'm so alone," he cried to the bitter, unfeeling wind.

Ben saw it affected Clay, too. Even when they gathered in the big house Christmas Eve and shared presents with the Adams clan, Ben felt alone, isolated, apart from the others.

Maybe that's what's sent the captain riding the far range, Ben thought. *It's somehow easier being alone when you're not confronted by those who aren't.*

A blue norther ushered in the new year, 1868. Long daggers of ice collected on the eaves of the bunkhouse, and the wind whined through cracks in the wall, sending shivers through the occupants. For a brief time Ben thought the earth would be swallowed up by a massive monster carved of frost and snow, but in time the storm, as all others before it, passed.

Ben turned sixteen. There was no celebration as there might have been if he'd stayed on the farm back home. In truth, Ben had no idea which particular morning it happened. Tom Adams kept no calendar about, and except for marking Sunday with prayers and a pause in their labors, every day was much the same as another. But though the date was uncertain, the changes that came upon Ben were not.

He grew taller, and his shoulders at last began to broaden. Whiskers appeared on his chin and above his upper lip, and though the application of a razor once a week sufficed to sweep them away, Ben welcomed them as a sign of approaching manhood.

Clay delighted in sporting a thickening moustache, and it vexed Ben to no end when his friend taunted and teased him about his own sparse growth.

"Be patient," Clay advised. "It'll grow in time, Ben. Ten years ought to do it."

Ben only scowled and concentrated on his chores. But except for working a few new colts and moving cattle around the range, there was little to occupy his time.

Spring arrived rather earlier than expected. Late February swung back and forth from wet and dreary to sunny and clear. By March the buffalo grasses were green, and wildflowers again adorned the hillsides. Soon it would be time to collect the cattle, brand yearlings, and prepare a trail herd.

Ben welcomed the work. He'd grown restless, and his new and untried muscles longed for the challenges of hard labor. They came soon enough. Adams had every cowboy on the ranch riding from dawn to dusk, collecting the livestock in four great camps along the river. Soon the air filled with the cries of bawling bull calves given to the knife. The stench of cowhide pressed with hot branding irons mingled with the odor of dung heaps and sweating men.

Ben spent most of his time cutting calves out of the herd so cowboys could mark their flesh with the TA brand and add the distinctive Adams ear notch. Later, when the others were busy culling steers for the trail herd, Ben assisted Tom Adams and a burly cowboy named Stu Jepson in converting ten wild mustangs into saddle horses.

Jepson had the build of a blacksmith. His arms and shoulders were too massive for his trim waist and slender hips. He tended to walk hunched over, a kind of menacing hulk of a man both feared and admired at the same time. Those powerful arms and shoulders were deceptive, Ben discovered. Stu Jepson didn't bend the mustangs with whip or blade. Instead, he used a firm hand, a fierce determination, and a rare talent for melding his spirit with that of the horse.

"Any fool can whip a horse till his heart breaks," Jepson explained to Ben. "He winds up with an animal that's fit for carryin' him along on a sunny day's ride down a wide road. Me, I'd as soon walk as ride an ox. These horses'll take you where you've got to get, and they'll do it when the rain's crashin' down on you, when they're as cold and worn through as you are. That's when you need a horse, boy, and if you touch his spirit, make him one with you, then his rider'll know he's got a mount beneath him."

Jepson had a thousand secrets, and he shared but a few of them. For one thing, the iron-shouldered wrangler smelled more of mustang than most of the horses themselves. He slept with the horses, even ate with them. Sometimes Ben was convinced Stu Jepson *was* a mustang.

"Those horses think so, too," Jepson explained. "That's the real secret, son. Once horses get so they're not mad at you, they'll generally come to cooperate. When they let one man ride 'em, they're apt to allow another."

Ben followed Jepson's technique, talking to the mustangs and letting them carry him around as dead weight. He often rode bareback, sometimes with success. Other times he'd find himself pitched halfway across the corral.

"At least you made a fair landing," Jepson would say, grinning a little more each time. "Next time try to stay atop him, though."

"I was trying this time," Ben would answer.

At supper he related his latest adventures to Clay.

"I don't know if you're staying atop those mustangs any better, Ben, but you are coming to smell powerfully like old Jepson. That may come in handy working horses, but I'd as soon you had a bath before you come to the bunkhouse tonight.''

Ben laughed, then set off for the river with Clay at his side.

Working the horses was a labor of love for Ben. He lacked Jepson's strength and experience, yet he astounded Adams and the cowhands with a knack for gentling the cantankerous ponies and convincing them to tolerate saddle, bit, and rider. However, Ben came to miss the company of Clay Hamilton and even the gruff Captain Clint Avery. As the days passed, and the time neared when the crew would set off on the long trail to Kansas, Ben felt more and more cut off from his former companions.

Tom Adams noticed the change.

"You seem unhappy, Ben," the rancher said as they stowed their tack in the barn. "I thought you'd enjoy working with Stu and me down here."

"I do," Ben said.

"Don't show it much."

"I guess that's true. Partly it's because I know it'll be over pretty soon. And, too, I kind of miss the freedom of the range, the races with Clay and the others."

"I figured you might take to regular ranch work."

"I ought to," Ben said, shaking his head. "It's only these last months that I've done anything else."

"Would you like to stay on here, Ben? I need another wrangler. Stu wants to raise a string of cow ponies, and I've agreed to let him do it. He'll need help, though."

"Thanks for asking, Mr. Adams," Ben said, forcing a smile onto his face. "But Clay and the captain'll be going to Kansas. So will I."

"You don't belong with those two, son."

"I do," Ben objected. "Mr. Adams, it's been good being here, almost like family. It's not the same, though. I know you think you're looking out for me, and I appreciate that, but I have to go my own way."

"Not with Avery. Please, Ben, I've known his kind all my life. They're in a hurry to get themselves killed. Or somebody else."

"Maybe," Ben admitted. "But it's my choice to make, isn't it?"

Adams grumbled to himself and walked away a few feet. Then he turned and gazed into Ben's solemn eyes.

"What made you throw in with Avery in the first place, Ben? You two are about as alike as fire and water."

"He helped me once," Ben whispered. "I owe him."

"How long are you going to honor that debt?"

"As long as I feel it's not been paid."

"I pray it doesn't help you to an early grave, Ben Haskell. That's how it happens all too often."

"I pray so, too, Mr. Adams. But if that's how it works out, well, I've already lived a year longer than I might have."

Ben didn't explain, and Adams asked no more questions. There was a finality in Ben's eyes just then that marked the debate as closed. Sixteen or sixty, Ben Haskell had made up his mind.

Chapter 7

The long trail to Kansas was fraught with peril. Tom Adams had a mere fifteen men to urge two thousand reluctant longhorns across hills and streams, through wicked ravines, and over land tortured by cactus and rattlesnakes. Any moment a horse might fall prey to a prairie dog hole. The sun came close to frying men's brains in June, and there would be days between water holes when the dust and the stench would choke him.

They were not even out of Young County when trouble appeared. Ben was riding on the herd's left flank, jabbering away at the lumbering longhorns, when a single bare-chested Indian appeared on a low ridge fifty yards away. Ben had barely digested the fact when the lone Indian was joined by six others.

"Comanches!" the other flank rider, a tall snaggle-toothed cowboy named Joley, cried in alarm.

Ben said nothing. Instead, he turned his horse and threaded his way into the herd. Comanches or not, they wouldn't be able to charge through a thousand steers.

Joley's outcry alerted Tom Adams to the crisis. The rancher rode down from the head of the herd, collecting riders along the way. Ben was working his way in the opposite direction when Clay appeared.

"Trouble's back there, Ben," Clay announced with a grin. "Don't you think we ought to lend a hand?"

"There are Comanches on that ridge," Ben said, gesturing to where the Indians had appeared. "Comanches, Clay!"

"Then I guess we'd best go see what they want."

Ben tried to protest, but Clay had already started making his way through the nervous longhorns toward the left flank. There was little to do but trail along behind.

The Indians, meanwhile, remained atop the ridge. Another five had joined the first group, and all twelve now started down the slope together. The sight of a dozen armed Comanches made Ben sorry he'd followed Clay. But Clay only slapped his horse into a gallop and hurried to where Adams and Avery were organizing the men.

Adams had collected half the crew when Clay and Ben arrived. The rancher seemed prepared to send them out against the approaching Indians, but Avery objected.

"Mr. Adams, that's just crazy," the captain argued. "Even if you bleed those Indians some, these cows of yours'll be scattered over most of Texas. Take you all summer to collect 'em."

"And what would you do?" Adams asked angrily.

"I'll show you. Give me Clay and a couple of men, and we'll turn those Comanches back on their heels, keep 'em occupied, so to speak. Fuller, there, has got a steady eye, and Ben can hold his own. You get the herd turned and we'll join you later on."

"Fuller?" Adams asked. "Ben?"

"I'll go," Fuller volunteered.

"Ben?" Clay asked.

Ben stared at the long line of Indians closing in on the herd. He couldn't understand how anyone preparing an attack could be so calm. But then Avery showed no panic, either.

"Ben, why don't you come along with me?" Adams suggested, looking at the others for a volunteer.

"No, I'll go," Ben said, sighing as he steadied his trembling fingers.

"Take my Spencer," Joley said, passing the carbine to Ben. "Watch yourself, too, son."

Adams nodded, then motioned for the rest of the outfit to follow. Avery immediately started toward the Comanches, and Ben pulled in behind Clay.

Lord, help us, Ben thought as he rode toward the Indians. The short Spencer repeater would be a help, but it wouldn't aim and fire of its own accord. Ben hadn't shot at anything save squirrels and rabbits in close to a year, and then he'd had time to prepare himself. He'd taken aim and shot point-blank. These Comanches would be moving — fast. And they'd be firing back.

"What we're going to do," Avery explained, "is ride into 'em like a bunch of hungry wolves! Shoot and scream and get their attention. Then lead 'em back up that ridge."

"And if they don't follow?" Ben asked.

"Then Mr. Tom Adams will be short some cattle," Avery said, laughing. "Let's go, boys!"

Avery cried out so that the clouds must have shook, then waved his pistol in the air and charged. Clay hooted and raced in pursuit. Ben and Fuller brought up the rear.

The Comanches froze and stared in surprise. Avery killed the first two before they realized what was happening. Clay swept through the line as well, firing wildly as he went. A third Comanche slumped in his saddle.

By the time Fuller arrived, the Indians were ready. One drove his spotted pony against Fuller's bay mare and clubbed the cowboy across the forehead. Ben guided his horse with his knees and swung the Spencer toward the nearest Comanche, then fired. The shot struck the Indian in the cheek and toppled him from the saddle. Ben continued on through the gap in the Comanches and raced to catch up with his comrades.

The air behind him filled with cries and shouts. He could hear horses thundering wildly up the hillside. Ben dared not glance back, though. His sole chance lay in catching Clay and the captain.

It seemed as if an eternity passed before Ben reached the crest of the ridge. He couldn't even see Clay's shadow the last hundred feet. But the moment Ben's horse stumbled atop the ridge, the air exploded with rifle fire. Behind him a pony shrieked, and as he turned to face the attacking Comanches, he saw one was writhing on the ground about twenty yards away, and two horses were now riderless.

"Ben, boy, over here!" Avery cried as Clay kept up a rapid fire on the Indians. "Hurry, you fool!"

Ben slapped his horse into motion. Then the loud report of a rifle boomed across the ridge, and the animal shuddered.

Oh, Lord! Ben thought as he felt the poor pony's blood on his fingers when he stroked the animal's neck. The horse managed to stumble ten more yards before collapsing. Ben barely was able to jump free. He then grabbed his carbine and worked his way toward Clay.

The young Georgian had settled into a nest of rocks and was firing steadily at the Indians milling around a hundred fifty yards downhill. Avery was five yards ahead. The captain's horse had collected a pair of bullets and was also near death.

"Doesn't look any too good, eh, Ben?" Clay asked as

he reloaded his rifle. "Comanches aren't much fun to fight afoot. So I hear, anyway."

"Sure aren't the friendliest sort," Ben added. "I saw some men got captured by 'em once. Wasn't pretty."

"Scalped?"

"And worse," Ben said grimly as he opened fire on a large, stumpy-legged Comanche who seemed to be organizing his companions. The shot missed badly.

"I was in a fix like this once before," Clay muttered, taking aim on the same Indian. The shot struck a second warrior three feet away.

"You got through that one. Maybe we'll survive this, too."

"Don't get your hopes ahead of you," Clay declared, pulling up his trouser leg to reveal a jagged-looking scar just below the knee. Ben had noticed it before, but Clay never spoke of how it had happened.

"Knife?" Ben asked.

"Yank saber," Clay explained. "Captain said I was lucky there was no surgeon about, else they'd have cut my leg off for sure. As it was, one of the boys had a sister who sewed it up just like a torn pair of britches, and I knitted pretty well."

"Hope your luck holds."

"Me, too," Clay said, managing a grin.

The Indians backed away a bit, and Avery trotted over.

"Got ourselves trapped real nice this time, eh, Captain?" Clay asked.

"Three riders and one horse," Avery grumbled. "Did you see what became of Fuller, Ben?"

"Got clubbed across the head," Ben answered. "He was on the ground. I can't see why they'd leave him alive."

"We cut 'em up some, boys, but when they come this time, we'll have a fight of it on our hands for sure."

"Ben could take my horse, go for help," Clay suggested.

"Adams'll have his hands full with the herd," Avery declared. "No, it's best one of us take that horse and try to get another two mounts."

Ben expected Clay to head for the horse, but instead Clay nodded and turned back toward the Indians. Avery then walked slowly to Clay's horse, mounted the animal, and sped off.

"You should've gone!" Ben protested. "That was your horse, and besides —"

"Captain's a born cavalryman," Clay explained. "He's twice the shot mounted that I am. We can hold out here awhile, Ben."

Sure, we can, Ben thought. *About as much chance of that happening as a snowstorm freezing those Comanches to their horses!* No snow came, but the instant Avery rode off, the remaining warriors screamed to high heaven and charged up the hill.

Ben had never seen anything quite like it. The Comanches rode hard, their bare chests hugging their ponies as they swung lances or war axes and shouted angrily. Clay shot the first two and Ben hit the fourth. The others raced on up the hill like a summer grass fire. The lead rider jumped from his horse and landed squarely in front of Clay. Ben shot him through the head. The next slammed into Ben full force, and the two rolled across the ground together, a single ball of sweat and flesh and fury. Ben soon lost his carbine. The Indian raised a hatchet, but Ben wrestled it away. Then out of nowhere a knife sliced through Ben's shirt and bit into the soft flesh just below the collarbone.

"Ahhh!" Ben screamed, kicking the Indian away. The Comanche grasped the knife with both hands and prepared to propel it into Ben's chest. Clay's rifle blew a half-inch hole in the Indian's throat, and the Comanche dropped to his knees, choking on his own blood.

The sight of three of their number bleeding out their lives was too much for the others. The thick-waisted leader waved a blanket in the air and raced back down the ridge. Those still mounted followed. The others scrambled to cover and began working their way toward horses.

"Lord, Ben, they ripped open your chest!" Clay cried as he finished the bleeding Comanche. "Are you dead?"

"Should be," Ben said, tearing apart what was left of his shirt and trying to inspect the wound.

"Leave that to me," Clay said, taking a canteen from the dead pony at his feet and splashing cool water on Ben's bloody chest. "Doesn't look too bad. Likely the knife struck the bone."

Ben lay back and closed his eyes. By the time Clay had a bandage of sorts in place, Clint Avery was back with two spare horses.

"They look to've killed you, Ben!" the captain exclaimed. For the first time Ben detected genuine concern in the old soldier's eyes. "Clay, you'd best get this young hero mounted and back to the trail camp."

"And you?" Clay asked.

"I plan to settle with those Comanches a bit. They owe me for my horse, and for what they did to young Ben there as well."

"I count five dead," Clay argued.

"The one who shot my horse got away," Avery said coldly. "I'll see he pays. Besides, it'll be best to have those Indians afoot so they don't hit the herd again."

"What about Fuller?" Ben asked.

"Nothing we can do for him," Avery explained. "Those Comanches made a fair mess of that cowboy. I threw a blanket over his face, and I'll dig him a hole later on."

Clay walked over then and removed the saddles from the dead mounts. After saddling the two pintos Avery had roped, Clay returned to Ben's side.

"Come on, Ben," Clay said, helping his wounded friend rise. "Let's get back to the others. I don't much like it here."

Ben nodded, then staggered along to the horses. Soon the two young cowboys were riding toward the mountain of dust that marked the location of the TA trail herd.

Tom Adams and the whole outfit celebrated the victory over the Comanche raiders — all save Avery, Fuller, and Ben. The captain hadn't returned, Fuller was dead, and Ben lay in the back of the cook wagon, beset by pain and boiling over with fever.

"I never should've let you stay back there, Ben," Adams chided himself. "You're not much older than my own boy, and scarce any taller."

"Don't worry about Ben," Clay told the rancher. "He's a survivor. We both are. Oh, you may carve us up now and then, but we'll get along in time."

"I hope so," Adams grumbled. "A man only has so many second chances when he travels the trail north, and I'd judge you two used up a couple today."

Two days later when Avery rejoined the drive, Ben was up and walking. His head was still fuzzy from loss of blood, and Adams refused to let him ride. Still, the fever passed, and Ben began to feel as if he'd live.

That was good. The crew had been whittled down to fourteen, and the hardships were only just beginning.

"There are more rivers to cross between here and Kansas than you ever dreamed of," Adams told Ben. "And longhorns don't take to baths any better than young cowboys do. I do believe it's easier to run steers into a hailstorm than to force 'em across the river.''

Unfortunately, Ben had a chance to find out. They managed to swing far enough west to avoid the Trinity, but the Wichita, two forks of her, more than made up for that. The treacherous Red River was even worse.

The Red River that June was little more than a half mile of quicksand sliced down the middle by a plodding rope of blue water a hundred feet wide. For a small price, an old Chickasaw Indian would mark the best crossing, but even then steers would wander a bit and simply sink from sight. The Red River just sucked them into the bowels of the earth.

Ben couldn't help but display respect for that river. Steers weren't the only of God's creatures that could be swallowed by that sand-colored muck. To make matters worse, a leather hat lay in the midst of the quicksand, and old Henry Sykes was quick to point out how its owner was likely just below the surface.

"The thing is, Ben, what gets sucked down always comes back up," Henry explained. "In time. Most of the men bob up — their bones, anyhow. Mud kind of digests the rest of 'em.''

"I was up here one time with a young cowboy got himself caught in quicksand," Joley declared. "We got a rope to him and pulled him out. Lord, I swear, that sand sucked his clothes right off. Peeled him like a potato. Even sucked his toenails off.''

"Lucky he still had his toes," Henry remarked. "I saw a cowboy once lost a whole foot to quicksand.''

Ben and Clay exchanged doubtful looks, then laughed heartily.

"You boys wouldn't be doubtin' the word of a Texas cowboy, would you?" Joley asked angrily.

"Doubt you?" Ben asked. "Never.''

He swallowed a burst of laughter and went on with his work. And though he judged there was less than a dime of truth in the stories, he did keep a wary eye on the quicksand.

As for hail, no sooner were the longhorns on the far bank of the river than the skies darkened, and the wind whipped up with the force of a cyclone. Trees blew over, and hailstones the size of pistol balls came raining down from every direction.

"It's like being wasp-stung!" Clay cried as he struggled to find shelter from the stinging stones.

Ben threw a heavy poncho over his shoulders and pushed his hat down over his ears. It seemed there was no end to the torments one faced on the trail to Kansas.

Chapter 8

Hailstones, river crossings, Comanches — they were but a few of the trials Ben was to face as the TA herd crept ever northward. Twice thunderstorms sent the whole herd stampeding out of control. Better than a hundred steers were lost, and whole days were spent rounding up strays. The sole saving grace was that other outfits fared no better, and sometimes strays from other herds could be added to make up for some of the trail loss.

The Chisholm Trail across the Indian Nations stretched nearly three hundred fifty miles on the map Tom Adams checked nightly. The route of the TA outfit added another fifty or so, and Ben felt he personally rode three times that, what with rousting strays out of tangled brush and racing back and forth to pass messages from Adams to old Henry Sykes in the cook wagon and back again. To top that, he began riding ahead with Avery to scout the trail.

"Sometimes I think I was born riding a horse," Ben remarked to Clay after scouting a crossing of the Cimarron River. "I'm getting so bowlegged I may have to start sleeping straddling a log."

"I know," Clay said, laughing at the thought. "These days when I cross a creek, my front side's got to wait another half hour for my backside to reach the far bank."

But whenever the youngsters grew tired and discouraged, the veteran cowboys would speak of trail's end, of the wild and exciting times awaiting them in Abilene or Wichita.

"They've got the prettiest women in Kansas," Joley boasted. "And there's not a one's not friendly. They'll lather you up and scrub you so there's not a sore spot left in your body. Then they'll show you the finest time in creation."

Ben and Clay spoke long and often of Abilene.

"Most likely it's just high talk, like about the quicksand and cyclones," Ben declared.

"Don't you even think that, Ben Haskell," Clay warned. "If it wasn't for that talk, I'd have buried myself certain a hundred miles back."

Once into Kansas, different problems confronted the drovers. First, Texas longhorns had spread tick fever among domestic cattle, and farmers all over Kansas were up in arms. Twice the TA crew had to detour miles out of the way to stay clear of quarantine lines backed by companies of shotgun-wielding farmers.

The other danger was posed by bands of renegade drovers, ex-cavalrymen from both sides of the late war, and all other manner of scoundrels and no-accounts known to Kansas. Most of them could have earned an honest wage employing their talents with a rope and pistol for one of the drives headed north. But instead they waited a few days from the railheads and prepared to swoop down on a herd, ambush its trail crew, and drive the stock along to the cattle pens.

Famed rustlers like Blackjack French could collect the profits for five or six different herds in a single summer so long as they were careful to choose a buyer in Abilene who wasn't too particular about buying stolen cattle. After all, any fool could tell the same man couldn't trail half a dozen different herds the same summer.

The first outlaws the TA outfit happened across offered to buy the stock.

"We'll take those steers off your hands for ten dollars a head," claimed a tall, long-nosed stranger dressed in the remnants of a federal corporal's uniform. "Cash money, right here and now."

"I could've sold 'em for that back home in Texas," Adams grumbled. "You crazy? The price in Abilene's closer to thirty."

"You aren't in Abilene," the tall man reminded Adams. "And if you figure to return to Texas, you ought to take my offer."

"Oh?" Avery asked, pulling his Colt revolver and running his fingers along the cold barrel. "I'd sure hate to see somebody get himself killed making threats."

"We've already fought Indians and battled the weather, mister," Adams added. "We don't plan to give away what we've sweated for, died for."

"More could die," the tall stranger suggested.

"You among 'em," Avery declared. "Look, friend, there are lots of herds headed up this trail. You boys'd do well to give us some room. I'm tired and hungry and I've got a boil on my backside. You ride up on this herd, and I'm liable to shoot you out of pure spite."

The tall rider drew back when Avery suddenly swung the pistol around so that it pointed directly at a certain long nose.

"I hear you," the tall man said. "We'll meet another day, perhaps."

"If we do, it'll be the sorriest day of your life," Avery promised.

The very next day Blackjack French himself appeared. French was well over six feet tall, weighed close to three hundred pounds, and if he wasn't enough to get a body's attention, a full dozen grim-faced riders rode behind him.

"We can make this easy, or we can make it hard," French said, chewing on the nub of a dollar cigar. "You turn over the herd and ride away, or we'll come and take it."

"You can try!" Avery barked. "Others have. They're all dead."

"Big talk," French said, spitting out his cigar. "We'll be by, friend. Count on that."

After French departed, Henry Sykes explained the fat man's reputation.

"Maybe someone ought to ride along to Wichita, summon a sheriff," Adams suggested. "Or maybe we should team up with another outfit."

"No," Avery objected. "First off, he'll have somebody watching for riders. It's a sure way to get a man killed. As for teaming up, that'd be fine if anybody was close by, but I haven't noticed anyone. Besides, there's a better way."

"Oh?" Adams asked.

"We go find 'em," Avery explained. "We hit 'em before they can pick the ground. I'll take Clay and Ben. We'll sting 'em hard, then come back and get the herd along to Abilene."

"You'll need more help," Adams argued. "Three men wouldn't be enough, and Ben's just a boy, still."

"We were enough for those Comanches," Avery reminded them. "Besides, if French should slip past us, you'll still have a good-sized crew."

And so once again Ben rode into battle with Clint Avery

and Clay Hamilton. This time was different, though. There would be no wild melee like with the Comanches. Instead, Avery located French's camp and laid a neat little ambush for the rustlers.

Ben tied the horses off in a small ravine. Then he and Clay took up positions on the right of several large boulders. Avery took the left. When French broke camp the next morning, his men rode down the trail straight toward the TA outfit — and right into Avery's trap. The first horseman was less than ten feet away when Avery shouted to fire. Ben and Clay opened up with repeating rifles, and Avery fired a shotgun. The concussion tore into the raiders. French himself was killed in the first volley, and half the others were hit as well. In less than five minutes Blackjack French's feared band was crippled. The wounded crept into the cover of some nearby cottonwoods, and the others collected the dead.

"I warned you!" Avery boasted. "Don't give me cause to come back."

After that, the TA herd had no trouble from anyone. Avery's only complaint came in Abilene, where he discovered one of French's men had dragged the burly bandit's corpse into town and claimed a five-hundred-dollar railroad bounty from the marshal.

Once the herd reached Abilene, there were but two days of hard work remaining. First, Tom Adams had to find a buyer for the stock. He had little trouble contracting the whole two thousand, though, and immediately afterward the cowboys began coaxing their reluctant steers into the maze of chutes and corrals leading to the waiting cattle cars.

It was hot, dust-choked labor, and Ben grew to hate it rather quickly. Every inch of him from hair to toes was caked with dust, and he emerged from the pens a slender, gray-haired monster.

"It's time you boys were paid," Adams announced, and even old Henry Sykes did a bit of dancing.

With coin in his pocket and a town to explore, Ben

prepared to set off on a great adventure. Tom Adams drew him aside, though.

"Ben, do you know where your life's leadin' you?" Adams asked.

"Here and there," Ben said, spitting the dust out of his mouth. "Now that I've been through the Nations and into Kansas, who knows? Clay's talked of the Dakotas, maybe even California."

"Most men I've known born Texans tend to go back home."

"I've got no home," Ben grumbled. "Lost it a couple of years ago, and I'm not sure I wasn't born to wander anyway. It's a fair life."

"Is it? Ben, can you tell me you relish this killin'? I never knew a boy with a finer talent for horses, with a gentler touch for livestock. I saw your eyes when you rode back from ambushin' French, after you tangled with the Comanches. You can't tell me you find it to your likin'."

"Killing's not supposed to be easy," Ben said, gazing off down the street. "Pa wrote it in a letter once. It's about the only one I ever got from him. He was killed pretty soon after that, you see. He said it was hard killing men, but it was necessary sometimes. A man has a duty, you know. That's all I've done."

"So far. Look, Ben, killin' gets easier. Look at Avery. Is that what you want to be — a cold-hearted killer? It may be too late for young Clay, but it's not for you. Don't let 'em turn you cold and cruel. Blackjack French likely started out that way. Come back to Texas with me, stay the winter at the TA. It's a good life. Later on, you can buy some land, find yourself a little gal in Newcastle, and build a future."

"Maybe," Ben said, scratching his dusty hair. "The thing is, Mr. Adams, I appreciate the offer an awful lot. You and Miz Adams have been really kind to me. I've learned a lot from you. But I owe Clay and the captain."

"You don't owe 'em anything."

"Yes, I do," Ben declared. "It's a heavy debt, and it's a long way from cashed out. I'll speak with them about coming back, but if they choose to go elsewhere, I'm afraid I'll be going along, too."

"Well, you have to do as you think best," Adams said sadly. "But the world has a way of turnin', son. You ever need a place to hang your hat, come along back to the TA."

"I appreciate that, Mr. Adams."

Adams nodded, and Ben raced off to catch up with Clay.

Their first stop was a bathhouse on the edge of town. By the time the two young cowboys arrived, twenty tubs were already filled with laughing, cigar-smoking trail hands. Ben picked out a wooden tub on the far wall, and Clay sat alongside and began stripping off his dusty rags.

"Where do we put our things?" Clay asked a small, dark-haired boy who was carrying pails of hot water around the room.

"You hold on to your valuables," the boy answered. "Everything else just drop alongside the tub. We'll get 'em scrubbed for you, what's worth cleanin'. I can get you a shirt, maybe some trousers, at the mercantile for a dollar."

Ben looked at his ragged clothes and agreed quickly. Except for his boots and belt, he didn't have a stitch of clothing without at least ten holes worn through. Clay was little better off, and once the two scrambled out of their clothes, the bucket boy made off with the rags, holding them cautiously at arm's length for fear something might crawl out of them.

Another boy brought water to fill the tubs, and soon Ben and Clay were lounging about in the comfort of wonderfully warm water. They lathered off weeks of dust and grime.

"I didn't realize you had yellow hair, Ben," Clay joked. "It's been black since the Red River."

"Don't let it trouble you," Ben answered. "I didn't remember myself."

Ben was enjoying the water so much he didn't notice when a young girl of fifteen or so appeared.

"Shave you for two bits?" she asked Clay.

Clay turned and smiled. Ben pulled himself down deeper in the tub and turned pink with embarrassment.

"You I'll do for a dime," she told Ben. "Hardly worth spreadin' the soap, really."

Clay laughed, and Ben frowned.

"How'd you get in here, anyway?" Ben asked. "This is a man's bathhouse."

"If it was, they wouldn't let you in, sonny," she retorted. "Besides, I'm the best barber in Abilene. As for it bein' a man's place, I've shaved and doctored men and boys most of my life. I ceased bein' impressed with a plucked chicken like you a long time back."

When she laughed, her bright blue eyes lit up, and Ben couldn't help liking her for it. What's more, she was right about the shave. Her hand was steady, and she even clipped their hair for another two bits. Ben judged that more than fair, especially since his hadn't been cut since winter.

The boy arrived shortly with the new clothes, and after paying what was owed for the shave and haircut, clothes and bath, Ben waited for the girl to leave so he could dress. She seemed in no hurry.

"You keep busy here, do you?" Ben asked.

"Sometimes," she said. "Whenever we get a new outfit hits town, I do a fair business."

"I was thinking maybe you'd care to have dinner with

us tonight,'' Ben said, eyeing Clay. ''We've got money. I plan to have myself the biggest supper I can buy, and I'd be glad to share it with you.''

''Best save it for yourself,'' she said, poking him in the ribs. ''I do believe they've starved you on the trail.''

''Should've seen him when he was skinny,'' Clay said, rising less than bashfully from the tub and wrapping a towel around his waist. ''We'd like you to come, just the same.''

''You'll pay?'' she asked.

''For everything,'' Ben declared.

''And just what does that mean?'' she asked angrily. ''Huh? Just what were you plannin' to buy?''

''Nothing but supper,'' Ben said, shrinking from her raised fist.

''Please, miss,'' Clay said, doubling over with laughter. ''Ben here wouldn't know about anything else. It's just, well, he hasn't known many girls, you see, being raised on a farm and all.''

''And where were you raised?'' she asked Clay. ''A New Orleans fancy house?''

Clay laughed, then shook his head.

''Not raised there,'' he told her. ''But I've been a visitor.''

''I imagine you have,'' she said, reaching slyly into her barber's kit and taking out the razor strop. Then, quick as lightning, she swatted Clay's rump with the strop. He hopped back and rubbed the sore flesh. The girl, meanwhile, made a mock bow at Ben and said, ''I'll be happy to meet you at Barney's Café at seven. My name, by the way, is Angelina.''

''I'm Ben Haskell,'' Ben announced. ''This is my sometimes friend, Clay Hamilton.''

She nodded to Clay, then flashed a big smile at Ben. Before he could speak another word, though, she hurried off to the far side of the bathhouse to shave some other cowboy.

"And here I thought I'd be the one showing you the ropes, Ben," Clay muttered as Ben finally pulled himself out of the tub. "Lord, Ben, you're a wonder!"

Angelina Martel served as Ben's guide the next two weeks in Abilene. She kept him out of the hands of the more polished and hard-hearted ladies who inhabited the drab, unpainted houses on the far side of the railroad tracks or the tents down along the river. Angelina also knew where a good meal could be had cheaply, where a bag of oats for a horse didn't cost a week's wages, and where a bit of quiet might be found in the midst of the clamorous little railhead town.

Ben found her company a welcome change from the boasting of the other cowboys. For the first time he could recall, he had days to spend as he chose, and money in his pocket to provide the means. But for the most part, he chose to devote that time to riding along the river or visiting the diverse outfits that wandered in and out of Abilene. One morning he might chat with a railroad foreman, and he'd swap tales with miners or buffalo hunters that afternoon. He avoided only the farm families that disembarked from the westbound trains. He saw in the eager faces of the children and the sober, stern gazes of their parents the life he would never again know.

"I'm an orphan, too," Angelina told Ben. "I'd guess half the gals over ten in Abilene are. Some pick up honest work, cookin' and cleanin' and such. Others take the high road to Miss Molly's or sign on with the Kansas Prairie Flowers. Those girls grow old fast, though, and I've got plans."

Ben enjoyed listening to Angelina talk of the fine clothes and big house she would own one day. They both knew it was a distant dream, of course, but dreams were hard to come by in Kansas, and even a borrowed glimpse of something better was an improvement over roaming the saloons or sitting at Clint Avery's elbow as the captain gambled his way through the long, hot days and endless nights.

"Maybe we should head back to Texas," Ben told Clay finally. "Mr. Adams would welcome us."

"Captain won't winter in a bunkhouse again," Clay declared. "So long as his luck holds, he won't venture far from the Silver Dollar Saloon."

"And what about you?"

"I guess I'm pretty much used to following the captain, Ben. You could go along back, though. Nobody'd hold it against you."

"No," Ben said, sighing. "If I went back there by myself, I'd about be another boy to Miz Adams, and I can't ever be anybody's kid again. Too much's happened. The two of us, well, we could kind of be partners of a sort."

"I can't leave the captain to himself," Clay mumbled sadly. "I did think maybe we could try our hand in the Colorado gold camps, though."

"Me, I'd rather rope mustangs."

"That's 'cause you're half horse yourself," Clay said, cheering a bit. "I'll speak to the captain. We've been here a long time now. He could be restless, too."

But Avery was content to drink his whiskey and play cards with the new bands of Texas drovers who daily found their way into Abilene.

It was about this time that Angelina introduced Ben to old Maurice Dumas. Mo, as people called him, had hunted and trapped most of the country west of the Mississippi. Lately he'd hunted buffalo for the Northern Pacific Railroad, supplying the work camps with beef and selling hides, heads, and horns for a pretty profit back East.

"There's a hundred men's fortunes lumberin' around on buffalo hooves," Mo proclaimed. "A good man with a Sharps rifle can make his living in one week if he's got a proper crew of cutters and curers. You eat well enough, and if you stay clear of those pesky Comanches and Cheyennes, you can get downright rich."

It wasn't the hunting that appealed most to Ben, though. Mo's stories of high mountains and virgin streams, of clear, crisp air, and a boundless horizon made Ben's mouth water.

"I'm bound to go with him," Angelina declared. "My brother Aaron and I, both."

"Your brother?" Ben asked in surprise. "I didn't know you had one."

"He works at the bathhouse, too. Truth is, the sun will do him some good. He's turned so feeble you'd swear he was a ghost."

"You never told me . . ."

"Ben, you grow all close-mouthed and sorrowful whenever somebody talks about family. Besides, Aaron's close to eleven now, and he doesn't depend on anybody. If he was a little bigger, nobody'd guess he was a boy at all."

He's like me, then, Ben thought.

Maurice Dumas planned to head back to the buffalo valleys in a week, and Ben devoted at least a few hours of each day to helping the grizzled old-timer with his horses or loading supplies onto wagons.

"Angelina says you've got a fair eye with a rifle, Ben," Mo said mid-week. "Ever fired a Sharps?"

"No, sir," Ben confessed.

"Like to give her a try?"

"I would," Ben declared. "I never shot anything with that big a bore, but I guess I can handle it as well as I did that dragoon Colt of Pa's."

Mo looked over the huge pistol Ben pulled from his belt and grinned.

"I'd so say, boy," Mo agreed. An hour later they

rode out to the river, and Ben fired a Sharps buffalo rifle for the first time. The recoil sent him flying, and old Mo broke out laughing.

"It has a pop to it," Ben said as he picked himself off the ground. "But I'd bet I could get used to it."

"I'd guess so. And if you've got the urge, Ben, I'd take you with me to the Republican River. Truth is, I need shooters, and Angelina says you have a pair of friends, both of 'em soldiers of a fashion."

"Yes, sir."

"I treat my people right. I pay for shot and powder, and I pay the crew. They get half the take to split among 'em."

"That would seem fair," Ben agreed.

"Then I take it you'll ride with me?"

"I'd like to," Ben said with darkening eyes. "Thing is, I'm a sort of partner. I'd have to convince the others."

"Well, I leave in three days, Ben. I'd need to know in two."

Ben nodded, then set to work immediately on Clay.

"It does sound fine," Clay admitted, "but what'll the captain say?"

Avery said no. He'd grown extremely lucky at the card table, and there was little hope of prying him away from such a profitable pursuit.

"I'm driven to distraction by all this waiting and watching," Ben told Clay. "When's he going to tire of it? In November, when snow's frozen the grass and left us to starve?"

"Ben, I said you could go," Clay muttered. "Nothing's holding you here."

"You know better'n that," Ben answered. "I owe you and the captain, both."

Clay nodded, and the two young men sat together on

a bench outside the saloon and whittled blocks of hickory. Then gunshots splintered the swinging doors of the Silver Dollar, and Ben and Clay took cover.

"It's the captain!" Clay shouted as he gazed inside. "He's shot somebody!"

Ben followed Clay through the door. As the powder smoke cleared, three cowboys stood opposite Avery, their hands poised beside pistols. Avery's own smoking Colt stood ready to fire. A dead cowboy rested on the floor, his own pistol clutched in his hand.

"Charlie was right," the cowboy in the middle asserted. "You've been uncommon lucky, and it would seem five kings are a few too many for a square deck of cards."

"I don't need to cheat," Avery argued. "But if you mean to call my hand, just go ahead and reach for your pistol. I can shoot three as easy as one."

"Have to be mighty handy," the man on the right said, staring hard at Avery. "Three men and four bullets would be long odds, even if nobody was shooting back."

"Three against three, on the other hand, is a different tally altogether," Clay called, leading Ben around to Avery's side.

"Is at that," the middle cowboy agreed, relaxing his arm. "You take your money, Avery, but we'll be around. Even a couple of pups won't help you next time."

Avery collected the money and motioned the boys on along to the door. The captain backed out of the room with drawn pistol.

"They meant what they said," Clay declared as Avery led the way down the street. "We'd best clear out."

"That's all right with you, isn't it, Ben?" the captain asked. "You were all lathered up about hunting buffalo anyway. Where's this Dumas fellow?"

Ben tried to grin, but he was still shaking from the sudden eruption of gunfire. He led the way to the livery and then to Mo Dumas. A bargain was made, and by week's end, Ben was following Clay and Avery a mile ahead of Mo's lead wagon, bound for the Republican River and a new life as a buffalo hunter.

Chapter 9

Ben Haskell came of age on the buffalo killing grounds of western Kansas. For three long years he, Clay Hamilton, and Clint Avery made their living roaming from the banks of the Republican River down to the Arkansas and back again, hunting with old Mo Dumas and devouring the unbridled freedom of an age rapidly vanishing. The railroad continued to creep ever westward, and the buffalo herds, which once blackened the prairies in summer, were vanishing in a sea of whitened bones. Deadly Sharps rifles killed in a single afternoon enough buffalo to feed a band of Kiowa or Cheyenne for two winters, and the wind seemed to whisper the death chant of the humped beasts even as the nomadic tribes fell prey to federal cavalry and reservation epidemics.

Ben was nineteen that warm summer of 1871. He'd grown tall, a hair over six feet, and if he remained a bit thin, there was nothing frail about him. His leathery shoulders had broadened, and he had the quick eye of the hunter he'd become.

Clay had changed less. He was a bit leaner, perhaps, but otherwise he was still the sandy-haired, bright-eyed young man Ben had met that awful morning back in Jack County. Clay had added a close-trimmed beard to his cheeks and chin, as well as a darker moustache to his upper lip. Even so, he looked no older than his twenty-one years, and often he appeared younger.

If anyone had aged, it was Clint Avery. Three years roaming the wild Kansas plain, most of it camped off away from his companions, had brought lines to the man's forehead and a deep scowl to his face.

In addition to Ben, Clay, and Avery, Mo Dumas employed an aging Cheyenne grandmother with the dubious name Prairie Willow, together with her daughter, Winter Dove, and three grandchildren. Angelina and Aaron Martel were also along. Mo was accustomed to sending Avery out to scout the trail ahead. Ben and Clay usually rode out as well whenever fresh buffalo sign was spotted. Mo drove the lead wagon, while Angelina drove the second and tended the cooking and washing. Young Aaron, barely fourteen and little more than a scruffy tangle of dark brown hair and greasy white flesh, brought up the third wagon and tended the stock. The Indians preferred riding their spotted ponies or trailing along on foot when the horses tired.

There were bigger outfits scouring the plains for buffalo, but few brought in more hides more often than old Mo's crew. His Indians could skin a full-grown bull quick as lightning, and his shooters approached their craft with rare skill and patience. Maurice Dumas had a rare knack for knowing the habits of the buffalo, and the Martels kept the crew well fed and the animals sound of foot and long of wind.

By early June the two hide wagons were better than half

full. The supply wagon, which also contained pickled tongues and long strips of dried meat, carried provisions for six more weeks. Ben hoped they wouldn't be needed. Mo had sent Clay and him out to scout to the north. Old Prairie Willow had the little ones sharpening their knives. Mo had a nose for finding the buffs, and Ben had grown to expect a herd anytime Mo sent them riding.

Clay was the first to sight them, and he waved Ben over. To the untrained eye the dark blobs on the flat terrain ahead might have appeared to be clumps of brush or large boulders. Ben knew better. Up there were fifty or sixty prowling buffalo dispersed across a couple of acres.

"Small herd," Clay said, "but then we haven't run across much else lately."

"I know," Ben agreed. "I'll head back and get the others."

"Hurry along, Ben. Those woolies won't wait forever."

Ben grinned his answer, then turned his horse toward Mo's wagons and set out to pass along the word.

It took less than a hour to locate the wagons. In another hour, Ben found Avery and led the way to the buffalo. The herd continued grazing peacefully, and Clay led the way to a small hill topped by three cottonwoods. It made a perfect blind, and the hunters hid their horses and took out rifles.

There was an art to setting up the kill. Ben and his companions were old hands at it. Avery located the prime bull, while Ben and Clay picked out the likely successors. Avery's Sharps boomed out, and the lead bull fell headfirst to the prairie. Instantly the herd began to turn a slow circle. As Avery reloaded the big rifle, Ben marked the emerging leader of the herd and shot it dead.

The confused animals turned another circle while Ben reloaded. Avery continued to fire at will. Clay, however, picked out the third leader and fired. Once again the lead bull fell. Sometimes the herd would circle for hours while one bull after another tried to emerge as the leader. Other times, like now, the buffalo would halt and resume their grazing so long as no bull hurried the others into motion.

In a way, it was sad, Ben supposed. The hunt was a little like killing off the head of a family, then shooting the others until only orphans remained to be picked off at will. Once the buffalo ceased their panic, a man might shoot as long as he had shot and powder.

Prairie Willow once told Ben how the Indians would only hunt the mature animals. No Cheyenne would think of shooting a calf. Mo Dumas made no distinctions.

"Boys as well as men want buffalo coats," the old-timer explained. "And after all, what chance would they have out here all alone? Somebody else would just happen by. Why should they make a profit off our labor?"

Even old Mo regretted leaving so much meat to spoil, but there was only so much time to smoke it, and with millions of longhorns heading up the trails from Texas, nobody much cared for the taste of buffalo steak.

"They say the white man has an angry God," Prairie Willow said. "This must be so. The Cheyenne pray to the buffalo spirit for strength and power, so this angry God of yours comes to take that power from us."

Ben sometimes raced ponies with little Joseph Hawk, Prairie Willow's lone grandson. The boy was maybe nine, and though his heart was light enough when racing his horse against Ben Haskell, the buffalo kill always cast a dark shadow across the youngster's eyes.

"My father is dead," Joseph once told Ben.

"Mine, too," Ben explained. "It happened back East in the war."

"My father was a warrior," Joseph said sadly. "This

I will never be. The buffalo spirit is angry, and when I grow tall, it will turn its head from me, and I will never ride the warrior path.''

"Maybe it's just as well," Ben declared, shaking his head sadly. "There's only death and killing — sadness. Your heart would grow dark."

"You have walked that way?"

"Yes," Ben said, frowning. "A long time now."

"Ah, but you hunt," Joseph said, proudly touching Ben's shoulder. "Many buffalo have you killed."

Yes, killed, Ben thought each time he raised the heavy Sharps and pulled the trigger. A farmer raised corn or wheat. Ben's crop was death.

It had become oddly casual, the killing, Ben told himself. Once his hands had shaken after the hunt. Now he fired, reloaded, and fired again. He did it without thinking, with no remorse. And when Angelina tried to dismiss it lightly, his eyes turned even darker.

"That's the worst part of it," he'd told Clay. "I don't even think about it anymore."

"Better that way," Clay declared. "You take it to heart, it'll eat your insides out. Better to take the captain's path. Shoot when it's called for, and don't cry for the dead. It doesn't do much good, you know."

Ben remained unconvinced, though. If Clint Avery was so sure of himself, why did he keep his distance, avoid even Clay? Ben suspected it was because the captain feared letting another person creep into that hard heart. Avery would never again grieve for anyone, for he'd never care.

They shot sixty-two buffalo. It took the better part of four hours, and Avery spent another hour walking amid the writhing animals, finishing off the wounded. The prairie seemed to run with their blood, and the smell alone was enough to draw every wolf and buzzard in Kansas.

Just before nightfall the wagons arrived. Prairie

Willow and her family immediately set out to strip the fallen creatures of their heavy coats. Little Joseph cut off heads and collected tongues. Sometimes when Aaron finished tending the stock, he would collect tails to sell in Dodge City to passengers on the railroad.

Angelina kept the supply wagon far upwind, and she insisted both hunters and hiders wash before approaching the camp. Whenever possible she located her wagon near a river or small stream so it was possible to get a good scrubbing.

"Serves me right for takin' on a white woman," old Mo grumbled. "Indians aren't half the trouble. 'Course, they don't cook half so good, either."

Ben rather appreciated Angelina's rules. They'd ridden by other camps plagued by flies and visited by coyotes and wolves. Besides, he never liked the sight of blood on his hands, and the sooner it was washed away the better.

It seemed strange to Ben that they should be able to kill a herd in a single afternoon, but that it took days for the skinning and even longer for the hides to dry and the meat to smoke. By then he, Clay, and Avery would be off scouting another herd, of course, but if one was found, it would be days before the wagons could be brought along and the shooting begun.

"No point to lettin' a hide rot," Mo had told them years before. "Only shoot when your skinnin' crew's at hand."

And so when Ben located a paltry herd of fifteen head just north of the Arkansas River, he gathered Clay and Avery, then rode off to tell the others. By the time the outfit had gathered and the hunt began, scouts from other outfits had located the animals as well.

Fifteen buffs, only three of which were full-grown bulls, could be cut down in short order, and that was exactly what happened. They didn't even circle. The three bulls went down in a single volley, and the others were killed rapidly. Only one bull calf made an attempt to escape. Ben found himself admiring the game little creature and refused to fire. Avery shot the calf dead a minute later.

Then Olin Hartman appeared. Hartman had as many as twenty hunters working for him at a time, but they never matched Mo Dumas's success. The herds were vanishing quickly now, and Hartman found it harder and harder to produce a profit at season's end. Fifteen animals were little enough, but when he brought his crew to the herd and discovered Mo Dumas's shooters had already been there, the tough Swede bellowed out in anger.

"That was my herd!" Hartman cried. "My scouts found 'em, and they were mine to shoot!"

"There wasn't anybody here when we arrived," Ben answered. "I was here days ago. It was our shot, and we took it."

"You won't live to enjoy it," Hartman warned as he formed his hunters in a line.

Ben turned as always at such times to Clint Avery. The big bore Sharps wasn't the ideal weapon for dueling, but Avery directed his at Hartman.

"Hartman, you'd do better to mind your own affairs," Avery warned. "I've fought often and well. Those boys of yours don't look as if they could hit a buffalo rump from five feet. Save yourself some grief and ride away."

Hartman wasn't about to back off, though. Instead, he pulled a pistol and fired in Avery's direction. The captain then motioned Ben and Clay to a rocky knob above the river. As Hartman's band charged, Ben and Clay raced for the protection of the rocks. Once there, they fired rapidly. Avery was already there, and the three big rifles emptied a like number of saddles.

"Nothing to this," Avery boasted as he reloaded. "Easier than buffalo by half."

The confused hunters made a second charge, but Ben shot Hartman's horse from under the big Swede, and two more hunters were also hit. Furious, Hartman limped away, waving for his men to follow.

"Never heard of such foolishness," Avery declared when the survivors left the scene. "Four men dead, and for what?"

Ben shared the sentiments. The dead hunters were mostly young cowboys. One still had a braided lariat on his horse. The lure of the hunt had drawn them from a hard life and led them to an early grave.

"I played cards with this one in Dodge," Avery announced as he turned one of the dead face up. "Name was George, I believe. Didn't have any luck at cards, either."

Ben frowned. If there'd been a spade handy, he would have dug a grave. As it happened, though, the sound of gunfire a mile or so away drew his attention instead. Ben turned to Clay, and Avery ran for the horses. All three had the same notion. Hartman had gone after old Mo and the wagons.

A spring's labor was riding along in those wagons, and what was more, friends were at risk. Ben flew to his horse, mounted up, and raced toward the three wagons as if the furies were after him. Avery was only a yard behind, and Clay was even closer.

The three horsemen topped a low ridge and spotted the two hide wagons rumbling along at high speed. A single rider was firing at old Maurice, and the old man was answering with a new Winchester repeater. Avery drew out his Sharps and headed that way. Ben turned away and raced to where the supply wagon stood near the Arkansas a quarter mile away. Hartman and the other attackers were there.

Ben never in his life rode any harder. He could feel the hot breath of his horse and knew the poor animal was killing itself to get him to the wagon. Once there,

Ben jumped to the ground, raced to the back of the wagon, and crept into the bed.

Joseph Hawk was there, firing a rifle steadily at the attackers. Ben took a second rifle, then tore open the canvas wagon cover and opened fire on the encircling raiders. First one, then a second, fell to the accurate Winchester.

"Swede, they'll kill all of us!" a fearful voice cried out.

Hartman raised his head to answer. Clay Hamilton arrived at that very instant. The Georgian drew a pistol and fired point-blank at the big Swede. Hartman toppled to the earth, and those of his men who could retired quickly.

Once the shooting died down, Ben crawled out of the wagon and tried to assess the damage. The front of the wagon was riddled with bullets, but little Joseph was unhurt. Ben himself bled from where a pair of splinters had gashed his left arm. It wasn't serious, though.

Maurice brought the other wagons down, and Joseph raced out to see to his mother and grandmother. Even old Prairie Willow was unhurt, though.

"Where's sis?" Aaron asked suddenly as he climbed down from the trailing wagon.

Ben felt something cold grip his heart. Joseph immediately pointed toward the river, and Ben raced Aaron to the spot. Angelina lay in a pool of blood beside a water bucket.

"Oh, no, sis," Aaron mumbled as he cradled her head. Ben shook violently, then knelt beside his dead friend and closed her empty eyes.

"I'll kill 'em!" Aaron screamed. Before he could run up the hill, however, Ben pulled him back.

"No," Ben whispered. "We'll dig a grave, say a prayer for her. She'd like it along here, by the river."

Aaron nodded.

"I'll get a shovel," Clay offered.

"No, I'll do it," Aaron said. "See that there are some flowers, Ben. She was partial to 'em."

"I see some daisies," Ben said softly. "I'll dig some up, and we can plant 'em atop the hill."

Young Aaron dug a trench on the hillside, and Ben carried Angelina there. She was surprisingly light for someone with so much backbone. He'd miss her warm words and her soothing broths, the quiet observations she made about flowers and birds and stars.

Ben planted the daisies, then remained with Aaron beside the grave while Maurice led the others to where the buffalo lay waiting to be skinned.

"Your horse's got a pulled tendon," Aaron finally spoke. "He won't do any riding for a time."

"No," Ben mumbled. "But he's luckier'n some."

"Yeah. Think it hurt much, Ben?"

"No, I don't think she even knew what happened. I suppose that's a blessing. Still, I know she'd rather've gone fighting."

"I don't think it much matters," Aaron declared. "You're dead all the same. You figure we shot the ones who did it?"

"Hartman, anyway, and he's the one who was back of it. The others were just poor dumb cowboys, not so different from me."

"You're not dumb. You can read."

"I have to be dumb to be out here," Ben said, rising to his feet and walking to the river. His hands were caked with blood — his own and Angelina's. He wanted to be sick. Instead, he shed his clothes and dove into the river.

"What're you doin'?" Aaron asked.

"Getting clean," Ben said with reddening eyes. "I have to get the blood off. God, I'm so weary of the powder smoke and the blood stench. And the dying!"

"I know," Aaron added, stumbling to the river. As the boy stripped off his shirt, Ben saw the tears streaming down Aaron's cheeks.

That's good, Ben thought. *He can cry. Me, all I can do is die a little more inside. And go on.*

Chapter 10

With Angelina dead, Ben had little heart for the buffalo hunt. Avery located another small herd, and when the wagons were at last full, Ben rejoiced at the chance to head for Dodge City.

They arrived in Dodge in early July.

Dodge City in '71 was the queen of the trail towns. To the east, law had begun to curb the wildness of the Texas drovers. Churches and schools appeared. In Dodge, though, gambling, loose women, and strong drink reigned supreme. Men were still shot dead over the appearance of an extra ace of spades or a smudge of cigar ash on the back of a queen of diamonds.

Ben hoped the trip to town would revive something in him, restore direction or faith or hope. But a hot bath and two sips of whiskey did no more for him than that dip in the Arkansas.

Old Mo was the lucky one. He had his Indians to look

after and the price of the hides to negotiate. Work, if not a remedy, at least provided a welcome distraction.

Clay occupied himself at Miss Belle's House of Amusements down on the Arkansas.

"Come along with me, Ben," his friend beckoned. "I'll see you meet somebody real nice. She'll take your mind off your troubles."

But in truth Ben knew whoever it was, she was certain to put him in mind of Angelina.

"Go ahead, Clay," Ben replied. "My horse's leg's still bad. I think I'll take him over to the livery and have the smith give him a look."

"It's a fool's errand if you ask me," Clay remarked. "Bad tendon's not going to get better anytime soon. If Aaron's poultice couldn't ease the swelling, no smith will."

"Well, nobody ever accused me of being sensible where horses were concerned," Ben admitted. "Get us a room at the hotel, will you? I'm apt to be along late."

"With any kind of luck, so will I," Clay replied. "You get the room."

Ben nodded and forced a weak smile on his face. He then took his poor lame horse down the street to a livery. But when he explained his problem, the stableboy shook his head.

"Mister, we just feed 'em and hire 'em out. Place you want's Mr. Sayles's outfit up on Kansas Street. He knows horses better'n anybody hereabouts, and he does most of the shoin' in Dodge."

"Thanks," Ben said, tossing the lad a quarter. Ben then led his pony back to where Kansas Street branched off Front Street. Sayles & Sons was a freight company. Ben had the devil's own time finding their horse barn. Even then he found only a boy no older than Aaron Martel tending the animals.

"Is Mr. Sayles about?" Ben asked.

"He's gone to Hays on business," the boy explained.

"Can I help you?"

"I wouldn't think so," Ben grumbled.

"Your horse's got a bad tendon," the boy said, hopping down from his perch atop a stall and approaching the horse with caution. "You rode him too hard, I'd guess. He's not a lot of horse, you know. He'd be pressed to carry me at a hard pace for long, and I'm scarce a hundred pounds."

"I didn't have much choice," Ben growled. "Was somebody's life at stake. You think I'd treat a horse hard by choice? Look at him! He's been cared for."

"Has at that," the boy agreed. "Bring him on in. Let's see what a bit of liniment will do."

Ben led his horse into an empty stall, and the boy fetched a bottle from a shelf in the tack room. Ben watched as the lad rubbed the lotion into the horse's sore leg. The mustang stomped about a moment, then began to calm.

"Heats up the muscles, loosens the tendons," the boy explained. "I'd keep it up three, four times a day till it gets better. If I'm any kind of judge, it will, too."

The horse dipped its head, and the boy stroked its nose. Ben couldn't help smiling.

"For a youngster, you sure know horses," he declared.

"I'm fourteen," the boy answered angrily. "As for horses, my pa's had me working stock since I could walk."

"Your name Sayles?"

"Sam Sayles. Who'd you be?"

"Anyone," Ben muttered. "My name's Ben Haskell."

"You sound Texas. You here with a drive?"

"Do I look it?" Ben asked. He was dressed in buckskins and a buffalo-hide vest. Only his boots hinted of the old days, driving cattle to Kansas.

"Hide hunter?"

Ben nodded, and the boy frowned.

"Pa says you fellows'll starve the Indians, and you kill off the buffalo so none'll be left."

"I'd say it's so."

"Then how come you do it?"

"Man's got to make his living somehow," Ben explained. "It hasn't been the worst life, though lately I have to admit it's made me weary."

"Can't do a man much good, shooting and killing all day. Me, I like handling stock."

"I did that once," Ben explained. "Broke wild mustangs back in Texas."

"Yeah?"

"It was a fair life."

"How came you to leave it?"

"I had friends heading to Kansas. I owed 'em."

"Well, if you're tired of hide hunting, come back around. Pa hires a lot of men these days, provided they don't ride their horses to death."

"Sensible of him, Sam. You got a bottle of that liniment I can take with me? I don't think they have any at the livery."

"You're not taking him anywhere," Sam replied. "I'll keep him right here till that leg's well."

"That's kind of you. How much I owe you?"

"Don't think I asked anything," Sam said, frowning. "Consider it a favor."

"I'd be happier if you'd let me pay. I don't care much for being in debt."

"Tell you what. We've got some horses my sister bought off a bunch of Texas cowboys. I'd judge 'em half wild by their eyes. Care to lend a hand gentling 'em?"

"I may not be here long."

"One day. Come down in the morning. Fair?"

"Sure," Ben said, shaking the boy's hand.

Ben then headed toward the hotel. He got as far as the

El Dorado Saloon before stopping. Clint Avery argued loudly with a pair of Texas cowboys, and Ben tried to lend a hand.

"Stay clear, son," a fierce-looking cowboy said, clamping a heavy hand on Ben's shoulder. "They're just havin' a bit of a disagreement about a card game. Jack over there's certain to see it stays calm."

Ben caught sight of a tall, burly man with a five-pointed star pinned to a leather vest. Avery appeared to be in no danger, though he did seem terribly old just then. The captain's bloodshot eyes and wrinkled face made him appear older than his forty-five years. He moved like an old man, and he no longer spread fear in his enemies as he once had.

Ben turned away and continued on his way. When he arrived at the Richmond Hotel, he spotted a familiar brand on the rump of a big sorrel stallion tied to the hitching rack.

"TA," Ben mumbled.

"You say somethin'?" a young cowboy asked, stepping out of the shadows.

"No, not really," Ben answered. "I just recognized the brand."

"Oh?"

"TA. Tom Adams. How is he?"

"Who'd be askin'?"

"Ben Haskell. I rode for him three years back. Might say he sort of took me in like a father for a time. He and Miz Adams are special that way."

"Tom's dead," the cowboy announced. "Fell off his horse and got stepped on. Rib went through a lung, and that was that."

Ben staggered to the hitching rack and leaned against the wooden bar for support. He'd always thought if worse came to worst he could ride for Tom Adams. Now it seemed that dark shadow of death was again devouring the good Ben knew.

"Does his family know?" Ben asked sadly.

"Henry Sykes sent a wire. You know Henry?"

Ben nodded. "Fine cook, old Henry."

"Best I ever knew. What do you do up here now? Don't look to be a drover."

"I hunt buffs," Ben mumbled. "Or I did. Now I guess I'm just another drifter."

"Blamed too many of those already," the cowboy declared. "Few bosses like Tom about, and that's a certain truth."

"Yes," Ben agreed.

"Heard of any work to be had?"

"Not a lick," Ben told the young man.

"Then I suppose I'd best head home pretty soon."

If you do, Ben thought, *you'll be one of the luckier ones.*

Chapter 11

Ben, as promised, appeared at Sayles & Sons the following day, eager to help with the horses and cast from his mind the memory of Hartman's raiders. It seemed life was always the same. Whenever a hint of brightness appeared, death and darkness cast it aside. He couldn't seem to escape the ghost of Angelina's smile, especially with little Aaron haunting the streets of Dodge City, his sad, mournful eyes reflecting Ben's own pain.

Ben hoped working the horses would break the spell, chase away the gloom. But as he climbed atop the corral fence and studied the lean cow ponies and the spotted mustangs prancing about, he found himself remembering Buffalo Springs, the rustlers at the TA Ranch, the Comanches, and even Olin Hartman.

"Well, what d'you think?" Sam Sayles asked, climbing up on the fence beside Ben. "Mangy bunch, huh?"

"The brown one with the splash of white on his nose looks prime," Ben responded. "The mustangs will prove steady enough, but they won't be much use in your trade."

"Pa will sell them off to some farmer," Sam said, laughing. "He buys up strings all the time. I've never known him not to get his price sooner or later. Besides, that spotted one with the white chest looks sound."

"Could be. Especially with the right handling."

"Well, that's your job, isn't it?"

"Guess so," Ben admitted, hopping down from the fence and starting toward the white-chested pony. "Come on, boy, let's get after it."

Ben labored long and hard at the corral. Except for a brief break around midday for some dried beef and biscuits provided by Sam, he devoted the entire day to the mustangs.

Toward nightfall Jim Sayles appeared. Except for having the same dark hair as Sam, he was as unlike his son as could be imagined. The older Sayles was tall, broad-shouldered, and thick-waisted. Ben suspected the freighter could move whole wagons with one massive arm.

"So, have we hired on a new wrangler, Sam?" Sayles asked. "I thought that was your personal folly."

"Ben's been working the mustangs," Sam explained. "Kind of a bargain we made. His horse has a bad tendon, and I'm looking after it."

"Seems a mighty poor bargain, a day's hard work for a bit of horse doctoring," Sayles declared.

"Truth is, it's a welcome change," Ben explained. "I used to work mustangs back in Texas."

"And now you hunt with Mo Dumas," Sayles said, grinning at Ben's surprise. "Don't look so startled. I've got eyes. You've been in and out of Dodge quite a bit the past year or so, son."

"My name's Ben Haskell," Ben said sourly. "If my debt's cleared, I guess it's best I head along."

"Hold on, Ben," Sayles called. "Didn't mean to run you off. Truth is, I've heard good things about you, and I see you've got a knack with the stock. You say your debt's squared. Well, I figure mine isn't. Go with Sam and wash up. My Nola's as fine a cook as there is in Kansas, and she'd welcome an extra guest. Let's feed you, at least. If you ask me, you could use some fleshing out."

Ben started to object, but Sam pointed toward the nearby house.

"No point to arguing," Sam whispered. "You are *skinny*, and Ma does a fair job with roast beef. Come on. I'll show you where you can scrub up."

Ben started to turn away, but Clay hadn't returned the night before, and Avery was still occupied at the El Dorado. Only Aaron and old Mo would want company, and Ben needed no more ghosts about. He nodded to Sayles and followed Sam toward the house.

The roast beef lived up to its reputation, and Ben enjoyed it tremendously. He felt a bit uneasy at the table, though. Sam's sister, Kate, and five younger brothers were there, all jabbering away with their father, swapping jests and taunts as families were prone to do. Ben ached at the sounds of laughter. It had been four years since he'd seen or heard from Catherine or Michael. The sense of loss was overwhelming.

"Can I help with the plates?" Ben offered when everyone had finished.

"That's no chore for company," Nola Sayles told him. "Sam, you and Jerome can tend to that. Kate, why don't you show Ben, here, the house?"

Ben started to explain it had grown late and he should return to the hotel, but Kate stepped toward him with eager, sparkling blue eyes, and he couldn't resist her outstretched hand. He took it, feeling the warmth that flowed from live flesh. He had been too much in the company of Angelina's ghost lately.

"I know you can't have any interest in seeing Ma's house," Kate said, leading the way through the hall and out into a grassy area beyond the back door. "It's quiet out here, though. Would you care to sit and talk?"

"I really should head back to the hotel," Ben explained.

"Am I that ugly?" she asked. "I know I'm only sixteen and a half and scarcely a match for the belles down the other side of the tracks, but surely I'm not such bad company that you want to leave straightaway."

"It's not you," Ben said, sighing. "It's me."

"Oh? And here I thought you a shade on the handsome side. True, your ribs stick halfway through your skin, but a few dinners here will change that."

"Just what would you know about my ribs?"

"I watched you working the horses. Sam likes you. He's not such a good judge of soap or linen napkins, but he's got a fair eye where horses and men are concerned. Pa, too."

"And what's he say about me?"

"That maybe you've got a talent with horses. And that you've got a lot of secrets."

"So you're curious, eh?"

"Maybe. And there aren't a lot of young men in town these days fit to walk the river with. Most are poor lonely cowboys, and they flock to the fancy houses and saloons. Not many pass their days working horses."

"I made a bargain with Sam, and I pay my debts."

"That's just as rare. Tell you what. You share one of your secrets, and I'll share one of mine."

"And what secrets could you have, Kate?"

"You first."

"All right. I'm from Texas. I have a sister back there we call Cate, short for Catherine with a C. Four brothers and two more sisters, too. So, you see, I'm no lone cowboy without a home."

"Yes, you are," she said, glancing down for a moment at his boots.

"And what's your secret?" Ben asked.

"I'm the lone girl of seven children, and I can outride, outwork, and outshoot the lot of them."

"So, I don't suppose that brings you a lot of callers."

"Not a lot," she whispered nervously.

"Well, I've only known one girl very well who wasn't a sister or a neighbor. She's dead."

"How?"

"Shot a week back by raiders. I miss her, and I see her face all the time."

"Tell me about her," Kate said, taking Ben's hand and clasping it firmly. He did. And afterward they walked through her mother's garden until Jim Sayles announced it was time they returned inside.

"It's late," he told Ben. "Maybe you'd like to come again, though."

Ben gazed into Kate's eyes, read a second invitation, and nodded.

Then he left the Sayles's house and returned to the hotel. Clay was waiting, eager to share the tale of his own adventure. Afterward, Ben told of his walk with Kate.

"You do have all the good fortune, Ben," Clay grumbled. "Short of being a banker or owning the railroad, Jim Sayles is as rich a man as you could find in western Kansas."

"And?"

"Even if she's ugly, Kate's got to be a good catch."

"I'm not marrying her," Ben said, laughing.

"You sure?"

As the days in Dodge stretched into a week, Ben became less certain. When he was not helping Sam and his brothers Tommy and Jerome with the horses, Ben would wrestle Taylor, Grant, and Andy, or help Mrs. Sayles hang laundry or replace shingles. Ben was clearly burrowing his way into their hearts, and as he and Kate strolled along the river or picked wildflowers on the hillsides beyond town, he began to let the memories of Texas and Angelina fade. The ghosts would never truly leave, he knew, but something rich and fine was coming to take their place in his nightly dreams.

"She's a keeper, Ben," Clay told him after they had attended Sunday supper at the Sayles's house. "So, have you asked her?"

"How can I? I don't know where I'll be in a week's time. I have no trade, and I —"

"Ben, you know that doesn't count for anything. It's not often a man stumbles across good in this life, and it's best to grab hold and hang on."

"But what about Mo?"

"He left two days ago," Clay explained. "I told him we'd had enough."

"And Captain Avery?"

"His luck's running hot, Ben. He's still at the El Dorado."

"What'll we do?"

"Well, I figure between us we've got a thousand dollars saved. We could buy ourselves a ranch out in Colorado, maybe, raise horses. And once you get the nerve to ask Kate, we can head out there. I never planned on wandering all my life. I'll find a gal myself before long, and we can raise an army of kids."

"If I ask Kate, will you stand up with me?"

"If you don't, I'm liable to ask her myself."

Ben grinned, and the two old friends walked briskly back to the hotel.

The next morning Ben led Kate out to the river.

"I'm none too familiar with fine words and poetry, Kate," he told her. "I'm not so much to look at, either.

But I know how to work hard, and I can be relied on."

"And?"

"I'd have you share my life," Ben said, clasping her hands. "If you'll consent to being my wife, I'd like to speak to your pa."

"If you don't do it pretty soon, he's likely to string you up on the nearest oak, Ben Haskell. What's taken you so long?"

"Does that mean yes?"

"Sure does," she said, holding him tightly.

The wedding took place the next Sunday. Ben stood stiffly in a dark black suit bought only two days before. Clay was no less nervous. Kate wore her mother's ivory-colored gown, and her smile lit the small chapel more brightly than the fifty candles scattered about the room.

Once the vows were exchanged, Jim Sayles led his new son-in-law aside for a moment.

"I know you've got your heart set on a ranch out West, Ben, but I've got another proposal to send your way," Sayles said, resting a heavy hand on Ben's slender shoulder. "For a long time now I've wanted to stretch my business into Colorado. The territory's rich with gold and fine land, and the railroad's got little interest in the middle of the state. I've picked out a place on the Arkansas, up in the high country, but I need a man to operate the place who can outlast the winter and fight the outlaws."

"I've grown weary of fighting," Ben answered.

"There's killing like the kind you've been doing, and there's protecting your home and family," Sayles argued. "It would bring in a steady income, and it'd be a big help to me. In a year I'd lend you Sam."

"I'd need help now, too. Can I ask Clay?"

"I'd be disappointed if you didn't. He seems a good one. And as for the horses, you could raise those, too. Land's cheap up that way. If things go as I expect, you could wind up founding a town, bringing a future to that valley."

"There are worse ways to start a marriage," Ben said, grinning. "Does Kate know?"

"I asked her first. She's no one to surprise, Ben. You'll come to learn that soon enough."

Ben laughed, then set off to locate Clay.

"Well, I always thought it'd be fine to ride into the high country," Clay responded. "When you finish your present obligations, we'll speak to the captain."

Ben nodded, then captured Kate from the gang of admirers who had collected around her.

"You agreed?" she asked as they climbed into a carriage that would take them to a waiting train and then to Kansas City for a brief escape from the frontier.

"So long as Clay goes along," he answered.

"That's good. You'll need a friend out there."

Yes, Ben agreed, wondering how Avery would respond.

The day Ben and Kate returned to Dodge City, he and Clay walked to the dingy El Dorado Saloon to speak with Clint Avery. They found the captain sitting alone at a corner table, sipping whiskey and shuffling a deck of cards.

"We missed you at the wedding," Ben declared.

"Oh, that's for family," Avery grumbled. "Old women cry, and kids can toss rice and pull pranks."

"You are family of a sort," Ben explained.

"No, I lost my family," Avery said, his eyes growing darker by the minute.

"Captain, Ben and I've done some thinking," Clay broke in. "Seems Jim Sayles wants to extend his freight line into Colorado. You know I've always wanted to see the Rockies. I thought we might head that way, raise some horses, and operate a depot."

"Sounds a fair idea," Avery declared.

"Think you could break off from here, go with us?" Clay asked.

"You don't need me," Avery said, setting the cards down and looking at his young companions. "War's been over better'n five years, Clay. You're not a stubble-cheeked kid afraid of his shadow anymore. It's time you boys found a home, and it appears to me this might be just the place."

"But, Captain," Clay objected.

"Go, boys," Avery said gruffly. "You can take care of your own affairs. I can sure tend mine. Time you headed on."

"You sure?" Ben asked.

"Aren't you, Ben? You've got a wife now. In time there'll be little ones. Hold 'em close, son. There's a world of harm waiting out there to snatch 'em away. And never forget, once they're gone, they never return."

Ben shook Avery's outstretched hand. All ten fingers trembled, and for the first time Ben could recall, Clint Avery rubbed away a tear from his eye. The old sour face soon returned, though. Ben turned and left Clay to say his farewell in private.

The final week of August, Ben led a long line of wagons westward down the Arkansas. He'd left towns before, many of them and often. But this time he wasn't riding off a wanderer, content to cast his fate on the whimsy of a gypsy wind. This time Kate was with him. Clay brought up the rear, and four teamsters completed a fine outfit. A bright future waited, and Ben was eager to mold it in his strong, confident hands.

"Colorado and destiny!" Clay had said, toasting their departure with a final sip of corn whiskey.

Colorado and a different, better life, Ben had thought. It was his fervent hope.

Chapter 12

The year 1876 was a remarkable one. The United States marked its one hundredth anniversary with parades, fireworks, and the admission into the union of the new state of Colorado. Five years earlier Ben Haskell and Clay Hamilton had set up a small freight depot and way station on the Arkansas River. From a log warehouse and station a town had grown, nestling in the mountains on the eastern fringe of the Continental Divide. They'd called it Saylesville after Kate's father.

Saylesville in 1876 was a town of almost a hundred inhabitants. A year earlier Ben had turned the freight office over to Sam Sayles and concentrated instead on a booming mercantile supplying the small ranches and mining settlements along the Arkansas and north and south along the Divide. Ben also had his ranch — seventeen hundred acres of pasture bounded by a pair of gurgling creeks. Clay Hamilton operated a livery and gunsmith shop adjoining the mercantile.

Sometimes Ben had a hard time recalling his wandering days. He doubted he was really alive before meeting Kate and heading to Colorado. Clay sometimes spun tales of hunting buffalo or battling Comanches, but Ben was content to relish the present and forget the past. Texas was a lifetime away.

Those five years in the mountains had been good ones. The town had grown and prospered. New neighbors had become fast friends. Most important, Kate had borne two fine sons: four-year-old Benny, and little Michael, three. She was expecting a third child momentarily — they hoped for a girl — and if there'd ever been as bright a summer, Ben didn't know when it might have been.

Yes, there had been a few problems. Three years before, a fire had burned half the town. Twice raiders had struck. The first group stole a shipment of ore from the Cottonwood Mine, but the culprits were ambushed later by a posse of angry miners. The second group of outlaws had tried to hold up the new Denver and Western Bank. A clerk shouted an alarm, and the bandits were slaughtered as they attempted to escape from town.

The foundation for a courthouse had been laid at the top of a new town square. The old log schoolhouse would be replaced by a more permanent structure. The church was finally receiving a brass bell, and Ben himself had constructed a steeple where the bell would soon hang.

Civilization had arrived. With law, education, and religion, the community would surely grow.

"It's time," Virginia Hamilton, Clay's bride of three years, declared. Her two-year-old, Bobby Lee, sat on one knee, while she cradled baby Clinton on the other.

"I don't know, Ginny," Clay replied. "I kind of miss the old days. We didn't meet in any church, you know."

"Watch that talk, Clayton," she scolded. "Your

boys have ears. They're wild enough without their father reminding them of his heathen ways."

"Motherhood does that," Clay whispered to Ben. "Makes 'em turn religious."

"A small price to pay," Ben said, smiling at Kate's enlarged middle. "God bless the children. What would we be without 'em?"

The others sighed, and Kate caught Benny's arm seconds before he tossed an apricot at his younger brother. Ben meant what he'd said, though. The little ones provided purpose, a sense of direction, to their lives. When winter gripped the Rockies hard, sending great blizzards of snow and sheets of ice to torment the people of Saylesville, Ben held his boys close and shared some half-forgotten story. Other nights the children would sing or play, and the brightness of their smiles and the life in their songs chased away even January's gloom.

In September Kate had her child, another boy, and they called the little one Clayton Samuel in honor of Ben's best friend and Kate's oldest brother. The child seemed sure to share his older brothers' tendency toward Ben's light hair and deep blue eyes. Only in their strong affection for music did the boys mirror Kate.

"The next one had best be a girl," she fumed when the doctor pronounced her fit to leave her bed. "Hear me, Lord? There are enough Haskell boys about to torment this town! Give us a girl to restore order."

Ben laughed heartily.

"Well, the ranch does want hands," he told Kate. "I asked your father, and he said your line leans to boys. I have three sisters myself, so don't blame me. The fault's clearly with you."

Kate fumed and frowned, but Ben knew she doted on the boys as she had on her brothers. A girl would be nice, though, he decided.

In October a long, steady stream of gold seekers funneled through Saylesville. There'd been a strike forty miles to the west, and all manner of folk abandoned their homes and families to stalk the elusive yellow mineral.

Ben kept a close watch over his store. At night he slept behind the counter while Kate and the boys rested safely upstairs. Twice a rock shattered the door glass, and renegades tried to rob the place. Each time Ben's sudden appearance, shotgun in hand, sent them fleeing.

Around the middle of the month Ben was unloading supplies from a freight wagon when a pair of men approached down the street. The first was a worn-out tin panner riding a thin, weatherbeaten old mule. The second wore a heavy buffalo cloak over his shoulders. His thick beard was speckled with gray, and his steel-cold eyes seemed familiar. He drew his horse to a halt and extended a wrinkled, withered hand toward Ben.

"Captain Avery?" Ben gasped.

"Heard you were up this way," Avery responded. "I thought maybe you could put up old Cyrus and me for the night, maybe offer us a meal. The cards turned on me a year back, and I've not had much luck hunting gold."

"You appear to've done right fine, though," Cyrus added. "These your boys, eh, Avery?"

"This is young Ben," Avery said. The trace of pride Ben might have expected was absent. Instead, there was a hint of despair mixed with frosty regret. Avery's eyes seemed to plead for a kind of forgiveness, as if requesting food and shelter from old friends was the worst kind of crime.

"Clay's working the livery," Ben said, setting aside his work and trotting to the door. "Come on in and warm yourself, Captain. I've got a boy inside helps with the store. I'll have him take your horses down the street."

"We'll need our goods," Cyrus said, protecting his

dented pan and provision bag as if they were life itself.

"Bring 'em along inside, then," Ben suggested. "The rest'll be at the livery when you're ready to leave. Clay won't let anyone mess with it."

"It's safe," Avery told his companion. "Let's go along inside. My toes must be frostbit. There's snow already in the high country," he added for Ben's benefit.

"Make yourselves comfortable by the stove," Ben said, pointing the two weary men to the big Franklin stove in the center of the room. "After I get through outside, I'll take you up to see Kate and the boys."

"Young ones?" Avery asked.

"Three of 'em, Captain, and Clay's got a pair himself. Looks like we're raising ourselves a company of cavalry."

"Good ranch crew anyway," Avery said, grinning as he warmed his hands. "You go along with your business, Ben. We'll do fine here."

Ben sent young Jeremiah Hollis down to the livery with the animals, then resumed his labors. After a few minutes, Avery, still bent by the cold and damp, came out to help.

"No need, Captain," Ben said, setting a barrel of nails on the mercantile's wooden porch. "It's little enough to keep one man occupied."

"I never knew you to turn down help, Ben Haskell," the captain declared, laughing. "You sure didn't in the old days."

"A lot of snow's fallen since then," Ben remarked.

"Yes, but a man never completely changes."

Ben supposed not, for he quit arguing and allowed Avery to help unload the wagon. In half an hour they had the stock moved inside and meted out to its appropriate shelves. Ben then walked upstairs and brought down Kate and the boys.

"We'll have to have a celebration," she declared.

"After all, Captain Avery, you weren't able to come to the wedding, and you haven't even met Virginia, Clay's wife. I'll get a ham ready, and we'll make merry."

"Don't stir up trouble on our account, ma'am," Avery said. "We're just a pair of old renegades escaped the mountains."

"Nonsense," Kate argued. "We seldom get company, and you're as close to family as Ben's ever invited to supper. I'll go tell Ginny straightaway."

And so it was settled. That night served as a reunion of sorts. Clay and Virginia arrived with their youngsters. Old Cyrus and Avery were the guests of honor, and Ben himself led in Benny and Michael, while Kate served up dinner. Baby Clinton rested in a crib nearby, and Avery's eyes were seldom far from the infant.

After a brief prayer, the company ate their dinner quietly. Gradually, though, Avery began to share a story or two of bygone days. First there was the story of Olin Hartman's raid on the wagons. Then Avery's smile broadened, and he tilted back his chair.

"I'll never forget the first time I saw young Ben," the captain began. "Was just Clay and I riding then. We happened along this farm down in Texas. All we wanted was a dip of well water, but this tow-headed boy with one arm in a sling calls out for us to halt. Lord help me, he had one of those dragoon Colts — cannon of a gun he could hardly hold steady. Hammer's cocked back, and he's ready to blow us to high heaven!"

"Why?" Kate asked.

Avery turned to Ben, who looked away.

"Ben?" she asked.

"We had trouble," Ben explained. "Some men killed my ma."

"We settled the score, though, didn't we, boy?" Avery boasted, taking a flask from his pocket and drawing a liberal sip. "Wasn't the only time. Why, when we went to work on that ranch, there was rustler trouble. We . . .''

Avery remembered in detail all the bloodiest episodes of the year Ben had passed riding the range from Texas to Kansas. The talk of killing and Avery's penchant for strong drink quickly soured Kate. She rounded up the children and put them to bed early. Virginia excused herself as well and carried her boys back to the room Kate kept ready for company.

"Guess they don't have the stomach for such things," Avery declared, emptying his flask. "They don't know how it was, do they?''

"They don't need to know," Ben said sternly. "I put all that behind me.''

"You never put it behind you," Avery said bitterly. "Killing's part of you, just like your heart or your arms. It'll come back.''

"No," Ben said. "I was little more than a boy back then. I had no place to go, nobody to lean on.''

"You could've stayed at the Adams place," Avery countered. "You rode with us because it was fresh, because you enjoyed the freedom and the power.''

"I owed you," Ben declared. "I pay my debts.''

"Glad to hear that, boy," Avery said, rising from the table. "I got a plan, and I'll need help. Cy here's got a claim up north a ways. Says it's swamped with nuggets.''

"That's right," Cyrus agreed. "Gold enough to paint the Rockies yellow.''

"If that's so, why do you look as though you couldn't come up with a silver dollar to pay for your supper?'' Ben asked.

"Well, the gold's there, sure enough," Cy went on. "Four men could dig a few thousand in a week.''

"It's late in the year to head into the mountains, Captain," Clay argued. "We've got families to look after.''

"We'd be back in a month," Avery explained. "And rich!"

"If it's that easy, you'll have no trouble finding volunteers," Ben said, gazing at Clay. "I can't. I lost a family once. I won't leave Kate."

"It's how things are," Clay added.

"I guess it's been a long time since we were an outfit, huh?" Avery asked.

"Sorry, Captain," Clay said somberly. "We've got roots here."

"You could, too," Ben went on to say. "Stay here. There's more work than I can ever get done."

"Keep a store?" Avery cried. "Not likely."

"I've got a ranch out there with horses to work," Ben explained. "There are worse lives."

"No, I was never one to stay in one place," Avery grumbled. "Besides, Cy and I aim to get rich."

"Sure do!" Cyrus shouted.

"Well, we wish you luck," Clay spoke, rising from the table and shaking the captain's hand. "And if it comes to naught you know where to find us."

"Oh, we'll be along," Avery promised. "Just to watch your eyes pop out when we flash a couple of fist-sized nuggets."

"We'll have a drink to your good fortune, then," Clay declared. "Best of luck to the both of you."

"Sure," Cy grumbled.

Avery only looked out the window at the distant mountains.

Avery and old Cy slept downstairs that night. In the morning Ben fixed them up with a month's provisions and a pack mule. When the two men departed town, Ben suspected it was the last he'd see of either. Winter was already descending on the Rockies, and the years were bearing down hard on Clint Avery.

Chapter 13

There was no sea of gold in the Rockies waiting for Clint Avery and old Cy. In truth, they panned less than a thousand dollars' worth. By spring Cy spent his share on whiskey, and he died a broken man shortly thereafter. Avery's share financed a year of card play. The old luck seemed elusive now, though, and soon the captain was once again wandering the little towns along the Arkansas, hunting bounties on petty criminals or selling his services to Wells Fargo or gold mines.

So it was that while Clint Avery clawed at the earth in hopes of finding wealth, a thick vein was discovered two years later on the Haskell ranch by a cowboy digging fence posts.

"Strange how things work out," Clay observed. "Here the captain heads north, when there's gold not a stone's throw away."

Avery was less amused by the fact. And as ore shipments to Denver smelters brought stacks of bank notes in response, the captain frequented Saylesville less and less often.

The mine proved the making of the town. In the beginning Ben entrusted the digging to Clay Hamilton. Clay rounded up a crew of a dozen men, and they blasted into the hillside and collected ore. In time, forty men labored at two shafts, and a small village of cabins sprang up to house the miners and their families.

Ben's newfound wealth brought changes with it. He moved Kate and the children into a new house on the outskirts of town. He also turned the store over to Kate's spinster cousin, Alice Meeker. Clay was too busy managing the mine to operate his livery, and the stable and gunsmith shop had been sold.

By early autumn, 1883, Saylesville was preparing to celebrate its tenth year. A spirit of optimism permeated the town. Hammers resounded throughout the afternoon, adding new houses and shops along side streets. There was talk the railroad would soon add a spur line from Pueblo. The steeples of four churches reached skyward, and Sunday mornings rang with the clanging of bells as a thankful populace turned out to worship.

The celebration was the idea of the ladies at the Methodist church. They soon convinced the Baptists, and in a week the women coaxed their neighbors into talking the town council into a history pageant, a parade, a carnival, and, to top it all off, a picnic for the entire town.

Kate was enthralled with the event. Though she now had six children to tend and a large house to manage, she found time to write most of the pageant.

"Who else knows more about Saylesville than me?" she asked. "This town is named for my father, and I was here when you and Clay nailed the first planks in place."

Ben ordinarily found little use for such foolishness, but he did enjoy seeing Benny and Michael portraying bearded explorers. It was just as much fun watching little Bobby Lee Hamilton decked out in the buckskin breechclout and hawk feathers of a Ute Indian.

Kate had enlisted her entire brood in the project. The younger ones — Allison, Richmond, and Jefferson — played the parts of squirrels.

"I'd say they were born to the role," Ben declared. "I never saw three kids more at home climbing trees and stirring up a racket."

In spite of Kate's goading, though, Ben refused to take a part in the festivities. He turned down the chance to give a founding father's speech, declined to narrate the pageant, even shook off an offer to oversee the fireworks display.

"This is your town as much as anybody's," Kate chided him.

"Maybe," he admitted, "but I'm little good at speeches or dramatics. You hold up the family honor, Kate. I'll see the mine keeps running."

Actually, though, Clay did that. Once a week the two old friends would share thoughts and make decisions, but it was usually a matter of Ben approving Clay's ideas. So it was that, while Kate and the children practiced the pageant, Ben met with Clay at the mine's business office in Saylesville.

"I can't see where it would hurt to hold off this next shipment a week," Clay pointed out. "With all this hoopla, it seems to me we'd do well to hold off sending the ore to Denver or bringing in a payroll."

"We've got a contract, Clay," Ben pointed out. "We have to send at least two loads. As for the payroll, folks will want to have money to spend at the carnival. Henry Belton doesn't keep enough at the bank to handle our needs."

"Then at least let's disguise it a bit," Clay suggested. "Send the bills on the regular stage."

"Three of those coaches have been robbed in the past six months."

"Hire extra guards."

"Won't that be a little like posting an announcement, Clay?"

"What about sending it with one of Sam's teamsters?"

"Better," Clay said, digesting the notion. "Split it up. Send it with the mercantile's supplies, half with the first wagon and the rest with the second."

"That ought to confuse folks, all right. You'll still want to hire an escort."

"Sure, but it would be best to hire a couple of really steady men."

"Sam's got a pair of men he's used before. I'll arrange it."

"Good," Ben said, resting easy knowing Clay would tend to the details.

In the days to come, Ben found it harder and harder to concentrate on business, though. Men hammered giant banners into place across the fronts of hotels, the courthouse, even the jail. Virginia and Kate borrowed half the men from the mine to construct tables, and Sam Sayles's teamsters were hard pressed to bring in barrels of flour, sugar, and fruit for the picnic. Steers and hogs for the barbecue were penned up in back of the Baptist church, and women frantically put the finishing touches on pageant costumes.

Ben did personally attend to one detail. Sheriff Gentry Boyd was concerned about the number of visitors flocking to Saylesville.

"You know how carnivals draw no-accounts," Boyd told Ben. "I've seen it before. Just last year on Independence Day I locked up three pickpockets and a fleece artist."

"Find yourself a couple of extra deputies, Sheriff," Ben suggested. "Don't worry about the money. The mine will foot the expense. Pick some men you can trust, though."

"I thought maybe you could lend me some of the boys from the mine, too. Kind of make 'em unpaid carnival rangers."

"Fine. Let me know who you want."

"There's one more thing, Ben," the sheriff added.

"Yes?"

"This payroll you're bringing in. I know the men want their pay, but couldn't you change the timing? There'll be all manner of extra folks in town, and —"

"Clay worries about it, too," Ben confessed, "but we'll have some guards on the road, and I'll see about hiring two or three to watch the office in town, too. The bank's already put on extra guards, I understand."

"Started yesterday."

"Good. Then let's do what we can and try to enjoy this madness. It'll be another ten years before we do this again."

"I hope," Boyd said, shaking his head.

Ben hoped so, too, though he was careful not to say so when Kate was around. Each night after supper he was treated to a new performance by his part of the pageant, and if Benny and Michael found their costumes were a bit tight and made their skin itch, then Ben only laughed and said that was all the more realistic.

"Back in my cowboy days, I went whole months without baths," he told the boys. "Out hunting buffs, we took a dip in a river or creek when one was handy, but the camp always smelled musty and foul anyway. We couldn't wait to hit Dodge City and get a real bath."

"Uncle Clay was with you when you did all that, wasn't he?" Benny asked. The eleven-year-old had taken to asking a hundred questions a day of late, and Michael was little better.

"That's right," Ben said, knowing Clay had spun tales of those adventures a hundred times over the years.

"Tell us about it," Michael pleaded.

"Please, Pa," little Allison said, taking her mangy squirrel's head off her pretty six-year-old face and grinning at her father. The girl's sparkling eyes melted Ben every time, and he soon gathered little Richmond and Jeff to his side and began a tale of scouting the herd. He didn't explain the icy chill the killing brought to his heart, the cold cruelty of slaughtering even the youngest. Instead, he painted a picture of swift horsemen and daring exploits.

"Ah, I knew we should've been buffalo hunters," Benny complained.

"Wasn't my idea to be a trapper," Michael pointed out.

"Shh!" Ben warned. "Your ma'll hear. Truth is, the buffs were pretty well finished by the time we came here."

"How come, Pa?" Michael asked. "There are still plenty of deer around."

"Men got greedy, I suppose," Ben explained. "People back East wanted buffalo hides for coats, and hunters took off for the plains, shot any they could find."

"Not the babies?" Allison asked.

"All of 'em," Ben mumbled. "Some say it was to chase the plains tribes onto reservations. I don't know. It's what happened. We can be sad about it now, but back then it's just what people did."

The children stared at him sadly, and Ben knew they didn't understand a bit of it. Well, they were young, and the world was still new. He prayed it would remain so a while longer.

"So, little ones, have you had your story?" Kate asked, joining them at last.

"It was a good one," Michael declared.

"About the buffalo," Benny explained as he hugged his mother.

"Then it's time you got your rest," Kate declared. "School tomorrow, and pageant practice afterward."

The older ones groaned. Ben hoisted little Clay on one shoulder, then collected four-year-old Richmond. Benny and Michael led Jeff, the youngest at three, while their mother carried her jewel, Allison.

It's a strange menagerie we've raised, Ben thought. Rich, his tired eyes peeking out from a furry head, seemed so wonderfully at peace. Clay wriggled like a worm, and the brave frontiersmen, Michael and Benny, seemed clearly far too young to break a trail, much less found a future state.

Ben helped Kate defrock the younger ones first. Rich could usually undress himself, but the long afternoon pageant rehearsal had exhausted him, and Ben didn't mind peeling the squirrel outfit from the boy's bony frame. After nestling Rich and Jeff in the feather bed they shared, Ben gave Allison her good-night kiss, then set off with little Clay for the third bedroom down the hall of the big house.

Michael and Benny were shooting buffalo from the cover of their beds, and Ben sat for a while and watched. That room was taking on the appearance of a bunkhouse, what with discarded boots on cedar chests and shirts of all sizes scattered about the floor. He'd have to speak with the youngsters soon, for Kate was losing patience.

"I never intended to raise a family of hogs," she'd said only the day before.

"Time to say prayers and catch some sleep, boys," Ben declared as he set a weary Clay on a corner of his bunk. "No more buffalo hunting tonight."

"Pa, did you really do all those things?" Benny asked as he peeled off his buckskin vest and scratched his reddened chest. "Break wild mustangs and chase Indians — all of it?"

"I did," Ben said, pulling the youngster close.

"Wish we could," Michael grumbled.

"I don't," Ben said, sitting beside Clay on the bed.

Benny huddled against Ben's other side, and Michael climbed up on the bed and rested his chin on Ben's shoulder. The closeness was overpowering.

"Was it hard, Pa?" Benny whispered.

"Hard and lonely," Ben told them. "That was the worst part, being alone all the time. Oh, there were others there, but it wasn't like having your ma or you kids around. Sometimes I'd feel so hollow I thought I'd die."

The boys instinctively burrowed under an arm and clung to a shoulder. Their warmth chased off the memories and brightened Ben's dour face.

"All that's behind me now," Ben said, falling back onto the bed and wrestling the three urchins. "Forever."

He tossed them in his hands and tickled their bellies until Kate appeared to put an end to the foolishness.

"Out of those costumes!" she ordered. "You rip open those seams, Michael, and I'll sew 'em right to your skinny hide! It's time you were all asleep."

The boys nodded obediently, and Ben gave them each a final hug before following Kate out of the room.

"I believe they've taken their roles to heart," she whispered. "I pray we're not raising hooligans."

"No chance of that," Ben said, clasping her hand. "Truth is, they're better than I've got a right to expect."

"Ben?"

"It's your doing, Kate. You've got a green thumb where growing children's concerned."

"I'd say their father's had a hand in it. You give them a chance to work off the raw edges."

Ben smiled. The chill he'd felt when recalling times gone by had passed into memory. The house filled with a wonderful warmth. He was a world away from the old hardness, the cold loneliness of wandering the plains, living from moment to moment and hoping to outlast his enemies. He'd found that wondrous peace, and he was thankful.

Chapter 14

Ben was going over Clay's ledgers at the mine office around ten in the morning when Clint Avery walked through the door. The old cavalryman was in his fifties now, silver-haired and weathered by time and hardship. Ben stood up instantly and extended his hand.

"Town's astir," Avery commented as he shook Ben's hand. "Got quite a lot going on, it'd seem."

"Tenth anniversary celebration," Ben said, sighing. "Kate and Virginia are all caught up in it. The kids, too. You should see Bobby Lee all painted up like a Ute!"

"I thought to have a word or two with young Clay."

"You mean *old* Clay," Ben said, laughing. "Around here young Clay's my seven-year-old. Old Clay's out at the mine. Care to ride out and have a look around?"

"Don't want to interrupt your work."

"Nonsense," Ben said, grabbing his hat and heading for the door. "Glad to have an excuse to ride a bit."

Avery brightened slightly. Once outside, though, Ben

found himself studying the captain. Avery was dirty and bedraggled, a tired old warrior struggling to survive in the December of his life. Only the hard, unrelenting gaze in his eyes remained of the gray-clad rider Ben had met sixteen long years before.

Ben picked up a horse at the livery, saddled the animal, and mounted up. Avery sat atop a gray gelding, waiting with a patience that startled Ben. The old Avery would have been mumbling curses and fidgeting at the delay. Well, the years had their way of tempering a man.

They rode along the Arkansas and on into the hills a bit before coming to the mine. Clay was supervising the loading of the ore shipment.

"Well, Ben, Captain, this is a surprise indeed!" Clay called, jumping down from the front wagon and trotting over to his old friends. "Just a bit more to do here. Then maybe we can visit a bit."

"I'll show him around," Ben said, dismounting. "Captain, you haven't seen the mine, have you?"

"No," Avery admitted. "I've had the itch to see her, though."

"Then come along," Ben said, leading the way toward the first shaft.

Ben conducted Avery through the shafts and tunnels that ate their way into the mountain. Miners swung picks and chipped away at the gold-yielding ore. Others collected the ore and loaded it in small trolleys.

"If you don't mind, I'd as soon move back outside," Avery said after a short time. "I don't find darkness much comfort at my time of life. I figure I'll have all the darkness I could ever wish for soon enough."

Ben laughed, but Avery appeared deathly serious. They made their way back outside. By that time Clay had the ore wagons loaded and on their way.

"Extra guards, huh?" Avery asked, pointing to the

four mounted escorts leading the wagons from the mine.

"Lots of thieves out this way lately," Ben explained. "Can't be too careful."

"No, and that's a fact," Avery agreed. "Last few months I've been up in the Wyoming Territory, operating as bounty agent for the Union Pacific. You'd be amazed at how many bands have taken to robbing express coaches."

"Was that good work?" Ben asked.

"Not so bad in summer, but winter's brutal up that way. I decided to head south for my health."

"You're out of work, then."

"Well, I can still earn supper money at the gaming tables, and I hire myself out here and there."

Ben frowned. Avery was clearly having a rough time, but the old man had pride. He wouldn't ask for work.

"Could be Clay's got a spot for you here," Ben said, leading the way to where Clay was tallying the day's shipment.

"I didn't come here to beg a job," Avery grumbled. "I'll have no such talk. Let's find ourselves a bottle and talk about old times."

Ben didn't have the heart to confess he'd rather leave old times to themselves. There were few warm memories for him back in Kansas or Texas. But when they met Clay, he ushered them to his office.

"I always keep a bottle by for special occasions," Clay explained, rummaging around a drawer until he located a bottle of Kentucky bourbon. "Let's just see if this doesn't go down smooth as rabbit fur."

Clay poured three generous portions, then raised his own glass.

"To old friends, good memories, and better tomorrows," he proclaimed.

Ben lifted his glass and touched the rim to Clay's.

Avery did the same. Ben sipped the powerful liquor. It burned his throat, and his eyes watered. He'd never been a heavy drinker, and Kate had close to sworn him off spirits. Clay treated his glass respectfully as well. Avery downed his, then refilled the glass.

"Been a long time since I tasted the likes of this, Clay," the captain said, putting away the second glass. "Up at Laramie and in the depots west of there, corn squeezings are about the best you can find."

"I'll see you have a couple of bottles to keep you warm this winter," Clay promised. "I'll arrange it with Hicks over at the Diamond C."

"That's fine of you, son."

"Now, tell us how long you'll be here," Clay went on. "You have to stay for the celebration. The kids are all taking part in the pageant, and we'll have fireworks, barbecued spare ribs, and whole sides of beef. You'll be here a week at least."

"Can't promise that," Avery mumbled. "A man's got to make his living, you know."

"Well, at the very least you'll come to supper," Clay declared. "Ginny rarely has company, and she's bursting her corset to show off the new house."

"I'd like to come," Avery replied. "Give me a chance to see the boys, too."

"Ben, can you come, too?"

"I'll ask Kate."

"Ask?" Avery cried in disbelief.

"She's putting in long days, Captain," Ben explained. "They've got her helping with this and that. She devotes the whole afternoon to working with the little ones on that pageant. Rich and Jeff are small yet, and she likes to have them in their bed early. I'd guess we could come for supper, though she may feel the need to leave early."

"Then it's settled," Clay said, pouring himself another drink. "Ben, why don't you take the captain to the hotel, see he's got a good room. We'll meet around six. All right?"

Ben nodded and rose to his feet. Avery poured himself another bourbon, drank it hurriedly, then downed a fourth. Ben noticed the old man showed not a trace of drunkenness, though. In truth, Avery seemed as straight in the saddle as ever and not a bit more talkative.

As they rode to town, Ben pointed to the growth of Saylesville, to new houses, the sawmill down at the river, to the dairies, hog farms, and ranches spreading across the valley.

"Country's closing in, Ben," Avery observed. "No far horizons left anymore. No buffalo."

"Not so many renegade killers, either," Ben added. "All in all, it seems a fair trade."

"I wonder," Avery grumbled.

At the hotel Ben greeted Charlie Gamble, the desk clerk, and requested an upstairs room.

"One with a view of the mountains, Charlie," Ben added.

"Room twenty-four," Gamble said, handing over the key. "With all that's going on, I'm asking five dollars a night now, Ben."

Avery frowned, but Ben placed a twenty-dollar bank note on the counter.

"He's my guest," Ben explained. "Anything else he needs, you put it on a tab and send it to the office."

"I pay my own way," Avery objected.

"You already have," Ben said, gripping the old man's trembling hand. "Long ago. I'd put you up at the house, only Kate's got everything turned upside down, and the kids would likely prove a vexation."

"Well, I thank you," Avery said, stepping away. Ben nodded, then turned toward the door. It was hard for a man like Clint Avery to admit obligation.

When Ben informed Kate of the dinner invitation, she scowled.

"You know how I feel about that old man," she said, folding her hands and shaking her head. "I don't like the way he boasts of murdering people. He drinks too much, and he prompts others to do the same. He scares the children. Ben, he smells of trouble, and I've got enough concerns just now."

"Just dinner, then?" he pleaded. "Afterward you can head along home."

"And the children?"

"You know he wants to see them, Kate."

"Let him come watch the pageant. If you feel strongly about it, let Benny and Michael come. I'll ask Sarah Kingsley to stay with the little ones."

"All right," Ben agreed. "It will make things a little easier on Virginia."

They arrived at the Hamilton house promptly at six. Almost immediately Benny and Michael raced off with Bobby Lee and Clint to partake in a bit of devilment. Ben led Kate into the parlor, and they joined Clay and Avery in a glass of peach wine.

"The captain's been telling us about Wyoming," Clay said, nodding to his silver-haired guest.

"Mountains there are so tall they block out the sun," Avery said. "Land's still virgin green. No fences, no smoky sawmills or foul-smelling smelters."

Avery's eyes flashed brightly, then grew duller as he reminded them of the changes that had come to Colorado. Finally, he spoke of stalking the killer of a stationmaster's family. Kate excused herself and went to help with dinner preparations.

"She's a sensitive gal, eh?" Avery asked Ben.

"She's as strong as they come, Captain," Ben declared. "She doesn't like to think much about the old days. She wasn't part of that, and I'm glad. I want better for my kids . . . for myself."

"Wasn't anything better," Avery grumbled.

"There was — and is!" Ben argued. "I'm sorry you haven't shared these times, Captain, because I'd wish you an easier life. There's comfort knowing you have a bed waiting for you at night, that there are those who care that you share their table and their hopes."

Avery's face paled, and Clay refilled the wineglasses and nervously proposed a new toast.

"To good fortune for all of us," Clay spoke.

"Yes," Ben agreed, raising his glass.

"To all of us," Avery echoed finally. But Ben could tell the old man was a thousand miles away and drifting further into the past. It was a relief when Virginia announced dinner was ready.

They ate quietly. Twice Virginia introduced new topics into the conversation, but aside from a brief sample of the history pageant provided by Benny, Michael, and Bobby Lee, a plague of silence haunted the room. Kate excused herself early and conducted her boys homeward. Ginny enlisted her sons' help in clearing the table, while Clay escorted Ben and Avery back to the parlor.

"Guess we let things get a bit out of hand," Clay said, taking a seat beside the fireplace. "I had in mind a better time for all of us."

"Me, too," Ben added.

"Was my doing," Avery declared. "I should hold my tongue when I'm around the ladies."

"It's the times," Clay grumbled. "Change is always on the wind nowadays, and it's easy to set aside what's gone before. Not many enjoy recalling those hard days we knew so well."

"Can't blame 'em," Avery said, taking a deep

breath. "You boys have life by the tail. Shoot! You're apt to wind up owning all of Colorado. Me, I've not found the door to your good fortune, so I try to pick out the best parts of a withered past."

"There's time yet," Ben added quickly.

"Maybe, but the curtain's dropping, boys. I haven't walked luck's trail lately. I'm on the outs with the law up north."

"How?" Clay asked.

"I was after Pete Cameron, a Kansas skunk who liked to shoot stationmasters in the back. I found him in a Cheyenne saloon, and we went at it. Thing is, the room was crowded, and when all was said and done, Cameron wasn't the only one got himself killed. A pair of cowboys went down, too. Cameron probably shot 'em. I hit what I aim at. Still, Cameron was dead, and I was alive. They've posted me."

"So you need a job," Ben said, laughing. "We hire all kinds of men, Captain. I told you before we can find a place for you at the mine."

"I don't have much affection for dark places," Avery reminded them. "Still, I heard maybe you might hire some extra guards for your Denver payroll wagons."

"How'd you know about that?" Clay asked nervously. "Nobody's to know."

"Somebody always does, though," Avery said, grinning. "Same trouble the Union Pacific has. Secrets are hard to keep."

"I guess so," Clay said, scowling.

"Well, I wouldn't guess many to know," Avery went on. "I've turned gray, boys, but my hand's as steady as ever. I have a sharp eye for trouble, and I'm here to tell you I can be trusted with your dollars. Let me carry this burden for you. I've done it before — often."

Clay turned to Ben.

"We've trusted you with our lives, Captain," Ben

said. "I'd guess this to be kind of a small matter. Consider yourself hired."

"Have you signed on anybody else?" Avery asked.

"No," Clay admitted. "Sam Sayles is sending a couple of riders down from Denver, but once the wagons get here, I thought we'd add a couple of men."

"I know three good hands hanging around Pueblo," Avery explained. "I could wire 'em."

"Do it," Clay advised. "So, we're back in business, so to speak."

"Yes," Avery said, grinning. "Been a while, too. Maybe later we can have a celebration of sorts."

"Consider that a promise," Clay answered. "Ben?"

"Certainly."

They stayed another hour in the parlor, laughing and talking about other times. Ben finally excused himself and headed home. It gave him a fine feeling knowing Clint Avery would for a short time at least know peace. And having Avery guard the payroll meant Clay could rest easier.

Chapter 15

The day of the celebration arrived at last. Ben was up early, coaxing the boys into their pageant costumes and seeing that they had something to eat. Kate managed to get herself and little Allison ready, but cooking was beyond her.

"I expected you to be a trifle uneasy," Ben told her, "but you're shaking worse than an aspen leaf in October."

"I know," she said as she tried to get her fingers into a glove. "Everyone's expecting so much, though, and I —"

"Everything will be fine," Ben assured her. "Now let's get these young vagabonds down to the square before they drive me to distraction."

Kate nodded, and they lined up the children, counted heads, then began the half-mile walk into town.

Others might have driven a carriage or ridden horses, but Ben had no intention of adding to the confusion already plaguing the streets of Saylesville. Once the fireworks began, any untended horses would likely run halfway to Kansas, and runaway buggies would imperil anyone in the streets.

And so the Haskells walked. Kate was obviously glad, for it afforded her a chance to collect her thoughts. The children delighted in showing off their costumes for any and all. Allison, in particular, curled her squirrel's tail and chattered away. Rich and Jeff bounced around a bit as well, but their mouths remained largely silent. Not so the older ones. Michael especially waved his wooden hunting knife, and Benny waved an equally harmless rifle. Little Clay, promoted to a bear at the last moment, bellowed and clawed the air.

"I feel like I've raised a carnival," Ben said, laughing as the bear took a swipe at its father.

"Well, it will soon be over," Kate reminded him. "And they are having a fine time."

Ben nodded. He supposed that made everything worthwhile.

By the time they passed the mine office, Clint Avery was there with his three hirelings from Pueblo. Kate gripped Ben's arm, and the children grew quiet. Except for Benny, they moved along behind their father, letting Ben shield them from the rough-looking men. Kate seemed especially dismayed at the sight of a revolver resting on Avery's hip.

"I should've told you," Ben whispered. "We hired him to guard the payroll."

"From the look of those men, you should hire guards to watch the guards."

Ben grinned and led her along. In truth, the men did look rather more like a gang of road agents than might be considered prudent, but Clint Avery usually knew what he was about. Ben bet they could shoot straight and think fast. That, after all, mattered more than looks or charm.

When Ben escorted his family onto the square, a village fair was already in progress. Children tossed rings toward poles, while their elders heaved horseshoes. Booths selling everything from fresh-baked pies and apple fritters to embroidery and quilts occupied the western corner of the square. Just opposite, carpenters had constructed a stage. Kate and the children headed in that direction.

If there was a man, woman, or child alive within fifty miles of Saylesville who wasn't crowded onto that square, Ben didn't know who it might be. Townspeople, friends, relatives, even placer miners from out of the Rockies had gathered to enjoy the festivities. Jim and Nola Sayles had arrived to visit their son and daughter and to watch the grandchildren perform. Ben devoted a few minutes to their company before welcoming the governor's entourage.

"Quite a party you folks are putting together," the governor proclaimed.

"Well, it's a wonder what a bunch of ladies can do when they put their heads together," Ben explained. "It does provide a good excuse for everybody to set aside work and devote a day to family, though, and I guess that's always a good idea."

"We're beginning the historical review now!" Mrs. Parkinson, the school's upper-grade teacher, boomed out then, and Ben hurried toward the stage. Kate would never forgive him if he wasn't close to the front. He'd just settled in at the right-hand corner when Bobby Lee Hamilton stepped out, painted face, feather headdress and all. Kate then began reading her script, and to the delight of everyone, the children played their parts in high fashion.

Indians, hunters and trappers, miners and missionaries — all stepped out in turn as Kate read the story of Saylesville. It might not have been as accurate as Mrs. Parkinson had wished, and the costumes occasionally had mishaps, but the pageant was clearly a great success.

At the play's conclusion, a mob surrounded Kate, praising and commending her efforts. Ben tried to gather the little ones, while their mother basked in the sunshine of the whole town's accolades. The children had remained in place on the stage when their parts concluded, and they'd grown restless. As a result, or perhaps because they had escaped the watchful eyes of the elders, they now embarked on a series of pranks. Bobby Lee took a pocket knife and scalped a bit of Susan Shaw's ponytail. As revenge, Susan then untied the vital string securing Bobby's breechclout and provided the pageant's most embarrassing moment. While the audience either laughed heartily or fought frantically to restore control, children raced about engaging in mock warfare or grabbing one another's tails or wings.

Ben wasn't sure what might have happened had not Mrs. Parkinson taken charge. The crusty-faced old woman bellowed out so that the mountaintops heard her, and the boys and girls halted. Their parents then managed to draw them aside.

Kate and her mother collected Allison, Jefferson, Richmond, and little Clay, leaving Ben to clamp one hand each on Benny and Michael.

"We're going home long enough to rid ourselves of the animal world," Kate explained with a grin. "You suppose you can bring those vagabonds along later?"

"Sure," Ben agreed. "I thought we might go down to the pond and watch the sailboats race."

The boys jumped at the notion, and Kate waved them along.

Briar Pond, as it was called, provided a rare island of tranquility that noisy morning. Many of the town's older boys had devoted a great deal of time and skill to crafting wooden models of fine sailing craft. They gathered at the edge of the pond to race their boats.

Younger children and interested spectators gathered at the far end and watched the race. A light breeze soon carried the boats on their way. Aside from one sloop, which sank in the first minute, the boats made good headway toward the far edge of Briar Pond

Benny and Michael cheered as, out of the fleet, a sleek clipper ship broke free. Wind filled the boat's delicate sails, and the ship cut through the water. It won by a good five feet, and everyone cheered. Afterward a sizable portion of the younger crowd shed trousers and shirts, then splashed their way into the shallows.

"Can we go in, Pa?" Benny pleaded.

"Yeah, Pa?" Michael piped in.

Ben nodded, then said, "Stay within a few feet of shore, though, and fold your costumes so they don't get torn. It's only for a short time, too."

The boys wasted no time in shedding the hot buckskins and cumbersome boots. As they splashed about the pond with their friends, Ben found himself remembering similar times back home with his own brothers, swimming the creek, embarking on this foolish escapade or that. Those pleasant times were often forgotten, buried by the pain and sorrow that had followed. It was what he hated most about his youth.

Benny and Michael splashed around in the pond for half an hour. Ben might have let them stay longer if he hadn't observed men setting out food on the tables back at the square.

"Come on, boys," Ben commanded. "Time to head home and get ready for the picnic. Come along. You wouldn't want to miss out on all those ribs!"

Benny sprang to his feet and splashed his way to the bank. Michael followed a bit more reluctantly. They then pulled on their boots, collected their costumes, and headed homeward in their soggy drawers, every bit as comical a sight as Bobby Lee Hamilton trying with little success to keep that strip of doeskin from exposing more of his flesh than was desired.

"Pa, this is one bad thing about not living at the ranch," Benny grumbled. "Out there we used to swim the whole afternoon if we wanted, and we didn't even have to wear drawers."

"You would now that you've got a sister with eyes," Ben told the boy. "Nobody ever said progress didn't have a price."

"You figure we could go up into the mountains and make camp sometime, like you and Uncle Clay used to do when you were riding with the captain?" Benny asked.

"Yeah, Pa," Michael said, resting a wet hand on his father's hip. "We could even shoot a bear, maybe."

"I don't think a bear would take kindly to that idea," Ben told them. "Might eat you, instead."

"You wouldn't let that happen," Michael said confidently. "Think we could go up there?"

"Maybe come spring," Ben told them. "Winter's coming soon, and that's no time to be camped in the mountains."

"I guess," Benny grumbled.

They soon reached the house, and Ben had them upstairs, dried, and dressed shortly. Then they returned through town to the square.

Kate had saved places at a table for Ben and the boys. Her parents sat among the children. Sam Sayles and his young wife, Zenia, held hands at the far end opposite Ben and Kate. It was a rare family gathering, and the children relished the opportunity to boast about their morning performances.

The food, as expected, was wonderful. Virginia Hamilton had been baking cakes and pies all week, and

Sheriff Boyd had supervised the barbecue. In addition, pots of baked beans, stewed potatoes and greens, carrots, corn, squash, and other assorted vegetables were available. Ben doubted the mounds of food could be eaten by an army, but an hour after the first table was set out, surprisingly little remained.

The afternoon entertainment consisted of a carnival of booths and various entertainments, all topped off by a fireworks display. Ben left the four youngest children to their grandparents, aunt, and uncle. Ben and the oldest boys walked back to the stage and listened to Kate perform in the Heritage Choir. He might have been suspected of bias, but he clearly believed Kate's lively soprano was the best voice in the company.

After the choir completed its performance, Ben located Clay, and the two men took their three oldest boys on a tour of the carnival booths. Clay won a fine pocket knife for shooting six of seven targets with a rifle, and Ben proved the champion archer, sending his arrow into the bull's-eye twice in four shots.

"Must have some Indian in him," the booth's manager declared, handing Ben a fine painted elk-hide shirt.

"That's what Bobby Lee needed this morning," Benny said, laughing.

"Yeah," Michael agreed. "It would've covered what needed covering."

Bobby Lee was a bit sunburned to begin with, and he now turned scarlet as a mountain sunset.

"Don't let 'em rile you," Ben said, squeezing the nine-year-old's shoulder. "I still think your costume was the best."

"Too bad he wasn't wearing it," Benny quipped.

It was well that Clay had earlier disarmed his Ute son, else there might have been a second scalping.

They continued to enjoy the other carnival booths even

though they met with less success at them. Michael hooked a small compass in the pot-luck pond; otherwise, the booths got the better of the Haskells and Hamiltons. Ben had deemed it time to take a rest, and the five of them spread out on the grassy square and relaxed.

"Look there," Clay called as the first rocket burst overhead. Another and another followed, and the boys cheered loudly.

"You mind looking out for Bobby Lee a bit?" asked Clay, who was turned back toward the street. "I see the wagons pulling in. Think I'll go see how the captain's doing."

"He'll do fine," Ben told his old friend. "Enjoy the fireworks."

"Captain told me this morning he was heading out for a while once he saw the payroll delivered to the bank," Clay explained. "I want to say my good-byes and make sure he knows there's work waiting here for him."

"Wait and we'll go along."

"Stay with the boys," Clay urged. "They don't want to miss the rockets."

The three youngsters stared at Ben with pleading faces, and he surrendered.

"Anyway," Clay added, "I won't be more'n a few minutes. You behave for your Uncle Ben, hear, Bobby Lee?"

The nine-year-old nodded respectfully, and his father started toward the mine office.

"That was a big one!" Michael announced as a cackle of fireworks exploded. Rockets flew in every direction at once, it seemed, and children tossed firecrackers into the street and at birds and squirrels. One mischievous scoundrel even set off a string of firecrackers under old Rufus Ornstead's boot, sending the old man howling and hopping about.

"Can we get some firecrackers, Pa?" Benny begged.

"Seems to me you boys have been up to enough nonsense today," Ben scolded them. "Firecrackers aren't toys, you know. They've got gunpowder in 'em, and I've seen a man lose an eye when one went off in front of his face."

"We'll be careful," Michael pleaded.

"No!" Ben replied. "Let's go see if we can locate your ma and buy ourselves some apple fritters. How's that sound?"

The one tonic for restless boys was a taste of sugar, and the offer of fritters freed Ben from the fireworks notion. Rockets continued to burst overhead, and that, for the time being, would suffice.

Chapter 16

Clay had been gone half an hour when a loud series of pops drew Ben's attention to Main Street.

"Sounds like somebody's setting off firecrackers back there, Pa," Benny said.

"So it seems," Ben said. He knew better. Those were gunshots.

"We could set some off back there, too," Michael said. "There aren't many horses around today, Pa."

"No," Ben said gruffly. "Benny, I want you to take your brother and Bobby Lee back to the carnival booths. Find your ma or grandpa. Stay with them till I come back. Understand?"

"No," Benny said, shaking his head. "What's wrong? Can't we go with you?"

"Do as I say, son," Ben said, dropping to one knee and gripping the boy's shoulders. "There'll be plenty of time to explain later on."

Benny seemed reluctant to go, and the other boys

were clearly confused. Something in Ben's eyes, something unseen in twelve long years, convinced them to go, though. And Ben turned slowly and started up Main Street toward the mine office.

It had been a long time since he'd scouted the countryside in search of trouble. Moving up Main Street was even a greater challenge, too. There were no convenient boulders or oaks behind which he could hide. Worse, he had no idea who might pose a danger. The street was alive with men and women hurrying along. Children played tag around wagons and near storefronts.

The gunfire had stopped as suddenly as it had begun, and Ben fervently hoped he would soon spot Clay and the captain hurrying to the square to report a foiled attempt on the payroll.

Ben's first stop was the bank.

"You hear anything like gunshots?" Ben called to Hank Paulson, the guard.

"Just firecrackers, Mr. Haskell," Paulson replied. "Kids been shootin' 'em off all mornin'."

"Seen the sheriff? Clay Hamilton?"

"Mr. Hamilton was by a bit ago. He was askin' about Sheriff Boyd, too."

Ben nodded, then hurried along toward the mercantile.

The store, being his first business, remained near Ben's heart. So it was that he continued to carry a set of keys to the place long after he'd turned over the day-to-day operations to Alice Meeker. He entered through the back door, then climbed the stairs so that he could look out onto the street without revealing himself.

The two freight wagons stood quietly outside the mine office. Not so much as a pebble stirred in the street. He saw no hint of either Gentry Boyd or Clay, nor of Avery and his guards.

They've either made a quick strike and gone, or they're still inside, Ben told himself.

He made his way back downstairs, then unlocked the

gun cabinet and took out a shiny new Colt revolver and a Winchester rifle. He loaded all six cylinders of the pistol, then stuffed his pockets with leftover shells. Then he rammed fifteen bullets into the Winchester's magazine and grabbed a box of rifle reloads.

Ben took a deep breath and unlocked the door. He left it to swing open just a crack. Then, as he prepared to step out into the deserted street, he heard the back door bang shut.

Instantly Ben turned. His thumb had already cocked the hammer on the pistol when he detected Benny's horrified face framed by the door.

"Lord, help me!" Ben cried, turning the barrel away from the boy and easing the hammer back to its harmless position. "Son, I told you to stay at the square."

"I know," Benny said, hurrying to his father and holding on with two trembling hands. "But then I thought how Uncle Clay hadn't come back, and —"

"Listen to me," Ben said, shaking the boy hard. "I don't know that there's trouble, but it seems likely. No matter what else, you stay here! Understand!"

"Yes, Pa," Benny mumbled. "But what if —"

"Stay here no matter what!" Ben barked. "I can't do any good if I have you to worry about, son. I've got to know you're safe."

Benny's eyes widened, and he hung on Ben's shoulder. Ben pried his son's fingers loose and slipped through the door.

Out on the street, Ben saw nothing. He hugged the shadows, scanning both directions at once. The mine office was only thirty more feet away. No one was about. Then Clint Avery stepped out from the office door, and Ben relaxed.

"Lord, Captain, I'm glad to see you," Ben said, sighing. "You hear some shooting?"

"No, boy," Avery answered. "You?"

"I sure thought so. Seen Clay?"

"He came by to say his farewells. I'm headed back to Pueblo for a bit. Got a job lined up guarding freight."

"I thought you had a job here," Ben said. "You sure everything's all right?"

"Couldn't be better."

"And you saw Clay?"

"Walked off with the sheriff a few minutes ago. You expect trouble, Ben? Seems like you're traveling with a heavy load."

"Guess I am," Ben said, resting the rifle against the side of an empty carriage and setting the box of shells beside it. "Got any coffee made inside? I could sure use a cup."

"Sure, Ben. Come on."

Ben took one step into the street, then stopped. It was all wrong. Avery seemed suddenly nervous. Next Ben spotted a pair of shadows. One hinted there was a man behind the front wagon. Another shadow marked a rifleman just behind the corner of the office. There appeared to be a third just in back of Avery in the doorway.

"What's wrong, Ben?" the captain called.

"Oh, I was just thinking about that coffee. You never cared much for coffee past noon. I've got a bottle of good Irish whiskey at the store. Why don't you come along and share a farewell glass with me? For old time's sake."

"Well, I suppose that would be all right," Avery agreed, stepping on into the street. Ben made a half turn, then spun around and fired his pistol twice into the doorway. The first shot went wide. The second slammed into the lurking gunman's right cheek and killed him instantly.

"Get clear, Captain!" Ben shouted.

" 'Fraid I can't, Ben," Avery answered, pulling a pistol and firing. Ben felt an explosion of hot lead tear through his lower left leg, and he collapsed in the center of the street. Avery returned to the doorway, and the other two opened up. In spite of the pain and confusion, Ben dragged himself across the street and took shelter behind a water trough.

"Leave it be, Ben!" Avery pleaded. "What's the money mean to you? You got all you could spend in ten lifetimes. Leave us to go our way, and you'll live to see tomorrow."

"Where's Clay?" Ben asked angrily as he took aim at the outlaw firing from in back of the wagon.

"Wasn't as lucky as you," Avery answered. "Stumbled up just about the time Berringer shot your sheriff. Had no choice."

Ben felt something inside himself die. The two men he thought he could count on most in the world were gone. Clay was shot, likely dead, and Clint Avery had gone outlaw.

"Toss your gun out, and we'll be on our way!" Avery yelled.

Ben reloaded the pistol's empty chambers and screamed out a defiant "No!"

"Looks like we'll have to do it the hard way," Avery grumbled. He then vanished inside the office, and Ben took the opportunity to tear off the sleeve of his shirt and fashion a bandage for his leg.

"Old man, you've gone sentimental," Ben mumbled, tightening the binding. The bone seemed intact. Avery hit what he aimed at, didn't he? It would have been as easy to kill. The captain hadn't lost all sense.

Ben knew he had an edge of sorts, too. Outnumbered though he was, he knew that town. He'd built the office, and there was just the one way in or out. Moreover, someone was bound to hear the shots. Why hadn't he thought to send Benny for help?

Suddenly the street exploded with rifle fire. Splinters from the trough showered down on him, and he fired blindly in reply, cursing the overconfidence that had made him leave the rifle across the street.

"Just like old times, eh?" Avery called. "You never did care much for shooting, did you, Ben? That was Clay's strong suit. And mine."

The firing heated up again, and the gunman at the wagon made a break for the far side of the street. Ben watched him go, then fired three times. The first shattered the outlaw's left elbow. The second lodged in the spine, sending him writhing to the street.

"Ollie?" the one behind the office called. "Ollie?"

Ollie was past caring now, though. The odds had narrowed.

"You hold your ground well enough, Ben," Avery called. "But you can't be long on bullets. Bet you wish you had that box of shells across the street."

"Make a break for it, friend!" the gunman at the corner urged. "That was my brother you killed!"

"Come see how many bullets I've got left!" Ben answered, making a quick check. He was down to the four shots left in his pistol and three spare bullets in his pocket. It took only two. But as the firing resumed, he felt obliged to answer. Seven dwindled to five and then to four. Ben loaded the last three in the empty chambers. His heart was heavy.

If only my leg could carry me back across the street, Ben thought. When he gazed at the buggy, though, he saw something that sent a sliver of fear down his spine. Benny was there. The boy cautiously took the Winchester from its resting place, then grabbed the box of shells.

No, Ben prayed. As if in answer to the plea, Avery raced from the office and jumped behind three barrels across the street. The hothead at the corner crept over behind the wagon and climbed into the bed. They would soon have a good view of the trough, so Ben crawled along the side of the building and crept into the mine office.

"Lord, you're a welcome sight," Clay called from the corner. Ben warmed at the sound of his friend's voice, but when he spotted Clay's bloodstained trouser leg and the pool of blood alongside, the hope began to fade.

"Clay, I —"

"Watch the door!" Clay urged. "Sorry I'm no help to you. I walked right in on it, no gun, feeling naked as little Bobby Lee up on that stage."

Ben watched the street carefully. It seemed impossible. Avery and his companion were most concerned with getting the back wagon into motion. Ben worried that Benny might grow reckless, and he knew Clay was bleeding his life away a few feet from him.

"Ben, we'll be heading along now!" Avery called.

The two raiders opened up on the office, shattering the front window and knocking pictures from the walls. Glass flew everywhere, and splinters gashed Ben's shoulders and forehead.

"I'm going after him!" the one in the wagon declared.

Ben used two of those last bullets to discourage the attempt. He then made his way to Clay, tightened a makeshift binding Avery had likely applied, then slid back to the door. Avery made a rush toward the wagon, and little Benny took the opportunity to dart toward the mine office.

"No!" Ben screamed as Avery turned and fired. Benny was flying across the street one minute, both hands gripped around the cold steel rifle barrel. Then Avery's bullet slammed into the boy's chest, and Benny fell like a rag doll in a puppet show.

"Pa?" the boy muttered as he tossed the rifle toward the door. Ben watched the pain-filled face as blood trickled out the corner of his mouth. The rifle was three feet away. Ben sprang out the door, dove for the gun, and rolled over. As the two outlaws rose in the wagon, Ben opened up a torrent of fire from the street as he crawled toward his son. The horses hitched to the front wagon reared up, and Ben somehow lifted Benny in his arms and carried the boy into the office seconds before the animals raced down the street over the very spot where the boy had lain.

Dust obscured the scene, and Ben dropped to his knees as pain surged through his leg. Ben kept his eyes on the street as he ran his fingers across Benny's bloody chest. When the dust cleared, Ben saw that the second wagon was gone, too. Avery had escaped.

"Is it bad?" Clay asked, dragging himself over.

"I don't know," Ben said, shredding the boy's shirt and fixing a bandage around the small, suddenly frail chest.

"It was the captain," Clay muttered in disgust. "The captain!"

"I know!" Ben mumbled bitterly as he fought to stop the lifeblood from flowing out of his boy's chest. "I know it! I'll get him, Clay. You know I will."

"Tend your boy first," Clay said.

Only now did Ben notice how dim Clay's eyes had grown.

"Clay?"

Clay Hamilton didn't answer. He smiled faintly, then fell over on one shoulder. Ben felt tears wander down his cheeks. Pain and hate and murderous rage filled his chest.

"I promise you, Clay!" Ben vowed. "I'll see he pays!"

Chapter 17

A stunned silence settled over Saylesville. What should have been the brightest day in the town's short history was transformed into the darkest of nightmares. Sheriff Gentry Boyd was dead. Clay Hamilton wasn't expected to last the night, and little Benny Haskell lay unconscious in Dr. Carl Sanders's surgery. Ben himself passed a long night at the hotel, his leg painted in iodine and wrapped in a mile of white bandages.

"How's Benny?" Ben asked when he limped into the doctor's small office just after dawn the next morning.

"I did what I could," the doctor explained. "I carved a bullet out of that boy's chest, close enough to the heart to have killed nine out of ten. Truth is, I don't know what's kept him breathing."

"He's small, but he's got solid timbers, Doc," Ben declared. "He won't give up without a fight."

"I've seen it before," the doctor said, nodding his

head. "If they get through the first few hours, the young ones often as not come back strong."

"But not always."

"No, but then they're not all Haskells. I know a dozen men who'd run the other way at the first shot. They say you carried that boy into the mine office after that Avery fellow put a bullet through your leg."

"I wasn't thinking much about me just then."

"Well, you give Benny time. Rest that leg, too. Bullet may have passed along through, but that doesn't mean the flesh didn't feel it some."

"You don't have to tell me that, Doc," Ben said, running his fingers along the bandaged leg. "It's been letting me know for hours now."

"Well, you haven't been listening or you'd lie down and let it heal some."

"I will," Ben promised. "First, I want to see Benny. And Clay."

"Later," the doctor argued. "Let 'em rest. Mary Talbot brings me breakfast. If you'd like, I'll get her to bring you some, too."

Ben agreed.

A little later the doctor allowed Ben to peek into the surgery room. Benny lay wrapped like a coccoon, his small face ashen. His chest scarcely moved. It was as if death hovered nearby, eager to snatch the small boy away.

"Clay's awake," the doctor said, pulling Ben away from the room and leading the way to a small back room nearby. Clay rested on a metal bed. His face was pale and drawn, and his eyes gazed down at where the toes of his left foot should have been outlined by the sheet.

"Thought you might be by," Clay mumbled in a shaky voice. "Funny after all those months fighting

Yanks and then six years roaming the range, fighting Comanches and shooting buffs, I should lose a leg to a friend."

"He's not a friend anymore," Ben barked. "He's a snake and a murderer."

"How's Benny?"

"Poor. Still alive, though."

"Got both legs at least," Clay said, staring up at the ceiling. "Ben, you got to let it be."

"Let what be?"

"The captain. There are others who'll take to the trail. You're shot up yourself, and Benny's going to . . ."

"Benny won't even know I'm here," Ben argued. "It's got to be done, Clay. Avery wrote his own law, remember? Well, he's hurt me and mine, and I'll see he pays."

"No gimp-legged mine operator's going to catch Captain Avery," Clay grumbled. "He's got more ways of ambushing trackers than you'll ever know. Ben, all you'll do is get yourself killed."

"No, I'll do what has to be done," Ben said, sitting beside Clay's bed a moment. "Clay, I never had a friend I could depend on outside of you. Shoot! I hardly knew my brothers, it seems. You don't mean to say you can forgive him?"

"I've still got my life," Clay whispered. "And who knows? With a leg gone, maybe folks'll believe I did fight in the war."

"If Avery rides away from this, sooner or later you'll start thinking about it, and so will I. There'll be a sore festering, spoiling all the good things hereabouts. We'll wonder if the kids are safe, and we'll be looking over our shoulders expecting the captain to come back."

"He'll expect you to follow, Ben!"

"Expect? He'll know. Won't be me looking over a shoulder, Clay. And when I finish, it will be over."

"Lord, Ben, you'll need help."

"A Winchester rifle and a couple of good horses are all I need."

Clay grew weary then, and Ben left. Outside, Virginia and the two boys huddled with Dr. Sanders.

"He looks pretty good for a man who's bled half to death," Ben announced. "I wouldn't worry, Ginny. Bobby Lee, Clint, your pa's going to be all right."

The boys looked hopeful, and Virginia leaned against Ben's shoulder. The doctor clearly was less optimistic.

"How's little Benny?" she whispered.

"Time will tell, right, Doc?" Ben asked.

Yes, Ben thought, limping to the door and crossing the street. He stopped at the mercantile to collect two rifles and several boxes of shells. He also pulled a pair of woolen blankets, rope, and tinned food for the trail.

"Hey, Joshua," Ben called.

A tow-haired lad of fourteen trotted over, and Ben handed over the supplies.

"Bundle all this and take it to the livery this afternoon," Ben instructed. "Tell Ed Wade to find the best two surefooted horses he can find. Get him to have one saddled and the other ready by sunrise tomorrow. Understand?"

"Yes, sir," the boy agreed. "Mr. Haskell, you goin' after 'em, are you? I'd be proud to ride along. There are others, too."

"This isn't a deer hunt, Josh," Ben said, staring out at the street. Men were already replacing the broken front window at the mine office. Others collected fragments of broken glass or washed blood off the porch planks.

"You think maybe Benny'd like a mouth organ?" Josh asked. "I was showin' him how to play mine a while back, and he blew it a bit. I don't have brothers, you know."

Ben nodded, then gripped the youngster's shoulder.

Boys like Josh, youngsters with no home or family, were all too frequent in Colorado, and the unexpected kindness moved Ben close to tears.

"I think he'd be proud to have one from you, son," Ben told the boy. "You'll remember to take care of the horses?"

"Count on me, Mr. Haskell."

Ben grinned at Josh, then started toward the door. Jim Sayles was waiting with a buggy.

"Didn't buy much," the freighter declared.

"Just looking in on the business," Ben explained.

"I saw. Ben, Sam and I have men riding guard for us all the time. They can track an old coot like Avery and bring him to bay in no time. Your place is with Kate and the kids."

"You don't know Avery. I do," Ben declared. "You can't convince me that if someone had shot Sam back in '71 you wouldn't have grabbed a rifle and gone after the man."

"It's been a long time since you were hunting buffalo, son."

"I know," Ben admitted. "I thought I'd put it all behind me. But the old knack came back easily enough."

Sayles frowned, then gave the horses a nudge. The buggy rolled on out of town, and Ben concentrated on what he would tell Kate.

"No!" she shouted when he told her. "Ben, I never liked that man. There's something sinister about his eyes. He'll kill you."

"He'll try."

"Oh? And just what do you think will keep him from getting the job done? Ben, I've watched some of the women in town who've lost husbands to Indians or mining accidents or fevers. I can't raise six children alone."

"Could be there'll only be five," he grumbled. "And

if Avery kills Michael or Allison? A father's got a duty to his kids."

"He has to stay alive."

"I intend to."

"Ben, I know you think you can do this, but you're wrong. You're angry, and that will lead to mistakes. Your leg needs another week at least before you dare trust it on the trail."

"A week?" Ben gasped. "He's got a day's lead already, Kate. Give Avery a week, and he'll be in Canada. I won't let him do this — shoot my boy, maybe kill Clay Hamilton, rob our payroll, and turn my life upside down. No!"

"Listen to me, Ben Haskell," Kate said sternly. "No matter what happens to Avery, Benny will still be shot. Clay's going to be short a leg. As for the money, we can get along without it."

"It's not the money," Ben told her. He limped back and forth across the room, then slammed his hand against the wall. "Don't you see, Kate? I have to do something. I can't sit on Benny's bed and watch him lie there, half dead, knowing it's my fault. I'm the one trusted Avery. Was me left the rifle behind. Benny was hit helping me."

"Then hire some men. Post a bounty."

"He isn't going anywhere bounty killers will find him. He's got a thousand ways of wriggling away from pursuers, Kate, but I know him. I'll be the one to find him. And when I do, I'll make sure he's never able to hurt anyone, not ever again."

"Please, Ben," she said, clasping his hands. "Don't you understand? I need you here with me, to hold while I wait for Benny to get better. The little ones need you to comfort them, to assure them everything's all right."

"It's not," he grumbled. "But it will be."

Kate stared at him with sad eyes. She'd never grant

him her blessing, but he knew she was reconciled to his leaving. So after spending some time with the children, he began collecting clothes for the journey.

Michael and little Clay helped him hone his skinning knife and fill a provisions bag. They brushed his boots and folded the flannel shirts required for winter tracking.

"Be careful, Pa," Michael said as Ben stuffed each item in a rucksack. "It gets cold up there, and there are wolves, I've heard."

"I guess we didn't have our trip up there together yet, huh?" Ben asked.

Michael curled up on his father's knee, and Ben picked up the boy like so much fluff. Clay wrapped his small hands around Ben's good right leg.

"I'll be back," Ben promised. "We'll have that trip in the spring, when the trout are running."

"Benny'll be better by then," Michael said, rubbing a tear from his eye.

"You help your ma and see the little ones say their prayers."

"We will," Clay promised.

After a quiet supper, Ben and Kate rode back into town to check on Benny. The boy remained unconscious; nevertheless, Ben spent a few minutes alone at his side.

"I'm going to get him, son," Ben whispered, touching the boy's cool toes. They were so very small. There had seemed to be more of Benny when he was racing around the hillside, terrorizing neighbors and younger brothers and sister. All Ben saw now was a small frail child, the seed that would blossom into a good man if given the chance.

"I love you, Benny," Ben added, kissing the boy's damp forehead. "Lord, You watch him, give him strength. He's too good, too fine, to leave just yet. We need him a while longer."

Ben tucked the sheets in and nestled them under the boy's chin before leaving. He then turned the boy over to Kate.

"I told you to give that leg some rest," Dr. Sanders complained when Ben closed the door to the surgery room and hobbled over to a chair beside the office door.

"I will, Doc — after I'm through."

"Ben, you go out there lame like this, anything's liable to happen. The leg could give way. Infection could set in, and you'd go out of your head with fever."

"Take care of Benny, Doc," Ben said, frowning. "He's such a little boy, but he's got heart."

"That's in his favor," the doctor noted. "More than's in yours."

"Justice favors me," Ben said. "It'll be enough."

"I pray so," Kate said, opening the door and stepping through it. "Doc, I want to stay with Benny tonight."

"Certainly, Kate," Dr. Sanders agreed. "I suppose Ben won't leave you for a bit yet."

"Dawn," Ben declared.

"And just who's going to mind the little ones?" the doctor asked.

"Kate's folks are here. I'm certain they'll stay till I finish."

"You're so sure of yourself," Kate growled. "You don't know what's going to happen!"

"Yes, he does!" Clay called from the back room. "You do what you have to, Ben. Finish it!"

Ben rose to his feet and limped to the door. Virginia opened it, and he looked inside at his old friend. Clay's face was without color. He looked dead. He only barely managed to lift his fingers from the bed to acknowledge Ben's presence.

"Is he . . ." Ben started to say.

"He's alive," Virginia said, tears streaking down her cheeks. "You get him, Ben. Kill him slow so he feels what my Clay's feeling. Kill him and leave him to the crows."

He gripped her arm, and she fell against his shoulder, weeping. Dr. Sanders came in and helped her to a chair. Ben swallowed hard, then left.

"I'll be here," Kate said, her voice more than a little shaky. "We've seen each other through eight births. I suppose it's fitting we should share this moment of trial."

"I'll be back, Kate, quick as I can."

"You just come back," she said, dabbing her cheeks with a handkerchief.

"I will," he promised.

Chapter 18

Ben spent a restless night back at the house. He wasn't alone. Terrible nightmares plagued Clay and Allison. Michael crept into Ben's room around midnight and passed the rest of the night sleeping at the foot of his father's bed.

An hour before the sun broke on the eastern horizon, Ben was up and about. He shook Michael awake, then led the groggy child down the hall.

"You'll help your grandma look after the little ones, won't you?" Ben asked. "With Benny laid up, you'll be the oldest. See your ma gets some rest, too."

"You're going away now, aren't you?" the boy asked.

"Yes, son. I'll be home soon, though. Then we'll have some fine times."

The youngster nodded, and Ben pulled him close. Ben then walked from room to room, kissing each of the children good-bye.

"Be careful, Pa," Allison urged.

"I will, honey," he assured her.

Jim Sayles drove Ben into town at daybreak. The horses were waiting at the livery, and Ben tied his provisions bag behind the saddle and mounted up. Leading the spare animal, he set off toward the river.

The heavy wagon had cut a clear trail along the Arkansas. Avery and his companion had run their horses hard, and the ruts scarred the riverbank. Ben followed cautiously. Avery was fond of doubling back on his pursuers, and a clear trail smelled of a trap. Ben threaded his way through the pines and aspens on the far hillside and kept a watchful eye.

Midday was approaching when Ben located the wagon some ten miles from town. Two of the four horses grazed nearby. One had a lame foreleg.

Well, he won't get far on a pair of draft horses, Ben thought. But the trail might prove challenging. It was hard to hide a wagon, but horses could practically disappear in the rocky ground above the river. He expected Avery might turn immediately toward the high country or else conceal his trail in the river. The captain did neither.

Ben followed the two thieves' trail through a grassy meadow. Nestled into the foothills ahead was a small trading post. Ben spotted the draft animals securely penned in a corral back of the barn.

Well, I guess you weren't expecting me after all, Captain, Ben thought as he eased his way into the nearby pines. He took time to tie off his spare horse before riding on toward the trading post. He pulled out the Winchester and rested it on his knee.

Ben scannned the scene for signs of Avery or the other outlaw. He found none. In fact, the trading post appeared deserted. Not so much as a sparrow stirred. Ben climbed off his horse when he was still a hundred yards distant. He then continued onward, using the horse as a shield against any possible gunfire from the long cabin up ahead and keeping his rifle ready.

Ben could feel his heart pounding as he closed those hundred yards. This was the kind of snare a wily old fox like Avery would set. The windows remained closed, though, and Ben reached the door without incident. He released the horse's reins and banged on the door.

"You so feeble you cain't open a door, friend?" a voice called from inside. "Come along in."

Ben nudged the door ajar, then ducked aside. When no one fired, Ben kicked the door and charged inside.

"Whoa, friend!" called a silver-haired old-timer clothed in buckskins. "You've no call to wave that rifle around!"

"Where's Avery?" Ben asked, his face growing scarlet as he searched the room for signs of crouching gunmen.

"Who?" the old man asked.

"Clint Avery! The man who brought those horses!" Ben shouted, pointing through a window toward the draft animals prancing about the corral.

"Gone since mornin'," the trader explained. "Swapped those two and five hundred dollars for a pair of mountain mules. Those nags he brought in wouldn't take a man far in this country."

"So you helped him out," Ben grumbled.

"I make my livin' doin' that. Any law against it?"

Ben glared angrily, then asked, "They say anything?"

"You the law?" the trader asked, fidgeting with an empty beer mug. "Five hundred's a fair price for two mules."

"You see a badge?" Ben asked. "I don't care about the money, mister. I want those two men! They like to kill my best friend, and they shot my boy! He's only eleven years old, for God's sake. If you know anything, tell me."

"I mind my own business," the trader said. "I'll pour you a beer, and my wife can fix you something to eat. Elsewise, you're on your own."

"I have a long memory," Ben growled, raising the rifle barrel until it pointed directly at the old man. "The way I feel right now, I don't think you'd find it any too healthy to be at cross purposes with me."

"Put your gun down, friend. You'll not get answers from a dead man."

Ben's fingers shook with anger, and he gripped the rifle harder. Then a side door opened, and a wrinkled old woman charged toward the bar.

"Tell him, Henry!" she hollered. "You heard what he said! They shot a sheriff, too. I heard old Pixton boast about it to the other one."

Ben gripped the rifle tightly. His eyes caught fire. The trader stepped back until he touched the wall and could retreat no farther.

"Mister, I never knew that Frank Pixton to do a real day's work in his whole life," the woman muttered. "It'd be a shame for anybody else to get killed 'cause of him. I don't know th'other one, but if he's travelin' with Pixton, he's like as not a bad one."

"Where'd they go?" Ben asked, easing the rifle down to the floor. "Which way?"

"Into the mountains," the woman said. Her husband's face turned white, but she wasn't to be silenced. "I know they paid you to hush up, Henry, but I won't shield a child-shooter. You know our own Jeff was but twelve when the Cheyennes killed him!"

"Hannah!"

"I'm goin' to tell him!" the woman declared, slamming her hand down on the bar. "Mister, they took the old miners' trail, headed to Sawyer's Pass. Left early this mornin', they did, but you can catch 'em."

"Hannah, you mind your tongue!" the old-timer warned.

"You mind yours!" Ben shouted, raising the Winchester to his shoulder and aiming at the trader's forehead. "One more word, and I'll see you don't trade any mules to killers ever again."

The trader shuddered, then reached for something below the bar. In spite of his stiff leg, Ben bounded over and slammed the butt of his rifle across the old man's face. A shotgun discharged, blowing a hole in the far side of the bar.

"Please, mister, don't kill him," the woman pleaded. "He's a fool, but he won't cause you any more trouble."

Ben leaned over the bar and gazed down at the stunned trader. His face was swollen purple. Ben grabbed the shotgun and a Colt that was also hidden behind the bar. He then tossed the weapons toward the door and turned to the woman.

"You said I could catch 'em," Ben said. "How?"

"There's an old Ute trace," she told him. "Not easy riding, but a man moving fast with a fire in his insides could get to Sawyer's Pass before daybreak. Pixton won't, not riding those mules. He and the other one didn't look to be in much of a hurry, either. They'll make camp somewhere tonight. You wait for 'em at the pass. They're bound to come through."

"How do I locate the trace?"

"I'll show you," she said, taking a sheet from a nearby ledger and sketching a rough map. "Just follow the trail. You look to know your way about. You find those two, shoot quick and sure. They may not be much on riding these mountains, but they can both shoot."

"I know," Ben said, touching his leg. "So can I."

"I see," she said, frowning. "Hold on just a minute."

Ben paused just short of the door. The trader staggered to a chair near the corner of the bar, and Ben kept his rifle ready. The old woman rummaged around, searching shelves and chests. She filled a provisions sack with half a loaf of bread, some dried beef, and strips of linen bandages.

"Lord help you, young man," she said as she handed Ben the sack. "You watch your back, too. Pixton never waits for a man to turn, and he does his best work from ambush."

Ben nodded. So Avery and Pixton were two of a kind. It didn't matter. If the old woman was right, Ben would be at the pass first. He unloaded the pistol and tossed the bullets out the door, then tossed the shotgun after it. He then backed out of the building, collected his horse, and cautiously headed back to where the spare horse was tied.

After changing mounts, Ben followed the old woman's map up the mountainside. Soon he located the beginning of the Ute trace. Clearly the trail was rarely traveled. Underbrush obscured its beginning, and as Ben made his way down the narrow trace, he often found it blocked by landslides or fallen pines. The going was slow, but the path was straight. The miners' trail down below wound its way through the lowlands, along creeks and through meadows. It was easy riding in the beginning, and Ben wondered how he would gain any time. But while the Ute trace began steep and hard, it soon reached a ridge and followed it toward Sawyer's Pass.

Ben drove himself along, pausing only to change horses. He made an afternoon supper of the beef and bread the old woman had stuffed into the provisions bag. By nightfall he found himself descending the ridge toward the broad opening in the mountains that was surely Sawyer's Pass.

Ben scouted the pass with great care, but he saw no signs of recent passage. He masked his own trail carefully, then made camp in a rocky outcropping on the far slope.

He dared not build a fire, and a can of cold beans was

scant nourishment. As night settled in, the long ride from Saylesville took its toll on Ben. His leg throbbed, and he had to slice open the leg of his trousers to redress the wound. It was red and festering. His head was hot, too. He prayed the fever would pass, but he knew it was less than likely.

He spread his blankets beneath a towering spruce. The scent of pine needles mingled with a nearby spring to flavor the air with sweetness. As Ben burrowed into the deep bed of pine needles, he was reminded of home, of Kate and the children. The stillness of the night was such a contrast with the sounds of children's feet running along the floorboards, of small voices singing or shouting or bidding their father good-night.

Ben missed listening to their prayers. He longed to tuck a blanket under Benny's chin, to see the boy's bright eyes sparkle with boyish exuberance. Ben's cold fingers reached for Kate's warm shoulder.

He was alone.

As he closed his eyes, old memories visited his dreams. He walked the smoke-stained hall of the house back in Jack County, remembering his mother's terrified eyes the moment she felt the cold blade of the killing knife. He felt the pain of his broken arm, smelled the stench of blood, trembled as he saw once more the faces of those killers — the murderers of his childhood.

Buffalo Springs haunted him as well. The sounds of pistols exploding in the crowded saloon shook him awake. His wide eyes stared at the moon overhead, but they saw murder committed. He relived every minute of the gunfight down to prying his mother's locket from her killer's hand.

Ben reached over to where his shirt lay. The locket even now rested in his pocket. He'd tried to give it to Kate, but she'd declared it brought him luck.

"Keep it with you, Ben. It's kept you safe."

It was all Ben had of his mother, of Jack County and

the world of skipping rocks across near-forgotten creeks and chasing Michael around the barn. All those golden times had been devoured by the blood and death that had followed.

Ben spit a bitter taste from his mouth. The sweetness had come again, only to be smothered by death and pain and blood.

"Avery, you're out there," Ben spoke to the engulfing darkness. "I can smell you. Tomorrow, we'll be settling this."

Chapter 19

Ben was accustomed to rising early. The mountains to the east hid the sun, but the first crack of yellow on the far ridge found Ben saddling his horse and packing up his camp. A half mile away a thin wisp of white smoke on the mountainside marked another camp. Ben watched in disbelief. Had Avery lost his mind? Could he believe no one would follow?

Ben soon had his answer. Through the swirling mists appeared two men on horseback. The campfire was a trick, just another of Avery's deceptions meant to slow the pursuit, delude their thinking. Meanwhile, Avery and his partner, the man the trader's wife had called Pixton, slapped their mules up the slope toward the summit of Sawyer's Pass.

So, Ben thought, *it's come to pass, Captain. I'm here, and you're coming.* Ben wondered if Avery could even imagine the fearful boy who'd pointed that ancient dragoon Colt so many years ago could now be waiting on the mountainside, preparing to deal death. And Ben couldn't help wishing that broken-armed boy back in Jack County had fired at the gray-clad rider with the cold, arrogant eyes.

How different life might have been! But now was no time for regrets or recollections. Ben cradled his Winchester, stuffed both pockets with boxes of shells, and headed through the pines toward the pass. Even now the two killers were only a quarter-mile away.

"Be patient," Avery had always urged. "Don't give yourself away. Hold your fire until they're atop you, boy, then kill 'em sure."

I will, Ben promised.

The riders drew close. Ben could hear them.

"I still don't see how you could've talked me into tradin' for these fool mules!" Pixton complained. "Captain, you got most of us shot up in town, and then you give half a thousand dollars to that old fool Henry Carson for these sorry mules! Ernie said you were smart. He must have had a snootful of whiskey to think so."

"Wasn't me shot the sheriff!" Avery argued. "I said to go in slow, do it quietly. Then you open up on young Clay. That boy didn't even have a gun!"

"Wasn't me shot the kid," Pixton reminded Avery. "A man shoots a sheriff, he finds himself posted. You shoot a kid, half the state'll be ridin' out after us."

"Don't you worry," Avery said, laughing so that chills ran down Ben's spine. "I got the one who'd come after us."

Ben longed to cry out. The raiders were less than a stone's throw away now, though. Pixton led the way. Ben aimed his rifle at the grizzled, buckskin-clad no-account. A brisk wind carried their foul smell to Ben's nostrils. He gripped the rifle firmly, with the old confidence, and squeezed the trigger.

It seemed the mountain itself exploded. Pixton was

lifted from his horse. He sat on the ground, stunned, as Avery fought to control his mule. Ben rammed the rifle's lever down and back up, advancing a second shell into the firing chamber. He fired again, this time at Avery, but the captain turned at that instant, and the bullet slammed into the poor mule instead. The animal collapsed, and Avery scrambled away.

In spite of his bandaged leg, Ben moved through the pines as if born to them. He was a flash of brown coat, a glimpse of boot, or a dash of leather hat. His leg plagued him at every step, but pain could be set aside when murder was at hand.

"Who's up there?" Pixton cried out as he clutched his belly. Blood stained his shirt and trousers. The Winchester had torn a gaping hole in the outlaw's midsection.

"Pixton?" Avery called from a pile of boulders left by a recent rock slide. "You hit bad?"

"Bad?" Pixton asked, screaming. "I'm dead, Captain! And I don't even know who's killed me."

"Utes?" Avery yelled. "You up there! You Ute? Fool Indians likely don't even know who we are!"

"They've killed me!" Pixton cried, holding his insides together with one hand, while he tried to pull himself to his feet and fire a pistol with the other. The gun spit bullets in six diverse directions. None found a human target, but startled animals scurried here and there, and birds sang out in alarm. Ben took careful aim, then fired. Pixton's head snapped to one side, and he fell stone-cold dead.

"Pixton!" Avery shouted again. "Lord, he's killed you!"

Ben limped away into the thick underbrush. A puff of white smoke left by his rifle marked its shooter's position, and soon Avery sent a pair of bullets that way.

"Who's up there?" Avery called again. "Listen, friend, I've got ten thousand dollars for you in my saddlebags. We can come to an understanding, I'm sure. You've got to be a clever tracker to've gotten here ahead of us. Make a bargain. Reward on my poor old head's got to be paltry, and you can drag old Pixton in to show 'em you were in earnest."

Ben crept closer. He was less than fifty feet away now. He could smell Pixton's corpse.

"Tell me who you are!" Avery shouted. "If it's not enough, take Pixton's share. He won't need it. I know where you can get more. Be reasonable. We can bargain!"

"Like you did with Clay?" Ben asked as he moved cautiously through the high grass past Pixton and on up the slope overlooking Avery's boulders.

"Lord! You must be Ute!" Avery cried. "No, wait. I know you. Lord, it can't be! I shot you! No!"

"Who else?" Ben asked.

"Can't be!" Avery shouted. "Ben, boy, it's me, the captain. You know how easy it is for a man to make a mistake. You can take the money along. We only spent five hundred dollars, and you've likely got that back from old Henry. Elsewise, you'd never found us. I do believe you must have Ute in you to've slipped past us in the dark. I kept watch through the night, but I never figured anyone'd be up here ahead of us. Come on out now. Let's make amends."

"Not likely," Ben said, firing his rifle into the boulders. The shot whined through the rocks, bouncing off one and then another, tormenting the trapped Clint Avery.

"Ben, I saved your life a hundred times. You'd got yourself killed for sure in Buffalo Springs. And what about when the Comanches hit the Adams outfit?"

"You rode off and left Clay and me to fend for ourselves."

"Don't you see?" Avery yelled. "If I hadn't, you'd

never've lived to see sixteen. Was me made you strong, boy!"

"No, Captain. Was you taught me your law, remember? If somebody hurts me or mine, I'll see they get hurt in turn. Right?"

"Ben, I'm an old man. I couldn't last another winter camped up here in the mountains without a pinch of gold dust to my name. You had money."

"I'd given it to you, had you asked!"

"Given?" Avery shouted. "I never waited for you to ask, Ben. You were a son to me."

"Was I?" Ben cried, his fingers trembling as they fired again. "A son? My son lies near death, maybe is dead now, all because you rode into Saylesville with my trust and shot Clay, shot me!"

"Then I guess there's no getting around it, boy!" Avery said, his voice growing somber. Ben knew the old cold determination was taking root. "Best come down and get me, boy — if you've got it in you! I'm betting you don't."

You're betting your life, Captain, Ben thought. *And your luck's been running poor of late.*

Ben moved slowly, cautiously, toward the boulders. He set aside the rifle and pulled his Colt from its holster. This was close-in fighting, and the winner would be determined by who saw first and shot first and hit first. Ben was younger, fresher, more familiar with the lay of the land. Avery was weary, but a trapped old badger was to be feared and respected, and Clint Avery was nothing if he wasn't crafty.

Twice Ben thought he had located his prey. First it proved to be Avery's tattered leather vest. The second time Ben found the saddlebags. A hastily scratched note bade Ben to take the money and return.

Spare a tired old man, the note concluded.

Ben never gave the notion a second thought. Avery

was just the man to stalk him the entire way and shoot from ambush.

It's an old game, this, Ben thought. He recalled scouting out the buffalo, setting up the shot skillfully, readying himself to shoot. The only difference was that this time instead of a dumb, half-blind buff, Ben was chasing a killer, the cleverest anybody in Colorado ever came up against.

Ben searched the boulders. Avery wasn't there. The wily old fox had escaped the snare. Suddenly Ben felt ill at ease. Who was the hunter now? Who stalked whom?

Ben took a deep breath and backtracked. He checked the saddlebags. The money — most of it, anyway — was there. He moved back to where the Winchester rested. He checked the magazine. A favorite trick of Avery's was emptying a man's gun, leaving him defenseless in a fight. Seven shells remained. Ben loaded another eight.

The silence was deafening. Even the birds seemed nervous, anxious for the battle to resume. It didn't. Instead, Ben climbed the hillside, gazing out for some sign of the captain. A mule honked and stomped, and Ben had his answer. Avery was frantically trying to control the animal and get mounted, but the shooting had clearly shattered the mule's nerves. Ben fired his rifle at the mule's tail, and the animal bucked Avery away and escaped up the trail. Avery instantly dove for cover as a second shot splintered a pine limb just overhead.

"Here!" Avery shouted, flinging a second set of saddlebags toward Ben. "There! You've got the money now! Leave me be!"

"You wouldn't, Captain!" Ben answered. "You taught me well."

"I'll make you pay, Ben!"

"I already have. I paid for trusting you. I didn't lose a leg like Clay, but I watched my son get himself shot to pieces."

"You're good at the game, aren't you?"

"I wasn't born to it," Ben replied. "You introduced me to it. I slipped away, and you brought me back. I owe you for that, too."

"You best get clear, Ben! I'll kill you this time."

"Go ahead and try," Ben taunted the old man. "I've got the high cards, Captain. You've drawn a dead man's hand."

"Not yet!" Avery yelled, making a dash up the hill. Ben raised his rifle, took aim, and fired. The shot smashed into the captain's right hip, shattering the bone. Avery's leg simply gave way, and he struggled to drag himself along. Blood flowed freely, and Ben fired again. The shot splintered the stock of Avery's rifle, and the old man's hands were peppered with wooden fragments.

"Ahhhh!" Avery cried.

"Give it up, Captain!" Ben shouted as he fired again. The shot tore away a spruce limb just to the left of Avery's ear.

"Finish it!" Avery screamed, pulling himself up next to a tree and shaking a defiant fist. Ben lowered his rifle, and Avery's quick right hand drew a pistol and opened fire. Ben managed to duck an instant before the bullet whined over where his head had been.

"I can wait," Ben said, taking shelter in some nearby rocks. "You're not going anywhere. The way you're bleeding, you won't last too much longer. Soon as you pass out, I'll be over there."

"What is it, Ben? You want to see me hang? That it? I've grown old waiting for my luck to turn. I lost everything I ever held dear when I was younger'n you. Look at me, boy! All that's left is a few rags and my pride. You would take even that."

"There's no shame in working at a mine."

"Handout. Now you offer me worse. You'd have your town to gather 'round like at one of those carnival booths, watching Captain Clint Avery dangle from a gallows. Children could laugh and throw rocks. Afterward, some city undertaker can sell pictures of me, my neck all stretched and my eyes bulging out. No, Ben, whatever I've done, I never earned that."

Avery staggered to his feet again. This time he aimed the pistol not at Ben but at himself. It fired, and the old rebel slumped against a tree.

Ben approached with caution nurtured by years of pain. Avery wasn't dead. The pistol lay at his feet, and blood flowed from the hip and an ugly wound in the neck. The captain remained alert, though.

"Well, Ben?" the old man begged. "Finish it!"

"I won't," Ben said, glaring at the face that had never offered comfort or solace. Clint Avery had taught murder and countenanced deceit.

"Yes, you will," Avery said, a grin suddenly appearing on his dying face. "You'll do it just like I would. It's easy — as easy as watching a kid trot out into the street with a rifle and a box of shells. All you have to do is wait, take aim, then shoot. I don't see how I could miss. He was small, though, so I suppose it wasn't as easy as . . ."

Ben fired. His hand worked the lever, and he fired again. Again. Again until the bullets chased the haunting grin from Avery's face and sent his body crashing lifeless to the ground.

"You could've been a father to me, Captain," Ben muttered angrily. "To Clay and me both. But you hardened your heart to life, to the good in it anyway, and you doomed yourself to this, a lonely death in a distant place.

"A man who lives by your law, Captain, is bound to die by it. I've got a better one. Hold dear the ones that matter and pray they come to no harm. Fight if you must, but never invite death into your house. It has a way of becoming an unwelcome guest."

Chapter 20

Ben buried the killers together near the boulders, then started back to Saylesville. He rode as long as his two stout horses could manage, then made camp along the Ute trace that night, too weary and shaken to cover another mile.

Home was clearly on his mind as he dined again on cold tins of beef. He missed Kate more than ever, and he longed to sit the little ones on his knee and feel their small hearts beating rapidly. He saw little Benny in his dreams, heard Clay's hoarse laughter. All would be well if only he got back.

He approached the house slowly. For the better part of three days now he'd lived on horseback. His leg troubled him more than ever in spite of another change of dressings. Back on the Arkansas he had washed and drained the wound, but it likely wanted Doc Sanders's attention.

Ben got no closer than fifty yards when he heard a fierce shout.

"Ma, it's him!" Michael cried. "Pa's back!"

Allison and little Clay raced out of the door, followed by Jeff and Richmond. Ben nudged his horse into a gallop, and he met the four youngsters halfway.

"Pa, you're back!" Allison yelled as Ben lifted her up onto the horse and she embraced her father.

"I promised," he said, hugging her tightly and feeling her tears mingle with his own.

"Did you get him?" Michael asked from below.

"He's dead," Ben said, frowning. "I guess you could say he got himself. Killers have a way of doing that."

Ben helped Allison back down, then dismounted. The little ones each grabbed a leg or leaned against him, and Ben pulled them close to him. Kate stood in the doorway, and he dragged the little mob along in that direction.

"I believe they're glad you're home," she said, clasping his hand. "There's someone else eager to see you, though."

He kissed her and shook the children loose long enough to hold her tightly. Then Kate led him into the sitting room. There, in a makeshift bed near the front window, rested little Benny, his pale face punctuated by two dazzling blue eyes.

"Son," Ben said, stumbling to the side of the bed and letting the child's small fingers intertwine with their father's. "You all right?"

"Doc says I shouldn't walk around just yet. He says Uncle Clay's getting a pegleg," Benny added as he grasped his father's hand and smiled. "Doc says all I'll have is a skinny scar, and you won't even see that till summer, when I can shed my shirt."

"Does it hurt much?" Ben asked as Kate ushered the other children outside.

"Not too much. Not anymore."

I know, Ben thought as Kate sat beside them and

brushed the boy's hair from his eyes. *Haskells bear pain well so long as they can lean on each other some.*

"Pa, I've been waiting on you," Benny whispered. "I'm glad you're home."

"So am I," Ben told the boy.

Yes, home, Ben thought, as Kate rubbed her eyes and Benny began babbling about hunting deer in November. *Home.* Was there a more beautiful word in any language?

The door cracked open, and ten eyes gazed in on their parents and brother. Ben smiled. The glow in his chest told him the answer. He'd known it all along.

William Appel

BRINGS TO YOU HIS NEWEST AND MOST EXCITING NOVELS YET!

THE
WHITE JAGUAR

WHITE POWDER. GREEN DEATH. BLACK EVIL.

_____ CDN 7701-0571-8 $4.95
_____ US   7701-0493-2 $3.95

WaterWorld

Out of dark dreams and cold hallucinations a questionable death surfaces.

_____ CDN/US 7701-0530-0 $3.50

The Watcher Within

A prisoner of fear against an Angel of Madness.

_____ CDN/US 7701-0552-1 $3.50

Prices subject to change without notice

BOOKS BY MAIL

320 Steelcase Rd. E.   **210 5th Ave., 7th Floor**
Markham, Ont., L3R 2M1   **New York, N.Y. 10010**

Please send me the books I have checked above. I am enclosing a total of $_____ (Please add 1.00 for one book and 50 cents for each additional book.) My cheque or money order is enclosed. (No cash or C.O.D.'s please.)

Name _____
Address _____ Apt. _____
City _____
Prov./State _____ P.C./Zip _____

(WA86)

JOHN BALL
AUTHOR OF **IN THE HEAT OF THE NIGHT** INTRODUCING, **POLICE CHIEF JACK TALLON** IN THESE EXCITING, FAST-PACED MYSTERIES.

WHEN RAPE IS THE CRIME, EVERY MAN IS A SUSPECT. EVEN THE NEW . . .
____ **POLICE CHIEF**   7701-03561/$2.95

A MIDNIGHT RENDEZVOUS BECOMES A DATE WITH DEATH.
____ **TROUBLE FOR TALLON**
                                7701-0357X/$2.95

BOOKS BY MAIL
320 Steelcase Rd. E.,
Markham, Ontario L3R 2M1

210 5th Ave., 7th Floor
New York, N.Y., 10010

Please send me the books I have checked above. I am enclosing a total of $_____ . (Please add 1.00 for one book and 50 cents for each additional book.) My cheque or money order is enclosed. (No cash or C.O.D.'s please.)

Name _____

Address _____ Apt. _____

City _____

Prov./State _____ P.C./Zip _____

Prices subject to change without notice.   (LTM8)

CLASSIC MYSTERIES

from

Gladys Mitchell

FEATURING

Dame Beatrice Adela
Lestrange Bradley

____ **DEATH-CAP DANCERS —**   7701-04010/$2.95
All they wanted was a vacation in the English countryside. Until they discovered that murder never takes a holiday . . .

____ **HERE LIES GLORIA MUNDY —**   7701-04037/$2.95
Gloria Mundy has a nasty habit of turning up when she is least wanted — even after she's dead!

____ **RISING OF THE MOON —**   7701-04304/$2.95
The moon sheds light on the horrors of the night . . . and on two small boys who see too much!

____ **SPOTTED HEMLOCK —**   7701-04835/$2.95
College pranks turn to deadly deeds in . . . SPOTTED HEMLOCK.

____ **UNCOFFIN'D CLAY —**   7701-04029/$2.95
Dirty deeds in Dorset turn up secrets buried deep in . . . UNCOFFIN'D CLAY.

Prices subject to change without notice

BOOKS BY MAIL

320 Steelcase Rd. E.   210 5th Ave., 7th Floor
Markham, Ont., L3R 2M1   New York, N.Y. 10010

Please send me the books I have checked above. I am enclosing a total of $_____ (Please add 1.00 for one book and 50 cents for each additional book.) My cheque or money order is enclosed. (No cash or C.O.D.'s please.)

Name _____

Address _____ Apt. _____

City _____

Prov./State _____ P.C./Zip _____

(GM/1)

PaperJacks *Presents*

BILL PRONZINI

THE "NAMELESS DETECTIVE"

____ **BONES** — An old grave opens a new case of murder. 7701-0451-7/$3.50

____ **LABYRINTH** — One smoking pistol points to a clear case of conspiracy. 7701-0432-0/$3.50

____ **HOODWINK** — A Pulpwriter's Convention becomes the setting for Real-life blackmail and murder. 7701-0549-1/$3.50

____ **SCATTERSHOT** — A wedding, a jealous wife, and murder add up to one shattering affair. 7701-0601-3/$3.50

Available at your local bookstore or return this coupon to:

BOOKS BY MAIL

320 Steelcase Rd. E.   210 5th Ave., 7th Floor
Markham, Ont., L3R 2M1   New York, N.Y. 10010

Please send me the books I have checked above. I am enclosing a total of $_____ (Please add 1.00 for one book and 50 cents for each additional book.) My cheque or money order is enclosed. (No cash or C.O.D.'s please.)

Name _____

Address _____ Apt. _____

City _____

Prov./State _____ P.C./Zip _____

Prices subject to change without notice   (PROZ/LR)

ANGEL EYES

by W.B. Longley
Adult Western at
its Finest

PaperJacks is pleased to present this
fast-paced, sexy western series.

____ # 1 THE MIRACLE OF
REVENGE
7701-0326X/$2.95

____ # 2 DEATH'S ANGEL
7701-0343X/$2.95

____ # 3 WOLF PASS
7701-0362/$2.95

____ # 4 CHINATOWN JUSTICE
7701-0374X/$2.95

____ # 5 LOGAN'S ARMY
7701-04126/$2.95

____ #6 BULLETS & BAD
TIMES
7701-04193/$2.95

____ # 7 SIX-GUN ANGEL
7701-0434-7/$2.95

____ # 8 AVENGING ANGEL
7701-0497-5/$2.95

BOOKS BY MAIL
320 Steelcase Rd. E.,
Markham, Ontario L3R 2M1

210 5th Ave., 7th Floor
New York, N.Y., 10010

Please send me the books I have checked above. I am enclosing
a total of $_____ . (Please add 1.00 for one book and
50 cents for each additional book.) My cheque or money order
is enclosed. (No cash or C.O.D.'s please.)

Name _____

Address _____ Apt. _____

City _____

Prov./State _____ P.C./Zip _____

Prices subject to change without notice.   (CP100)

WAYNE D. OVERHOLSER

WESTERNS

____ **BUNCH GRASS** — Chuck Harrigan wanted peace — but he'd have to start a war to get it!
7701-0515-7/$2.95

____ **GUNPLAY VALLEY** — A wealthy cattleman turns a peaceful land into a flaming valley of death.
7701-0551-3/$2.95

____ **THE LONG WIND** — Dawson rides off the wind-swept prairie into a fiery war!
7701-0449-5/$2.95

____ **RETURN OF THE KID** — A small town becomes the battleground for a very deadly family feud.
7701-0623-4/$2.95

Available at your local bookstore or return this coupon to:

 BOOKS BY MAIL
320 Steelcase Rd. E.,
Markham, Ontario L3R 2M1

210 5th Ave., 7th Floor
New York, N.Y., 10010

Please send me the books I have checked above. I am enclosing a total of $_____ . (Please add 1.00 for one book and 50 cents for each additional book.) My cheque or money order is enclosed. (No cash or C.O.D.'s please.)

Name _____
Address _____ Apt. _____
City _____
Prov. State _____ P.C. Zip _____

Prices subject to change without notice   OVER LR

FREE!!
BOOKS BY MAIL
CATALOGUE

BOOKS BY MAIL will share with you our current bestselling books as well as hard to find specialty titles in areas that will match your interests. You will be updated on what's new in books at no cost to you. Just fill in the coupon below and discover the convenience of having books delivered to your home.

PLEASE ADD $1.00 TO COVER THE COST OF POSTAGE & HANDLING.

BOOKS BY MAIL

320 Steelcase Road E.,
Markham, Ontario L3R 2M1

IN THE U.S. -
210 5th Ave., 7th Floor
New York, N.Y., 10010

Please send Books By Mail catalogue to:

Name _____
(please print)

Address _____

City _____

Prov./State _____ P.C./Zip _____

(BBM1)